Measuring and Evaluating School Learning

Measuring and Evaluating School Learning

THIRD EDITION

Lou M. Carey
University of South Florida

Allyn and Bacon
Boston ■ London ■ Toronto ■ Sydney ■ Tokyo ■ Singapore

Vice President, Publisher: Paul A. Smith
Editorial Assistant: Shannon Morrow
Marketing Manager: Brad Parkins
Editorial-Production Administrator: Annette Joseph
Editorial-Production Coordinator: Susan Freese
Editorial-Production Service: Omegatype Typography, Inc.

Text Design: Denise Hoffman
Electronic Composition: Omegatype Typography, Inc.
Composition Buyer: Linda Cox
Manufacturing Buyer: Suzanne Lareau
Cover Administrator: Linda Knowles

Copyright © 2001, 1994, 1988 by Allyn & Bacon
A Pearson Education Company
160 Gould Street
Needham Heights, MA 02494

Internet: www.abacon.com

Between the time website information is gathered and then published, it is not unusual for some sites to have closed. Also, the transcription of URLs can result in unintended typographical errors. The publisher would appreciate being notified of any problems with URLs so that they may be corrected in subsequent editions. Thank you.

Many of the designations used by manufacturers and sellers to distinguish their products are claimed as trademarks. Where those designations appear in this book and Allyn and Bacon was aware of a trademark claim, the designations have been printed in caps or initial caps.

Library of Congress Cataloging-in-Publication Data

Carey, Lou.
   Measuring and evaluating school learning / Lou M. Carey. — 3rd ed.
      p.   cm.
   Includes bibliographical references (p.) and index.
   ISBN 0-205-32388-X
   1. Educational tests and measurements—United States.   I. Title.

LB3051 .C36   2001
371.2'6'0973—dc21   00-035566

Printed in the United States of America

10 9 8 7 6 5 4 3 2 1   RRDV   05 04 03 02 01 00

Permissions Credits

Figure 15.4 is adapted from *TerraNova Technical Bulletin 1,* copyright © 1997 CTB/McGraw-Hill. Reproduced with permission of The McGraw-Hill Companies, Inc.

Tables 15.2, 15.3, and 15.5 and Figures 15.5, 15.7, 15.13, 15.14, 15.15, 15.20, and 15.21F are adapted from *TerraNova Spring Norms Book,* copyright © 1997 CTB/McGraw-Hill. Reproduced with permission of The McGraw-Hill Companies, Inc.

Figures 15.10, 15.11, 15.12, 15.18, and 15.19 and Tables 15.6 and 15.7 are adapted from *TerraNova Information Systems,* copyright © 1997 CTB/McGraw-Hill. Reproduced with permission of The McGraw-Hill Companies, Inc.

BRIEF CONTENTS

v

CONTENTS

PART II   Developing Classroom Assessments

5 Writing Objective Test Items   121

6 Constructing and Using Essay and Product Development Tests   167

PART III   Analyzing and Evaluating Student Progress

10 Evaluating Group Performance   273

11 Analyzing Test Items, Tasks, and Tests   301

14   Grading and Reporting Student Progress   411

Measuring and Evaluating School Learning focuses on the information and skills teachers need to design, develop, analyze, and interpret tests; to use test results in planning, monitoring, and evaluating instruction; and to evaluate student progress. It is directed to undergraduate education students who are preparing to teach, and to graduate students who want to improve their teaching and testing skills. It can also serve as a reference for educators in schools, universities, businesses, and government agencies.

The book assumes that readers have had little, if any, instruction in educational measurement, evaluation, or statistics. The Practice Exercises require readers to be familiar with the curriculum and skills in their fields, with basic learning principles, and with the application of these principles to their disciplines.

Testing is an integral part of the teaching and learning process, and it provides teachers with vital information. When tests are anchored to the instructional goals in the curriculum, teachers can conduct formative evaluations using (1) readiness tests to determine whether students have the knowledge and skills necessary to begin a unit of instruction, (2) pretests to identify skills that need to be emphasized during instruction, and (3) practice tests to monitor skill development, identify instructional needs, and pace instruction. Finally, posttests can be used to summatively evaluate student progress and locate inadequacies in instruction.

■ Changes in the Third Edition

Since its conceptualization, *Measuring and Evaluating School Learning,* has presented a systems-based approach to classroom assessment. Teachers have been required to consider their students' characteristics, their school districts' curricula, and their schools' environments and resources in designing and developing their tests. This third edition has built on this systems foundation and now anchors these critical concepts to recent reform movements related to learner-centered and curriculum-centered classroom assessment and teacher accountability.

Expansions related to learner-centered assessment include developing and adapting tests for a classroom of diverse students, including those for whom English is a second language (ESOL) and those with a variety of exceptionalities. Related to curriculum-centered assessments, national, state, and professional society standards for student achievement in both the cognitive and affective domains are used throughout the textbook. Students are linked to websites for these groups and encouraged to visit the sites, analyze and compare the standards, and actually use the standards as they complete the learning exercises prescribed in this book. The cognitive learning theories already included in curriculum analysis are expanded to include constructivist theories in the design and development of classroom tests. To address the arena of alternative assessment more centrally, the chapters in this edition have been sequenced differently. Following the first section on designing learner-centered and curriculum-centered classroom assessments, the text addresses the development of all types of classroom assessment that are anchored to the standards.

The chapters on analysis and evaluation support classroom decision making and information management from both continuous-progress and group-paced models. They include formative and summative evaluation models, and they address norm-referenced and criterion-referenced teacher judgments. Finally, within the area of communicating students' progress, portfolio assessment is still central, and grading and reporting strategies include both classical and mastery-style report cards.

Teacher accountability is also an important issue for teachers, schools, and communities today, and teachers need to monitor their own effectiveness with the pupils they are assigned. This text addresses measures of teacher effectiveness using student achievement data from both classroom tests and commercial standardized tests. The section on student-mastery assessment includes strategies for aggregating mastery data into measures of teacher effectiveness in the classroom. Within the chapter on standardized testing, the previous section on value-added assessment using scale scores has been expanded to include a personal assessment, teacher effectiveness measure called the Instructional Quality Index.

■ Plan for the Text

Measuring and Evaluating School Learning presents the following four-part process for constructing and using tests:

- Part I—Designing Learner-Centered and Curriculum-Centered Classroom Assessments
- Part II—Developing Classroom Assessments
- Part III—Analyzing and Evaluating Student Progress
- Part IV—Communicating Student Progress

Part I, Designing Learner-Centered and Curriculum-Centered Classroom Assessments, includes locating and sequencing instructional goals, describing the characteristics of new groups of students, analyzing instructional goals, designing classroom tests, and writing test item or task specifications. Part II, Developing Classroom Assessments, includes writing test items and constructing tests; constructing and using essay, product development, and active performance tests; constructing and using behavior observation forms and attitude questionnaires; and developing and administering tests for nonreaders, including primary, ESOL, and exceptional students. Part III, Analyzing and Evaluating Student Progress, includes using data generated from tests to evaluate group performance, evaluate test quality, evaluate an individual student's achievement from a criterion-referenced and norm-referenced perspective, and evaluate instruction. Part IV,

Communicating Student Progress, includes analyzing and evaluating student progress using portfolios, grading and reporting student progress, interpreting students' performance on standardized tests, and conducting value-added assessments.

This systems-oriented text is constructed using sound principles of learning. First, chapters are sequenced in the natural order that tasks are undertaken by teachers in the classroom. For example, early chapters describe procedures for beginning a school year, including analyzing the curriculum and the characteristics and needs of new students. These chapters are not intended to substitute for courses in curriculum or educational psychology; instead, they serve to remind readers of relevant prerequisite information and tasks and provide the critical context for a course in classroom testing. These chapters also provide the foundation for learner-centered and curriculum-centered classroom assessment. From these curriculum-learner anchors, the text illustrates, in order, design, development, analysis, evaluation, and reporting procedures.

Second, each chapter begins with a list of learning outcomes (Objectives) to focus readers' attention. Third, applicable concepts, principles, and procedures are introduced for each phase of the process and accompanied by an array of examples and illustrations. For the novice, these examples and illustrations facilitate learning new capabilities and promote transfer of these capabilities to students' disciplines and teaching areas. Fourth, a single concrete example, based on the instructional goal of writing a paragraph, is used throughout the text to demonstrate procedures and to illustrate the linkages among the phases of design, development, analysis, evaluation, and communication.

Fifth, beginning with Chapter 2, the discussion in each chapter concludes with the following sections: Computer Technology, a presentation of technological advances in the testing field; Summary, an overview of key concepts and procedures; Practice Exercises, problems and activities that facilitate learning and transfer; and Feedback, responses to exercises to aid in understanding. Another unit within the Practice Exercises, called Enrichment, is especially useful in facilitating transfer of newly acquired skills and information. Because learners' responses to many of the Practice Exercises and Enrichment activities will vary, these sections can serve as a basis for classroom discussion and further elaboration.

Following the Enrichment section is a Rubric students can use to evaluate the design and development products they create during their study. The main goal of the course is for students to learn and to internalize the criteria for quality test design and development. As teachers progress, using these rubrics for self-evaluation is important for developing skill in creating assessments and in evaluating assessments provided by others for their use. Finally, each chapter presents Suggested Readings, providing additional sources for readers who may wish to pursue further given topics.

■ Use of Computer Demonstration Programs

The preparation of preservice and inservice teachers should include experience with the emerging technologies that are shaping the "best practices" models of professionalism. As computers and computer applications become commonplace fixtures in the classroom, it is critical that both new and experienced teachers develop the skills and dispositions for using technological support. The value of integrating computer technology with effective classroom testing and management of student progress has been demonstrated in schools nationwide.

To provide preservice and inservice teachers with the opportunity to learn about these technological advances, this third edition of *Measuring and Evaluating School Learning* includes several features. A section called Computer Technology (found in each chapter except 15) offers guidance and examples of computer applications for the principles and procedures introduced in that chapter. In addition, to give readers real experience with computer applications in classroom measurement and evaluation, websites for available commercial item banking, test production, progress record management, and gradebooks are listed. These materials are all available for a trial period, and many are available free to classroom teachers. These shareware programs provide students with a medium in which they can experience actual computer applications.

Students may use the test item banking programs to gain technical experience through comparing the example item banks, designing and developing their own computerized test item banks, assembling a variety of tests from their item banks, printing tests they have created, and printing student feedback reports for their tests.

Students may use the sample gradebook programs to review the program features, enter pupil performance data, enter grading criteria, enter weighting factors to tailor composite scores according to a plan, and convert raw scores to a variety of derived scores. Students can become familiar with all the features and operations of these electronic gradebooks.

The sample programs are available for IBM and Macintosh computers. They are menu driven, and operation is made easy with HELP features and onscreen prompts. Examining these item bank and gradebook programs during this course on measurement and evaluation of pupil progress will help teachers integrate these technological advancements into both their perspectives on testing and their routine work as classroom teachers.

■ Approach to Learning and Teaching

Measuring and Evaluating School Learning is intended for all students enrolled in measurement courses for teachers. Such students typically are from a variety of disciplines, including language arts, mathematics, science, social studies, physical education, business education, elementary education, and special education. Because these students have diverse backgrounds, they do not have the discipline expertise required to analyze correctly the instructional goals in secondary school curricula for disciplines other than their own. For example, students who are expert in American government, chemistry, or music can be expected to understand illustrations and apply skills in these disciplines. However, students lacking expertise in these areas will be at a disadvantage. Because similar problems surface, regardless of the discipline, areas chosen for illustration and exercises were purposefully selected from common knowledge disciplines. All students, regardless of their majors, will be able to analyze such goals correctly and find such analyses quite challenging.

Students must be able to look beyond the content of the goals used as examples in this text in order to concentrate on the learning, measurement, and evaluation principles and procedures involved. After applying these skills using basic examples, students will be prepared to transfer them to their own disciplines for class projects or for their own work. Completing the activities prescribed in the Enrichment section of the Practice Exercises for each chapter will also help students transfer the skills to their own disciplines.

These common knowledge examples also have an advantage for teachers of this course. Like students, our areas of expertise beyond measurement and evaluation are diverse. Using basic skills examples enables us to provide many illustrations, adequate guidance, and corrective feedback to students as they perform the tasks.

■ Acknowledgments

Many individuals participated in the formative evaluation of this book. I would like to acknowledge my colleagues—Roger Wilk, Tary Wallace, and James Carey—who field-tested versions of the text with their classes and provided valuable criticism on content, organization, presentation, and effectiveness.

Students in my classes also used field-tested versions and provided valuable guidance. The following students deserve special mention: Sue Beck, elementary education; Mark Lange, English education; John Myrick, physics education; Allison Salisbury, biology education; and Katie Winterhalter, mathematics education. Working as a small field-test group, these individuals applied each chapter to their majors and substantially influenced the final version of the text. Their contributions have undoubtedly increased its relevance for other students who want to learn testing principles and procedures.

Additional thanks go to CTB/McGraw-Hill Publishing Company for their permission to reproduce sample materials from the TerraNova achievement tests.

The preparation of this third edition was guided by comments received from those individuals who reviewed the book for Allyn and Bacon: Virden Evans, Florida A&M University; David McMullen, Bradley University; and Royal Van Horn, University of North Florida.

And once again, thanks go to those individuals who reviewed the previous editions: Tony Allen, University of Rhode Island; James Applefield, University of North Carolina at Wilmington; Robert M. Brashear, Western Michigan University; William L. Deaton, Auburn University at Montgomery; Steve Dunbar, University of Iowa; Louise Fleming, Ashland University; Richard Jaeger, University of North Carolina at Charlotte; James R. MacCluskie, Edinboro University of Pennsylvania; Don Mizokawa, University of Washington; Bruce Rogers, University of Northern Iowa; John Sanderston, University of Virginia; Landa Trentham, Auburn University; and Gaylen Wallace, University of Missouri at St. Louis.

Measuring and Evaluating School Learning

Introduction

Teachers choose their careers in the classroom for a variety of reasons. Some enjoy a particular subject, some have been inspired by teachers they had when they were students, and others enjoy helping people learn. Few, if any, enter the profession because they want to design and develop tests or interpret test results. Testing, however, plays a vital role in teaching. It also can help you refine your teaching skills throughout your career.

Effective teachers must be proficient in testing, and proficiency in testing requires the synthesis of many different skills. Teachers must know about their discipline; about the nature of learning; and about their students' language skills, interests, and experiences. They must be able to write clearly, summarize and analyze data, and make comparisons and inferences to interpret test results. In applying testing principles and procedures, they must use their professional judgment and make informed decisions about their methods and instruction. Because teaching is a decision-based activity, the quality of instruction will depend on teachers' ability to gather, interpret, and use relevant information.

This text illustrates a systematic process of test development, use, and interpretation. Each chapter begins with a list of objectives that will help direct your study. The objectives are followed by relevant concepts, principles, and procedures. Many tables and figures illustrate the concepts and procedures, and a Summary section concludes each chapter. To help you develop your testing skills, each chapter ends with a comprehensive set of Practice Exercises. Many of these exercises require judgment and interpretation; thus, they will help you formulate questions you may want to ask during class discussions. Each set of Practice Exercises also includes suggestions for enrichment activities. These suggestions will help you transfer the skills to your discipline and classroom. As you read the text and complete the exercises, you will learn how to plan for new classes, create and use classroom tests, and report on students' overall progress. Many chapters also include a rubric that you can use for self-reflection and evaluation as you design and develop classroom tests.

The first phase, design, consists of four activities: identifying and sequencing instructional goals, describing student characteristics and needs, analyzing instructional goals, and designing overall assessments as well as test item or task specifications. The information you gather and the decisions you make during this first phase become the basis for all subsequent activities.

In the second and third phases of the process, you will develop classroom assessments and evaluate your students' performances. The information you gather during these phases will help you improve both your tests and your instruction. The last phase is communication. Many teachers will prepare portfolios of students' work to illustrate student progress. In addition, you will need to grade and report your students' progress and to interpret their performance on standardized tests. Figure 1.1 illustrates these four phases and indicates the chapters that describe each activity. The remaining sections of this chapter present an overview of each phase.

◾ Designing Learner-Centered and Curriculum-Centered Classroom Assessments

The design phase begins with two questions: What are you expected to teach in this course? and Whom are you expected to teach? To answer the first question, consult your school district's curriculum guide and your state's curriculum standards, the lists of goals and objectives recommended by professional societies, and the manuals for standardized tests adopted by your district. After you have identified and compared instructional goals and objectives from these different sources, sort the goals by topic and then sequence the ones you will use. The list of sequenced instructional goals will guide your test design and development activities for each unit of instruction.

The best source of information about your students' achievement characteristics is the students' permanent school records. These records contain standardized test scores, grades, and other pertinent information. After you decide which information you need, prepare a form on which you summarize the group's achievement characteristics. This group summary will help you design appropriate tests, establish minimum standards for performance, and interpret test results. Other valuable sources of information include the students' parents and previous teachers, guidance counselors and school psychologists, school social workers and nurses, English-as-a-second-language (ESOL) specialists, and special education faculty. These professionals can inform you about students' interests and special needs. Added to the achievement information, a profile of your students will begin to develop.

With the instructional goals in hand and the characteristics of students in mind, you are ready to analyze the goals to identify the skills students will need in order to demonstrate mastery of your instructional goals. You should separate each goal into subordinate tasks and then sequence the tasks in some logical order. This activity, which is called *goal analysis* or *task analysis,* produces a framework of tasks that becomes the foundation for both your lessons and tests.

FIGURE 1.1

Designing and Developing Learner-Centered and Curriculum-Centered Classroom Assessments

Phase 1

Designing Classroom Assessments

| Locate and sequence performance standards and goals. Ch. 2 | Describe students' characteristics and needs. Ch. 2 | Analyze goals for enabling and prerequisite skills. Ch. 3 | Design tests for formative and summative evaluation of progress. Ch. 4 | Design test item task specifications (i.e., objectives). Ch. 4 |

Phase 2

Developing Classroom Assessments That Are Congruent with Curriculum Standards and Students' Needs

| Develop objective tests. Ch. 5 | Develop essay and product tests, and scoring rubrics. Ch. 6 | Develop active performance tests, scoring rubrics, and procedures. Ch. 7 | Design and develop attitude and behavior observation instruments. Ch. 8 | Develop/adapt tests for non-readers, ESOL, and students with special needs. Ch. 9 |

Phase 3

Analyzing and Evaluating Student Progress and Instruction

| Analyze and evaluate group performance. Ch. 10 | Analyze and evaluate items and tests. Ch. 11 | Describe a student's group-relative progress. Ch. 12 | Evaluate a student's mastery of goals. Ch. 12 | Use students' mastery data for self-evaluation of instruction. Ch. 12 |

Phase 4

Communicating Student Progress

| Use portfolios to evaluate student progress. Ch. 13 | Grade and report students' progress. Ch. 14 | Interpret standardized test performance. Ch. 15 | Conduct value-added assessments of student progress. Ch. 15 | Use value-added assessment for self-evaluation. Ch. 15 |

- - - - - Reflects feedback of information for revisions and refinements

The next step in the process is to design your assessments. The types of assessments you design will depend on the kinds of decisions you want to make. You might decide to use readiness tests and pretests, which will provide information about your students before you plan instruction. You might want to administer other formative evaluation assessments, such as practice tests to allow students to rehearse the skills and to monitor their progress during instruction. Regardless of whether you use these formative types of tests, you will probably need to design summative evaluation posttests to evaluate the students' progress as well as the quality of your instruction. Your purpose and the decisions you wish to make should guide your design activities.

Test designs are called *tables of test specifications* or *test blueprints*. To develop a table of test specifications, you should consider not only the purpose for the test but also the objectives for the unit, student characteristics, the classroom environment, resources available for testing and scoring, the time available for the test, and ways to produce valid and reliable scores. You can then use this information to select the specific knowledge and enabling skills from the goal framework to be measured, prescribe the best test item format, and determine the number of test items or performance tasks to include for each skill.

Finally, you will need to develop a list of test item or task specifications for each enabling skill selected for your test blueprints. These item specifications are sometimes called *instructional* or *learner objectives*. The item specifications should specify the conditions or the circumstances under which the students will demonstrate their mastery of the skills. To create appropriate specifications or objectives, consider the achievement characteristics of the group, the task's content and specified behavior, the classroom environment, and available resources. In certain instances, you may also need to include criteria for judging the quality of a group's performance.

■ Developing Classroom Assessments

With the table of specifications and item task specifications complete, the design process gives way to the development phase of classroom assessment. In the development phase, you will consider the criteria for developing all types of classroom assessments and match the particular format used to your performance standard and instructional goal.

Criteria for Quality Assessments

Regardless of whether the format of an assessment is objective, product, or performance, there are at least four general areas of quality criteria that are applied in the development of classroom assessments. These include curriculum-centered, student-centered, school environment-centered, and professional-centered criteria.

Curriculum-centered assessment has three important areas of quality criteria for test development. The first is ensuring alignment among the test item or task and the conditions, behavior, and content in the test item specification, or objective. The second criterion is ensuring that the performance level of the standard assessed is relevant to the level typically applied in the students' environment. The third is ensuring adequate assessment for both formative and summative evaluation of the learners' progress.

Learner-centered quality criteria for test development can be classified into four general areas. The first is accommodating the achievement characteristics or developmental level of the learners, including their vocabulary and reading levels. The second is creating assessment contexts and situations that are familiar to the learners. Another is avoiding cultural, gender, and other forms of bias in developing items and tests. The fourth criterion is determining that the assessment format and administration procedures are adapted to accommodate students with special needs.

School environment-centered criteria are in one main area called *feasibility.* First, you must carefully consider the number of students you are assigned and, based on this number, the time required to develop, administer, score, and provide formative or summative feedback for a particular item or test format. You also must consider the resources and facilities available to support the planned assessment.

Professional-centered criteria for assessment development include qualities related to your personal professional skills. The first criterion relates to your writing ability, including the clarity and precision of word choice and the accuracy of grammar, punctuation, and spelling used in items and directions. The second is more difficult, but just as important, and it relates to your creativity and inventiveness in developing assessment simulations and tasks that engage the learners above the knowledge and comprehension levels. Another criterion relates to your skill in structuring items and task directions according to formatting rules that are designed for clarity.

Classroom Assessment Formats

Objective Tests   Quality criteria for formatting six different types of objective-style items are included in this category. The student-generated response formats include short-answer items and completion items. Student-selected response items include several varieties of alternative response items, two types of matching items, and multiple-choice items.

Essay, Product, and Active Performance Tests   Criteria for developing alternative classroom assessments are related to creating assessment instructions, the items or tasks, scoring rubrics, and scoring procedures for cognitive skills.

Behavior and Attitude Assessment   Many state and school district achievement standards today include information and skills related to acquiring appropriate attitudes and behaviors for health and citizenship. Theoretically based criteria and procedures for analyzing curriculum-based attitudes are addressed in this format. In addition, criteria for formatting behavior observation forms and self-report attitude questionnaires are included. Methods for conducting the observations and scoring the assessments are described and illustrated.

Adapting Assessments for Students with Special Needs   In the area of assessment, all nonreading students are classified as students with special needs. This broad group includes (1) very young children who have yet to develop the skill; (2) students who do not yet speak English or students who are just beginning to speak and read academic English—that is, students who use English as a second language (ESOL); and (3) students with a variety of physical, emotional, and psychological needs. Criteria for adapting classroom assessments to meet these students' needs are related to creating and using teachers' scripts; graphical or illustration student response forms; translations, dictionaries, and other test helpers; and technology. In addition, administration procedures for both individuals and groups as well as scoring procedures are included in this book.

■ Analyzing and Evaluating Student Progress

Test results can be used to describe and evaluate a group's overall performance, the test, an individual student's test performance, and instruction, in that order. To make judgments about quality, you will need some standard or criterion against which to compare results. These criteria are developed using your interpretation of the complexity of the skills measured and the achievement characteristics of the students tested. When measures indicate that students have performed as well as or better than anticipated, you can conclude that instruction and the test were effective. However, if students' performance falls short of anticipated levels, then you have evidence that the instruction, and perhaps the test, should be questioned.

Indicators you will use to evaluate a group's overall test performance include the shape and location of the raw score distribution; measures of central tendency, including the mean and median; and measures of variability, including the range and standard deviation. As before, the complexity of skills measured and the achievement characteristics of the group are used to set standards for performance. The actual measures are compared with the anticipated ones to determine the quality of the group's performance.

When evaluating the quality of an objective test, the performance indicators used include each item's difficulty index and discrimination index. Using these indices, any items that are found questionable are reviewed further by employing a distractor analysis. Items judged defective following this review are eliminated, and test scores are adjusted accordingly before evaluating instruction or an individual's performance. The overall quality of a test is judged by using indices of the test's internal consistency, which provide a general indication of test score reliability.

The third type of analysis involves evaluating each student's test performance. Each student's performance is described by comparing it to the overall group's performance and by determining the number of skills mastered. Before you make your final judgment, compare each student's performance with her or his previous achievement to determine whether students have equaled or surpassed their previous records. By combining students' mastery performances into a group composite, you will be able to identify quickly the particular students who need enrichment and those who need review or remediation on specific skills. Finally, you can locate skill areas in which instruction was good, acceptable, and inadequate.

When evaluating the quality of instruction, items are sorted by objective or goal. The difficulty and discrimination indices are then compared for sets of items. When the students' performance does not meet anticipated levels for all or most items within a skill set, then instruction related to the skill is questioned.

■ Communicating Students' Progress

Schools and teachers strive to communicate clearly the current status of their students. Communication with students, parents, and colleagues can take many forms, including portfolios, mastery charts, grades and report cards, and standardized test performance.

Portfolios and Mastery Charts

Teachers often collect students' work into portfolios to enable achievement progress reviews by teachers, students themselves, and parents. Besides individual portfolios, many teachers use mastery charts to monitor a student's progress in the instructional goals taught during a course or grade level. Once mastery charts are completed for all members of a class, teachers can evaluate the quality of their instruction by determining the percentage of students who mastered each main component of a product or performance. Group performance information can be used to monitor and improve the quality of instruction for each instructional goal in the curriculum guide.

Grading and Reporting Progress

Students' grades should accurately summarize and reflect their performances during each term, semester, and year. To ensure this accuracy, you will need to consider the instructional goals and objectives covered during a term, those measured by each posttest, each student's posttest scores, the district's grading policies, and the proportion each test will contribute to the final grade. In addition, you may need to synthesize individual scores into a composite score and either establish or locate standards for converting composite scores into term grades. Today, most teachers use computer-based gradebooks to accommodate all of this information and aid their work.

Interpreting Standardized Test Performance

Every teacher should be able to interpret students' scores on standardized tests. Chapter 15 describes (1) the nature, the purpose, and the construction of standardized tests; (2) the purpose for the norm group; (3) the normal distribution and its relationship to standardized test scores; (4) the relationship of the scores to each other; (5) the procedures for interpreting scores on a student's profile; and (6) the procedures for conducting a student- and classroom-level assessment of each student's growth from year to year.

■ Computer Technology

Today, it is common for teachers to use computer-based test item banks, test scoring programs, and gradebook programs to aid in their testing and information management tasks. Although the user's manuals that accompany these programs provide invaluable information for operating the programs, they do not provide, nor do they intend to provide, the information necessary to learn to design and develop a quality testing program. Once you understand the basics of designing and developing a quality testing program, however, these computer-based programs and manuals will prove invaluable for easily implementing your designs, developing your items, assembling your tests, scoring the tests, obtaining achievement summaries for a class, and producing reports of an individual's or group's progress.

The manner in which computer-based testing and grading programs are used by teachers to aid in their testing and information management tasks is described in each chapter of this text. There are many commercial test item bank, scoring, and gradebook programs available today on various websites. The Computer Technology sections in each chapter link the testing, scoring, and grading procedures introduced in the chapter to the capabilities of the commercial programs.

Many teachers ask what considerations are important when choosing a computer-based testing program for themselves. Figure 1.2 lists some general criteria you can use to evaluate the suitability of available programs. After you have studied this text and tried some of the web-based programs to design and develop your own tests, you will undoubtedly be able to develop a more sophisticated list of selection criteria for yourself.

If the school system in which you work does not provide computer support for classroom testing, scoring, grading, and record keeping, you may want to take advantage of the low cost and availability of personal computers. There are many programs from a variety of publishers that are designed for use on a personal computer. You will be able to review programs that cover a wide range of capability, complexity, and cost, and choose the programs that best suit your needs and budget. Teachers with sufficient levels of interest and skill in computers sometimes choose to develop their own test management programs and use any of the popular spreadsheet programs for record keeping and grading. Whatever your level of computer skills and however you choose to use technology in your classroom, you will find that computer support can be a valuable time saver in your testing program.

■ Documenting the Process

The documents related to planning, designing, developing, summarizing, analyzing, and evaluating tests presented in this text are closely related and they build one on the other. Although each chapter provides many examples and illustrations, the book uses one instructional goal to illustrate how the decisions you make at any stage in the process influence your decisions at other stages. Thus, you will undoubtedly want to compare the documents developed at different stages. The primary documents for each phase of activity for the sample instructional goal are repeated in Appendices A

FIGURE 1.2

General Considerations for Selecting a Computer-Based Testing and Information Management System

I. General Considerations
   A. What types of computer-based testing, scoring, and gradebook programs are provided by your school district for use by teachers?
   B. What type of technical assistance is available for users of a given system?
   C. What types of computer, storage, disk configuration, and printer are required to operate the system?
   D. What types of test scanning and scoring programs are available in the school or school district, and are they compatible with gradebook programs you may be considering? (Scanning and scoring programs usually link directly with gradebook programs from the same publisher.)
   E. What item banking assembly programs are available for the scanning and scoring services available to you?

II. Linking Testing and Instruction
   A. In the item banking program, are there multiple ways to classify and store items that will enable you to track them by curricular standard, instructional goal, enabling skill, learning level, text chapter, reading level, test purpose, and so on?
   B. Is there a way you can use a test plan or blueprint to retrieve items from your test item bank?

III. Creating Items
   A. Does the program support the development of objective-style test items?
   B. Does the program support the development of essay and problem-style test items?
   C. Does the program support the development of alternative-style tests, including product tests, live performance tests, attitude and behavior rating scales, and checklists?

IV. Scoring Tests and Updating the Item Bank
   A. Is there a scoring program linked to the item bank program?
   B. Can you automatically update item data in your item bank each time you score tests?
   C. Does the scoring program support the development of student progress reports and a gradebook?

V. Test Performance Analysis
   A. Does the scoring program provide indices of group performances, including score distributions, measures of central tendency, and measures of variability?
   B. Does the scoring program provide information about the norm-referenced and criterion-referenced performance of individual students on a test?
   C. Does the program provide indices of item quality, including difficulty, discrimination, and distractor quality?
   D. Does the program provide indices of overall test quality?

VI. Gradebook
   A. Does the program link the scoring program to a gradebook program to enable automatic entry of students' scores into a gradebook?
   B. Does the program enable you to convert students' raw scores to common scale scores for weighting?
   C. Does the program enable you to weight scores and calculate cumulative scores for a term?
   D. Does the program enable you to use various marks for communicating students' progress (e.g. A–D, Credit/No Credit, Mastery/Nonmastery)?
   E. Does the program assign grades according to your weighting plan and grading criteria?
   F. Does the program produce a variety of reports of students' performance and progress?

through K to help you avoid flipping through the chapters to make your comparisons. For example, if you want to compare the table of test specifications described in Chapter 4 with the documents on which it is based, turn to the Appendices. Appendix A contains the instructional goal framework and Appendix B contains the table of test specifications developed from the goal framework. Appendix C contains the objectives or test item or task specifications for the skills prescribed in the table of test specifications. If you want to see samples of tests developed from the test item specifications in Chapter 4, see Appendices D through G. Appendices I through K contain the analysis and evaluation documents that are based on the planning, design, and development documents.

■ Summary

In its narrowest applications, this book is about designing, developing, and using classroom measures of students' progress. In this text, however, testing and alternative assessment are viewed in a broader sense, as an integral part of the teaching and learning process. Classroom assessment must flow directly from sound curriculum design and can even help sharpen your thinking about curriculum and focus your efforts in planning instructional methods, materials, and activities. It is more than just tools for grading. Classroom assessment is a method for collecting information that improves your professional judgment about the quality of your instruction and the needs of your students. In its broadest applications, this book is about one of the foundations of the teaching profession: the systematic collection and use of information for guiding decisions about your teaching and your students.

SUGGESTED READINGS

American Federation of Teachers, National Council on Measurement in Education, & National Education Association. Standards for Teacher Competence in Educational Assessment of Students. Washington, DC <http://www.libfind.unl.edu/buros/article3.html>.

Cain, R. W., & Kenney, P. A. (1992). A joint vision for classroom assessment. *Mathematics Teacher, 85,* 8: 612–615. <http://www.enc.org/reform/journals/enc2201/nf_2201.htm>.

Kubiszyn, T., & Borich, G. (2000). *Educational testing and measurement* (6th ed., pp. 1–17). New York: John Wiley & Sons.

Lynn, R. L., & Gronlund, N. E. (2000). *Measurement and assessment in teaching* (8th ed., pp. 1–26). Englewood Cliffs, NJ: Prentice-Hall.

Worthen, B. R., White, K. R., Fan, X., & Sudweeks, R. L. (1999). *Measurement and assessment in schools* (2nd ed., pp. 1–54). New York: Addison-Wesley Longman.

Planning for New Classes

Curriculum-Centered Objectives

- Identify sources of instructional goals for a course.
- Determine the congruence among instructional goals found in various sources.
- Describe how to sequence instructional goals for a course.

Learner-Centered Objectives

- Describe how class groups are formed.
- Define the terms *heterogeneous* and *homogeneous* and relate them to group achievement levels.
- Determine which information to use in assessing the achievement characteristics of a class group.
- Design a form for summarizing group achievement.
- Use student achievement data to describe previous performance levels of newly assigned class groups.
- Locate and describe students' special needs that may require accommodation during assessments.
- Identify individuals who can provide information about accommodation for special needs during assessments.

Two of a teacher's first tasks at the beginning of a new school year are to determine what he or she is expected to teach and to whom. Although these tasks might at first appear to be unrelated to testing activities, they provide the foundation necessary for determining what skills to test and for interpreting the test scores obtained. This chapter describes these two planning activities. The first activity is to identify and sequence instructional goals for a course, and the second is to describe the characteristics and needs of assigned class groups.

■ Planning for Curriculum-Centered Assessment

Education is a highly complex system that requires curriculum planning and coordination. Curriculum plans are communicated through national and state performance standards and district curriculum guides listing instructional goals that students in a given grade level and subject are expected to achieve. These standards and goals are produced by a team that usually includes classroom teachers, curriculum specialists, professional society members, and university-level content experts. Teams developing curriculum in vocational subjects commonly include experts from business and industry as well.

State performance standards and curriculum guides serve as a foundation to plan and coordinate two main activities at the state, district, and school levels: instruction and testing. At the state level, the standards are used to coordinate instruction across school districts, to adopt the most relevant instructional texts, and to provide a foundation for statewide achievement tests. School administrators at the district level use the state guides as one resource for developing their own more comprehensive curriculum guides. The district guides are then used to coordinate instruction across schools and grade levels and to select instructional texts for each subject and grade. Related to testing, the guides are used to select the most appropriate standardized tests and to develop districtwide achievement tests. Classroom teachers use the district's curriculum guide to identify and sequence the instructional goals assigned for their subject and grade level, to plan instructional units and lessons, and to develop achievement tests that measure students' progress. Curriculum standards and guides help ensure that important instructional goals are not inadvertently omitted, that unintended repetition is avoided, and that a direct match exists among the standards, the instruction provided, and the tests used to measure students' progress.

Today, most states publish their standards on the World Wide Web. Most school districts also publish their curriculum guides, at least in the basic skills subjects. If standards are provided for your subject they will define your primary teaching responsibilities. Sometimes, however, these guides either are not provided or are not as complete as you would like. If a curriculum guide is not provided for your subject, you should prepare one yourself. If the one provided is sketchy and incomplete, you will need to expand or clarify the instructional goals included. In either situation, you can turn to a variety of resources for help.

Sources of Instructional Goals

Instructional goals can be located in various places. As noted, some state departments of education provide performance standards for specific subjects, particularly subjects dealing with basic skills. These standards are one valuable source of instructional goals. The publications of professional associations that describe goals and standards for your discipline may be useful as well, and professional society standards for many disciplines are readily available on the Internet. You can also turn to textbooks and other instructional materials adopted for your subject. Scanning several adopted texts should give you an overview of the goals different authors consider important.

The teacher's and administrator's manuals for standardized achievement tests that will be administered to your students are another good source of instructional goals. These documents often describe not only goals but related instructional objectives as well. They describe the specific form of the test and the grade in which each objective is tested. They also key each objective to published instructional materials.

Elements of an Instructional Goal

The instructional goals listed in curriculum guides are broad statements of learning outcomes that indicate both the behavior and the instructional content students are to acquire. Although it is often not the case, the behaviors included in an instructional goal should be observable and measurable. They should describe overt student behaviors that demonstrate whether students acquired the desired knowledge or skill. Words typically used to describe overt behaviors include *list, select, define, recite, sequence, summarize, classify, predict, solve,* and *explain.* Terms such as *understand, appreciate,* and *comprehend* are often found in standards produced by committees of parents, community members, and political task forces. Teachers convert these global behaviors to observable ones because such terms do not clearly indicate how students will demonstrate that they have acquired the desired skill or information. Although the underlying purpose of instruction is to produce understanding and comprehension, instructional goals are written or refined to communicate how students will visibly demonstrate these internal processes.

The second part of an instructional goal identifies the content of the instruction. This content may be a topic, such as punctuation, capitalization, mixed fractions, or the Constitution. The content part of the goal identifies the topic and the particular portion of the topic to be studied.

The sample instructional goals listed in Figures 2.1, 2.2, and 2.3 were selected from elementary and secondary school curriculum guides in language arts, mathematics, and special education, respectively. Notice that regardless of the subject area considered, each goal listed in the three tables includes both the desired student behavior and the instructional content to be learned. Note also that the behaviors included describe overt actions rather than such terms as *comprehends* and *understands.*

Comparing Instructional Goals from Different Sources

Comparing the instructional goals from a variety of sources can often be useful. You may compare your district's guide with (1) the state or national standards; (2) the text and instructional materials for the class; (3) the recommended goal lists of professional associations; and (4) the goals and objectives measured on mandated, standardized achievement tests. In making such an analysis, you may find some instructional goals recommended in all your resources. You may also discover that some goals in your district's curriculum guide are included in only a few, or none, of the other sources.

FIGURE 2.1

Sample Instructional Goals for Language Arts at Various Grade Levels

1. Sequence a group of four pictures.
2. Arrange four sentences into a meaningful paragraph.
3. Alphabetize any given list of words.
4. Use guide words to locate specified words in a dictionary.
5. Write a story using a logical organizational pattern.
6. Paraphrase a written passage.
7. Distinguish between fact and opinion.
8. Determine the cause and effect of an event or action.
9. Infer tone and mood from a written passage.
10. Use regular plural forms of nouns.
11. Capitalize proper nouns.
12. Capitalize appropriate words in titles.
13. Match nouns and pronouns.
14. Select the appropriate tense of regular verbs in context.
15. Make subjects and verbs agree.
16. Write declarative sentences.
17. Write interrogative sentences.
18. Write compound sentences using a comma, semicolon, and colon.
19. Use a comma to separate words in a series.
20. Use an apostrophe to form contractions.
21. Associate words that are the same or opposite in meaning.
22. Form derived words using prefixes and suffixes.
23. Determine the meaning of a word in context.
24. Identify metaphors and similes.

FIGURE 2.2

Sample Instructional Goals for Mathematics at Various Grade Levels

1. Add whole numbers with regrouping.
2. Subtract whole numbers with regrouping.
3. Multiply whole numbers with regrouping.
4. Divide whole numbers with regrouping.
5. Add proper fractions having like denominators.
6. Subtract proper fractions having unlike denominators.
7. Multiply proper and improper fractions.
8. Read and write mixed decimal numbers through hundredths.
9. Add, subtract, multiply, and divide mixed decimal numbers.
10. Round a number having two decimal places to the nearest whole number.
11. Write equations to solve word problems.
12. Solve word problems involving money.
13. Solve word problems involving time.
14. Solve word problems involving temperature.
15. Solve word problems involving length.
16. Solve word problems involving liquid capacity.
17. Solve word problems involving mass.
18. Solve word problems involving percentages.
19. Calculate probabilities.
20. Calculate the mean.
21. Find the perimeters of given objects.
22. Find the areas of given objects.
23. Read graphs including ordered pairs and coordinates.

The other documents may also recommend goals that the assigned curriculum guide does not. When the same instructional goal appears in multiple sources, it is undoubtedly one that content experts consider very important. When a goal appears only in the district's curriculum guide, it is one that local curriculum specialists and teachers consider important for the district. If the district's curriculum guide and the adopted text

FIGURE 2.3

Sample Instructional Goals for Exceptional Students at Various Grade Levels

A. Goals for Students Who Are Educable
1. Match identical symbols (letters and numerals).
2. Discriminate colors.
3. Discriminate sounds.
4. Copy upper-case and lower-case letters.
5. Write own name and address.
6. Compare objects by size, dimensions, quantity, position, or sequence.
7. Write letters of the alphabet when named.
8. Demonstrate self-care skills in personal hygiene.
9. Demonstrate self-care skills in health and safety.
10. Demonstrate appropriate peer group interactions.

B. Goals for Students Who Are Trainable
1. Distinguish basic sensory qualities (hot-cold, wet-dry, burning smell, hard-soft, spoiled-fresh).
2. Name and locate body parts.
3. Demonstrate self-help in safety situations.
4. Demonstrate self-help in dressing.
5. Demonstrate general work skills.
6. Demonstrate appropriate work relations.

exclude goals appearing on mandated, standardized tests, you may want to insert these goals in your curriculum guide as an addendum.

If goals from various sources are worded differently but imply the same behavior and content, you may consider them the same. The language arts instructional goals for the fifth grade shown in Table 2.1 were taken from three different sources. Notice that, although the wording is different, their intent is the same. Because the goals prescribed in the state guide and the test manual are more complete than the one in the district guide, they could be used to clarify and expand the district's goal statement.

TABLE 2.1

Language Arts Instructional Goals

Goal Source	Goal
District curriculum guide	Uses context clues to supply the meanings of words
State-level standard	Infers the meanings of words in context using (a) example clues, (b) direct explanation clues, (c) synonym clues, and (d) compare and contrast clues
Teacher's manual for a standardized test	Selects the definitions for multimeaning words in context and uses context clues to identify word meanings

TABLE 2.2

A Comparison of Instructional Goals from Different Sources

Goals in Curriculum Guide	Other Sources
1. Sequence a group of four pictures.	T(5), S
2. Arrange four sentences into a meaningful paragraph.	I, T(5), S
3. Write a friendly letter.	I, S

Note: T(5) = Standardized test (month usually administered)
     S = State curriculum standards
     I = Adopted instructional materials

To help you remember the sources of similar goals, assign symbols to your sources and key them to your curriculum guide. When an instructional goal from another source matches one in the district guide, place the symbol for that source in the margin beside the goal. You may also want to edit the district's goal to include any clarifying information found in other sources. If you decide to add goals to the curriculum guide, note the source in the margin beside each one. Referencing other sources in your curriculum guide will help you evaluate the completeness of the curriculum guide, determine the guide's congruence with adopted instructional materials and standardized tests, and perhaps sequence goals for your new class.

Table 2.2 provides an example of the congruence between a school district's curriculum guide and three other goal sources. Goals similar to Goal 1, "Sequence a group of four pictures," appear on the standardized test and in the state curriculum guide. The adopted text does not include instruction for this goal. The second goal is included in the text, the standardized test manual, and the state curriculum. The third goal appears in the text and the state curriculum but not on the standardized test. A teacher reviewing this analysis should recognize that Goal 1 presents an instructional problem to be solved. Because the adopted text does not include instruction for this goal, the teacher will undoubtedly need to develop or locate all instruction related to it.

Sequencing Instructional Goals

Once you have a list of instructional goals for the course, cluster them by topic and sequence them. This planning activity can help you decide where to begin instruction and how to proceed during the year. When you have finished, your curriculum guide will have all your instructional goals ordered in the sequence you plan to present them. The guide can direct your instructional activities throughout the year and help you develop records to monitor students' mastery of your instructional goals.

The several strategies you can use to sequence instructional goals differ in importance. Three of the most important considerations in selecting a sequence are the relationships among the goals, the dates when standardized tests are administered, and the sequence of topics in the textbook. The most important consideration is the relationship among the goals. Some goals are hierarchically related, meaning that certain skills must be learned before others. For example, the goal "Recognize nouns" is a prerequisite to the goal "Differentiate between common nouns and proper nouns." In another hierarchical relationship, the goal "Add without regrouping" must precede the goal "Add with regrouping." The first sequencing strategy is to identify and sequence all goals in the guide that are hierarchically related.

Once goals are ordered according to their hierarchical relationships, the next important consideration is the timing of any standardized tests that all your students are required to take. Your goal sequence should permit you to teach the skills these tests measure before the tests are administered. The third consideration, text order, is one of convenience. To the degree possible, goals should be ordered to correspond to their presentation sequence in the textbook.

Even after sequencing goals in the curriculum guide using these three strategies, some goals may remain to be sequenced. These remaining goals can be sequenced using such factors as complexity, familiarity, chronology, or potential motivation. When you have completed your goal analysis and sequencing, you will be ready to consider the students who have been assigned to your class.

■ Planning for Learner-Centered Assessment

Most teachers are assigned new class groups at the beginning of each school year. The characteristics of the students in each group will affect all instructional activities, including the analysis of the instructional goals, lesson development, the selection of resource material, the delivery of instruction, the writing of test items, and the interpretation of test performance. Because each class will be different, you should assess the achievement levels of each group, identify any special needs, and tailor your instructional and assessment activities accordingly.

Assignment of Class Groups

In forming class groups, school administrators consider several factors in addition to previous achievement. They usually try to balance the number of students in each class, the number of males and females in a group, the number of mainstreamed and other exceptional students, and the cultural and racial mix at each grade level. They must also consider scheduling for such elective subjects as art, band, chorus, and special programs. All of these factors affect administrative decisions concerning class groups, but none of these factors is as important to the teacher as the students' previous achievement levels.

The school district's philosophy influences how classes are grouped. Some districts attempt to tailor instruction to the needs of students who are similar in previous achievement. Such districts form separate class groups of high, medium, and low achievers. In other districts, each class group has a representative number of students from each achievement level. Some districts use a combination of the two methods, depending on the subject and grade level. Given all the philosophical and practical trades that administrators made in forming your classes, it is important for you to identify the achievement characteristics of each group.

Homogeneous and Heterogeneous Groups

Information about a group's previous achievement will help you establish expectations for group performance. As you observe students' progress, compare these expectations with the students' actual performance and then refine your judgments about their work.

In analyzing student characteristics, you should first determine whether a group is homogeneous or heterogeneous in achievement. A *homogeneous* group contains students who are similar in a given characteristic. For example, a group that is homogeneous in previous achievement contains students with similar histories of either high, average, or low achievement. A *heterogeneous* group contains students who are dissimilar in a given characteristic. A group that is heterogeneous in achievement contains students with a wide range of previous performances.

Homogeneous and *heterogeneous* are not absolute descriptors. They are relative terms, much like such adjectives as *tall* and *average*. We might ask, How tall is tall, how average is average, and how homogeneous is homogeneous? A class group with only high-achieving students is easily classified as homogeneous. When compared to the first group, a class containing average and above-average students would be heterogeneous. On the other hand, this class would be more homogeneous than a group whose scores ranged from very low to very high.

Throughout the school year, teachers continuously ask themselves, How are my students doing? You can usually answer this question by comparing students' current achievement with their previous work. For example, if you have been assigned a group that is heterogeneous in previous work, you may expect a wide range of scores on your first test. For a homogeneous group of high achievers, you might anticipate a narrow range of high test scores, and for a homogeneous group of low achievers, a narrow range of lower test scores.

After you administer your first test, you can compare the students' scores with your expectations. If the two fall within the same range, you can tentatively conclude that the group is performing normally. If the students did not perform as expected, note the incongruity, seek reasons, and wait for more information on subsequent tests.

Class Summary Forms

The availability of computers for producing current records has enabled many school districts to provide teachers with a summary of each newly formed group's previous achievement. These performance summaries usually contain the grades each student in the class received on semester exams and final course grades in the same or closely related courses. They also frequently contain students' standardized test scores in such basic subjects as mathematics and language. These forms will help you determine whether each group is heterogeneous or homogeneous in previous achievement.

Although interpreting grades previously earned on semester exams and in courses is rather straightforward, some information about interpreting the commonly reported standardized test scores will be useful. The standardized test scores included on the permanent record indicate how well the student performed relative to a comparable norm group of students. Note the particular standardized test scores used to indicate each student's performance levels. Undoubtedly, either stanine or percentile scores will be reported, and sometimes both scores are included in the record. If stanine scores are used, they can be interpreted as follows:

1. Stanines range from a low score of 1 to a high score of 9.
2. Stanines of 1, 2, and 3 reflect below-average achievement in the subject compared to the norm group.
3. Stanines 4, 5, and 6 reflect average-level achievement compared to the norm group.
4. Stanines 7, 8, and 9 reflect above-average achievement compared to the norm group.

If percentile scores are reported, they can be interpreted as follows:

1. Percentile scores range from a low score of 1 to a high score of 99.
2. Any given score indicates that the student scored better on the test than that percentage of students in the norm group. For example, a percentile score of 86 means that the student who earned this score surpassed 86 percent of the students in the norm group.
3. Generally, percentile scores at 25 and below are considered to indicate below-average achievement compared to the norm group.
4. Percentile scores between 25 and 75 are considered to reflect average achievement.
5. Percentile scores at 75 and above are considered to signify above-average achievement compared to students in the norm group.

Using either the stanine or the percentile score, each student's performance can be classified as below average, average, or above average in the basic skills measured by the test.

Table 2.3 contains two abbreviated summary forms that a science teacher might have developed for two classes. A complete form would include data for many more students. In addition to science grades, the teacher summarized the students' English and math grades from the previous year, their most recent standardized test scores, and their grades on the previous year's semester exams in science.

Describing Class Groups

Given a summary form for a group of students, you are ready to interpret the information and describe the class. You will want to determine whether the class is heterogeneous or homogeneous, and if homogeneous, whether it is above average, average, or below average in previous achievement. You can then use this information to establish your initial expectations for the group's performance. Differences in assigned groups will influence how you analyze instructional goals, plan lessons, and write test items.

In analyzing a class group, consider their performance levels in each category of data, such as previous grades, standardized test scores, and semester exam scores. Then, with their performance within a category described, compare their performance

TABLE 2.3

Class Summary Forms

	Group I							
	Previous Grades			Standardized Achievement Test Stanine Scores[a]			Districtwide Semester Sci. Exams	
Students	*Eng.*	*Math*	*Sci.*	*Lang. Mech.*	*Read.*	*Math*	*S1[b]*	*S2*
Abrams	C	C	C	5	5	6	C	C
Brown	C	C	C	5	4	5	C	C
Crown	C	B	C	6	5	6	C	B
Davis	C	C	C	5	5	5	C	C
Evans	B	B	B	6	6	7	C	B
Flynn	C	B	C	6	6	6	B	C
Good	C	C	B	5	5	5	C	C
Hayes	B	C	C	5	6	5	C	C
Jones	C	C	C	4	5	5	C	D
Kelly	D	C	D	4	4	4	D	C

	Group II							
	Previous Grades			Standardized Achievement Test Stanine Scores[a]			Districtwide Semester Sci. Exams	
Students	*Eng.*	*Math*	*Sci.*	*Lang. Mech.*	*Read.*	*Math*	*S1[b]*	*S2*
Allen	A	B	B	9	9	7	B	A
Boyd	C	B	C	6	6	7	B	C
Carter	C	C	C	4	5	5	C	C
Doyle	A	A	A	9	9	9	A	A
Egan	B	A	B	6	7	8	B	B
Fowler	C	C	B	6	6	6	C	B
Graham	B	B	C	7	6	7	B	C
Howe	D	D	C	3	3	4	D	C
Johnson	F	D	D	2	3	3	F	D
Keller	C	B	B	7	7	6	B	B

[a]Stanine scores range from 1 to 9. Compared to norm group:
  Scores 1, 2, and 3 indicate below-average achievement.
  Scores 4, 5, and 6 indicate average achievement.
  Scores 7, 8, and 9 indicate above-average achievement.

[b]S1 = Semester one of previous year; S2 = Semester two of previous year.

across categories to determine whether the information across categories is similar or incongruent. If the performance levels across all categories indicate the same range of performance, then you can be relatively sure you have an accurate description of the class. However, if you note incongruent performance across categories, consider this in establishing your initial expectations.

Consider how a science teacher might interpret the data in Table 2.3. The first clue about Group I's makeup comes from their grades in English, math, and science. Most students earned grades of C, along with an occasional B and D. This similarity of performance suggests a homogeneous, average group. The group's standardized test (stanine) scores range from 6 to 4 in language and reading, and all but one score in mathematics fall into the average range. Semester exam grades in science also indicate a homogeneous group of average performance. All three categories of performance reflect the same range of achievement for the group; thus, a teacher looking at these data may reasonably expect Group I to be a homogeneous class that will continue to achieve at an average level.

The data for Group II, however, indicate a different pattern of previous achievement. Grades range from A to F, stanine scores range from 9 to 2, and semester exam grades range from A to F. All three categories of performance reflect consistent, heterogeneous achievement for the group. The teacher might thus anticipate a wide range of achievement from this class group.

Unfortunately, in some school districts, the teacher is given only a list of students' names for each new class. It is very difficult to begin planning for a group without any information about the students' achievement characteristics. Should you find yourself in this situation, request that the school provide the necessary information. If your request is not honored, review your students' permanent records to obtain the background information. At a minimum, summarize the standardized achievement test scores in language and mathematics to determine whether the group is homogeneous or heterogeneous in these basic skills. Once you have decided on the information you want, find out where and how it is recorded on one student's record. Using this record as an example, you can design a form that will help you summarize and interpret the rest of your data.

In interpreting students' records, be careful not to develop inflexible expectations for the group. Previous performance is not a sure indicator of how individuals will perform in a new situation. A year's maturation, a new group of students, and a new teacher are all factors that can affect individual performances. In turn, these changes can produce different results for a portion, if not for all, of the class.

Accommodating Students' Special Needs

Classrooms today have very diverse groups of students, and many of the students have special needs that may affect your assessment program. When examining students' permanent records for previous achievement data, you should also seek information about students' physical and psychological conditions as well as their home language, since these factors may influence their test-taking behaviors. Physical conditions such as dyslexia as well as hearing, sight, psychomotor, or speech impairments must be accommodated for both paper-and-pencil and performance tests. Psychological conditions may also influence students' behavior during tests, such as attention-deficit hyperactivity disorder (ADHD) and extreme performance anxiety. Students who do not speak or read English well must be accommodated, as well, during assessments if they are to succeed.

Conditions that require accommodation during assessments are typically noted in students' permanent records, and you should plan ahead to accommodate your students with special needs as you design your tests and administration procedures. If you are unfamiliar with particular conditions of your students and unsure about how to accommodate them, schedule appointments with resource persons to learn more about tailoring testing strategies for unique situations. People who can help you plan appropriate procedures for your students with special needs include parents, previous teachers, the school psychologist and counselors, the school nurse, English-as-a-second-language (ESOL) specialists, and special education teachers who may have experience working with similar students. A conference with the student may also provide you with ideas and strategies for designing appropriate assessments and procedures. General strategies for accommodating students with special assessment needs are presented in Chapter 13.

■ Computer Technology

At the beginning of a school term, create a computer-based list of students, often called a *class roster,* for your class or classes. A class roster includes students' names, identification numbers, telephone numbers, e-mail addresses, grading codes, and special comments. In addition to the identification information, the class roster includes spaces for students' test scores.

Why should you create a class roster? The class roster will enable you to record automatically your students' scores on each examination, to create quickly interim or midterm reports of individual students' progress for parents, and to determine rapidly either students' grades or the particular instructional goals they have mastered, partially mastered, or not mastered during a term. Performing these tasks for each student without a computer requires many hours of work. With a computer, recording, grading, and reporting can be accomplished in a fraction of the time required to perform these tasks by hand.

If you choose to use commercially available gradebook programs, there are three ways to enter new student information into your class roster. First, you can have your students mark the information about themselves on computer-readable scan sheets, and then have the computer read the information directly into the program. Second, using a computer keyboard, you can type the necessary information into the class roster yourself. Third, you can enter data into the roster from a computer disk. Many schools today provide teachers with computer files that list pertinent information about new students in each of their classes. Once your roster is created for a class, you may enter new students or delete students who have dropped your class at any time during a grading term.

Figure 2.4 contains a sample class roster for a new group of students. The top of the form identifies the class, the time and days the class meets, the teacher's name,

FIGURE 2.4

A Sample Student Roster

Course: 701
Course: AM HISTORY
Day/Time: M-F 10:00

Instructor: Karen Hauser
Term/Year: Spring 01

28 students in this roster

	ID#	Student Name	Phone	Comments
1	432-34-3233	Augustine, Katy	813 974 3220	
2	544-25-6564	Bailey, Brooke	813 988 9209	Special Diet
3	436-26-7783	Carey, Edward	813 968 9592	
4	246-35-7811	Cromer, Cindy	813 989 4255	Entered 10/30
5	590-22-5619	Deddens, Robert	813 974 3400	Sight impair
.				
.				
.				

the term and year, and the total number of students in the class. The first column contains the record number, the second includes the students' identification numbers, the third column lists the students in alphabetical order, the fourth contains the telephone numbers, and the last column includes any special comments the teacher wants to note for each student. This particular record is for seventh-grade American history with the assigned course number 701. The class meets Monday through Friday at 10:00 A.M. The teacher's name is Karen Hauser, the record is for spring term, 2001, and there are 28 students in the class. Examine the instructions for several commercial programs available either in your school district or on the Internet and choose one that best suits your needs. Many teachers create their own computer-based rosters and gradebooks using spreadsheet programs.

■ Summary

Two planning activities can help a teacher prepare for new classes. The first is to establish the instructional goals for a course, and the second is to describe the characteristics of assigned classes.

Instructional goals are general statements of intended learning outcomes that describe the behavior the student is to demonstrate and the content to be learned. Sources of instructional goals include the state's curriculum performance standards (available on the Internet), the school district's curriculum guides, professional associations' recommended lists of instructional goals and objectives, adopted instructional texts, and the teacher's or administrator's manual for required, standardized achievement tests. Compare the instructional goals in all these sources and add goals and objectives from state guides and standardized tests that are not found in the district's curriculum guide. You may then cluster the goals by topic, sequence them by logical order, and assign each goal to specific terms and semesters, depending on when students will be tested on each goal.

Knowing the previous achievement levels of a new class can help you set initial expectations for class performance, analyze instructional goals, develop and pace lessons, write test items, and interpret group performance.

Many school districts provide teachers with class summary forms that can be used to describe the characteristics of a new group. Using the data in these forms, you can determine whether each assigned group is homogeneous or heterogeneous in previous achievement. This determination will aid in planning instruction, designing tests, and interpreting students' performance. Be cautious in forming opinions about new class groups, however, and be willing to reinterpret students' progress depending on your own experiences with the group.

You should also seek information about your students' special needs that may require assessments and procedures tailored to their needs. Students who have special needs should be accommodated to give them fair opportunities to succeed.

Today, computers aid teachers in performing record-keeping tasks. At the beginning of the school year, you can create a computer-based student roster for each class that contains students' names and other information such as student identification numbers, telephone numbers, e-mail addresses, and special needs that require accommodations. With the roster, it is easy to manage students' mastery records and to produce interim and term summary reports of achievement for individual students and class groups.

■ PRACTICE EXERCISES

I. Identifying Instructional Goals
   A. Who usually decides what skills will be taught in a given subject and grade level?
   B. List the types of people usually included on a school district's curriculum team.
   C. List potential resources you can use to identify the instructional goals for a course.
   D. List three reasons for matching district curriculum guides with state guides, goals and objectives for standardized tests, and adopted textbooks.

II. Identifying Elements of an Instructional Goal
   A. Name the two parts of an instructional goal and describe the function of each part.
   B. Identify the behavior and content in the following instructional goals by underlining the behavior with two lines and the content with one line.
   1. Name synonyms for given words.
   2. Name antonyms for given words.
   3. Alphabetize any given list of words.
   4. Retell a story in own words.
   5. Recite a paragraph verbatim.
   6. Add three-digit numbers with regrouping.
   7. Solve story problems using addition.
   8. Name the capital city for each state.

C. Analyze the following instructional goals and revise those that need clarification or improvement. (There is no one correct way to revise these goals. Revised goals should include both observable behavior and content.)
   1. Understands currency of different denominations.
   2. Punctuate.
   3. Identify one-half, one-third, and one-fourth of a given area.
   4. Understand how to measure the length, width, and height of a given object.
   5. Identify the main idea in a paragraph.
   6. The mean and median.

III. Determining Congruence among Goals from Different Sources
   Column A lists six mathematics goals taken from district curriculum guides. Column B lists mathematics goals from state curriculum guides. Although the state goals are worded differently, some match the goals in the district guides. Indicate matching goals by placing the letter of the state goal in the space preceding the number of the district goal.

	Column A	*Column B*
_____	**1.** Determine equivalent amounts of money.	a. Given a fraction, identify an equal decimal number.
_____	**2.** Write fractions as decimal numbers.	b. Determine the correct change for a given purchase.
_____	**3.** Calculate the lowest form of given fractions.	c. Multiply mixed fractions.
_____	**4.** Add fractions.	d. Equate coins and dollar bills of different denominations.
_____	**5.** Subtract fractions.	e. Reduce fractions.
_____	**6.** Use multiplication to solve mixed-fraction problems.	f. Select the money required to equal a given amount.

IV. Sequencing Goals
   A. List four strategies for sequencing instructional goals.
   B. Use the following procedure to cluster and sequence the set of instructional goals listed in Figure 2.5:
      1. Divide the goals into three categories of similar goals and title each category.
      2. Write the names of the categories in the order you would present them to students.
      3. Sequence the goals within each category in the order you would present them to students.

V. Describing Groups
   A. List four factors that school administrators usually consider when they form class groups.
   B. Which of the four factors listed in item A (above) will have the most influence on teachers when they plan instruction and interpret student performance?
   C. What do the terms *heterogeneous* and *homogeneous* mean when applied to group achievement?
   D. List the four types of information that would help you determine if a class were heterogeneous or homogeneous in achievement.
   E. If you were designing a form to summarize a group's previous achievement, what would the rows and columns on your form indicate? Show how you might design your form.

FIGURE 2.5

Exercise for Sequencing Instructional Goals

Goals

1. Locate the subject of a simple sentence.
2. Select verbs to show future tense.
3. Match singular subjects with singular verbs.
4. Locate the predicate of a simple sentence.
5. Match plural subjects with plural verbs.
6. Select verbs to show present tense.
7. Identify simple sentences.
8. Select verbs to show past tense.

Goal Categories (Topics)   Goal Sequence (by Number)

F. Table 2.4 presents achievement data for a newly formed English class. Use the information in the table to describe the class.
   1. Previous English grades
   2. Standardized achievement test in language skills
   3. Districtwide English exam
   4. Congruence among indicators
   5. Special assessment needs and possible accommodations.
G. If you were the teacher for the class in Table 2.4, how might you expect the group to perform during the coming year?

VI. **Enrichment**
   A. Obtain state and school district curriculum guides for the subject and grade level you teach or plan to teach. Review the types and sequencing of instructional goals and the scope of the subject the goals define.
   B. Ask teachers and administrators in a school how class groups are formed there.
   C. If you can obtain permission to review a district's class summary form for a newly formed class in your subject, analyze the data provided on the form, describe the group in terms of its achievement characteristics, and predict the general level of achievement you would expect for the class.
   D. Locate any students with special needs and talk with their teachers about assessment accommodations for them.

TABLE 2.4

Data Summary Form for an English Class

Students	Special Needs	Previous Year's English Grades	Standardized Achievement Test (Stanines[a])	Districtwide English Exam[b] (% Correct)
1. Allen, B.		C	3	72
2. Bonito, B.	Sight	C	2	60
3. Brown, L.		D	3	75
4. Carter, D.		C	3	78
5. Donovan, T.		D	1	43
6. Evans, R.		C	3	64
7. Fischer, A.	Sight	C	2	74
8. Garcia, J.	ESOL (4)	C	2	62
9. Good, T.		B	3	68
10. Graham, N.		B	3	76
11. Hanson, A.		C	3	75
12. Howe, R.		C	2	70
13. Kelley, N.		D	3	73
14. Miller, C.		C	2	64
15. Otto, J.		C	2	60
16. Potter, G.		D	1	53
17. Scott, H.		C	2	68
18. Smith, J.	ADHD	C	2	72
19. Taylor, B.		B	3	78
20. Washburn, M.		D	1	46

Average Score = 67%

Range = 78 − 43 = 35

[a]Stanine scores range from 1 to 9. Scores of 1, 2, and 3 are considered below average; 4, 5, and 6 average; and 7, 8, and 9 above average.

[b]The district has set a minimum passing score for the exam of 70 percent.

■ FEEDBACK

I. Identifying Instructional Goals

    A. State departments of education and school district curriculum teams write performance standards and curriculum guides that describe the instructional goals and objectives for a given subject and grade level. When guides are not provided by the state or district, teachers create their own.

    B. Curriculum teams usually include classroom teachers, curriculum supervisors, university-level content experts, and representatives from the community, business, and industry.

    C. Resources include district curriculum guides, state curriculum guides, assigned textbooks and other instructional resources, professional societies' recommendations for instructional goals, and teachers' or administrators' manuals for mandated standardized tests.

    D. Matching goals in a school district's curriculum guide with other sources will permit you to:

        1. Identify matching goals and objectives.

        2. Identify goals and objectives that are unique to the district.

        3. Identify important goals and objectives not found in the district guide.

II. Identifying Elements of an Instructional Goal

    A. Instructional goals contain the desired student behavior and the content of the topic that students will learn.

    B. Behavior and content are underlined with two lines and one line, respectively, in the following instructional goals:

        1. Name synonyms for given words.

        2. Name antonyms for given words.

        3. Alphabetize any given list of words.

        4. Retell a story in own words.

        5. Recite a paragraph verbatim.

        6. Add three-digit numbers with regrouping.

        7. Solve story problems using addition.

        8. Name the capital city for each state.

    C. The instructional goals may be clarified as follows:

        1. Equates coins and bills with their defined values.

        2. Some possible clarifications include:

            a. Selects the correct punctuation to end a sentence.

            b. Uses quotation marks, commas, and ending punctuation to punctuate direct quotations correctly.

            c. Punctuates the greeting and closing of a letter.

            d. Uses commas to separate items in a series.

        3. This goal includes both the behavior and content.

        4. Measures the length, width, and height of an object using metric and English scales.

        5. This goal includes both the behavior and content.

        6. Possible goals include:

            a. Define the mean and median of a set of scores.

            b. Calculate the mean and median of a set of scores.

            c. Interpret the mean and median of a set of scores.

            d. Plot the mean and median of a set of scores.

III. Determining Congruence among Goals from Different Sources

The district and state curriculum guides contain these matching goals:

1. d	**4.** no match
2. a	**5.** no match
3. e	**6.** c

IV. Sequencing Goals

    A. The four strategies for sequencing instructional goals include:

        1. Group goals according to topics.

        2. Once you have grouped goals by topic, identify any hierarchical relationships among the goals in each set. If a hierarchy of goals exists, place prerequisite goals first.

     3. If the goals show no hierarchical relationship within a set, sequence each set according to either their order in the textbook or the dates the standardized tests will be administered.

     4. Other logical factors, such as chronology, complexity, concreteness, familiarity, or motivation potential, can be used to sequence goals not organized using the preceding strategies.

B. The instructional goals listed in Figure 2.5 may be categorized and sequenced in this manner:

Goal Category	*Goal Sequence*
1. Identify complete sentences.	$1 \rightarrow 4 \rightarrow 7$
2. Match subjects and verbs.	$3 \rightarrow 5$
3. Select verb tense.*	$6 \rightarrow 8 \rightarrow 2$

     * The goals in this category are not hierarchically related and may be presented in any order.

V. Describing Groups

  A. Factors in class assignments include gender balance, racial or cultural balance, the scheduling of elective subjects, and previous achievement levels.

  B. The previous achievement levels of students will have the most influence on teachers.

  C. Heterogeneous groups contain students who vary or are dissimilar in achievement. Homogeneous groups contain students who are similar in achievement.

  D. You might want to collect:

     1. Previously earned grades in the same subject.

     2. Previously earned grades in language and math skills if these subjects are important for the subject to be taught.

     3. The most recent standardized test scores.

     4. Grades on previous semester exams in the same subject.

  E. Your form should be tailored to the types of information you decide to collect. Create a row for each student in the group and a column for each type of information you plan to record.

  F. The information in Table 2.4 shows that:

     1. Students' grades ranged from *D* to *B*, with most students receiving *C*'s; 5 students received *D*'s; 12 students *C*'s, and 3 students *B*'s. Based on grades alone, the group appears to be relatively homogeneous and average in achievement.

     2. Students' scores on the standardized achievement test in language ranged from 1 to 3; 9 students received a score of 3, 8 received a score of 2, and 3 a score of 1. Their performance was homogeneous and below average.

     3. Students' scores on the districtwide English exam were low. The average score earned by the class was 67 percent; the scores ranged from 43 to 78 percent. Half the students passed the exam at a relatively low level, and half failed.

     4. The three indicators of performance are relatively congruent, although the assigned grades appear to be somewhat higher than would be predicted by the test scores.

     This information should lead you to conclude that the group is relatively homogeneous and below average in previous English achievement.

     5. Two students in the class have sight impairments noted. The teacher will need to determine whether large-print tests, individualized oral test administration, or another form of accommodation will be necessary. J. Garcia, the level-4 ESOL student, may need to have a Spanish-English dictionary and additional time for her exams. Her

English may be better this year, and she should be assessed for possible reassignment to an above-average achievement class. J. Smith, the ADHD student, may require a quiet environment, more direction, or more time for completing assessments.

G. You might expect the group's test performances to be limited in range and toward the low end of the scale.

SUGGESTED READINGS

Darling-Hammond, L. (1997). *The right to learn: A blueprint for creating schools that work.* San Francisco: Jossey-Bass.

Dick, W., Carey, L. M., & Carey, J. O. (2001). The systematic design of instruction (5th ed., pp. 15–31, 88–114). New York: Addison-Wesley Longman.

Lambert, N. M., & McCombs, B. L. (Eds.). (1998). *How students learn: Reforming schools through learner-centered education.* Washington, DC: American Psychological Association.

Nitko, A. J. (1996). *Educational assessment of students* (2nd ed.). Columbus, OH: Merrill.

Polloway, E. A., & Patton, J. R. *Strategies for teaching learners with special needs* (6th ed.). Columbus, OH: Merrill.

Worthen, B. R., White, K. R., Fan, X., & Sudweeks, R. L. (1999). *Measurement and assessment in schools* (2nd ed.). New York: Addison-Wesley Longman.

Consult the following educational materials for further information on planning new classes:

The curriculum guides from a local school district for the grades and subjects you plan to teach.

The instructor's manual for the standardized test adopted for the school district in which you teach or plan to teach.

Sample permanent records for students in a local school district.

Hill, C. (2000). *Developing educational standards.* <http://putwest.boces.org/Standards.html#Section2>. This is an annotated and frequently updated list of Internet sites with K–12 educational standards and curriculum frameworks documents. The site is maintained by Charles Hill and the Putnam Valle Schools and the Wappingers Central School District in New York. This valuable website enables us to view what's new in learning standards across school disciplines and to compare and contrast curriculum standards across the United States that are produced by state education departments, subject area groups, U.S. government, professional societies, research centers and laboratories, state-focused groups, as well as other nations' standards groups.

The Joint Committee on Testing Practices. <http://www.ncme.org/related/jctp.ace>. The Joint Committee on Testing Practices (JCTP) provides "a means by which professional organizations and test publishers can work together to improve the use of tests in assessment and appraisal." JCTP groups have developed *The Code of Fair Testing Practices in Education, Test User Qualifications: A Data-Based Approach to Promoting Good Test Use and Responsible Test Use: Case Studies for Assessing Human Behavior, The ABC's of School Testing, Test Taker Rights and Responsibilities,* and is developing guidelines for testing persons with disabilities.

The Joint Committee on Fair Testing Practices. *Code of fair testing practices in education.* <http://www.ericae.net/code.txt>.

Analyzing Instructional Goals for Instruction and Tests

- Define the following six levels of learning commonly found in curriculum guides: knowledge, comprehension, application, analysis, synthesis, and evaluation.
- Given a list of instructional goals, classify each goal by the level of learning required.
- Define the following five types of learning commonly included in curriculum guides: intellectual skills, verbal information, cognitive strategies, motor skills, and attitudes.
- Given a list of instructional goals, classify each goal by the type of learning required.
- Given an instructional goal, identify the framework of subordinate skills required to perform the goal and sequence of skills.

Chapter 2 presented procedures for identifying and sequencing instructional goals and suggested methods for describing assigned groups of students. This chapter reviews goal analysis techniques that are essential prerequisites to effective instruction and evaluation. Goal analysis provides a foundation for developing and interpreting classroom achievement tests that should be directly related to the instructional goals for the course. Goal analysis identifies the type of learning involved, the subordinate skills required to achieve the goal, and the relationship among the subordinate skills. Such an analysis will help you relate the subordinate skills to your instruction and achievement tests. You can also use a goal framework to evaluate adopted textbooks and to select supplementary instructional materials. This chapter includes two sections. The first section summarizes the six levels of learning defined by Bloom, Madaus, and Hastings (1981) and the five types of learning described by Gagné (1985). The second section describes common instructional goal analysis procedures. If this is your first exposure to learning analysis, you may want to obtain the texts listed at the end of the chapter. They will provide more detailed information about the classification and analysis of instructional goals. Both theorists described in this analysis chapter ascribe to cognitive learning theories and related procedures. Analyzing state and district performance standards is better suited to cognitive-based methods. Constructivist theories, important in learner-centered assessment, will be addressed in the next chapter.

■ Levels of Learning

During the early 1980s, Bloom, Madaus, and Hastings (1981) identified six learning levels that educators often use in writing instructional goals and objectives. These levels help clarify the depth of skills students are to acquire and the kinds of responses that will demonstrate students' skills and knowledge. The six levels of learning appear in Table 3.1.

The first level, *knowledge,* involves the recall or recognition of information that has been learned. This level is sometimes referred to as rote memory or repetition. For example, a student who memorizes and repeats the statement, "In 1492, Columbus sailed the ocean blue," would be participating in a knowledge task. Other examples include memorizing and repeating poems or lines from a play; recalling dates and persons associated with important events; and recalling formulas, rules, procedures, facts, and definitions. No mental process other than remembering is involved.

TABLE 3.1

Six Levels of Learning Defined by Bloom, Madaus, and Hastings

Level of Learning	Definition
Knowledge	Recalling or recognizing specific elements in a subject area
Comprehension	*Translation:* putting a concept or message into different words or changing from one symbolic system to another
	Interpretation: seeing the relationships among the separate parts of a communication
	Extrapolation: going beyond a literal communication and making inferences about consequences
Application	Using rules, principles, procedures, generalizations, and formulas to solve problems
Analysis	Separating a unit into its component parts so the relationship among the parts is made clear
Synthesis	Arranging and combining separate elements to form a whole
Evaluation	Using criteria and standards to make judgments about the value of ideas, products, and procedures

The second level, *comprehension,* involves paraphrasing information or translating a given message into one's own words. Students participating in a comprehension task might explain the meaning of the sentence, "In 1492, Columbus sailed the ocean blue," with such statements as "Columbus began exploring in 1492" or "Columbus discovered America in 1492." Converting a story problem into a formula, converting a formula into words, inferring the main idea from a paragraph or story, and paraphrasing a definition are other comprehension tasks. Any translation, interpretation, or inference that demonstrates a student's understanding of a communication falls into this learning category.

At the *application* level, students solve problems by applying rules, principles, generalizations, or procedures. Using formulas to solve numerical problems, following rules of grammar and spelling, and constructing an object according to a plan are application tasks. At this level, students are expected to demonstrate their understanding of a rule, a principle, or a procedure by applying it to a task or problem.

The fourth level of learning, *analysis,* involves dividing a concept or unit into smaller parts so the parts and the relationship among them is clear. Dividing a story into the components of plot, characterization, and setting and then describing the relationship of these components is one example of analysis. Conducting a literature search for a term paper or a research project is another. In this chapter, you will learn how to divide an instructional goal into its subordinate skills and how to sequence the skills according to their relationship. These activities also represent the analysis level of learning.

At the fifth level, *synthesis,* the learner combines and integrates separate elements according to their relationship. This reassessment of components permits the learner to organize, summarize, and explain information and to make predictions. Assembling information for an essay or a position paper is one example of synthesis. The person writing the document must consider the ideas to be expressed, the interest and skills of the intended readers, the desired mood, and the appropriate writing style. The final product should reflect the writer's synthesis and interpretation of these elements. Original research also involves synthesis-level learning. The researcher analyzes the literature, identifies the variables, and synthesizes the relationships among the variables through statements of hypotheses. The procedures and instruments used to conduct the study constitute the researcher's interpretative summary of the context, the variables, and the relationships among the variables. The literature, the current hypotheses, the procedures used, and the research results are synthesized to make up the discussion and conclusions.

The sixth level of learning, *evaluation,* involves using criteria and standards to judge the quality and the value of ideas, products, or procedures. Criteria used to judge quality include such factors as accuracy, precision, economy, consistency, assumptions, evidence, and organization. In turn, these criteria become the basis for standards of work quality.

Teachers often expect students to judge the quality or worth of their own and others' work. Students can learn to evaluate many types of work, including their own essays, papers, artwork, and term projects; other people's articles, artwork, and term projects; speeches, plays, books, and movies; commercial products; events they have planned or sponsored; and instruction and tests.

Teachers use the six levels of learning to clarify and interpret the behavior specified in instructional goals and to write their own goals and objectives. Considering the level of learning ensures that the desired behavior in the goal or objective clearly communicates the level of learning intended. The levels can also be used to ensure that achievement tests include items that measure student performance relevant to instructional goals.

Types of Learning

Another learning theorist, Robert Gagné (1985), identified five types of learning that are reflected in most current state and district learning standards. The types of learning are intellectual skills, verbal information, cognitive strategies, motor skills, and attitudes. A summary and examples of each type of learning appear in Table 3.2. The following sections of the text explain intellectual skills and verbal information and describe methods you can use to identify subordinate skills for instructional goals of each type. Many goals used as examples reflect basic skills because the content is obvious. Focus thus can be placed on definitions and procedures used in goal analysis. After reading about each type of learning, you should be able to apply the procedures to goals in your own subject area.

Cognitive strategies are mentioned here and included in Table 3.2 to provide a complete summary of Gagné's types of learning; however, cognitive strategies are not described in detail because they are analyzed for instruction and testing in much the same way as are the higher levels of intellectual skills, with the notable exception being that the performance of cognitive strategies normally implies independent thinking and original solutions to novel problems. Motor skills and attitudes are also included here, but both are described in more detail in later chapters.

Intellectual Skills

When we use symbols to interact with our environment, we are applying intellectual skills (Gagné 1985). To understand or make sense of phenomena we encounter, we *differentiate* among objects and ideas, generalize our learning by *classifying,* and *solve problems* that perplex us. Intellectual skills also enable us to *explain* why things happen and to *predict* what will happen under given circumstances. Our use of intellectual skills produces visible results, but the mental processes we use are not observable. Intellectual skills are also referred to as *procedural knowledge* or learning how to do something. The procedures involved, however, are mental rather than physical. Intellectual skills include the reading, language, and arithmetic goals commonly referred to as *basic skills.* They thus make up a large portion of school learning.

Intellectual skills are divided into four subcategories that form a hierarchy of simple to complex skills. The most basic skill is *discrimination* learning, which serves as a foundation for the development of *concrete concepts.* In turn, concrete concepts permit the formation of *defined concepts,* and both types of concepts are required for the development of *rules.* The following paragraphs explain each of these subcategories.

TABLE 3.2

Gagné's Five Types of Learning

Type of Learning	Definition	Example
Intellectual Skills	The use of symbols to interact with the environment. Often called *procedural knowledge,* intellectual skills are used to interpret phenomena and solve problems. Subcategories are: 1. Discriminations—differentiating among objects as similar or different 2. Concrete concepts—using physical characteristics to classify objects into categories 3. Defined concepts—using a definition to classify objects, events, or conditions into categories 4. Rules—following a mental procedure to solve a problem or create a product 5. Principles—combining two or more concepts and describing the relationships among them to explain observed phenomena or to predict an outcome	1. Learning that rectangles are not the same as squares 2. Learning that an object is a square because it has four equal sides that are closed and form right angles 3. Learning that the founder of an organization is the person primarily responsible for the existence of the organization 4. Learning to calculate the circumference of a circle, punctuate sentences, write a short story 5. Explaining erosion or predicting the weather
Verbal Information	1. Associating objects, events, symbols, or conditions with their names 2. Remembering facts and repeating or recounting information	1. Learning that the symbol + means to add, the symbol 2 is two, a particular person is called John, and the word *fever* indicates an abnormally high body temperature 2. Recalling that John had a fever on Saturday, the words to a particular song, and that given authors wrote fiction
Cognitive Strategies	Managing one's own internal mental processes of learning, remembering, and thinking, often toward the development of unique solutions to new problems	1. Planning a group activity in such a way that all group members feel they are making important contributions 2. Devising a strategy in chess to counter a novel sequence of moves 3. Inventing a mnemonic to help remember new terms for a biology exam 4. Applying physical principles of inertia to explain patterns of social change

(continued)

TABLE 3.2	Continued	
Type of Learning	**Definition**	**Example**
Motor Skills	Physical procedures that require movement, precision, and timing, and that include simultaneous or sequential steps. Learning complex motor skills requires both knowledge of the steps and practice.	Playing the piano, riding a bicycle, operating machinery and equipment, tying knots and buttoning buttons, sewing, and painting
Attitudes	Mental states that govern our choices and behavior. An attitude has three main elements: 1. Affective—a person's positive or negative feelings toward something 2. Behavioral—the way a person acts or behaves 3. Cognitive—knowing about or how to do something. This component may include intellectual skills, verbal information, and motor skills. It usually includes information about cultural expectations, rewards, and consequences for behaving in a prescribed manner	Respecting the property of others 1. Having a positive feeling about oneself and other people who show respect for the property of others 2. Obtaining permission to use another's property; exercising care and following directions when using borrowed property; returning property undamaged and quickly 3. Learning expectations for behavior with borrowed property; learning the rewards of and consequences for acceptable and unacceptable behavior; and learning how to use the borrowed property correctly

Discrimination   In discrimination learning, a student compares objects on the basis of their physical properties. At its simplest level, discrimination is the ability to recognize that two objects are the same or different. For example, a child learning to tell the difference between nickels and dimes must use the physical characteristics of the coins to determine whether they are the same or different. Being able to tell the difference between letters of the alphabet and between numbers are other examples of discrimination learning.

Concepts   Two types of concepts make up this category: concrete concepts and defined concepts. A *concrete concept* refers to objects whose physical properties permit us to recognize, classify, and generalize. Learning a concrete concept involves distinguishing the physical characteristics that make an object a member of a class. For example, children learn to classify neighborhood animals as dogs by first learning to recognize the distinguishing characteristics of dogs. Once they recognize these unique characteristics, they can correctly classify a dog when they see one. They learn to distinguish bottles, boxes, cans, and numerous other objects by their physical properties.

A *defined concept* includes more than physical properties in its definition. It may have physical characteristics as a component, but the definition will also describe a relationship between or among objects. For example, *teacher* and *father* are defined concepts. We cannot classify people as teachers or fathers if we know only their physical characteristics. We also need to know what they do and how they relate to other people. To determine whether someone fits into the category of teacher or father, we must know how these terms are defined.

Vase is another example of a defined concept. We can define a vase as an object that holds cut flowers or cut plants. This definition permits us to relate a vase to a class of objects (containers) and to discriminate cut flowers or cut plants from their growing counterparts. The word *holds* tells us what the vase does or is used for and thus describes the relationship between the objects. Using this definition, we can identify as vases all sorts of different containers, including tin cans, wine bottles, crystal containers, pitchers, and baskets. We can also discriminate between containers that are vases and those that are flower pots. For example, if we see a pitcher being used as a vase, we would not say to ourselves, "That is not a vase." Instead, we would probably think, "That is an interesting vase." We recognize the pitcher's change in function because it now matches our definition of vase.

Other examples of defined concepts include *leader, honesty, fairness, principle,* and *dangerous.* To classify examples of these concepts, a person must know how each concept is defined. Some definitions will be brief and straightforward; others will be complex statements of related features, uses, relationships, and characteristics. The clearer and more precise a definition, the more accurately a person will be able to classify examples of the concept.

Rules   *Rules* are propositions that govern our behavior toward stimuli and cause us to respond in a given or expected way. We follow rules to perform skills correctly (Gagné 1985). Language and mathematics are two examples of rule-governed skills. If we want to use language correctly, we must follow rules of spelling, sentence construction, punctuation, subject and verb agreement, capitalization, and so forth. The rules for addition enable us to add numbers correctly, regardless of their nature, quantity, and size.

A rule may be brief, as in "Capitalize proper nouns," or it may be a long procedure, like the ones needed to do long division and to calculate a standard deviation. Rules are composed of two or more concepts. For example, the rule, "Capitalize proper nouns," is made up of three concepts: capitalize, proper nouns, and nouns. Before students can follow this rule, they must learn all three concepts. They must be able to follow the rules for capitalizing words, for classifying words as nouns, and for classifying the subset of nouns called *proper nouns.* To classify nouns and proper nouns correctly, students must know how these concepts are defined. Once they know the concepts involved, they are ready to learn and apply the rule for capitalizing proper nouns.

Principles are rules used to explain and interpret phenomena and to predict what will happen in given circumstances. They explain why events happen by combining two or more concepts and their relationships. The relationships of the concepts may be causal (one concept causes another concept) or correlational (one concept is positively or negatively related to another). "Poor eating habits usually result in digestive problems" exemplifies a commonly accepted principle that has a causal relationship between the named concepts. "Cigarette smoking is positively related to various health disorders" is an example of a correlational principle. We use these principles to predict what will happen if someone consistently overeats, eats the wrong foods, or smokes cigarettes. When individuals who have poor eating habits or who smoke cigarettes develop health problems, we then explain their condition using the commonly believed principles. Like rules, principles may be brief and straightforward or they may be lengthy with many concepts and their relationships. For example, you might use a principle to explain how a group of students performed on a test or to predict how one would perform. The concepts included in your principle might be (1) student's ability, (2) student's motivation and effort, (3) the quality of the instruction provided, and (4) the quality of the test administered. The principle might be expressed as follows:

$$\text{High Test Achievement} = \text{High Student Ability} + \text{High Motivation and Effort} + \text{Quality Instruction} + \text{Quality Measure of Achievement}$$

With this principle in mind, you would explain observed high test achievement as resulting from or as caused by the presence of this combination of factors. If you believed these factors to be present before administering an achievement test, you would undoubtedly predict high achievement on the test.

Verbal Information

Gagné (1985) identified a second type of learning as verbal information. Verbal information involves learning names or labels, facts, and collections of information that are sometimes called *bodies of knowledge.* Unlike intellectual skills, which represent procedural knowledge, verbal information represents declarative knowledge. Much of what is taught in school is verbal information. When students learn to name the parts of the body, repeat historical facts, or memorize poems, they are learning verbal information.

Names and Labels   Learning the names for objects, events, ideas, and symbols involves consistently associating the name with a given object, event, idea, or symbol. For example, the symbol *9* is always called nine, the symbol + means to add, a particular teacher is Mr. Jones, the word *red* refers to a particular color, and $\overline{X}$ is the symbol for an average score. We often learn the name for an object at the same time as we learn its distinguishing characteristics. A person who learns the name for an object, however, may not be able to generalize the properties of the object and to recognize other examples of the same concept. Thus, to name or label something, a person must simply remember the name of a given object, event, idea, or symbol when it is encountered.

Facts   Verbal information also includes facts, such as knowing that a particular building is the library, that the library is the newest building in town, that it contains more books than any other library in the state, and that it is open from eight o'clock in the morning until nine o'clock at night.

Verbal information and intellectual skills appear to work in a symbiotic way. Verbal information helps us communicate our intellectual skills, and intellectual skills help us organize and structure our verbal information. Although verbal information appears to be a simpler form of knowledge than do intellectual skills, it is not necessarily subordinate. For example, students could more easily communicate or verbalize the concrete concept *boat* if they knew the name of a floating vehicle that carries cargo or people. At the same time, they do not have to know the name *boat* to classify examples. Likewise, they can learn that the name of a particular object is *boat* without being able to classify other examples of the concept.

■ Procedures for Analyzing Instructional Goals

Based on Bloom's (1956) definition, *analysis* is the intellectual process of separating a unit into its component parts so the relationship among the parts is made clear. In instructional goal analysis, the unit is the instructional goal, and the purpose for the analysis is to identify the information and tasks, often called *subordinate skills,* required to perform the goal. In addition, the subordinate skills should be sequenced to illustrate the relationships among them. Instructional goal analysis can be relatively complex, even for experts in a discipline; however, it can be made easier by using common analytical procedures.

There are a variety of analysis procedures that teachers can use to analyze instructional goals in their curriculum guides. Three of the most commonly employed procedures are the matrix diagram, tree diagram, and flowchart. No one of these procedures works best for every instructional goal within a discipline, and some teachers prefer to work with one strategy rather than another. The following sections describe each of these procedures.

The Matrix Diagram

The matrix diagram is a two-dimensional structure of rows, columns, and intersecting cells. The basic structure of the matrix diagram is illustrated in Figure 3.1. The columns, labeled A through D, can be used to analyze and sequence one dimension in the analysis. The rows, labeled I through IV, can be used to analyze and sequence a second dimension. The intersecting cells, labeled I.A through IV.D, can be used to note relationships between each row-by-column set. A matrix diagram can have any number of rows and cells, and the appropriate number is determined during the analysis process.

A Matrix Diagram

	A	B	C	D
I	I.A	I.B	I.C	I.D
II	II.A	II.B	II.C	II.D
III	III.A	III.B	III.C	III.D
IV	IV.A	IV.B	IV.C	IV.D

The Tree Diagram

The second analysis procedure is the tree diagram, and its structure is illustrated in Figure 3.2. The trunk on the far left side of the diagram (I) usually contains the behavior and content in the instructional goal. The branches in the second level (I.A and I.B) are typically used to name the key subordinate skills in the goal. The third level of branches (I.A.1 through I.B.2) is used to break down each of the key subordinate skills named in the second level. Each successive level is used to break down further the identified subordinate skills.

The Tree Diagram

The Flowchart

The third analysis procedure is the flowchart. Flowcharts are similar to tree diagrams but they differ in two key ways: orientation and flexibility. A tree diagram is oriented horizontally on the page, whereas the flowchart is organized vertically, with the instructional goal at the top of the page and the most basic subordinate skills at the bottom. The flowchart is more flexible than the tree diagram in that it can be constructed to illustrate single and simultaneous operations, decision points, and iterations. A flowchart diagram is illustrated in Figure 3.3.

The structure of the flowchart implies the type of instructional goal best suited to this analysis format: physical or mental procedures such as sports, operating equipment, performing mathematical operations, or solving problems (e.g., scientific method). The placement of tasks in the diagram, the shape of the boxes, and the direction of the arrows all communicate the relationships among the tasks. For example, A.1 and A.2 are hierarchically related to A in Figure 3.3. The hierarchical relationship is indicated by the vertical placement of the tasks and the upward direction of the arrow connecting the tasks. Tasks A and B are chronologically related, with A being performed before B. The chronological relationship is indicated by the horizontal placement of the tasks and the direction of the arrows. Tasks C and D occur simultaneously, and this is indicated by their vertical placement on parallel, horizontal lines. Task F is diamond shaped, and the diamond indicates a decision point in the procedure. If the decision is yes, then the performer advances to steps G, H, and I. If the decision is no, the performer takes a different path through steps J and K. The broken line connecting tasks I and A and the direction of the arrow indicates an iteration or return to the previous step.

An Example

The instructional goal, "Write a paragraph," is used to illustrate goal analysis using a matrix diagram, tree diagram, and flowchart. This particular goal was chosen for the

The Flowchart Goal Analysis Procedure

example because it appears in curriculum guides from primary grades through graduate school; thus, it can be used to exemplify the educational mandate or *continuous quality improvement*. It is also interdisciplinary since teachers, regardless of their subject area, are concerned with students' ability to express ideas within a discipline. In addition, students' progress on this goal can be assessed using both objective tests and alternative assessments. Finally, it is an example with which all teachers are familiar, regardless of whether their area of expertise is in physics, art, special education, or any of the myriad of specialties that comprise education. Analyzing instructional goals in an unfamiliar content area makes the analysis process more difficult than necessary, so the instructional goal of writing a paragraph is used in the examples that follow.

■ Using a Matrix Diagram to Analyze Intellectual Skills

The two-dimensional matrix analysis procedure is particularly useful for classroom teachers since instruction is comprised of both learning and content. One dimension can be used to analyze and sequence learning tasks, and the other can be used to identify and sequence the main concepts in any given domain. The intersecting learning-by-content cells can be used to note interrelationships between particular levels of learning and areas of content. The following steps can be used to analyze an instructional goal using a matrix analysis procedure:

1. Identify the levels of learning appropriate for the instructional goal, and sequence them in the columns from most basic (left) to most complex (right).
2. Identify the concepts (content) contained in the instructional goal, and sequence them in the rows.
3. Integrate the learning and content elements by noting particular relationships in the intersecting row-by-column cells.

Each of these steps is described in the following sections.

Analyze Levels of Learning

Since the instructional goal, write a paragraph, is an intellectual skill, the elements of an intellectual skill can be used to create the column headings in the matrix. Translating Bloom's and Gagné's categories into useful goal analysis categories requires some analysis and interpretation. The categories included and their sequence are a matter of professional judgment, and they are often modified to suit both a particular instructional goal and the teacher's "sense of sequence."

Both Bloom's and Gagné's categories of intellectual skills have a defined order from simple to complex, and the column headings should generally reflect this order.

Their categories are quite broad, however, and further analysis is usually required to create the most useful matrix. For example, Bloom's knowledge category and Gagné's concepts category can be further broken down using the basic informational questions, Who? What? Where? When? and Why? For the paragraph goal, the questions What? and Where? can be equated to the *physical characteristics* of a paragraph (concrete concepts). The question Why? can be equated to the *functional characteristics* of a paragraph (defined concepts), and How? can be equated to the *quality characteristics* of a paragraph (defined concepts). For other instructional goals, you might need different basic categories of information or concepts, and you should choose those that are, in your professional judgment, best suited to the goal you are analyzing.

Figure 3.4 contains two sample matrix diagrams with sequenced levels of learning for intellectual skill goals. The top matrix contains columns that are based on Bloom's categories. They are reconfigured, however, to suit better the task of analyzing instructional goals. Knowledge and comprehension are clustered together, and the categories of state/recall physical (A), functional (B), and quality (C) characteristics are included within these two categories. The application category is next and, following rules based on characteristic combinations, students are to discriminate between examples and nonexamples (D) of a concept. Column (E) is the evaluation of given examples, which requires both analysis and synthesis of the physical, functional, and quality characteristics for making judgments about the quality of a paragraph. The

FIGURE 3.4

Sample Column Headings Based on Bloom's and Gagné's Levels of Intellectual Skills

Bloom's Levels: Knowledge, Comprehension, Application, Analysis, Synthesis, Evaluation

	KNOWLEDGE AND COMPREHENSION			APPLICATION	ANALYSIS AND SYNTHESIS	
	A State/Recall Physical Characteristic	**B** State/Recall Functional Characteristic	**C** State/Recall Quality Characteristic	**D** Classify Examples & Nonexamples	**E** Evaluate Given Examples	**F** Produce Examples
CONCEPTS/ CONTENT						

Gagné's Levels of Intellectual Skills: Concrete and Defined Concepts, Rules, Principles

	CONCRETE CONCEPTS	DEFINED CONCEPTS		RULES		
	A State/Recall Physical Characteristic	**B** State/Recall Functional Characteristic	**C** State/Recall Quality Characteristic	**D** Classify Examples & Nonexamples	**E** Evaluate Given Examples	**F** Produce Examples
CONCEPTS/ CONTENT						

last column, (F), is also listed under analysis and synthesis since these skills are also required for the production of a paragraph.

The bottom matrix is based on Gagné's levels of intellectual skills. The first column (A) contains concrete concepts, or the physical characteristics of the concept to be learned. Information included in this column answers the questions, What does "it" look like? and Where is it located? Both the second and third columns contain defined concepts. The particular defined concepts considered appropriate for the production of a paragraph are the functional and quality characteristics. Functional characteristics answer the questions, What are "its" purposes? and Why is it important or needed? The quality characteristics category contains information about qualities and values beyond form and function. The three columns on the right (D, E, and F) are all under the rules heading since students must synthesize concrete and defined concepts into rules for classifying examples and nonexamples, evaluating given examples, and producing examples.

Notice the double line between columns C and D in both sample matrices. This line signals the difference between recall-type tasks and higher-order tasks that require intellectual processing such as analysis and synthesis. Notice also that evaluation is located before production in both matrices. This is due to the fact that teachers want students to recognize the quality characteristics of paragraphs and use them in evaluating given paragraphs as practice for integrating them into their plans for producing original paragraphs.

Some teachers prefer using Bloom's categories for analyzing instructional goals, whereas others are more successful using Gagné's categories. In your work, use the system you find most comfortable. Further, you should not hesitate to alter the content or order of the categories for given instructional goals. These categories are to be used as guides, and they can be tailored to fit a particular goal or group of students.

Analyze Content

The second dimension in the matrix is content, and main areas of content are placed in the row headings. The procedure for identifying the row headings is to analyze the intellectual skill instructional goal in order to identify its concepts, rules, or principles. The steps in analyzing the goal for the matrix rows are the following:

1. State (or locate) the rule for a paragraph.
2. Underline the key concepts in the rule.
3. Determine the relationship among the key concepts.
4. Sequence the concepts based on the identified relationships.

Rule and Key Concepts   The rule for writing a paragraph with key concepts underlined could be stated as follows:

A <u>paragraph</u> is a series of sentences on one topic. It typically contains a <u>topic sentence, supporting sentences,</u> and a <u>concluding sentence.</u> The first sentence of a paragraph is usually indented.

The concepts in the paragraph rule that are not underlined describe either physical or functional characteristics of a paragraph, and they can be addressed during the analysis of the key concepts.

Relationship   The next step in the analysis process is to determine the relationships among the key concepts selected. In this example, topic sentences, supporting sentences, and concluding sentences all name types of sentences contained in paragraphs. Further, they typically have a chronological relationship with topic sentences placed first, supporting sentences placed in the center, and concluding sentences located at the end of the paragraph.

Sequence   The final step is to sequence the key concepts in the matrix rows based on their identified relationships. Among the three types of sentences, they would be placed in the rows from top to bottom based on their natural sequence. The teacher has some leeway, however, in whether to place the concept paragraph first or last in the sequence. For this example, it is placed first in order to form a foundation for the three types of sentences contained in it. Figure 3.5 contains the matrix diagram with the levels of learning inserted in the column headings and the discipline-based content inserted in the row headings. The concept and rule labels have been omitted in the column headings for convenience.

Integrate Learning and Content

The third step in the analysis is to integrate the learning levels and content. You could list the major learning outcomes for the paragraph instructional unit by simply integrating

FIGURE 3.5

Sample Matrix Diagram for the Intellectual Skill "Write a Paragraph"

CONCEPTS/ CONTENT	A State/Recall Physical Characteristics of:	B State/Recall Functional Characteristics of:	C State/Recall Quality Characteristics of:	D Classify Examples and Nonexamples of:	E Evaluate Given Examples of:	F Produce Examples of:
I. Paragraph						
II. Topic Sentence						
III. Supporting Sentences						
IV. Concluding Sentences						

the row and column headings. For example, combining all the column headings with the first row heading in Figure 3.5 produces the following learning outcomes:

I.A   State/Recall the physical characteristics (appearance) of a paragraph
I.B   State/Recall the functional (purpose) characteristics of a paragraph
I.C   State/Recall the quality characteristics of a paragraph
I.D   Classify (or generalize to new material) examples and nonexamples of paragraphs
I.E   Evaluate given paragraphs
I.F   Produce paragraphs

Notice that learning outcome I.F is the instructional goal, "Write a paragraph." Combining all column headings with all row headings in the matrix (I.A through IV.F) automatically produces a comprehensive list of the general student learning outcomes (behavior and content) for the instructional unit on paragraphs. This is an important list of outcomes since it forms the foundation for the unit's objectives or item specifications, which will be discussed in a later chapter.

With the matrix diagram completed to this point, you have the foundation for analyzing the relationships between each row and column heading. Any relationships identified, that are judged reasonable for the target learners, can be paraphrased in the intersecting cells. During the integration process, teachers often find that some cells contain several interconnecting relationships while others are scant or blank. You may find that some of the cells are no more than a summary of other cells. You may also decide to add another column or row or to delete an existing one. These findings should not be disconcerting, however, since the matrix is simply a guide for the goal analysis.

Figure 3.6 contains the complete matrix diagram for the paragraph instructional goal. Notice that the cells I.C and I.E are left blank. They are blank because the paragraph quality characteristics are elaborated in cells II, III, and IV.C, and the evaluation skills are elaborated in cells II, III, and IV.E. If you had chosen to repeat these quality characteristics and evaluation tasks in row I, it would not have been incorrect, just redundant. The particular criteria listed in column C, the particular judgments listed in column E, and the specific types of paragraphs listed in column F reflect the unique choices of the teacher. Other teachers might have stressed different types of paragraphs to be written or emphasized different criteria.

■ Using a Tree Diagram to Analyze Intellectual Skills

Similar to the matrix analysis procedure, the product resulting from the tree diagram analysis should be a list of the subordinate tasks required to perform the instructional goal. The task statements should contain both the behavior (learning) and the content.

The tree diagram procedure is somewhat more difficult for teachers to use because it provides less guidance during the analysis process. Without guidance, teachers are tempted to include prerequisite skills, such as writing a complete sentence or

FIGURE 3.6

FIGURE 3.6

Sample Matrix Diagram Analysis for the Instructional Goal "Write a Paragraph"

CONCEPTS/ CONTENT	A State/Recall Physical Characteristics	B State/Recall Functional Characteristics	C State/Recall Quality Characteristics	D Classify Examples and Nonexamples	E Evaluate Given Examples	F Produce Examples
I. Paragraph	Series of sentences Indented	Express ideas on one topic		Correct vs. not indented Many topics		Time Series Feelings Procedure Description
II. Topic Sentence	Typically first Indented	Introduce topic	Relevance Scope Interest	Topic vs. Supporting Concluding	Correct vs. flawed by: Relevance Scope Interest	Time Series Feelings Procedure Description
III. Supporting Sentences	Middle sentences	Elaborate topic	Relevance Sequence Transition	Supporting vs. Topic Concluding	Correct vs. flawed by: Relevance Sequence Transition	Time Series Feelings Procedure Description
IV. Concluding Sentences	Typically last	Conclude/ summarize topic	Transition Relevance Sums up Scope	Concluding vs. Topic Supporting	Correct vs. flawed by: Transition Relevance Conclusion Scope	Time Series Feelings Procedure Description

punctuating sentences. Although you could correctly argue that such tasks are subordinate to writing paragraphs, they are prerequisites that should be mastered before entering a unit of instruction on paragraph construction.

Some teachers find the tree diagram procedure more complex to use; others prefer it because of the freedom and lack of structure. Suggested steps for using a tree diagram are the following:

1. In the far left margin, and centered between the top and bottom of the diagram, write the instructional goal.
2. State clearly the main rule or principle that is required to perform the goal and underline the key concepts in the rule (or rules in the principle).
3. Analyze the relationships (e.g., hierarchical, chronological, importance, abstractness, etc.) among the key concepts and sequence them in the next column according to the identified relationships.
4. Transform each key concept into a learning task by adding an appropriate level of learning required to perform the task. Anchor the key learning tasks to the instructional goal using the tree branches.

5. Analyze each of the key learning tasks by asking yourself, What must a learner know or be able to do in order to perform this task? Subordinate tasks identified should be listed in the next column and connected using the tree structure.
6. Keep identifying subordinate skills for each level until you reach a level you believe all students in your target group have mastered.

A sample tree diagram is illustrated in Figure 3.7. Notice that the contents are similar to those included in the matrix diagram.

Using a Flowchart to Analyze Intellectual Skills

The flowchart procedure can also be used to analyze the paragraph instructional goal. As noted previously, one main difference between tree diagrams and flowcharts is the orientation of the diagram on the page and the use of arrows to indicate relationships among learning tasks. Figure 3.8 contains the paragraph instructional goal analyzed using a flowchart. The goal, write a paragraph (I), appears at the top of the chart, and the four key subordinate skills are to discriminate between paragraphs and nonparagraphs (I.A), write topic sentences (I.B), write supporting sentences (I.C), and write concluding sentences (I.D). The upward arrows from these four skills to the instructional goal indicate that they are hierarchically related to the goal. The relationship among these four tasks is chronological rather than hierarchical, and the structure of the flowchart illustrates their sequential nature. The remaining tasks in the flowchart are all hierarchically related to these four main subordinate skills, and the hierarchical nature is again illustrated using the upward arrows.

Notice the similarities between the subordinate skills identified using the matrix, tree diagram, and flowchart procedures. They are similar because the content of the goal and the intellectual skills required to perform the goal were integrated during the analysis process.

Analyzing Instructional Goals That Are Verbal Information

Students will learn and remember verbal information more easily if it is organized in a meaningful way and presented as interrelated or connected facts and names. Gagné has recommended creating frameworks (*schemata*), which cluster similar facts and information, and providing a meaningful context for learning labels and names. For example, instead of presenting important historical figures in chronological order, a teacher might group them according to the nature of their accomplishments. Notable writers, inventors, politicians, and explorers could all be presented in their turn. In introducing new vocabulary, a teacher could present groups of related words, such as those associated with food and eating, work, recreation, and travel. Two schemata for presenting verbal information related to geography and biology appear in Figure 3.9.

FIGURE 3.7

Sample Tree Diagram for the Instructional Goal "Write a Paragraph"

FIGURE 3.8

Sample Flowchart Analysis of the Instructional Goal "Write a Paragraph"

FIGURE 3.9

Matrix Diagram for Organizing Verbal Information Related to Geography and Biology

A. Geography: Countries Located in the Americas

MAIN CONTENT AREAS	A Name	B Capital city	C Size in sq. miles	D Location on map	E Population	F Climate
I. Countries in North America	I.A	I.B	I.C	I.D	I.E	I.F
II. Countries in Central America	II.A	II.B	II.C	II.D	II.E	II.F
III. Countries in South America	III.A	III.B	III.C	III.D	III.E	III.F

B. Biology: Human Body System

MAIN CONTENT AREAS	A Name/Recall Physical Characteristics	B Name/Recall Functional Characteristics	C Name Location of System in Body
I. Circulatory	I.A	I.B	I.C
II. Respiratory	II.A	II.B	II.C
III. Digestive	III.A	III.B	III.C
IV. Nervous	IV.A	IV.B	IV.C
V. Muscular	V.A	V.B	V.C
VI. Skeletal	VI.A	VI.B	VI.C

Each diagram separates information into categories, and columns and rows provide space for related information and examples.

Although the goal analysis procedure is time consuming, it is a necessary prerequisite to writing item specifications or objectives, developing lesson plans, evaluating instructional materials, developing relevant tests, and diagnosing students' problems. If you have difficulty analyzing and sequencing subordinate skills for instructional goals, the skills probably have become automatic for you. This state of automatic performance enables you to perform efficiently with little conscious thought about what you are doing. Although automatic performance makes routine tasks easier, it also makes the analysis of subordinate skills for an instructional goal more difficult. New teachers often comment that they really had not understood their subject until they tried to teach it to someone else. This and similar comments indicate the automatic nature of the skills these teachers are trying to communicate. Before they can effectively convey these skills to other people, teachers must mentally relearn each skill by breaking it down into all of its component skills.

Personally, you may prefer either the flowchart, the tree diagram, or the matrix analysis method for analyzing the intellectual skill instructional goals in your curriculum guide. If you are using one method and experiencing difficulty with your analysis, try another. Procedurally oriented goals, such as those for performing long division, seem easier to analyze using the flowchart procedure, whereas creation-oriented goals, such as writing a sentence, paragraph, essay, or research report, seem easier to analyze using the matrix analysis method.

■ Computer Technology

Current computer-based, word-processing programs make the goal analysis process much easier to perform than prior paper-and-pencil methods. The matrix tables can be created using the table function. With the table feature, you can create the number of columns and rows that you need, and add or delete either as your framework develops. The row-by-column intersecting columns expand automatically to provide the space needed as you enter information. In addition, column widths can be expanded or reduced as needed.

Teachers who choose to use flowchart or tree diagram analysis methods will enjoy the drawing features in word-processing programs. Especially useful are the text boxes, type resizing features, and the arrow and line capabilities. Another great feature is the ability to move text boxes, or enabling skills, around the screen as the teacher identifies yet another skill that should be inserted.

Possibly the best feature for both matrix and flowchart production is the text editing and moving features. These features allow formative evaluation and refinement of one's designs both before and after instruction. It also promotes sharing of goal frameworks among teachers within a school and across a district. Many school districts currently have a website where teachers can post and share their goal frameworks. This teacher-to-teacher web-based sharing of materials can be expected to increase in the future.

■ Summary

Instructional goals link classroom instruction and assessments to state performance standards and school district curriculum guides. They provide a focus for instruction and describe the learning outcomes for units and lessons. To develop lessons and tests, you should first clarify each instructional goal for a course according to the level of learning (Bloom, Madaus, and Hastings 1981) and the types of learning involved (Gagné 1985). Using the Bloom, Madaus, and Hastings classification strategy, cognitive goals can be identified as being either knowledge, comprehension, application, analysis, synthesis, or evaluation. Knowledge is the most basic level, and evaluation is the most complex. Using the Gagné classification strategy, goals can be classified as intellectual skills, verbal information, cognitive strategies, motor skills, or attitudes.

Gagné suggests procedures for analyzing each instructional goal based on its classification. Intellectual skill goals that are rules or principles should be separated into their discrete concepts and the relationships among the concepts. Defined concepts can be separated into their subordinate concepts and the relationships among them. Concrete concepts are separated into the unique physical properties that define the class. Dividing each intellectual skill into its subordinate tasks and sequencing the tasks according to their relationship result in a learning hierarchy, or task analysis. These analyses can be performed using either a matrix, tree diagram, or flowchart.

Gagné makes the following suggestions for analyzing verbal information:

1. Names and labels should be placed in a meaningful context.
2. Facts should be organized into bodies of knowledge or schemata of related facts using tables that help clarify the relationships among the facts.

His suggestion for organizing names and labels so they are placed in a meaningful context would result in placing these tasks, when possible, on the task analyses beside or near the named concepts. This means that verbal information will appear on the frameworks for intellectual skills, cognitive strategies, motor skills, and attitudes.

■ PRACTICE EXERCISES

I. Levels of Learning

Match each task listed in Column A with the appropriate level of learning listed in Column B. You may refer to Table 3.1 for definitions of each term in Column B.

Column A	*Column B*
_____ **1.** Calculate the average score for a set of test scores.	a. Knowledge
_____ **2.** Break a rule or principle into its separate elements and describe the relationships among them.	b. Comprehension
	c. Application
	d. Analysis
	e. Synthesis
_____ **3.** Use specified criteria to judge the quality of a product.	f. Evaluation
_____ **4.** Use the relationships among a variety of elements to combine them into a whole.	
_____ **5.** Paraphrase a fact, a definition, or a procedure.	
_____ **6.** Recall the verbatim definitions for a given list of concepts.	
_____ **7.** Write the formula for calculating a standard deviation.	
_____ **8.** Write a technical report for a given target audience.	

II. Types of Learning

A. In your own words, define Gagné's five types of learning and write at least one instructional goal or behavioral objective from your content area that fits each type of learning: intellectual skills, verbal information, cognitive strategies, motor skills, and attitudes.

B. Read the following list of instructional goals in Column A and classify the type of learning each represents from Column B.

Column A

_____ **1.** Write a persuasive essay with a unique line of reasoning.

_____ **2.** Recite a short poem.

_____ **3.** Choose to work independently on school assignments.

_____ **4.** Name common traffic signs.

_____ **5.** Choose to be punctual.

_____ **6.** Bounce a ball.

_____ **7.** Name the capital city for each state.

_____ **8.** Write a paragraph containing a topic sentence, supporting facts, and a concluding sentence.

_____ **9.** Button a shirt.

_____ **10.** Alphabetize any given list of words.

_____ **11.** Select the correct coins to make any given amount of money up to 99 cents.

_____ **12.** Name all 50 states in the United States.

_____ **13.** Interpret a state map.

_____ **14.** Organize homework, projects, and study time to ensure adequate preparation for final exams.

Column B

a. Intellectual skills

b. Verbal information

c. Cognitive strategies

d. Motor skills

e. Attitudes

III. Instructional Goal Analysis

A. For the instructional goal, "Write compound sentences," perform the following:

1. Create an intellectual skills analysis matrix using column headings similar to those in Figure 3.4.

2. Determine the row headings you will need.

3. Analyze the goal by determining what information should be included in intersecting cells. Check your goal matrix with the one in Figure 3.10F in the Feedback section.

Note: Do not worry if your frameworks do not include enough detail or are different from those of other students. A sketchy framework is better than none at all, and your ability to analyze goals will improve with practice. Creating good frameworks takes time and experience. After developing and using a framework, you will want to make changes that reflect your classroom experiences with students.

    B. Verbal Information. Develop a table that includes information students will need to "Name common traffic signs." Your table should include sign colors, sign shapes, and sign names. (See Figure 3.11F for feedback.)

IV. Enrichment

    A. Choose an instructional goal for a subject you know well. Identify the analysis procedure for the type of goal you choose and develop a framework of the subordinate skills required to achieve the goal. Ask another person who is familiar with the subject to critique your work.

■ FEEDBACK

I. Levels of Learning

1.	c	**5.**	b
2.	d	**6.**	a
3.	f	**7.**	a
4.	e	**8.**	e

II. Types of Learning

    A. Definitions (If you are unsure about the appropriateness of your instructional goals or objectives, you may want to discuss your examples with classmates or with the professor.)

        Intellectual skills involve the use of symbols to interact with the environment. Intellectual skills are mental procedures used to interpret phenomena and solve problems. They include discrimination, concrete concepts, defined concepts, and rules.

        Verbal information, often called *declarative knowledge,* involves associating objects, symbols, events, or conditions with their names. It also includes remembering facts and repeating or recounting information.

        Cognitive strategies are the mental processes by which we control thinking and construct or choose novel solutions to problems.

        Motor skills are physical tasks that require movement, precision, and timing. They often take the form of physical procedures having a series of steps to be performed either simultaneously or in a prescribed sequence.

        Attitudes are mental states that govern our choices and behavior. Attitudes have three main components: affective, behavioral, and cognitive.

    B. Classification

1.	c	**5.**	e	**9.**	d	**13.**	a
2.	b	**6.**	d	**10.**	a	**14.**	c
3.	e	**7.**	b	**11.**	a		
4.	b	**8.**	a	**12.**	b		

III. Instructional Goal Analysis

    A. The steps in identifying the content are to: (1) state clearly the rule for compound sentences, (2) underline the key concepts in the rule, and (3) sequence these concepts from the least to most complex in the left column of the goal analysis matrix. The rule is: A *compound sentence* contains two *simple sentences* connected using a *comma* preceding a *coordinating conjunction.* The goal analysis matrix is in Figure 3.10F.

    B. The verbal information for naming common traffic signs is in Figure 3.11F.

FIGURE 3.10F

Goal Analysis Framework for the Intellectual Skill "Write a Compound Sentence" (Problem III.A)

MAIN CONTENT AREAS	RECALL			PERFORM		
	A Name/Recall Physical Characteristics	**B** Name/Recall Functional Characteristics	**C** Name/Recall Quality Characteristics	**D** Classify Examples and Nonexamples	**E** Evaluate Good vs. Poor Examples	**F** Produce Examples
I. Comma	Period with tail	Alert reader		Comma vs. 1. period 2. semicolon		Comma
	I.A	I.B	I.C	I.D	I.E	I.F
II. Simple Sentence	Subject, predicate	Communicate simply, clearly	Complete	Simple vs. 1. compound 2. complex	Complete vs. incomplete	Simple sentence
	II.A	II.B	II.C	II.D	II.E	II.F
III. Coordinating Conjunction	Word between two simple sentences	Combine two simple sentences	Imply relationship between two sentences	Conjunction vs. 1. subject 2. verb 3. comma	Match relationship vs. mismatch relationship	Best for given pair of sentences
	III.A	III.B	III.C	III.D	III.E	III.F
IV. Compound Sentence	Two simple sentences joined with comma, coordinating conjunction	Combine simple sentences to smooth message, reduce jerkiness	1. Two interrelated simple sentences (e.g., first introduces idea and second elaborates, explains qualifies, refutes) 2. When needed, proper noun of second sentence changed to pronoun 3. Relevant coordinating conjunction	1. Compound vs. a. simple b. complex c. simple with dual subjects d. simple with dual objects 2. Comma vs. no comma 3. Conjunction vs. no conjunction	1. Related vs. unrelated simple sentences 2. Proper nouns converted vs. unconverted 3. Coordinating conjunction relevant vs. irrelevant	1. Convert two simple to one compound 2. Elaborate given simple sentence into compound by adding second simple sentence
	IV.A	IV.B	IV.C	IV.D	IV.E	IV.F

FIGURE 3.11F

Analysis of the Instructional Goal "Name Common Traffic Signs"

Name of Sign	Shape of Sign	Colors of Sign
Stop	Octagon	Red with white
Yield	Triangle, tip down	
Do not enter	Circle within square	
Action prohibited		
Warning, road conditions	Diamond	Yellow with black
Warning, railroad	X within circle	
Warning, no passing	Triangle with tip pointing to right	
Warning, school zone	Triangle top, rectangle bottom	
Warning, construction	Diamond	Orange with black
Warning, maintenance		
Regulatory sign	Rectangle or square	White with black
Information sign		
Railroad crossing	Crossbuck	
Public recreation	Rectangle	Brown with white
Park signs		
Motorist service signs	Rectangle	Blue with white
Directional information	Rectangle	Green with white

■ **R U B R I C**

Rubric for Assessing Instructional Goal Frameworks

0	1	2	3	**A. Matrix Instructional Goal Framework**	**Comments**
				A. The concepts in my goal framework are:	
				1. Important key concepts for the instructional goal	
				2. Logically ordered	
				B. The levels of learning are:	
				3. Clearly identified	
				4. Appropriate for the named instructional goal	
				5. Logically ordered, simple to complex, left to right	
				C. The intersecting Concept × Learning Level cells contain paraphrased details that:	
				6. Are appropriate for the named class group	
				7. Guide teacher during development of instruction and tests	
0	1	2	3	**B. Flowchart/Tree Diagram Instructional Goal Framework**	**Comments**
				1. My instructional goal is included, clearly stated, and observable.	
				2. Main steps in the procedure for accomplishing the goal are included and logical.	
				3. Substeps for accomplishing each main step are included and logical.	
				4. Each enabling skill (step) includes both observable behavior and content.	
				5. Enabling skill codes clearly illustrate a logical teaching/learning progression.	
				6. Placement of enabling skills on the page and arrows illustrate a logical teaching/learning progression from simple to more complex skills.	
				7. The level of detail provides clear guidance for designing/developing tests.	

Note: 0 = None
1 = Needs Improvement (NI)
2 = OK
3 = Good

Shaded cells are not scored.

REFERENCES

Bloom, B. S. (1956). *Taxonomy of educational objectives: The classification of educational goals, Handbook I: Cognitive domain.* New York: David McKay.

Bloom, B. S., Madaus, G. F., & Hastings, J. T. (1981). *Evaluation to improve learning.* New York: McGraw-Hill.

Gagné, R. M. (1985). *The conditions of learning and theory of instruction.* New York: Holt, Rinehart and Winston.

SUGGESTED READINGS

American Psychological Association. (1997) *Learner-centered psychological principles: A framework for school redesign and reform.* Washington DC. <http://www.apa.org/org/ed/lcp.html>.

Bruning, R. H., Schraw, G. J., & Ronning, R. R. (1995). *Cognitive psychology and instruction* (2nd ed., pp. 155–179, 211–235). Englewood Cliffs, NJ: Prentice-Hall.

Dick, W., Carey, L. M., & Carey, J. O. (2001). The systematic design of instruction (5th ed.). New York: Addison-Wesley Longman.

Gagné, R. M., & Driscoll, M. P. (1988). *Essentials of learning for instruction.* Englewood Cliffs, NJ: Prentice-Hall.

Gallagher, J. D. (1998). *Classroom assessment for teachers (pp. 99–126). Columbus, OH: Merrill.*

Lynn, R. L., & Gronlund, N. E. (2000). *Measurement and assessment in teaching* (8th ed., pp. 51–72). Englewood Cliffs, NJ: Prentice-Hall.

McCombs, B. L., & Whisler, J. S. *The learner-centered classroom and school: Strategies for increasing student motivation and achievement.* San Francisco: Jossey-Bass.

Oosterhof, A. (1999). *Developing and using classroom assessments* (2nd ed., pp. 21–33). Columbus, OH: Merrill.

Thorndike, R. M. (1997). *Measurement and evaluation in psychology and education* (6th ed., pp. 488–492). Columbus, OH: Merrill.

Tombari, M., & Borich, G. (1999). *Authentic assessment in the classroom* (pp. 33–50). Columbus, OH: Merrill.

Worthen, B. R., White, K. R., Fan, X., & Sudweeks, R. L. (1999). *Measurement and assessment in schools* (2nd ed., pp. 188–203). New York: Addison-Wesley Longman.

Designing Test and Test Item Specifications to Help Ensure Validity and Reliability

O B J E C T I V E S

- Define *measurement, test, evaluation,* and *criterion-referenced test.*
- Define *test validity* and describe test design considerations that help ensure valid decisions based on test results.
- Define test *reliability* and describe test design considerations that help ensure reliable test results.
- Divide subordinate skills in the goal framework into prerequisite and enabling skills.
- Define *entry behaviors test, pretest, practice test,* and *posttest* and describe how each type of test provides information teachers need for their planning and evaluation decisions.
- Define *table of test specifications* and describe how such a table is developed and used to help ensure the validity and reliability of test scores.
- Develop a table of test specifications for an entry behaviors test, a pretest, a practice test, a unit posttest, and a comprehensive term examination.
- Convert subordinate skills into test item or task specifications (or objectives) by adding performance conditions and, when needed, criteria for acceptable performance.

■ Measurement, Tests, and Evaluation

Three terms frequently used in this text are *measurement, test,* and *evaluation.* Although these terms are related, there are important differences among them. The term *measurement* refers to quantifying or assigning a number to express the degree to which a characteristic is present. Some common characteristics measured for people include height, weight, and skill attainment. The number or measure used to express height is based on a scale of feet and inches; the measure for weight is expressed as pounds; and the measure of skill attainment is a score that reflects the number of items answered correctly or points earned on some type of achievement test. Using any of these measures, people can be ranked on scales that reflect the degree to which they possess the characteristic.

Measures of a characteristic are obtained using measuring instruments. A yardstick is the instrument used to obtain a measure of height; a weight scale is the instrument used to obtain a measure of weight; and an assigned set of tasks to be performed, called a test, is the instrument used to obtain a skill measure. The quality or stability of the instrument used to obtain a measure will influence the accuracy of the measure.

Evaluation is the procedure used to determine the quality of something. Decisions about quality require criteria or standards that can be applied to judge worth. Once you have a measure of some characteristic, you can compare the measure against established criteria or standards to determine whether it reflects an excellent, good, adequate, poor, or unacceptable level of the characteristic. Both the measures and the tests, or instruments, can be evaluated. For example, some criteria for evaluating a measure of height are based on group norms (e.g., he is quite tall compared to other boys his age); some on cultural expectations (e.g., he is too short to be considered for that role in the play); and others on health (e.g., her growth rate and height reflect physiological problems). Standards for judging a measure of weight are also based on group comparisons, cultural expectations, and health. Likewise, standards for evaluating a skill measure are based on group comparisons (e.g., above average, average, or below average compared to other people with similar experience and training) or on a level set to reflect high accomplishment of the skill itself (e.g., typing 60 words a minute with no mistakes).

Instruments used to obtain measures are also evaluated. One criterion for judging the quality of an instrument is the consistency with which it produces the same measure under the same conditions. For example, a weight scale that produced three different weight measures for the same person at 10-minute intervals would be an inadequate instrument, whereas one that indicated the same weight each time would be considered good. Likewise, a skill test that resulted in very different scores for the same person on the same day would be judged an inadequate test. This criterion is called *reliability of test scores*. The scores generated from teachers' tests should be reliable if they are to be useful.

A second criterion for evaluating a test or instrument is whether it actually measures the characteristic it is supposed to measure. A yardstick would be an inadequate instrument to measure weight, and a test focused on tennis rules would not provide an adequate measure of a student's ability to play the game. This criterion is often called *validity*. Are the scores produced by a particular test valid for the purpose of the test? Teachers' tests should produce scores that result in valid decisions about students and instructional quality. Other less important criteria used to evaluate a test include costs and practicality. Tests that consistently measure what they are supposed to measure, yet are either too expensive or too cumbersome for a given situation, would be judged inadequate for the circumstances.

Teachers use measures of student achievement to evaluate (1) students' progress throughout a term or year, (2) the quality of their tests, and (3) the quality of their instruction. Schools use measures of students' achievement, behavior, and attitudes to evaluate the quality of the curriculum and the overall program. Because measures of an individual's performance are the building blocks of evaluation, accurate evaluation at the classroom, school, and district levels cannot be accomplished without accurate measures. Likewise, accurate measures cannot be obtained without quality tests. This chapter presents methods you can use to design tests most likely to produce accurate measures of students' achievement.

Criterion-Referenced Tests

Chapter 3 described procedures you can use to analyze your instructional goals and identify subordinate skills for the goal frameworks. A goal framework of subordinate skills, sometimes called a *domain,* provides the foundation you need to design both your instruction and your classroom tests. Three names are generally used for tests based on the carefully identified and sequenced set of skills in a goal framework: *criterion-referenced tests, domain-referenced tests,* and *objective-referenced tests.* The set of skills in the framework is the criterion, or standard, used to judge students' progress on an instructional goal. The term *criterion-referenced test* simply means that the items on the test are referenced to or drawn from a carefully specified set of subordinate skills that make up the goal. On a *domain-referenced test,* the test items are referenced to or drawn from a carefully delineated domain of tasks. Thus, students' performance on such tests is referenced to the criterion set of skills or domain. For *objective-referenced tests,* the subordinate skills in the goal framework are converted to measurable item specifications (or objectives) before test construction.

Whether an objective-referenced test is also criterion referenced depends on the foundation for the objectives used. Objective-referenced tests based on a loosely connected set of objectives are not criterion-referenced tests. They do not become true criterion-referenced tests by simply specifying a cut-off score or criterion for passing or by selecting the number of items that must be answered correctly for each objective measured.

Four major factors need to be considered in the test design process. The first factor is to design tests most likely to yield valid results for the decisions you need to make. The second is to design tests most likely to provide reliable, or consistent, results. The third factor is the main purpose for the test, and the fourth is the type of test that best suits the prescribed purpose. This chapter describes each factor and how it influences design considerations. Decisions made during the design stage are recorded in matrices called *tables of test specifications.* These tables are used to record the sample of subordinate skills to be included on each test, the best item format to use for each skill selected, and the number of items to be selected for each skill. Procedures for developing tables of test specifications are described.

Validity and Test Design

The term *validity* refers to the appropriateness of inferences made from students' test results. If a test adequately measures the subordinate skills and goals it is intended to measure, the students' test scores should be valid for the inferences based on these scores. The tests you administer are more likely to result in valid decisions if you consider validity as you design the test. To help ensure that your tests provide valid measures of student progress, consider the following five questions during the design process.

1. *How well do the subordinate skills selected for the test represent the instructional goal framework?* Ensuring that the skills measured accurately reflect the goal framework or domain involves a particular form of validity called *content validity.* A goal framework usually includes subordinate skills that represent different, but related, content areas and different levels of skill. For example, the instructional goal on writing paragraphs includes skills related to four content areas: paragraphs, topic sentences, supporting sentences, and concluding sentences. Different levels of learning are also commonly found among the subordinate skills in a goal framework. Some subordinate skills require students to recall names, facts, characteristics, rules, or principles. Other skills require students to apply this information in order to classify, analyze, synthesize, solve, or create something. For example, both recall- and application-level skills are included in the goal on writing a paragraph. Students need to recall the rule for writing paragraphs and the rules for writing each type of sentence within a paragraph. They also need to be able to apply these rules and definitions for classifying the types of sentences, evaluating sentences, and writing paragraphs. In designing a test that will have good content validity, subordinate skills should be selected to represent each main content area and level of learning included in the goal framework. Inferences made about students' achievement of an instructional goal that are based on a test that is not representative of the instructional goal framework are likely to be invalid or incorrect.

2. *How will test results be used?* You are more likely to obtain valid test results if, during the design process, you consider the planning and evaluation decisions you need to make. Related to planning instruction, you may want to determine whether you will need to develop remedial instruction, whether you need to develop lessons for all the skills in the framework or only a subset of them, or whether you need to develop review or enrichment lessons for the unit. Evaluation decisions will be necessary regarding the appropriateness of the instructional goal for a given group of students, the quality of your lessons, or students' achievement in order to assign grades. Considering the use of test results during the design stage will help you select, for each test, the most appropriate skills from the goal framework.

3. *Which test item format will best measure achievement of each skill?* A variety of item formats can be selected, and some types measure the behaviors prescribed in subordinate skills better than other types. The more closely students' responses match the behavior specified in the task, the more likely their scores will validly reflect their achievement. Objective item formats that require students to select an answer from among a set of alternatives may be best for measuring student performance on some subordinate skills. Other skills in the goal framework may be measured best by requiring students to supply a missing word or complete a sentence. Still others may be measured best by essay questions, product development, or some type of active performance. In designing a test, the behavior specified in the subordinate skill should be considered carefully when selecting the most appropriate item.

4. *How many test items will be required to measure performance adequately on each subordinate skill?* Objectives that require students to recall names, facts, characteristics, or definitions usually require only one item to determine whether the student can recall the required information. However, if students are to apply this information to classify examples or solve a problem, then several items will be needed for them to demonstrate their application skills. For example, only one item would be needed to test whether students can recall the definition for a common noun; several items would be needed to determine whether students can discriminate consistently between common nouns and other parts of speech. When designing tests, you should consider the complexity of each objective selected and then prescribe an adequate number of items to measure the objective.

5. *When and how will the test be administered?* Considering the purpose for the test will help you design a test schedule and administration procedure most likely to result in scores that are valid for the decisions to be made. Tests used for formative evaluation and planning decisions, such as whether instruction on prior, hierarchically related goals are needed for a group and which skills need to be emphasized during a unit, should be scheduled and administered before planning lessons for the unit. These preliminary tests need not be announced in advance because students are not expected to prepare for them; they can be administered informally during a class session or as a homework exercise.

Other formative evaluation tests are used to provide students with an opportunity to practice skills after instruction, to evaluate the quality of lessons, or to determine whether review or enrichment is needed and these tests should be administered following initial instruction. They can be administered informally as a class exercise, as a small group activity, or as individual tests. They also can be administered during a class period or as a homework assignment. Summative evaluation tests used to evaluate students' overall achievement and grade their progress should be administered following all instruction and review, and they should be announced in advance to enable students to prepare for them. They also should be administered during a class period, whenever possible, to ensure that each student's score reflects only his or her efforts. Tests used for the purpose of assigning students' grades that are administered unannounced, before the conclusion of instruction, or in an unsupervised setting may not accurately reflect students' achievement. Thus, decisions based on these scores may be invalid.

■ Reliability and Test Design

Reliability refers to the consistency or stability of the test scores obtained. For example, if a student received a low score on a test taken in the morning, the teacher should be able to expect similar results if the student were to take the same or an equivalent test in the afternoon. Similar test scores would suggest that the test was reliable. If the student received a substantially higher or lower score the second time, the test would be unreliable. Valid inferences about students' performance cannot be made when test scores are unreliable.

Because students' test performances are influenced by many factors—including variations in memory, motivation, attention, and fatigue—absolute reliability (i.e., obtaining the exact same score twice) is unlikely. Test scores should be stable enough, however, to permit accurate judgments about students' mastery of the objectives.

Although you will not be able to eliminate fluctuations in test scores, you can help ensure that your tests will produce the most reliable scores possible. When designing a test, follow these five steps.

1. *Select a representative sample of subordinate skills from the goal framework.* The better your skills represent the entire framework, the more reliable the scores will be. For example, a test covering a goal framework that has 10 skills ranging from easy to difficult should include test items that reflect each skill. If two different forms of the test are to be used, the second form should also contain items for every skill. The two test forms should produce relatively consistent scores because both cover the entire framework of knowledge and skills. On the other hand, one test containing items for the 5 easiest skills and a second test reflecting the 5 most difficult skills would produce very different scores. If time is available to measure only a subset of skills from the framework, then they should be selected to represent both the easy and difficult skills.

2. *Select enough items to represent adequately the skills required in each subordinate skill.* Enough test items should be included for a skill to cover all the possible situations implied in that skill. For example, if students are to select common nouns from among a list of words that includes nouns and other parts of speech, enough items should be prescribed to include all categories of nouns that students will encounter. One or two items that relate to only one category, such as persons, would not adequately measure students' mastery of the skill. A test that included only one or two items in one category of nouns and one that included several items from all four categories are likely to produce very different scores.

3. *Select item formats that reduce the likelihood of guessing.* Students who do not know an answer may guess. If they guess correctly on one form of a test and incorrectly on the second, their scores will not be stable. When guessing is possible, the reliability of test scores will be lower than if guessing were not possible.

4. *Prescribe only the number of items that students can complete in the time available.* Test scores will be more reliable when students are given enough time to complete the test. Students' emotional states during a test can influence their performance, and hurrying causes some students to become careless. To increase the reliability of scores, adjust the length of the test to match the time available for its completion.

5. *Determine ways to maintain positive student attitudes toward testing.* Students' attitudes about a test can affect their motivation and effort, and test planning should identify ways to ensure positive attitudes. For example, you should plan to inform students of a test's date and time, the purpose for the test, and how the results will be used. Never plan to use tests as a punishment or as a substitute for unplanned lessons. Such misuses produce poor motivation and may result in unreliable scores.

Types of Subordinate Skills

The subordinate skills in the instructional goal framework can be divided into two categories: skills students should have mastered during a previous unit or year and skills that should be the primary focus for current instruction. Subordinate skills in the goal framework that should have been previously mastered are commonly called *prerequisite skills.* Subordinate skills that constitute the primary focus for current instruction are called *enabling skills.*

Before beginning to design tests for a unit of instruction, divide the subordinate skills in the goal framework into prerequisite and enabling skills. This division is based on your best judgment about whether a particular skill or set of skills in the framework was mastered by students during previous instruction. For example, students may already know the physical and functional characteristics of paragraphs and know how to apply these characteristics for classifying examples and nonexamples. They may not have mastered the quality characteristics for evaluating paragraphs and for producing good examples. In this case, skills related to physical and functional characteristics and to discrimination of examples would be classified as prerequisite skills. Enabling skills would be those for quality characteristics, evaluation, and production of paragraphs. The existence of prerequisite skills in a goal framework has implications for the type of achievement tests you design.

Types of Tests

Teachers develop and administer four types of achievement tests: entry behaviors tests, pretests, practice tests, and posttests. Each type is administered for a different purpose, and the purpose helps determine which subordinate skills will be selected for the test and when the test is administered.

Entry Behaviors Tests

Teachers use entry behaviors tests (also known as *readiness tests*) to determine whether students have mastered the prerequisite skills they need to begin a unit of instruction. The skills selected from the goal framework for an entry behaviors test include only those classified as prerequisite skills. These tests are administered before planning any unit lessons. Teachers use results from entry behaviors tests in three ways:

1. They determine whether the instructional goal is appropriate for a given group of students. If none or few of the students in a class have mastered the prerequisite skills, then the goal is probably too complex for the class.
2. They determine whether remedial instruction is necessary. If several students in the class have not mastered the prerequisite skills, then these students will need remedial instruction.
3. They group students in the class for instruction in the unit. Students can be grouped according to whether they have mastered prerequisite skills. Thus, instruction can be tailored to students' needs.

It is not always necessary to design an entry behaviors test. If none of the subordinate skills in the goal framework is classified as a prerequisite, or if you have recently taught the prerequisites and are familiar with students' mastery of them, then no entry behaviors test is needed. Additionally, if you have a homogeneous group of high-achieving students, you may safely assume that they have mastered the subordinate skills classified as prerequisite. However, if you have a heterogeneous group and are unfamiliar with their skills in the area, then consider designing an entry behaviors test to determine whether remedial instruction is warranted. Students may struggle with the enabling skills in a unit of instruction, not because the materials and instruction are poor, but because they do not possess essential prerequisite skills. Without testing the group on these skills before instruction begins, a teacher may not detect the real cause of students' problems until it is too late.

Pretests

Pretests are also administered before instruction, and results are used to plan lessons for the unit. When adequately designed, they include all the subordinate skills classified as enabling skills in the goal framework and thus provide an overview of students' skills for the entire unit. The teacher can use this information to plan review for any skills previously mastered and to develop lessons emphasizing skills that remain to be learned. Pretest data can also be used to group students who already have mastered most of the enabling skills and students who have not.

Pretests are not always necessary. If the enabling skills in a goal framework are not likely to have been encountered during previous instruction at school or at home, then it is reasonable to assume that instruction should be developed for each skill. However, if students are likely to have encountered previous instruction on any of the enabling skills, then a pretest will help you identify these skills and develop efficient instruction by focusing lessons on skills that remain to be learned. Sometimes students benefit from a pretest even if the teacher does not. Pretests can help students identify important skills to be learned, guide their study, and help them review for posttests.

If you decide that both an entry behaviors test and a pretest would be useful for a particular unit, you can combine them into one test, because both need to be administered before planning instruction. However, items for each test should be scored separately because each serves a different purpose. A total score on the entire test will not help you determine who is ready for the instruction or how the lessons should be designed.

Practice Tests

Teachers often administer informal practice tests during and immediately following instruction on a limited set of enabling skills. These tests are completed either in class or as homework. Data from these tests may be used in at least four ways. First, the teacher may determine the effectiveness of the instruction, identify skills that most students have not mastered, and seek new ways to present additional instruction. Second, students may be regrouped according to their mastery of the skills. Third, the data may help the teacher diagnose misconceptions and problems that students may have developed during instruction. Fourth, practice test results may be used for developing review materials and posttests. Students can also use these tests to determine whether they have learned required skills, to help them formulate questions, and to guide their study for exams.

To make adequate judgments, both teachers and students need detailed information; thus, practice tests should be designed to cover only a limited number of the enabling skills and their corresponding objectives. Because these tests are meant to provide practice for students and to help teachers plan, they should not be used to determine course grades.

Posttests

Posttests are given after instruction is completed; they help a teacher determine the effectiveness of instruction, evaluate student progress, and assign grades. The teacher can use posttest data to identify ineffective elements of the instruction and to improve the lessons for subsequent classes.

Any test used to assign term grades—whether a short quiz, an exam covering an entire unit, or a comprehensive exam over several units—is a posttest. Quizzes usually include the enabling skills for one or two lessons; unit exams cover a representative sample of all the enabling skills in a unit; and comprehensive exams contain a few of the most important enabling skills for each of several units. The enabling skills selected for a comprehensive exam are usually at the highest level of learning for each unit and should encompass all other enabling skills in the goal frameworks.

Because posttests are used to assign term grades, they should represent students' best efforts. The teacher should inform students of test dates and content to be covered. Unannounced tests, including pop quizzes, are inappropriate because they may not be valid reflections of students' learning. Unannounced quizzes fall into the category of practice tests.

■ Designing Tests Using Tables of Test Specifications

Once you have determined the types of tests you will administer, you will need to write a prescription for each type. Developing tables of test specifications will help you construct tests most likely to produce reliable scores that are valid for the decisions to be made. The process involves the following four steps:

1. Prescribe the types of tests needed to support your decisions during a unit of instruction.
2. Select the most representative subordinate skills from the instructional goal framework for each type of test prescribed.
3. Specify the number of items required to measure students' performance as accurately as possible on each subordinate skill.
4. Estimate the time required for students to answer the total number of items specified for each skill and for the test.

Specify the Types of Tests
for an Instructional Unit

Usually, there is a fixed amount of time available for instruction in a given course and for units of instruction within the course. Teachers must balance this fixed time between class time devoted to instruction and learning and class time devoted to testing students' skills. Some teachers administer only posttests because they believe that the amount of instructional time should be maximized and testing time should be minimized. Although such a rationale appears at first to be prudent, it might be a naive approach leading to ineffective instruction and inadequate learner achievement. For example, providing even the best-quality instruction for enabling skills will result in inadequate posttest performance by students who do not possess the mandatory prerequisite skills for entering the instruction (e.g., instruction on writing paragraphs when they cannot write simple sentences). Likewise, devoting time to introducing and rehearsing enabling skills that were mastered in a previous class is inefficient for teachers and often boring for students. The balance between teaching and testing time should be carefully considered if instruction is to be maximally efficient. In fact, many educators argue that good tests are an integral part of instruction and an important learning aid for students; thus, time spent on testing is also time spent on learning.

There are several criteria for helping you to decide whether you will need readiness tests, pretests, and/or practice tests in addition to posttests. They include (1) the complexity of the instructional goal, (2) the characteristics of the target learners, and (3) the school-based considerations of time and curriculum.

Goal Complexity   Instructional goals that are judged to be complex and hierarchical may require a variety of types of tests if teachers are to maximize students' potential for achieving the goal. Readiness tests support judgments about appropriate levels of goal complexity for given student groups and judgments about grouping students for instructional effectiveness. Helping students acquire complex skills may necessitate several practice tests in a variety of formats to enable students to store the skills in memory and to retrieve them when needed. These tests also enable teachers to detect and correct students' misconceptions and errors in applying the skills. When instructional goals are complex intellectual skills, teachers will undoubtedly prescribe multiple types of tests for efficient management of the instructional unit.

Learners' Characteristics   The characteristics of target students should also figure into determining the number and types of tests needed. If a group is homogeneous and consists of high, average, or low achievers, the teacher may be able to predict accurately the learners' status on prerequisite and enabling skills. On the other hand, if the group is rather heterogeneous, the teacher may increase instructional efficiency by testing students' achievement of subordinate skills and then grouping by achievement levels on the skills. Estimating students' achievement of prerequisite skills might be risky when students come to the classroom from a variety of previous classes and teachers. Regardless of whether you believe you need readiness tests or pretests, you will need practice tests to ensure that learners have adequate opportunities to rehearse new skills and knowledge. You will also need a variety of posttests to support the evaluation of your students' progress.

School-Based Considerations   School-based considerations for determining the types of tests for a particular instructional unit include the importance of the goal in the curriculum, the number of class periods available for a unit, and the length of individual class periods. Related to the curriculum, if the same goal (e.g., writing a sentence) were considered a basic life skill and included across several years of the curriculum, then teachers would undoubtedly prescribe tests for prerequisites and enabling skills to identify students' current skill levels and to aid their lesson planning and evaluation activities. The time available for the total unit will also enter into the decision. If you have only three class periods to devote to a particular goal, then the notion of including readiness tests, pretests, practice tests, and posttests becomes absurd. Considering the time available during a single class session and the possible need for changing learners' focus and activity in order to maintain their attention may help you determine whether to include some form of practice test as a routine part of the daily lesson structure.

Select Prerequisite and Enabling Skills

Both the purpose for the test and the interrelationship among the prerequisite and enabling skills in the goal framework must be considered when designing tests to help ensure validity and reliability. The following paragraphs illustrate the design process used to specify subordinate skills for a table of test specifications for each of the four types of tests.

Readiness Tests   Since the purpose for readiness tests is to measure learners' mastery of prerequisite skills for a given instructional goal, the *most* representative set of objectives for a readiness test would include every subordinate, prerequisite skill in the instructional goal framework. Figure 4.1 contains a skeletal replication of a hypothetical instructional goal matrix.

1. The first three columns in each row (A, B, and C) reflect recall-level skills related to identifying physical, functional, and quality characteristics.
2. The last three columns in each row (D, E, and F) reflect performance-level skills related to classifying examples and nonexamples, evaluating the quality of given examples, and producing acceptable examples.
3. Skills within each row progress hierarchically from left to right in one area of content, with left-side skills subordinate to right-side skills within a row. Skills also tend to progress hierarchically in the last column from skill I.F, lowest level, through skill IV.F, highest level.

Since the most representative set of prerequisite skills for a readiness test would include all prerequisite skills, then the table of specifications for this hypothetical unit should prescribe the prerequisite skills represented by cells I.A through II.F in Figure 4.1. A readiness test that measures all these prerequisite skills should yield scores that have very good potential for aiding valid decisions about who is and who is not ready for the unit. These scores should also be reliable since all prerequisites are included; students could reasonably be expected to earn a similar score regardless of the particular items used to represent each of these prerequisite skills.

FIGURE 4.1

Hypothetical Instructional Goal Analysis Matrix

MAIN CONTENT AREAS	RECALL LEVEL			PERFORM LEVEL		
	A Name/Recall Physical Characteristics	**B** Name/Recall Functional Characteristics	**C** Name/Recall Quality Characteristics	**D** Classify Examples and Nonexamples	**E** Evaluate Examples	**F** Produce Examples
I. Prerequisite Skills	I.A	I.B	I.C	I.D	I.E	I.F
II. Prerequisite Skills	II.A	II.B	II.C	II.D	II.E	II.F
III. Enabling Skills	III.A	III.B	III.C	III.D	III.E	III.F
IV. Enabling Skills	IV.A	IV.B	IV.C	IV.D	IV.E	IV.F

Note: Shaded rows reflect prerequisite skills, or skills students should have mastered prior to entering the instructional unit.

Sometimes, due to management constraints, you cannot prescribe that every prerequisite skill in the goal framework is included on a readiness test. However, you should still try to prescribe the most representative subset of prerequisite skills possible in order to maximize the potential for obtaining reliable test scores and for making valid decisions about who is prepared to begin instruction on the enabling skills. Some subsets of prerequisite skills from the goal matrix have more potential for yielding reliable scores and valid decisions than others. Two rules to follow in sampling among all prerequisite skills in the framework include:

1. Select skills from all relevant rows in the goal framework, ensuring that all content areas are represented in the test.
2. Select skills from the right-hand side (performance-level skills) since these performance-level skills are likely to encompass the subordinate recall-level skills.

Using these two rules for sampling among the two rows of prerequisite skills in Figure 4.1, you could reduce the number of skills included on the readiness test from 12 to 6 and specify only the prerequisite skills from cells I.D through I.F and II.D through II.F. You can see in Figure 4.1 that these are the highest-level skills in each content row and that both content rows are represented; thus, this prescription would more than likely yield reliable test scores and enable valid decisions about who is ready for instruction on the enabling skills.

Assuming that selecting any other 6 of the 12 prerequisite skills would result in the same level of representation would be inaccurate. Suppose that the 6 skills were instead selected from cells I.A through I.F in Figure 4.1. Selecting these 6 prerequisites would totally eliminate the second, and possibly more complex, strand of skills, which would very likely reduce the validity of decisions about who was prepared to enter the unit. Likewise, specifying skills I.A through I.C and II.A through II.C, or the first three cells in each content row, would also be an inferior representation of skills that would yield very questionable test scores for determining students' readiness.

Suppose you could only include two skills in the readiness test rather than six skills. You could help ensure the best representation of skills by selecting one skill cell from each content area and by selecting that cell from the far right side of the goal framework. In Figure 4.1, the most ideal skills to select for this circumstance would be skills I.F and II.F. If learners could produce examples or solve problems in each content area, then you could validly conclude they were ready for the unit. In summary, a test that measures prerequisite skills from all content areas and that contains higher-order skills has more potential for yielding reliable test scores and for supporting valid judgments about learners' readiness than tests representing only some content strands or lower level skills.

Pretests   The purpose for pretests is to determine which ones of the enabling skills have been previously mastered. This information is used to plan lessons efficiently in that enabling skills previously mastered by all students can simply be reviewed, whereas skills that most students fail to perform adequately must be introduced, elaborated, and rehearsed during the unit. This purpose for the pretest implies that the individual student and group status on every enabling skill in the goal framework should be measured. Related to the example skills in Figure 4.1, then, the pretest would ideally include skills A through F in Row III and skills A through F in Row IV.

Recall the manner in which the number of skills measured on the readiness test was reduced and the representativeness of the skills measured for determining pupils' readiness for the unit was maintained. Could you reduce the enabling skills measured on the pretest to only skills III.F and IV.F in Figure 4.1 and still have pretest scores valid for lesson planning decisions? No. Measuring only these 2 skills would indicate who had and who had not mastered the instructional goal, but it would not reveal which of the other 10 skills were mastered. For those students who could not perform skills III.F and IV.F, you could not efficiently develop lesson plans to aid their acquisition of the instructional goal. In designing pretests, you might want to follow the strategy of including all the enabling skills on the test that time will allow. When you must compromise, again follow the strategy of sampling from all major content areas and from all higher-level skills in those areas.

Practice Tests   The purposes for practice tests are to enable learners to rehearse and transfer new skills learned in a lesson and to help students and teachers monitor learning progress during instruction. Based on these purposes, a single practice test typically measures fewer enabling skills than the other three types of tests. It is often focused on a single lesson or two and administered during or immediately following instruction. A unit of instruction may have only one pretest or posttest, but it typically has several practice tests that measure different portions of the enabling skills.

Determining exactly how to select enabling skills for practice tests requires knowledge of the enabling skills in a unit and their interrelationships. For illustration purposes, suppose you decide to design four practice tests for the hypothetical unit in Figure 4.1. The first practice test might include enabling skills III.A through III.F, and the second one might focus only on enabling skills III.E and III.F for additional rehearsal and transfer. Likewise for the enabling skills in Row IV, perhaps the third practice would encompass the recall skills in cells IV.A through IV.C, and the final practice test might measure the performance skills in cells IV.D through IV.F. In designing actual practice tests, you must consider the complexity of enabling skills, how they are divided for lessons within the unit, and the amount of class time that is available for rehearsal and feedback.

Posttests   The purpose for posttests is to describe students' achievement of the enabling skills and instructional goals. Most teachers have latitude in how unit-level examinations are designed, which means that one can observe many different styles of posttests. Some teachers prefer administering a series of smaller examinations, each of which covers a portion of the enabling skills in the unit. Such small, focused examinations are often called *quizzes*. Other teachers prefer a combination of focused quizzes and a comprehensive unit examination that measures performance on all enabling skills. Yet others administer no posttests besides a comprehensive unit-level exam. Regardless of the strategy you prefer, unit posttests should either collectively or singly measure all the enabling skills in a unit.

A comprehensive posttest for a unit would resemble a comprehensive pretest in that it measures all the enabling skills in the unit. In fact, if you were asked to discriminate between a pretest and posttest for a unit, you should not be able to tell which is which. The only difference would be in how the students' scores from the two tests were used. Similar to the pretest, a comprehensive posttest design from the hypothetical unit in Figure 4.1 would include as many of the enabling skills as time allowed, and ideally all skills, III.A through IV.F, would be represented on the test. Should you need to sample among them, the same rule of prescribing skills from each content area and from the higher-level skills would be followed. A teacher who chose to administer two posttests might include only skills from content row III on one exam and only skills from content row IV on the other. Another strategy might be to administer three posttests with the following enabling skill prescriptions:

Test 1:   Row III, skills A through F
Test 2:   Row IV, skills A through F
Test 3:   Skills III.F and IV.F

Term and Semester Posttests   When designing comprehensive term and semester examinations that measure enabling skills and goals from across many units of instruction, the same rule of representativeness should be followed. Suppose that the hypothetical unit of instruction in Figure 4.1 was to be combined with 22 other instructional units for the semester examination. Following the rule of representativeness, which enabling skills would you select to represent this unit in the comprehensive exam? Hopefully, you would choose skills III.F and IV.F or simply IV.F if III.F is hierarchically subordinate. Should these skills not be measurable on the semester exam because of test format policies in the school (e.g., only objective-style tests), you might choose instead skills III.E and IV.E or singly IV.E if III.E is hierarchically subordinate. With the subordinate skills prescribed for an examination, you are ready to select the particular objectives that will be used to guide the process of teaching and measuring each skill.

Specify the Number of Items for Each Subordinate Skill Chosen

A test should include enough items for each skill to ensure that the skill is measured adequately. There are several criteria to use in determining how many items should be prescribed for a subordinate skill. They include:

1. The complexity of the skill selected
2. The possibility of correctly guessing an answer
3. The possibility of committing inadvertent errors in answering an item
4. The students' attention span
5. Class time available

Basically, ask yourself, How many times must students correctly perform a skill for me to be reasonably sure that they have mastered it?

Consider first the issue of enabling skill complexity. You would not need to administer many test items to be sure that students remember the name of something. This is a very simple recall-level skill, and you would undoubtedly specify only one or possibly two items. On the other hand, classifying examples of concepts in several categories is quite a bit more complex, and you would undoubtedly specify several items to ensure that students could accurately and consistently perform this skill across all categories.

The ease of correctly guessing an answer is a second factor to consider in determining the number of test items to prescribe. When learners have a 50-50 chance of correctly guessing the answer to an item, then you will need to prescribe more items. For example, students have a 50 percent chance of guessing correctly whether the term *Coca Cola* is a proper noun. If only this single item is presented and the student answers it correctly, then you really do not know whether the student possesses the skill or simply guessed correctly. Increasing the number of instances presented for classification reduces students' ability to appear skilled when they are not.

On the other hand, suppose you present students with only one item related to a skill they have thoroughly mastered. There are any number of circumstances, such as misreading the directions or not understanding an irrelevant term in the item, that might cause students to miss the single item presented. Should the students miss the item, your test data will not help determine whether students do not have the skill or inadvertently missed the item due to some other factor.

This discussion might lead you to conclude that more is always better when prescribing the number of items for each objective, but this is not the case. Considering the time available for the total test and the potential for tiring students during the test, you will need to compromise and specify only the number of items you believe will help ensure that students' scores on the total test validly reflect their true achievement status on the skills measured.

Prescribe a General Test Item or Task Format

To help ensure curriculum-centered assessment, select the general test item or task format that best enables a student's authentic demonstration of achievement for each enabling skill and instructional goal selected for a test. The purpose for prescribing the general test format at this point in the design is to create the most valid assessment possible and to aid your estimations of the time and resources required to administer and score it. The basic decision you are making is whether to create an objective, product, or live performance test or to develop an assessment that includes some combination of these formats. Another decision you will need to make is whether to administer the assessment on one day, on two days, or over many days.

Some test item formats are better for assessing some skills than others. You may apply several criteria in choosing the type of item or task format you believe is best. These criteria are related to requirements for authentic demonstrations of enabling skills and goals, students' developmental levels, the purpose for the test or information needed, and available classroom resources.

Curriculum-Centered Criteria   To ensure authentic demonstrations of the enabling skills and goals, examine the behavior and content in each enabling skill and ask yourself, Why is this skill important? How is it typically applied in the students' environment? and What is the *best* or most authentic way for them to demonstrate their achievement of this skill? For example, if an enabling skill reflects verbal information, the most efficient assessment format would undoubtedly be an objective test item format. Students can demonstrate their knowledge and comprehension of a wide variety of concepts in a relatively short period of time using an objective item format. Many higher-order skills related to problem solving and evaluation can also be assessed best using simulated or illustrative materials and objective-style test items for responding. On the other hand, if students need to provide lengthy answers or develop a product of some type, such as a research report or a bookcase, then you will undoubtedly prescribe an essay or product assessment format. Alternatively, students might need to demonstrate their achievement through a live performance, such as speaking before an audience or playing the violin. When live performances of achievement are required, then you will most likely prescribe a performance assessment format.

Learner-Centered Criteria   Related to students' developmental levels and needs, you must prescribe a format type that enables them to demonstrate their achievement without becoming confused or fatigued by the format. You might choose to prescribe an objective format with oral questioning and responding for very young nonreaders. You might also choose "oral essays" for students at any age level who have difficulty writing responses. When students have developed adequate writing skills, you might prescribe written essays requiring demonstrations such as analysis of Internet, televised, or live government proceedings. To be most valid, the assessment format must fit the students' ability to understand what you want them to do and to understand how to respond.

Instruction-Centered Criteria   The manner is which data and information from a particular assessment are going to be used by teachers, students, and parents should be considered when you select the most appropriate item or task format. For example, readiness tests and pretests are used to determine whether to enter a particular instructional unit and to tailor lesson plans to student needs, thus they should have a format that is economical to administer and score. Practice assessments are often completed cooperatively by students in the classroom or as homework assignments, and they can take any number of formats. They should, however, be formatted in a similar manner to the posttest, or the congruence of formative evaluation with feedback to summative evaluation with grading is questionable. The format of posttests should enable as authentic an assessment as possible, since scores from these tests will be used to grade and communicate students' progress.

School-Centered Criteria   The economics of your classroom will influence the format of items and tests that you design. For example, consider the format of assessments that can be administered and scored by a single music teacher who teaches 300 students daily, or the physical education teacher who teaches 250 students each day. Under these classroom conditions, it does not make sense to prescribe authentic, individual, live-performance tests that require even 10 minutes for each student. Imagine the total time required for assessment and feedback for just one instructional goal. Now imagine the science, math, social studies, or English teacher who has five classes each day, perhaps very heterogeneous classes, with 35 or more students in each class. If authentic assessment is beginning to appear complex, imagine the teacher who is told that there is no money for copying or reproducing assessments, for purchasing or creating illustrative or resource materials for higher-order skills assessments, or for scoring, analyzing, and managing assessment data for 175 students each day. Ideal, authentic assessment requires resources. Schools that have reasonable class sizes and resources will undoubtedly have teachers who design authentic assessments. Those who do not will have teachers who create the best possible assessments under their economic circumstances.

Estimate the Time Required for the Overall Test

Even with the general test item format selected, approximating the time required for students to complete a test always constitutes a best-guess situation. However, with knowledge of students' typical work speed, the format of an item, and the number of items per objective, you will be able to obtain a ball-park figure for the total time a test will require. This last step in developing the table of test specifications is important because it can illustrate whether you have prescribed more items from an ideal perspective than your students can possibly answer in the allotted time. When students earn low scores on exams related to fatigue or inadequate time to complete the test, you will be compromising the reliability of your scores and the validity of your decisions.

The table of test specifications should include time estimates for answering all items prescribed for each objective and for the total test. These items can be estimated by using the following process:

1. Consider the complexity of the subordinate skill.
2. Consider the amount of time required for students to study and interpret any stimulus material that might accompany the items.
3. Consider the amount of time required for students to respond to each item.
4. Multiply the total amount of time required to answer each item by the number of items prescribed for each skill.
5. Sum the times estimated for each skill to project the total amount of time required for students to answer the items.
6. Add to this item-based estimate the administration time required to introduce the test, distribute the test, and collect materials when students have finished.

When the estimated time for the examination fits your ball-park figure of time allocated for the test, the table of test specifications is complete. Should any of the time estimates represent impossible allocations for the time available or the attention span of the students, you may either reduce the number of items specified or administer the prescribed test in more than one test session. Reducing the number of items may not be the wisest approach to solving the problem, since the skills and items were prescribed to maximize score reliability and decision validity.

An Example

The instructional goal on writing paragraphs is used to illustrate tables of test specifications for a unit of instruction. Sample tables of test specifications for the pretest, unit posttest, and practice tests are included in Figure 4.2. The readiness test is omitted from the figure, since it is based on objectives from a prior instructional unit on constructing sentences.

There are many different ways to format tables of test specifications. Some teachers use a copy of their instructional goal framework as the foundation for the table, whereas others create a different format. The basic test design information about a particular test that needs to be recorded in a table of test specifications includes the following:

1. The levels of learning to be assessed on a particular test (recall and/or higher order)
2. The specific enabling skills selected for the test from the instructional goal framework
3. The number of items or tasks needed for each enabling skill chosen and for the overall test
4. The general format of test items or tasks needed for each enabling skill selected (e.g., objective style, product development, and live performance)
5. The amount of time the teacher estimates will be required for students to answer questions or perform the tasks prescribed for each enabling skill and for the overall test

FIGURE 4.2

Tables of Test Specifications for the Intellectual Skill "Write a Paragraph," Based on the Goal Framework in Figure 3.6

PRETEST

		RECALL-LEVEL SKILLS						HIGHER-ORDER SKILLS				
Skills	# Items	Item Task General Format*			Time	Skills	# Items	Item Task General Format			Time	
		OB	PD	PF				OB	PD	PF		Totals**
I.A	1	X			.5	I.D	2	X			1.0	Sk: 18
I.B	1	X			.5							Itm: 28
II.A	1	X			.5	II.D	2	X			1.0	Mn: 20
II.B	1	X			.5	II.E	3	X			3.0	
II.C	1	X			.5							
III.A	1	X			.5	III.D	2	X			1.0	
III.B	1	X			.5	III.E	3	X			6.0	
III.C	1	X			.5							
IV.A	1	X			.5	IV.D	2	X			1.0	
IV.B	1	X			.5	IV.E	3	X			3.0	
IV.C	1	X			.5							

UNIT POSTTEST

		RECALL-LEVEL SKILLS						HIGHER-ORDER SKILLS				
Skills	# Items	Item Task General Format			Time	Skills	# Items	Item Task General Format			Time	
		OB	PD	PF				OB	PD	PF		Totals*
I.A	1	X			.5	I.D	2	X			1.0	Sk: 22
I.B	1	X			.5	I.F	4		X		40.0	Itm: 43
II.A	1	X			.5	II.D	2	X			1.0	Mn: 69
II.B	1	X			.5	II.E	4	X			3.0	
II.C	1	X			.5	II.F	3		X		3.0	
III.A	1	X			.5	III.D	3	X			1.0	

(continued)

Skills	# Items	OB	PD	PF	Time	Skills	# Items	OB	PD	PF	Time	
		Item Task General Format						Item Task General Format*				
III.B	1	X			.5	III.E	3	X			2.0	
III.C	1	X			.5	III.F	3		X		6.0	
IV.A	1	X			.5	IV.D	2	X			1.0	
IV.B	1	X			.5	IV.E	3	X			2.0	
IV.C	1	X			.5	IV.F	3		X		3.0	

PRACTICE TEST 1: Topic Sentence, Relevance

	RECALL-LEVEL SKILLS						HIGHER-ORDER SKILLS					
Skills	# Items	Item Task General Format			Time	Skills	# Items	Item Task General Format			Time	
		OB	PD	PF				OB	PD	PF		Totals*
II.A	1	X			.5	II.D	1	X			1.0	Sk: 6
II.B	1	X			.5	II.E	7	X			3.0	Itm: 14
II.C	1	X			.5	II.F	3		X		3.0	Mn: 18

PRACTICE TEST 2: Topic Sentence, Scope, and Relevance

	RECALL-LEVEL SKILLS						HIGHER-ORDER SKILLS					
Skills	# Items	Item Task General Format			Time	Skills	# Items	Item Task General Format			Time	
		OB	PD	PF				OB	PD	PF		Totals*
												Sk: 2
						II.E	12	X			24.0	Itm: 15
						II.F	3		X		9.0	Mn: 33

PRACTICE TEST 3: Supporting Sentences, Relevance

	RECALL-LEVEL SKILLS						HIGHER-ORDER SKILLS					
Skills	# Items	Item Task General Format			Time	Skills	# Items	Item Task General Format			Time	
		OB	PD	PF				OB	PD	PF		Totals*
III.A	1	X			.5	III.D	2	X			1.0	Sk: 6
III.B	1	X			.5	III.E	4	X			8.0	Itm: 11
III.C	1	X			.5	III.F	2		X		9.0	Mn: 19

PRACTICE TEST 4: Supporting Sentences (Sequence)

Skills	# Items	Item Task General Format			Time	Skills	# Items	Item Task General Format			Time	Totals*
		OB	PD	PF				OB	PD	PF		
						III.D	2	X			1.0	Sk: 3
						III.E	4	X			8.0	Itm: 8
						III.F	2		X		9.0	Mn: 18

PRACTICE TEST 5: Supporting Sentences (Transition)

Skills	# Items	Item Task General Format			Time	Skills	# Items	Item Task General Format			Time	Totals*
		OB	PD	PF				OB	PD	PF		
						III.D	2	X			1.0	Sk: 3
						III.E	4	X			8.0	Itm: 8
						III.F	2		X		9.0	Mn: 18

PRACTICE TEST 6: Concluding Sentences

Skills	# Items	Item/Task General Format			Time	Skills	# Items	Item Task General Format			Time	Totals*
		OB	PD	PF				OB	PD	PF		
IV.A	1	X			.5	IV.D	1	X			5.0	Sk: 6
IV.B	1	X			.5	IV.E	7	X			7.0	Itm: 14
IV.C	1	X			.5	IV.F	3		X		9.0	Mn: 18

PRACTICE TEST 7: Concluding Sentences, Scope, and Relevance

Skills	# Items	Item Task General Format			Time	Skills	# Items	Item Task General Format			Time	Totals*
		OB	PD	PF				OB	PD	PF		
												Sk: 2
						IV.E	12	X			24.0	Itm: 15
						IV.F	3		X		9.0	Mn: 33

(continued)

FIGURE 4.2   Continued

PRACTICE TESTS 8–11: Writing Paragraphs

			HIGHER-ORDER SKILLS				
	Skills	# Items	Item Task General Format			Time	
8. Writing descriptive paragraphs			OB	PD	PF		**Totals for Each Test***
9. Writing time series paragraphs							**Sk: 2**
10. Writing procedural paragraphs	IV.E	12	X			24.0	**Itm: 15**
11. Writing expression of feeling paragraphs	IV.F	3		X		40.0	**Mn: 64**

*For general item formats, OB = objective-style items, PD = essay or product assessments, and
PF = live-performance assessments.

**For Totals, Sk = enabling skills, Itm = items, and Mn = minutes. Time estimate totals are rounded up to
nearest minute.

The example table of test specifications format illustrated in Figure 4.2 includes
all this required information.

Levels of Learning   Two general levels of learning are named in the top row:
Recall-Level Skills and *Higher-Order Skills*. All enabling skills selected for a particular test that are verbal information or knowledge-level learning (definitions, terms,
facts, etc.) are recorded in the left side of the table in the recall-level skills columns.
All tasks selected for a test that are higher-order skills (e.g., generalizing, evaluating,
solving problems, creating products, performing, etc.) are recorded in the higher-
order skills columns. Separating the recall-level skills from the higher-order skills in
a table of test specifications helps teachers to ensure a balanced test.

Notice in Figure 4.2 that both general skill levels are included for the pretest
and the posttest. This signals that the teacher plans for both tests to be comprehensive, enabling him or her to identify students' status and needs at the beginning and
at the conclusion of the unit's instruction. Now examine the skill levels included for
the planned practice tests. Practice tests 1, 3, and 6 include both recall-level and
higher-order skills. These will undoubtedly be the first practice tests used during instruction for each concept area to help ensure that students practice and acquire both
the knowledge and the skills included in the domain. Notice that practice tests 2, 4,
5, and 7 include only the higher-order skills in the domain, signaling that these particular higher-order skills require multiple practice with feedback opportunities.
Note also that practice tests 8 through 11 are rehearsals for writing whole paragraphs. These practice tests reflect the instructional goal, assess only the highest-
order skills in the framework, and signal the teacher's concern with the complexity
of the goal and the need for multiple opportunities for rehearsal. All 11 practice tests
together illustrate the teacher's commitment to students' active participation during
instruction.

Enabling Skills Selected   The column labeled *Skills,* on the far-left side of each skills level, is used to record the enabling skill code from the instructional goal framework. Including the enabling skill code links your test designs and actual tests to their instructional goal framework. It also helps you monitor whether your test is balanced by content area and learning level.

Notice that every concept row in the instructional goal framework (I–IV) is included in both the pretest and posttest, helping to ensure content validity on both tests. Related to the levels of learning, however, the teacher is not requiring students to write paragraphs (I. F) on the pretest; he or she will examine only enabling skills for writing paragraphs. The instructional goal itself is often eliminated from pretests because of time constraints associated with obtaining feedback from product or live performance pretests. Using objective-style pretests whenever possible allows more time for planning lessons for the unit that are tailored to the observed needs of the students. If teachers know that all students have previously mastered the enabling skills for writing a paragraph and simply need to refine their writing skills, then they will logically eliminate the pretest from the assessment design. Eliminating the pretest based on students' skill levels, teachers would possibly begin unit assessment activities with practice test 2, writing relevant topic sentences.

Considering the practice tests, notice that they relate to different concept rows. Each of practice tests 1 through 7 covers enabling skills from single concept areas, linking enabling skills to related lessons. Creating lesson-level practice tests provides the interactive exercises necessary to engage students *during* instruction. Practice tests 8 through 11 cover the entire domain of writing a paragraph, and they enable critical rehearsal and feedback during instruction.

The Number of Test Items or Tasks   The next column, named *# Items,* is used to record the total number of test items or tasks that students will need to complete for each enabling skill chosen. The basic rule of thumb used in determining the number of items prescribed in this example was to include only one item for verbal information or knowledge-level skills and multiple items for the more complex higher-order skills. The exact number of items or tasks to choose for a particular enabling skill is a matter of professional judgment.

Notice in Figure 4.2 that, regardless of the type of test, only one test item is specified for each recall-level skill chosen. On both the pretest and posttest, two items are prescribed for classification-level skills (D), and three items are prescribed for evaluation-level skills. These skills are more complex, with multiple facets to assess. Similarly, students will be required to write three of each type of sentence, and on the posttest, they will be asked to produce four paragraphs.

Item or Task Formats   The next columns in each section are titled *Item / Task General Format.* At this point, you should study the behavior and content named in the enabling skill and ask yourself, How would this skill be assessed most validly? In some instances, an objective item format would be best; for other skills, a product development or live performance task would best suit the enabling skill. In the example, the Xs in the column labeled *OB* (objective) indicate that an objective-style test item format is prescribed to assess the students' knowledge or skill. An X in the column named *PD* indicates that the students must develop a product of some type. In this case, they must develop topic, supporting, and concluding sentences, and they must write original paragraphs to demonstrate their progress in writing paragraphs. An X in the column labeled *PF* indicates the students must give a live performance. A general rule of thumb for prescribing the item or task format is that objective item formats are typically used for verbal information or knowledge-level enabling skills. For higher-order skills, you will need to be more thoughtful in selecting the format. For example, some problem-solving tasks may require a lot of creativity and mental gymnastics, while the eventual solution or answer can be written in one small space or selected from a list. Others require development or performance. Be thoughtful. Choose the general format you believe will best assess the students' current achievement status in the enabling skill.

Considering the various tests in Figure 4.2, notice that the teacher has prescribed only objective items for the pretest. This is to ensure timely scoring and adequate time for planning lessons tailored to students' observed needs. For the unit posttest, all objective item formats are prescribed except for the enabling skills that require students to write sentences or paragraphs, and a product (PD) item format is prescribed for these skills. For the practice tests, objective-style items are prescribed for all enabling skills except those that require students to write sentences or paragraphs.

Time Requirements   The sixth column, named *Time,* is used to record the amount of class time the teacher estimates it will take for students to answer the questions and perform the tasks prescribed for each enabling skill. Estimating the amount of time required for students to complete certain tasks on a test is often difficult until you gain testing experience with a particular group of students.

Regardless of the test type in Figure 4.2, the teacher is estimating 30 seconds for reading and answering each recall-level item. Time estimates for the higher-order skills are varied and based on skill complexity. For example, a total of 40 minutes is prescribed on the posttest for writing four paragraphs, and 6 minutes are prescribed for evaluating three sets of supporting sentences. Notice on practice tests 8 through 11, however, that the teacher is prescribing 40 minutes for each paragraph. This is undoubtedly due to the instructional activities planned during the practice tests (e.g., student self-rating, peer rating, editing, and revising activities). The differences in time allotted illustrate the fact that designing tests is difficult if you do not know how you will administer a test or how you will use the assessment activity or test results in support of learning and instruction.

Totals   The far-right column in each section of Figure 4.2, *Totals,* contains the total number of enabling skills (Sk) assessed on a particular test, the total number of items (Itm) to be developed or selected, and the total number of minutes (Mn) for students to complete the test.

In the example, there are 18 skills and 28 items included on the pretest. The posttest will cover all the enabling skills on the pretest plus the instructional goal, thus 22 skills are included. The posttest contains more items than the pretest, 43, and the teacher estimates 69 minutes for students to finish. Based on this length of time, the posttest will undoubtedly be administered in two separate testing sessions to avoid student fatigue. Notice that each practice test will include fewer enabling skills and items than either the pretest or the posttest.

Designing Comprehensive Term or Semester Exams

Teachers frequently want to measure students' progress on several instructional units. Such comprehensive tests should be balanced by content areas and learning levels. Because several different frameworks of skills will be tested, prescribing test items that represent all of the enabling skills is not feasible. A table of specifications can help you manage the process of test development and design a test that best represents all the units covered.

Although skipping the development of a table of specifications for a comprehensive exam may save time, it is not recommended. Using items from previous unit tests will not ensure that the comprehensive posttest is balanced according to content, learning levels, and representative enabling skills. A posttest developed without appropriate prescriptions may produce scores of limited use and interpretation, thus compromising the entire project.

As you develop a table of specifications for a comprehensive posttest, you should consider the following six elements: (1) balance among the goals selected for the exam, (2) balance among the levels of learning, (3) the test format, (4) the total number of items, (5) the number of test items for each goal and level of learning, and (6) the enabling skills to be selected from each goal framework. A table of specifications incorporating these factors will help ensure a comprehensive posttest that represents each unit and is balanced by goals and levels of learning.

In constructing the table, first consider the balance among the goals to be represented on the exam. Study the goals and their respective frameworks and determine the relative complexity of the goals. The more complex a goal, the more emphasis it may need. For example, if 10 goals of approximately equal complexity are represented, the items for each goal may account for 10 percent of the total test. If 5 goals are more complex than the others, test items for these goals may take up a larger proportion of the test, with the 5 less complex goals represented by a smaller percentage of items. Regardless of the rationale you use to determine percentages, you should record the proportion of items for each goal in your table of specifications.

Once the appropriate balance among goals is established, turn to the second important element—balance among the levels of learning within each goal. When allocating the proportion assigned for a goal among the levels of learning, remember that recall-level skills are often subsumed within higher-order skills. Additionally, recall-level skills are less complex than higher-order skills and thus can be measured using fewer items. Therefore, you will usually want to assign a greater portion of the items allocated for each goal to higher-order skills. A caution is in order, however. If only higher-order skills are included on a test, and students fail to answer these items correctly, you may have difficulty interpreting their scores. You will not be able to detect whether they missed the items because they did not know the rule or definition or because they knew it but had trouble generalizing it.

Table 4.1 contains three tables of test specifications that balance 10 goals differently by goal and by level of learning. The specifications for Test A indicate equal emphasis among the 10 goals; however, 80 percent of the items require higher-order skills. The prescription for Test B emphasizes 5 of the 10 goals and indicates that 75 percent of the items test higher-order skills. The chart for Test C specifies uneven percentages for the 10 goals and requires that 100 percent of the items test higher-order skills. The different balances in goals and levels of learning in Tests A, B, and C will potentially result in different student scores for the three tests and different inferences about students' achievement. The most appropriate balance among goals and levels of learning can best be determined by studying the relative complexity of the goals to be measured and assigning a portion of the test to each goal accordingly. Then, with each goal assigned a portion of the test, you can select the proportion for each level of learning within the goal.

Once you have weighted all the goals and learning levels to be covered, you then select a test format. Depending on the instructional goals to be measured, you may decide on an objective test, an essay exam, a product development project, an active performance measure, or some combination of these formats. In making your decision, review the behaviors specified in the instructional goals to be measured and the general item formats prescribed in the tables of test specifications for each unit.

You are now ready to prescribe the total number of items to be included on the exam and the number of items allocated for each goal. In selecting the total number of test items, consider two factors: the time available for testing and the required level of performance.

The time available for testing depends on the length of the class period and on students' attention spans. Students should be able to complete the test within the class period and before they become fatigued.

The required level of performance will also help determine the total number of questions on the exam. Recall-level items typically require less time than higher-order-skill items, whatever the test format. Items that ask students to solve problems, analyze or synthesize information, or evaluate examples all require more time than do items that require students to remember a term, fact, definition, rule, or principle. Essay questions require more time than either selected-response or short-answer items.

Suppose, for example, that your class period is 50 minutes long. Of this time, approximately 10 minutes will be needed to distribute the tests, give instructions, and collect the tests; 40 minutes remain. If you estimate that students can answer an average of one short-answer question per minute, then your test can include a maximum of 40 short-answer items. If you plan to administer an essay test, and predict that each question will require approximately 12 minutes to answer, then you can include only three essay items. A test that contains a combination of short-answer and essay questions should allow enough time for each type of question.

After you have determined the total number of test items, then determine the number of items for each goal. For example, if each of 10 goals is to represent 10 percent

TABLE 4.1

Partial Test Specifications for Three Comprehensive Posttests, Weighted by Goal and Learning Level

Goal	Percentage of Items	Percentage Recall[a]	Percentage Higher-Order Skills[b]
Test A			
1	10	2	8
2	10	2	8
3	10	2	8
4	10	2	8
5	10	2	8
6	10	2	8
7	10	2	8
8	10	2	8
9	10	2	8
10	10	2	8
Total	100%	20%	80%
Test B			
1	14	3	11
2	6	2	4
3	14	3	11
4	6	2	4
5	14	3	11
6	6	2	4
7	14	3	11
8	6	2	4
9	14	3	11
10	6	2	4
Total	100%	25%	75%
Test C			
1	14		14
2	6		6
3	10		10
4	8		8
5	12		12
6	8		8
7	16		16
8	6		6
9	14		14
10	6		6
Total	100%	0%	100%

[a]The Recall category prescribes remembering and comprehension items.

[b]The Higher-Order Skills category prescribes classification, evaluation, problem-solving, explanation, prediction, product development, and live performance items.

of the test, and you have a total of 40 questions on the test, then the total number of items can be multiplied by the allocated proportion to determine the appropriate number of items (.10 × 40 = 4). Each goal would be represented on the test by four items.

The number of items allocated for each goal can then be divided between recall and higher-order items. If you choose to measure only higher-order skills for one goal, then all four of the assigned items would be designated for higher-order skills. If you choose to emphasize higher-order items, but also want to include some recall items for another one of the goals, then you probably would assign three of the available items to higher-order skills and one to recall.

Table 4.2 illustrates a partially completed table of test specifications that prescribes the total number of test items, the percentage and number of items for each of 10 goals, and the distribution of items according to learning level. For this comprehensive exam, 25 percent of the items measure recall-level skills and 75 percent measure higher-order skills.

The final step in developing a table of specifications is the selection of enabling skills from each goal framework. Because the number of items for each goal must be limited, you should select the enabling skills that best represent each goal. For example, the test specifications in Table 4.2 limit the number of recall-level objectives

TABLE 4.2

Partial Table of Test Specifications Prescribing Percentage and Number of Items for Each Goal and Level of Learning

| | Levels of Learning | | | |
Goals	Recall[a] No. of Items (Columns A–C)	Higher-Order[b] No. of Items (Columns D–F)	Total No.	Percentage of Total Items
1	1	3	4	10
2	1	3	4	10
3	1	3	4	10
4	1	3	4	10
5	1	3	4	10
6	1	3	4	10
7	1	3	4	10
8	1	3	4	10
9	1	3	4	10
10	1	3	4	
Total	10	30	40	
Percentage of total items	25%	75%		100%

[a]The Recall category prescribes remembering and comprehension items.

[b]The Higher-Order category prescribes classification, evaluation, problem-solving, explanation, prediction, product development, and live performance tasks.

for each goal to one. Only three items for each goal can be included at the higher-order skill level. In selecting higher-order enabling skills, you have three options: develop three items for one enabling skill, write one item for one enabling skill and two items for another, or write one item for each of three enabling skills. Try to choose the option that will result in the best measurement of student achievement on the goal.

An Example

Suppose you developed a table of test specifications for comprehensive term and semester examinations in language arts, and you decide the following:

	Total Items	Percentage for Paragraph	Total Items for Paragraph
Term Exam	40	20	8
Semester Exam	50	10	5

Figure 4.3 contains the table of test specifications for the paragraph portions of these tests, and the following section explains the paragraph prescriptions for each test.

Comprehensive Term Exam   The term exam will cover several instructional goals besides the one for writing paragraphs. Due to the limited number of items available for this unit, the teacher specified only evaluation- and writing-level objectives. Even with this limitation, the time required to administer this portion of the term exam is estimated at 64 minutes; thus, the teacher may need to administer the term exam in sections. One strategy might be to include the objective-style items with objective items from the other units and administer the paragraph writing assessment on a separate day.

Comprehensive Semester Exam   The semester exam will cover units taught during one-half of the school year, and there will be only five items devoted to the paragraph unit. With this limitation in mind, the teacher prescribed only writing-level skills. Three short-answer items are prescribed, and students will be required to write two paragraphs. With total testing time estimated at 51 minutes for just the paragraph items, the teacher may need to separate the objective items and paragraph writing items to ensure that students do not become fatigued during the exam.

Once you have completed tables of test specifications, you are ready to begin writing test item specifications.

■ Writing Test Item or Task Specifications (Objectives)

A test item or task specification is similar to an *instructional, performance, learning,* or *behavioral* objective. These terms are all used in curriculum and instruction to identify statements of learning outcomes that are anchored to the enabling skills in an

FIGURE 4.3

A Sample Table of Test Specifications for Term and Semester Exams for the Instructional Goal "Write a Paragraph"

COMPREHENSIVE TERM EXAM

RECALL-LEVEL SKILLS						HIGHER-ORDER SKILLS						
Skills	# Items	Item Task General Format			Time	Skills	# Items	Item Task General Format			Time	
		OB	PD	PF				OB	PD	PF		Totals**
						I.F	2		X		40.0	Sk: 7
						II.E	1	X			2.0	Itm: 8
						II.F	1		X		6.0	Mn: 64
						III.E	1	X			2.0	
						III.F	1		X		6.0	
						IV.E	1	X			2.0	
						IV.F	1		X		6.0	

COMPREHENSIVE TERM EXAM

RECALL-LEVEL SKILLS						HIGHER-ORDER SKILLS						
Skills	Items	OB	PD	PF	Time	Skills	Items	OB	PD	PF	Time	Totals**
						I.F	2		X		40.0	Sk: 4
						II.F	1		X		3.0	Itm: 5
						III.F	1		X		5.0	Mn: 51
						IV.F	1		X		3.0	

*Sk = enabling skills, Itm = items, and Mn = minutes.

instructional goal framework. Recall from courses in curriculum, instructional design, and learning that performance objectives typically contain four parts: conditions, behaviors, content, and, when required for accurate scoring, criteria. Performance objectives are sometimes called *item or task specifications* in this text because there is a specific focus to this book: designing the most appropriate test items and tasks for given enabling skills and instructional goals. Very prescriptive objectives are synonymous with *test item and task specifications*. In contrast, general objectives that are sometimes encountered in curricular materials, such as "given instruction in Chapter 4, the student will be able to describe the three branches of government," are not acceptable prescriptions for designing a classroom test. The objectives, or item and task specifications, need to be much more prescriptive and describe the format of the test item. A prescription or specification is well written when two teachers can follow it to create very similar test items or tasks. The following sections describe the four parts of objectives or test item and task specifications.

Conditions

Conditions is a term used to indicate the information, tools, equipment, or other resources students will be given when they are asked to perform the skill. Conditions are used to prescribe the stimulus that will be provided for the task and to limit the task's scope and complexity so that it is reasonable for given students. They also refine the general item format prescription to describe a particular item format.

To prescribe the stimulus for a subordinate skill, consider the behavior in the skill and what students will need in order to demonstrate that behavior. Consider how the conditions in the following examples prescribe the stimuli students will be given to perform the subordinate skills:

Conditions	*Subordinate Skills*
1. Given the name of a concrete concept, . . .	1. . . . list the distinguishing properties of the concept.
2. Given a prototype of a concrete concept, . . .	2. . . . list the distinguishing properties of the concept.
3. Given a list of the distinguishing properties of a concrete concept, . . .	3. . . . name the concept.
4. Given several examples and nonexamples of a concept, . . .	4. . . . classify examples of the concept.
5. Given several examples of a concrete concept, . . .	5. . . . analyze the examples and list their common characteristics.

Although, at first glance, the stimuli appear to be obvious, this is not always the case. Notice, for example, that subordinate skills 1 and 2 are the same, yet the conditions are different. In example 1, students will be given the name as a stimulus, whereas in example 2, they will be given an actual object with which to work. The differences in these stimuli will change the nature of the task. When given the name as a stimulus, students will need to search their memories to recall the distinguishing characteristics they have learned, with no clues provided. On the other hand, the actual object will provide clues but it may also cause unskilled students to confuse unique characteristics with others not used to define the class. For example, birds, dogs, and fish all have two eyes. Being precise in prescribing the stimulus helps ensure that test items measure the intended behavior.

In setting performance conditions, you should also consider the sophistication, achievement levels, and special needs (e.g., ESOL, varying exceptionalities) of students in the group. You can vary the conditions in an item specification so that the required performance matches the skill level of your students. Consider the subordinate skill, "Locate specified places on a state map." The conditions you specify will determine the complexity of this task. Notice how the following three conditions affect the difficulty of the task:

Conditions
1. Given a simplified state map with no more than 10 identified points, . . .
2. Given a simplified state map with 20 to 30 identified points, . . .
3. Given a commercially prepared state map, . . .

Subordinate Skill
. . . locate specified places on the map.

Notice that the basic stimulus remains the same: given a state map. However, qualifiers are added to each condition to limit the complexity of the stimulus and the behavior. The first condition would be most appropriate for lower elementary grades; the second for upper elementary grades; and the third for junior high, senior high, or adult students. Although the basic skill of locating specified places on a state map remains the same, the conditions have an important effect on the complexity of the task.

Figure 4.4 lists three learning tasks and five related item specifications. The two specifications for the task, "Capitalize proper nouns," prescribe different conditions. For the first condition, students are given sentences without proper nouns capitalized. For the second, they are given a list of words containing common nouns and proper nouns.

The item specification for the second task, "Estimate the distance between specified places on a map," includes three conditions: a simplified map, a ruler, and a simplified mileage scale.

The item specifications for the third task, "Add numbers," has conditions that limit the digits in each number, the numbers in each problem, and whether regrouping is required.

■ Using an Instructional Goal Framework to Generate Test Item Specifications

The instructional goal framework is the foundation for creating test item specifications for a unit of instruction. The procedure for developing item specifications is illustrated using the hypothetical instructional goal framework in Figure 4.5. This table could represent either an intellectual skill or a verbal information goal, depending on the behaviors listed in the column headings at the top of the table. Every cell in a goal framework that contains paraphrased information connecting a content-by-learning task pair could have at least one test item specification. Therefore, in Figure 4.5, there could be one or more item specifications constructed for the cells I.A, I.B, I.C, and so forth for every cell. Synthesizing the information from the goal framework and adding realistic conditions for the students' characteristics should produce the appropriate test item specifications for the instructional goal.

FIGURE 4.4

Item Specifications for Three Learning Tasks

Task: Capitalize proper nouns.

Conditions	*Subordinate Skill*
1. Given sentences without proper nouns capitalized, . . .	. . . locate and capitalize the proper nouns.
2. Given a list of words containing common and proper nouns, . . .	. . . locate and capitalize the proper nouns.

Task: Estimate the distance between specified places on a map.

Conditions	*Enabling Skill*
1. Given a simplified map with 10 to 12 identified places, a ruler, and a scale with one inch equal to 10 miles, . . .	. . . estimate the distance between specified places, . . .

Task: Add numbers.

Conditions	*Enabling Skill*
1. Given two whole numbers of two digits that do not require regrouping, . . .	. . . add the numbers.
2. Given two whole numbers of two digits that require regrouping, . . .	. . . add the numbers,

---

FIGURE 4.5

Hypothetical Instructional Goal Framework for Identifying Test Item Specifications

CONTENT AREAS	LEARNING TASKS					
	A	**B**	**C**	**D**	**E**	**F**
I.	I.A	I.B	I.C	I.D	I.E	I.F
II.	II.A	II.B	II.C	II.D	II.E	II.F
III.	III.A	III.B	III.C	III.D	III.E	III.F
IV.	IV.A	IV.B	IV.C	IV.D	IV.E	IV.F

In addition to constructing one or more test item specifications for individual cells within the framework, you may combine cells to prescribe more complex items when appropriate. It is often unnecessary to combine cells when the instructional goal is an intellectual skill, since such cells are naturally combined due to the hierarchical nature of skills in the framework. For instance, writing topic sentences requires the synthesis of many subordinate skills. When the goal matrix represents a schemata of verbal information, however, you may want to combine cells when deriving objectives. Combination enabling skills typically form the basis for essay test questions that require the analysis skills of comparing and contrasting or the synthesis skills of describing and discussing.

In combining matrix cells, it is best to combine cells within a single row or within a single column of the framework to create these "supra-objectives." For example, you might want to create a synthesis-style objective from Figure 4.5 by combining cells I.A, I.B, and I.C within content area I. An item specification for such a combination of cells might require students to describe or discuss a concept by synthesizing information about its physical characteristics, uses, and qualities. Such a combination specification might prescribe discussing one country by location, climate, population, and government system, or prescribe discussing the circulatory system by physical, functional, and location characteristics.

Besides combining cells within a row for deriving test item specifications, cells may be combined within columns. A combination of cells from a column in the matrix will integrate information within one level of learning but across interrelated concepts in the content rows. An objective might be created that combines cells in the first column of Figure 4.5, or cells I.A, II.A, III.A, and IV.A. If these cells were each related to naming the form of government in various countries, then the item specification would relate to comparing the countries by their forms of government. Combining cells on the diagonal in the goal framework (e.g., cells I.A, II.B, III.C, and IV.D) typically does not make sense because such a combination would mix both learning task levels and main content areas, which is an illogical integration.

In summary, test item specifications are written based on the cells in the instructional goal framework. Every cell that contains information that interconnects concepts and learning tasks can have at least one item specification, and each cell may have more than one. Item specifications may be created by combining relevant cells within a concept area (e.g., describe, discuss) or across content within a learning task area (e.g., compare, contrast).

An Example

The completed table of test specifications in Figure 4.2 was used to derive the test item specifications listed in Figure 4.6 for the paragraph instructional goal. The first six columns contain information repeated from the table of test specifications, and the last column contains the actual test item prescriptions. The item format specifications, sometimes called *conditions* or *givens,* are written first. They prescribe and vary the stimulus material that students will have for performing the task, and they tailor the complexity of the task for a particular group's needs.

The conditions are followed by the behavior and content of the anchor enabling skills. The enabling skills are italicized in the table to help you visually separate the test item formatting conditions from the skills. There is at least one test item specification for each enabling skill prescribed for the posttest, and many of the higher-order enabling skills have multiple item formats specified. There are objective test item formats calling for both written and selected response items. There are also product development or creative writing task specifications for students' production of four- to six-sentence

FIGURE 4.6

Table of Test and Test Item Specifications for the Paragraph Unit Posttest Illustrated in Figure 4.2

UNIT POSTTEST

RECALL-LEVEL SKILLS					
Skills	**# Items**	**Item Task General Format**			**Test Item Specifications (Performance Objectives)**
		OB	**PD**	**PF**	**Time**	

Skills	# Items	OB	PD	PF	Time	Test Item Specifications (Performance Objectives)
I.A	1	X			.5	I.A.1 Given a description of the appearance (or physical characteristics) of a paragraph, and a list of terms related to paragraphs, *select the paragraph as the term being described.*
I.B	1	X			.5	I.B.1 Given a description of the purpose (functional characteristics) for a paragraph, and a list of terms related to paragraphs, *select the term being described.*
II.A	1	X			.5	II.A.1 Given a description of the appearance (physical characteristics) of topic sentences, and a list of terms related to paragraphs, *select the term being described.*
II.B	1	X			.5	II.B.1 Given a description of the purpose (functional characteristics) of a topic sentence, and a list of terms related to paragraphs, *select the term being described.*
II.C	1	X			.5	II.C.1 Given a description of the quality characteristics of a topic sentence, and a list of terms related to paragraphs, *select the term being described.*
III.A	1	X			.5	III.A.1 Given a description of the appearance (physical characteristics) of supporting sentences, and a list of terms related to paragraphs, *select the term being described.*
III.B	1	X			.5	III.B.1 Given a description of the purpose (functional characteristics) of supporting sentences, and a list of terms related to paragraphs, *select the term being described.*
III.C	1	X			.5	III.C.1 Given a description of the quality characteristics of supporting sentences, and a list of terms related to paragraphs, *select the term being described.*

(continued)

FIGURE 4.6   Continued

Skills	# Items	Item Task General Format			Time	Test Item Specifications (Performance Objectives)
		OB	PD	PF		
IV.A	1	X			.5	IV.A.1 Given a description of the appearance (physical characteristics) of concluding sentences, and a list of terms related to paragraphs, *select the term being described.*
IV.B	1	X			.5	IV.B.1 Given a description of the purpose (functional characteristics) of concluding sentences, and a list of terms related to paragraphs, *select the term being described.*
IV.C	1	X			.5	IV.C.1 Given a description of the quality characteristics of concluding sentences, and a list of terms related to paragraphs, *select the term being described.*

HIGHER-ORDER SKILLS						
Skills	# Items	Item Task General Format			Time	Test Item Specifications (Performance Objectives)
		OB	PD	PF		
I.D	2	X			1.0	I.D.1 Given a series of complete and incomplete paragraphs, correctly indented, *locate the complete paragraphs.*
II.D	2	X			1.0	II.D.1 Given a complete paragraph, correctly indented, *locate the topic sentence.*
II.E	4	X			3.0	II.E.1 Given an incomplete paragraph with the topic sentence, omitted, and given three to four optional sentences to complete the paragraph, *choose the best sentence to complete the paragraph.* II.E.2 Given (1) a complete paragraph with the topic sentence flawed by *relevance,* (2) a list of possible judgments about the sentence that includes "no flaw present," as well as (3) the criteria for quality sentences, *choose the problem with the sentence.*
II.F	2		X		3.0	II.F.1 Given an incomplete paragraph, missing the topic sentence, *write the sentence to complete the paragraph.*
III.D	2	X			1.0	III.D.1 Given a complete paragraph, correctly indented, *locate the supporting sentences.*

Skills	# Items	Item Task General Format			Time	Test Item Specifications (Performance Objectives)
		OB	**PD**	**PF**		
III.E	3	X			2.0	III.E.1 Given (1) a complete paragraph with the supporting sentences flawed by *interest value for reader,* (2) a list of possible judgments about the sentences that includes "no flaw present," as well as (3) the criteria for quality sentences, *choose the problem with the sentences.*
						III.E.2 Given (1) a complete paragraph with the supporting sentences flawed by *relevance,* (2) a list of possible judgments about the sentences that includes "no flaw present," as well as (3) the criteria for quality sentences, *choose the problem with the sentences.*
						III.E.3 Given a complete paragraph with either supporting sentences flawed by *transition,* and given a list of possible judgments about the sentences that includes "no flaw present," as well as the criteria for quality sentences, *choose the problem with the sentences.*
III.F	3		X		6.0	III.F.1 Given an incomplete paragraph, missing the supporting sentences, *write the sentences to complete the paragraph.*
IV.D	2	X			1.0	IV.D.1 Given a complete paragraph, correctly indented, *locate the concluding sentence.*
IV.E	3	X			2.0	IV.E.1 Given an incomplete paragraph with the concluding sentence omitted, and given three to four optional sentences to complete the paragraph, *choose the best sentence to complete the paragraph.*
						IV.E.2 Given (1) a complete paragraph with the concluding sentence flawed by *relevance,* (2) a list of possible judgments about the sentence that includes "no flaw present," as well as (3) the criteria for quality sentences, *choose the problem with the sentence.*
IV.F	3		X		3.0	IV.F.1 Given an incomplete paragraph, missing the concluding sentence, *write the sentence to complete the paragraph.*

(continued)

FIGURE 4.6   Continued

| | | Item Task General Format | | | | Test Item Specifications (Performance Objectives) |
Skills	# Items	OB	PD	PF	Time	
						INSTRUCTIONAL GOAL
I.F	4		X		40.0	I.F.1 Given a topic requiring a description of something, *write a 4- to 6-sentence paragraph.*
						I.F.2 Given a topic requiring a time series (chronology), *write a 4- to 6-sentence paragraph.*
						I.F.3 Given a topic that is a procedure for doing something, *write a 4- to 6-sentence paragraph.*
						I.F.4 Given a topic that is an expression of feelings or attitude, *write a 4- to 6-sentence paragraph.*

Note: OB = objective-style items, PD = essay or product assessments, and PF = live-performance assessments.

paragraphs. Notice also that enabling skill I. F is included at the end of the table. This was done to illustrate that skill I. F is the highest-level skill included in the unit, although the placement of skills within the table of test item specifications is a matter of preference. Figure 4.6 includes only a sample of the test item specifications that can be written for the paragraph instructional goal framework.

At this point in the development process, test items can be written for the enabling skills in the instructional goal framework, but before writing tests, it makes sense to learn some general criteria for writing items in any format that will help ensure valid, reliable test results.

■ Using Quality Criteria to Create Test Items and Tasks

Regardless of whether test items or tasks are intended to be objective, essay, product, or live performance, there are at least four general areas of quality criteria that are applied in the development of classroom assessments. These include curriculum-centered, learner-centered, school-centered, and professional-centered criteria.

Curriculum-Centered Criteria

Curriculum-centered assessments have two important areas of quality criteria for test development. The first is ensuring congruence among the test item or task and the conditions, behavior, and content prescribed in the test item specification, or objective. A second criterion is ensuring that the performance level of the standard assessed is relevant (authentic) to the level typically applied in the students' environment.

Congruence of Items with Objectives   Congruence between test items and item specifications (objectives) helps ensure that test scores are valid. When writing items, pay careful attention to the behavior, content, and conditions prescribed in the item specifications.

Behavior   The response format selected for test items should match the behavior prescribed in the specification. It is important to note whether the student needs to define, list, select, solve, construct, perform, or evaluate. As you write each item, consider alternative ways the student might respond to demonstrate the behavior, and then write the items to solicit the prescribed behavior.

Content   The content subsumed in each enabling skill may be simple or quite complex. Instances of content selected for test items should clearly reflect all facets of the content students are likely to encounter. For example, if you were selecting instances of proper nouns, you would need to select some related to person, places, and things. Writing items related to only one or two areas of content would be insufficient.

In writing test items, be careful not to confound the rules or principles measured. Items that measure two or more skills at once will be difficult to interpret because the student may select the correct answer for the wrong reason. For example, when measuring students' ability to capitalize a proper noun, the word used to measure this skill should not be placed first in a sentence. Students may respond correctly using the rule for capitalizing sentences rather than the one for capitalizing proper nouns.

Finally, you need to ensure that the instances of content you select for items are precise and relate only to the content measured. Using nouns again as an illustration, words that have multimeanings, such as *park, season,* and *field,* can be either nouns or verbs. Students will respond to multimeaning words depending on how they define them. If multimeaning words are used, they should always be placed in a context in which their meaning is precise.

Conditions   Many intellectual and motor skills can be measured only in a situation that allows students to demonstrate their skill. In order to preform, operate, analyze, synthesize, or evaluate, students must be given appropriate resources. Test items that require supplementary resources are called *context-dependent* or *interpretive* items.

For most teacher-made tests, the conditions specified in the test item specification can be matched closely or realistically simulated. The conditions, which describe what students are to be given, can specify a variety of resource materials. They may require that students be provided with such materials as short stories, pictures, charts, diagrams, data tables, models, slides, specimens, or particular products. They may also specify such equipment as computers, saws, dissecting tools, sewing machines, weighing instruments, or automobiles. In addition, conditions sometimes include facilities, such as the school library or a learning resource center. The resource materials provided to students during testing must be congruent with the conditions specified in the test item specification. These materials are just as critical to valid measurement as is the nature of the items.

Of all the quality criteria for designing test items, the congruence between the elements of the objective or item specification and the elements of the test item is the most critical. When objectives and test items are not congruent, then something besides the intended objective is most likely measured by the item.

Authenticity of Tasks   Enabling skills are typically assessed within a context or situation designed to make the students' performances as realistic and interesting as possible. Solving real problems, predicting outcomes, or explaining phenomena present and visible in their lives will provide a better assessment of students' capabilities and aid transfer of the skills learned in class to the outside world. For example, if students are entering the work world, simulations and examples related to obtaining or keeping a job would be authentic for them. On the other hand, work contexts would be inappropriate for young children. If students are to conduct an experiment, one on a topic of interest to them would be superior to one that is abstract or unfamiliar.

Learner-Centered Criteria

Learner-centered quality criteria for test development can be classified into two general areas. The first is accommodating the characteristics and needs of the learners, including adapting assessments and procedures to accommodate students with special needs. A second is avoiding cultural, gender, and other forms of bias in developing items and tests.

Accommodating Learners' Characteristics and Needs   There are several criteria related to designing tests that are congruent with learners' characteristics and needs. Table 4.3 lists criteria for test development and the rationale for each. Accommodating each criterion while developing items and tests will help ensure the validity of your test results. Regardless of whether students know the answer to a question or can perform a task, they should be clear about what is asked, and they should feel that the item or task and format are appropriate for them.

Freedom from Bias   Test items and resources should be free of stereotyping and of cultural, racial, and gender biases. People described in the items and resources should positively reflect the cultural, racial, and gender characteristics of students in the group. The contexts and problem situations used should also be appropriate for males and females and for the cultural groups represented in the class. Students who are offended by items or unfamiliar with cultural-dependent contexts used may be less able to answer correctly, thus reducing the accuracy of the scores. Carefully designing items with potential bias in mind should help eliminate unconscious stereotyping and biases.

You should also avoid using contextual material that may unnecessarily arouse students' sensitivities. Contextual reference to such topics as religion or church, political affiliations, or sexual behaviors are not appropriate in items unless the *content*

TABLE 4.3

Learner-Centered Considerations as Criteria for Test Development

Criteria Classroom assessments should be congruent with students':	Rationale
Language, vocabulary, and reading levels, including special language considerations for students who do not speak English as a home language (ESOL) and students with special needs.	Students should always know what they are asked to do in a test item or in task directions, regardless of whether they know the answer or can perform the skill.
Attention span and work habits related to age and ability levels.	Fatigue and hurrying behaviors can influence the students' accuracy in answering test items.
General life experiences, areas of familiarity, cultural backgrounds, and understandings.	Testing new information and skills in an unfamiliar context inappropriately increases the difficulty of the assessment for students.
Age and interests, including appropriate/ interesting materials, situations, and contexts.	Materials clearly geared for much younger or older students do not gain students' interest and motivation. They can cause students to consider the skills assessed to be irrelevant for their needs.
Familiarity with different test item formats (e.g., objective items, oral assessments, live performances, interpretative exercises, laboratory examinations, and timed tests).	Testing new information and skills in an unfamiliar format inappropriately increases the difficulty of the assessment for students.

of the instructional goal specifies religion, politics, or sexual behavior. Consider the following item intended to measure verb choice:

1. Fritz _____ to church last Sunday.
    a. go
    b. gone
    c. went

The religious context used in this item is inappropriate and may arouse the sensitivities of students who do not attend church or who do so on different days.

School-Centered Criteria

As noted previously, school-centered criteria are clustered in one main area called *feasibility.* Before developing assessments, you must carefully consider the number of students you are assigned and, based on this number, the time required to develop, administer, score, and provide formative or summative feedback for a particular item or test format. If you do not have the time available for a particular format, given your student load, then you should choose a more economical format prior to spending your time developing the logistics and materials for an assessment that you cannot manage. Teachers with 35 students in five classes each day, or 175 students, will have difficulty grading frequently lengthy essays, performance tests, and research papers.

Another consideration is the turnaround time between administering an assessment and reporting the results to the school office. Product and performance tests that require a lot of time to administer and score often cannot be administered at the end of a term. The end of a grading period typically means that you must administer tests in all classes within a day or two. You will also need to have all tests evaluated and graded, with grades reported to the school office within another one- or two-day period. Because of time constraints at the end of a term, many schools even prescribe objective term examinations.

A third feasibility area to consider is the availability of resources and facilities to support planned assessments. Besides your time, quality tests often require equipment, specimens, illustrative and simulated materials, resource personnel, and adequate paper and copy services. Another resource to consider is scoring services that provide individual student scores, group scores on each test item and the overall test, and enabling skill mastery scores. Schools that do not have adequate student-teacher ratios, time, and materials typically have less than the ideal classroom assessments. As you design your own tests, create the best tests feasible, given your school's resources.

Professional-Centered Criteria

Professional-centered criteria for assessment development include qualities related to the teacher's professional skills and ethics. These criteria are in six main areas, including clarity, professional appearance, creativity, application of item task formatting rules, accuracy of measures, and ethics.

Clarity   The clarity of items also affects the validity and reliability of a test. To ensure valid measures, items should be carefully constructed to avoid ambiguity and unintended complexity. Clearly written items allow students to focus their attention on the actual skill being measured. The language should be clear and precise; grammar, sentence structure, and punctuation should be correct. Each item should pose only one question. Questions that contain multiple ideas or that address several issues will confuse students of any age. Irrelevant or extraneous materials should be avoided. Instructions for responding should be clear, explaining how students are to respond as well as how resource materials are to be used.

To help ensure reliability, items should have only one correct or clearly best answer. Including more than one correct answer confuses students and can result in inconsistent answers, scoring, analysis, and interpretation.

Professional Appearance   The second criterion relates to the professional appearance of assessments. Regardless of whether they are objective, essay, product, or live performance, posttests should be typed, proofread, and well formatted within and across pages. Assessments are used to judge to students' status and progress, and they should have a professional appearance. They should not be hastily handwritten on the board or overhead transparencies.

Creativity   The third criterion is just as important, and it relates to the teacher's creativity and inventiveness in developing assessment simulations and tasks that are authentic and that engage the learner above the knowledge, comprehension, and application levels. Many teachers are very creative in test development, whereas others appear to need technical assistance.

Formatting Rules   Another criterion relates to the teacher's skill in structuring items and task directions according to prescribed formatting rules that are designed to enhance task clarity. Regardless of the item format, a student must be clear about the question or directions and the nature of the response prior to encountering the need for a response. Some students become anxious during assessments, and these formatting rules are designed to reduce anxiety and enhance their ability to perform with confidence. The next chapters on test item and task development address these commonly accepted formatting rules.

Accuracy of Measures   Some items may measure students' skills more accurately than others. Factors related to the accuracy of measures are the novelty of items, susceptibility to guessing, susceptibility to cheating, and familiarity with item and test format.

The novelty of items and resources used on a test can influence test validity. Test items should not simply duplicate those previously used in classroom instruction or on earlier tests. Whenever feasible, novel items should be used each time an enabling skill is measured. Otherwise, students may answer the questions correctly by remembering the correct answer from a previous unit test, practice test, or pretest. To ensure that students can preform the skill and are not simply recalling a previous instance, novel items should be used. The duplication of test items can lead to incorrect inferences about students' achievement levels.

Novelty of resource materials and equipment is a different matter. Resources, such as charts, stories, pictures, and data tables, should contain novel information, but the organization and kinds of information as well as the degree of complexity and detail included should remain the same as that used during instruction. Such resources as computers, saws, sewing machines, and dissecting tools should not be changed for tests. Students should be tested using the same equipment they used to practice, particularly if changing equipment might increase the complexity of the task.

Guessing behavior tends to affect the reliability of test scores. While writing items, consider the probability of students answering the question by guessing correctly. Test items that require students to select an answer are most susceptible to this problem. For example, students who do not know the answer to a two-choice item still have a 50 percent chance of answering correctly. Items containing three, four, or five choices reduce the probability of guessing correctly, but guessing remains a factor nevertheless. Items that require students to write rather than select answers also reduce the likelihood of guessing correctly.

Inadvertent clues in the item directions, or resources, also increase the probability that students will correctly guess an answer. For example, it is relatively easy for students to classify proper nouns in a list of words where all proper nouns are capitalized and all common nouns are not. Some students may use the capital letter rather than the meaning of the word to select the correct answer. To avoid this clue, you should capitalize all words in the list, capitalize no words in the list, or capitalize only some proper nouns and some common nouns. Removing potential clues from items will increase the reliability of students' scores.

Another factor that affects score reliability is the ease with which students can cheat on a test. When students are seated close together and their responses are brief, they can easily copy answers form other students' tests. When writing items that are susceptible to cheating, you should use strategies to reduce the likelihood of its occurrence. One such strategy is to create multiple forms of the test that contain the same questions but use a different item sequence on each form. With answers reordered, students' ability to locate corresponding answers at a glance will be eliminated.

Finally, students' familiarity with the item format and test medium can influence their scores. Their first experience with an essay, multiple-choice, matching, oral, or public performance exam should not be on a posttest. Likewise, testing procedures that require students to respond using such resources as a machine-scored answer sheet or a computer should not be introduced on a posttest. Students should practice using unfamiliar item formats and responding resources in a nongraded situation, such as a pretest or practice test, to avoid creating unnecessary confusion and anxiety during a posttest.

Ethics   Your assessment responsibilities require commitment to professional ethics, from assessment development through evaluating and communicating student progress. Related to development, there are many compromises you will need to make between the ideal assessment for the curriculum and student and the resources you have available. First, always create the best assessment program possible within your resources. Second, develop enough alternative forms of your posttests to diminish students' opportunities to "share" answers within and across your classes. Unethical test behavior on the part of students is often created and tolerated by teachers who do not create adequate tests and testing climates. For example, a teacher who administers the same posttest across classes within a day should not be surprised when students appear to be better prepared in the afternoon. Teachers who administer the same test year after year, and send completed tests home, should not be surprised that younger children in a family appear better prepared.

Related to using classroom assessments, in addition to using summative evaluation assessments for grading students' progress, your program should include formative evaluation assessments to support student learning and to improve instructional quality. Always evaluate the quality of your assessments and instruction using students' performance on your tests. Tests should never be used to punish an unruly or unprepared student or class, and they should never be administered as a class-activity substitute for inadequate lesson preparation. And last, grades based on your assessments should be used as descriptions of a student's status rather than as rewards or punishments for classroom behavior. Tests and grades should not be used as a means of controlling students' behavior.

With these quality criteria for developing tests in mind, you are ready to consider the formatting criteria for objective, essay, product, and live performance assessments. Suggestions for formatting each type of assessment are presented in the next three chapters.

■ Computer Technology

Creating tables of test specifications and tables of test item specifications for classroom tests is best accomplished using the *table* function in computer-based word-processing programs. Teachers can create the number of columns and rows required to create a table, and they can easily edit or duplicate information from one test type to another.

One design and development consideration of importance at this point in the process is to code carefully the instructional goals, enabling skills, and test item specifications in your tables. These codes are used to link your test designs back to your state's or district's curriculum standards. They are used to link your enabling skills to items in your computer-based test item banks and to your tests. They are also used in the feedback loop to link students' mastery performance on your tests back to the curriculum in the state and district standards. Careful coding at this point creates the linkages for tracking design, development, student performance analysis, and mastery reporting.

Another benefit of using computer files to create and refine test designs is that they can be shared among teachers within a building and district. Many districts are now creating websites for teachers to post and share instructional and assessment materials they develop. Computer-based tables of test and item specifications are easily placed on a website, and teacher-to-teacher sharing will only increase in the future, given the current and expected communications capabilities.

■ Summary

Carefully designed classroom tests can help you make correct decisions about the quality of your instruction and student progress. Test results can be used to tailor instruction and review for a particular group of students, evaluate the quality of instruction, and identify portions of your lessons that need improvement. Test results are also used to determine whether a group or individuals within a group have the prerequisite skills to begin a unit of instruction; provide students with practice during instruction; evaluate student progress; and determine students' mastery of instructional objectives.

During the design of classroom tests, you need to be concerned with the validity of your decisions based on test scores and the reliability of test scores. *Validity* refers to the appropriateness of inferences made from test scores. *Reliability* refers to the consistency or stability of scores obtained from a test. If the scores are unreliable, decisions or inferences based on them are dubious. Tests must be designed carefully to yield reliable scores and valid decisions about learner performance.

Factors related to ensuring the content validity of a test include how scores will be used; how well the subordinate skills selected represent the goal framework; the test item formats that would best measure students' achievement of each enabling skill; and the number of items required to measure achievement of each enabling skill.

To help ensure reliable test scores, follow these five steps during the design stage: (1) select a representative sample of subordinate skills from the goal framework; (2) select enough items to represent adequately the skills required in the objective; (3) select item formats that reduce the likelihood of guessing; (4) prescribe only the number of items students can complete in the time available; and (5) determine ways to maintain positive student attitudes toward testing.

The subordinate skills in an instructional goal framework should be divided into prerequisite skills (skills students should have mastered before entering a unit of instruction) and enabling skills (skills that comprise the main focus of instruction for a unit).

Teachers typically design four types of tests to help them with planning and evaluation activities. Entry behaviors tests help determine whether students possess the prerequisite skills needed for a unit of instruction. Pretests provide data useful in developing lesson plans. Entry behaviors tests and pretests are often combined and administered before instruction is planned. Practice tests are usually informal instruments administered during instruction to help ensure active student engagement. The data from practice tests permit you to evaluate students' progress, assess the quality of instruction, and provide corrective feedback to students. Posttests are administered after instruction, and the data are used to evaluate student progress, assign grades, and refine the instruction.

Careful planning and the development of tables of specifications substantially increase the likelihood of valid decisions and reliable test scores. The steps in developing test specifications for one unit of instruction are as follow:

1. Prescribe the types of tests needed to support your decisions.
2. Select the most representative set of subordinate skills from the goal framework for the types of tests prescribed.
3. Specify the general item or task format (objective, product, performance).
4. Specify the number of items for each subordinate skill.
5. Estimate the time required for students to answer the total number of items for each objective and for the test.

Teachers who want to test students on their mastery of goals from several units of instruction should design test specifications for a comprehensive posttest. The six steps in this procedure are:

1. Construct a matrix that lists all instructional goals to be measured.
2. Review the goal framework and tables of specifications for each goal listed, and insert the appropriate levels of learning across the top of the matrix (recall and/or higher-order skills).
3. Determine the overall portion of the test to be devoted to each goal and to each level of learning and record this information in the matrix.

4. Review the table of test specifications for each goal, note the item formats prescribed in each table, and select the best test format(s).
5. Use the selected test format, the time available for administering the test, and the skills of the students to determine the total number of test items.
6. Determine the number of items for each goal and for each level of learning and record this decision in the table.

The instructional goals and their subordinate skills, identified through task analysis, should be converted into test item specifications. Item specifications include the subordinate skill and the conditions. The stimulus required for the prescribed behavior and the skill level of target students help determine the conditions a teacher decides to include in item specifications. Appropriately written item specifications provide valuable guidelines for developing test items.

In writing test items and directions for tasks, your primary concerns should be the validity and reliability of the resulting scores. Effective criteria for achieving these qualities include curriculum-based, learner-based, school-based, and professional-based considerations. Related to the curriculum, test items should be congruent with the test item specification, or objective, and they should be authentic representations of how the skill is applied in the students' environment. Learner-based item and task development criteria include congruence with the learners' characteristics and needs as well as freedom from gender, cultural, or racial bias. School-based criteria are all related to feasibility of tests and procedures, and include time related to teacher-student ratio, turnaround time from test administration to score reporting, and resources for test development, administration, scoring, and reporting. Professional-based criteria include considerations of item and task clarity, the professional appearance of assessments, the teacher's creativity and skill with item formatting rules, creating accurate measures, and assessment ethics.

■ PRACTICE EXERCISES

I. Designing Test and Item or Task Specifications
   A. Test scores that accurately reflect students' mastery of instructional goals and lead to appropriate inferences about students' achievement are called _____ test scores.
   B. Test scores that are consistent and that provide a stable indication of students' performance are called _____ test scores.
   C. List four factors that affect the validity of test scores and that should be considered during test design activities.
   D. List five steps a teacher can take during test planning to help ensure reliable test scores.
   E. The subordinate skills in the goal framework that students should have mastered prior to beginning a unit are called _____ skills.
   F. The subordinate skills in the goal framework that will be the main focus of instruction during a unit are called _____ skills.
   G. List five ways teachers use test results to help plan instruction.
   H. List four ways teachers use test results to help monitor student progress.

I. Figure 4.7 includes a column for each of the four types of tests described in the chapter. The left-hand column contains statements that describe one or more tests. Match the descriptions with the appropriate type of test by checking the correct test columns. Check your responses in the completed version of Figure 4.8F in the Feedback section.

J. Design Test Specifications. Suppose you need to design the tests to support an instructional unit on writing compound sentences. This is a fundamental goal of schooling that is taught across elementary, secondary, and university levels. The instructional goal framework is located in the Feedback section of Chapter 3 in Figure 3.10F.

   1. Prescribe the types of tests that should be developed for the unit.
   2. Divide the subordinate skills in Figure 3.10F into prerequisite and enabling skills.
   3. Design a pretest, four practice tests, and a posttest for the unit using tables of test specifications.

   You may compare your test designs with those illustrated in Figure 4.9F in the Feedback section.

K. Assume you wanted to design a comprehensive posttest that could include only 45 items. Also assume that only 20 percent of the test would be devoted to the compound sentence unit.

   1. How many items on the test would relate to compound sentences?
   2. Given that you are limited to this number of items, select the major skill areas and objectives you would include, the item format you would use, and the number of items you would include for each objective.

FIGURE 4.7

Types of Tests and Their Descriptions

Descriptions	Entry Behaviors Test	Pretest	Practice Test	Posttest
A. Main purpose for test				
1. Plan instruction				
2. Evaluate instruction				
3. Revise instruction				
4. Monitor student progress				
5. Grade student performance				
B. When test is administered				
1. Before planning lessons				
2. During instruction				
3. After instruction is completed				
C. Subordinate skills included on a test				
1. Only prerequisite skills				
2. A representative sample of enabling skills from the goal framework				

II. Test Item Specifications

Write item or task specifications based on the coordinating conjunction (III) and compound sentence (IV) rows of the instructional goal matrix in Figure 3.10F. Recall that when using the matrix analysis procedure, subordinate skills are created by synthesizing the information from row and column headings and from intersecting row-by-column cells. Compare your list of item specifications with those included in Figure 4.10F in the Feedback section.

III. Criteria for Writing Test Items and Tasks

A. Name two quality characteristics of all test items.
B. List the four primary criteria areas for producing test items and tasks to ensure these quality characteristics.
C. Criteria are used while writing test items to help ensure that the items result in valid and reliable measures of students' achievement. In the following exercise, match each recommendation to its criterion area.

Criteria Areas
a. Curriculum-based criteria   **c.** School-based criteria
b. Learner-based criteria   **d.** Professional-based criteria

Recommendations
_____ **1.** Include only one question in each item.
_____ **2.** Use a response format for items that is appropriate for the prescribed behavior.
_____ **3.** Exclude extraneous material from the item.
_____ **4.** Construct items to minimize guessing correctly.
_____ **5.** Use a familiar context.
_____ **6.** Select or develop resources that accurately reflect the conditions.
_____ **7.** Select instances of content that are clearly examples and nonexamples.
_____ **8.** Use vocabulary that is readily understood.
_____ **9.** Include instances that cover the scope of content that students are likely to encounter.
_____ **10.** Select an item format that is familiar.
_____ **11.** Use correct grammar and punctuation.
_____ **12.** Construct items to reduce the probability of guessing the correct answer.
_____ **13.** Use contexts that are free from cultural, racial, and gender stereotypes.
_____ **14.** Ensure adequate time and resources for item or tasks.

IV. Evaluating Test Items

A. The left column contains sample test item specifications, the center column contains target grade level(s) for students, and the right column contains sample objective test items. Using the primary criteria, judge the quality of the item presented. In judging the item, make the following responses:
a. Flawed by objective congruence (curriculum based)
b. Flawed by target student congruence (learner based)
c. Flawed by bias (learner based)
d. Flawed by feasibility (school based)
e. Flawed by clarity (professional based)
f. The item has no apparent flaws

Specification	*Grade Level*	*Item*
IV.A.4 Given the term *concluding sentence,* recall its physical characteristics.	Primary (K–2)	1. Where is the concluding sentence typically located in a paragraph? _____
IV.A.2 Given the physical characteristics of a concluding sentence, recall its name.	Intermediate (3–6)	2. The sentence that comes last in a paragraph is called the _____ sentence. 3. **T F** The last sentence in a paragraph is called a topic sentence.
IV.B.2 Given the term *concluding sentence,* recall its function characteristics.	Middle School (6–8)	4. The purpose of the concluding sentence in a paragraph is to: **a.** Introduce the subject **b.** Elaborate the subject **c.** Entertain the reader **d.** Summarize the ideas
IV.D.1 Given a complete paragraph, correctly indented, locate the concluding sentence.	High School (Basic)	5. Mark the letter before the **concluding sentence** in the following paragraph on your answer sheet. (a) Each time we elect a president, we turn into a nation of advice oracles. (b) From every rooftop and laptop, someone's shouting out another set of instructions for the president-elect. Words of council, caution, and exhortation fill every newspaper and talk show. (c) At heart, we are a know-it-all society. 6. The purpose of the concluding sentence in a paragraph is to: **a.** Introduce the subject **b.** Elaborate the subject **c.** Entertain the reader **d.** Summarize the ideas 7. Mark the letter before the **concluding sentence** in the following paragraph on your answer sheet. (a) Mr. Garcia, the janitor, works very hard at school. (b) He arrives at 5:30 A.M., before any one else, to start his day. (c) By midmorning he often walks two miles completing his chores. (d) It is hard for him to complete his schedule of tasks each day because students and teachers always call him to solve their problems around the school. (e) By the end of the day, he is not finished and is always exhausted, but he is also proud of the positive contributions he makes for so many people.

B. *Curriculum-Based Criteria.* For the next four examples, evaluate the congruence between the item specifications and test items. Use the responses below to indicate your judgments. You may use more than one response for each item.

a. The item specification and item(s) *are* congruent.

b. The item specification *conditions* and item *stimulus material* are *not* congruent.

c. The item specification *behavior* and item *response directions* are *not* congruent.

d. The item specification *content* and item *directions* and/or *stimulus material* are *not* congruent.

Objective	*Item*
1. Given a list of words containing common and proper nouns with all words capitalized, identify the proper nouns.	*Directions:* Place a check (✓) in the space before the proper nouns in the following list.

_____ 1. french fries
_____ 2. Burger King
_____ 3. Whopper
_____ 4. Big Mac
_____ 5. hamburger
_____ 6. McDonalds

2. Given a specified liquid capacity amount, state an equivalent amount of liquid in the specified unit.

Directions: For each of the liquid measures named in column A, identify an equivalent amount for the unit of measure specified in column B.

	A		B
1.	16 tablespoons	= _____	cup(s)
2.	3 cups	= _____	quart(s)
3.	2 quarts	= _____	gallon(s)
4.	8 quarts	= _____	gallon(s)

3. Given a lower case letter, write the corresponding upper-case letter from memory.

Say, "For each of the letters I write on the board, circle the capital letter that matches it on your paper."

Letters on Board	*Responses on Answer Sheet*
f	B G E F C
a	B C P T A
l	I L J T M

4. Given simple sentences containing proper nouns without the proper nouns capitalized, locate the proper nouns.

Directions: Underline the words in the following sentences that should be capitalized.

1. he arrived early at school with his father.
2. they all enjoyed the picnic.
3. Barney went to the game with Mary and Fred.
4. seattle is located in the northwest.

V. Enrichment

For the goal analysis framework you have developed in your own content area, construct a table of test specifications for:

A. An entry behaviors test.

B. A pretest.

C. A practice test.

D. A unit posttest.

Using the general item format prescriptions in the table of test specifications, convert selected enabling skills into test item specifications by adding conditions.

■ F E E D B A C K

I. Designing Test and Item or Task Specifications

   A. Valid

   B. Reliable

   C. Factors related to validity include:

       1. The purpose for the test and how the results will be used.

       2. How well the subordinate skills selected represent the goal framework.

       3. The match between the behavior described in the subordinate skill and the test item format.

       4. The adequacy of the number of items used to measure performance on each subordinate skill.

   D. The five steps for reliability are to:

       1. Select a representative sample of subordinate skills from the goal framework.

       2. Select item formats that adequately represent the skills required in each item specification.

       3. Select item formats that reduce the likelihood of guessing.

       4. Include only the number of items that students can comfortably complete.

       5. Determine ways to maintain positive student attitudes toward testing.

   E. Prerequisite skills

   F. Enabling skills

   G. Teachers use test results to help them:

       1. Determine whether prescribed instructional goals are at the appropriate level for students.

       2. Separate the enabling skills that have been previously mastered from those that must be learned.

       3. Plan remedial, enrichment, and review activities.

       4. Evaluate the quality of the instruction.

       5. Revise instruction.

   H. In monitoring students' progress, teachers use test scores to help them:

       1. Determine who is ready to begin a unit of instruction and who should receive remedial instruction prior to beginning a unit.

       2. Identify subgroups of students to receive remedial or enrichment activities.

       3. Identify students who have mastered the enabling skills for a unit.

       4. Assign grades.

   I. The completed version of Figure 4.8F follows.

FIGURE 4.8F

Test Types and Purposes

Descriptions	Entry Behaviors Test	Pretest	Practice Test	Posttest
A. Main purpose for test				
1. Plan instruction	X	X		
2. Evaluate instruction			X	X
3. Revise instruction			X	X
4. Monitor student progress			X	X
5. Grade student performance				X
B. When test is administered				
1. Before planning lessons	X	X		
2. During instruction			X	
3. After instruction is completed				X
C. Subordinate skills included on a test				
1. Only prerequisite skills	X			
2. A representative sample of enabling skills from the goal framework		X	X	X

J. Design Test Specifications
  1. Tests should include a readiness test, a pretest, several practice tests, and at least one posttest.
  2. Referring to Figure 3.10F, the prerequisite skills should include Row I, skills I.A through I.F, and Row II, skills II.A through II.F, all pertaining to the content areas of commas and simple sentences. The enabling skills should include all the remaining cells, III.A through IV.F, pertaining to coordinating conjunctions and compound sentences.
  3. Review the test specifications for a pretest, four practice tests, and a posttest in Figure 4.9F.
K. Your comprehensive posttest would include:
  1. Nine items related to compound sentences.
  2. See the comprehensive term exam specifications at the bottom of Figure 4.9F. All the objectives prescribed are at the classification and evaluation levels. These objectives require selected response item formats due to administration and scoring time constraints that are always present at the end of a term or semester.

II. Test Item Specifications
Figure 4.10F contains item specifications for Row III and Row IV of Figure 3.10F.

FIGURE 4.9F

Table of Test Specifications for the Intellectual Skill "Write a Compound Sentence"

PRETEST

		Item Task General Format*						Item Task General Format				
RECALL-LEVEL SKILLS						**HIGHER-ORDER SKILLS**						
Skills	# Items	OB	PD	PF	Time	Skills	# Items	OB	PD	PF	Time	Totals**
III.A	1	X			.5	III.D	4	X			4.0	Sk: 12
III.B	1	X			.5	III.E	4	X			4.0	Itm: 38
III.C	1	X			.5	III.F	4	X			8.0	Mn: 43
IV.A	1	X			.5	IV.D	8	X			8.0	
IV.B	1	X			.5	IV.E	8	X			8.0	
IV.C	1	X			.5	IV.F	4	X			8.0	

POSTTEST

		Item Task General Format*						Item Task General Format				
RECALL-LEVEL SKILLS						**HIGHER-ORDER SKILLS**						
Skills	# Items	OB	PD	PF	Time	Skills	# Items	OB	PD	PF	Time	Totals**
III.A	1	X			.5	III.D	3	X			3.0	Sk: 12
III.B	1	X			.5	III.E	3	X			3.0	Itm: 30
III.C	1	X			.5	III.F	3	X			3.0	Mn: 37
IV.A	1	X			.5	IV.D	5	X			5.0	
IV.B	1	X			.5	IV.E	5	X			10.0	
IV.C	1	X			.5	IV.F	5	X			10.0	

PRACTICE TEST 1: Simple Sentence and Coordinating Conjunction

		Item Task General Format*						Item Task General Format				
RECALL-LEVEL SKILLS						**HIGHER-ORDER SKILLS**						
Skills	# Items	OB	PD	PF	Time	Skills	# Items	OB	PD	PF	Time	Totals**
III.A	1	X			.5	II.D	4	X			3.5	Sk: 5
III.B	1	X			.5	III.D	8	X			7.0	Itm: 15
III.C	1	X			.5							Mn: 12

PRACTICE TEST 2: Coordinating Conjunction

RECALL-LEVEL SKILLS						HIGHER-ORDER SKILLS						
Skills	# Items	Item Task General Format*			Time	Skills	# Items	Item Task General Format			Time	
		OB	PD	PF				OB	PD	PF		Totals**
						III.D	8	X			6.0	Sk: 3
						III.E	8	X			6.0	Itm: 24
						III.F	8	X			6.0	Mn: 18

PRACTICE TEST 3: Compound Sentences

RECALL-LEVEL SKILLS						HIGHER-ORDER SKILLS						
Skills	# Items	Item Task General Format*			Time	Skills	# Items	Item Task General Format			Time	
		OB	PD	PF				OB	PD	PF		Totals**
IV.A	1	X			.5	IV.D	15	X			12.5	Sk: 4
IV.B	1	X			.5							Itm: 18
IV.C	1	X			.5							Mn: 14

PRACTICE TEST 4: Compound Sentences

RECALL-LEVEL SKILLS						HIGHER-ORDER SKILLS						
Skills	# Items	Item Task General Format*			Time	Skills	# Items	Item Task General Format			Time	
		OB	PD	PF				OB	PD	PF		Totals**
						IV.D	10	X			6.0	Sk: 3
						IV.E	10	X			8.0	Itm: 30
						IV.F	10	X			10.0	Mn: 24

COMPREHENSIVE TERM EXAM

RECALL-LEVEL SKILLS						HIGHER-ORDER SKILLS						
Skills	# Items	Item Task General Format*			Time	Skills	# Items	Item Task General Format			Time	
		OB	PD	PF				OB	PD	PF		Totals**
						IV.D	2	X			1.5	Sk: 2
						IV.E	5	X			7.5	Itm: 7
												Mn: 9

*For general item formats, OB = objective-style items, PD = essay or product assessments, and PF = live-performance assessments.

**For Totals, Sk = enabling skills, Itm = items, and Mn = minutes. Time estimate totals are rounded up to nearest minute.

FIGURE 4.10F

**Table of Test Item Specifications for the Instructional Goal
"Write Compound Sentences"**

RECALL-LEVEL SKILLS					
Skills	**# Items**	**Item/Task General Format**			**Time**	**Test Item Specifications (Performance Objectives)**
		OB	**PD**	**PF**	
III.A	1	X			.5	1. Given a description of the physical characteristics (appearance) of a coordinating conjunction, *recall its name.*
III.B	1	X			.5	1. Given a description of the functional characteristics (purpose) of a coordinating conjunction, *recall its name.*
III.C	1	X			.5	1. Given a description of the quality characteristics of a coordinating conjunction, *recall its name.*
IV.A	1	X			.5	1. Given a description of the physical characteristics (appearance) of a compound sentence, *recall its name.*
IV.B	1	X			.5	1. Given a description of the functional characteristics (purpose) of a compound sentence, *recall its name.*
IV.C	1	X			.5	1. Given a description of the quality characteristics of a compound sentence, *recall its name.*
HIGHER-ORDER SKILLS					
III.D	3	X			3.0	1. Given simple sentences, complex sentences, and compound sentences, *indicate whether each sentence has a coordinating conjunction, and if so, locate it within the sentence.*
III.E	3	X			3.0	1. Given compound sentences with coordinating conjunctions that match and do not match the relationship between the sentences, *evaluate the congruence of the conjunction.*
III.F	3	X			3.0	1. Given two simple sentences, *name a coordinating conjunction that logically can be used to combine the sentences into a compound sentence.*
IV.D	5	X			5.0	1. Given simple sentences, complex sentences, and compound sentences, *locate the compound sentences.*
IV.E	5	X			10.0	1. Given two simple sentences, *evaluate their relationship and determine whether they can be combined into a compound sentence.*

\multicolumn{6}{c}{**HIGHER-ORDER SKILLS**}					
Skills	**# Items**	\multicolumn{3}{c}{**Item/Task General Format**}	**Time**	**Test Item Specifications (Performance Objectives)**
		OB	**PD**	**PF**		
IV.E (contin-ued)						2. Given two simple sentences, *evaluate their relationship and determine the best placement of the sentences (first or second) when combining them into a compound sentence.* 3. Given compound sentences with the subject of the second simple sentence converted (e.g., pronoun) and not converted, *evaluate the quality of the sentences.*
IV.F	5	X			10.0	1. Given two simple sentences, *convert them into compound sentences.* 2. Given the term compound sentence, *write one on a topic of choice.*

Note: OB = objective-style items, PD = essay or product assessments, and PF = live-performance assessments.

III. Criteria for Writing Test Items and Tasks

A. Two quality characteristics of all test items are *validity* of decisions made based on test scores and *reliability* of test scores.

B. The four primary criteria areas are curriculum-based, learner-based, school-based, and professional-based criteria.

C. Designing Test Items

1. d	**5.** b	**9.** a	**13.** b
2. a	**6.** a	**10.** b	**14.** c
3. d	**7.** a	**11.** d	
4. d	**8.** b	**12.** d	

IV. Evaluating Test Items

A. Test Item Specifications and Objective Test Items

1. b	**5.** b
2. f	**6.** a
3. f	**7.** c
4. a	

Note: The Hispanic gentleman in the scenario is stereotyped as a janitor. Notice that changing the word *janitor* to *principal* works very well in the paragraph.

B. Specifications and Test Items

1. b

2. a

3. c

4. b, d

Rubric for Assessing Tables of Test and Test Item/Task Specifications

0	1	2	3	I. Tables of Test Specifications	Comments
				A. Enabling skill codes are inserted from your instructional goal framework.	
				B. Appropriate number of items prescribed given the:	
				1. Stated purpose for the test (e.g., pretest, practice, posttest)	
				2. Age level	
				3. Special needs of the learner	
				4. Level of learning implied in the enabling skills.	
				C. Minutes prescribed are appropriate for enabling skill and number of items.	
				D. Balance and coverage of content areas are appropriate for comprehensive posttest (grading students' mastery).	
				E. Balance and coverage of levels of learning are appropriate for comprehensive posttest (grading students' mastery).	
				F. General item formats prescribed are congruent with enabling skill behaviors.	
				G. The enabling skill, item, and time totals are accurate for the overall test.	
0	**1**	**2**	**3**	**II. Tables of Test Item/Task Specifications**	**Comments**
				A. The conditions:	
				1. Specify the information/resources students will be given.	
				2. Specify the complexity of the assessment task.	
				3. Imply the item or task formats.	
				B. The behaviors:	
				4. Are congruent with the anchor enabling skill.	
				5. Imply level of learning required (describe, classify, execute, produce, solve, etc.) rather than manner in which student will respond (circle, underline, etc.).	
				C. The content:	
				6. Is congruent with anchor enabling skill.	
				D. The overall test item specification is:	
				7. Detailed enough to enable colleagues to create congruent test items for them.	
				8. Parsimonious (unnecessary and redundant information excluded).	

Note: 0 = None
    1 = Needs improvement (NI)
    2 = OK
    3 = Good
    Shaded cells are not scored.

SUGGESTED READINGS

Dick, W., Carey, L. M., & Carey, J. O. (2001). *The systematic design of instruction* (5th ed., pp. 116–138). New York: Addison-Wesley Longman.

Gronlund, N. (1999). *How to write and use instructional objectives* (6th ed.). Columbus, OH: Merrill.

Kubiszyn, T., & Borich, G. (2000). *Educational testing and measurement* (6th ed., pp. 45–79). New York: John Wiley & Sons.

Lynn, R. L., & Gronlund, N. E. (2000). *Measurement and assessment in teaching* (8th ed., pp. 73–168, 557–562). Englewood Cliffs, NJ: Prentice-Hall.

Nitko, A. J. (1996). *Educational assessment of students* (2nd ed., pp. 36–62, 100–122). Columbus, OH: Merrill.

Oosterhof, A. (1999). *Developing and using classroom assessments* (2nd ed., pp. 11–20, 35–44). Columbus, OH: Merrill.

Thorndike, R. M. (1997). *Measurement and evaluation in psychology and education* (6th ed., pp. 96–168). Columbus, OH: Merrill.

Thorndike-Christ, T. (1997). Assessment and educational decisions. In R. M. Thorndike, (Ed.), *Measurement and evaluation in psychology and education* (6th ed., pp. 194–214). Columbus, OH: Merrill.

Tombari, M., & Borich, G. (1999). *Authentic assessment in the classroom* (pp. 51–67). Columbus, OH: Merrill.

Worthen, B. R., White, K. R., Fan, X., & Sudweeks, R. L. (1999). *Measurement and assessment in schools* (2nd ed., pp. 55–180, 203–207). New York: Addison-Wesley Longman.

CHAPTER 5

Writing Objective Test Items

- Describe the formatting criteria for the following objective test items: completion, short answer, alternate response, clustered alternative response, matching, keyed, and multiple choice.
- Use the primary criteria and the formatting criteria to evaluate objective test items.
- Write objective test items following primary and formatting criteria.
- Assemble an objective test and write directions for responding to the items.

With the item specifications written for each enabling skill in the instructional goal framework, you are ready to begin writing test items that can be used to judge students' mastery of the enabling skills and instructional goal. This chapter includes the formatting criteria for each type of written and selected-response objective test item and procedures for formatively evaluating objective items.

Objective test items require students to write or select a correct or best answer. These items are called *objective* because they can be *scored* more objectively than any other type of item used to measure students' performance. Written-response items include sentence completion and short-answer questions. Selected-response items include alternative-response, matching, keyed, and multiple-choice items.

Objective test items are popular with classroom teachers for several reasons. First, a teacher can use them to measure many types of learning, from verbal information to the use of rules and principles, and many levels of learning, from knowledge through evaluation. Second, a wide range of content can be measured because the items can be answered relatively quickly. Third, objective tests are easier to administer, score, and analyze than are other types of tests. Fourth, they can often be adapted for use with computers and can be scored and analyzed by machine. Finally, fewer scoring errors are likely to be made, yielding scores generally more reliable than those from other types of tests.

Despite their positive features, objective tests cannot be used to measure many of the skills found in curriculum guides. For example, objective test items cannot measure students' ability to write a report, deliver a speech, construct a mobile, operate equipment, paint a picture, or play the piano. Although objective items can measure certain aspects of these skills (e.g., related terminology, rules, or procedures), actual performance tests provide a more valid measure of these skills.

■ Developing Written-Response Test Items

Written-response test items require students to recall information from memory or to apply a skill before they write the answer. These items have several positive features. Because no alternatives are provided from which students can select an answer, students are less likely to guess correctly. By analyzing students' original responses, you can identify misconceptions and problems students have. The ability to identify misconceptions will help you tailor review materials to real problems and write plausible distractors for subsequent selected-response test items. Written-response items are very versatile because they can be constructed in a variety of formats and used to measure both verbal information and intellectual skills. The following list of possible uses is not exhaustive, but it illustrates the versatility of these items. Students may be:

1. Given a definition and asked to write the name of the concept defined
2. Given the name of a concept and asked to write a brief definition for it
3. Given the name of a concept and asked to list its unique characteristics
4. Asked to supply a missing word or words in a given definition, rule, or principle
5. Given a resource paragraph and asked to recall specific details from the paragraph, supply correct punctuation, reorder information, or edit it
6. Given a written passage to analyze and then asked to list the main ideas and the relationship among them
7. Given an incomplete paragraph and asked to write an introductory or concluding sentence for it
8. Given a product and asked to list its qualities and inadequacies
9. Asked to view materials, such as slides or specimens set up at different test stations, and then to write short answers for questions posed about each exhibit

Despite their versatility, written-response items have their limitations. First, the item must be clearly written to produce the anticipated answer. More than one logical answer to an item will cause scoring problems and may reduce reliability. You must decide whether to accept logical, yet unanticipated, answers, whether to reduce credit for misspelled answers, and how much credit to allow for incomplete answers. Second, written answers cannot be machine scored. Scoring items, synthesizing answers by objectives, and analyzing individual and group responses all take time. Even though written-response items are time consuming and more difficult to score reliably, they should be the item format of choice when the behavior in the enabling skill requires a written response.

Completion Items

The distinguishing characteristic of completion (sometimes called *fill-in-the-blank*) items is that the items are complete sentences that have key terms replaced with a blank. An example completion item is: "Tests administered prior to instruction that measure students' performance on enabling skills are called _____." The following are suggestions for writing clear, effective items in this format.

1. *Remove only key words from the statement.* A statement containing too many blanks does not adequately communicate the desired answer. For example, the item, "_____ _____ are words that refer to particular _____, _____, or _____," would be quite confusing to students. This ambiguity can be corrected in either of the following ways:

   a. Proper nouns are words that refer to particular _____, _____, or _____.
   b. Words that refer to particular persons, places, or things are called _____.

2. *Place blanks for key words near or at the end of the statement.* Students should be able to anticipate the correct missing word before they encounter the blank. Placing the blank near or at the end of a statement does not change the meaning of the sentence, but students may find the item easier to read and answer.

The following suggestions will help you structure a completion item. First, write the complete statement. Second, select the key word or words you wish to eliminate. Third, if the key word is not located toward the end of the statement, rewrite the statement so the key word comes toward the end and replace it with a blank. Finally, read the statement with the words removed to ensure that enough information remains to guide students to the desired answer. The following series of statements illustrates these steps:

   a. Write statement: Nouns are words that refer to persons, places, things, or ideas.
   b. Select key word: *Nouns* are words that refer to persons, places, things, or ideas.
   c. Rewrite statement: Words that refer to persons, places, things, or ideas are called _____.

3. *Eliminate the possibility of several plausible answers.* Often, incomplete sentences can logically be completed using several different words. For example, the item, "Proper nouns are words that refer to _____ persons, places, or things," would likely produce a variety of responses. Students might insert the word *particular, specific, given, proper,* or *some.* When there are several plausible answers to an item, replace the word that was taken out and remove another instead. A much superior item would be, "Words that refer to particular persons, places, or things are called _____."

4. *Eliminate clues to the correct answer.* Students will find clues to answers in blanks that are the length of desired words, in a blank preceded by *a* or *an,* and in the use of singular or plural verbs. You can eliminate these clues by making all the blanks the same length; by using *a(an)* instead of either *a* or *an;* and by avoiding singular or plural verbs that may suggest a correct response.

5. *Paraphrase statements taken from instructional materials.* Test items that consist of verbatim statements taken from text promote rote memorization and tend to reduce students' need to read for comprehension. A much better test item would paraphrase key ideas in the text.

6. *Reduce scoring time by using answer sheets or other devices that simplify scoring.* Scoring completion items is time consuming, but there are several ways to make the task easier. Many teachers have students use a separate answer sheet with blanks numbered to correspond with those on the test. Another method is to make a column of blanks in either side margin of the test itself. Both techniques shorten the time required to score students' responses.

Short-Answer Items

Short-answer items are very versatile, and there are several ways in which they can be formatted. One type of short-answer item is a complete statement or question that requires students to insert a word, a phrase, or a sentence. Examples include:

1. Briefly define the term *proper noun.* _____
2. What are words that refer to *particular* persons, places, or things called?
   _____
3. John had $5.00. He bought a model kit for $2.56 and glue for $1.29. He paid 5% sales tax on his purchase. How much money did he have left?
   $_____
4. In the story *Habits,* describe why Clarissa may have acted as she did.

   _____

   _____

A second type of short-answer item frequently appears on mathematics tests. A group of items is presented with one set of directions. See Figure 5.1 for an example.

F I G U R E   5 . 1

Short-Answer Items with One Set of Directions

Directions: Use the sign in each problem to find the answer.

(1) 56	(2) 78	(3) 56	(4) 80	(5) 24	(6) 52
+ 43	+ 25	− 43	− 45	× 12	× 46

A third type of short-answer format is association items that require students to associate a given stimulus with a response. Students are asked to associate a word, a symbol, or a picture with something else. The directions explain what the association should be. The examples in Figures 5.2 through 5.5 illustrate this format.

FIGURE 5.2

Short-Answer Association Items: Stimulus and Response

Directions: Write a matching capital letter for each letter given.

a _____   m _____

e _____   q _____

i _____   u _____

FIGURE 5.3

Short-Answer Association Items: Stimulus and Response

Directions: The names of several traffic signs appear below. <u>Draw the traffic sign</u> that matches each sign name in the blank provided.

1. Stop _____

2. Yield _____

3. Do not enter _____

4. Railroad crossing _____

5. School zone _____

FIGURE 5.4

Short-Answer Association Items: Stimulus and Response

Directions: Name parts of flowers. For each line in the diagram (1–4), write the <u>name</u> of the part indicated by the line.

1.

2.

3.

4.

FIGURE 5.5

Short-Answer Association Items: Stimulus and Response

Directions: Write the <u>time</u> each clock indicates: minutes after the hour; minutes before the hour.

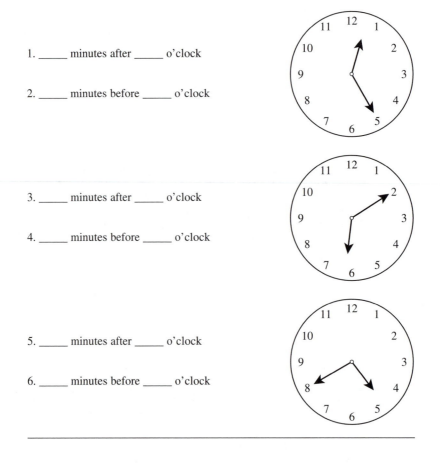

1. _____ minutes after _____ o'clock

2. _____ minutes before _____ o'clock

3. _____ minutes after _____ o'clock

4. _____ minutes before _____ o'clock

5. _____ minutes after _____ o'clock

6. _____ minutes before _____ o'clock

The following three suggestions will help you prepare good short-answer items.

1. *Provide a blank for each item that suggests whether the response should be one word or several (i.e., a phrase or sentence).* If you expect a one-word answer, the blank should be the length of one word. To avoid providing clues, make all word-sized blanks the same length. If the answer is a phrase or sentence, the blank or space should not permit students to write more than that. Some students will feel compelled to fill whatever space is allowed and will write an essay when a short answer is asked for.

2. *Specify the units required in the answer.* If the answer is to be in inches, dollars, or some other unit, specify the unit both in the question and beside the blank. Other-

wise, some students may use alternative or inappropriate units in their answers. Clearly indicated units help ensure that an incorrect answer was not the result of misreading or misunderstanding the question.

3. *Ensure that the directions for a cluster of items are appropriate for all items in the set.* If one set of directions is used for a set of items, ensure that all items included are compatible with the directions. When a set of associations is to be made, state the basis for the association and the type of response sought. Include only homogeneous stimuli in the set.

■ Developing Selected-Response Test Items

Selected-response items require students to choose an answer from a given set of plausible, alternative choices. Because each item must include one or more incorrect alternatives, selected-response items can be difficult to construct. Incorrect alternatives, sometimes called *distractors* or *foils,* should not be tricky or obscure and should not contain material unfamiliar to the students. Instead, they should represent plausible misconceptions that students may have developed. Because the correct answer appears in each item, students have a better chance of guessing correctly than they would with written-response items, and their potential for guessing correctly is increased when distractors do not appear reasonable.

Despite these drawbacks, using selected-response items has several advantages. First, each item requires students to choose among alternative responses that they may not have considered otherwise. These items can require students to make fine distinctions among several plausible answers. Therefore, teachers can use them to test aspects of students' skills that cannot be tested with other item formats. Second, students can answer more selected-response items than written-response items in the same period of time. Thus, a selected-response test can measure a wider range of skills than can a written-response test, when the two testing times are equal. Third, selected-response tests can be adapted for computer administration, or scoring can be done by machine. The following sections describe different types of selected-response items and present suggestions for item development.

Alternative-Response Items

Alternative-response items give students a choice of two responses. Each item presents a statement that students are to judge. The directions may ask students to make such decisions as whether the statement is true or false, correct or incorrect, or fact or opinion. The alternative-response format is desirable because it can be used to measure several types and levels of learning. For example, it can be used to:

1. Test students' ability to recall information. Students can be asked to determine whether a definition, a rule, or a principle is stated correctly.
2. Determine whether students can use a definition to classify examples and nonexamples of a concept.

3. Determine whether students can judge the correctness of given analyses or syntheses material.
4. Assess students' ability to evaluate material. For example, after reviewing selected materials, students can be asked whether they agree or disagree with given evaluations of the materials.
5. Apply principles in order to judge the accuracy of statements of causality or correlation.

In spite of its versatility, students have a 50 percent chance of guessing the correct answer to an alternative-response item. To reduce the potential for guessing correctly, some teachers modify the format by asking students to change an underlined word or words in an item if they believe the item is incorrect as stated. The students are directed to write the correct information either above the underlined word or in a blank provided beside the item. The following example illustrates a traditional and a modified true-false item.

Traditional
T   F   1. A served tennis ball that strikes the net before landing in the appropriate area is called a net ball.

Modified
T   F   <u>let</u>   1. A served tennis ball that strikes the net before landing in the appropriate area is called a <u>net</u> ball.

Because it reduces the probability of guessing, the modified alternative-response item results in more valid and reliable test scores than does the traditional item. Students may recognize that the statement in a traditional item is incorrect, but they still may not know the correct answer or the reasons they thought the statement was wrong. With the modified format, students must first recognize that the statement is false and then supply the correct information. Although this modification reduces the probability of guessing correctly, it also increases scoring time. It can no longer be totally machine scored unless the test is administered by computer. The desirability of this modification will depend on the time and resources available for scoring.

The following suggestions for developing alternative-response items deal primarily with the directions for items and with the statements students are asked to judge.

1. *Explain judgments to be made in the directions.* Alternative-response items can be used to have students make a variety of judgments, such as true-false, yes-no, correct-incorrect, and fact-opinion. The nature of the required judgment should be clearly described.

2. *Ensure that answer choices logically match the necessary judgments.* For example, if students are to determine whether statements are *true* or *false,* the best answer choices are *true* and *false.* If a statement logically requires a *yes* or *no* answer, the item

should offer students these two choices. If students are to determine whether a statement reflects fact or opinion, the two answer choices should be *fact* and *opinion.*

3. *Explain in the directions how students are to record their answers.* Without explicit instructions, students are likely to respond in a variety of ways. Directions should indicate whether students are to circle letters or words, fill in circles or spaces on a machine-scored answer sheet, or write words in blanks beside the items.

4. *Include only one idea to be judged in each statement.* Statements that include several ideas or that are only partially true will confuse students and affect their answer choices. A simple sentence with clear, precise wording at an appropriate vocabulary level is most appropriate. One exception to this rule is an item intended to check students' ability to detect causality or correlation.

5. *Word statements in a positive manner.* Negatively stated items are more complex and difficult to interpret than are positive statements. Negative words, such as *no* and *not,* add confusion that can reduce both the validity and reliability of students' responses. In effect, such items may be measuring the students' ability to read carefully rather than their objective-based skills. For example, students attempting to respond to the statement, "The word *boy* is not a noun," would have to recall the definition for nouns and then determine whether the word *boy* fits the definition. If they decided that the word was a noun, they would then need to note the word *not* and select false as the correct response. Some students may know that the word *boy* is a noun, miss the word *not* in the statement, and incorrectly mark the statement as true. If there is a legitimate reason for including negative words in a statement, they should be underlined or written in all capital letters to attract students' attention.

6. *Avoid designing questions to trick students.* Teachers who intentionally create items meant to trick students may also be tricking themselves. Such items not only confuse students but may also make the students' scores uninterpretable. A teacher using trick items would not be able to determine whether the instruction was effective or whether students were ready to begin the next lesson.

7. *Avoid providing clues to the correct answer.* Unintended clues help students guess the correct answer to test items. Any type of pattern, either in the directions, items, or responses, will guide students toward the right responses. An obvious example is the use of statements that are either all true or all false. Some students will quickly detect and accept this pattern, whereas other students will distrust the pattern of their answers and change some of them to the alternative. Less obvious, but still detectable, patterns can affect test results. Such patterns include the consistent use of true and false statements of different lengths, the obvious preference for one answer type, and the alternate placement of true and false items. For example, students will quickly recognize a pattern in which true statements are always longer than false ones. To avoid providing these types of clues, you should make statements of both types approximately the same length, review the list of statements to ensure that one type is not dominant, and review the sequence of responses to ensure that no pattern exists.

A final type of clue is the use of determiners or qualifiers, such as *always, never,* and *absolutely.* A statement that includes these and similar words strongly suggests an answer of false or no. This type of clue is one of the easiest to avoid.

Table 5.1 contains poor and improved examples of test items for the item specification, "Given the definition of a noun, identify it as such." The item specification appears at the top of the table. The suggestions discussed in this section are listed on the left. The second column provides examples of items that do not incorporate these suggestions, and the third column shows revisions of the same items.

Clustered Alternative-Response Items

A useful modification in the alternative-response item is called the *clustered alternative-response format.* The purposes for this format are to eliminate redundancy in items and to reduce reading time. These items include a common set of directions and short items of only one or a few words. For example, the following set of repetitive items could easily be clustered.

T F 1. The word *house* is a noun.
T F 2. The word *happy* is a noun.
T F 3. The word *bird* is a noun.
T F 4. The word *ran* is a noun.

To reduce the redundancy, redesign the items to appear as follows:

Directions: Identify nouns. For each of the following words, circle <u>YES</u> if the word <u>is</u> a noun and <u>NO</u> if the word <u>is not</u> a noun.

Yes No 1. house
Yes No 2. happy
Yes No 3. bird
Yes No 4. ran

The following suggestions will help you write good clustered alternative-response items:

1. Ensure that every item in the cluster is congruent with the response directions.
2. Ensure that only one of the two response options can be correct for each item.
3. Ensure that the instances included adequately sample the content in the objective.
4. Ensure that no clues are provided through patterns of answers or the number of items included in each category.

Figure 5.6 contains 12 clustered alternative-response items for the skill "Given a list of words containing nouns and other parts of speech, select words that are nouns." Using the suggestions as a guide, review the directions and cluster of items in Figure 5.6 to see whether you can locate potential problems.

TABLE 5.1

Alternative-Response Test Items for the Item Specification (Objective) "Given the Definition of a Noun, Identify It as Such"

Suggestion	Item		Improved Item
Ensure that answer choices logically match the judgments to be made.	**1 2**	1. Nouns are words that refer to people, places, things, and ideas.	**T F** 1. Nouns are words that refer to people, places, things, and ideas.
Include only one idea in each statement.	**T F**	1. Nouns are words that refer to people, actions, places, conjunctions, things, and modifiers.	**T F** 1. Nouns are words that refer to people, places, things, and ideas. **T F** 2. Nouns are words that refer to actions, conjunctions, and modifiers.
Use clear, precise wording.	**T F**	1. Words used in the English language to reference persons we are speaking or writing about are called *nouns*.	**T F** 1. Words that refer to people are called *nouns*.
Statements should clearly relate to one of the alternatives.	**T F**	1. Words that refer to any physical object are sometimes called *nouns*.	**T F** 1. Words that refer to physical objects are nouns.
Make the wording of statements positive.	**T F**	1. Nouns are not words that refer to action.	**T F** 1. Nouns are words that refer to action.
Make both correct and incorrect statements about the same length.	**T F**	1. Nouns are words that refer to persons, places, things, and ideas.	**T F** 1. Nouns are words that refer to persons, places, things, and ideas.
	T F	2. Nouns are words that refer to actions.	**T F** 2. Nouns are words that refer to actions, conjunctions, and adjectives.
Avoid specific determiners, such as *always* and *never.*	**T F**	3. Nouns are words that refer to conjunctions.	
	T F	1. Nouns are words that always refer to people.	**T F** 1. Nouns are words that refer to people.

Initially, it appears that all the items in the set are congruent with the directions (suggestion 1). However, each word in the list cannot be answered correctly with only one of the options (suggestion 2). Of the words chosen for the list, both *farm* and *park* fail to meet this criterion because they can be either nouns or verbs. Some students may visualize *park* as a place, whereas others may interpret it as an action. Some may visualize *farm* as a place, whereas others may define it as what a farmer does to obtain crops. This means that both responses could be correct for these terms, thus creating scoring problems.

FIGURE 5.6

Clustered Alternative-Response Test Items for the Item Specification "Given a List of Words Containing Nouns and Other Parts of Speech, Select Words That Are Nouns"

Directions: Identify nouns. Each of the following words is either a noun or some other part of speech. If the word is a noun, circle <u>yes</u>. If the word is not a noun, circle <u>no</u>.

Words	Noun	Not a Noun
1. farm	yes	no
2. mouse	yes	no
3. library	yes	no
4. happy	yes	no
5. swiftly	yes	no
6. man	yes	no
7. tall	yes	no
8. aunt	yes	no
9. park	yes	no
10. book	yes	no
11. took	yes	no
12. where	yes	no

According to the third suggestion, the words in the cluster should adequately sample the content of the enabling skill. Two items, *man* and *aunt,* refer to persons. *Farm, library,* and *park* refer to places, and *mouse* and *book* refer to things. There are no examples included to represent the idea category of nouns. Therefore, the list does not adequately cover the content.

Finally, you should look for potential clues in the cluster. Clues might be found in the order of items in the list, in the number of instances included in each content category, and in the number of nonexamples. In Figure 5.6, nouns related to persons, places, and things are dispersed throughout the list, and nonexamples are interspersed as well, so no clue is provided there. The number of instances for each category is varied—two words relate to persons, three to places, two to things, and five to nonexamples. Therefore, no clues related to the number of items in each category are provided.

Several adaptations could be made to the directions for responding to the clustered items in Figure 5.6 to simplify responding and scoring. One would be to instruct students simply to place a check (✓) in the blanks before words that are nouns and to make no mark in the blanks before words that are not nouns. Another set of directions could be used to adapt these items for machine scoring. Students could be instructed to darken response 1 on the answer sheet for items that are nouns and to darken response 2 for items that are not nouns. If answer sheets are to be used, it is a good idea to modify the cluster of items as well to help students remember which space on the answer sheet corresponds to the response they wish to make. The list of words could be modified for machine scoring, as illustrated in Figure 5.7.

Word List Modified for Machine Scoring

Directions: Identify nouns. Each of the following words is either a noun or some other part of speech. If the word is a noun, darken ① on your answer sheet beside the item number. If the word is <u>not</u> a noun, darken ② on your answer sheet beside the item number.

Word	Noun	Not a Noun
1. farm	①	②
2. mouse	①	②
3. library	①	②

Matching Items

Matching items are another popular selected-response format. These items require students to match information in two columns. Items in the left-hand column are called *premises*, and those in the right-hand column are called *responses*. Students are required to locate the correct response for each premise.

Although this format cannot be used to measure all levels and types of learning, matching exercises permit a teacher to measure many related facts, associations, and relationships quickly. It is an excellent way to measure students' ability to associate terms with their definitions, associate symbols with their names, name parts of an illustration, relate dates with names or events, match individuals with their accomplishments, and classify examples of concepts. Additionally, this item format is easily adapted for machine scoring. The one difficulty teachers have with the matching format is identifying multiple, plausible responses for each premise in the set. The following suggestions for writing matching items address the directions, the premises, and the responses:

1. *Provide clear, informative directions.* The directions should describe the types of items in each column and the basis for matching them. The directions should also indicate how and where responses are to be made and whether a response can be used more than once.

2. *Ensure that a set of premises is homogeneous and includes the more difficult reading material.* A set of premises should contain items that present the same kind of information (e.g., either authors, inventors, explorers, or politicians). Information on a variety of topics should not be included. If long phrases or sentences are to be used, they should be placed in the *premise* rather than the *response* column. For example, if definitions and symbols are to be matched, the premise should be

the definition and the shorter symbol the response. The set should be limited to four to six items to help avoid irrelevant complexity.

3. *Ensure that responses are homogeneous, brief, and logically ordered.* Like the set of premises, the set of responses should be homogeneous; unrelated information is not likely to function well as distractors. The set of responses should contain more than one plausible response for each premise to avoid students guessing the correct answer through the process of elimination. Because students will reread the responses several times while matching items in the set, the responses should be as brief as possible. The responses should be arranged in chronological, alphabetical, or numerical order to help students locate their chosen answers and to help avoid pattern clues.

4. *Avoid one-to-one correspondence between premises and responses.* A different number of premises and responses should be included in a set. For example, if there are only four of each included, when three of the four items are matched, the answer to the fourth becomes automatic. This problem can be avoided in one of two ways. First, the set can be designed so that one response is correct for two or more of the premises. Second, more responses than premises can be included in the set. Either solution helps avoid the problem. The directions should always indicate whether a response can be used more than once.

Figure 5.8 contains a set of matching items for the instructional goal "Name common traffic signs." The set, which measures students' ability to associate traffic sign names with their shapes, applies the suggestions just outlined. The directions describe the enabling skill, the types of information in the columns, the basis for matching items, and how to mark responses. Both the *premise* and *response* columns contain homogeneous material. Notice that sign colors have not been included in the response list. Mixing colors and shapes would break the homogeneity of the list and substantially and unnecessarily increase the complexity of the item. Although there are eight premises and eight responses, multiple premises match the same response in order to avoid providing clues. The matching format is an efficient way to measure the verbal information skills in this goal.

Keyed Items

Keyed items are similar in format to matching items. Like matching items, they include a set of responses for several different questions. Unlike matching items, the sets of premises and responses are placed one above the other, rather than side by side, to facilitate spacing on the page. The suggestions for writing matching items also apply to keyed items. Figure 5.9 provides an example of this format. The homogeneous set of responses appears above the item statements. Each item asks for the name of a learning level, and to avoid clues, there are more responses than items. Notice that the responses are placed in the defined order of complexity from knowledge to evaluation to help students locate the answer they choose. The definitions, presented as items, are mixed in their order of complexity.

FIGURE 5.8

Matching Items for the Instructional Goal "Name Common Traffic Signs"

Directions: Match traffic signs with their names. Column A contains the names of common traffic signs. Column B contains the shapes of traffic signs. For each sign named in Column A, select the matching shape in Column B. Place the letter of the matching shape in the blank before the name of each sign. A response may be used more than once or not at all.

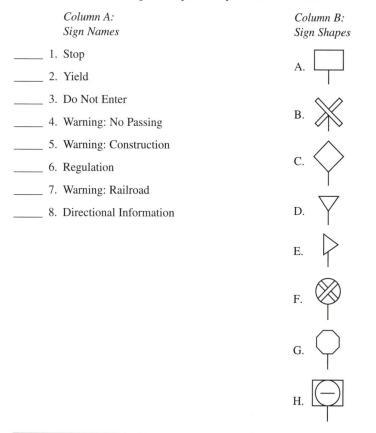

Column A:
Sign Names

_____ 1. Stop

_____ 2. Yield

_____ 3. Do Not Enter

_____ 4. Warning: No Passing

_____ 5. Warning: Construction

_____ 6. Regulation

_____ 7. Warning: Railroad

_____ 8. Directional Information

Column B:
Sign Shapes

■ Writing Multiple-Choice Items

Multiple choice is one of the selected-response test item formats, but it is given its own section in this chapter because it is the most popular and most frequently used of the selected-response formats. It commonly appears on classroom tests in all grade levels and subjects and is used almost exclusively on standardized tests. Although multiple-choice items can be formatted in several ways, these items have certain common characteristics: an initial stem that introduces a problem or asks a question and a list of three or more alternative responses following the stem. The list of responses includes a correct answer and several incorrect answers.

FIGURE 5.9
Keyed Items That Measure Knowledge of Bloom's Levels of Learning

Directions: Define Bloom's levels of learning. The following items contain descriptions of Bloom's levels of learning. The responses name the levels of learning. Place the letter for the correct learning level in the blank before each description.

Responses
a. Knowledge
b. Comprehension
c. Application
d. Analysis
e. Synthesis
f. Evaluation

_____ 1. Divide a communication into its component parts and describe the relationship among the parts.

_____ 2. Use prescribed criteria to judge the quality of a product.

_____ 3. Recall the exact definition of a term.

_____ 4. Use rules and principles to solve a problem.

_____ 5. Paraphrase a given idea.

   The versatility of multiple-choice items has caused teachers to select this item format more than any other. A test made of such items can be an excellent diagnostic tool with the following advantages:

1. Multiple-choice items can measure both verbal information and intellectual skills. Within the intellectual skill category, they can measure all levels, from knowledge through evaluation.
2. These items can be used to focus students' attention on particular aspects of a problem.
3. By providing multiple responses, these items can force students to choose among alternatives that they may not have otherwise considered.
4. By instructing students to select the best answer, these items can measure students' ability to make fine discriminations.
5. Multiple-choice items permit the use of more than one correct alternative in a set of responses (e.g., Both A and B are correct).
6. They enable measurement of a wide range of content in a relatively short time period.
7. They can be reliably scored.
8. They are easily adapted for machine scoring and for computer administration and scoring.
9. Multiple-choice items are easily compiled into item banks.

At the same time, multiple-choice items have their limitations. First, like other objective items, they cannot directly measure attitudes or motor skills that require demonstration and active performance. However, they can measure the intellectual skills and verbal information that support attitudes and motor skills. Second, students who do not know the correct answer to a multiple-choice question can sometimes guess correctly. Third, teachers usually have difficulty in thinking of plausible incorrect answers that reflect students' actual misconceptions and problems. Incorrect alternatives that are illogical to students diminish the diagnostic value of these items as well as the validity of the test results. The following suggestions for writing multiple-choice items relate to the stem, the responses, and the placement of items.

The Stem

The stem of a multiple-choice item poses a problem or asks a question; it can be formatted in several ways. The most common format is a complete sentence or question. Using this format, the stem resembles the short-answer item except that students select rather than write their answers. A second popular format is the incomplete statement that students complete by selecting one of the responses. This stem format closely resembles the completion item. A third widely used format embeds the stem in the directions. The stem in this case poses a single problem for a series of items that contain only responses. This format avoids repeating the same problem numerous times. Figure 5.10 contains an example of each of these stem formats.

FIGURE 5.10

Common Formats for the Stem of a Multiple-Choice Item

I. *Complete Question*

What level of learning requires breaking a message into its parts and showing the relationships among the parts?
a. Knowledge
b. Comprehension
c. Application
d. Analysis
e. Synthesis

II. *Incomplete Statement*

The level of learning that requires breaking a message into its parts and showing the relationships among the parts is called:
a. Knowledge
b. Comprehension
c. Application
d. Analysis
e. Synthesis

III. *Common Stem Embedded in Directions*

Locate the nouns in the following sentences. Place the letter of the words that are nouns in the blank before the sentence.

_____ 1. The plump squirrels ran up and down.
             a   b   c   d

_____ 2. The band was energetic and noisy, if not melodious.
             a   b   c   d

Many teachers prefer stems that are complete questions or statements, such as those in examples I and III, to the incomplete statement format illustrated in example II. Complete questions and statements provide all the information students need to answer the question before they consider the response choices. Students may need to read an incomplete statement several times before they understand what is being asked. The complete question or statement is usually less confusing to them and therefore more efficient. When the incomplete statement format is used, all information required to formulate the responses from memory should precede the colon. In other words, students should not need to read the responses in order to determine the nature of the question.

Regardless of the format used for stems, the suggestions for writing them are the same as those for writing other objective items. The wording should be clear and precise, and the punctuation should be accurate. If negative words are necessary, they should be underlined or highlighted to ensure that they will not be overlooked. When embedding the stem in directions, the stem or problem should precede the directions for marking responses.

Responses

The responses for a multiple-choice answer consist of a correct answer and two or more incorrect answers, which are called *distractors* or *foils*. The responses can be designed using a variety of formats. They may be symbols, words, phrases, or sentences that are listed vertically beneath the stem (the traditional format). However, responses can also be embedded in contextual material, such as sentences, paragraphs, or articles. They can be the labeled parts of pictures, illustrations, or data tables. When testing young children or nonreaders, responses may be a series of pictures or illustrations. They may also consist of a set of real objects, such as rocks, tools, equipment, slides of specimens, or beakers of liquid. In addition, an object can have its parts labeled as responses. Examples of these response formats appear in Figure 5.11.

Correct Responses   Good correct responses should be brief, clear, grammatically consistent with the stem, and clearly labeled with a number or letter. Information taken from the textbook should be paraphrased. Key words from the stem should not be repeated in the correct answer as this will provide a clue. When it is necessary to repeat a key word in the correct response, then the same word should be included in at least one of the distractors. An item should contain only one best answer, even when two or more of the options are correct. A single-answer choice can be used to combine multiple correct options into a best answer—for example, "Both A and B are correct" or "All of the above are correct." Although multiple correct answers add to the versatility of the multiple-choice item, do not use them simply because you cannot think of good distractors for the item.

Distractors   Ideally, an item should enable you to differentiate between students who know the correct answer and those who do not. Quality distractors that reflect common misconceptions and problems are more likely to help you make this differentiation. If unskilled students can immediately eliminate incorrect responses, the item is not functioning as it should.

FIGURE 5.11

Response Formats for Multiple-Choice Items

Type of Response	Test Items
1. Vertical list of symbols, words, phrases, or sentences following a stem	What is the name of a word that refers to a person, a place, or a thing? a. A noun b. A pronoun c. An adjective d. An adverb
2. Set of pictures or illustrations	Teacher says, "Color the square."
3. Labeled parts of an illustration or picture	*Directions:* Locate direction in a map. The map in Figure 1 has its edges labeled A, B, C, and D. Choose the edge that answers questions (1) through (4). _____ (1) Which edge is north? _____ (2) Which edge is west? _____ (3) Which edge is south? _____ (4) Which edges bound the northeast? *Figure 1*
4. Labeled objects	At station 1 you will find a set of four leaves. Each leaf is labeled either A, B, C, or D. Which leaf was taken from a *deciduous* tree? (Assume four different leaves are labeled and placed at station 1.)

5. Embedded in sentences	*Directions:* Find the *verbs* in the following sentences. Write the letter under the verb in the space before the item number.
	
	_____ 1. Beth ran swiftly down the path.
	          A B C D E
	_____ 2. John felt superb after the award.
	          A B C D E

6. Embedded in paragraphs, stories, or articles	*Directions:* Read the following paragraph and decide whether you think all the sentences in it relate to the topic. If you find a sentence that does *not* fit the topic, underline it. I can see so many things on a hike in my neighborhood. The trees, bushes, and flowers in my neighbors' yards are always interesting because they change with the seasons. Sometimes I can even see people in their yards mowing the grass, pruning the bushes, or weeding the flower beds. I enjoy planting flowers. Once I saw workmen sawing down a large oak tree and loading it into a big truck. I decided to sit down and watch them work. It was interesting to see how the appearance of the yard and house changed as more and more of the tree was removed. I see something different every time I take a walk.

Quality distractors are much more difficult to write than is the correct response. One problem is the difficulty of identifying misconceptions and problems the students are likely to have. Plausible distractors can be found in the content of other enabling skills in the same or related lessons, in questions students ask in class about your presentations or their homework, and in students' written responses on pretests and practice exercises. If you analyze the nature of their questions and errors, you will be able to construct quality distractors that help detect persistent problems.

Even though you may have identified actual misconceptions to use as distractors, several factors can reduce their attractiveness to unskilled students. The use of unfamiliar words or ideas unrelated to the lessons, the lack of homogeneity in the list of responses, and grammatical incompatibility between the distractor and stem can cause students to avoid otherwise attractive distractors. One strategy for increasing the attractiveness of a distractor to students who are guessing is to repeat a key word from the stem in a distractor. Students who are using key words as clues to the correct answer will be drawn to this option.

Machine-Scored Responses   When machine-scored answer sheets are used, students can become confused and mark the wrong space. Marking errors affect both the validity and reliability of the scores. Labeling the test responses so that they correspond to the response letters and numbers on the answer sheet will reduce the probability of marking errors. For example, answer sheets are designed so that either letters or numbers can be used to identify responses. One type of response will appear at the top of the column, and the other type will appear within the circles, parentheses, or brackets beside the item number. The following example illustrates such an arrangement:

		Responses			
Item	*A*	*B*	*C*	*D*	*E*
1.	①	②	③	④	⑤
2.	①	②	③	④	⑤
3.	①	②	③	④	⑤

As students continue down the answer sheet, they will have more and more difficulty using the response codes across the top of the column (in this example, A, B, C, D, and E). Thus, using the response codes beside the items on the answer sheet when constructing your items is a better method. One caution should be made. If the options beside the item number are numbers (as illustrated), and the answer to the question is also a number between one and five, then students are likely to confuse the answer number with the response code number. The following example illustrates this problem:

Question: 1. 2 + 0 = _____   *Correctly coded:*   1. 1   2   ③   4   5
             1. 0   *Misplaced:*   1. 1   ②   3   4   5
             2. 1
             3. 2
             4. 3
             5. 4

When numbers are used to code the responses, students will often darken the numbered space that matches the numeric answer rather than the correct answer code. For such items, use the letter codes across the top of the column or match the answer code and response numbers if possible. Other types of items on the same test can require students to use the more convenient numbered responses.

Editing Items

Once the stem, correct response, and distractors are written, then evaluate the entire item. Words repeated in each response should be removed and placed in the stem to avoid unnecessary redundancies. The set of responses should be sequenced logically using an alphabetical, chronological, numerical, or procedural order whenever possible. Additionally, check to see whether clues to the correct answer have been provided. The following mistakes are common in writing multiple-choice items that provide clues:

1. Only the correct response repeats a key word from the stem.
2. Distractors are consistently longer or shorter than the correct answer.
3. The correct answer is more technical and detailed than the distractors.
4. Answer options that indicate multiple responses, such as "Both B and D are correct," appear only when these options are the correct answers. If other test items do not include these options as distractors, students will quickly identify the pattern.
5. The correct response frequently appears in the same position in the set. Some teachers consider the first and last positions too obvious, and they tend to place the correct answer in the middle. Using a logical sequencing strategy for the responses, such as alphabetical or numerical, will help you avoid such detectable patterns.

Item Format and Placement

Practice in writing multiple-choice items will help you gain the skill necessary to write good diagnostic items. The following suggestions for item format and placement can help you develop multiple-choice tests that are easy for students to use.

1. List single-sentence, phrase, or word responses vertically beneath the stem and begin each response on a separate line.
2. Underline and code responses embedded in a sentence or paragraph.
3. Place the stem and all responses on the same page.
4. Place resource materials that cannot be included on the same page on a separate, unattached page for easy reference.
5. Label resource materials with titles, such as Figure 1 or Table 1, so they can be clearly identified in the directions.
6. Place directions for locating and using resource materials before the resource materials.
7. Place resource materials included on the same page before the related items.

8. For items requiring the use of real objects, set up work stations with numbers that correspond to related items on the test.
   a. Sequence work stations to match the order of items on the test.
   b. Label each object or part of an object to match a response code on the test paper.

Writing Objective Test Items

With the primary criteria and the formatting criteria for each type of objective test item in mind, you are ready to begin writing items. These test items should be linked to the item specifications you have written for the enabling skills in your instructional goal. Selected item specifications for the paragraph instructional goal contained in Figure 3.6 are used to illustrate the link between objective test items and specifications. Table 5.2 contains sample test items for the selected specifications. The first column in the table includes the code and item specification objective. The second column contains the types of items that can be created to assess students' acquisition of the skill, and the third column includes sample test items. When you have the item specifications before you as a reference while you write items, you are more likely to create items that are congruent with them.

In addition to linking items to item specifications, you should construct items at the appropriate language and complexity level for your students. Notice the three multiple-choice items at the end of Table 5.2. All three items can test the skill, "Locate the topic sentence in a paragraph." They differ, however, in the complexity of the subjects addressed, vocabulary level, sentence complexity, and the responding behavior. Elementary-age pupils would have difficulty responding to the first two items, and most senior high level students would be bored with the paragraph on baking cupcakes. Senior high students with lower reading abilities, however, may have more success with the second paragraph than the first.

You should also take care during item construction not to stereotype characters included in your scenarios. Notice in the second multiple-choice item that a boy, not a girl, is baking the cupcakes. Without conscious effort, many teachers illustrate girls helping around the house or providing an audience for others, while boys are depicted adventuring, earning cash, or being admired for some accomplishment.

Assembling an Objective Test

With the test items written and each objective test designed to serve a particular purpose, you are ready to assemble your tests. The order in which items are placed on the test is important, and there are three criteria to consider before determining item order. These criteria include ensuring that the item order does not

1. Contribute to inadvertent test complexity for students taking the test.
2. Provide students with unintended clues to the correct answers.
3. Make scoring the test or analyzing students' performance more difficult than necessary.

TABLE 5.2

Objective Test Items Linked to Test Item Specifications for the Instructional Goal "Write a Paragraph"

Item Specification Code	Item Format	Item
II.B.1 Given the term *topic sentence,* recall its functional characteristics.	Short Answer	■ What purpose does the **topic sentence** serve in a paragraph? _____ ■ Why are **topic sentences** included in a paragraph? _____
II.F.1 Given an incomplete paragraph that is missing a topic sentence (time series, feelings, procedure, or description), write a topic sentence to introduce the paragraph.	Short Answer	**Write Topic Sentences.** For the following incomplete paragraphs, write topic sentences to introduce them. Please write your sentences in the blank provided on your answer sheet. 1. _____ One product that always surfaces on TV at Christmas is the "Clapper" that can turn off and on lights and appliances with a clap of the hands. Another relatively late comer, yet persistent cyclical product, is the "Chia Pet" that grows plants into an animal shape when seeds and water are added to the planter. A third holiday cycle product is the Remington "micro-shave" that "shaves as close as a blade or your money back." If the number of people who receive these products as gifts is proportional to the number of commercials aired for them around the holidays, a lot of clean-shaven men with bushy pottery pets who are clapping on and off their razors will ring in the new year.
II.B.2 Given the functional characteristics of a topic sentence, recall its name.	Completion	■ The sentence that **introduces the subject** of a paragraph is called the _____ sentence. ■ The sentence that tells what a paragraph is about is called the _____ sentence. ■ The introductory sentence of a paragraph is called a _____ sentence.
	Alternative Response	■ **T F** Topic sentences conclude the information presented in a paragraph. ■ **T F** Topic sentences introduce the subject of a paragraph.
II.A, II.B, III.A, III.B	Matching	**Characteristics of Paragraphs.** Column A contains descriptions of the types of sentences found in a paragraph, and Column B contains sentence names. Match each description with the type of sentence described. Place the letter of the sentence name in the space before each description. **You may use each name more than once or not at all.**

(continued)

TABLE 5.2 Continued		
Item Specification Code	**Item Format**	**Item**
		Column A *Column B* _____ The middle sentences a. Complex sentence in a paragraph b. Compound sentence _____ Introduces the subject c. Concluding sentence _____ Typically comes last d. Supporting sentence in a paragraph e. Topic sentence _____ Elaborates the subject _____ Summarizes the ideas in a paragraph _____ Typically comes first in a paragraph
	Keyed	**Recognizing Characteristics of Paragraphs.** Darken the letter indicating the type of sentence in the space beside the item number on your answer sheet. *Types of Sentences* a. Complex sentence b. Concluding sentence c. Simple sentence d. Supporting sentence e. Topic sentence What sentence is 1. Used to elaborate the topic of a paragraph? 2. Most typically located first in a paragraph? 3. Used to summarize the ideas in a paragraph? 4. Typically located last in a paragraph? 5. Used to introduce the ideas in a paragraph? 6. Usually located in the middle of a paragraph?
II.B.3 Given the term *topic sentence* and a list of possible functional characteristics related to the concept, choose those for a topic sentence.	Multiple Choice	1. What is the function of a topic sentence in a paragraph? a. Elaborate the topic b. Conclude the topic c. Introduce the subject d. Provide transition within the paragraph 2. The purpose of the topic sentence within a paragraph is to provide: a. Indention b. Relevance c. An introduction d. An ending 3. What is the role of the topic sentence in a paragraph? a. Present ideas on one topic b. Introduce the subject c. Sequence information d. Express feelings

Item Specification Code	Item Format	Item
II.D.1 Given a complete paragraph, correctly indented, locate the topic sentence.	Multiple Choice (Modified)	**Locate Topic Sentence.** For each of the following paragraphs, locate the topic sentence and darken the letter preceding the topic sentence for that item on your answer sheet.

1. Which of the following sentences is the **topic sentence** of the paragraph?

   (A) The president's priority is to revive the nation's economy and citizens' incomes, and many economists believe he should start by changing some federal regulations. (B) Their research shows that agricultural subsidies cost consumers and taxpayers almost 6 billion dollars a year more than they benefit farmers. (C) Regulated minimum prices for milk cost consumers 500 million dollars a year, and sugar growers reap more than 1 billion tax dollars through price supports. (D) More startling, the federal paperwork to monitor our regulations costs Americans an estimated 100 billion dollars a year, and state and local governments add another 22 billion dollars. (F) The total cost of federal regulations is estimated at 392 billion annually, or $4,000 for each household. (G) It seems the president might benefit by examining federal regulations as one important step in economic recovery.

2. Underline the **topic sentence** in the following paragraph.

   To save our tax dollars, the president should change some laws. For example, the law that protects farmers' incomes costs us 6 billion dollars. The law that protects dairy farmers costs us 500 million dollars a year. The law that protects sugar farmers costs us more than 1 billion dollars every year. The paperwork we must complete to see that such laws are kept costs us about 100 billion dollars a year. The total cost of these laws is about 392 billion dollars each year, or $4,000 for each household. If the president really wants to save our tax dollars, he should look at these laws.

3. Underline the **topic sentence** in the following paragraph.

   Jerry is very good at baking cupcakes. He puts the mix from the box into a bowl. Then he adds an egg and some milk. He stirs it all with care. He pours his mix into cupcake papers that he has placed into a cupcake pan. While they are baking, he mixes the icing. As soon as they cool, he adds the icing. When he makes cupcakes, his father calls him "the chef."

To the degree possible, cluster together items that measure the same enabling skills and instructional goals. This strategy is beneficial for both examinees and teachers, since it helps provide students with a context for items on the test, and it aids teachers in analyzing students' mastery of enabling skills and goals. When items for one goal are scattered throughout the test, they must be rearranged for mastery analysis.

Occasionally, however, items for one goal will need to be scattered throughout the test to avoid providing clues to the correct answer. One example where scattering items would be necessary is a comprehensive capitalization test that measures capitalizing the first word of a sentence, the pronoun *I,* proper nouns, and so forth. If you place these goal-based items together on a test, students could quickly detect the error patterns in the items.

Writing Directions for Objective Test Items

Directions help clarify for students what they are to do and how to indicate their chosen response. Two criteria are important for ensuring that directions aid rather than confuse students. The first relates to the order of information provided in directions and the second has to do with highlighting or separating directions from items on the test.

Order of Information   The best order for presenting directions is the following:

1. State the skill measured.
2. Describe any resource materials required to answer the item (e.g., maps, charts, paragraphs).
3. Describe how students are to respond.
4. Describe any special conditions.

The following example directions illustrate this order:

Capitalize proper nouns. The following paragraph contains both common and proper nouns. Locate the common and proper nouns that have capitalization errors and <u>underline</u> each noun that is wrong. Some sentences may have more than one mistake, and other sentences may have no errors.

Highlight Directions   Directions should be highlighted to enable students to locate them easily before they begin to answer a set of questions and to review them while they are answering the questions. There are many ways to highlight directions, including placing a box around them, using all capital letters, using bold print, or changing the page margins. The following example illustrates the procedure:

Directions: Create compound sentences. The following test items each contain two simple sentences. In the space provided just below each pair of sentences, write one compound sentence for each set of simple sentences. In writing your compound sentences, you may want to (1) change some proper nouns to pronouns or (2) omit some of the words in the simple sentences for clarity. Take care that the coordinating conjunctions you choose clarify the relationships between the simple sentences.

■ Formative Evaluation of Items

Even though objective items are written carefully, the first draft of a test may contain many errors. Before administering any posttest, a draft copy should be evaluated to locate and remove potential problems. Some errors in item construction are more critical than others. The primary consideration in evaluating an item is its congruence with the enabling skill and test item specification. Without this congruence, criteria such as the appropriateness of the item for target students, the feasibility of the format, the clarity of item wording, and the accuracy of measures are irrelevant. The second most important consideration is the congruence of the item with the characteristics and needs of target students. Once you are sure items meet these two criteria, next consider whether subtle biases exist and, if so, eliminate them. After bias, you should consider the clarity of each item and check to see whether the items are likely to result in accurate measures. Finally, determine whether the item meets feasibility and professional criteria.

In addition to the criteria and their order of importance, consider who would be the best judge of each criterion. Table 5.3 lists each criterion and the individuals who can judge it. Like the criteria, the evaluators are listed in their order of importance because some may be better judges than others for each factor.

Curriculum-Based Criteria

Congruence between Items and Objectives   The primary consideration in evaluating a test item is its congruence with its enabling skill and item specification. Colleagues are recommended as the primary evaluators of this criterion; authors are recommended as secondary reviewers because they will tend to see both what they intended to include in the item and what they actually included. This tendency may cause them to overlook important problems, whereas colleagues, unaware of authors' intentions, can judge only what is present. Whether the item is being evaluated by colleagues or by the author, the following procedure is recommended for judging the congruence between items and item specifications:

1. Place the item specifications and item side by side.
2. Break down both the item specifications and the item into their separate elements.
3. Relate comparable elements in the specifications and item.
4. Judge whether comparable elements are congruent.

Table 5.4 illustrates the first two steps in the procedure. The item specification contains three elements: conditions, behavior, and content. The item also contains three elements: response directions, content, and stimulus material.

The third step is to relate comparable elements in the specifications and the item. The conditions in the specifications should be compared with the stimulus material in the item; the behavior in the specification should be compared with the response direction; and the content in the specification should be compared with the content specified in the directions and in the stimulus material.

TABLE 5.3

Criteria and Evaluators for Formative Evaluations of Test Items

Criteria Areas in Order of Importance	Criteria	Evaluators in Order of Importance
Curriculum-based criteria	■ Congruence between item specifications and items ■ Authenticity and relevance	Curriculum specialists Colleagues Author
Learner-based criteria	■ Congruence with the learners' characteristics and needs ■ Freedom from gender, cultural, or racial bias	Target students including representatives from gender, cultural, and racial groups and students with special needs Author Colleagues
Professional-based criteria	■ Teacher's personal skills with item and task clarity, teacher's creativity, teacher's skill with item formatting rules ■ Creating accurate measures, assessment ethics, and professional appearance of assessments	Author Colleagues Target students, including representatives from gender, cultural, and racial groups and students with special needs
School-based criteria	■ Feasibility of tests and procedures including development time related to teacher-student ratio; turnaround time from test administration to score reporting; and resources for test development, administration, scoring, and reporting	Colleagues Author Administrators

The fourth step is to judge whether comparable elements are congruent. Stimulus material in the item should match the material prescribed in the conditions. For example, if the conditions prescribe that students be given a paragraph with the topic, supporting, and concluding sentences out of order, then the stimulus material in the item should be an unorganized paragraph. The behavior in the response directions should be compatible with the behavior in the specifications. For instance, if the behavior prescribed sequencing the sentences in a paragraph, then the response directions should include comparable behaviors, such as reorder, reorganize, rearrange, or even sequence. The content in the specifications should match the content in both the directions and the stimulus material. If the content in the specifications prescribed a chronological sequence, then the directions should specify chronological order and the sentences included in the paragraph should have a clear chronological relationship.

TABLE 5.4

Specifications and Items Separated into Elements

Specifications	Item
Given a list of words containing nouns and other parts of speech, select words that are nouns.	*Directions:* Locate the nouns in the following list, and place a check beside each one.

_____ 1. sun		_____ 5. library
_____ 2. run		_____ 6. religion
_____ 3. boy		_____ 7. flower
_____ 4. happy		_____ 8. smooth

Objective Elements	Item Elements
Conditions: Give a list of words containing nouns and other parts of speech,	*Response directions:* Locate Place a check beside
Behavior: select	*Content:* nouns
Content: words that are nouns.	*Stimulus materials:*

_____ 1. sun	_____ 5. library
_____ 2. run	_____ 6. religion
_____ 3. boy	_____ 7. flower
_____ 4. happy	_____ 8. smooth

The elements for the specifications and items on discriminating between nouns and other words are compared in Table 5.5. The specifications elements are included in the first column, the item elements are included in the second column, and the judgments about congruence are included in the last column. Based on these comparisons, these items and their specifications would be judged congruent.

Now consider the specifications and sample items in Table 5.6. The first column contains the specifications with its elements separated, the second column contains items that are not congruent with the specifications, and the last column contains items that are congruent. Consider first the incongruent items. Notice that the conditions prescribed in the specifications do not match the stimulus material. The conditions specify that the sets of simple sentences be complete with proper capitalization and punctuation. However, the items in the stimulus material are already combined into compound sentences. The stimulus material in the items in the third column are congruent: two separate simple sentences are presented.

Consider next the behavior prescribed in the specification and that included in the directions. The specifications prescribe that students rewrite the sentences, whereas the item directions in column two tell students to punctuate only. Rewriting would

TABLE 5.5

Comparison of Elements in Item Specifications and Test Items

Specifications Elements	Item Elements	Congruent?

Conditions
Given a list of
words containing
nouns and other
parts of speech,
	Stimulus Materials
	1. sun
	2. run
	3. boy
	4. happy
	5. library
	6. religion
	7. flower
	8. smooth
		Yes
		1. A list of words is provided.
		2. The list contains five words that
		   are clearly nouns.
		3. The list contains three words
		   that clearly are not nouns.

Behavior
select
	Directions for Responding
	Locate
	
	Place a check beside
		Yes
		1. Students must discriminate
		   between nouns and other words.
		2. They can demonstrate their
		   selections by checking their
		   nouns.

Content
words that are nouns.
	Directions
	Nouns
	
	Stimulus Materials
	1. sun
	2. run
	3. boy
	4. happy
	5. library
	6. religion
	7. flower
	8. smooth
		Yes
		1. The content in the objective and
		   item directions is the same.
		Yes
		1. Nouns included in the list refer
		   to persons, places, things, and
		   ideas; thus, they are
		   representative of the content.
		2. Other words presented represent
		   verbs and adjectives.

require students to punctuate; select a coordinating conjunction, if needed; omit the ending punctuation in the first sentence; and omit the beginning capital letter in the second sentence. Obviously, rewriting the sentences is more complex than punctuating given compound sentences that already have these modifications. Thus, the behaviors in the specifications and items are not congruent. The rewrite response specified in the third column is congruent with the specifications.

Last, compare the content in the specifications with that included in the items. The specifications name compound sentences, the directions for the items in the second column specify compound sentences, and the stimulus material in the second column contains compound sentences. Thus, these items and the specifications are congruent in content even though they are not congruent in conditions and behavior. The items in the third column also contain content congruent with that in the specifications.

TABLE 5.6

Example Item Specifications with Incongruent and Congruent Test Items

Specifications	Incongruent Item	Congruent Item

1. Given sets of two simple sentences, complete with their first words capitalized and their ending punctuation, <u>rewrite</u> them as <u>compound sentences</u>.	*Directions:* <u>Punctuate</u> the following <u>compound sentences</u>.
	1. John is taller than Paul but Bill is taller than John.
	2. Jill really enjoys the animals at the zoo but she likes the elephants best.
		Directions: <u>Rewrite</u> the following sets of simple sentences to form <u>compound sentences</u>.
		a. John is taller than Paul.
		b. Bill is taller than John.
		1. _____
		   _____
		a. Jill really enjoys the animals at the zoo.
		b. She likes the elephants best.
		2. _____
		   _____

Learner-Based Criteria

Congruence between Items and Students' Characteristics   After ensuring that items and item specifications are congruent, you should next evaluate the appropriateness of items for given students. For this review, you will need from one to three students typical of the target population. If you have a homogeneous group, the judgments of one student should suffice. However, if you have a heterogeneous group, you might want one student who is above average, one who is average, and one who is below average in achievement to review the items.

Ask the student reviewers to read the directions, to underline all words they do not understand, and to inquire about any instructions that are unclear. They should then read and respond to each item. Again, they should underline any words that are unfamiliar and inquire about questions that confuse them. Based on their inquiries and on their responses to items, you can locate unfamiliar, ambiguous, or awkward material and rephrase it as needed. Although it is not important for these students to know the correct answers to items, it is important for them to understand what they are to do (directions) and the meaning of the questions. If these students can respond as you intend, then you can assume that the items are appropriate for similar students in your classes. You might also ask these student reviewers to show you answer clues that they find in either the directions or the items, because students can often find clues that escape teachers.

If you have no student reviewers available, review the items for their appropriateness yourself, since you are the one most familiar with the characteristics of students in your classes. In addition, colleagues who teach similar students can be asked to evaluate the appropriateness of the language and examples for their students.

Freedom from Bias   The best persons to judge whether test items are free from bias are your colleagues and perhaps members of particular groups such as women, men, different racial or ethnic representatives, or different religious or political groups. It is important when asking colleagues and group representatives to evaluate test items for bias that you specifically tell them the purpose for the review. Bias can be so subtle that you are unaware that it is creeping into your items, and reviewers are unaware that it is in the items without consciously looking for it.

Professional-Based Criteria

Clarity of Items   The fourth criterion is the clarity of items. In judging your writing skills, the most appropriate evaluators are your colleagues. The items may appear clear and grammatically correct to you, but colleagues can independently judge what you actually wrote instead of what you intended to write. These evaluations are especially tricky because many reviewers do not simply indicate errors in items; instead, they often rephrase the items to suit themselves. This problem usually can be avoided by providing reviewers with the following instructions: First, mark *errors* in grammar and punctuation; second, eliminate unnecessary words or phrases; and third, rephrase items that remain unclear after the first and second steps are complete.

The best colleagues to use for this review are those who judged the congruence between your items and objectives. This preliminary exercise helps clarify your intentions and helps critics avoid rewriting items so they are no longer congruent with the objective.

If colleagues are not available to assist with this review, evaluate the items for clarity yourself. This is best done after enough time has passed for you to forget what you intended to express.

Accuracy of Measures   You are the best person to judge the potential of your items for producing accurate measures. You are the only one who knows whether an item is novel or repeated; you know as well as anyone whether particular item formats are amenable to guessing behaviors; and you know the seating arrangements in your class and whether students can readily obtain answers from other students.

Item Formatting Criteria   Besides these primary criteria, remember that several recommendations were presented for formatting each type of objective item, and these suggestions also provide criteria for formatively evaluating your items in each format. The only individuals who can judge whether your items are correctly formatted are people familiar with the suggestions for writing each type of item. People unfamiliar with item formatting rules will tend to focus on the general clarity of your items rather than on their structure.

School-Based Criteria

Feasibility   The most appropriate evaluators of feasibility are colleagues familiar with your time and resource constraints. Related to time, do you have the available time to develop, administer, score, and provide constructive feedback? For resources, do you have the materials and classroom or school setting requirements available? Sometimes, the most "ideal" test must be modified because it is not feasible, given your teaching situation and resources.

■ Computer Technology

Many teachers do not simply create the exact number of test items required to create one test according to the prescriptions in a table of test specifications. Instead, they develop many items for their instructional goal frameworks by using computer-based test item banking programs. Test item banks enable you to anchor items to your enabling skill codes and create items in all the objective formats described in this chapter. They also enable you to use your tables of test specifications and enabling skill item codes to retrieve the banked items for multiple forms of a particular test with item order scrambled or item responses scrambled. Once the items are developed, entered in the bank, and edited, many alternative tests can be created in a matter of minutes.

Many distributors provide commercially produced item banks available from the Internet as *shareware*, meaning that you can download the program onto your personal computer, examine it for a limited period of time, and license yourself as a user if the program seems to suit your needs. For example, consider the following excerpt from a commercially available item banking program that you can download from the Internet from Russell Stevens of Russ & Ryan EdWare **<http://www.rredware.com/russ8.htm)>.**

Test Maestro for Windows   Test Maestro is an advanced test-generating program that will automatically create fully formatted tests from a test bank of questions you enter or import. It includes a full-featured word processor for composing the questions. Questions may use different fonts, font sizes, bold facing, italics, color, sub and superscripts, paragraph alignments, borders, etc. Test questions may be fully formatted. There is no restriction—you can enter whatever type of question you want. There is full support for inserting pictures (wmf, dib, bmp, ico), as well as . . . objects. Thus you can insert Clip Art, Excel spreadsheets, Excel charts, Word documents, Word equations and tables, Visio drawings, etc. If you prefer, you can use your existing word processor to create or edit the questions.

All of the questions and tests are stored in an encrypted, password protected database for security. Questions are stored by user defined subjects. Each subject may include units such as chapters, lessons, blocks, and sections. Each unit may be given a descriptive unit name. Numerous fields are available for recording the question description, author information, reference information, teacher comments, the correct answer, type of question, and targeted grade level. You may specify whether you want the question to include a leader blank for entering the answer and the length of the leader blank.

To add questions to a test, you just drag and drop the questions you want to include. You can drag and drop them in any desired order or the program can randomize the order if you need to print several versions of the test. The program can print out a test booklet that may be used when selecting questions from your local test bank or imported test bank. After selecting the questions you want to include on an exam, they are automatically flowed into the layout you select (up to 4 columns).

Whether you teach in kindergarten or graduate school, you should examine available test item banking programs available in your school, district, or over the Internet. You can select one for yourself and begin to build your testing materials.

■ Summary

In writing objective items, your primary concerns should be the validity and reliability of the resulting scores. Important factors in achieving these qualities are the congruence between the item and the item specifications and characteristics of target students, the feasibility, the clarity of language used, the accuracy of the measure, and your ethics related to test development and use. In addition to these primary considerations, there are several suggestions for writing items using each format.

Objective tests typically consist of written-response and selected-response items. Written-response formats include completion and short-answer items; selected-response formats include alternative-response, matching, keyed, and multiple-choice items. Several features of these items make them desirable for classroom tests. First, they can be used to measure several types and levels of learning. Second, a wide range of content can be tested in a relatively short period. Third, each format has several variations for flexibility. Finally, objective tests can be scored more reliably and quickly than can other types of tests.

Written-response items can be used to measure a variety of types and levels of learning, minimize the probability of students guessing correctly, and help teachers analyze misconceptions and problems that students have. These items can either be single statements and questions that require an answer or clusters of items with one set of common directions. Clustered items usually have words, phrases, pictures, or symbols that act as stimuli. Two drawbacks of written-response items are lengthy scoring time and the difficulty of scoring items objectively.

Selected-response items require students to select an answer from a given set of alternatives. They are versatile and can be used to measure several types and levels of learning. One unique feature is that a well-constructed selected-response item can measure students' abilities to see different facets of a problem and to make fine discriminations. These items can be administered quickly, and a wide range of material can be tested. In addition, they can be hand-scored quickly, adapted for computer administration, or adapted for machine scoring. Formats include the alternative-response item that requires students to select one correct answer from two alternatives, the matching item in which students match a set of premises and responses, the keyed item that requires students to use the same set of responses for a group of items, and the multiple-choice item that requires students to choose responses from among three or more alternatives.

The rubric at the end of this chapter can be used for formatively evaluating objective test items. The first section of the checklist names criteria for evaluating test items regardless of their particular format, and the remaining sections name criteria for evaluating each type of objective test item.

Computer-based test item banks enable you to use all the objective-style items described in this chapter. In fact, they are quite easy to enter into an item bank and edit once they are entered. In addition to your items, you can link exhibits, such as passages, tables, or graphs, to the items. Many teachers work independently to create their item banks, but working in teams to create large, flexible item banks for a grade level or subject is becoming more popular.

■ PRACTICE EXERCISES

A. **Match the physical descriptions of test items in Column A with the names of objective test items in Column B. Place the letter preceding the name of the item in the space preceding the description. You may use any answer more than once or not at all.**

Column A

_____ **1.** A test item that contains a stem and three to five alternative responses.

_____ **2.** A set of test items preceded by a single list of three or more response options that are used to answer all items in the set.

_____ **3.** A complete statement with one or two key terms omitted and replaced with a blank.

_____ **4.** A complete statement that students are to judge as true/false, correct/incorrect, fact/fiction, etc.

_____ **5.** Two columns of elements that students are to equate.

_____ **6.** An item for which students must supply a term, phrase, number, sentence, or other brief response.

Column B

a. Alternative response
b. Completion
c. Keyed
d. Matching
e. Modified alternative response
f. Multiple choice
g. Short answer

B. **The following items are statements about formatting criteria for objective test items. For each statement, identify the type of item described. You may use each answer more than once or not at all, or you may have more than one answer for an item.**

Responses

a. Alternative-response items
b. Clustered alternative-response items
c. Completion items
d. Keyed items
e. Matching items
f. Multiple-choice items
g. Short-answer items

Statements

_____ **1.** Remove only key words from a statement.

_____ **2.** Avoid specific determiners.

_____ **3.** Ensure that the directions for a cluster of items are appropriate for all items in the set.

_____ **4.** Avoid designing questions to trick students.

_____ **5.** Eliminate the possibility of several reasonable answers.

_____ **6.** Include only one idea to be judged in each statement.

_____ **7.** Specify the units (e.g., lbs, inches, miles) required in an answer.

_____ **8.** Avoid double negatives.

_____ **9.** Ensure that the premises are homogeneous and contain the more difficult reading material.

_____ **10.** Ensure that responses are homogeneous, brief, and logically ordered.

C. **The following items relate to formatting criteria for multiple-choice items. Place the letter corresponding to the best answer in the blank beside the question number.**

_____ 1. Which of the following characteristics is *unique* to multiple-choice items?
  a. A complete statement that asks a question or poses a problem
  b. A complete statement that is correct in grammar and punctuation
  c. A set of three or more responses from which a student must select the answer
  d. An item that matches the conditions, behavior, and content specified in the objective
  e. Both c and d are correct

_____ 2. What part of a multiple-choice item contains the problem statement?
  a. Distractor
  b. Foil
  c. Responses
  d. Stem

_____ 3. Which of the following terms is used for incorrect responses?
  a. Distractor
  b. Foil
  c. Response set
  d. Stem
  e. Both a and b are correct

_____ 4. Which of the following statements reflects a *positive* feature of multiple-choice items? They can be used to measure:
  a. Various types of learning including attitudes.
  b. Students' ability to make fine discriminations.
  c. A student's unique or novel solutions to a problem.
  d. Both a and b are correct.

_____ 5. Which of the following statements reflects *limitations* of multiple-choice items? They *cannot* be written to:
  a. Measure complex intellectual skills.
  b. Measure several levels of learning.
  c. Diagnose misconceptions and problems students have.
  d. Avoid the probability of students guessing the correct answer.
  e. Measure the intellectual skills that are subordinate to a motor skill.

Directions: The following items may have more than one correct answer. Indicate the responses that apply.

_____ 6. Which of the following characteristics does a good stem have?
  a. It is congruent with the behavioral objective.
  b. The vocabulary, the context, and the complexity are appropriate for the students being tested.
  c. It clearly poses the question or problem.
  d. The grammar and punctuation are correct.

_____ 7. Which of the following suggestions would help you develop correct responses for multiple-choice questions?
  a. Repeat key words from the stem in the answer.
  b. Use statements as they appear in the textbook.
  c. Do *not* use such options as "Both A and B are correct" as the answer.
  d. Ensure that the answer is grammatically consistent with the stem.

_____ **8.** Which of the following suggestions would help you write good distractors?
   a. Construct responses that are plausible to students.
   b. Ensure that distractors are grammatically consistent with the stem.
   c. Include common misconceptions and problems students may have with the skill measured.
   d. Construct them to be either longer or shorter than the correct answer.

_____ **9.** Which of the following characteristics does a good set of responses have?
   a. They are homogeneous.
   b. They all contain the same key words from the stem.
   c. When the responses are numerals, the answer code should also be a numeral for consistency.
   d. They are placed in a logical order.

_____ **10.** Which of the following statements describes clues commonly found in multiple-choice items?
   a. Distractors are consistently longer or shorter than the correct answer.
   b. Using such responses as "Both A and C are correct" only when this is the correct response.
   c. Key words in the stem appear in one or more of the distractors.
   d. The correct answer frequently appears in the same position in the set.

_____ **11.** Which of the following suggestions would help you arrange multiple-choice items on a test?
   a. List responses horizontally on a line.
   b. Place resource materials between the directions and the questions when they are on the same page.
   c. Place resources that require a lot of space, or that are needed for questions on several pages, on a separate, unattached page.
   d. For economy, place some or all of the responses on the page following the one containing the stem.

D. Evaluate the formatting of the following completion, alternative-response, matching, and keyed items. Write any problems you identify on a separate sheet.

1. Completion Items

   Directions: Reading a map. Complete each statement by writing the missing word or words in the blank provided.

   a. The top of the map is traditionally _____.
   b. The _____ contains the names of symbols used on a map.
   c. The _____ is used to locate towns on a map.
   d. The _____ of town names is included in an _____.

2. Short-Answer Items

   Directions: Reading a map. Use the map in Figure A to answer the following questions. Write your answer in the blank before each question. (Assume that the map is appropriate for target students.)

   _____ miles   **a.** Use the mileage scale and your ruler to estimate the number of miles between Carter and Doyle.
   _____ miles   **b.** How far is it from Hyatt to Bryne?
   _____   **c.** What is the name of the city to the north of Jackson?

3. Alternative-Response Items

   Directions: Reading a map. Circle T if the statement is true and F if it is false.

   T F **a.** A map legend identifies symbols used in a map and can be used to locate particular cities.

   T F **b.** The direction arrow on a map does not usually point north.

   T F **c.** The map legend always contains the direction indicator and the mileage scale.

4. Matching Items

   Directions: Reading a map. Place the letter from Column B in the space before the matching item in Column A.

Column A	*Column B*
_____ **1.** Legend	a. A sphere that contains a map of the earth
_____ **2.** Grid	b. An alphabetical list of places contained on a map
_____ **3.** Index	c. A key or legend used to identify symbols on a map
_____ **4.** Globe	d. An organization that provides maps
_____ **5.** AAA Automobile Club	e. A matrix of lines running through the map top to bottom and side to side

5. Matching Items

   Directions: Reading a map. The items in Column A describe aids that can be used to interpret maps. Identify the aid in Column B that each item describes. You may use each of the responses in Column B more than once or not at all.

Column A	*Column B*
_____ **1.** An alphabetical list of cities and towns	a. Legend
_____ **2.** Lines that divide the face of the map into blocks	b. Grid
_____ **3.** A key that contains map symbols and their names	c. Index
_____ **4.** A table that contains the names of major cities and the distances between them	d. Mileage scale
_____ **5.** A line marked off in miles	e. Mileage table
_____ **6.** An aid used to locate specified towns	
_____ **7.** An aid used to estimate distance between small towns	
_____ **8.** An aid used to locate types of highways	

E. Write Objective Items

Using your own paper, write two objective test items for each of the following test item specifications based on the compound sentence enabling skills in Figure 3.10. Select any objective item format that you believe will appropriately assess the behavior stipulated in the specifications. Before beginning to write the items, imagine a particular group of students. Then write the items so they are appropriate in vocabulary, content, and complexity for the group. You may want to use the item writing criteria in the rubric at the end of this chapter to guide your item development. Compare your items with the sample ones included in the Feedback section; they were created for students in the upper elementary grades.

Code   *Test Item Specifications*

III.B.1   Given the term *coordinating conjunction,* state its role or function.

III.B.2   Given a description of the function of the coordinating conjunction, name the word described.

III.D.1   Given a compound sentence, locate the coordinating conjunction.

III.D.2   Given a compound sentence with various elements of the sentence underlined and numbered (e.g., subject, verb, comma, and coordinating conjunction), locate the coordinating conjunction.

III.E.1   Given two simple sentences and a coordinating conjunction, judge whether the conjunction is logical.

III.E.2   Given (a) two simple sentences joined by a comma and a blank space and (b) a list of alternative coordinating conjunctions, choose the most logical conjunction.

III.F.1   Given two simple sentences separated by a comma and a blank space, write an appropriate coordinating conjunction in the space.

F. Enrichment

Using the test item specifications you have developed from your own content area, complete the following activities:

1. Write appropriate objective test items.
2. Evaluate your test items for:
    a. Congruence with the test item specifications
    b. Congruence with the characteristics of your target students
    c. Bias of any kind
    d. Feasibility
    e. Clarity (grammar, punctuation, precision)
    f. Accuracy of measure (novelty, clues) and ethical development and use
    g. Formatting suggestions
3. Ask a colleague to evaluate your items and directions and suggest revisions. Have the evaluator compare the items with your objectives.
4. Have any available target students read the items and mark any directions and items that they do not understand. Additionally, have them circle any words that they cannot define.
5. Use your colleague's suggestions and students' remarks to revise the directions and items.

■ FEEDBACK

A. Descriptions and Names of Test Items

1. f	**4.** a
2. c	**5.** d
3. b	**6.** g

B. Formatting Objective Items

1. c	**6.** a
2. a	**7.** g
3. all formats	**8.** a
4. all formats	**9.** e
5. c, g	**10.** d, e, f

C. Formatting Multiple-Choice Items

1. c	**4.** b	**7.** d	**10.** a, b, d
2. d	**5.** d	**8.** a, b, c	**11.** b, c
3. e	**6.** a, b, c, d	**9.** a, d	

D. Evaluate Objective Items. The sample items reflect the following problems:

1. Completion Items
  a. The item is vague and many answers are possible.
  b. The blank is at the beginning of the item.
  c. The blank is at the beginning of the item, and there are two correct answers (index, grid).
  d. The first blank is placed toward the beginning of the item and does not require a key term. Additionally, the word *an* preceding the second blank suggests that the response begins with a vowel.

2. Short-Answer Items
  a. This item contains no major problems.
  b. This item does not indicate how students are to determine the mileage. Instructions about whether they should use a mileage table, mileage scale, or miles printed along the highway should be added.
  c. This item should be clarified as several towns are likely to be north of the one specified. Adding such information as "the first town north of Jackson" would help clarify the item.

3. Alternative-Response Items
  a. The statement includes more than one idea.
  b. The item contains an unnecessary negative word.
  c. The item contains the determiner *always* and two ideas.

4. Matching Items. These items contain many problems.
  a. The directions:
    (1) do not explain the contents of the premise or response list.
    (2) do not describe the basis for matching the items.
    (3) refer to columns that are not titled.
    (4) do not specify if a response can be used more than once.
  b. The premises:
    (1) are shorter than the responses.
    (2) do not all have more than one plausible answer for each premise.
    (3) are not homogeneous. Although both premises and responses are all related to maps, the sets are not homogeneous.

5. Matching Items. The examples have these weaknesses:
  a. The questions and the answers are placed in the same order.
  b. Item four contains the word *table*, which matches the word *table* in the answer, thus providing a clue to the answer.

E. Write Objective Items

Code	Item Specifications	Items
III.B.1	Given the term *coordinating conjunction,* state its role or function.	**1.** What **purpose** does the coordinating conjunction serve? _____ **2.** What is the role of the coordinating conjunction in a compound sentence? _____

III.B.2   Given a description of the function of the coordinating conjunction, name the word described.

3. The word that links two simple sentences to form a compound sentence is called a/an _____.

4. The term that bridges two simple sentences and shows the relationship between them is called a/an _____.

III.D.1   Given a compound sentence, locate the coordinating conjunction.

Directions: Underline the **coordinating conjunction** in the following sentence(s):

5. The boat rolled and twisted in the storm, and the passengers feared for their lives.
6. The cat passed by the butcher shop for breakfast each morning, but today there was no one there.

III.D.2   Given a compound sentence with various elements of the sentence underlined and numbered (e.g., subject, verb, comma, and coordinating conjunction), locate the coordinating conjunction.

Directions: **Locate Coordinating Conjunctions** in the following sentences. Mark the letter beneath the coordinating conjunction on your answer sheet beside the item number.

7. <u>Jill</u> had to finish <u>painting</u> the deck <u>before</u> she
     A   B   C

   was allowed to talk with her friends, <u>so</u> she
                                        D

   painted faster <u>than</u> she ever painted before.
                  E

8. The <u>pep rally</u> was fun on Friday, <u>because</u> all
        A   B

   the girls and boys <u>who play</u> on any team
                      C

   were <u>honored</u> by the student <u>body</u>.
          D   E

III.E.1   Given two simple sentences and a coordinating conjunction, judge whether the conjunction is logical.

Directions: Evaluate the coordinating conjunctions in the following sentences. If the conjunction **logically connects** the two simple sentences, mark **(1)** on your answer sheet beside the item number. If the conjunction forms an **illogical link,** mark **(2)** on your answer sheet.

9. Everyone was gathered on the lawn outside the science museum, but there was a lunar eclipse tonight.
10. The earth's shadow moved slowly across the moon's surface, and soon the entire moon was dark.

III.E.2   Given (a) two simple sentences joined by a comma and a blank space and (b) a list of alternative coordinating conjunctions, choose the most logical conjunction.

Directions: **Evaluate Coordinating Conjunctions.** For each of the following sentences, choose the **best** coordinating conjunction from the list beneath the sentence. Mark the letter of your choice beside the item number on your answer sheet.

11. Benjamin Franklin is known for discovering electricity, _____ he also was renowned for editing Poor Richard's Almanac.
    a. and
    b. because
    c. however
    d. thus

12. Deep-sea fishing can be a lot of fun, _____ you must be careful not to get too much sun.
    a. and
    b. because
    c. but
    d. moreover

III.F.1   Given two simple sentences separated by a comma and a blank space, write an appropriate coordinating conjunction in the space.

Directions: **Supply Coordinating Conjunctions.** Read each of the following compound sentences carefully and identify the relationship between the two sentences. Based on this relationship, write the best coordinating conjunction in the blank to link the two sentences.

13. We were going to plant a rose garden this spring, _____ the price of roses is too high.

14. Sara was a wonderful pitcher, _____ she occasionally hit a home run.

■ R U B R I C

Rubric for Evaluating Objective Test Items

GENERAL CRITERIA FOR ALL TEST FORMATS		

Yes	No	
___	___	**I. Curriculum-Based Criteria (directions, stems, and responses)** A. Are items congruent with the conditions, behavior, and content of the task specification?
___	___	B. Is task-situation authentic and relevant to curriculum and environment?
___	___	**II. Learner-Centered Criteria (directions, stems, and responses)** A. Are items congruent with the language (including ESOL), context, developmental level, and special needs of learners?
___	___	B. Are items free from biasing material related to gender, cultural/ethnic groups, and religious and political ideas?
___	___	**III. School-Based Criteria (feasibility)** A. Are development and administration time available related to teacher-student ratio?
___	___	B. Is turnaround time available from test administration to score reporting?
___	___	C. Are resources available for test development, administration, scoring, and reporting?
		IV. Professional-Based Criteria A. Are directions, stems, and responses clear related to:
___	___	■ Grammar?
___	___	■ Spelling?
___	___	■ Expression?
___	___	■ Order of information?
___	___	B. Is the task creative and interesting?
___	___	C. Are materials and procedures professional appearing?
___	___	D. Is the task likely to yield accurate measures? E. Ethics related to test development:
___	___	■ Have you used the best items possible within your resources?
___	___	■ Are the students' opportunities to "share" answers within and across your classes limited?
___	___	■ Are enough items and instruments included to allow formative as well as summative evaluation?
___	___	■ Have you made provisions to evaluate the quality of your assessments and instruction using students' performance data? F. Ethics related to administration and use:
___	___	■ Are tests administered as a substitute for inadequate lesson preparation?
___	___	■ Are tests used as rewards or punishments for classroom behavior?
___	___	■ Are tests and grades used as a means of controlling students' behavior?
___	___	■ Are tests used to punish an unruly or unprepared student or class?
		(Note: A "no" response in section IV.F is correct.)

(continued)

FORMATTING CRITERIA FOR WRITTEN-RESPONSE TEST ITEMS

Yes	No	
____	____	**I. Completion Test Items**
____	____	A. Are only key words removed from a statement?
____	____	B. Is all information required to answer a question presented *before* any blanks are provided for answering the question?
____	____	C. Has the possibility of several reasonable answers been eliminated?
____	____	D. Have all clues to the correct answer been eliminated?
		E. Have key statements taken from instructional materials been paraphrased?

II. Short-Answer Test Items

A. Do blanks for each response suggest the length of anticipated answers?
B. Are the units required for an answer specified (e.g., lbs., yds.)?
C. Are directions for a cluster of items appropriate for all items in the set?
D. Does a statement of the skill measured (e.g., "Identify nouns") precede explanations of materials provided *and* directions for answering the question(s)?

FORMATTING CRITERIA FOR SELECTED-RESPONSE TEST ITEMS

I. Alternative-Response Items

A. Are judgments to be made explained in the directions?
B. Do answer choices logically match the judgments?
C. Does each statement include only one item to be judged?
D. Are statements worded positively?
E. Are questions avoided that purposefully may trick or mislead students?
F. Are clues to the correct answer avoided?

II. Clustered Alternative-Response Items

A. Is every item in the set congruent with the response directions?
B. Is only one of the two options clearly correct?
C. Do instances contained in the set adequately represent all aspects of the content in the objective?
D. Are clues through patterns of answers, number of items, length of items, and so on avoided?

III. Matching Items

A. Do directions indicate the skill measured?
B. Do directions indicate the basis for matching elements in the columns?
C. Does the column on the left side (premise) contain homogeneous content (from one general area)?
D. Does the column on the left side (premise) contain the more difficult or lengthy reading material?
E. Are the responses located in the right-hand column?
F. Are the responses homogeneous?
G. Are the responses as brief as possible, and more brief than the elements in the left column?
H. Are the responses logically ordered in the list (e.g., alphabetically, chronologically, procedurally)?

		FORMATTING CRITERIA FOR MULTIPLE-CHOICE TEST ITEMS

Yes	No	**I. The Stem**
———	———	A. Does the stem contain all the information required for the learner to formulate a correct answer from memory?
———	———	B. Are any negative words in the stem underlined for emphasis?
———	———	C. Do common stems that are embedded in directions contain, first, the skill measured; second, a description of the item if needed; and third, instructions for how to mark answers?

		II. The Correct Response: Does the correct response:
———	———	A. Grammatically fit the stem?
———	———	B. Contain paraphrased rather than textbook language?
———	———	C. Have only one correct or best answer?
———	———	D. Contain the options "All of the above are correct" or "None of the above are correct" only when logical?
———	———	E. Contain "All of the above are correct" and "None of the above are correct" for *both* correct responses and for distractors?
———	———	F. Avoid key terms from the stem whenever possible?
		G. Appear similar to the distractors in:
———	———	a. Technical detail?
———	———	b. Specificity?
———	———	c. Length?
———	———	H. Vary in position within the set of responses across a group of items?

NA	Yes	No	**III. The Distractors: Do the distractors:**
———	———	———	A. Reflect common misconceptions and problems?
———	———	———	B. Logically answer the problem posed in the stem?
———	———	———	C. Grammatically fit the stem?
———	———	———	D. Repeat key words from the stem to attract students who are guessing?
———	———	———	E. Avoid repeating common words or phrases?

			IV. The Set of Responses: Does the set of responses:
———	———	———	A. Contain homogeneous material/ideas?
———	———	———	B. Reflect logical ordering (e.g., alphabetical, chronological, procedural)?
———	———	———	C. Avoid the confusion between the numeric responses 1 through 5 and the response codes one through five?
———	———	———	D. Use the response codes directly adjacent to question numbers on answer sheets?

REFERENCE

Stevens, R. (2000). *Test Maestro for windows.* Spruce, MI: Russ and Ryan Edware. <http://www.rredware. com>.

SUGGESTED READINGS

Dick, W., Carey, L. M., & Carey, J. O. (2001). The systematic design of instruction (5th ed., pp. 140–174). New York: Addison-Wesley Longman.

Gallagher, J. D. (1998). *Classroom assessment for teachers* (pp. 130–196, 205–284). Columbus, OH: Merrill.

Kubiszyn, T., & Borich, G. (2000). *Educational testing and measurement* (6th ed., pp. 81–109). New York: John Wiley & Sons.

Lynn, R. L., & Gronlund, N. E. (2000). *Measurement and assessment in teaching* (8th ed., pp. 169–233, 372–374). Englewood Cliffs, NJ: Prentice-Hall.

Nitko, A. J. (1996). *Educational assessment of students* (2nd ed., pp. 123–159, 218–238). Columbus, OH: Merrill.

Oosterhof, A. (1999). *Developing and using classroom assessments* (2nd ed., pp. 63–70, 85–120). Columbus, OH: Merrill.

Thorndike, R. M. (1997). *Measurement and evaluation in psychology and education* (6th ed., pp. 443–484, 493–495). Columbus, OH: Merrill.

Tombari, M., & Borich, G. (1999). *Authentic assessment in the classroom* (pp. 68–118). Columbus, OH: Merrill.

Worthen, B. R., White, K. R., Fan, X., & Sudweeks, R. L. (1999). *Measurement and assessment in schools* (2nd ed., pp. 183–279). New York: Addison-Wesley Longman.

Test item banking software distributors on the Internet, including shareware and freeware:

Russ and Ryan Stevens. Edware. <http://www.rredware. com>.

Softseek. <http://softseek.com/Education_and_Science/ Teaching_Tools>.

Constructing and Using Essay and Product Development Tests

- Define *essay* and *product development tests.*
- Describe the types of skills typically measured using essay and product development tests.
- Discuss the positive and negative features of essay and product development tests.
- Write essay questions and product development instructions.
- Select and include relevant information in directions.
- Define *global scoring* and describe its uses.
- Define *analytical scoring* and describe its uses.
- Develop rubrics for analytical scoring, including checklists and rating scales.
- Use a rubric to score given products.
- Describe typical errors associated with constructing and scoring essay and product development tests.
- Describe benefits of students using rubrics to evaluate and reflect on their own work.

Curriculum guides often contain complex instructional goals that require students to demonstrate their ability to create a unique response. In constructing unique responses, students need to determine how they will approach a given problem, plan and organize their responses, and present their ideas. Objective tests do not require students to produce original pieces of work that demonstrate these capabilities.

Often, these complex goals can be measured with essay questions, which typically require students to discuss, analyze, compare for similarities and differences, synthesize, or evaluate. For example, students may be asked to discuss a product, a procedure, an event, a political action, a natural phenomenon, historical characters, a scientific experiment, a piece of literature, or a philosophical viewpoint. They may be expected to analyze and describe the components of a concrete or defined concept, rule, or principle,

167

or to analyze and describe the steps in a procedure or the components in a system. Essay questions also can be used to measure their ability to compare or contrast concepts, theories, systems, procedures, events, people, and numerous other subjects. They can measure students' abilities to synthesize pieces of literature, articles, events, or other phenomena. In addition, students may be asked to evaluate the quality of a product or event, the execution of some procedure or motor skill, or an instance of behavior.

Some instructional goals, such as higher-level intellectual skills and cognitive strategies, cannot be adequately measured by either objective or essay questions. To demonstrate their skill, students need to develop some type of product either with pencil and paper or by some other method. Such products include letters, themes, poems, abstracts, term papers, flowcharts, computer programs, original songs, photographs, videotapes, maps, bookcases, blueprints, and drawings. Each student's product will be unique and will vary in complexity, originality, and accuracy. Even when students are following detailed instructions, their responses will vary.

Both essay and product development tests require students to synthesize many enabling skills in their responses. For example, students writing a summary of a book must form sentences and paragraphs, write legibly, select ideas and information, and organize their presentation. One advantage of these tests is the teacher's ability to separate and comment on particular elements of students' responses, such as their approach, organization, logic, and accuracy.

Unfortunately, this type of testing has several major drawbacks. First, a teacher must spend considerable time selecting the task, writing the instructions, scoring the products, analyzing students' work, and evaluating both individual and group performance. Second, more class time is usually required for essay and product exams than for objective-style exams, which often limits the breadth of the material tested. Third, because responses vary, only experts can make the fine distinctions that determine whether an answer is acceptable. Responses cannot be machine scored or given to an aide or student assistant for scoring. Finally, scoring is less reliable on these exams than on objective exams for several reasons. Teachers' standards may shift during scoring, and fatigue can cause lapses in concentration. Scoring bias is another serious problem. Some teachers tend to be lenient, whereas others consistently give all the students average or below-average marks. Teachers' perceptions of individual students also can bias the scores they assign. In addition, students with excellent verbal and organizational skills can bluff an answer and often receive better scores than less verbally skilled students whose answers contain superior content. In spite of these limitations, essay and product development tests provide the best means of determining whether students can actually perform complex skills, such as writing paragraphs and themes, conducting and reporting scientific experiments, or critiquing literature and plays.

■ Analyzing Instructional Goals That Require Essay or Product Development Responses

The same procedures described in Chapter 3 for analyzing instructional goals that are intellectual skills and verbal information are used to analyze instructional goals that require product development. Recall that intellectual skills goals are typically analyzed using a goal matrix diagram, tree diagram, or flowchart to identify key enabling skills. Objective tests are used to assess students' mastery of enabling skills in the goal framework, whereas essay and product development exams are usually used to determine whether students can synthesize all the enabling skills to perform the goal.

The instructional goal is typically located in the far right column (Produce) of the goal matrix, at the far left of a tree diagram, and at the top of a flowchart, and one or more task specifications (objectives) should have been written for the goal during the analysis process. These objectives prescribe the conditions appropriate for performing the goal.

The criteria for judging students' essays and products are located in the goal analysis framework. In a matrix analysis, they are located in the first three columns of the matrix, and they include the physical, functional, and qualitative characteristics of a product that are specified for a particular group. In the tree diagram and flowchart, they are typically located toward the basic ends, and they include the characteristic descriptions of a product. You may wish to review the goal analysis frameworks in Chapter 3 to examine the enabling skills that describe the physical, functional, and qualitative characteristics of paragraphs. The matrix diagram is located in Figure 3.6, the tree diagram is in Figure 3.7, and the flowchart is in Figure 3.8. When scoring a student's product, such as a paragraph, drawing, or bookcase, you need to question whether the product (1) has the prescribed physical characteristics, (2) functions as intended, and (3) includes the quality characteristics specified to an acceptable degree for the developmental level of the target students.

Essay tests are really just one specific type of product development test, so the foundation for essay questions is also the instructional goal matrix. Essay questions typically require students to describe, explain, contrast, compare, analyze, and so forth. Recall from Chapter 4 that essay questions are usually created by combining cells in the goal framework. For example, students can describe something by combining the cells within an enabling skill concept strand, and they can compare for similarities and differences the physical, functional, and qualitative characteristics of concepts within these columns of the matrix. Related to the geography goal matrix in Figure 3.9, students might be asked to describe a particular country in North America (Row I), and you would score their answer by the particular number of identifying facts the students could recall (e.g., the capital city [I.B], location on map [I.D], area size [I.C], population size [I.E], climate [I.F], etc.). On the other hand, you may want students to compare the similarities and differences among North, Central, and South American countries using characteristics such as area size, population size, gross national product, or form of government. Once you have located the skills you want to measure on the goal analysis framework, you are ready to write questions and instructions and to develop scoring procedures.

■ Writing Questions and Instructions

Many of the suggestions for writing objective test items also apply to essay questions and instructions for product development. Questions and instructions should match the behavior, content, and conditions prescribed in the objective; the vocabulary, complexity, and context should be appropriate for target students; and questions and instructions should be clearly written using correct grammar and punctuation.

An essay question or set of instructions should describe the type of response that you expect. For example, if students are to compare two things, the instructions should begin with the word *compare*. If they are to critique something, the instructions should begin with the word *critique*. Students should know the meaning of these words and how to demonstrate these skills. If all or some students do not understand what these terms are, their responses may reflect their misunderstanding of what they are told to do.

Providing Guidance

The amount of guidance in the question or instructions depends on the skill being measured and the sophistication of the students. Related to the skill, instructions may require students to discuss or compare things using components they select themselves, or the instructions may specify which components they are to use. Students may have to select and use evaluation criteria, or they may be given the criteria to apply. Related to students' characteristics, older students and high achievers tend to work well with minimum guidance. However, younger students and average or below-average achievers need more structure in the directions.

Students' responses will depend on the amount of guidance in the instructions. Consider the amount of guidance provided in the three essay questions included in Figure 6.1. The questions in the left-hand column have the content removed to illustrate the item format. Any content could be substituted for the letters *X* and *Y* and the letters *a, b,* and *c.* The questions in the right-hand column use the same format, but content is included in each.

FIGURE 6.1

Degrees of Guidance in Essay Questions

---

1. Compare *X* and *Y.*

2. Compare *X* and *Y* for the following:
   a.
   b.
   c.

3. Compare the similarities of and differences between *X* and *Y* for the following:
   a.
   b.
   c.

1. Compare *pretests* and *posttests.*

2. Compare *pretests* and *posttests* for the following:
   a. The test's relationship to the goal framework
   b. The time the test is administered
   c. Uses for test scores

3. Compare the similarities of and the differences between *pretests* and *posttests* for the following:
   a. The test's relationship to the goal framework
   b. The time the test is administered
   c. Uses for test scores

Notice that the three sets of instructions vary considerably in the amount of guidance provided. The first question requires students to decide which aspects of the pretest and posttest they will compare and how they will compare them. This is the most complex question because students must determine all the elements in their response. The lack of guidance will produce greater variety in students' answers.

The second question provides more guidance. Students are told which aspects of pretests and posttests they are to compare. The third set directs students' responses even more by specifying that students compare similarities and differences. Each question is of value. The amount of guidance to include in an essay question depends on whether you want students to recall the facets to be compared or whether you want to provide them. In determining the appropriate amount of guidance, you should always consider what skills you want to measure and the skill level of students being tested.

The amount of guidance to include is also a consideration when writing instructions that require development of a product. For example, the instructions for producing a paragraph can vary considerably in the amount of guidance provided. Consider the following three sets of instructions:

1. Write a paragraph about a fire drill.
2. Write a paragraph about a fire drill. Your paragraph should include:
   a. A topic sentence
   b. At least four supporting sentences
   c. A concluding sentence
3. Write a paragraph that describes fire drill procedures. Your paragraph should include:
   a. A topic sentence
   b. At least four supporting sentences
   c. A concluding sentence

Each set of directions will undoubtedly produce very different paragraphs. The second set is more specific than the first and the third more specific than the second. The third set limits the topic to fire drill procedures and specifies the number and types of sentences to be included. To determine which set of instructions would be best, first decide how much guidance should be provided for a particular group of students and what skills you want to measure. Specific instructions like those in the third set would not be appropriate if you wanted to measure whether students remembered to include topic and concluding sentences in their paragraphs. However, they would be appropriate for measuring students' skill in ordering events in a prescribed procedure (such as a fire drill). Regardless of the test's purpose, the directions must include enough information to provide clear and unambiguous guidance for the task.

Providing Organizational Information

Besides specifying the nature of the task to be performed, instructions can include additional information to help students determine the relative importance of different questions or sections of the test. Information that can help students organize their work includes (1) the length and scope of the response sought, (2) the number of points each question is worth, and (3) the time available for completing the test or the recommended time students should spend on each question. This type of information is incorporated in the paragraph test in the following example:

1. Write a paragraph that describes fire drill procedures. Your paragraph should include 6 to 10 sentences. Be sure to include:

   a. A topic sentence (5 points)
   b. At least four supporting sentences (8 points)
   c. A concluding sentence (4 points)

You will have 20 minutes to write and revise your paragraph.

The paragraph is a relatively small product, but other intellectual skills products are quite complex, span a long period of time, and require quite detailed instructions. Figure 6.2 contains sample directions and organizational information for the term project in a classroom measurement and evaluation course. The directions are quite detailed, yet many students request additional information prior to beginning work and intermittently throughout their projects. The directions provide the basic understandings for how students are expected to proceed, what they are expected to produce, and when their products are due.

◾ Developing Scoring Procedures

Teachers typically use two types of scoring procedures to evaluate the quality of students' responses to essay questions and products. With *global* scoring (also called *holistic* scoring), the teacher uses general impressions to judge the quality of an answer or product. A teacher using *analytical* scoring divides a response into its relevant components and evaluates each part separately.

Global Scoring of Essay and Product Tests

Global scoring is appropriate whenever a test is *not* used to provide corrective feedback to students or to evaluate instruction. Its purpose is to sort students' responses into categories that indicate quality. For example, global scoring would be sufficient for a writing test used to place students in an English class. When a teacher has many papers to score, and it is not important to communicate the nature of the errors, global scoring is adequate.

The procedure for global scoring consists of the following seven steps:

1. *Establish the scoring categories you will use.* For example, you may have responses that fall into such categories as pass or fail; good, adequate, and poor; or excellent, good, adequate, poor, and unacceptable. The number of categories you select depends on the purpose for the evaluation and on your ability to place similar

FIGURE 6.2

Sample Instructions for One Product in a Classroom Measurement and Evaluation Course

Directions for Developing Your Item Bank and Producing Tests

1. Form a discipline/major-based team (no more than four members per team) with classmates.

2. Using a local school district curriculum guide (or State Curriculum Standards), choose an instructional goal for a small unit of instruction (about same in scope as writing a paragraph).

3. Create page 1.0 of your project:
   a. Name team members and your major areas of study.
   b. Describe the instructional goal selected by your team and its source.
   c. Describe the achievement characteristics of students for which your instruction/tests are intended.

4. Create page 2.0 of your project:
   a. Use an analytical procedure (matrix diagram, tree diagram, flowchart, etc.) to create a goal framework for the instructional goal you have chosen. Name your goal framework (e.g., **Table 1: Goal Framework for the Instructional Goal** _____). See Figures 3.6, 3.7, and 3.8 in the text.

5. Create page 3.0+ of your project:
   a. Develop Tables of Test Specifications for an Instructional Goal that includes:
      (1) The enabling skill codes from your instructional goal framework
      (2) The number of items that should be used to determine a learner's mastery level for each objective
      (3) The time required for students to answer the prescribed questions or perform the tasks.
      (4) The general format of the items (objective, product, performance)
   b. Name your test specifications (e.g., **Table 2: Tables of Test Specifications for the Instructional Goal** _____). See Figure 4.2 in the text.

6. Create page 4.0+ of your project:
   a. Develop prescriptions for individual items or tasks. Name these prescriptions (e.g., **Table 3: Test Item Specification for Enabling Skills for the Instructional Goal** _____). See Figure 4.6 in the text.

7. Create an item bank for your instructional goal:
   a. Go to the computer lab, register as a member of this class, sign up for creating an item bank, and purchase one floppy disk for each team member and one to submit as part of the term project. (Purchase the type recommended by the lab assistant for use with the item banking program.)
   b. Enter the item bank program, and name an item bank for your instructional goal.
   c. As a team, develop a set of descriptor codes for the items in your bank. Your descriptors might include the following categories: enabling skill code, learning level of the skill, concept or topic, grade level, test use (e.g., pretest, practice test, unit exam, term exam), reference chapter, etc. Create item descriptors that seem most reasonable to you as a team.
   d. Enter your item descriptor categories into your item bank.

(continued)

     e. Each team member should create (enter into the item bank) the number of test items specified in 5.a.(2) above for each enabling skill in the goal framework. Use the item format most appropriate for each test item specification in your set. Link appropriate graphics, tables, charts, textual material, rating scales, and checklists to the items in your bank. Remember to maintain a backup copy of your bank.

     f. When you have completed your portion of the bank, print a reference copy of your entire bank.

  8. Have a team meeting to *evaluate* the items in your item bank. Date: _____

     a. The items for all enabling skills should be written by this team meeting. During the meeting, members should exchange items so that all items are evaluated by all members of the team. The rubrics for quality items should be used to evaluate items. Descriptors for items should also be reviewed to ensure the compatibility of descriptors and items across authors. Evaluators should write their suggestions for item improvements directly on the author's item printout.

  9. Revise items based on colleagues' critiques. Item authors should reenter their item banks, locate, and edit their items based on evaluators' comments.

 10. Assemble tests for the unit. All tests prescribed in Table 2 of your project should be assembled, printed, and submitted as a portion of the term project.

     a. Each team member should use his or her own integrated item bank to assemble the pretest, the practice tests, or a unit posttest. As a team, all prescribed tests should be assembled, printed, and submitted as part of the project.

 11. The pretest for your team should become **Table 4,** and it should be named appropriately. The practice tests should become **Tables 5** and **6** and named appropriately. The unit posttest should be the last table in your project. You should submit a copy of your item bank disk as part of the project.

 12. Team projects are due on _____ .

responses consistently into the same category. If you create too many categories or do not carefully define each category, you will find scoring difficult.

    2. *Characterize a response that fits each category.* If, for example, you were to use the three categories of excellent, adequate, and poor, you should describe the particular characteristics that a response should have to be classified into one of the categories. What characteristics should be present for a response to be considered excellent? What would be absent or present in an adequate response? What would be absent in a poor response? Listing these characteristics helps you classify responses more consistently.

    3. *Read each response rapidly and form an overall impression.* During the reading, look for the characteristics you used to describe each rating category.

    4. *Sort the responses into the designated categories.*

    5. *Reread the papers that have been placed within a category.* After all papers have been classified, you should consider only those within a set for their comparability.

6. *Move any clearly superior or inferior responses to other categories.*

7. *Assign the same numerical score to all responses within a category.* For example, papers in the excellent category can be assigned a score of 5, those in the adequate category can be assigned a score of 3, and so forth.

Although global scoring is relatively fast and reliable, two limitations make it less appropriate for classroom tests. First, it does not provide students with adequate feedback about their work. Most students will want to know why they received the assigned score and will not be satisfied with a global rating. Second, global evaluations do not permit the teacher to analyze the responses and identify specific instructional problems. Thus, students do not have the information they need to correct their mistakes, and teachers cannot classify errors and relate them to problems in their lessons.

Analytical Scoring of Product Tests

Analytical scoring is a superior method for instructional purposes, but it is more time consuming than global scoring. This procedure helps a teacher focus on relevant aspects of students' responses and provides a systematic way to assign partial credit. Just as important, it allows students to see where they lost points. Using this method, teachers can summarize the group's performance on main components, analyze errors, and use error analysis to evaluate and revise instruction.

At the same time, analytical scoring also has some disadvantages. First, constructing a scoring instrument and marking responses take considerable time. If the teacher has not identified and sequenced all the components desired in an answer in the order they are likely to appear in students' responses, searching for these components in students' work will take even longer. Second, developing a flexible scoring procedure that accommodates unanticipated responses can also be difficult. Teachers using analytical scoring may struggle with the problem of scoring correct, unusual answers that do not fit the structure and that cannot be compared to other students' responses.

Analytical scoring can be simplified by using a rubric that indicates the desired elements of a response and the number of points to be awarded for each. To construct such a form, first identify and order the desired components and subcomponents of each response. The major components you select should always be based on an instructional goal and its framework of subordinate skills. In addition to these skills, you may want to use other elements, such as the students' approach, organization, and originality, to judge their work. Some teachers believe that grammar, neatness, punctuation, and spelling should always count whereas others choose not to emphasize these elements in every task. If you choose to include elements not contained in the goal framework and not included in instruction for the unit, you should inform students of this intention in the test directions.

Figure 6.3 includes a hypothetical goal analysis matrix with two main concept areas and six levels of learning. Main components for the product include I. First Concept and II. Second Concept. The characteristics listed in columns A, B, and C make

FIGURE 6.3

Hypothetical Instructional Goal Analysis Framework

CONCEPTS/ CONTENT	A State/Recall Physical Characteristics of:	B State/Recall Functional Characteristics of:	C State/Recall Quality Characteristics of:	D Discriminate between Examples and Nonexamples	E Evaluate Given Examples	F Produce Examples of:
I. First Concept	1. _____ 2. _____	1. _____	1. _____ 2. _____ 3. _____			
II. Second Concept	1. _____	1. _____ 2. _____	1. _____ 2. _____ 3. _____			

up the subcomponents that are included within each main component. The skeleton of the hypothetical analytical scoring form with the main concepts and their characteristics included is outlined in Figure 6.4. Notice that the top of the form has a title, a space for the student's name, a space to record the date, and a space to record the student's score. The far left column, labeled Criteria, contains the enabling skills codes (e.g., I.A.1), the main concepts (main components), and the key characteristics of the concepts (subcomponents) that are to be judged.

Pay careful attention to how you word or phrase the criteria in your rating form. All criteria should be either positively or neutrally worded. The wording of some elements should not reflect positive features of a product while others reflect negative feature or errors. Consistency in the direction of the criteria is critical for maintaining congruence between the criteria and your ratings of students' products. For example, one criterion should not be "good sequence" while another is "poor transition." A rating of yes for each of these criteria would result in a nonsensical score for students. With the analytical scoring form completed to this point, you are ready to decide how to score each of the subcomponents identified. There are two basic rating choices for rubrics in analytical scoring: checklists and rating scales.

Checklists   A checklist permits you only two categories to judge the quality of each component or subcomponent of a student's product. These two categories might be the presence or absence of a given characteristic, or they might be the acceptability or unacceptability of a characteristic present in the work.

When using a checklist to score a student's product, simply check each subcomponent that is present or that is acceptable in the product. The check marks can be summed to obtain a total score for the student, and this sum of checks is compa-

Main Components and Subcomponents in an Analytical Scoring Form

TITLE OF THE TEST	
Name _____	Date _____ Score _____
Criteria	
I. First Concept	
A.1 Physical Characteristic 1	
A.2 Physical Characteristic 2	
B.1 Functional Characteristic 1	
C.1 Quality Characteristic 1	
C.2 Quality Characteristic 2	
C.3 Quality Characteristic 3	
II. Second Concept	
A.1 Physical Characteristic 1	
B.1 Functional Characteristic 1	
B.2 Functional Characteristic 2	
C.1 Quality Characteristic 1	
C.2 Quality Characteristic 2	
C.3 Quality Characteristic 3	

rable to a student's raw score on an objective test. Raw scores can be converted to percentage correct scores by dividing the number of acceptable components by the total number of criteria used to evaluate the product and then multiplying by 100. Figure 6.5 contains the hypothetical evaluation criteria from Figure 6.4 configured into a checklist. In the example, the teacher has left space for comments on the far right. Sample check marks are inserted to illustrate how raw scores and percentage correct scores are obtained.

One note to keep in mind about checklists is that when planning to use scores for grading purposes, you must remember that the points assigned to each component of the checklist should be proportional to the importance of the component. The scoring in the example checklist in Figure 6.5 would indicate that all components are considered to be of equal importance, because each check mark is worth one point. If, however, you judged several components of the product being evaluated to be two or three times as important as the other components, then a check mark by those components would be worth two or three points instead of one point. This way of scoring a checklist will automatically assign the most weight to the components that you judge to be most important.

FIGURE 6.5

A Skeleton Checklist for Analytically Scoring Students' Products and Essays

TITLE OF THE TEST			

Name _____	Date _____ Score _____8_____ /(12) _____67_____ %

Yes	No	Criteria	Comments
		I. First Concept	
✓		A.1 Physical Characteristic 1	
✓		A.2 Physical Characteristic 2	
	✓	B.1 Functional Characteristic 1	
✓		C.1 Quality Characteristic 1	
	✓	C.2 Quality Characteristic 2	
✓		C.3 Quality Characteristic 3	
		II. Second Concept	
✓		A.1 Physical Characteristic 1	
	✓	B.1 Functional Characteristic 1	
✓		B.2 Functional Characteristic 2	
✓		C.1 Quality Characteristic 1	
✓	✓	C.2 Quality Characteristic 2	
	✓	C.3 Quality Characteristic 3	

Checklists can be used to evaluate written products such as term papers, and they can be used to evaluate other types of student products, such as a bookcase or a picture frame constructed in an industrial arts class, a dress or meal produced in a home economics class, or a mobile constructed in either a math or art class. For example, students being tested on the goal "Construct a mobile" would need to construct mobiles to demonstrate their skill even though the principles involved could be measured at the knowledge and comprehension levels using an objective test. The instructional goal framework should be used as the basis for both objective tests and the product evaluation form. A goal framework that a math teacher might develop is illustrated in Figure 6.6. Figure 6.7 is a corresponding checklist for evaluating students' mobiles. Notice that the criteria included on the checklist are observable and reflect the teacher's judgment of major components that should be included. An instructional goal framework and checklist created by an art teacher would undoubtedly be different from these examples because art teachers would need to include additional enabling skills related to the artistic quality of the mobile.

FIGURE 6.6

Instructional Goal Framework for Constructing a Mobile

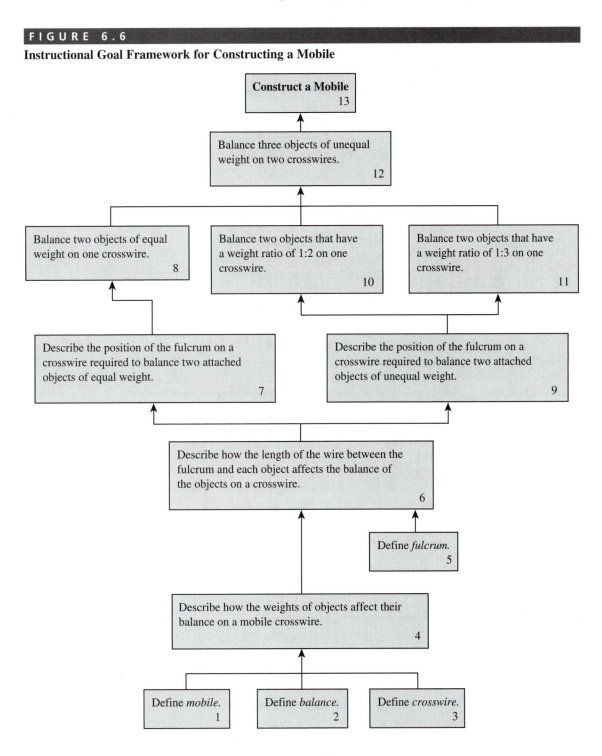

Checklist for Evaluating Mobiles

Name _____ Date _____ Score _____
                                                                Total   (15)

I. Mobile with 1:1 weight ratio between two objects
  _____ 1. Objects correctly selected by weight
  _____ 2. Objects correctly positioned on crosswire
  _____ 3. Fulcrum found on crosswire

II. Mobile with 1:2 weight ratio between two objects
  _____ 1. Objects correctly selected by weight
  _____ 2. Objects correctly positioned on crosswire
  _____ 3. Fulcrum found on crosswire

III. Mobile with 1:3 weight ratio between two objects
  _____ 1. Objects correctly selected by weight
  _____ 2. Objects correctly positioned on crosswire
  _____ 3. Fulcrum found on crosswire

IV. Mobile having three objects of unequal weight and two crosswires
  _____ 1. Objects correctly selected by weight
  _____ 2. Wires correctly selected by length
  _____ 3. Objects attached to correct crosswires
  _____ 4. Objects positioned correctly on crosswires
  _____ 5. Fulcrum found on lower crosswire
  _____ 6. Fulcrum found on upper crosswire

Notice in the example in Figure 6.7 that assigning one point for each check mark will automatically give Part IV of the checklist twice as much weight as Part I, II, or III, because Part IV has six components instead of three. For judging this product, however, the natural weighting built into the checklist is probably appropriate, because the double-wire mobile is more complex than any of the single-wire mobiles.

Rating Scales   The rating scale, an extension of the checklist, lets you judge not only the presence or acceptability of a characteristic but also its degree of quality. A rating scale contains all the main components and key subcomponents identified from the instructional goal framework. Similar to the checklist, these components should be stated in a consistently positive or neutral manner so that a low or high rating has the same meaning across all criteria. In addition, the rating scale has a sequence of numbers that represent degrees of quality for each product characteristic. The lowest end of a rating scale may have either the number 0 or 1. A rating of 0 is used *only* when a component or characteristic can be totally absent from a student's product. It should never be used to represent an unacceptable level of a characteristic that is present in a student's work. Remember that the purposes for the ratings are evaluation and communication—not demoralization!

There is no clear limit for setting the high end of the rating scale, but there is a good rule of thumb for determining one. You should never include more quality categories than you can clearly differentiate and consistently (reliably) rate. Teachers are probably most consistent with checklists where they are judging the acceptability or unacceptability of a particular characteristic. They can remain relatively reliable in their judgments when they add one more category, so there are three levels of quality to judge for a single characteristic. Three levels typically are used to reflect unacceptable (1), acceptable (2), and good (3) levels of a characteristic in a product. Four quality levels usually reflect unacceptable (1), acceptable (2), good (3), and excellent (4). Above this level, you should be very cautious. Only very complex characteristics can be judged consistently using four or more quality characteristics.

The number of quality levels you prescribe for each characteristic depends on the nature and complexity of the particular concept and characteristic to be rated. For example, judging whether a paragraph is indented does not require three or four levels of quality differentiation. Indentation is basically a checklist, yes/no, type of characteristic. Likewise, rating whether a student has the topic sentence properly located within a paragraph is also very straightforward, and a three- or four-point rating scale would be very difficult to use consistently to judge this characteristic. On the other hand, rating characteristics such as the sequence of information presented in a message or the quality of transitional words and phrases used in the message is more complex and can warrant differentiated levels of quality.

This paragraph example provides an opportunity for illustrating yet another quality characteristic you should consider in the construction of product and essay rating scales. The components and subcomponents in the rating scale do not need, nor should they necessarily have, the same number of quality points. The symmetrical four- or five-point rating scales included on attitude surveys and questionnaires, although attractive, are most often inappropriate for scoring products since the criteria differ by concept and characteristics.

Finally, once you have settled on the appropriate number of quality categories for each characteristic, it is a good idea to identify verbal descriptions for each of the numerical points on the scale. These verbal or qualitative descriptions will help you be more consistent in using the quantitative levels in your scales. For example, a rating of 0 could have the descriptor "Not Present." This particular label would help ensure that you only assign a score of 0 for missing ideas or components and not for inadequate examples. The better the descriptors fit the positive and negative features of individual components in your rating scale, the more consistent your ratings will be and the better they will communicate strengths and weaknesses to students.

In summary, the best rating scales for instructional purposes are those that include a thorough list of main components and subcomponents, but include a limited and appropriate number of quality levels to be differentiated for each component. Such a rating scale not only focuses the rater on the important elements of a product and aids consistent judgment but it also communicates expectations and judgments better to students.

Figure 6.8 contains a hypothetical rating scale developed from the checklist in Figure 6.5. Notice that the components and subcomponents are the same as for the checklist. The checklist has been expanded from two rating categories to three for the majority of the subcomponents. Note also that quality descriptors are provided above the quality levels at the top of the rating scales.

To use such a rating scale, you would locate each component in the product and then locate each subcomponent prescribed within the main category. For example, if you were rating topic sentences in a paragraph (a main component), you would first locate the topic sentence. With it in view, you would then rate its physical characteristics, how well it functions within the paragraph, and whether it meets the

FIGURE 6.8

A Skeleton Rating Scale for Analytically Scoring Students' Products and Essays

TITLE OF THE TEST			
Name _____ Date _____ Score __25__ / (30) = __83__ %			

Criteria	Not Present 0	Present 1	Adequately Developed 2	Well Developed 3
I. First Concept (15)				
A.1 Physical Characteristic 1	0	①		
A.2 Physical Characteristic 2	0	1	②	
B.1 Functional Characteristic 1	0	1	2	③
C.1 Quality Characteristic 1	0	1	2	③
C.2 Quality Characteristic 2	0	1	②	3
C.3 Quality Characteristic 3	0	1	2	③
II. Second Concept (15)				
A.1 Physical Characteristic 1	0	①		
B.1 Functional Characteristic 1	0	1	②	
B.2 Functional Characteristic 2	0	1	2	③
C.1 Quality Characteristic 1	0	1	②	3
C.2 Quality Characteristic 2	0	1	2	③
C.3 Quality Characteristic 3	⓪	1	2	3

qualitative characteristics prescribed for a particular student group. You indicate your rating of each subcomponent by circling the quality-level number that best reflects the level of work.

These ratings for each subcomponent can be summed to obtain the student's raw score on the product. In the example, the student earned 14 of the 15 points available for the first concept and 11 of the 15 points available for the second one. The student's raw score is 25. The percentage correct score is obtained by dividing the student's assigned points (25) by the total possible number of points on the rating scale (30) and then multiplying by 100. The student's percentage correct score is 83. For grading purposes, it is important to understand that the score of 83 percent does not necessarily mean that the student has mastered the skill at an 83 percent level. It means only that the student was credited with 83 percent of the points available on the rating scale. *If* the points available for each of the components (e.g., 1, 2, or 3) reflect the relative importance of the components, *then* you can feel more comfortable using the 83 percent score for grading purposes.

Analytical Scoring of Essay Tests

The preceding examples illustrate the development of checklists and rating scales for scoring students' products. An extension of these same procedures is used to develop analytical scoring forms for essay tests. Scoring forms for essay tests differ somewhat because these tests usually contain several questions that represent broader content areas. The basic procedure for developing the scoring form for each essay question is the same as that previously described—that is, (1) identify and sequence the main components and subcomponents for each essay question, (2) determine whether a checklist or rating scale would be most useful, and (3) develop the scoring form according to a plan.

The rating form for an essay test might contain a rating scale for each question, a checklist for each question, or a combination of the two formats. In fact, the rating plan for one question might contain some components to be checked as present and others to be rated on a quality scale. Consider the hypothetical rating form in Figure 6.9 for a four-question essay test. A checklist containing five components is used to score the first question; the second and third questions are scored using rating scales that contain 16 points each; and a checklist worth 6 points is used to score the fourth question. Using such a form, the topic of each question can be inserted beside the question number, and the components can be inserted beside the capital letters. The number of points a student earns can be inserted in the space beside each question and then multiplied by a desired weight, if additional weighting is needed to balance the questions. In the example, weights were chosen to increase the value of questions 1 and 4 to approximate the value of questions 2 and 3.

Using such a rating form to score the questions on an essay test will help you be more objective during scoring, show students where they earned and lost points, and aid your analysis of the group's responses, which is necessary for evaluating instruction and planning review sessions. It will also reduce the time you spend scoring students' tests, since you can illustrate where and why they lost points without rewriting their answers for them.

FIGURE 6.9

Hypothetical Rating Form for an Essay Test Containing Four Questions

---

Name _____ **Date** _____ **Score** _53.5 of 62 = 83%_

Question 1 (Checklist, 5 Points)   *Points* × *Weight* = *Score*
Present   Component
___✓___ A. _____   4   ×   3   =   12
___✓___ B. _____
___✓___ C. _____
_____ D. _____
___✓___ E. _____

Question 2 (Rating Scale, 16 Points)
Components   Ratings
                    (1)   (2)   (3)   (4)
A. _____   ____   ✓   ____   15   ×   1   =   15
B. _____   ____   ____   ✓
C. _____   ____   ____   ____   ✓
D. _____   ____   ____   ✓
E. _____   ____   ____   ✓

Question 3 (Rating Scale, 16 Points)
Components   Ratings
                    (1)   (2)   (3)   (4)
A. _____   ____   ____   ✓   14   ×   1   =   14
B. _____   ____   ✓   ____
C. _____   ____   ____   ____   ✓
D. _____   ____   ✓   ____
E. _____   ____   ____   ✓

Question 4 (Checklist, 6 Points)
Present   Component
___✓___ A. _____   5   ×   2.5   =   12.5
_____ B. _____
___✓___ C. _____
___✓___ D. _____
___✓___ E. _____
___✓___ F. _____

Evaluating Checklists and Rating Scales

Before you use a checklist or rating scale to score students' work, evaluate the form and revise it if necessary. First, select two or three students' responses or products and rate their work using the form. Determine whether the components on the form are observable and whether they are listed on the form in the sequence they most frequently occur in the products. Delete components that are not observable, change the sequence of components if necessary, and add components observable in the products that you may have inadvertently overlooked. When adding components, be sure they are appropriate for the instructional goal measured and not an artifact of the particular subset of responses you have chosen. Adjust students' scores on the few products rated to reflect any changes made in the rating form. Second, score each paper again. It is good to allow some time to lapse between the two ratings so that you forget the scores assigned the first time. Compare the two ratings you assigned each paper and locate any inconsistencies. Where inconsistent scores occur, either revise the form to include fewer categories of quality that need to be differentiated or write more descriptive titles for each of the categories.

You might also ask a colleague to rate the same papers using the form. Compare your ratings with those of your colleague, discuss any inconsistencies, locate ways in which the form can be changed to improve consistency, and revise the form as needed. Once you begin to score students' work, do not alter the form. Any changes at this point may produce inconsistent ratings.

Avoiding Common Errors in Test Development, Scoring, and Grading

Development Errors

In producing essay and product development tests, teachers tend to commit two kinds of errors. First, some teachers teach skills at the lower levels of learning and test them at the higher levels. You should not teach lessons at the knowledge and comprehension levels and then expect students to perform at an application level on the test. Likewise, you should not teach at the comprehension level and then write tests to measure skills at the analysis, synthesis, or evaluation levels. If students are required to develop a product or analyze a piece of literature, they should have been instructed at these levels and given ample opportunity to practice these skills before the posttest. To avoid this problem, make sure that novel items used on the posttest mirror those used on practice tests.

Teachers also err in constructing essay and product development tests when the items or directions do not provide adequate guidance. One way to ensure that items and directions are clear and the task posed is feasible is to construct the evaluation form before you administer the test. Constructing the evaluation form will help ensure that you have a clear notion of what you are asking students to do. After the evaluation form is complete, recheck your questions and directions to see whether they provide adequate guidance for the responses you anticipate.

Essay tests can include several questions that require relatively brief answers, or they may contain only one or two questions that require lengthy responses. Whatever the number of questions, the entire class should be directed to answer all the questions included on the test. One relatively common practice in developing essay tests, which is *not* recommended by test specialists, is to provide several questions on an essay test and allow students to select a subset of questions to answer. This practice would be similar to letting students answer 20 of 30 objective items. Both essay and objective test items represent only a few of those a teacher could construct, and the same sample should be used to evaluate all students. When students' responses are not comparable, your ability to evaluate your instruction and students' performance is compromised.

Scoring Errors

Two common scoring errors are inconsistency and bias. Even when teachers use checklists and rating scales, they can score students' responses inconsistently. They may become stricter or more lenient as they work through a set of papers, and their attitudes can change when they become tired, hurried, or bored. You can avoid such inconsistencies in several ways. First, instead of marking all the essay questions on one student's paper, score all the students' responses to one question before going on to the next question. Complete the scoring of one question during one marking period rather than in several. After you have completed all the papers on each question, check your consistency by again scoring the first few papers. If a student's first and second scores are the same, your scoring was probably consistent for all students. Noticeable inconsistencies in marking might indicate that your attitude, rather than the quality of students' work, determined test scores. If the scores are different, you should rescore the tests.

Besides attitude, the inclusion of too many quality categories for each component can lead to inconsistent scoring. For example, the paragraph rating scale in Figure 6.10 lists only main components with no physical, functional, or quality characteristics. The rating scales for each main component have eight quality levels for each component with only two descriptor categories. Although it would take little time to develop such a scale, the probability of the teacher's marking paragraphs inconsistently is high. It would be more difficult to identify distinct quality descriptors for all eight category numbers. It would also be difficult to differentiate consistently between adjacent categories (e.g., determining when a student should receive a 3 instead of a 4 or a 6 instead of a 7). When inconsistencies are present, you might want to revise your rating scale and use strategies to minimize potential attitude shifts before rescoring tests.

F I G U R E 6 . 1 0

Rating Scale with Inappropriate Quality Categories

Component	Rating		
	Inadequate		Excellent
I. Topic Sentence	1 2 3 4 5 6 7 8		
II. Supporting Sentences	1 2 3 4 5 6 7 8		
III. Concluding Sentence	1 2 3 4 5 6 7 8		

Scoring bias is another common problem. Some teachers give all the students high test scores regardless of quality. Others give all average or all very low marks. In your own marking, compare the range of scores you assign with the heterogeneity or homogeneity of the group. If you have a homogeneous group of students, a small range of high, average, or low scores may accurately reflect the quality of students' work. If you are assigning similar scores to a heterogeneous group, however, your marking may be biased.

Teachers' opinions of individual students can also bias their scoring. Teachers are often inclined to score particular students' papers more leniently than they score others, and disruptive or uncooperative students sometimes receive scores lower than they deserve. Students who are struggling can evoke a great deal of sympathy, and teachers who want to encourage their efforts may score these students' papers quite leniently. However you choose to justify unearned scores, keep in mind that they are, indeed, unearned.

Because teachers are often unaware of their bias, they may find it difficult to avoid. Test specialists recommend that teachers maintain objectivity by disassociating students' names from their responses. For example, you could instruct your students to put their names on the backs of their papers or you could cover their names with removable labels until you finished scoring the papers. Students could also write their names and an identifying number on a separate sheet of paper and indicate only the identifying number on their work. If you have difficulty scoring papers that do not identify the student, your impressions of students are probably influencing the way you score. If this is the case, you should keep in mind that you are scoring responses and not individuals.

Another common error sometimes observed in scoring essay tests is to use *subtractive* rather than *additive* scoring. Subtractive scoring occurs when a teacher decides subjectively that a test will be worth a given number of total points, divides these points equally among the questions on the test, and then scores students' answers by subtracting a subjective number of points from each answer for errors and omissions present in the answers. Students' raw scores are obtained by subtracting the negative points from the total number of points allocated. To illustrate subtractive scoring, a teacher may administer a four-question essay test and decide that the total exam will be worth 100 points, with 25 points allocated to each of the four questions. Before grading begins, all students have a score of 100 in the exam. As the teacher reads each answer, points are subtracted from the total for omissions and errors. For one omission, a student's score may be reduced by 2 points, for an error it may be reduced by 5 points, and 1 point might be subtracted for each spelling error. The sum of the negative points the student earns is then subtracted from the total points allocated to determine the student's score on the question. If the student made one omission, one content error, and misspelled five words, the score for the question would be $25 - 12 = 13$. This method of subtractive grading is very subjective, does not clearly communicate to students the strengths in their answers, and tends to result in inconsistent scoring across items on one student's test and across students in the class on one test item.

Additive scoring, on the other hand, enables teachers to allocate a specified number of points for each component of an answer, locate that component in the answer, and assign an appropriate number of the allocated points. Students' raw scores are then obtained by adding the points earned for each component. Additive, analytical scoring helps teachers be more objective, and it better communicates the strengths and problems in a student's answer.

A Grading Error

One common grading error is to count practice tests as posttests and include them in the term grade. This tends to happen more on essay and product development practice tests than on objective-style practice tests because of the time and effort required for essay and product tests by both the teacher and students. But the required effort is not what differentiates between practice exercises and posttests. The purposes of practice tests, regardless of the format, are to provide students with the opportunity to rehearse skills and to provide them with corrective feedback. Despite the degree of effort required, students' scores on essay and product development practice tests should not be considered when calculating term achievement grades.

■ Using Product Rating Forms as an Instructional Tool

Used as self-assessment tools, rating scales and checklists can help students identify and use appropriate criteria for developing their responses. During practice exercises, they can use an evaluation form to rate the quality of their work and to compare their ratings with yours. You can then discuss differences in ratings with students who have difficulty finding problems in their work. Students can also use the rating forms to evaluate example answers and products that you provide. They can discuss similarities and differences among their evaluations and between theirs and yours. Using the criteria when developing their responses for practice exercises and when reviewing work samples will help students focus on the important aspects of a skill. Such involvement should help them not only produce better work but also feel a greater sense of responsibility for the quality of their work and the scores they receive. This is an ideal form of guided self-reflection.

The use of product rating forms can also serve to keep cooperative learning activities and group projects on track. Notice in the instructions for developing a test item bank (Figure 6.2) that students are directed to use the test item checklists they were given during instruction. Using the checklists as a guide, students evaluate the items they have written as well as those written by their teammates. This evaluation activity during the production of term projects serves as instruction for students, and it results in superior item banks.

■ An Example

The instructional goal framework and item task specifications on writing a paragraph are used to illustrate the development of evaluation forms for rating the original paragraphs written by students. The product-level task specifications written for the instructional goal are the following:

I.F.1   Given a topic requiring a description of something, write a four- to six-sentence paragraph.

I.F.2   Given a topic that requires time series, write a four- to six-sentence paragraph.

I.F.3   Given a topic that is a procedure for doing something, write a four- to six-sentence paragraph.

I.F.4   Given a topic that is an expression of feelings or attitude, write a four- to six-sentence paragraph.

The following sections contain examples of instructions as well as checklist and rating scale rubrics.

Writing Instructions

The following instructions are for task specification I.F.3, "Write a paragraph that describes a procedure." Very few directions about the paragraph itself are given because the teacher wants to evaluate whether students remember to include all three types of sentences, order their sentences according to the procedure they describe, and use transitional words to illustrate sequence.

Write a four- to six-sentence paragraph that **describes how** to wash a dog. Use a clean sheet of paper, and write your name in the top, left corner of the page. Put today's date in the top, right corner of the page. You will have 20 minutes to write and revise your paragraph. You may want to outline your dog-washing ideas before you begin to write.

Developing Scoring Procedures

The instructional goal framework for writing a paragraph is repeated in Figure 6.11. There are four main concepts in the framework: paragraphs, topic sentences, supporting sentences, and concluding sentences. These main components will comprise the major sections of the evaluation form. Recall that the criteria for evaluating these main components should be located in the physical, functional, and qualitative characteristics columns of the matrix. The goal framework will be used to create checklist and rating scale rubrics for evaluating students' paragraphs.

A Checklist for Scoring Paragraphs   The main components in rows I, II, III, and IV and their subcomponents in columns A, B, and C are configured into the checklist in Figure 6.12. The title of the checklist reflects the instructional goal and the particular assignment within the goal. Space is also included at the top of the form for inserting students' names, the date, their raw scores, and the percentage of total points earned. This information is important later for monitoring students' writing progress and for sequencing writing samples in a portfolio of their work.

Matrix Diagram Analysis for the Intellectual Goal "Write a Paragraph"

CONCEPTS/ CONTENT	A State/Recall Physical Characteristics	B State/Recall Functional Characteristics	C State/Recall Quality Characteristics	D Discriminate Examples and Nonexamples	E Evaluate Given Examples	F Produce Examples
I. Paragraph	Series of sentences Indented	Express ideas on one topic		Correct vs.: Not indented Many topics		Time Series Feelings Procedure Description
II. Topic Sentence	Typically first Indented	Introduce topic	Relevance Scope Interest	Topic vs.: Supporting Concluding	Correct vs. flawed by: Relevance Scope Interest	Time Series Feelings Procedure Description
III. Supporting Sentences	Middle sentences	Elaborate topic	Relevance Sequence Transition	Supporting vs.: Topic Concluding	Correct vs. flawed by: Relevance Sequence Transition	Time Series Feelings Procedure Description
IV. Concluding Sentence	Typically last	Concludes/ summarizes topic	Transition Relevance Sums up Scope	Concluding vs.: Topic Supporting	Correct vs. flawed by: Transition Relevance Conclusion Scope	Time Series Feelings Procedure Description

The left side of the checklist includes spaces for indicating the presence or acceptability of each facet of students' paragraphs. The second column contains the four main components and their subcomponents extracted from the instructional goal framework. The last column includes space for commenting on students' paragraphs. This comment area can be used to praise particularly good characteristics and to point out areas the student needs to reconsider. Using a comments section with your checklists will help you avoid marking over or rewriting students' paragraphs.

Students' raw scores are obtained by checking the acceptable characteristics in the left column and then summing the check marks. The percentage of total points earned is obtained by dividing the student's raw score by the number of possible points (19) and then multiplying the quotient by 100.

A Rating Scale for Scoring Paragraphs   Figure 6.13 contains the paragraph checklist reformatted into a rating scale. The project title and other identifying information remains the same. Notice that the main components and subcomponents

FIGURE 6.12

A Sample Checklist for Rating Students' Original Paragraphs

WRITING PROCEDURAL PARAGRAPHS (WASHING A DOG)			
Name _____		Date _____ Score _____ (19) _____ %	
Yes	No	Criteria	Comments
		I. Paragraph	
_____	_____	A.1 Four to six sentences	
_____	_____	A.2 Indented	
_____	_____	B.1 Only one idea	
_____	_____	B.2 Describes procedure	
		II. Topic Sentence	
_____	_____	A.1 Location (first)	
_____	_____	B.2 Introduces topic	
_____	_____	C.1 Relevant to paragraph	
_____	_____	C.2 Appropriate scope	
_____	_____	C.3 Interest for reader	
		III. Supporting Sentences	
_____	_____	A.1 Location (middle)	
_____	_____	B.2 Elaborates topic	
_____	_____	C.1 Relevant to topic	
_____	_____	C.2 Sequence of ideas	
_____	_____	C.3 Transition	
		IV. Concluding Sentence	
_____	_____	A.1 Location (last)	
_____	_____	B.2 Summarizes	
_____	_____	C.1 Transition	
_____	_____	C.2 Relevance	
_____	_____	C.3 Scope	

also remain the same but they are moved to the first column of the form. The second column contains the descriptive categories and numbers to indicate quality levels. The comments column is again included to allow highlighting particularly good components as well as ones that need to be improved.

FIGURE 6.13

A Sample Rating Scale for Evaluating Students' Original Paragraphs

WRITING PROCEDURAL PARAGRAPHS (WASHING A DOG)					
Name _____ Date _____ Score _____ (44) _____ %					
Criteria	**No** **0**	**Vaguely** **1**	**Mostly** **2**	**Well** **3**	**Comments**
I. Paragraph (7)					
A.1 Four to six sentences	0	1 (Yes)			
A.2 Indented	0	1 (Yes)			
B.1 Only one topic		1	2		
C.1 Describes procedure		1	2	3	
II. Topic Sentence (10)	0	1 (Included)			
A.1 Location (first)	0	1 (Yes)			
B.2 Introduces topic		1	2		
C.1 Relevant to paragraph		1	2		
C.2 Appropriate scope		1	2		
C.3 Interest for reader		1	2		
III. Supporting Sentences (14)	0	1 (Included)			
A.1 Location (middle)	0	1 (Yes)			
B.2 Elaborates topic		1	2	3	
C.1 Relevant to topic		1	2	3	
C.2 Sequence of ideas		1	2	3	
C.3 Transition		1	2	3	
IV. Concluding Sentence (13)	0	1 (Included)			
A.1 Location (last)	0	1 (Yes)			
B.1 Summarizes		1	2	3	
C.1 Transition		1	2	3	
C.2 Relevance		1	2	3	
C.3 Scope		1	2		
Totals		( ) +	( ) +	( )	= _____

■ Computer Technology

Although some teachers believe that computer-based item banks are inappropriate for essay and product tests, this is not so. There are several options you can use to enter a checklist or rating scale into an item bank. Probably the easiest method is to enter the performance directions using an essay item format and then enter the accompanying evaluation form as a table or illustration linked to the item. Any time the item (directions) is printed, the rating scale or checklist will also be printed. Another method is to enter the evaluation form itself, using either the essay or problem format, and then classify it as a rubric with the user descriptors (e.g., subject, topic, test type) for easy retrieval. A third option would be to enter it as a figure that accompanies the item directions. Recall from Chapter 5 that you can link graphs, charts, and tables to designated items using the figure feature. Each time the directions are printed, the accompanying figure is also printed.

Besides test item banks, another marvelous assessment aid is computer-based spreadsheet programs such as Microsoft's Excel. Spreadsheet programs will speed your scoring tasks, enhance your record-keeping abilities, and aid in evaluating the effectiveness of instruction for the overall goal and individual enabling skills within the goal. In setting up your spreadsheet, you can use the top rows to identify the main components and subcomponents of the assessment and points assigned for each subcomponent. The left-hand columns of the spreadsheet can be used for students' names and identification numbers. As you score each subcomponent of an essay question or product, you can enter the earned score into the appropriate intersecting student-by-criterion cell in the spreadsheet. You can then enter formulas into the spreadsheet that will calculate each student's raw score and percentage correct score, saving hours of calculation time. You can also enter formulas that will weight subcomponents and main components and then calculate weighted raw and percentage correct scores for all students. These spreadsheet-based rubrics can then be printed for student feedback and maintained in a class file for gradebook and reporting records.

Using spreadsheet programs to record an individual student's points earned also helps you summarize exam scores to evaluate your instruction for the main elements of the instructional goal. You can sum across students' scores for each main component to determine the percentage of total points that was earned by a class. Using this percentage score, you can identify enabling skills where students' performances were best or possibly need improvement. After setting a criterion for effective instruction, you can compare the class summary percentage scores with your criterion for effective instruction to identify enabling skills where instruction might be improved.

■ Summary

Essay tests and product development tests measure students' skills in producing original responses. Essay questions can ask students to discuss, explain, analyze, summarize, or evaluate something. Product development tests can be used to measure students' skill in producing a variety of verbal products, such as paragraphs, book reports, and themes. Product tests can also be used to measure students' skill in creating such objects as mobiles, photographs, and maps.

Essay and product tests allow students to select their approach to a given problem, the information they will include, and the methods of organization and presentation they will use. (Such skills cannot be measured using objective tests.) These tests enable a teacher to determine both what and how students think. Test drawbacks include the time required to develop, analyze, and score them; difficulties in scoring responses consistently and without bias; and the advantage essay tests give to students with well-developed verbal skills.

The procedure for developing and using essay and product development tests consists of three phases: (1) writing questions and directions, (2) developing scoring procedures, and (3) scoring students' responses.

The criteria for developing valid and reliable test items also apply to essay questions and directions for products. The behavior, content, and conditions included should match those in the task specifications; the complexity, context, and vocabulary should be appropriate for students; and grammar, punctuation, and sentence structure should be correct. Good questions and directions also provide adequate guidance for responding. Questions and directions that provide little guidance require students to exercise considerable judgment in responding. A lot of guidance guarantees that students will address specific issues, but it also limits the approaches they can take. Considering the main purpose for your test and the skill level of students will help you select an appropriate amount of guidance.

Besides describing the task to be performed, you should provide information that can help students determine the scope of the anticipated responses. You might want to include such information as how long their response should be, the amount of time they should spend, and the number of points each question or section is worth. Developing an evaluation form before administering the test will help you evaluate the clarity and feasibility of your questions or directions.

Essay and product development tests can be scored using either global or analytical scoring methods. Global scoring provides information on the overall quality of students' responses. Analytical scoring provides information on the quality of specific components and subcomponents of a response. Although analytical scoring is more time consuming than is global scoring, it provides students with better feedback and teachers with specific information they can use to analyze and evaluate the quality of instruction.

Analytical scoring requires the use of rubrics that are either checklists or rating scales. Both rubric formats should list the components and, if needed, the subcomponents of a skill to direct your attention to particular aspects of a response. The components and subcomponents should be taken directly from the enabling and prerequisite skills in the instructional goal framework. A checklist allows you to mark the presence or absence of a component, whereas a rating scale enables you to differentiate various quality categories for each component using a scale. The number of quality categories included on the scale should not exceed the number you can consistently judge. Verbal descriptors should be written for each quality category. Once the checklist or rating scale is designed, review the number of points allocated to each component. If the value assigned does not contribute an appropriate amount to the total score, use weighting schemes to adjust the relative value of components.

When the evaluation form is complete, review the questions and directions to ensure that they provide students with the guidance necessary to produce the responses you anticipate. At this point, revisions can be made in the questions, directions, or evaluation form as needed. After the test is administered, the rating form should again be evaluated using a few tests. Determine whether the components listed are observable in students' responses, whether they are sequenced in the most efficient order on the form, and whether you can score responses consistently. Make necessary revisions before beginning to score students' work.

Teachers experience two problems when rating students' responses: inconsistent scoring and bias. Inconsistent scoring can be caused by shifts in attitude that may lead to stricter or more lenient scoring. It can also result when you include more categories of quality for each component than you can consistently judge or use vague descriptors for each category. Bias results from marking all students as good, average, or poor regardless of the quality of their work. Bias also results when you consider not only the nature of the response but also the characteristics of the student who made the response. After scoring all papers, rescore the first two or three to see whether you were consistent. Also check to see whether the range of scores assigned is reasonable given the heterogeneity or homogeneity of the group. If inconsistency or bias is detectable, you should rescore the papers.

Similar to objective-style items, essay questions and product development directions can be entered into a computer-based test item bank. Keeping test questions or directions and scoring forms in an item bank enables easy retrieval of the materials and convenient editing when changes are necessary. Additionally, scores from product tests are easy to enter into students' records for inclusion on interim and term progress reports.

■ PRACTICE EXERCISES

I. Develop and Score Product Tests
   A. Which of the following skills could be measured only with essay or product development tests?
   1. Recall verbal information.
   2. Design a solution to a problem.
   3. Discriminate among examples and nonexamples of a concept.
   4. Use a rule to solve a problem.
   5. Decide how two or more things should be compared and make the comparisons.
   6. Evaluate a rule, a principle, an object, or a product.
   7. Synthesize facts and information.
   8. Organize facts and information.
   9. Follow rules to produce an original piece of work.
   10. Recall, select, organize, and present information.

B. Figure 6.14 includes an instructional goal framework for outlining a passage. Use the framework to:

1. Write instructions for a test that measures students' skills in outlining given passages. Assume that the given passages each have three main topics, three secondary ideas, and no level-three or level-four ideas.
2. Write instructions for a practice test in outlining in which students will use a rating form to guide their practice.
3. Develop an evaluation form for scoring students' outlines. (See Figure 6.17F in the Feedback section.)

C. Score the three paragraphs entitled "Washing a Dog" in Figure 6.15 using the paragraph rating form in Figure 6.16. Assume the paragraphs were written by sixth-grade students.

FIGURE 6.14

Goal Framework for the Instructional Goal "Outline a Passage"

Components	Define Levels	Paraphrase Entries	Sequence Entries within Level	Label Entries	Align Entries in Outline
Main topics	Define main topics as key main ideas in total passage.	Use sentence or topic outline. Do not mix sentences and phrases in one outline.	Place entries in order defined by passage.	Use Roman numerals to label main ideas.	Place all main topics flush with left margin.
Secondary topics	Define secondary topics as key ideas within each main topic. There should be at least two entries.	Make all entries within a main topic parallel in structure. Structure may differ from that of main topics and from that of secondary topics for other main ideas.	Place secondary topics in order defined by passage.	Use capital letters to label secondary topics.	Indent secondary entries 5 spaces from left margin and align.
Level-three topics	Define level-three topics as key ideas *within* each secondary level topic. There should be at least two entries.	Make all entries within a secondary level topic parallel.	Place level-three topics in order defined by passage.	Label level-three topics with Arabic numerals.	Indent all level-three topics 10 spaces from left margin and align.
Level-four topics	Define level-four topics as key ideas *within* each level-three topic. There should be at least two entries.	Make all entires within a level-three topic parallel.	Place level-four topics in order defined by passage.	Label level-four topics with lower-case letters	Indent all level-four topics 15 spaces from left margin and align.

FIGURE 6.15

Three Paragraphs Entitled "Washing a Dog"

Paragraph 1

> One of my chors on Saturday is to wash my dog Rover. I use warm water to get him wet all over. Then I rub him with a special soap that doesn't hurt his eyes and keeps his coat glossie When he is clean, I rinse him twice to make sure all the soap is gone. After he shakes off most of the water, I rub him with a clean old towel. He thinks I do a good job.

Paragraph 2

> Put a wash tub in the yard. Fill it with water and sope. Put the dog in the tub. Scrub the dog. Rinse the dog with a hose. Stand back when the dog gets out of the tub.

Paragraph 3

> My dog hates to take a bath. When anyone gets out the tub she runs and hides. It is easy to find her because she always hides in the same place. You have to hold her the whole time or she will run away again. She shivers and barks the whole time. My cousin's dog likes to get a bath.

Record your scores for each paragraph in the last three columns of the form. When you have finished:

1. Compare the scores you assigned with those of classmates.
2. Discuss inconsistencies and try to determine why the scores were different.
3. If you attribute differences to inadequacies in the rating scale, suggest ways to improve the form.
4. Compare your scores to those in Figure 6.18F (in the Feedback section) that reflect the judgment of another rater.

II. Enrichment

Select a skill from your own field that can only be measured with an essay or product development test and do the following:

1. Analyze the skill to identify its subordinate skills and create a goal framework that illustrates the relationship among the skills.
2. Write a behavioral objective for the skill; be sure to include relevant conditions.
3. Write an essay question or questions or the instructions for product development. Include adequate guidance for the skill being measured and for the sophistication of target students.
4. Develop a scoring checklist or rating scale.
5. If you have students' work available, score their work using your form.
6. Revise the rating form if necessary.

FIGURE 6.16
A Sample Rating Scale for Evaluating Students' Paragraphs in Figure 6.13

WRITING PROCEDURAL PARAGRAPHS (WASHING A DOG)							
Name _____			Date _____	Score _____ (44) _____ %			
Criteria	**No** **0**	**Vaguely** **1**	**Mostly** **2**	**Well** **3**	**#1**	**#2**	**#3**
I. Paragraph (7)							
A.1 Four to six sentences	0	1 (Yes)					
A.2 Indented	0	1 (Yes)					
B.1 Only one topic		1	2				
C.1 Describes procedure		1	2	3			
II. Topic Sentence (10)	0	1 (Included)					
A.1 Location (first)	0	1 (Yes)					
B.2 Introduces topic		1	2				
C.1 Relevant to paragraph		1	2				
C.2 Appropriate scope		1	2				
C.3 Interest for reader		1	2				
III. Supporting Sentences (14)	0	1 (Included)					
A.1 Location (middle)	0	1 (Yes)					
B.2 Elaborates topic		1	2	3			
C.1 Relevant to topic		1	2	3			
C.2 Sequence of ideas		1	2	3			
C.3 Transition		1	2	3			
IV. Concluding Sentence (13)	0	1 (Included)					
A.1 Location (last)	0	1 (Yes)					
B.1 Summarizes		1	2	3			
C.1 Transition		1	2	3			
C.2 Relevance		1	2	3			
C.3 Scope		1	2				
Totals		( ) + ( ) + ( )					

■ **F E E D B A C K**

I. Develop and Score Product Tests

A. The following skills could be measured only with essay and product development tests: 2, 5, 9, and 10.

B. Instructions for a test of outlining skills.

   1. Read the article titled _____ . Make a <u>topic</u> outline of the information in the article. You have 20 minutes to complete the task.

   2. Instructions for a practice test of outlining skills.

   Make a <u>sentence</u> outline of the information in the article entitled _____ . You have 30 minutes to complete the following:

   a. Read the article.

   b. Review the rating form attached to the article that will be used to score your outline.

   c. Select and organize the information you think should be included.

   d. Write your outline.

   e. Use the rating form to:

   (1) review your outline and <u>correct</u> any problems you find.

   (2) <u>score</u> your outline.

   f. Turn in both your outline and your completed rating form when you have finished.

   3. See Figure 6.17F.

C. Compare your scores with those of classmates and students included in Figure 6.18F.

Rating Scale for Evaluating Outlines

Name _____ Date _____ Score _____

Total   (35)

I. Main Ideas	1	2	3
A. Main ideas identified	Secondary ideas included	Some ideas missing	All main ideas included
	1	2	3
B. Clearly paraphrased	Some meaning changed	Too brief/wordy	Clearly paraphrased
	1	2	3
C. Parallel structure	Mixed sentence/phrase	All sentences or phrases	Consistent word format
	1	2	3
D. Consistent order	Out of order	Most in order	All in order
	1	2	3
E. Consistent labels	Inconsistent	Consistent	
	1	2	
F. Alignment	Flush with left margin	Aligned	
	1	2	

II. Secondary Ideas			
A. Secondary ideas identified	Main ideas included	Some ideas missing	All secondary ideas included
	1	2	3
B. Related to main idea	Scrambled placement	Most within right topic	All within right topic
	1	2	3
C. Clearly paraphrased	Some meaning changed	Too brief/wordy	Clearly paraphrased
	1	2	3
D. Parallel structure	Mixed sentence/ phrase/word	All sentences, phrases, or words	Consistent word format
	1	2	3
E. Consistent order	Out of order	Most in order	All in order
	1	2	3
F. Consistent labels	Inconsistent	Consistent	
	1	2	
G. Alignment	Indented five spaces	Aligned	
	1	2	

FIGURE 6.18F

Ratings for Students' Original Paragraphs on Washing a Dog

WRITING PROCEDURAL PARAGRAPHS (WASHING A DOG)							
Name _____			Date _____	Score ____ (44) _____ %			
Criteria	**No 0**	**Vaguely 1**	**Mostly 2**	**Well 3**	**#1**	**#2**	**#3**
I. Paragraph (7)							
A.1 Four to six sentences	0	1 (Yes)			1	1	1
A.2 Indented	0	1 (Yes)			1	0	0
B.1 Only one topic		1	2		2	2	1
C.1 Describes procedure		1	2	3	3	3	1
II. Topic Sentence (10)	0	1 (Included)			1	0	1
A.1 Location (first)	0	1 (Yes)			1		1
B.2 Introduces topic		1	2		2		2
C.1 Relevant to paragraph		1	2		2		2
C.2 Appropriate scope		1	2		2		2
C.3 Interest for reader		1	2		2		2
III. Supporting Sentences (14)	0	1 (Included)			1	1	1
A.1 Location (middle)	0	1 (Yes)			1	0	1
B.2 Elaborates topic		1	2	3	3	3	3
C.1 Relevant to topic		1	2	3	3	3	3
C.2 Sequence of ideas		1	2	3	3	3	3
C.3 Transition		1	2	3	3	1	1
IV. Concluding Sentence (13)	0	1 (Included)			1	0	1
A.1 Location (last)	0	1 (Yes)			1		1
B.1 Summarizes		1	2	3	3		1
C.1 Transition		1	2	3	1		1
C.2 Relevance		1	2	3	3		1
C.3 Scope		1	2		2		1
Totals		( ) + ( ) + ( )			42	17	31

■ RUBRIC

Rubric for Evaluating Essay and Product Tests

		GENERAL CRITERIA FOR ALL TEST FORMATS
Yes **No**		**I. Curriculum-Based Criteria (instructions, directions, and rating forms)**
_____ _____		A. Are items or tasks congruent with the conditions, behavior, and content of the task specification?
_____ _____		B. Are items or tasks authentic and relevant to curriculum standard?
		II. Learner-Centered Criteria (instructions, directions, and rating forms)
_____ _____		A. Are items or tasks congruent with the language (including ESOL), context, developmental level, and special needs of learners?
_____ _____		B. Are items or tasks free from biasing material related to gender, cultural/ethnic groups, and religious and political ideas?
		III. School-Based Criteria (feasibility)
_____ _____		A. Are development and administration time available related to teacher-student ratio?
_____ _____		B. Is turnaround time available from test administration to score reporting?
_____ _____		C. Are resources available for test development, administration, scoring, and reporting?
		IV. Professional-Based Criteria
_____ _____		A. Are instructions, directions, and rating forms clear related to:
_____ _____		■ Grammar?
_____ _____		■ Spelling?
_____ _____		■ Expression?
_____ _____		■ Order of information?
_____ _____		B. Is the task creative and interesting?
_____ _____		C. Are materials and procedures professional appearing?
_____ _____		D. Is the task likely to yield accurate measures?
		E. Are scoring procedures ethical in that:
_____ _____		■ Work product rather than student is judged?
_____ _____		■ Ratings are reliable within and across students?
_____ _____		■ Quality levels applied appropriate for students' developmental level?
		FORMATTING CRITERIA FOR ESSAY AND PRODUCT TESTS
		I. Directions (directions and instructions)
_____ _____		A. Do directions provide appropriate guidance for students' skill level?
_____ _____		B. Do directions provide appropriate guidance for the skill measured?
_____ _____		C. Do directions provide adequate organizational information (e.g., time allowed, point values for tasks, length and scope of response sought)?

Yes	No	
		II. Global Scoring
____	____	A. Are there established scoring categories that will be used?
____	____	B. Are there only the number of scoring categories that can be consistently differentiated?
____	____	C. Are there clearly described characteristics of a response that fit each of the categories?
		III. Analytical Scoring—Criteria (Stems)
____	____	A. Are evaluation criteria congruent with the main concepts (components) in the instructional goal framework?
____	____	B. Are evaluation criteria congruent with the physical, functional, and qualitative characteristics included in the instructional goal framework (product development)?
____	____	C. Are evaluation criteria congruent with the main categories of information to be described (rows) or contrasted (columns) in the instructional goal framework (essay)?
____	____	D. Are evaluation criteria paraphrased clearly in the rating form?
____	____	E. Are evaluation criteria ordered/sequenced logically/conveniently for observation?
____	____	F. Are evaluation criteria stated either positively or neutrally so that both criteria and ratings are consistent in meaning?
		IV. Analytical Scoring—Checklists
____	____	A. Are there descriptors for categories (yes/no, acceptable/unacceptable) listed at the top of the rating column?
____	____	B. Are the blanks for checking clearly marked and conveniently located?
		V. Analytical Scoring—Rating Scales
____	____	A. Are there only the number of quality levels that can consistently be differentiated for each characteristic?
____	____	B. Are there verbal descriptors for each quality level?

SUGGESTED READINGS

Gallagher, J. D. (1998). *Classroom assessment for teachers* (pp. 205–284). Columbus, OH: Merrill.

Kubiszyn, T., & Borich, G. (2000). *Educational testing and measurement* (6th ed., pp. 11–127). New York: John Wiley & Sons.

Lynn, R. L., & Gronlund, N. E. (2000). *Measurement and assessment in teaching* (8th ed., pp. 235–288). Englewood Cliffs, NJ: Prentice-Hall.

Nitko, A. J. (1996). *Educational assessment of students* (2nd ed., pp. 160–175). Columbus, OH: Merrill.

Oosterhof, A. (1999). *Developing and using classroom assessments* (2nd ed., pp. 151–164). Columbus, OH: Merrill.

Thorndike, R. M. (1997). *Measurement and evaluation in psychology and education* (6th ed., pp. 287–306). Columbus, OH: Merrill.

Tombari, M., & Borich, G. (1999). *Authentic assessment in the classroom* (pp. 143–163). Columbus, OH: Merrill.

Worthen, B. R., White, K. R., Fan, X., & Sudweeks, R. L. (1999). *Measurement and assessment in schools* (2nd ed., pp. 280–328). New York: Addison-Wesley Longman.

CHAPTER 7

Constructing and Using Tests That Require Active Performance

OBJECTIVES

- Analyze instructional goals that require active performance.
- Select, paraphrase, and sequence the components to be observed in a performance.
- Develop rubrics, including checklists, rating forms, and evaluation procedures.
- Write instructions for a performance test.
- Describe procedures for formatively evaluating instructions and rating forms.
- Rate students' performances.

Many skills students learn in school involve some type of performance, such as delivering an oral report, driving a car, changing a tire, operating audiovisual equipment, and performing athletic skills. Teachers can rate and assign grades to these performances, just as they do for the skills measured by objective, essay, and product development tests. Performance tests enable teachers to analyze students' performances and to comment on such aspects as timing, speed, precision, sequence, and appearance. Like other types of tests, they provide a basis for evaluating the quality of instruction for separate aspects of the skill. For outgoing students, they are also motivational. Some students enjoy the opportunity to demonstrate their skill for the teacher and their classmates.

At the same time, performance tests have their disadvantages. First, because individuals must be evaluated separately, performance tests are time consuming. Second, teachers have to observe closely because important aspects of the performance may be rapid and difficult to see. Asking students to repeat a performance because something was missed may affect their performance negatively. Third, some students become extremely self-conscious and uncomfortable when they are asked to perform in front of the teacher or the group. If a teacher is not sensitive to the needs and feelings of these students, performance tests might actually inhibit learning and reduce the quality of performance. Finally, a teacher must have excellent classroom management skills in order to (1) maintain a positive atmosphere for the performing student, (2) keep other students engaged in some activity, and (3) focus attention on the performing student. In spite of these limitations, performance tests are the most appropriate method for measuring skills that require action.

The procedure teachers use to evaluate students' performance is similar to that for developing and scoring essay exams and products. Teachers should (1) define and analyze the expected performance, (2) select the components to be evaluated, (3) develop an evaluation form with procedures and instructions, (4) formatively evaluate the form and procedures, and (5) observe and rate students' performances.

The following sections describe general procedures for measuring students' performance. The particular steps you take as a teacher will depend on the content of your instruction, your classroom environment, and the characteristics of your students.

Analyzing Instructional Goals That Require Active Performance

The instructional goals that require active performances are both intellectual skills and motor skills. The analysis procedures for intellectual skills were described in Chapter 3, and motor skills were introduced at that point. The analysis of motor skills is explained in this chapter since evaluation of student's performances requires complete, accurate observation and rating forms for helping ensure the objectivity of teachers' judgments.

Gagné (1985) describes *motor skills* as those skills requiring the coordination of muscular movement, such as walking, running, jumping, and lifting. We acquire some of these skills by watching other people perform them, trying them ourselves, and refining them through trial and error. Complex motor skills—such as driving a race car, forming a clay pot on a potter's wheel, and blowing glass into predesigned forms—require instruction and considerable practice. In school, students use motor skills to form printed and cursive letters, draw pictures, operate scientific equipment, perform in athletic events, use tools and machines, play musical instruments, and sing in a chorus.

Many motor skills can be separated into action steps, which may take place sequentially or simultaneously. These steps, often called *part skills,* make up the complete performance or total skill. Students may learn and practice part skills separately, but they must eventually integrate them into practice of the total skill (Gagné, 1985).

A flowchart is used most often to analyze an instructional goal for a motor skill. During the analysis, you need to identify the total skill, the main part skills, and the proper sequence of the parts. Once the part skills are identified, each skill is further separated into required subskills.

A common method used for beginning the analysis of a motor skill is to videotape a performance of the skill by someone you would consider to be proficient. Then view the performance with the person and talk through the sequence of physical actions and mental activities that accompany the physical actions. At that point, you can begin to put your observations and notes into a flowchart of the part skills and subskills.

Figure 7.1 contains a partial analysis of the goal, "Execute a golf swing." The statement for the total skill appears at the top. Five part skills are listed next: grip the club, address the ball, execute the backswing, execute the downswing, and execute the follow through. In this partial analysis, only the overlap grip is broken down into subskills, which appear in their proper sequence. In a complete analysis, each of the five part skills in the top row would be broken down into subskills. Although some of the part skills might be taught separately, a person learning how to execute a golf swing eventually would have to integrate and practice all of the skills in one smooth, continuous motion.

FIGURE 7.1

Partial Analysis of the Motor Skill Goal "Execute a Golf Swing"

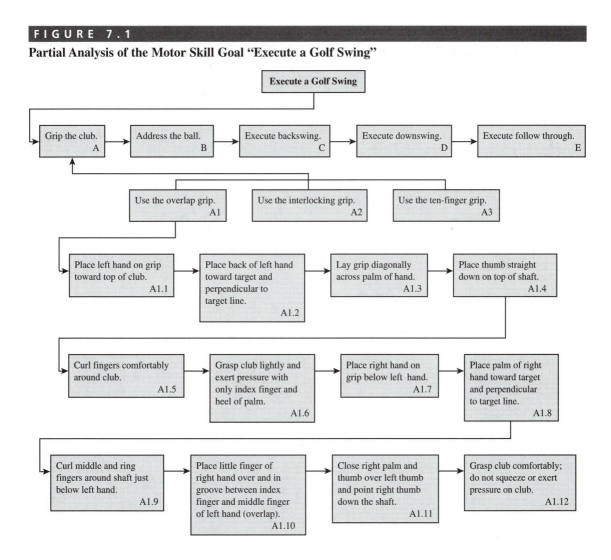

Some instructional goals do not fall neatly into a single category of learning; instead, they seem to integrate or combine levels. The instructional goal, "Make an oral presentation," is such a goal, and it includes both motor and intellectual skills. Figure 7.2 includes a matrix analysis for this combination goal. There are three main performance areas: physical expression, vocal expression, and verbal expression. There are five learning levels with three columns for descriptive characteristics (physical, functional, and qualitative), one for evaluation, and one for active demonstration. The discrimination of examples and nonexamples column was classified by the teacher as prerequisite skills for this unit and omitted. For example, all students learning to make oral presentations should be able to locate facial expressions, eyes, and so forth.

FIGURE 7.2

Instructional Goal Framework for the Goal "Make an Oral Presentation"

	A Identify/Recall Physical Characteristics	B Identify/Recall Functional Characteristics	C Identify/Recall Quality Characteristics	D Evaluate Instances	E Demonstrate
I. Physical Expression	■ Posture ■ Movement ■ Gestures ■ Facial expression ■ Eye contact I.A	■ Gain attention ■ Communicate comfort/ interest I.B	■ Posture: alert/ comfortable ■ Movements: fluid ■ Facial expression: pleasant ■ Eyes: encompass audience I.C	Effective vs. Ineffective: ■ Posture ■ Movements ■ Gestures ■ Facial expressions ■ Eye contact I.D	■ Effective physical expression while speaking before a group I.E
II. Vocal Expression	■ Voice ■ Intonation ■ Volume ■ Speed ■ Enunciation II.A	■ Gain and maintain audience attention/ interest II.B	■ Voice: steady/calm ■ Intonation: varied ■ Volume: varied ■ Speed: enables clarity II.C	Effective vs. Ineffective: ■ Steadiness ■ Calmness ■ Intonation ■ Volume ■ Speed II.D	■ Effective vocal expression while speaking before a group II.E
III. Verbal Expression	Message III.A	■ Gain attention ■ Inform ■ Entertain III.B	■ Words: fluid/precise ■ Avoids repetition ■ Ideas: complete/ sequenced III.C	Effective vs. Ineffective: ■ Fluidity ■ Precision ■ Repetition ■ Completeness ■ Organization III.D	■ Effective verbal expression while speaking before a group III.E

Another instructional goal that may appear to be only a motor skill is, "Serve a tennis ball." Certainly someone learning to serve a tennis ball must develop and combine several complex motor skills. At the same time, however, the person will need to know tennis serving rules and strategies. The person should also be able to identify parts of the playing court related to the serve. Finally, the person will need to acquire positive attitudes about cooperation, fair play, consideration of other players, and practice. Because the goal includes motor skills, intellectual skills, verbal skills, and attitudes, it is considered a combination goal. This type of goal requires a combination of analysis procedures.

Figure 7.3 contains a partial analysis for the goal, "Serve a tennis ball." Section I contains a partial analysis of serving procedures. Only step B, "Toss ball," is broken down into subskills. Section II, Intellectual Skills, lists serving rules a player would need to know. The list also includes serving strategies. Section III, Verbal Information, includes the names of parts of the court used during the serve, and Section IV identifies desired attitudes.

In analyzing instructional goals for active performances, you should use the analysis procedure or combination of analysis procedures that works best for a particular goal. Goals that are procedural will probably be most easily analyzed using a flowchart, whereas others that do not have sequential steps, such as oral presentations, may be more easily analyzed using a matrix or tree diagram. If you have difficulty analyzing a particular goal using one of the analysis procedures, switch to one of the others or try a combination.

■ Developing Performance Tests

Selecting and Organizing the Components to Observe

Many of the same procedures for developing essay or product rating forms can also be used to develop performance rating forms. With performance tests, however, you must be especially careful in selecting the components.

There are important differences in the procedures for evaluating products and performances. One is the timing of the observations and ratings. To evaluate performance, a teacher must observe and score students while they perform. Because students are usually tested individually, considerable class time must be reserved for performance and observation. Another difference is that the teacher always knows the identity of each student evaluated; thus, avoiding rater bias is more difficult. Another critical difference is that no tangible product remains for reconsideration and feedback unless the performance is videotaped. This means that judgments must be quick and that there is usually nothing except the rating form to show students. Finally, the speed with which some skills are performed restricts the time for observation and detailed analysis of components and subcomponents. This means that evaluation forms must be concise, components must be carefully ordered and easy to find, and score marking must be easy.

FIGURE 7.3

A Partial Analysis of a Combination Goal "Serve a Tennis Ball"

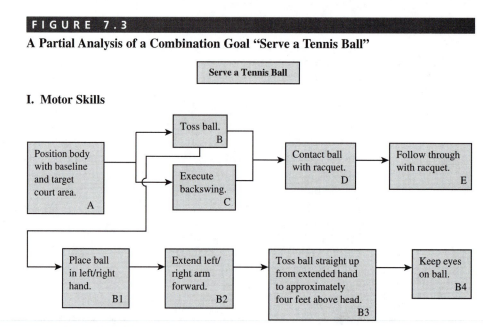

I. Motor Skills

II. Intellectual Skills

Demonstrate the following rules related to designated tasks:

Task

A   When serving into the left-hand court, the player must stand between the center mark and the right sideline.

A   When serving into the right-hand court, the player must stand between the center mark and the left sideline.

A   The player must keep both feet behind the baseline during each serve.

D   After the player contacts the ball with the racquet, the player's feet may touch the baseline.

Goal   When serving into either court, the ball must clear the net without touching it and land within the designated court area or on its boundary line.

Demonstrate the following strategies of serving:

1. Vary speed of ball.
2. Vary direction of ball.
3. Serve to opponent's demonstrated weak hand.

III. Verbal Information

1. Label court lines.
2. Label playing areas.
3. Label net.

IV. Attitudes

Affective Component
The player has positive attitudes toward skill development, fair play, and cooperation.

Behavioral Component
The Player:
1. Practices serves when given the opportunity.
2. Accepts the umpire's and opponents' calls.
3. Does not verbally or physically abuse self, equipment, or other people.

The following seven steps are recommended for selecting, sequencing, and paraphrasing the components:

1. Develop an instructional goal framework of the enabling skills and their sequence.
2. Select from the framework the skills you believe will be observable.
3. List these observable skills in the order you believe they will occur.
4. Watch several students who are proficient in the skills and compare the skills on your list with those you are able to observe.
5. Eliminate the skills you do not see and add any others you identify during the performance that are not contained on your list.
6. While the students are performing, check your sequence of components and reorder them if necessary.
7. After you have identified and sequenced the components, paraphrase your verbal descriptions of each component into one or two key words.

Developing Rubrics and Evaluation Procedures

Although you may choose to use either global or analytical scoring methods, analytical scoring is preferable. It is especially helpful for performance tests because global scoring does not usually provide a tangible product to mark and return to students. Analytical scoring enables you to focus on separate aspects of the performances and gather information needed to evaluate the instruction and help students understand their scores. You can use a checklist, a rating scale, or a form that combines the two. The form you develop depends on the type of performance you are observing.

To begin, identify a feasible number of quality categories for each component. If an action cannot be broken down into levels of quality, use a checklist that indicates only its presence or absence. On the other hand, if it is possible to distinguish levels of quality for some or all of the components in the time available, the use of a rating scale will provide better information. The quality categories should represent low to high levels of proficiency. For each category, write a descriptor of the characteristics used to classify an action. The more carefully you select and describe the categories, the more reliable your ratings will be. Assign a score to each category, with low numbers representing low quality and high numbers representing high performance levels.

One caution is in order. Only positive descriptors should be used with a checklist because mixing positive and negative descriptors will result in an uninterpretable score. Consider the meaning of a score of 2 in the following example:

	(0) No	(1) Yes
A. Good posture	_____	✓
B. Awkward movements	_____	✓
Total		2

Checking yes for the presence of each action results in a score that reflects good posture as well as awkward movements. Because a high score is meant to reflect only positive performance, each action should be stated positively. If the second criterion were restated as *Fluid movements,* a yes rating would reflect a positive performance for that criterion as well. If you need to rate distracting behaviors, such as lengthy pauses and hesitations or the overuse of certain words, the word *avoids* can be added to these components to make a yes rating a positive score.

Finally, as in working with checklists and rating scales in the previous chapter, the points assigned to each component should be proportional to the importance of the component if the score is going to be used for grading. If the importance of some components is not adequately represented, then a weighting scheme will need to be used.

Writing Instructions for Performance Tests

Before students are tested, they should understand exactly what they are to do and how they are to do it. Written directions ensure that each student receives the same information, which should include any special conditions of the performance. The suggestions for writing objective, essay, and product development tests are also appropriate for performance tests. The task described should match the behavior, content, and conditions in the objective. Language should be clear and precise, and the vocabulary should be appropriate for target students. It is especially important on performance tests to ensure that (1) the skill is not too complex for target students and (2) the conditions of performance are the same for all students.

After students have read the instructions, they should be allowed to discuss them and ask questions. During discussion, the teacher can clarify the task and correct misunderstandings for the entire group. The teacher can also explain what the students are to do and how they are to behave while individuals are being tested.

The requirement that a skill be tested in a novel or unfamiliar context does not apply to all performance tests. Many performance tests require students to demonstrate the skills in the same sequence and with the same equipment they used during instruction and rehearsal. Obviously, a student who has learned to drive a car with an automatic transmission should not be evaluated on the ability to drive a car with a standard transmission. For students' performance to be a valid indication of their skill, the testing situation should require the same equipment, content, sequence, and conditions as in the instruction.

■ Formatively Evaluating the Performance Test Form and Procedures

Taking the time for a formative evaluation of your form and procedures is critical to the success of performance testing. Remember that formative evaluation of a test means trying it out with target students under conditions that are similar to those you will find in the actual performance test. The purpose of the formative evaluation is to find potential problems and make appropriate revisions in the directions, content, forms, or procedures for the test.

You should not modify the instructions or the evaluation form for a performance test after the test begins. Certainly, you would not want to ask students to repeat a performance because the instructions were unclear or the evaluation form was cumbersome. To avoid an awkward situation, always evaluate and, if necessary, revise both the instructions and evaluation form you plan to use. One evaluation method is to observe students informally as they practice their skills. The information you gather during their rehearsals will help you modify both the assignment and the rating form.

A good place to begin the formative evaluation is with the task itself. Do the students' actions during rehearsal reflect an understanding of what they are to do? Are they able to demonstrate the desired actions in the time set aside for their evaluation? Can you observe and rate all the actions you have delineated? Are you able to differentiate all the quality categories you have included? Are the components in the best order? Answers to these questions will help you revise the form and estimate the amount of time needed to administer the test to all students.

■ Rating Students' Performances

Students who know they are being scored on a performance are bound to be influenced by the teacher's behaviors. Nonverbal expressions of anger, disappointment, displeasure, surprise, boredom, or fatigue will produce some type of reaction in students. Often, they will adjust their performance according to the behavioral clues they receive from you. Thus, as you evaluate students' performances, you should always appear positive, noncommittal, and interested in the task. Although you want students to perform well, you should also avoid verbal and nonverbal coaching during a performance. Such assistance, although appropriate during rehearsal, is not appropriate during a posttest.

Rating bias is especially problematic on performance tests. The limited time available for scoring each student's performance can contribute to rating patterns that are consistently generous, neutral, or critical on all components, even though the student was better in some areas than others. If you find that each student was rated consistently in all areas, it could reflect the presence of response bias. Being aware of this potential danger will help you differentiate the quality of different aspects of the performance.

Rating students' performances and behaviors requires both professional judgment and self-awareness. Unlike evaluating essay and product development tests, you usually cannot check previous ratings of the same performance to determine whether you are consistently judging behaviors. Review the range and location of scores you have assigned a class and determine whether they are realistic given the group's characteristics. When the range of scores appears restricted and inappropriately high, average, or low for a given group, your judgments may have been biased.

Eliminating personal bias from scoring is also difficult because students' identities are not separated from their performance. Thus, a teacher's perception of individual students can influence ratings. Obviously, the more a teacher's biases affect students' scores, the more the validity of the test is threatened. You can help avoid this tricky problem by not forming expectations for each student's performance. Although easier said than done, you can try to find positive indicators in a typically weak student's performance and problems in a typically strong student's performance. If you look only for the type of performance you expect, your ratings may not accurately reflect the performance.

A final problem in performance tests is the tendency of students to demonstrate their skills inconsistently. In athletic skills, they may be inconsistent in their ability to serve a tennis ball, shoot baskets, pitch a softball, or execute a particular dive. When such skills are being measured, students can be given several opportunities during the test to perform the skill, and the final score can be determined not only by judging their form and execution each time but also by judging the number of times they succeed in placing a serve or scoring a basket. Some teachers prefer to sum the total scores students receive on each trial and then determine an average score by dividing the sum by the number of trials. Inconsistencies also occur in other types of performances. For example, students delivering oral reports may initially demonstrate nervousness through trembling hands, looking only at their notes, and halting speech. However, as they continue their presentations, some may gain their composure, which will reduce or eliminate these types of behaviors. Others may begin in a composed manner and grow more nervous as they proceed. Inconsistent performance can be communicated to students using a rating category, such as *Sometimes Effective* or *Inconsistent.*

■ An Example

The instructional goal framework for the goal, "Make an oral presentation," in Figure 7.2 is used to demonstrate the development of a checklist and rating scale to evaluate students' active performance.

Paraphrasing Components and Subcomponents

The list of behaviors in Figure 7.4 shows how one teacher identified, sequenced, and paraphrased the components to be judged. Notice that the teacher selected only observable skills from the framework. Because the skills had no inherent order, the teacher decided on a sequence that would permit efficient observation.

Paraphrasing is an important aspect of writing component descriptors. Notice in Figure 7.4 that each component is paraphrased using only one or two words. This minimizes the amount of reading required during the students' performance.

Developing a Checklist

Figure 7.5 is a sample checklist rubric for evaluating an oral presentation. It contains only two rating categories, Needs Improvement and Yes. A teacher using this format would judge only whether the defined action was acceptable. Notice that an indicator of performance quality is added to each component statement; thus, checking the Yes column reflects a positive score. A student demonstrating all fourteen behaviors on the checklist would receive a total score of 14 on the test.

FIGURE 7.4

Behaviors to Evaluate during Oral Presentation

I. Physical Expression
   A. Posture
   B. Movements and gestures
   C. Facial expression
   D. Eye contact

II. Vocal Expression
   A. Calmness
   B. Intonation
   C. Volume
   D. Speed
   E. Enunciation

III. Verbal Expression
   A. Word flow
   B. Word choice
   C. Repetition
   D. Complete thoughts and ideas
   E. Organization

FIGURE 7.5

Checklist Rubric for Evaluating Oral Presentations

Name _____ Date _____ Score _____

Total   (14)

Criteria	Needs Improvement	Yes
I. Physical Expression		
A. Good posture	_____	_____
B. Fluid, natural movements	_____	_____
C. Effective facial expression	_____	_____
D. Good eye contact	_____	_____
II. Vocal Expression		
A. Calm voice	_____	_____
B. Good intonation	_____	_____
C. Good volume	_____	_____
D. Appropriate speed	_____	_____
E. Clearly enunciates	_____	_____
III. Verbal Expression		
A. Avoids hesitation	_____	_____
B. Effective word choice	_____	_____
C. Avoids repetition	_____	_____
D. Completes thoughts and ideas	_____	_____
E. Good organization of ideas	_____	_____
Total Score		_____

Developing Rating Scales

Figure 7.6 illustrates a rating scale rubric for an oral presentation. The components are listed in the left column and all quality categories are included in the right columns. Four general quality levels are used to rate all 14 components. The lowest rating is *Distracting,* which would indicate negative actions for the component. The second category, *Sometimes Effective,* would be used to score an action that was sometimes distracting and sometimes acceptable. The third category, *Generally Effective,* indicates that no distracting actions were observed and that the student was consistent in demonstrating the behavior. The fourth category, *Very Effective,* would be used for students who consistently demonstrated the skill in an effective, polished manner. As students are observed, the assigned rating can be circled. The student's total score could then be obtained by summing the circled numbers. A student who received a perfect rating in all 14 components would earn a total score of 56 points.

If the general categories of quality included in the rating scale in Figure 7.6 were not adequate to express the reasons for rating a particular component as distracting or effective, the rating scale could be expanded to allow for additional quality descriptors. For example, the facial expression component could be expanded to differentiate

---

FIGURE 7.6

Rating Scale Rubric for Oral Presentations

Name _____ Date _____ Score _____
Total   (56)

Component	Distracting	Sometimes Effective	Generally Effective	Very Effective
I. Physical Expression				
A. Posture	1	2	3	4
B. Movements/gestures	1	2	3	4
C. Facial expression	1	2	3	4
D. Eye contact	1	2	3	4
II. Vocal Expression				
A. Calmness	1	2	3	4
B. Intonation	1	2	3	4
C. Volume	1	2	3	4
D. Speed	1	2	3	4
E. Enunciation	1	2	3	4
III. Verbal Expression				
A. Word flow	1	2	3	4
B. Word choice	1	2	3	4
C. Repetition	1	2	3	4
D. Thoughts/ideas complete	1	2	3	4
E. Ideas organized	1	2	3	4

among different types of facial expressions. Such expressions as boredom, lack of expression, frowning, and nervousness could be distracting. In actuality, a student may exhibit one of these negative expressions but not others.

The expanded rating scale in Figure 7.7 enables you to differentiate among different types of facial expressions and better explain why students received a low rating in this area. The components are listed in the far left column. Negative and positive descriptions of expression border each end of the rating scale. Negative descriptors are listed down the left side beside low ratings, and positive ones are listed in the far right column beside high ratings. The ratings of *Distracting, Sometimes Effective,* and *Very Effective* are positioned in the middle columns. Such a scale would help you be more precise in marking your ratings and in communicating the meaning of each rating to students. Be careful, however, not to create a scale with so much

FIGURE 7.7

Expanded Rubric for Oral Presentations

Name _____ Date _____ Score _____
Total   (60)

Component	Negative Quality	Rating			Positive Quality
		Distracting	Sometimes Effective	Very Effective	
I. Physical Expression					
A. Posture	1. Slouched	1	2	3	Straight
	2. Awkward	1	2	3	Relaxed
B. Movements/ Gestures	1. Hands trembling	1	2	3	Hands steady
	2. Awkward gestures	1	2	3	Fluid gestures
C. Facial Expression	1. Bored	1	2	3	Interested
	2. Unexpressive	1	2	3	Animated
	3. Frowning	1	2	3	Pleasant
	4. Nervous	1	2	3	Relaxed
D. Eye Contact	1. With few people	1	2	3	With many people
	2. Reading notes	1	2	3	Looks at audience
II. Vocal Expression	A. Wavering/cracking	1	2	3	Steady/calm
	B. Monotonous	1	2	3	Varied
	C. Too loud/quiet	1	2	3	Natural
	D. Too rapid/slow	1	2	3	Natural
	E. Poorly enunciated	1	2	3	Enunciated well
III. Verbal Expression	A. Long pauses	1	2	3	Fluid
	B. Slang expressions	1	2	3	Precise vocabulary
	C. Needless repetition	1	2	3	Effective/varied
	D. Incomplete thoughts	1	2	3	Complete thoughts
	E. Poorly organized	1	2	3	Well organized

detail that it is cumbersome to use while observing a student's performance. To use the rating scale, simply circle the rating desired and sum the circled numbers to obtain the total score for each student. A student who received the highest possible rating in each category would earn a total test score of 60 points.

Computer Technology

Similar to essay and product tests, it is appropriate and convenient to put your instructions for active performance tests directly into your test item bank. You can use the essay- or problem-style item format to enter instructions for the required performance. Likewise, you can insert your rubric for scoring students' performances as a linked table or illustration. Also similar to objective, essay, and product items, your active performance instructions can be classified using your item categories (e.g., subject, topic, enabling skill code, etc.). Your active performance instructions, as well as your rating scales and checklists, can be edited at any time.

Spreadsheet programs such as Microsoft's Excel are also very useful for scoring students' performances, and many teachers use a portable computer to score students' performances as they occur. These programs have really streamlined the observing and scoring process, calculating and summarizing a student's enabling skill and overall scores, and locating strengths and possible performance problems for the entire class. Similar to scoring essay and product tests, a spreadsheet can be tailored to a particular rubric, and individual and class reports can be generated easily.

Summary

The procedure for evaluating students' performances and behaviors consists of four major steps: (1) analyze instructional goals and select the skills to include on the performance test; (2) prepare testing procedures, forms, and instructions; (3) try out the performance test and revise as needed; and (4) use the test to evaluate students' performances. Each of these four steps has several substeps:

1. To analyze goals and select skills:
   a. Use a matrix, tree diagram, or flowchart to analyze the performance goal. A combination of these procedures may be required since performance goals can contain procedures composed of motor skills, intellectual skills, verbal information, and even attitudes.
   b. Review the goal framework and select only those skills you believe can be observed during a performance.
   c. Observe someone performing the task and verify that the chosen skills are observable and that none has been omitted.
   d. Sequence the skills in the order they can be observed most efficiently.
2. To prepare testing procedures, forms, and instructions:
   a. Paraphrase each skill using only one or two key words. Either make all statements neutral or all statements positive.

     b. List the paraphrased actions or behaviors in the left column.

     c. Select the number of quality categories that you can consistently distinguish for each.

     d. Write a descriptor for each category and assign each a number, with low numbers representing inadequate performance or negative behaviors.

     e. Determine the relative value of each component rated and devise a weighting plan, if needed, so that the points available are proportional to the importance of each component.

     f. Plan testing procedures and write specific instructions to help ensure uniform performance conditions for all students.

3. To do a formative evaluation of the performance test forms and procedures:

     a. Ask a few students to read the instructions, and revise as needed if there are problems of accuracy or clarity.

     b. Try using the checklist or rating form during the students' practice sessions to review the skill components and rating categories. Revise as needed if there are problems observing skills or distinguishing different quality levels in the rating categories.

     c. While trying the checklist or rating scale during practice sessions, review your own ability to use the form in a smooth, timely manner. Revise as needed if it is confusing, tedious, or cumbersome.

4. To use the test forms and procedures to evaluate students' performances:

     a. Set up performance testing sessions that afford all students equal time and opportunity to demonstrate their skills.

     b. When judging students' behaviors that reflect an attitude, select a time when you are *not* fatigued, disappointed, or unhappy. Your own attitude will influence your interpretation of students' behaviors.

     c. Be aware of how your perceptions of individual students can influence the scores you assign. Take care to look for good qualities in the performance of students who usually score lower than others and look for problems in the performance of students who usually score high. This will help you avoid seeing what you expect to see when it is not there.

     d. When judging a performance test, be especially careful not to exhibit nonverbal gestures that will influence a student's performance.

     e. Be careful not to coach students during a performance posttest because coaching will tend to alter their performance.

     f. Use multiple trials of the performance when needed to improve the validity and reliability of the test.

     g. After summarizing the scores for a group, check to see whether the range and pattern of scores is realistic for that group.

     h. Use the checklists or rating scales and videotape (if appropriate) to provide corrective feedback and instructional guidance to students after the test.

By following these steps, you can evaluate students as objectively as possible; provide students with specific, corrective feedback; and have the information you need to evaluate the quality of your instruction.

■ P R A C T I C E   E X E R C I S E S

I. Analyzing Motor Skill Instructional Goals

Identify and sequence the steps students would need to achieve the goal, "Bounce a ball while standing still." Compare your answer with Figure 7.9F in the Feedback section.

II. Rating Students' Performances

A. Use Figure 7.1 to develop either a checklist or a rating scale for evaluating students' overlap grip. Compare your evaluation form with the example checklist provided in Figure 7.10F in the Feedback section.

B. Use Figure 7.3 to develop a rating scale for evaluating component B of that figure, *Toss ball.* Compare your rating scale with the example provided in Figure 7.11F in the Feedback section.

C. Use the instructional goal framework in Figure 7.8 to develop instructions and a rubric you could use to evaluate students' active performances in delivering persuasive speeches or serving as an advocate for some person or cause. Think of an age group you currently teach or plan to teach, and develop an assessment activity appropriate for work with that age group. Based on the framework:

1. Develop student instructions for an active performance assessment. See Figure 7.12F in the Feedback Section.

2. Develop a rating scale you could use to evaluate students' active performances. See Figure 7.13F in the Feedback Section.

III. Enrichment

A. Rating Student Performance

1. Select an active performance skill that is relevant for the subject and grade level you teach or plan to teach.

2. Analyze the skill to identify the main components and subcomponents within each main step.

3. Develop either a rating scale or checklist for the skill.

4. Use your evaluation form to rate students or other individuals as they perform the skill.

5. Evaluate the form's feasibility and convenience and revise it if necessary.

6. Use the rating form to develop an appropriate performance summary form.

■ F E E D B A C K

I. Analyzing Motor Skill Instructional Goals

See Figure 7.9F.

II. Rating Students' Performances

A. See Figure 7.10F.

B. See Figure 7.11F.

C. See Figures 7.12F and 7.13F.

F I G U R E   7 . 8

Instructional Goal Framework for the Instructional Goal "Write and Deliver a Persuasive Speech before the Class: Play the Role of Advocate"

Concepts	A Recall Physical Characteristics of:	B Recall Functional Characteristics of:	C Recall Qualitative Characteristics of:	D Classify Examples and Nonexamples	E Evaluate Given Examples	F Deliver an Oral Speech
I. Advocacy or Persuasive Speaking	Human speaker (Ethos)	Recommends to others a person, position, point of view, course of action				
II. Voice	Pitch, pace, loudness (adequate and varied) Articulation	Demonstrates confidence, commitment, and sincerity	Shows personal enthusiasm, interest, conviction, reasonable self-assurance, courage, preparation, intensity, flexibility, adaptability, sincerity, directness, and honesty			
III. Action	Good posture Demeanor corresponds to ideas stated Gestures spontaneous	Demonstrates confidence, commitment, and sincerity				
IV. Appearance	Good personal grooming Consistent with role/position	Demonstrates confidence, commitment, and sincerity				
V. Message	Language Topics Reasoning	Demonstrates competence, commitment, and sincerity	Preparation Convincing			

FIGURE 7.9F

Subordinate Skills for the Instructional Goal "Bounce a Ball while Standing Still"

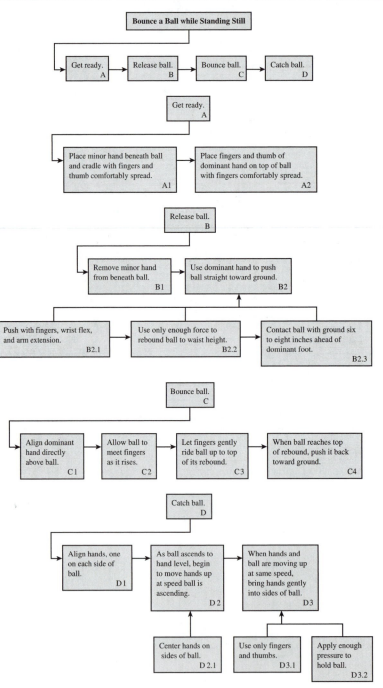

FIGURE 7.10F

Checklist for Rating and Overlap Grip

Name _Joseph Augustine_   Period ___2___   Date __10/15__   Score __12__
                                                                Total   (15)

No	Yes	Observed
		A. Placement of Left Hand
	✓	1. Hand toward top of club
	✓	2. Back of hand toward target
	✓	3. Back of hand perpendicular to target line
	✓	4. Grip diagonally across palm
	✓	5. Thumb down topside of shaft
	✓	6. Fingers curled comfortably
✓		7. Club grasped lightly
		B. Placement of Right Hand
	✓	1. Hand just below left hand
	✓	2. Palm facing target
	✓	3. Palm perpendicular to target line
	✓	4. Middle and ring finger curled around shaft
✓		5. Little finger overlapping left hand
	✓	6. Right palm and thumb over left thumb
	✓	7. Right thumb pointed down topside of shaft
✓		8. Club grasped lightly
Total	12	

Note: This checklist is for a right-handed person. For a left-handed person, the right and left hands would be reversed.

**Partial Rating Scale for the Toss Ball (B) Portion of Serving a Tennis Ball
(from the Instructional Goal Analysis in Figure 7.3)**

SERVING A TENNIS BALL				
Name _____	Date _____			Score _____
	Inadequate 1	Adequate 2	Good 3	**Comments**
A. Position Body				
B. Toss Ball				
B.1 Ball in hand	1	2		
B.2 Arm extension	1	2	3	
B.3.1 Ball trajectory	1	2	3	
B.3.2 Ball height	1	2	3	
B.4 Eyes on ball	1	2	3	
C. Backswing				
D. Contact Ball				
E. Follow-through				
Totals	( ) + ( ) + ( )			= _____

FIGURE 7.12F

Student Instructions for an Advocacy Speech

ADVOCACY SPEECH

1. Prepare and deliver a 6- to 8-minute speech of personal advocacy on the following topic:

   _____

2. Assume that your audience is made up of the following individuals or groups:

   _____

3. Examine the accompanying rating scale for criteria that will be used to evaluate your advocacy presentation.

4. You may not use notes at the podium or your chosen point of delivery. You may, however, prepare and use outlines or other "audience focus" reference materials that you project on a screen for your audience. These materials can serve as your prompts.

5. You should be ready to rehearse your presentation no later than _____.
   - Rehearsals will be videotaped for your review.
   - Use the accompanying rating scale to evaluate your presentation and adjust it as needed.

6. Formal presentations will begin on _____. Your presentation will be videotaped. After your presentation, please use the accompanying rating scale to rate your own delivery. Bring your rating to the debriefing session on _____.

FIGURE 7.13F

Rubric for Evaluating Students' Advocacy Speeches

ADVOCACY SPEECH			
Name _____ **Date** _____ **Score** _____			
Person/Cause Supported:			
I. **Voice**			
A. Pitch	High/Low	1 2 3 4	Pleasing
B. Pace	Fast/Slow	1 2 3 4	Pleasing
C. Loudness	Soft/Loud	1 2 3 4	Pleasing
D. Articulation	Slurred	1 2 3 4	Clear
II. **Action**			
A. Posture	Slouched	1 2 3 4	Alert
B. Demeanor	Inconsistent w. message	1 2 3 4	Consistent w. message
C. Gestures	Awkward	1 2 3 4	Confident
III. **Appearance**			
A. Grooming	Unkempt	1 2 3 4	Well groomed
B. Congruent with position	Incongruent	1 2 3 4	Congruent
IV. **Personal Qual.**			
	Bored	1 2 3 4	Enthused
	Nervous	1 2 3 4	Confident
	Insincere	1 2 3 4	Sincere
	Evasive	1 2 3 4	Direct
V. **Message**			
A. Language	Incongruent	1 2 3 4	Congruent
B. Reasoning	Flawed	1 2 3 4	Logical
C. Preparation	Sketchy	1 2 3 4	Thorough
D. Position	Weak	1 2 3 4	Convincing
Comments: _____			
_____			
_____			
_____			
_____			
Beginning Time: *Ending Time:* *Length:*			

■ R U B R I C

Rubric for Evaluating Live Performance Tests

		GENERAL CRITERIA FOR ALL TEST FORMATS
Yes	**No**	**I. Curriculum-Based Criteria (instructions, directions, and rating forms)**
——	——	A. Are criteria congruent with the conditions, behavior, and content of the task specification?
——	——	B. Are task-situations authentic and relevant to curriculum standard?
		II. Learner-Centered Criteria (instructions, directions, and rating forms)
——	——	A. Are criteria congruent with the language (including ESOL), context, developmental level, and special needs of learners?
——	——	B. Are criteria free from biasing material related to gender, cultural/ethnic groups, and religious and political ideas?
		III. School-Based Criteria (feasibility)
——	——	A. Are development and administration time available related to teacher-student ratio?
——	——	B. Is turnaround time available from test administration to score reporting?
——	——	C. Are resources available for test development, administration, scoring, and reporting?
		IV. Professional-Based Criteria
		A. Are instructions, directions, and rating forms clear related to:
——	——	■ Grammar?
——	——	■ Spelling?
——	——	■ Expression?
——	——	■ Order of information?
——	——	B. Is the task to be performed creative and interesting?
——	——	C. Are materials and procedures professional appearing?
——	——	D. Is the task likely to yield accurate measures?
		E. Are scoring procedures ethical in that:
——	——	■ Performance rather than student is judged?
——	——	■ Ratings are reliable within and across students?
——	——	■ Quality levels applied are appropriate for students' developmental level?
		FORMATTING CRITERIA FOR LIVE PERFORMANCE TESTS
		I. Directions (directions and instructions)
——	——	A. Do directions provide appropriate guidance for students' skill level?
——	——	B. Do directions provide appropriate guidance for the skill measured?
——	——	C. Do directions provide adequate organizational information (e.g., time allowed, point values for tasks, length and scope of response sought)?

(continued)

■ R U B R I C   Continued

Yes	No	
		II. Global Scoring
____	____	A. Are there established scoring categories that will be used?
____	____	B. Are there only the number of scoring categories that can be consistently differentiated?
____	____	C. Are there clearly described characteristics of a response that fits each of the categories?
		III. Analytical Scoring—Criteria (Stems)
____	____	A. Are evaluation criteria congruent with the main concepts (components) in the instructional goal framework?
____	____	B. Are evaluation criteria congruent with the physical, functional, and qualitative characteristics included in the instructional goal framework?
____	____	C. Are evaluation criteria congruent with the main concepts to be performed in the instructional goal framework?
____	____	D. Are evaluation criteria paraphrased clearly in the rating form?
____	____	E. Are evaluation criteria ordered/sequenced logically/conveniently for observation?
____	____	F. Are evaluation criteria stated either positively or neutrally so that both criteria and ratings are consistent in meaning?
		IV. Analytical Scoring—Checklists
____	____	A. Are there descriptors for categories (yes/no, acceptable/unacceptable) listed at the top of the rating column?
____	____	B. Are the blanks for checking clearly marked and conveniently located?
		V. Analytical Scoring—Rating Scales
____	____	A. Are there only the number of quality levels that can consistently be differentiated for each performance area?
____	____	B. Are there verbal descriptors for each quality level?

REFERENCE

Gagné, R. M. (1985). *The conditions of learning and the-ory of instruction.* New York: Holt, Rinehart and Winston.

SUGGESTED READINGS

Darling-Hammond, L., Ancess, J., & Falk, B. (1995). *Au-thentic assessment in action.* New York: Teachers College Press.

Kubiszyn, T., & Borich, G. (2000). *Educational testing and measurement* (6th ed., pp. 158–178). New York: John Wiley & Sons.

Lynn, R. L., & Gronlund, N. E. (2000). *Measurement and assessment in teaching* (8th ed., pp. 259–288). En-glewood Cliffs, NJ: Prentice-Hall.

Nitko, A. J. (1996). *Educational assessment of students* (2nd ed., pp. 243–278). Columbus, OH: Merrill.

Oosterhof, A. (1999). *Developing and using classroom assessments* (2nd ed., pp. 133–150, 151–164). Columbus, OH: Merrill.

Popham, W. J. (1999). *Classroom assessment: What teach-ers need to know* (2nd ed., pp. 266–284). Boston: Allyn and Bacon.

Thorndike, R. M. (1997). *Measurement and evaluation in psychology and education* (6th ed., pp 287–306). Columbus, OH: Merrill.

Tombari, M., & Borich, G. (1999). *Authentic assessment in the classroom* (pp. 100–118). Columbus, OH: Merrill.

Wortham, S. C. (1995). *Measurement and evaluation in early childhood education* (2nd ed., pp. 122–147, 179–195). Columbus, OH: Merrill.

Worthen, B. R., White, K. R., Fan, X., & Sudweeks, R. L. (1999). *Measurement and assessment in schools* (2nd ed., pp. 280–328). New York: Addison-Wesley Longman.

Constructing and Using Measures of Students' Attitudes and Classroom Behavior

- Analyze instructional goals that are attitudes.
- Develop rubrics and evaluation procedures.
- Describe procedures for rating students' behavior.
- Develop questionnaires to gather students' self-reported attitudes.

In addition to measuring students' achievement of verbal information, intellectual skills, cognitive strategies, and motor skills, teachers are often expected to assess students' attitudes and classroom behavior. Rating attitudes and behaviors can be much more difficult than judging achievement. Attitudes and behaviors, such as the attitudes toward learning and classroom conduct, are abstract and difficult to define. In judging a skill, a teacher has to make very few syntheses and inferences. When judging attitudes and behavior, however, a teacher must classify individual instances of behavior over time and synthesize them into a general impression of the underlying attitude. These actions often require inferences about intentions and motives, which are very difficult. The same action or statement can be interpreted many different ways, depending on the context, tone of voice, facial expression, or physical mannerism accompanying the behavior. Because human social behavior is interactive, a teacher must be aware of the effects that the actions and reactions of other group members can have on individual students. Teachers should also have some sense of how their own attitudes and behaviors influence those of students.

Gagné (1985) defines *attitudes* as internal states that influence an individual's choice of personal action. According to Gagné, an attitude consists of three elements:

1. An *affective* component includes the positive and negative feelings a person has.
2. A *behavioral* component is made up of behaviors or acts that result from a person's feelings and knowledge.
3. A *cognitive* component consists of a person's knowledge about how to do something and the rewards or consequences for doing it.

Our feelings about people, things, events, and concepts affect our behavior. Learning theorists propose that human beings acquire many of their attitudes by watching and mimicking people they respect or want to emulate. In our society, teachers are expected to play an important role in developing their students' attitudes. For example, most teachers would encourage their students to demonstrate the following attitudes:

1. A negative attitude toward cheating
2. A positive attitude toward learning and toward participation
3. A positive attitude toward classroom and community rules for acceptable behavior
4. A negative attitude toward drug use, smoking, and other activities that are considered dangerous or harmful
5. A positive attitude toward thorough, careful work
6. A positive attitude toward responsible behavior

This chapter describes procedures for (1) locating attitudes and behaviors teachers are expected to monitor and assess, (2) analyzing attitudes to identify their affective and behavioral components, (3) developing forms to assess students' classroom behaviors, (4) rating students' behavior and actions in the classroom, and (5) developing questionnaires that students can use to assess their own attitudes and behavior.

■ Identifying Attitudes to Be Evaluated

Most curriculum guides focus on the achievement of verbal information, intellectual skills, and motor skills, and they do not always identify the student attitudes and behaviors that teachers may be asked to report. This information usually appears on the school district's report card. Occasionally, related information will be included in a student or teacher handbook. Report cards typically indicate categories of attitudes to be rated, and the handbooks explain school policy and rules of student conduct. Some teachers add rules to those specified by the district to suit their subject area, classroom environment, and particular students.

Students to be rated on certain attitudes and behaviors need to understand the meaning of each category of behavior on a report card. Teachers required to judge attitudes and behaviors should define them for students and explain how the ratings will be done.

To define a district's affective goals to students and parents, a teacher must first understand the categories and have evaluation procedures already developed. The most appropriate place to begin is with the information on the report cards. Although report cards often vary from school to school, and typically from district to district, most list attitudes or behaviors on which students are to be rated. Consider the secondary-level report card shown in Figure 8.1. In addition to grading achievement, teachers in this district are required to evaluate a student's citizenship, attitude toward learning, and study habits for each grading period. Teachers using such

FIGURE 8.1

Secondary School Report Card for One Semester

STUDENT PROGRESS REPORT

_____   _____   _____
(Name)   (School District)   (Year)

_____   _____
(School)   (Home Room)

Course Per Teacher	Grading Period I					Grading Period II					Semester I	
	GRD	CIT	ATL	SH	ABS	GRD	CIT	ATL	SH	ABS	EX	SAG
1												
2												
3												
4												
5												
6												
7												

Abbreviations	Grade Codes	
PER = Class period during day	A = Excellent (93–100%)	I = Incomplete work
GRD = Achievement grade	B = Good (85%–92%)	P = Pass
CIT = Citizenship	C = Fair (77–84%)	S = Satisfactory
ATL = Attitude toward learning	D = Poor (69%–76%)	N = Needs improvement
SH = Study habits	F = Failure (68% and below)	U = Unsatisfactory
ABS = Absences (frequency)		
EX = Semester exam score		
SAG = Semester average grade		

report cards must decide what attitudes and behaviors a mark in each category would reflect.

Figure 8.2 illustrates behaviors that elementary-level teachers in two different school districts are expected to rate. Besides achievement grades in the subjects studied, teachers using Report Card A must comment on students' conduct, citizenship, and work habits. Rather than including just these general categories, *Citizenship* is divided into five specific behaviors that must be rated and *Work Habits* includes four separate categories. Teachers report students' progress in each area using the ratings of satisfactory, needs improvement, and unsatisfactory. Elementary Report Card B includes nine categories of behavior that are not organized according to areas. Similar to Report Card A, teachers use *Satisfactory, Needs Improvement,* and *Unsatisfactory* to rate each of the nine areas. A comparison of the nonachievement categories

FIGURE 8.2

Attitudes and Behaviors Rated on Two Elementary-Level Report Cards

Report Card A		Report Card B	
Attitude/Behavior	Rating	Attitude/Behavior	Rating
I. Conduct		1. Practices self-discipline	
		2. Works independently	
II. Citizenship		3. Works well in group	
A. Respects authority		activities	
B. Uses self-control		4. Makes good use of time	
C. Respects property		5. Respects persons and	
D. Respects others' rights		property	
E. Obeys school rules		6. Is thoughtful and considerate	
		7. Completes classroom	
III. Work Habits		assignments	
A. Listens attentively		8. Completes homework	
B. Works quietly		assignments	
C. Follows directions		9. Respects authority	
D. Completes assignments			

Scale:
S = Satisfactory
N = Needs improvement
U = Unsatisfactory

Scale:
S = Satisfactory
N = Needs improvement
U = Unsatisfactory

included on the secondary and two elementary examples shows that these three school districts are interested in reporting similar types of behaviors to students and parents.

To identify attitudes that you will need to consider during a grading period, go first to report cards and state, district, and school handbooks. Then add any particular attitudes and behavior that are required in your subject area, such as safety habits in an industrial arts class or chemistry laboratory.

■ Analyzing Instructional Goals That Are Attitudes

Once you have located attitudes you are expected to teach or monitor and assess, you are ready to analyze them. Recall that they are comprised of an affective component that includes positive and negative feelings, a behavioral component that includes actions that reflect the feelings, and a cognitive component that includes verbal information and intellectual skills required to act in the desired manner. To analyze attitudinal goals, you should identify the relevant components for each of the three elements. This chapter addresses only the affective and behavioral components of an attitude since analysis of intellectual skills and verbal information was described in preceding chapters. The following steps can aid your analysis:

1. Generally define the attitudes to be taught and assessed.
2. Further define or operationalize each attitude by listing the positive feelings or beliefs your students should possess or acquire.
3. For each of the feelings you identify, list actions or behaviors that will demonstrate a student's status on the feeling. This collection of behaviors represents how you have operationalized the general attitude.

The following paragraphs describe and illustrate each of these steps.

Generally Define the Attitudes

The first step is to define the attitudes you are expected to assess. The purpose of this step is to differentiate among the various attitudes included in the curriculum guide and report card. For example, the secondary report card in Figure 8.1 has one attitude category called *Attitude toward Learning* and another called *Study Habits.* In what ways do students' attitudes toward learning differ from their study habits? Elementary Report Card A in Figure 8.2 includes both *Conduct* and *Citizenship.* If you were using this report card, how would you distinguish between the two? As a teacher in this district, you would need to determine what these terms mean and how they relate to each other, to the subject taught, to the classroom environment, and to your students. Your interpretations will undoubtedly differ from those of other teachers due not only to the abstractness of the terms but also to differences in students' ages, classroom environments, and subjects. Consider, for example, one teacher's definitions of the following categories:

1. *Citizenship* is the social interactions students have with their peers and with their teacher. It includes their individual contributions to the classroom society.
2. *Conduct* relates to observing established school and classroom rules of behavior (e.g., safety, property, and permissible actions).
3. *Attitude toward learning* relates to the student's approach to learning new ideas and skills.
4. *Study habits* relates to the procedures a student uses to accomplish assigned work.

Definitions such as these serve only as a beginning for the analysis process. With these general definitions in mind, you are ready to define further each attitude by identifying the positive feelings you believe are associated with each attitude.

List Associated Positive and Negative Feelings

No one or two feelings would be adequate to define an attitude. Attitudes are abstractions, sometimes called *constructs,* that must be defined using a set or combination of associated feelings. A person possessing one or two of the feelings in a set may or may not possess the attitude, but someone who possesses the entire set can reasonably be said to hold the attitude.

A good way to identify the best set of feelings for an attitude is to brainstorm and list all the possible associated feelings that you can imagine. With this so-called laundry list of feelings in hand, you can evaluate the list and eliminate those you consider redundant, irrelevant, more related to other attitudes, or inappropriate for a given group of students in a particular environment.

In considering feelings that are related to a student's approach to learning, one teacher settled on these six positive feelings: interest, curiosity, self-confidence, independence, perseverance, and a desire to improve one's skills and abilities. With the list selected, the next step is to identify behaviors that reflect a student's status on each feeling.

List Behaviors That Demonstrate Each Feeling

The six feelings described in the previous section partially explain the teacher's perceptions of students' attitudes toward learning. Generating a list of the behaviors students would exhibit in the classroom relative to each feeling would further operationalize the attitude. The best way to generate the list is to imagine the actions of a person who possesses and does not possess each positive feeling identified. As you consider the actions, brainstorm, and write down all the behaviors you can generate. Once you have exhausted your ideas, evaluate the list and remove actions you consider irrelevant, redundant, unobservable, or inappropriate for your age group and classroom environment. The behaviors that remain after your evaluation provide the basis for developing checklists and rating scales to evaluate students' behavior.

Table 8.1 contains the classroom behaviors the teacher considered relevant for the six feelings linked to students' attitudes toward learning. The left side of the table

---

TABLE 8 . 1

Teacher-Constructed List of Behaviors That Reflect a Student's Attitude toward Learning

Positive Behaviors	Negative Behaviors
1. Appears interested in the topics being studied	1. Appears disinterested in or bored by topics being studied
2. Shows curiosity by asking questions or seeking more information	2. Rejects ideas presented and does not seek additional information
3. Demonstrates confidence in ability to learn new information and skills; is eager to try	3. Lacks confidence in ability to perform new tasks; resists trying
4. Works independently	4. Quits working on tasks when not monitored
5. Demonstrates perseverance in accomplishing tasks	5. Becomes frustrated and quits before completing tasks
6. Seeks and accepts corrective feedback; adjusts performance accordingly	6. Rejects corrective feedback and resists adjusting performance

includes positive actions, and the right side contains associated negative behaviors for each of the feelings. This list of classroom behaviors represents the teacher's operationalization of the construct, attitude toward learning. With the attitude operationalized, the teacher has the necessary foundation for developing checklists or rating scales to observe and rate students' related behaviors in the classroom. From these behaviors, the teacher can infer the students' attitudes toward learning.

The process just described for analyzing attitudes might seem rather subjective to you. It is subjective, but not nearly as subjective as simply marking and communicating students' attitudes toward learning without carefully considering what you are judging. Defining attitudes as carefully as possible will enable you to reflect on your definitions and refine them, communicate better with students and parents about attitudes and classroom behavior, and identify attitudinal areas where instructional interventions appear warranted.

■ Developing Rubrics to Assess Classroom Behavior

The type of rating form you develop depends on the behaviors you are observing and the number of times you plan to evaluate students. The behaviors on your list probably range from very abstract to very concrete, and each type of behavior requires a different evaluation method. For example, you may wish to record the number of times a student fails to turn in a homework assignment or fails to bring required materials to class. If you assign homework 15 times during a grading period, your form should permit you to record the number of times a student either submits incomplete assignments or fails to turn in an assignment. The totals for each student can then be converted to descriptors, such as *Almost Always, Usually,* and *Rarely.*

Abstract behaviors, such as *Displays Interest in Topic,* are much more difficult to evaluate. A rating form might include two or three rating categories for such a behavior. For example, the categories *Disinterested/Bored, Easily Distracted,* and *Interested/Engaged* might be used to rate students on their interest. If you include too many categories for an abstract behavior, you undoubtedly will have difficulty scoring students consistently.

The following sections illustrate a sample checklist and rating scale the teacher could use to rate students' behaviors that reflect their attitudes toward learning.

Checklist

Figure 8.3 contains an observation checklist based on the behaviors listed in Table 8.1. There are three behaviors included for each of the six feelings. All the behaviors are positively stated such that a check mark in the *Typically* column reflects a positive action, and the sum of the check marks will reflect the level of a student's demonstrated attitude toward learning.

Notice the teacher has included space for rating the student's behaviors on three separate dates. Including space for three dates on one page has its benefits and its

FIGURE 8.3

A Sample Checklist Based on the Affective Feelings in Table 8.1

CLASSROOM BEHAVIORS REFLECTING STUDENTS' ATTITUDES TOWARD LEARNING			
Date _____ **Score** _____	**Date** _____ **Score** _____	**Date** _____ **Score** _____	**Name** _____
Typically	**Typically**	**Typically**	
_____ _____ _____	_____ _____ _____	_____ _____ _____	1. Student demonstrates *interest* and engagement in: a. Explanations and demonstrations b. Assignments c. Classwork
_____ _____ _____	_____ _____ _____	_____ _____ _____	2. Student demonstrates learning *curiosity* through: a. Asking questions b. Seeking additional resources in the classroom c. Locating additional materials in the library
_____ _____ _____	_____ _____ _____	_____ _____ _____	3. Student demonstrates *confidence* by: a. Volunteering to answer questions in class b. Offering to help others understand ideas c. Proposing alternative ideas/solutions
_____ _____ _____	_____ _____ _____	_____ _____ _____	4. Student demonstrates *independence* by: a. Beginning assignments without being asked b. Working alone without being monitored c. Completing assignments before they are due
_____ _____ _____	_____ _____ _____	_____ _____ _____	5. Student demonstrates *perseverance* by: a. Working through complex problems b. Returning to complex problems independently c. Not complaining about complex assignments
_____ _____ _____	_____ _____ _____	_____ _____ _____	6. Student demonstrates *desire to improve* by: a. Seeking corrective feedback from teacher b. Accepting corrective feedback c. Correcting errors and problems in work

drawbacks. From a beneficial perspective, it cuts down on the amount of paper the teacher needs to manage and keeps information together. The drawback is that seeing your previous ratings of the student may influence your judgments on subsequent occasions. To avoid this inadvertent influence problem, you may want to cover your prior ratings so you cannot see them until after you finish rating the student. Comparing your ratings across occasions after you have finished is sometimes quite informative.

Rating Scale

Rating scales can also be created from the list of positive and negative behaviors you generate for each attitude. Figure 8.4 illustrates one rating scale that could be developed for the list of behaviors in Table 8.1. The six feelings are listed in the left column as anchors, and each feeling has three levels of behavior listed on the right side. Notice that each level or number includes a behavioral descriptor to aid rating students' actions consistently.

You could also configure the behavioral rating scale to accommodate several evaluation dates by adding three or four columns to the right or left of the items and recording your rating in the column rather than circling your response. It is important

---

FIGURE 8.4

Rating Scale for Attitude toward Learning

Name _____ Date _____ Score _____

Total   (18)

Behavior	Rating		
1. Interest	Disinterested/ Bored	Easily distracted	Interested/ Engaged
	1	2	3
2. Curiosity	Does not seek additional information	Occasionally questions topic	Seeks resources, enrichment
	1	2	3
3. Confidence	Resists trying	Apologizes for questions/work	Eager to try
	1	2	3
4. Independence	Needs encouragement to begin	Quits working when unmonitored	Begins promptly, works independently
	1	2	3
5. Perseverance	Easily frustrated, usually quits	Occasionally frustrated and quits	Works steadily, completing tasks
	1	2	3
6. Accepts corrective feedback	Ignores comments, does not correct work	Occasionally argues, sometimes corrects work	Seeks correction, adjusts work
	1	2	3

to keep your descriptions of each value, however, to help ensure the consistency of your judgments.

Rating Students' Attitudes and Behavior

Rating students' behavior in the classroom can be quite complex; each teacher's observation forms, students, and classroom environment are different. This complexity is increased because each teacher has rather different notions about what constitutes good, acceptable, and unacceptable behavior in the classroom. Additionally, teachers' interactions with their students and students' interactions with each other are within a culture that is unique to the classroom and that has its own spoken and unspoken rules of conduct. Within the context of the classroom culture, some behaviors are acceptable under some circumstances and inappropriate in others, making the teacher's task even more complex. If you are unsure about a student's behavior or motives for a certain behavior, it is a good idea to withhold judgment until you have more information.

In determining what constitutes good behavior in your classroom, avoid *Never* and *Always* categories. Distinguishing consistently between good behavior and behavior that needs improvement for a given student can be difficult because most students fluctuate somewhere between these two categories. What you are attempting to communicate is whether a student's behavior is mostly good or whether it mostly needs improvement. This situation is reflected in behavioral checklists and rating scales that contain descriptors such as *Typically, Mostly,* and *Usually.* If you really feel the need for a category that includes the notion of *Always,* you might want to preface it with the term *almost.*

The inclusion of several areas of attitudes, conduct, and behaviors to be rated on report cards can be problematic for middle and high school teachers who see well over 100 students each day. These teachers encounter so many students daily that they sometimes do not have a clear picture of the behavior patterns and motivations of students unless they are particularly well behaved or ill mannered. If you find yourself in the situation of needing to rate and communicate students' conduct, yet are unclear about how to rate them, solve the problem by rating these students' actions and attitudes as satisfactory until you have specific reasons to do otherwise. To avoid this problem, establish a schedule and make notations of behavior and attitudes several times during a grading period.

The number of times during a term that students' behavior is formally rated must be determined. Although students are informally observed on a daily basis, formal observations need not be as frequent. The number of evaluations will depend on the nature of the behavior observed. Concrete behaviors, such as submitting or completing assignments and bringing required materials to class, should be recorded at the appropriate time. Behaviors that are used to infer attitudes, such as attitude toward learning and citizenship, are not usually measured as frequently. Certainly, you want to rate the behaviors you have chosen to reflect these attitudes more than once during a grading term. Multiple ratings help ensure that students' term marks reflect their attitude throughout the term, not just the week preceding report card distribution. Some teachers choose to rate students weekly, some biweekly, and others less frequently. The number of times you choose to rate students' behavior formally depends in part on the subject and on the students you teach. A good rule of thumb is to have at least three measures of behaviors that reflect attitudes. This helps ensure that the ratings students receive on report cards are not peculiar to a special set of circumstances.

Select times when you are fresh, unhurried, and in a positive mood to do your ratings. Because of the degree of inference required, teachers' ratings can reflect their own attitudes more than those of students. As with performance tests, rating bias can affect the validity of students' attitude scores. While rating students' behavior, you should be aware of the potential bias from rating patterns and from general impressions of students and try to be as objective as possible.

■ Developing Attitude Questionnaires

Some teachers convert their behavior observation forms into questionnaires to gather attitudinal information directly from students. In interpreting students' self-reported attitudes, however, you should keep in mind that students, similar to the rest of us, often mark responses they consider socially acceptable. Their responses may or may not reflect their actual feelings or beliefs. Because of this natural tendency, you cannot describe students' actual attitudes from questionnaires they complete themselves. What you can describe from these forms is how they are willing to tell you they feel. Comparing students' reported attitudes with those obtained through teacher observation can be very interesting and informative.

Converting observation forms to self-report questionnaires is quite straightforward since most of the analysis work was done during the creation of the teachers' observation forms. The following conversions remain to be done:

1. Instructions to the respondent need to be added.
2. The language used to describe the behaviors and rating categories should be phrased appropriately for the students' reading levels.
3. Wording to indicate that the students are judging themselves should be added.

Figure 8.5 contains a questionnaire based on the six key feelings included in Table 8.1. This questionnaire is a checklist that students use to indicate their most typical feelings. The example is developed for use with a mark-sensitive answer sheet that can be scanned and scored using a computer.

The instructions direct students to respond by shading either a 1 or a 2 on the answer sheet for each item. Students' scores can be obtained by summing the numbers they indicate for each item. For example, there are 18 items on the questionnaire, each worth a possible two points. A student who marked a 2 for each item would receive a score of 36, a student who marked all 1s would receive a score of 18, and a student who marked half 2s and half 1s would receive a score of 27.

Figure 8.6 contains a rating scale for students to use in describing their attitudes toward learning. It contains the same six key feelings described in Table 8.1 and three optional statements that relate to varying strengths or degrees of feeling in each of these key areas. Students' scores on this rating scale can be obtained by summing

FIGURE 8.5

A Sample Checklist Based on the Affective Feelings in Table 8.1

MY FEELINGS ABOUT LEARNING IN THIS CLASS

Instructions: This form contains statements that describe how students may feel about their work in school. Read each statement and decide whether it describes **your** feelings in this class **most often** or **not usually.** *Please use the answer sheet provided and a pencil to indicate your feelings. Insert your name and student number before you begin to answer.* If a statement does **not** describe how you usually feel, darken a (1) on your answer sheet. If it describes how you **most often** feel, darken a (2) on your answer sheet.

Not Usually	Most Often	
		A. I am very interested in:
1	2	1. The teacher's explanations and demonstrations
1	2	2. The homework assignments I am asked to complete
1	2	3. The projects and problems we work on in school
		B. I locate more information about the topics we study by:
1	2	4. Asking questions
1	2	5. Looking through resources in the classroom
1	2	6. Finding additional materials in the library
		C. In this class, I like to:
1	2	7. Volunteer answers to questions the teacher asks
1	2	8. Help others understand ideas
1	2	9. Suggest different ideas or solutions for problems we study
		D. When assigned work to do, I:
1	2	10. Begin my work without being asked
1	2	11. Continue working even when no one is watching me
1	2	12. Like to complete my work on time
		E. When asked to do tough assignments, I:
1	2	13. Work through them without being frustrated
1	2	14. Keep trying until I get them done
1	2	15. Keep working on them even after they are due
		F. I really want to do a good job, and I:
1	2	16. Ask the teacher how I can do better
1	2	17. Am pleased when the teacher shows me areas I can do better
1	2	18. Fix problems and mistakes I make in my work

A Sample Attitude Questionnaire Based on the Teacher Observation Form in Table 8.5

ATTITUDES ABOUT LEARNING AND STUDYING

Name _____ Period _____ Date _____

Instructions: Please describe your feelings about learning and studying in this class. In Column A below, there are terms that describe feelings about learning. In Column B, there are statements about how students sometimes feel. For each of the six feelings, circle the one statement that **best describes** your feelings **most of the time.**

Column A	Column B
A. Interest in Learning	1. I am usually very bored in class. 2. The things we study in this class are sort of interesting, but my mind keeps thinking about other things. 3. The things we study in class are pretty interesting, and I am rarely bored in class.
B. Curiosity	1. I do not want to know any more about the things we have to learn in this class. 2. I usually want to know more about the things we learn. 3. I almost always want to know more about the ideas we learn in this class.
C. Confidence	When I think about my work in this class, I think: 1. I am not good at doing the assignments. 2. I am sometimes good at doing the assignments. 3. I almost always do a good job.
D. Independence	When an assignment is made in this class, I usually: 1. Don't even start it until the very last minute. 2. Start working but quit when there is no one to help me. 3. Work along and finish the task on time.
E. Perseverance	When I try to do school work by myself and get stuck, I: 1. Usually get flustered and quit before I finish. 2. Sometimes get flustered and quit before I finish. 3. Usually keep working on the problem until I finish.
F. Desire to Improve	When the teacher criticizes my work, I: 1. Usually ignore the comments and do not correct the work. 2. Occasionally argue, and sometimes correct the work. 3. Ask for more information on how to fix it, and I almost always fix my mistakes.

the numbers circled by students. For example, if a student chose all statements preceded by the number 2, the score would be 12. You could also format such a rating scale for computer scanning and scoring if your class group is proficient using such forms. This modification would only require changing the instructions for how students are to respond.

Once you have developed and administered your checklists or rating scales, you will need to summarize students' scores for evaluating their behavior and attitudes. Chapter 12 describes procedures for summarizing responses to locate strengths and find problem areas requiring attention.

■ Computer Technology

Most teachers do not consider putting their behavior observation checklists or rating scales in their test item banks, but it is not difficult to do so. You may create an item bank just for the attitudes and behaviors you are expected to observe, rate, and report for a grading term. You might call this bank ATTITUDE and store your behavior observation and self-report instruments in the ATTITUDE item bank using the following strategy:

1. Use the essay- or problem-item format to enter the name and definition of the attitude to be rated (e.g., citizenship, attitude toward learning).
2. Enter the checklist or rating scale as a linked illustration or table.
3. Classify each attitude with item descriptors you create for your attitude item bank.

You may use the same strategy to create and store attitude rating scales that you design to gather students' responses about their attitudes. With your behavior checklists and rating scales stored in your item bank, you will only need to create them once. You can produce an original copy each time you need to use one, and you can edit or update your instruments at any time.

Similar to product and performance tests, spreadsheet programs may be used to facilitate scoring and data analysis. Simply enter the observation categories and quality points along the top of the spreadsheet and students' names along the side. You can then enter students' scores, add formulas for calculating total scores, and produce both individual and class reports easily.

■ Summary

Teachers are often expected to judge students' attitudes and to report these judgments to students as well as parents. It is sometimes difficult to locate these attitudes in the curriculum guide for a school district, but they can typically be found on report cards and in the school's handbook for teachers and students.

Gagné (1985) defines *attitudes* as internal states that influence an individual's choice of personal action. He suggests that attitudes have three parts, including an affective component, a behavioral component, and a cognitive component.

Analyzing attitudes from curriculum guides and report cards is quite different from analyzing intellectual or motor skills. The procedure used, sometimes referred to as *operationalizing* an attitude, has the following suggested steps:

1. Generally define each of the attitudes you must evaluate.
2. Compare the general definitions generated to ensure that you have differentiated adequately among the attitudes.
3. Further define each attitude by naming particular positive and/or negative feelings that are associated with the general attitude definition.
4. For each of these feelings, list behaviors that are demonstrable in the classroom that would best reflect the feeling.
5. Create a checklist or rating scale of these behaviors.

Checklists and rating scales should not include absolute rating categories such as *Always* and *Never*. Instead, they should contain categories that enable you to rate the general frequency of occurrences or the tendencies in students' behavioral patterns.

Students' attitudes and behaviors should be rated more than once during a term to ensure the ratings students are assigned reflect their behavior patterns and not behavior related to specific instances that occurred near the time of the ratings. You should always rate students' behavior when you are fresh, unhurried, and in a positive mood. This strategy will help ensure that students' ratings reflect more their attitudes than yours.

Rubrics used by teachers to observe students' behavior can be converted to questionnaires that students use to report their own feelings and attitudes. Teachers must be cautious in interpreting students' self-reported attitudes and feelings, since students tend to select socially acceptable responses that may or may not reflect their true feelings.

Both observation and self-report forms for assessing students' attitudes can be formatted for computer scanning and scoring. Using this equipment reduces the amount of clerical work required to score students' ratings. These forms can also be placed in a test item bank for easy editing and retrieval.

■ PRACTICE EXERCISES

I. Rating Attitudes and Behaviors
   A. Many school districts require teachers to report students' progress in citizenship. Develop a rating scale you could use to judge behaviors you believe reflect citizenship. In developing your rating scale, follow these steps:
   1. Write a definition for the term *citizenship* that can be used to guide your work.
   2. List all the positive feelings you believe are associated with the attitude as you have defined it.
   3. List the positive behaviors you believe reflect each feeling and the negative behaviors that demonstrate a student's lack of citizenship. Your list should be appropriate for the students and subject you teach or plan to teach.

4. Evaluate the list and remove behaviors that are redundant, unobservable in the classroom, irrelevant, or inappropriate for your situation.

5. Paraphrase and list selected behaviors on the left side of a sheet of paper. Check to ensure that all are either neutrally or positively worded.

6. Select rating categories for each behavior and write a verbal description for each.

7. Assign a number for each category with low numbers reflecting negative or inappropriate categories.

8. Design the form so you can rate students' behavior three times during a term. Compare your definition and rating scale with those included in Figure 8.7F in the Feedback section. Because definitions, subjects, grade levels, classroom environments, and target students vary, your form will undoubtedly differ from the example provided.

B. Using the steps outlined in I.A, develop a behavior rating scale for study habits. Compare the definition and rating scale you develop with the one in Figure 8.8F in the Feedback section.

C. For the attitude goal "Choose to be punctual" analyze the following (see Figure 8.9F for feedback):

1. The positive feelings (affective component) a student is expected to possess

2. The overt behaviors that will indicate whether a student chooses to be punctual

3. The verbal information (cognitive component) a student should possess (the information should include cultural expectations, rewards, and consequences)

4. A procedure for punctuality a student could follow

II. Enrichment

A. Rating Attitudes and Behaviors

1. Locate the attitudes and behaviors to be communicated on a report card for your subject and grade level.

2. Locate the rating categories for the attitudes and behaviors on the report card.

3. Define each attitude and behavior category.

4. Develop rating forms for evaluating the attitudes and behaviors.

5. If you are teaching a class, use the forms to evaluate the behavior of students in the class. Revise the form as needed for feasibility and convenience.

■ F E E D B A C K

I. Rating Attitudes and Behaviors

A. See Figure 8.7F.

B. See Figure 8.8F.

C. See Figure 8.9F.

FIGURE 8.7F

Definition and Behavior Rating Scale for Citizenship

Name _____ **Term** _____ **Score** _____

Total   (153)

Definition: Citizenship is the social interactions that students have with their peers and with their teacher. It includes their contributions to the classroom society.

	Observation Dates:			Total
I. Citizenship				
A. Self-discipline				
1. Minds own affairs	____	____	____	____
2. Controls emotions	____	____	____	____
3. Is honest	____	____	____	____
4. Is truthful	____	____	____	____
B. Interactions with peers				
1. Shows interest in classmates	____	____	____	____
2. Listens to classmates	____	____	____	____
3. Helps and encourages classmates	____	____	____	____
4. Shares resources and materials	____	____	____	____
5. Contributes to group activities	____	____	____	____
C. Interactions with teacher				
1. Listens when teacher is talking	____	____	____	____
2. Follows directions	____	____	____	____
3. Seeks guidance and help	____	____	____	____
4. Accepts suggestions and comments about classroom interactions	____	____	____	____
D. Support of a positive classroom environment				
1. Helps define and analyze class problems	____	____	____	____
2. Suggests solutions for class problems	____	____	____	____
3. Accepts responsibility for personal contributions to class problems	____	____	____	____
4. Helps maintain class property	____	____	____	____
Totals:	____	____	____	____

Scale: 1 = Rarely; 2 = Inconsistently; 3 = Almost always
Note: Write quality ratings in blanks opposite each behavior.

FIGURE 8.8F

Definition and Rating Scale for Study Habits

Name _____ Term _____ Score _____

Definition: Study habits are the procedures students use to accomplish assigned work.

Behavior	Observation Dates:	___	___	___	Total
I. Class preparation					
A. Reads assignments before class		___	___	___	___
B. Brings required materials to class		___	___	___	___
II. During presentations/demonstrations					
A. Listens		___	___	___	___
B. Takes notes		___	___	___	___
C. Follows instructions		___	___	___	___
III. During class work					
A. Organizes material		___	___	___	___
B. Works carefully and accurately		___	___	___	___
C. Uses time productively		___	___	___	___
	Totals	___	___	___	___

Number of homework
assignments during term: _____

IV. Homework
  A. Number submitted on time _____
  B. Number submitted complete _____
  C. Number accurate _____

Scale: 1 = Rarely; 2 = Inconsistently; 3 = Almost always

Note: Write quality ratings in blanks opposite each behavior.

FIGURE 8.9F

Analysis of Instructional Goal "Choose to Be Punctual"

Affective Component	Behavioral Component
The individual has a:	The individual chooses to:
1. Positive attitude toward planning and self-discipline 2. Positive attitude toward being punctual 3. Negative attitude toward inconveniencing others	1. Keep a calendar of appointments 2. Plan activities to enable punctuality 3. Arrive shortly before the scheduled beginning time 4. Begin scheduled activity on time 5. End activity on or before scheduled ending time

Cognitive Component (Verbal information)

Cultural Expectations	Rewards	Consequences of Habitual Lateness
1. We live in a time-oriented culture. 2. Punctuality is considered to be an indicator of a person's ability to plan and exercise self-control. 3. Other people expect a person to be punctual. 4. Other people dislike waiting for people who are not on time. 5. Being late is considered discourteous because it causes worry for your safety and demonstrates lack of regard for the feelings of other people	The individual gains increased respect from others because he or she has demonstrated: 1. Good planning skills 2. Good self-control 3. Respect for other people's time 4. Respect for other people's opinions 5. The ability to be dependable	The individual loses the respect of other people for being discourteous and undisciplined. The individual causes other people to worry. The individual causes other people to become annoyed and angry.

Cognitive Component (Procedure)

■ RUBRIC

Rubric for Evaluating Attitude and Behavior Observation Forms and Self-Report Questionnaires

		CRITERIA FOR EVALUATING ATTITUDE AND BEHAVIOR OBSERVATION FORMS
Yes	No	**I. Criteria (actions/behaviors)**
____	____	A. Are criteria congruent with the aspects in the overall definition of the attitude?
____	____	B. Are criteria unique, avoiding overlapping aspects/feelings/behaviors?
____	____	C. Are criteria clear reflections of positive or negative feelings?
____	____	D. Are criteria overt or observable behaviors in the intended context?
____	____	E. Do criteria contain only one action in each?
____	____	F. Are criteria worded neutrally or positively for consistency?
____	____	G. Are criteria reasonable for the age group observed?
____	____	H. Are criteria appropriate for the classroom environment and context (regular, laboratory, gymnasium, work-study, etc.)?
		II. Rating Scale
____	____	A. Are there only the number of quality categories (e.g., 1–4) that can be judged with consistency?
____	____	B. Does each quality category have a verbal descriptor?
____	____	C. Are terms such as *always* and *never* avoided as verbal descriptors?
____	____	D. Are spaces provided for multiple ratings when appropriate?
		III. Additional Criteria for Evaluating Self-Report Questionnaires
		A. Directions
____	____	1. Do the directions contain clearly written language appropriate for the age group?
____	____	2. Do the directions contain clearly written rationale or reason for asking students to self-report?
____	____	3. Do the directions contain clearly written instructions indicating whether responses are anonymous?
____	____	4. Do the directions contain clearly written instructions indicating whether responding is voluntary?
		B. Criteria (behaviors/feelings to be judged)
____	____	1. Do criteria clearly relate to affective or behavioral standards prescribed by curriculum standards, report cards, or student handbooks?
____	____	2. Are criteria clearly *not* an invasion of the students' privacy?
____	____	3. Are criteria free of biasing information or terms?
____	____	4. Are criteria worded clearly for the age group?
____	____	5. Do criteria contain only one feeling or action in each?

Yes	No	
____	____	C. Response scale
		1. Does the response scale contain only the number of quality categories that the age group can differentiate accurately?
____	____	2. Does the response scale contain verbal descriptors for each quality category?
____	____	3. Does the response scale contain verbal descriptors likely to be familiar to age group?

REFERENCE

Gangé, R. M. (1985). *The conditions of learning and theory of instruction.* New York: Holt, Rinehart and Winston.

SUGGESTED READINGS

Kubiszyn, T., & Borich, G. (2000). *Educational testing and measurement* (6th ed., pp. 452–480). New York: John Wiley & Sons.

Lynn, R. L., & Gronlund, N. E. (2000). *Measurement and assessment in teaching* (8th ed., pp. 315–343). Englewood Cliffs, NJ: Prentice-Hall.

Popham, W. J. (1999). *Classroom assessment: What teachers need to know* (2nd ed., pp. 28–350). Boston: Allyn and Bacon.

Thorndike, R. M. (1997). *Measurement and evaluation in psychology and education* (6th ed., pp. 351–392). Columbus, OH: Merrill.

Tombari, M., & Borich, G. (1999). *Authentic assessment in the classroom* (pp. 189–206). Columbus, OH: Merrill.

Worthen, B. R., White, K. R., Fan, X., & Sudweeks, R. L. (1999). *Measurement and assessment in schools* (2nd ed., pp. 329–380). New York: Addison-Wesley Longman.

Developing and Administering Tests for Nonreading, ESOL, and Exceptional Students

- Develop and administer group tests for students who are nonreaders.
- Develop and administer tests for students with limited reading skills.
- Develop and administer tests for students who speak English as a second language (ESOL).

Many students in the early elementary grades are nonreaders or limited readers. Although the preceding suggestions for designing and developing tests might seem irrelevant for teachers of these students, this is not the case. Such teachers do encounter some distinct technical problems; however, the suggestions for designing tests for readers also apply to designing tests for students with limited reading skills. For example, teachers still need to analyze instructional goals to create a framework of subordinate skills and create tables of test and item specifications to design readiness tests, pretests, practice tests, and posttests. At the point of test development, these teachers must make some significant departures. Rather than writing directions and questions for students to read, they need to write direction and item scripts that they read to students. Instead of writing responses for students to read, they must create other ways for students to demonstrate that they can recall a fact or perform a skill. They must also use different methods for administering their tests and for recording students' responses. The following sections contain recommendations for testing nonreaders and students with limited reading skills in groups and individually.

Tests that are designed and developed for students with limited reading skills should have the same qualities as tests created for all students—namely, the validity and reliability of test scores. The same four quality criteria recommended for creating objective, product, and performance tests are applied to assessments for students with limited reading skills to help ensure the validity and reliability of test results. Recall that these quality standards include curriculum-, learner-, school-, and professional-centered criteria.

■ Testing Groups of Nonreaders

Testing an entire class at once requires less time than administering the same test individually to each student in a class. Testing nonreaders simultaneously, however, requires care because following oral instructions is difficult for students. Without clear directions, the group becomes baffled and frustrated, their responses become meaningless, and you become convinced that group testing is not feasible for your class. Most classes can successfully take group tests when the tests are carefully developed and administered. Developing such tests requires writing a script for yourself, creating a response form for students, and using special techniques during test administration.

Writing the Introduction Script

Good tests for readers contain introductory remarks and instructions for completing the test; nonreaders need the same information. Because they cannot read the instructions themselves, you need to provide instructions orally. Your introductory remarks should include what the test is about and an explanation and accompanying demonstration of what students are to do. To help ensure that you have their attention, this information should be provided before response forms are distributed. Figure 9.1 provides an example introductory script for a test. Notice that the enabling skill measured is written at the top and that the script includes (1) a general statement of the skill to be performed, (2) a demonstration of the skill that shows what students will find on their response forms and how they are to respond, and (3) a call for questions from the group.

Before using such instructions with an entire class, you should field test the instructions with one or two students. Pay careful attention to the clarifying questions they ask and revise your instructions as needed. This trial will reduce the number of questions asked during the test, which will decrease the amount of time required for the test and help avoid frustrating the students.

Writing the Questions Script

You need to write a script for each question on the test. Students cannot reread a question they do not initially understand. Therefore, carefully ordering the directions, pausing to allow students time to perform a step, and repeating key information will help students perform the tasks with a minimum amount of confusion. Directions should be ordered in the following manner:

1. Tell students how to locate their place (e.g., "Find the star on your paper").
2. Tell them what kinds of objects they will find in that location (e.g., "See the boxes beside the star?").
3. Describe the skill measured (e.g., "Find the box beside the star with four marbles in it").
4. Tell them how to show that they can perform the skill (e.g., "Put an *X* on the box that has four marbles in it").

FIGURE 9.1

Teacher's Script and Student's Response Form for a Nonreader Group Test

Introduction and Directions

Enabling skill B.2: Given multiple sets of objects that contain up to 10 objects, select the set that contains a specified number of objects.

Introduction: "Today I want you to show me that you can count the number of marbles in a box. On the paper I will give you, you will see a picture of something that will help you find the right boxes. (Draw a typical locator symbol on the chalkboard.) Beside the cat you will find three boxes of marbles." (Draw three boxes of marbles on the chalkboard beside the object.)

"See, one box contains two marbles (point to correct box), one box contains one marble (point to correct box), and one box contains three marbles (point to box). Only one of the boxes beside the cat will contain the number of marbles that I say. If I asked you to find the box with one marble in it, you would find this box (point to box) because it is the only one *beside the cat* that has one marble in it. I want you to put an X on this box (put large X on box) to show me that you can find the box with one marble in it. Do you have any questions?"

Distribute response forms.

"Do you have any questions about your paper? Let's begin. I will read the questions, and you will mark your answers with an X."

Teacher's Question Script (Skill B.2)	Student's Response Form (Skill B.2)
	Name _____ Date _____ Score _____
1. "Find the star on your paper. Do you see the star? (pause) See the boxes beside the star? (pause) Find the box that has four marbles in it. Find the box that has four marbles in it. (pause) Place an X on the box that has four marbles in it." (pause)	
2. "Find the sailboat on your paper. Do you see the sailboat? (pause) See the boxes beside the sailboat? (pause) Find the box that has five marbles in it. Find the box that has five marbles in it. (pause) Put an X on the box that has five marbles in it." (pause)	
3. "Find the apple on your paper. Do you see the apple? (pause) See the boxes beside the apple? (pause) Find the box that has seven marbles in it. Find the box that has seven marbles in it. (pause) Put an X on the box that has seven marbles in it." (pause)	

This question script, with the recommended pauses and repetition inserted, appears in Figure 9.1.

Initially, you might think that creating such scripts constitutes busywork. However, writing a script has four benefits. First, it helps you avoid omitting important information needed for smooth test administration. Second, the script can be evaluated and refined to avoid the same problems in future test administrations. Third, it enables you to use teacher's aides to help with testing. Using your script, they can administer the test (1) to the class, freeing you to circulate among students and provide additional assistance when needed; (2) to individual students who were absent during the group test; and (3) to small groups or individuals who need to retake the test following additional instruction. Fourth, the script will be available when you need to measure the same skill for a new class.

Developing the Response Form

As you write the question scripts, you should develop the corresponding paper-and-pencil response form. Space for the student's name, the date, and the score should be included at the top. The illustrations on the form must match the information in the introduction and question scripts. The symbols used to help students locate their place should be familiar to the class. If they are familiar with numerals or letters, use them. If not, use such symbols as a star, ball, dog, cat, moon, bike, or sailboat. The responses in each set should be clearly separated and easy for children to distinguish. Similar to other selected-response tests, they should contain one clearly correct answer and one to three distractors that represent plausible misconceptions or errors. A sample response form is included in Figure 9.1

Administering the Test

Once the scripts and response form are developed, you are ready to administer the test. If you have a teacher's aide or parent volunteer available, he or she can provide valuable assistance with this challenging task. The person who reads the script should watch the group closely for clues about pacing and needed repetition. Having a second person who can circulate among students and provide additional attention (e.g., pointing to the correct location) will make the procedure progress more smoothly. If you have no help, seat those students you predict will need assistance close by you. The pauses built into the question scripts enable you to scan the entire group for potential problems.

■ Testing Individual Nonreaders

It is not always feasible to test a group of nonreaders; thus, individual tests might need to be given. This situation is common for special education teachers who provide individualized instruction and have each student in the class studying a different lesson. Developing individually administered tests requires a question script, sometimes objects that students manipulate, and a student response record. Keeping the required materials together in a test packet or kit will save time because you will need the same materials each time the test is administered. These kits can be labeled to identify the enabling skills or goals measured and the material enclosed. They can be filed in sequence with other test kits that measure subordinate skills related to the same instructional goal.

Developing the Script and Response Form

Unlike group-administered tests, the script for individually administered tests is usually included on the same form as the student response record. They can be included on the same form because the teacher both reads the script and records the student's responses. The form should contain space for recording the student's name, the date the test is administered, the objective measured, the script used to introduce the test, the directions/questions script, and space for recording the student's responses. Consider the example test form in Figure 9.2. The enabling skill measured and introduction script are included at the top; the directions/questions script is included on the left side; and spaces to record the student's responses are in the right-hand columns. Notice the space to record each response the student makes and spaces for repeating the test if necessary.

Manner of Responding

Because these tests are administered individually, a student can respond orally to your questions or can manipulate given objects to demonstrate skill. For example, a student can choose a specified picture from a set; sequence a set of pictures, numbers, or letters; count a specified number of objects; select a particular shape, letter, number, or color from a set; or classify similar objects in a set. Objects needed for a test should be kept in the test kit along with the script and response record.

Administering the Test

To begin the test, introduce the skill to be measured and answer any questions the student might have about what you want her or him to do. When there are objects to be manipulated, you will find that demonstrating the skill using a simple example is helpful. As with group tests, such a demonstration will help ensure that the student's errors relate to skill rather than to understanding your directions. Watch the student carefully and pace your test according to his or her ability to follow your directions.

As the student responds to each question, you should record *all* the responses. Recording only incorrect or correct responses will affect a student's attitude and may influence performance on subsequent items. For the same reason, incorrect answers should be marked or identified only after the test is completed.

In addition to how you record responses, the way you behave during the test is important; the student will watch you closely to detect your reactions to responses. You should remain pleasant and patient regardless of whether the student makes an incorrect response or asks to have information repeated a third or fourth time. Coaching,

FIGURE 9.2

Teacher's Script and Student's Response Record for an Individualized Test

Name _____

Enabling Skill A.4: Given a set of 10 objects, count out two sets of objects containing a specified number and sum the number of objects removed.

Introduction: "See the pile of <u>beans</u> I have given you? Today I want you to count the number of beans I say and take them from the pile. (Demonstrate with one bean and two beans.) Then I want you to tell me how many beans you have taken from the pile altogether. (Demonstrate $1 + 2 = 3$). Are you ready?"

Directions/Questions Script	Student's Responses	
	Dates Tested	
	9/12	9/30
1. "Take three beans from the pile and place them here."	3	3
2. "Take two beans from the pile and place them there."	2	2
3. "How many beans have you taken from the pile altogether?"	5	5
"Put the beans back in the big pile."		
4. "Take four beans from the pile and place them here."	4	4
5. "Take four beans from the pile and place them there."	4	4
6. "How many beans have you taken from the pile altogether?"	8	8
"Put the beans back in the big pile."		
7. "Take five beans from the pile and place them here."	✗	5
8. "Take four beans from the pile and place them there."	4	4
9. "How many beans have you taken from the pile altogether?"	✗	9
Total Correct Responses	7	9

rewarding (e.g., "Great, Johnny"), or criticizing behaviors will influence the validity of the measure.

Providing Corrective Feedback

Provide feedback to the student immediately following an individual test, if time permits. You can review errors the student made, explain or show why the response was incorrect, and demonstrate how the task is performed correctly. After this additional instruction, you might give the student an opportunity to perform the skill correctly and include the amount of verbal guidance or coaching the student appears to need. However, a correct response after coaching should not be counted as a correct answer on the test. The student's ability to perform the skill should be checked on another day to see whether the skill was remembered over time.

Testing Students with Limited Reading Skills

Nonreaders in the primary grades are but one group of students that has difficulty reading testing materials. Many students have problems reading assessment materials and following directions; two typical groups include ESOL students in the primary grades with limited English skills and special education students whose exceptionalities make reading difficult. When students have difficulty reading assessment materials and following directions carefully, teachers must make every effort to ensure that their students are assessed fairly. The assessment scores students receive should reflect their knowledge and skill in the content area assessed rather than their reading ability.

To ensure fairness in testing for students with limited reading skills, teachers often need to make several adaptations to their materials and procedures. These can include adaptations to the test format, administration procedures, or scoring procedures. Table 9.1 contains possible adaptations for tests and testing procedures for students with limited reading skills.

Testing Students with English as a Second Language (ESOL)

A fourth group of students that deserves special assessment consideration to help ensure the validity and reliability of their test scores is ESOL students. The differences in test development for ESOL students occur after the table of test specifications is completed and test formatting is started. The test items must be formatted to provide students with access to the information and skills being assessed, and the testing procedures, whether group or individually administered, must provide students with ample time and an accepting environment.

One caution is in order. Teachers must take care to differentiate between assessment and instructional activities for ESOL students. During assessment, the student *must* know what is being asked or what he or she is to do. Switching to English in testing before the student reads or speaks English is not helpful, and it leads to invalid, unreliable test results. If you have ESOL students in your class and you know that they are unable to read the tests you administer to other students, seek help immediately for your testing activities with these students.

Many school districts classify ESOL students into five levels, based on the students' skills in speaking and reading their home languages and English. Each of these levels is defined in the first column in Table 9.2, and considerations for formatting, administering, and scoring the tests are included in the remaining columns for each ESOL level.

TABLE 9.1

Considerations for Testing Students with Limited Reading Skills

Student Group	Test Format	Administration Procedures	Scoring Procedures
Typical students in the primary grades with limited reading skills	■ Simple sentences ■ Clear directions, including sample items to be worked together as a group ■ Ample space without crowding directions, stems, or responses ■ Familiar vocabulary ■ Familiar contexts ■ Limited number of enabling skills tested at one time ■ Limited number of items included in one session	Administer in a group-paced manner, with teacher reading aloud each item and students reading the same item silently with the teacher. Following the oral reading, students mark their answers. The group moves together to the next item.	Teacher marks students' correct and incorrect answers after all students have completed the test.
Special education students whose exceptionalities make reading difficult	■ Simple sentences ■ Clear directions, including sample items to be worked together as a group ■ Familiar and *age-appropriate* vocabulary ■ Familiar and *age-appropriate* contexts ■ Limited number of enabling skills tested at one time ■ Limited number of items	Group testing procedures are the same as above. Individual and small group testing procedures include: ■ Adjust for the specific needs of the students (e.g., hearing, sight, or other physical impairment; intellectual, emotional, or attention impairment) ■ Allow ample time for the test ■ Avoid verbal and nonverbal coaching ■ Mark all answers given and score accuracy later ■ Remain pleasant and patient throughout the test ■ Invite students to question unclear areas ■ Answer students' questions clearly unless questions infringe on the skill being tested	For group testing, the same as above. For individual and small group tests, the teacher marks answers given as correct and incorrect after students have completed the test.

TABLE 9.2

Test Design and Development Considerations for ESOL Students with Limited Reading Skills in English

ESOL Student Classifications	Test Format	Administration Procedures	Scoring Procedures
Level 1: Illiterate in home language and English	Similar to nonreaders of English: Directions and items are presented orally in home language using a teacher script.	Similar to nonreaders of English: Student responds orally, by using manipulatives, or by using a graphic response sheet.	Responses are scored correct or incorrect by language specialist.
Level 2: Limited in home language, non-English speaker	Similar to nonreaders of English: Directions and items are presented orally in home language using a teacher script.	Same as above.	Same as above.
Level 3: At grade level in home language, non-English speaker	Language specialists translate test into home language for student.	Student independently takes test, responding in home language.	Same as above.
Level 4: At grade level in home language, below 33rd percentile on standardized English test	▪ Directions and items should be formatted to reduce the reading load to the degree possible. ▪ Use simple sentences. ▪ Use familiar terminology.	▪ Allow ample time for student to complete the test (perhaps using two testing sessions). ▪ Invite students to inquire when they are unfamiliar with terminology or do not understand directions. ▪ Allow use of home language dictionary unless test itself is an English vocabulary test.	Responses are scored by regular teacher using criteria appropriate for the age and grade level.
Level 5: At grade level in home language, above 33rd percentile in standardized test in English	No special adaptations to the test are required.	Same as above.	None.

■ Summarizing and Analyzing Students' Responses

The suggestions for organizing, summarizing, and analyzing students' responses presented in Chapter 12 are appropriate for both individual and group tests. You summarize and analyze the data you recorded on students' records during individual tests or the data students created using their own response forms on group tests. From these group summaries, you can evaluate the quality of both your tests and your instruction.

Computer Technology

The creation of tests for nonreaders and students with limited reading skills using a computerized item bank and test assembly program is quite easy when compared to the process of creating them by hand. The scripts (items) you create can be entered into the item bank using the essay question or problem format. Your item scripts can then be classified and systematically stored through the program's item descriptors (e.g., subject, topic, enabling skill code, etc.). Students' response forms can be linked to your item scripts using the student feedback section or linked tables and charts feature.

Computerized script (item) storage and test assembly capabilities are especially useful for teachers of students who have limited reading skills or who are nonreaders. These capabilities provide teachers with the flexibility necessary either to assemble many different versions of a test or to create many very small tests that contain only a few items. In order to meet the needs of their students, these teachers tend to include fewer items on their tests. When considering readiness tests, pretests, practice tests, and posttests, however, they typically need a greater number of tests than other teachers. The item bank can help them assemble a variety of tests for the same instructional goal that will help meet the needs of their total class, different achievement-level groups within their class, or individuals who require specialized materials.

Special education teachers will also find computerized item banks invaluable. Their needs are different from those of typical classroom teachers since they tend to have fewer students, with each student at a different grade level or studying unique materials. Computerized item banks and assembly programs will enable these teachers to create any number of tests, each designed to meet the special needs of individual students. One adjustment special education teachers can make to maximize the utility of the item bank for themselves is to change one of the item descriptors to an age-level category. When using search criteria to locate items in the bank for a student at a particular age, teachers can add this search criterion to find the most appropriate items relative to context and vocabulary.

Summary

Nonreaders and students with limited reading skills can be tested in groups or individually. Group tests require you to write scripts for directions and questions, develop a student response form, and administer the test carefully. Suggestions for developing and administering these tests include:

Directions Script
1. Describe the skill to be measured.
2. Write a script for demonstrating the skill.
3. Ask for clarifying questions.

Questions Script
1. Sequence instructions in the following order:
   a. Tell students how to find the correct location on the response form.
   b. Describe what they will find in that location.
   c. Describe the skill to be performed.
   d. Tell students how to mark their response.
2. Include pauses between instructions that enable students to perform the specified task.
3. Repeat key information (e.g., the skill to be performed).

Response Form
1. Include familiar symbols that students can use to locate the correct response set.
2. Clearly separate the responses within and across sets.

Administration
1. Seat students you predict will need extra help close by you.
2. Read the directions script.
3. Demonstrate the skill to be performed.
4. Ask for clarifying questions.
5. Distribute the response form.
6. Call for questions.
7. Read the questions script.
8. Observe the group during pauses to identify potential problems.
9. Repeat any instructions as needed.

Individual tests for nonreaders require a form that includes a script for directions and questions, space to mark a student's responses, objects to manipulate (sometimes), and special administration techniques. The procedures for developing the script are the same as those described for group tests. Procedures for creating the response form and administering the test are:

Response Form
1. Include space to record the student's response to each task.
2. Include space for administering the test several times.

Administration
1. Read the directions script.
2. Demonstrate the skill to be performed.
3. Ask for clarifying questions.
4. Read the questions script, pausing and repeating information as needed.
5. Record all responses.
6. Remain pleasant and patient throughout the test.
7. Avoid using coaching, rewarding, or criticizing behaviors.
8. Mark incorrect responses only after the test is completed.
9. Provide students with corrective feedback immediately following the test, if time permits.

Tests for limited readers in the primary grades resemble the format of tests for readers. The main formatting difference is that these tests typically assess fewer enabling skills and use fewer items for one testing session, because group administration requires more time. The administration procedures differ in that teachers and students go through the test as a group, with the teacher reading each question aloud. Students follow the teacher, reading the question silently. The teacher pauses, usually rereading the question for those who remain unclear about the task or answer, and then pauses to allow time for students to respond. When teachers are sure that all students have answered, they move to the next question, again reading aloud for students.

Tests for exceptional students often need to be tailored to the special needs of each student. Teachers must be thoughtful about the particular needs related to each student's exceptionality, and develop their materials and procedures accordingly. For example, different formats and procedures are needed for students with physical impairments such as hearing or sight impairments. Different procedures still are needed for students who are exceptional based on their memory, emotions, or attention. Rather than listing each combination of possibilities, simply observe each student carefully, ask yourself what format and procedure would be most effective with that particular student, and then format your materials and procedures accordingly.

Tests for students whose home language is other than English are classified into five separate categories based on their language ability in their home language and in English. Testing materials and procedures are tailored to these language levels. ESOL students who do not speak or read English are tested by language specialists in their home language. ESOL students who speak and read English at the 33rd percentile or lower on a standardized test of English frequently take tests in a regular classroom with native English speakers. Teachers must adapt their administration, and sometimes their test formats, for these students to help ensure the validity and reliability of their scores. Most often, Level 5 ESOL students who score at the 33rd percentile or above on standardized English tests take the same classroom tests as all other students in their classes. Teachers must ensure, however, that these students have enough time to complete the test and that they understand the vocabulary and contexts used in the test items and in the resource materials.

■ PRACTICE EXERCISES

I. Group Testing Intellectual Skills for Nonreaders
Examine the partially completed instructional goal analysis and test item specifications in Figure 9.3. Based in these materials, develop a teacher script and student response form for testing students' mastery of the enabling skill II.F using test item specifications II.F.2.

II. Individually Testing Motor Skills for Nonreaders
Many teachers are concerned with students' eye-hand coordination and their motor development. One very good task for assessing students' status and progress in this developmental area is bouncing a playground ball while standing still, while walking, and while running. Using the goal analysis in Figure 9.4 for bouncing a ball while standing still, develop a checklist that can be used on four separate occasions during a term to assess students' status on this skill.

FIGURE 9.3

Matrix Diagram and Test Item Specifications for the Intellectual Skill "Write Lower-Case and Upper-Case Letters"

CONCEPTS/ CONTENT	A State/Recall Physical Characteristics of:	B State/Recall Functional Characteristics of:	C State/Recall Quality Characteristics of:	D Discriminate between Examples and Nonexamples	E Evaluate Given Examples	F Produce Examples of:
I. Lower-case letters				a through z		a through z
II. Upper-case letters				A through Z		A through Z

I.D Given a response sheet that contains lower-case letters in sets of 10, circle the letter in each set that is named by the teacher. To the degree possible, the letters included in each set should be similar in appearance.

I.F When each of the lower-case letters is named by the teacher, draw the letter named.

II.D Given a response sheet that contains upper-case letters in sets of 10, circle the letters named by the teacher. To the degree possible, the letters included in each set should be similar in appearance.

II.F.1 When each of the upper-case letters is named by the teacher, draw the letter named.

II.F.2 Given the illustration of each lower-case letter, write the corresponding upper-case letter.

III. Group Testing Limited Readers

Circle *T* for *True* and *F* for *False* statements about developing and administering tests for students with limited reading skills.

  A. When developing the test format for group testing limited readers, you should:

    T F **1.** Use simple sentences for developing stems and responses.

    T F **2.** Format the test to look similar to a test for readers.

    T F **3.** Ensure each page does not appear crowded.

    T F **4.** Format items to require as little reading or writing as possible unless you are developing a reading or writing test

    T F **5.** Require students to read independently to help them develop reading skills.

  B. When administering a test to students with limited reading skills, you should:

    T F **1.** Keep the group together.

    T F **2.** Read each item aloud for them.

    T F **3.** Not repeat items, because repeating items will encourage students to stop paying attention.

    T F **4.** Pause, allowing time for students to answer.

    T F **5.** Answer students' questions about the test during the test.

FIGURE 9.4

Subordinate Skills for the Instructional Goal "Bounce a Ball while Standing Still"

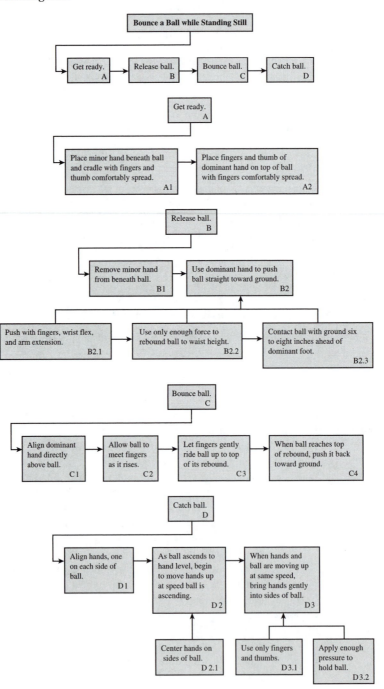

IV. **Testing Students Whose Home Language Is Other Than English (ESOL)**
Column A contains testing strategies and Column B contains each of the 5 levels of ESOL
Students. For each strategy, select the level of ESOL for which the strategy is appropriate.
You may select each level more than once for a strategy or not at all.

Column A	*Column B*
Testing Strategies	*ESOL Levels*

_____ A. Translate items to home language.   1. Level 1

_____ B. Orally read teacher script in home language.   2. Level 2

_____ C. Create test in English and read items along   3. Level 3
        with students.   4. Level 4

_____ D. Administer a written test in English for   5. Level 5
        students to complete independently.

_____ E. Seek assistance from a member of the
        student's community to translate your test
        into the student's home language.

V. **Enrichment**
   A. Locate a curriculum guide for preschool, kindergarten, or first grade and perform the fol-
      lowing:
      1. Choose an instructional goal from the guide that is either an intellectual skill, a motor
         skill, or a social development skill.
      2. Use either a matrix diagram, tree diagram, or flowchart to analyze the goal.
      3. Write item or task specifications for each enabling skill identified.
   B. For an existing test, adapt the test and administration procedures for students with phys-
      ical impairments.
   C. Using an existing test for students at your grade level, adapt the test for ESOL students,
      Level 4.

■ FEEDBACK

I. **Group Testing Intellectual Skills for Nonreaders**
See Figure 9.5F

II. **Individually Testing Motor Skills for Nonreaders**
See Figure 9.6F

III. **Group Testing Limited Readers**
A. 1 = T; 2 = T; 3 = T; 4 = F
B. 1 = T; 2 = T; 3 = F; 4 = T; 5 = T

IV. **Testing Students Whose Home Language Is Other than English (ESOL)**
A = 1, 2, and 3; B = 1 and 2; C = 4; D = 4 and 5; E = 1, 2, and 3

FIGURE 9.5F

**Teacher's Script and Students' Response Form for a Test
on Writing Upper-Case Letters**

Teacher's Script

1. "Today I want you to write capital letters on a special paper that I give you. While I pass out the papers, please get out a pencil that has a good point for writing your letters. Do not write on the paper I give you until I tell you how I want you to write." (Distribute response sheets.)

2. "Does everybody have a paper and a pencil?" (Pause while readiness determined.)

3. "Let's begin. See the line at the top of your paper beside the word *Name?*" (Point out line on sample response sheet on overhead projector so students can see example on projector screen.)

4. "Print your name on this line." (Print sample name in space for overhead display.)

5. "See the line beside your name where it says *Date?* On this line write the numbers *2-6* just like this." (Demonstrate on overhead.)

6. "Do you see all the lower-case letters on your paper?" (Point out letters on overhead.)

7. "I want you to write the capital letter for each lower-case letter."

8. "Write each capital letter on the line beside each lower-case letter." (Point to line beside letter on overhead.)

9. "Let's do one together. See the first letter? It is a lower-case *a*." (Point to *a* on overhead.)

10. "See the line beside the letter *a?* Let's write a capital *A* on the line to show that it belongs to the lower-case *a*." (Write a capital *A* on overhead.)

11. "Do you have any questions about what you are supposed to do?"

12. "Let's begin. Write the capital letter for each lower-case letter on your paper."

Students' Response Form

II.F.2 Writing Capital Letters for Given Lower-Case Letters

Name _____   Date _____

a _____   b _____   c _____   d _____   e _____

f _____   g _____   h _____   i _____   j _____

k _____   l _____   m _____   n _____   o _____

p _____   q _____   r _____   s _____   t _____

u _____   v _____   w _____   x _____   y _____

z _____

FIGURE 9.6F

Sample Checklist for Assessing Students' Ability to Bounce a Ball while Standing Still

BOUNCING PLAYGROUND BALL WHILE STANDING STILL				
Name _____	Date ___ Yes No	Date ___ Yes No	Date ___ Yes No	Date ___ Yes No
A. Getting ready				
1. Minor hand supporting underneath	— —	— —	— —	— —
2. Dominant hand over	— —	— —	— —	— —
3. Dominant hand relaxed, fingers curved	— —	— —	— —	— —
B. Release				
1. Remove minor hand	— —	— —	— —	— —
2. Push with "fingers" of dominant hand	— —	— —	— —	— —
3. Force adequate to rebound ball to waist	— —	— —	— —	— —
4. Ball bounces about 6 inches ahead of dominant foot	— —	— —	— —	— —
C. Bounce				
1. Dominant hand aligned above ball	— —	— —	— —	— —
2. Rising ball meets flexed fingers	— —	— —	— —	— —
3. Fingers "ride" ball to top of rebound	— —	— —	— —	— —
4. Push ball back to ground with flexed fingers	— —	— —	— —	— —
D. Catch ball				
1. Align hands, palms in	— —	— —	— —	— —
2. Hands move toward and ascend with ball	— —	— —	— —	— —
3. Hands move gently into ball	— —	— —	— —	— —
4. Use only fingers and thumb to contact ball	— —	— —	— —	— —

■ R U B R I C

Rubric for Evaluating Assessments for Nonreaders, Limited Readers, and ESOL Students

		GENERAL CRITERIA FOR ALL TEST FORMATS
Yes	**No**	**I. Curriculum-Based Criteria** (directions, scripts, and response forms)
_____	_____	A. Are items/tasks congruent with the conditions, behavior, and content of the task specification?
_____	_____	B. Are criteria task-situation authentic and relevant to curriculum and environment?
		II. Learner-Centered Criteria (directions, scripts, and response forms)
_____	_____	A. Are directions and items/tasks congruent with the language (including ESOL), context, developmental level, and special needs of learners?
_____	_____	B. Are items free from biasing material related to gender, cultural/ethnic groups, and religious and political ideas?
		III. School-Based Criteria (feasibility)
_____	_____	A. Are development and administration time available related to teacher-student ratio?
_____	_____	B. Is turnaround time available from test administration to score reporting?
_____	_____	C. Are resources available for test development, administration, scoring, and reporting?
		IV. Professional-Based Criteria (directions, scripts, and response forms)
		A. Are directions and tasks clear related to:
_____	_____	1. Grammar?
_____	_____	2. Spelling?
_____	_____	3. Expression?
_____	_____	4. Order of information?
_____	_____	B. Are tasks creative and interesting?
_____	_____	C. Are materials and procedures professional appearing?
_____	_____	D. Is the task(s) likely to yield accurate measures?
		E. Ethics related to test development:
_____	_____	1. Best items possible within your resources?
_____	_____	2. Students' opportunities to "share" answers within and across your classes are limited?
_____	_____	3. Includes enough items and instruments to allow formative as well as summative evaluation?
_____	_____	4. Provisions made to evaluate the quality of your assessments and instruction using students' performance data?
		F. Ethics related to administration and use:
_____	_____	1. Tests not administered as a substitute for inadequate lesson preparation?
_____	_____	2. Tests not used as rewards or punishments for classroom behavior?
_____	_____	3. Tests and grades not used as a means of controlling students' behavior?
_____	_____	4. Tests not used to punish an unruly or unprepared student or class?

CRITERIA FOR LIMITED READER (INCLUDING ESOL) TEACHER SCRIPTS, STUDENTS RESPONSE FORM, AND PROCEDURES		

Yes	No	**I. Teacher's Scripts**
____	____	A. Are scripts provided for the assessment?
____	____	B. Do scripts contain incorporated pauses to allow for student work?
____	____	C. Do scripts contain repetition to allow for better understanding?
____	____	D. Do scripts contain sample items to clarify the task for students?
____	____	E. Is information presented in the recommended order ([1] where to look, [2] what they will see, [3] description of the skill to be measured, [4] how to respond)?
____	____	F. Are scripts translated into home language for ESOL students Levels 1, 2, and 3?

		II. Criteria for Response Form: Does the response form contain:
____	____	A. Spaces for name, date, test title reflecting skill, and score?
____	____	B. Locator symbols that are familiar to the group?
____	____	C. Locator symbols, manipulative materials, illustrations, response sets, etc., that match the information provided on the teacher's script?
____	____	D. Response sets that are clearly distinguishable?
____	____	E. Response sets with one clearly best answer?

		III. Criteria for Administering Tests to Individuals: Does the administrator:
____	____	A. Greet the student and put him or her at ease?
____	____	B. Introduce and demonstrate the skill to be assessed?
____	____	C. Ensure the student understands the directions?
____	____	D. Pace the test according to the student's ability to follow?
____	____	E. Record all responses, not marking response accuracy during the test?
____	____	F. Refrain from verbal or nonverbal coaching during the test?
____	____	G. Maintain a pleasant, patient, accepting demeanor throughout the test?
____	____	H. Answer all students' questions that do not lead to revealing the answer?

		IV. Criteria for Tests for Limited Readers: Do the test forms:
____	____	A. Contain simple sentences?
____	____	B. Contain objective item formats that require less reading and writing (unless it is a reading or writing test)?
____	____	C. Contain type size appropriate for the students' development/needs?
____	____	D. Appear *not* to have ample space?
____	____	E. Assess a limited number of enabling skills (attention span)?

(continued)

■ RUBRIC   Continued

_____ _____		**V. Administering Tests for Limited Readers: Does the administrator:**
_____ _____		A. Keep the group together during the test?
_____ _____		B. Read each item aloud for the students?
_____ _____		C. Build repetition into the reading of the items?
_____ _____		D. Build pauses into the reading of the items?
_____ _____		E. Pace the test appropriately, allowing students time to respond?
_____ _____		F. Maintain good order and a good testing environment for students?

SUGGESTED READINGS

Cook, R. E., Tessier, A., & Klein, M. D. (1996). *Adapting early childhood curricula for children in inclusive settings* (4th ed., pp. 101–124, 127–136). Columbus, OH: Merrill.

González, J., & Darling-Hammond, L. (1997*). New concepts for new challenges: Professional development for teachers of immigrant youth.* Washington, DC: Center for Applied Linguistics

Ittenbach, R. F. (1997). Assessment and exceptional children. In R. M. Thorndike (Ed.), *Measurement and evaluation in psychology and education* (6th ed., pp. 394–418). Columbus, OH: Merrill.

Kubiszyn, T., & Borich, G. (2000). *Educational testing and measurement* (6th ed., pp. 417–478). New York: John Wiley & Sons.

Polloway, E. A., & Patton, J. R. (1997). *Strategies for teaching learners with special needs* (6th ed.). Columbus, OH: Merrill.

Schlam, L., & Cafetz, S. (1977). Using portfolios with language minority students. In R. B. Weiner & J. H. Cohen (Eds.), *Literacy portfolios* (pp. 288–304). Columbus, OH: Merrill.

Soodak, L. (1977). Using portfolios with students who have learning and behavioral-emotional problems. In R. B. Weiner & J. H. Cohen (Eds.), *Literacy portfolios* (pp. 260–284). Columbus, OH: Merrill.

Tombari, M., & Borich, G. (1999). *Authentic assessment in the classroom.* Columbus, OH: Merrill.

Wortham, S. C. (1995). *Measurement and evaluation in early childhood education* (2nd ed., pp. 149–176). Columbus, OH: Merrill.

Worthen, B. R., White, K. R., Fan, X., & Sudweeks, R. L. (1999). *Measurement and assessment in schools* (2nd ed., pp. 504–524). New York: Addison-Wesley Longman.

Evaluating Group Performance

- Set expectations for the distribution of test scores, measures of central tendency, and measures of variability based on
  a. The complexity of the tasks measured
  b. The achievement characteristics of the group
  c. The perceived quality of the instruction and the test
- Describe the group's performance by
  a. Creating a frequency distribution
  b. Calculating measures of central tendency
  c. Calculating measures of variability
- Evaluate the group's performance by comparing the anticipated to the calculated measures.

After you have administered and scored your test, you are ready to evaluate a group's performance. To evaluate performance, you need to calculate several measures of the group's performances and then compare these measures with criteria and standards you establish. You need to answer one basic question: Are these measures reasonable given the circumstances? There are four main factors to consider when establishing criteria for judging the reasonableness of the measures, including:

1. The complexity of the tasks measured
2. The achievement characteristics of the group
3. The quality of the instruction
4. The quality of the test

The first two factors are relatively fixed; that is, your instruction is not likely to change the nature of the task or the characteristics of the group. However, the quality of your instruction and test can make a difference in how students perform.

When estimating levels of performance, teachers generally assume that their instruction was effective and their test was good. Therefore, expectations for group performance are set using only the complexity of the tasks and the group's characteristics. Should the group's performance not meet the expected levels, then the instruction and test are usually reviewed to locate the cause for the discrepancy.

Three main areas of indicators are used to describe a group's test performance: (1) location and shape of the raw score distribution; (2) measures of central tendency, including the mean, median, and mode; and (3) measures of variability, including the range and standard deviation. The following sections present procedures for calculating and interpreting these measures to describe a group's performance. In addition, there are procedures for identifying criteria and setting standards for evaluating a group's performance. Practically speaking, calculating these group performance indicators by hand is tedious and unnecessary. However, basic paper-and-pencil methods are illustrated to ensure that you understand the logic behind the indices. Without this understanding, your ability to interpret the data would be affected. Whenever possible, obtain these indices from machine-scoring services or spread sheets and spend your time interpreting rather than calculating. When machine scoring is not feasible, use an inexpensive hand calculator with the capacity to compute measures of central tendency and variability from raw scores.

■ Describing the Distribution of Test Scores

To describe the distribution of test scores, you can use either a frequency table or a frequency polygon.

Creating a Frequency Table

Table 10.1 shows a frequency table for hypothetical objective test scores. The first column lists all the possible scores, starting with the highest and ending with the lowest. A second column indicates the number of times each score occurs. The third column indicates frequencies, or the total number of times each score appears. Notice that the term *raw score* and the symbol X are used to represent the number of items each student answered correctly. These widely accepted terms are used to represent students' individual scores throughout the chapter. Summarizing the scores on such a table will permit you to determine the highest and lowest scores quickly and to identify the score distribution pattern.

Creating a Frequency Polygon

A *frequency polygon* is a graph that provides the same information as a frequency table. Plotting a graph of the frequency of scores will help you determine the shape of the distribution, which you can then use to interpret the results. A frequency polygon has a horizontal axis and a vertical axis placed at right angles to each other. Each point on the horizontal axis represents a possible raw score, and each point on the vertical axis represents the frequency or the number of times each score occurs. To complete the graph, place a dot at the intersection of each raw score and its frequency. Figure 10.1 shows how the frequency of one score is plotted. The dot at the inter-

TABLE 10.1

Frequency Distribution of Objective Test Scores

	Raw Scores X	Tally	Frequency
Highest Possible Score	20	ЖТ	5
	19	III	3
	18	II	2
	17	II	2
	16	II	2
	15	III	3
	14	I	1
	13	I	1
	12	I	1
	•		
Lowest Possible Score	• 0		

section of a raw score of 5 on the horizontal axis and the frequency 4 on the vertical axis indicates that 4 students in the group answered 5 of 20 items correctly.

After you have plotted the frequency of each raw score, connect the dots to complete the polygon, as shown in Figure 10.2. This graph indicates that (1) everyone in the group answered more than eight and fewer than twenty items correctly, (2) one person correctly answered nine items and two correctly answered ten items, and (3) thirteen correct items was the most frequently earned score.

Figure 10.3 contains a frequency polygon for the raw scores summarized in Table 10.1. The slashes at the beginning of the horizontal axis indicate that no students earned raw scores from 0 to 11. The graph begins with a raw score of 12 and ends with 20, the maximum score possible.

Table 10.1 and Figure 10.3 both illustrate the distribution of raw scores for the class. To interpret this distribution, you need to understand the different shapes that distributions can take and what these shapes indicate.

General Shapes of Test Score Distributions

A test score distribution reflects one of several commonly observed shapes. It can be *symmetrical, skewed, unimodal, bimodal,* or *multimodal.* The normal distribution (sometimes called the *bell-shaped curve*), the rectangular distribution, and the U-shaped distribution illustrated in Figure 10.4 are all symmetrical. In a normal distribution, most scores are near the center of the distribution. The low and high ends of the score scale contain very small frequencies of scores. The rectangular distribution, while also symmetrical, indicates that an equal number of students received each score. There is no common area of performance. In the U-shaped distribution, a large

FIGURE   10.1

Plotting the Frequencies of Raw Scores

FIGURE   10.2

Completed Frequency Polygon

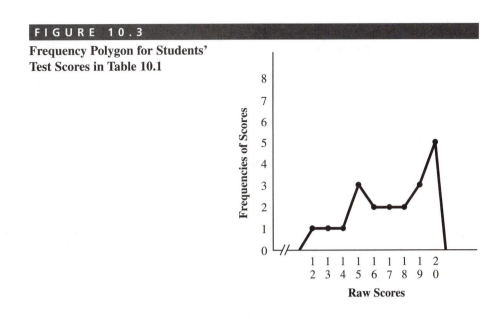

FIGURE 10.3

Frequency Polygon for Students' Test Scores in Table 10.1

FIGURE 10.4

Symmetrically Shaped Test Score Distributions

Normal Distribution (Bell-Shaped Curve)   Rectangular Distribution   U-Shaped Curve

number of scores occur at the low and the high ends, but none or few occur in the middle of the distribution.

In a skewed distribution, more scores occur at either the high or low end of the score scale. When most scores occur at the high end of the scale, the distribution is *negatively skewed.* Notice that in the negatively skewed distribution in Figure 10.5, the highest frequencies appear to the right of the midpoint on the raw score scale. If the curve were folded in half at the midpoint, the two sides of the distribution would not be equal. A negatively skewed distribution indicates that more students received high scores than low scores. For this reason, it is sometimes called a *mastery curve.*

A distribution in which most scores appear toward the lower end of the score scale is *positively skewed.* A positively skewed distribution is illustrated to the right

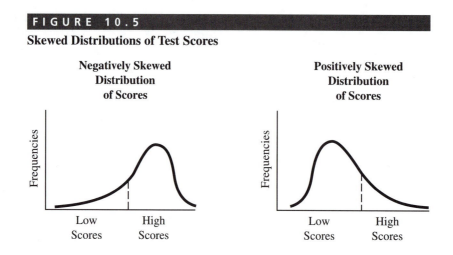

FIGURE 10.5

Skewed Distributions of Test Scores

in Figure 10.5. Such a distribution indicates that a test was difficult for most of the class.

Distributions can also be unimodal, bimodal, or multimodal. The raw score that occurs most frequently in a distribution is called the *mode*. If only one score appears most frequently, the distribution is unimodal. The bell-shaped curve in Figure 10.4 and the skewed distributions in Figure 10.5 are examples of unimodal distributions. If two scores, some distance from each other on the scale, have higher frequencies than the scores surrounding them, the distribution is bimodal. The center distribution in Figure 10.6 represents a bimodal curve. The right-hand illustration represents a multimodal distribution in which more than two scores have atypically high frequencies compared to the scores around them.

Interpreting a Score Distribution Using Its Location and Shape

To interpret test results, consider both the location and the shape of the distribution on the raw score scale. The distribution can spread out across the range of possible test scores, or it can cover only a small portion of the scale. Tall, narrow shapes indicate homogeneous group performance; a wide distribution of scores reflects heterogeneous performance. High, narrow distributions located at the upper end of the score scale represent high achievement; those toward the lower end of the scale suggest inadequate achievement. Consider the shapes and locations of the score distributions in Figure 10.7. Although all three distributions are unimodal, bell-shaped curves, each reflects a different level of performance. The distribution in Example A is short and wide, reflecting heterogeneous group performance. The one in Example B is high and narrow and located toward the high end of the scale, indicating homogeneous, high test performance. Such a distribution suggests that the group was made up of high-achieving students, or that the skills tested were very easy for the group, or that the instruction was very effective. The distribution in Example C is also tall and

Unimodal, Bimodal, and Multimodal Distributions of Test Scores

Width and Location of Score Distributions

narrow but located toward the lower end of the scale. This distribution indicates that the group contained low-achieving students, or that the skills tested were too complex for the group, or that the test, the instruction, or both were inadequate.

Evaluating a Group's Performance Using the Score Distribution

In order to use the observed score distribution to evaluate a group's performance, you need to judge whether the observed distribution is reasonable, given the circumstances. Two factors can be used to establish reasonable levels of performance: the complexity of the tasks measured by the test and the achievement characteristics of the group. Using your perceptions related to these two factors, estimate a reasonable score distribution for the situation. When the distribution you observe does not resemble one you anticipate, investigate the cause.

Consider the class that took the test illustrated in Figure 10.3. Suppose that based on their previous achievement the class was described as heterogeneous, and the skills measured by the test were described as relatively easy. In this case, you would expect to see a relatively wide distribution of scores to reflect the group's heterogeneity. However, since the tasks were considered relatively easy, the shape should be negatively skewed. Now, review the distribution obtained for the test in Figure 10.3. As expected, the distribution is relatively wide. It is also located in the top half of the raw score scale, making it negatively skewed. This means that the instruction was effective and the test good, as anticipated.

A score distribution considered reasonable for one group may not be acceptable for another. For example, if the class taking the test contained only high achievers, the teacher would undoubtedly be disappointed with the score distribution in Figure 10.3. Instead of this shape, the teacher would have expected a narrow, tall distribution located toward the high end of the scale. This mismatch between the anticipated and obtained distributions would cause the teacher to question the instruction and test.

■ Using Measures of Central Tendency

Measures of central tendency that identify the center of a score distribution include the mean and the median. The *mean* is a group's average raw score. The *median* is the central point in the distribution of scores that divides the group in half, with one-half the group earning scores above the median point and one-half the group earning scores below the median point.

Relating the Mean and Median to the Distribution of Scores

To interpret measures of central tendency, compare (1) the relative positions of the mean and median in the distribution, (2) their distance from the highest earned score, and (3) their distance from the highest possible raw score.

The illustrations in Figure 10.8 show the relative positions of the mean and median in three distributions. In Example A, which is normal and symmetrical, the mean and median occupy the same central point. In a negatively skewed distribution, like the one in Example B, the atypically low scores in the group produce a mean lower than the median. A positively skewed distribution, as the one in Example C, has a few extremely high scores that raise the mean above the median. These illustrations show that the mean is influenced by the size of each raw score in the distribution, whereas the median is not. Extreme scores raise or lower the mean, but they have no effect on the median. In the latter case, very high or very low scores are simply scores, regardless of their values. The relative position of the mean and median in a distribution helps you determine whether its shape is symmetrical or skewed, and if skewed, in what direction.

To assess the difficulty of a test for a group, compare the mean, the highest earned score, and the highest possible raw score for the test. When the mean is relatively close to the highest earned score, you have evidence that the overall group's performance was rather similar. Additionally, when the highest earned score is the same as, or close

FIGURE 10.8
Relative Positions of the Mean and Median in Score Distributions

A	B	C
Bell-Shaped Curve	**Negatively Skewed Distribution**	**Positively Skewed Distribution**

Mean ——————
Median --------

to, the highest possible score, you have evidence that the group performed similarly and well on the test. This situation is illustrated in Example A of Figure 10.9.

When the mean score is close to the highest earned score (X_H), yet the highest earned score is quite a bit below the highest possible score, then a different interpretation would result. This finding would indicate that the group's performance was rather homogeneous and that the test was rather difficult. This situation is illustrated in Example B of Figure 10.9.

Another pattern could emerge in which the highest earned and the highest possible scores were the same, or similar, yet the mean score was quite a bit below them on the scale. This result, illustrated in Example C, would tend to reflect heterogeneous group performance on relatively complex tasks.

Evaluating a Group's Performance

To evaluate the group's performance using measures of central tendency, you need to estimate reasonable values for the mean and median and compare the estimated scores with those observed. In deciding what to expect, you should again consider the difficulty of the tasks measured and the achievement characteristics of the group. For example, if you have a homogeneous group of high achievers and relatively complex tasks, then you would expect to find the mean and median relatively close to the highest possible score. When the tasks measured are judged to be relatively easy for such a group, you might expect to see these scores located even closer to the highest possible score. Your expected mean and median would be lower for a homogeneous, average group and even lower for a homogeneous, below-average group. When setting expectations for the mean and median, you should select an area in which these scores will fall rather than particular scores because estimating precise scores would be very difficult. When the mean and median fall outside a reasonable area, you have reason to question the instruction and test.

Now, use the measures of central tendency to evaluate the group's performance on the test illustrated in Table 10.1 and Figure 10.3. As previously described, the

FIGURE 10.9

Describing a Group's Performance Using the Mean, Highest Earned Score, and Highest Possible Score on a Test

A   Total possible points = 50
Highest earned score (X_H) = 50
Mean score ($\overline{X}$) = 43 (86%)

Raw
Scores
| | | | | | |
0   10   20   30   40   50

B   Total possible points = 50
Highest earned score (X_H) = 43 (86%)
Mean score ($\overline{X}$) = 38 (76%)

Raw
Scores
0   10   20   30   40   50

C   Total possible points = 50
Highest earned score (X_H) = 50 (100%)
Mean score ($\overline{X}$) = 38 (76%)

Raw
Scores
0   10   20   30   40   50

group is heterogeneous, and most of the tasks are relatively easy. These two factors would lead you to anticipate that:

1. The mean and median will be relatively close to the highest earned and the highest possible scores.
2. The mean will be lower than the median to reflect the anticipated negatively skewed curve.

The calculated mean is 17.15 and the median is 17.5. Comparing the mean (17.15) and the median (17.5) with the highest earned score (20) and the highest possible score (20), you find that the obtained scores fall within the area anticipated. Comparing the relative positions of the mean and median, you find that the mean is lower than the median, which reflects the anticipated negatively skewed distribution. Therefore, the measures of central tendency reflect that the group's performance on the capitalization test is reasonable given the circumstances.

Calculating the Mean and Median

Today, schools often provide scoring services that automatically calculate indices of central tendency and include them with score reports. Teachers who do not have these services available can instead obtain indices of central tendency automatically from their computer-based gradebooks. Most electronic gradebooks create a variety of test reports that include both histograms and measures of central tendency. Other teachers calculate the indices using the statistical functions within their spreadsheet programs. Although the likelihood of having to hand calculate group performance measures is small, you will be most comfortable interpreting the indices for yourself and others if you are completely clear about how they are derived.

To calculate the mean for a set of raw scores, add all the scores together and divide the sum by the number of students in the group. For example, if raw scores for a group of five students were 5, 6, 7, 8, and 9, you would calculate the mean as follows:

1. Add	2. Divide	
5	$\frac{35}{5} = 7$	7 is the mean score for the set of scores.
6		
7		
8		
+ 9		
35		

The following formula is used to represent this calculation:

$$\overline{X} = \frac{\sum X}{N}$$

In the formula, the symbol $\overline{X}$ represents the mean; the symbol Σ means to sum the raw scores, represented by X; and N is the number of scores, or students, in the group.

The median is a point that divides the distribution of scores in half. You can approximate a median by locating the middle score in an ordered set of scores. For example, the median for the scores 5, 6, 7, 8, and 9 is the middle score, or 7. For an uneven number of scores, the median is simply the middle score. The median for an even number of scores is a point halfway between the two middle scores. For example, the median for the scores 5, 6, 7, 8, 9, and 10 is halfway between 7 and 8, which are the two middle scores. Thus, the median for this set of scores is 7.5.

When there are several tied scores in a distribution, calculating the median is a bit more complex. In this situation, each score is considered to extend .5 point below and .5 point above the actual scores. For example, a score of 18 would extend from 17.5 to 18.5. The score 17.5 is called the *lower real limit* for the observed score 18. The median is calculated using the following formula:

$$\text{Median} = L + \frac{\frac{N}{2} - \text{Sum of students below the score containing the median}}{\text{Frequency of students at the score containing the median}}$$

where:

L = The lower real limit of the raw score containing the median
N = The number of students in the group

FIGURE 1 0 . 1 0

Calculating the Median

X	f	
20	I	1. The number in the group is 26 and half this number is 13. Therefore, the median will divide the scores such that 13 scores are below and above it.
19	I	
18	III	2. Count from the bottom of the distribution to locate the raw score that contains the thirteenth and fourteenth scores. In this example, the raw score 16 contains these scores.
17	IIII	
16	JHT	3. The median is then calculated using the formula:
15	IIII	
14	III	$$\text{Median} = 15.5 + \frac{\frac{26}{2} - 12}{5} = 15.5 + \frac{1}{5} = 15.5 + .20 = 15.70$$
13	II	
12	I	
11	I	
10	I	
N = 26		

Figure 10.10 illustrates the use of this formula to calculate the median for a set of scores.

Now, review the data for the test in Table 10.1 and calculate the mean and median. To find the mean, add all the raw scores together (ΣX). You should have five scores of 20, three scores of 19, two scores of 18, and so on. Next, divide the sum of the scores by 20, the number of students in the group. Your calculation should look like this:

1. Sum scores.

    20 + 20 + 20 + 20 + 20 + 19 + 19 + 19 + 18 + 18 + 17 + 17 +
    16 + 16 + 15 + 15 + 15 + 14 + 13 + 12 = 343

2. Divide the sum by the number of students.

$$\overline{X} = \frac{343}{20} = 17.15$$

The group's average score on the test is 17.15.

You may have already concluded that multiplying each raw score by its frequency and then adding the products is a faster way to obtain ΣX. Whenever you use a frequency table to calculate a mean, you can save time by doing some simple multiplication, as illustrated in Figure 10.11

Because there is an even number of scores (20), the median will be halfway between the two middle scores. The tenth score from the top of the distribution is 18, and the tenth score from the bottom is 17. Thus, the median is halfway between 18 and 17, or 17.5.

FIGURE 10.11

Calculating the Mean and Median Using a Frequency Table

1. Multiply each score by its frequency and sum the products.

Raw Scores X		Frequency f		Product f X
20	×	5	=	100
19	×	3	=	57
18	×	2	=	36
Median → 17	×	2	=	34
16	×	2	=	32
15	×	3	=	45
14	×	1	=	14
13	×	1	=	13
12	×	1	=	12
		ΣX =		343

2. Divide ΣX by the number of students (20) to obtain the mean value.

$$\overline{X} = \frac{343}{20} = 17.15$$

3. Count up and down the *Frequency* column to locate the point where 10 students' scores fall above it and 10 students' scores fall below it. In this example, the median is 17.5, or one-half the distance between the raw scores of 17 and 18.

■ Using Measures of Variability

The variability of performance among students in the group is indicated by the range and standard deviation. The range is the difference between the two extreme scores, and the standard deviation is a measure of how widely the scores in a group differ from the average score. Both measures reflect the amount that individual performances differ and thus describe the homogeneity or heterogeneity of a group's performance.

Interpreting the Range

One caution should be made about using the range to interpret a group's performance. Because the range is based only on the two extreme scores in a set, an atypical high or low score for the group will distort your interpretation. Atypical scores are called *outliers;* they reflect the performance of an atypical student rather than overall group performance. Thus, before calculating and interpreting the range, determine that the high and low scores are not extreme compared to the other scores in the distribution. If you find an outlier score on either end of your distribution, eliminate it and calculate the range using the next closest score to it in the set.

There are some rules of thumb you can use to interpret a range. A range that covers about one-quarter or less of the total raw score scale generally reflects homogeneous performance. Thus, if a test contains 40 items and the range is about 10, then the group's performance can be considered homogeneous. As the width of the range increases, so does the heterogeneity of the performance. A range spanning about one-third of the raw score scale indicates a somewhat heterogeneous group performance; one that spans about one-half or more of the raw score scale signals a very heterogeneous group performance. Therefore, for a 40-item test, a range of about 13 (or one-third of 40) would reflect somewhat heterogeneous group performance; a range of about 20 would reflect very heterogeneous performance.

As previously noted, the group's achievement characteristics and the complexity of the tasks measured should be considered when using the range to evaluate a group's performance on a given test. Again considering the data from the test in Figure 10.11, you would expect to see a range that spans between one-third to one-half the raw score scale because the group was previously described as heterogeneous. One-third of the raw score scale is 6.6, or 20 (items) divided by 3. The observed range is 9, or 20 minus 12 plus 1. Therefore, the observed range comes close to the expected range, indicating that the group's performance is heterogeneous. Like the performance indicators previously described, the range reflects that the group's overall test performance was as anticipated.

Interpreting the Standard Deviation

Two factors influence the size of the standard deviation: the range and the distribution of scores within the range. Because both the range and the standard deviation are measures of a group's variability, larger ranges will produce larger standard deviations. A wide range and standard deviation both reflect heterogeneous performance, and narrow ones reflect performances that are more similar.

For a given range size, the size of the corresponding standard deviation will vary based on the distribution of scores within the range. For example, the ranges and mean scores are the same in the score distributions illustrated in Figure 10.12, yet the score patterns within these distributions are very different. These different score patterns produce different standard deviations.

Most scores are close to the mean score in the rather bell-shaped curve in example A. In distributions in which there is a short distance between the mean and most other scores in the set, the standard deviation will be small for the range. A relatively small standard deviation for a given range reflects rather similar performance for most students in the group. The scores in the rectangular distribution, illustration B, are farther from the mean. The standard deviation for such a distribution will be larger than one for a distribution in which most of the scores are clustered in one area. A rectangular distribution reflects heterogeneous performance within the range with no area of similar performance. The bimodal, U-shaped distribution in example C produces the largest standard deviation because the distance between the mean and other scores in the set is greater. This distribution reflects two divergent groups within the class.

FIGURE 10.12

Three Score Distribution Shapes Having the Same Mean and Range but Different Standard Deviations

A
Bell-Shaped Curve
$\bar{X} = 15$
$R = 10$
SD = 1.92

B
Rectangular Distribution
$\bar{X} = 15$
$R = 10$
SD = 2.92

C
U-Shaped Curve
$\bar{X} = 15$
$R = 10$
SD = 5

You can estimate the distribution of scores within the range using a few quick calculations and comparisons. The largest possible standard deviation for any given range is the range divided by two. Such a large standard deviation would reflect a U-shaped distribution (see example C in Figure 10.12). Although so large a standard deviation is unlikely, you can use this figure as a basis of comparison for the obtained standard deviation value. The following rules will help you determine the variability of a group's performance within the range.

1. A standard deviation close to one-half of the range indicates that the group's performance is very diverse within the range.
2. A standard deviation close to one-third of the range reflects scores that are dispersed throughout the range.
3. A standard deviation spanning one-quarter or less of the range indicates that most scores are clustered within an area.

For example, if the range were 20, an observed standard deviation approaching one-half this value, or 10, reflects two diverse groups in the class. An observed standard deviation of around 6.6, or one-third of the range, reflects a more even distribution of scores throughout the range. However, a standard deviation of about 5 or less, one-quarter of the range, reflects a majority of scores clustered within an area.

Evaluating a Group's Performance

To evaluate a group's performance using the range and standard deviation, you should first decide what values you expect. Using the previously obtained information for the test data in Table 10.1 and Figure 10.3, you would undoubtedly expect a standard deviation somewhere around one-third to one-quarter of the range because, although the group is heterogeneous, the tasks were relatively easy. Given the range of 8 for the test, you would expect the standard deviation to be between 2.66 and 2, rather than between 2.66 and 4. Once you have selected an area for the standard deviation, you should compare it with the one obtained. The standard deviation calculated for the test is 2.48 and the expected standard deviation is about 2.66. Therefore, the scores are distributed as anticipated and reflect the heterogeneous nature of the group on relatively easy tasks.

Machine-scoring services, electronic gradebooks, and spreadsheet programs eliminate the tedium of calculating measures of central tendency and variability. These scores are provided on the computer printouts of student performance and need only be compared with those you anticipate.

Calculating the Range

Some measurement specialists define the range (R) as the difference between the highest score and the lowest score earned on a test. The formula for this calculation is:

$$Range\ (R) = X_H - X_L$$

Other specialists define the range as including all observed scores in the set. Using this definition, the formula for calculating the range is:

$$R = (X_H - X_L) + 1$$

The latter procedure ensures that the range extends to include all scores. For example, if the highest observed raw score on a test is 28 and the lowest is 12, then the range would be:

$$R = 28 - 12 = 16$$
$$R = (28 - 12) + 1 = 17$$

Whether you use the first or second calculation method is a matter of personal choice, although most teachers use the first one. For all practical purposes, the interpretation of the index would be the same.

Calculating the Standard Deviation

Because all scores in the distribution and the mean are used in calculating the standard deviation, the procedure is more complex. It involves the following series of steps:

1. Calculate the mean score ($\overline{X}$).
2. Subtract the mean score from each raw score (X) to find the deviation score (x).
3. Square each deviation score (x^2).
4. Add together all the squared deviation scores (Σx^2).
5. Divide the sum by the number of scores (N).
6. Find the square root of the quotient.

The formula for calculating the standard deviation is:

$$\sigma = \sqrt{\frac{\sum (X - \overline{X})^2}{N}} \quad \text{or} \quad s = \sqrt{\frac{\sum (X - \overline{X})^2}{N - 1}}$$

The first formula, using the symbol σ for the standard deviation and N in the denominator of the formula, is used when the group tested is the target population, which typically is the case for classroom teachers. The second formula, using the symbol s for the standard deviation and $N - 1$ in the denominator, is used when the group tested represents only a sample of the target population rather than the population itself. For the purpose of describing the variability of students' performance on a classroom test, it does not matter whether you use the population or the sample formula. The difference between the indices obtained using the two formulas will be negligible and not cause you to reach a different conclusion about the variability of your class on a test. The second formula, for a sample, is the one usually contained in calculators and spreadsheet programs.

Although the procedure for calculating the standard deviation appears complicated, you can easily master it with practice. Moreover, most hand calculators can automatically square numbers and calculate square roots.

Working through an example will help you understand the procedure. Given a set of five raw scores (5, 6, 7, 8, and 9), rank and list the scores from highest to lowest. Next, add all the scores and divide by the number of scores to obtain the mean. The sum of the five scores is 35, and the mean is 7, or 35 divided by 5. The next step is to calculate the deviation score (x), and the easiest way to do this is to set up a table of columns as follows:

Raw Scores (X)		Mean ($\overline{X}$)		Deviation Scores x
9	–	7	=	2
8	–	7	=	1
7	–	7	=	0
6	–	7	=	–1
5	–	7	=	–2

Notice that the mean score, 7, is subtracted from each raw score. The resulting differences are the deviation scores.

The reason for the next step, squaring each deviation score, now becomes obvious. The sum of 2, 1, 0, –1, and –2 is 0. Zero divided by the number of scores is also 0. To eliminate this problem, change all the negative deviation scores to positive numbers by squaring each score. Next, the squared deviations should be summed to obtain Σx^2. Your calculations should appear as follows:

$(X - \overline{X})$	x	x^2
9 – 7	2	4
8 – 7	1	1
7 – 7	0	0
6 – 7	–1	1
5 – 7	–2	4
	$\Sigma x^2 =$	10

Now you can calculate the standard deviation using the formula:

$$\sigma = \sqrt{\frac{\sum (X - \overline{X})^2}{N}}$$

You already have the numerator, 10, which is the sum of your x^2 column. Divide 10 by 5, which is the number of scores in the set. Your formula now is:

$$\sigma = \sqrt{\frac{10}{5}} = \sqrt{2} \quad \text{or} \quad s = \sqrt{\frac{10}{4}} = \sqrt{2.5}$$

Use your calculator to find the square root of 2, which is 1.41. This standard deviation of 1.41 for this set of scores is a measure of the distance between the scores and the mean of those scores. Because the computation includes the step where the sum of deviations from the mean is divided by the number of scores, the standard deviation *has the effect of* being the average amount that the scores deviate from the mean.

Table 10.2 presents the calculations needed to figure the standard deviation for the test data illustrated in Figure 10.3. The procedure illustrated is the one typically used when there are several tied scores in a data set. The first column (X) contains each raw score, and the second column (f) indicates the frequency of each raw score. The third column (x) includes the deviation of each raw score from the mean, or $X - \overline{X}$, and the fourth column (x^2) contains the squared deviation scores. The last column (fx^2) includes the squared deviation scores multiplied by the frequency with which each occurs in the data. Summing the fx^2 column, you will obtain the numerator in the formula, or $\Sigma(X - \overline{X})^2$. This sum divided by the number of students in the group yields the value 6.128, and the square root of this value is the standard deviation, or 2.48. If you were to use $N - 1$ as the denominator in the formula, then the standard deviation, s, for the test would be 2.54, a difference of .06 from σ.

An Example

Figure 10.13 contains raw scores for one version of the paragraph unit posttest prescribed in the table of test specifications in Figure 4.2. The objective portion of the posttest contains 43 items covering enabling skills I.A. through IV.F.

Scenario   Some skills measured by the paragraph posttest are relatively easy (recall and discrimination), whereas others are quite complex (evaluation and production). The class that took the test is somewhat heterogeneous, containing average and

TABLE 10.2

**Calculating the Standard Deviation for the Test Data
in Table 10.1 and Figure 10.3**

X	f	x	x^2	fx^2	
20	5	2.85	8.12	40.61	$\sigma = \sqrt{\dfrac{\Sigma(X - \overline{X})^2}{N}}$
19	3	1.85	3.42	10.27	
18	2	.85	.72	1.45	
17	2	−.15	.02	.05	$= \sqrt{\dfrac{122.56}{20}}$
16	2	−1.15	1.32	2.65	
15	3	−2.15	4.62	13.87	
14	1	−3.15	9.92	9.92	$= \sqrt{6.128}$
13	1	−4.15	17.22	17.22	$= 2.48$
12	1	−5.15	26.52	26.52	
			$\Sigma(X - \overline{X})^2 =$	122.56	

FIGURE 10.13

Group Performance Measures for a Paragraph Unit Posttest

$N = 20$

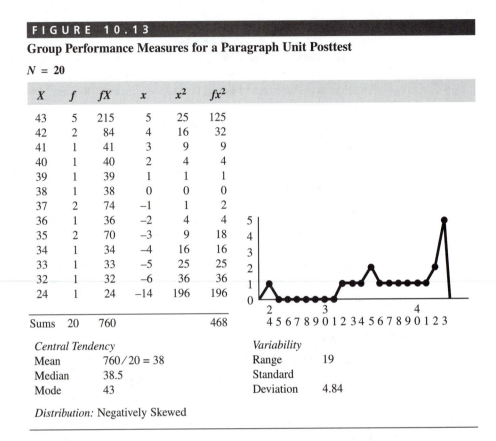

X	f	fX	x	x^2	fx^2
43	5	215	5	25	125
42	2	84	4	16	32
41	1	41	3	9	9
40	1	40	2	4	4
39	1	39	1	1	1
38	1	38	0	0	0
37	2	74	−1	1	2
36	1	36	−2	4	4
35	2	70	−3	9	18
34	1	34	−4	16	16
33	1	33	−5	25	25
32	1	32	−6	36	36
24	1	24	−14	196	196

| Sums | 20 | 760 | | | 468 |

Central Tendency
Mean   760/20 = 38
Median   38.5
Mode   43

Variability
Range   19
Standard
Deviation   4.84

Distribution: Negatively Skewed

above-average students. The class contains one mainstreamed student whose achievement is well below that of other class members. The paragraph posttest was administered following all instruction on paragraphs. The teacher expects the class to perform very well on the exam, with many students earning near perfect scores. A negatively skewed score distribution is anticipated, with the mean score located near the highest score. The mainstreamed student struggled through the instruction and is expected to score much lower than classmates. This student's raw score is expected to affect the mean, range, and standard deviation for the group.

Results   Notice in Figure 10.13 that the class contained 20 students ($N = 20$ or Σf). The raw scores are listed in the far left column, followed by the frequency for each one. Measures of central tendency, the distribution shape, and measures of variability are listed at the bottom of the figure. A frequency polygon of raw scores is also pictured in the figure.

The mean score, 38, represents 88 percent of the items included on the paragraph test ($38 \div 43 = .88$), which indicates that instruction was effective for the majority of the class. The median, 38.5, is higher than the mean, and it reflects a negatively skewed distribution of raw scores. The mode, 43, is a perfect score on the test.

As anticipated, the variability measures were affected by the mainstreamed student whose raw score of 24 could be considered an outlier for the class. The range, 19, is greater than one-third of the items included on the test ($19 \div 43 = .44$) and reflects quite heterogeneous performance. With the lowest score eliminated from calculations, however, the range would be 11. This value is approximately one-quarter of the 43 items, and it more closely reflects the teacher's observations of students' progress during the unit. This difference in ranges was great enough to warrant recalculation of the group's data with the outlier score removed.

Figure 10.14 contains the measures of central tendency and variability recalculated after eliminating the atypical raw score for the mainstreamed student. These modified group performance measures reflect better the overall group's posttest performance. The adjusted mean is 38.74, the median is 39, and the mode remains 43. Even without the mainstreamed student's raw score in the calculations, the distribution remains negatively skewed. The range is now 11, which reflects unanticipated homogeneous performance. The recalculated standard deviation is 3.71 (approximately one-third of the range reflecting the negative skew of raw scores).

Table 10.3 summarizes the group's performance on the paragraph test. The performance indicators are listed in the far left column, and the teacher's estima-

FIGURE 10.14

Paragraph Unit Posttest Data Recalculated after Eliminating Outlier Student's Raw Score

X	f	fX	x	x^2	fx^2
43	5	215	4.26	18.75	90.75
42	2	84	3.26	10.63	21.26
41	1	41	2.26	5.11	5.11
40	1	40	1.26	1.59	1.59
39	1	39	.26	.07	.07
38	1	38	−.74	.55	.55
37	2	74	−1.74	3.03	6.06
36	1	36	−2.74	7.51	7.51
35	2	70	−3.74	13.99	27.98
34	1	34	−4.74	22.47	22.47
33	1	33	−5.74	32.95	32.95
32	1	32	−6.74	45.43	45.43
Sums	**19**	**736**			**261.73**

```
          2           3              4
          4 5 6 7 8 9 0 1 2 3 4 5 6 7 8 9 0 1 2 3
```

Central Tendency
Mean $736 / 19 = 38.74$
Median   39
Mode   43

Variability
Range $43 - 32 = 11$
Standard
Deviation   3.71

Distribution: Negatively Skewed

TABLE 10.3

Summary of the Estimated and Observed Measures of Group Performance on the Paragraph Posttest (Outlier Removed)

Performance Indicator	Estimation Based on Relatively Easy Tasks and a Heterogeneous Group	Observation	Discrepancy
Location of highest earned score	Highest possible score	Highest possible score	None
Location of lowest earned score	Slightly more than half the number of items correct	32 (or 74%) of the items correct	Better than anticipated
Location of mean score	Close to the high end of the distribution	38.42 (or 84% correct)	None
Location of median score	Higher than the mean score	39	None
Location of mode	Toward the top of the scale	At the top of the scale	None
Range	Between one-third and one-half of the total number of items $\frac{43}{3} = 14.3$ $\frac{43}{2} = 21.5$	11	More narrow than anticipated
Standard deviation	Somewhere around one-third of the range $\frac{11}{3} = 3.66$	3.71	None
Distribution shape	Negatively skewed	Negatively skewed	None

tions for the class are listed in the second column. The observed results are listed in the third column, and any discrepancies between the estimated and observed measures are listed in the last column. Comparing the information summarized in the table, you can see that the teacher was very good in synthesizing factors that relate to group preformance since there are only two discrepancies between the estimated and observed measures. This teacher would undoubtedly conclude that the group's test performance was better than expected and very good for a heterogenous class.

◼ Computer Technology

If you have the appropriate automated equipment, computers can save you many hours of scoring time, and they can produce very useful reports for analyzing and evaluating a group's achievement and progress.

Procedures for Scoring a Test

Your tests can be scored by a computer quite easily and quickly if students record their responses to items on *mark sense sheets,* sometimes called *scan sheets,* and your school system provides automated scanning equipment. You create answer keys for scoring students' tests using a blank answer sheet to record the correct answer(s) for each item. Students' answer sheets are read by a scanner, and the answers they select are compared with those on the answer key. When a student's answer matches the answer on the key, the item is counted as correct. When the answer does not match the keyed answer, the distractor chosen is typically printed to facilitate distractor analysis. Through automation, hundreds of answer sheets can be scored and reports produced in a few minutes. Once a test is scored, there are several group performance reports provided, including students' raw scores and percentage correct scores, a histogram of scores, and measures of central tendency and variability.

Computer-based spreadsheets are very handy for calculating measures of central tendency and variability. Teachers who use spreadsheets to score product and performance tests can simply use the statistical functions within the spreadsheet rubric to calculate raw scores, percentage correct scores, and measures of central tendency and variability.

Computer-based gradebooks also can be used to obtain test score distributions as well as measures of central tendency and variability. Once you set up your gradebook by entering students' names, a test name, and raw scores for each student, the program does the rest and produces a variety of test reports that include group performance measures.

Various testing programs will provide printouts (reports) that differ in format, but most will include the standard descriptions of central tendency and variability that you have studied in this chapter. You will appreciate the ease with which the computer manages group performance data for you.

■ Summary

The following outline summarizes the procedure used to describe and evaluate a group's test performance.

    I. Describe and compare test results.
        A. Create a frequency table or frequency polygon of the test scores.
        B. Compare the location of the highest and lowest earned scores with the highest possible score and decide whether they are reasonable, given the complexity of the tasks measured by the test and achievement characteristics of the group.
        C. Calculate and compare measures of central tendency. (This is typically done by computer and not by hand or with a calculator.)
            1. Calculate the mean and note its position in the score distribution.
            2. Locate the median and note its position in the score distribution.

3. Locate any mode (or modes) and note its position in the score distribution.

4. Compare the mean, median, and mode and describe the distribution as being symmetrical or skewed based on these measures.

D. Compare the observed measures of central tendency and their location in the score distribution to those you would expect, given the complexity of the tasks and the achievement characteristics of the group.

E. Calculate and compare the measures of variability. (This is typically done by computer.)

1. Calculate the range.

2. Calculate the standard deviation.

F. Compare the variability measures with those you would expect, given the complexity of the tasks and the group's characteristics.

II. Note any discrepancies between measures you expected and those you observed.

III. Try to explain any discrepancies you find. Discrepancies are usually caused by misjudging the quality of instruction or the test. They are also potentially related to misinterpreting the complexity of the tasks or the group's achievement characteristics.

IV. Judge the group's performance as being better than expected, as expected, or lower than expected.

Computer-based testing programs can be used to score students' tests, calculate measures of central tendency and variability, and plot histograms that graphically represent a group's test performance. Teachers who can interpret these indices and graphics can obtain the information they need for class management from the student performance reports generated by the computer.

■ P R A C T I C E E X E R C I S E S

I. Measures of Central Tendency and Variability

A. Central Tendency

1. What is the name of the average score in a set of test scores?

   a. Mode

   b. Standard deviation

   c. Mean

   d. Median

2. Fifty percent of the scores fall below which point in a distribution?

   a. Mean

   b. Median

   c. Mode

   d. A score half way between the highest and lowest raw score

B. Distributions

Column A contains the location of the mean and median in a distribution of test scores. Column B contains the shapes of score distributions. Match the location of the mean and the median with the corresponding distribution shape.

Column A	Column B
_____ **1.** The mean and median are the same value.	a. Positively skewed
	b. Negatively skewed
_____ **2.** The mean is greater than the median.	c. Symmetrical, bell-shaped
	d. Symmetrical, rectangular
_____ **3.** The median is greater than the mean.	e. Both c and d

C. Variability

Column A describes distributions of scores within a range. Column B lists possible values of the standard deviation for a range of 9. Match each distribution with the standard deviation value that would reflect it.

Column A	Column B
_____ **1.** The majority of the scores in the set are located close to the mean.	a. $\dfrac{9}{2} = 4.5$
_____ **2.** The scores are spread throughout the range.	b. $\dfrac{9}{3} = 3$
_____ **3.** The scores are divided between the upper and lower end of the range reflecting a bimodal, U-shaped distribution.	c. $\dfrac{9}{4} = 2.5$

II. Score Distributions

Examine the following score distributions and name each type:

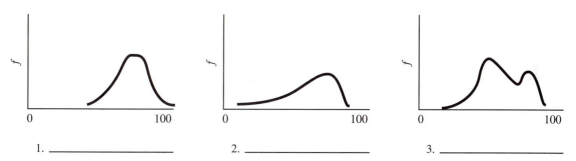

1. _____   2. _____   3. _____

III. Describe Group Performance

Using Figure 10.15 and a spreadsheet program for calculations, calculate group performance measures for a compound sentence posttest. There is a total of 42 items on this version of the posttest covering 12 enabling skills (III.A. through IV.F.). Check your work in the Feedback section.

IV. Enrichment

Use a test you have developed and administered to complete the following exercises:
1. Use information about the complexity of the tasks measured and the achievement characteristics of the group to estimate the group's performance. You should estimate:
   a. The areas in which the highest and lowest raw scores will occur.
   b. The area between the highest and the lowest scores in which the mean will be located.

FIGURE 10.15

Group Performance Measures for a Compound Sentence Unit Posttest

X	f	fX	x	x^2	fx^2
42	2				
41	2				
40	5				
39	2				
38	1				
37	1				
36	1				
35	2				
34	1				
33	1				
31	1				
27	1				

Sums ____ ____   ____

5
4
3
2
1
0
2   3   4
7 8 9 0 1 2 3 4 5 6 7 8 9 0 1 2

Central Tendency   *Variability*
Mean _____   Range ___ (~___% of items)
Median _____   Standard
Mode _____   Deviation ___ (~___% of range)

Distribution: _____

   c. The area in which the median will occur.
   d. The shape of the distribution.
   e. The range.
   f. The standard deviation based on the estimated range.
2. Determine the shape of the distribution, measures of central tendency, and measures of variability.
3. Use the observed measures to describe the group's performance.
4. Compare the anticipated and observed performances and try to explain any discrepancies.
5. If you do not currently use a spreadsheet program, examine one and use it to calculate measures of central tendency and variability.

■ FEEDBACK

I. Measures of Central Tendency and Variability
   A. Central Tendency
      1. c
      2. b

    B. Distributions
        1. e
        2. a
        3. b
    C. Variability
        1. c
        2. b
        3. a

II. Score Distributions
    The score distributions are:
        1. Bell-shaped
        2. Negatively skewed
        3. Bimodal

III. Describe Group Performance
    See Figure 10.16F.

FIGURE 10.16F

Group Performance Measures for a Compound Sentence Unit Posttest

X	f	fX	x	x^2	fx^2
42	2	84	4.5	20.25	40.50
41	2	82	3.5	12.25	24.50
40	5	200	2.5	6.25	31.25
39	2	78	1.5	2.25	4.50
38	1	38	.5	.25	.25
37	1	37	−.5	.25	.25
36	1	36	−1.5	2.25	2.25
35	2	70	−2.5	6.25	12.50
34	1	34	−3.5	12.25	12.25
33	1	33	−4.5	20.25	20.25
31	1	31	−6.5	42.25	42.25
27	1	27	−10.5	110.25	110.25

Sums 20   750   301.00

Central Tendency

Mean   750/20 = 37.5
Median   38.5 + [(20/2 − 9)/2] = 39
Mode   40

Variability

Range   15 (~36% of items)
Standard
Deviation   3.88(σ) (~26% of range)
           3.98(SD)

Distribution: Negatively Skewed

SUGGESTED READINGS

Gallagher, J. D. (1998). *Classroom assessment for teachers* (pp. 355–369). Columbus, OH: Merrill.

Kubiszyn, T., & Borich, G. (2000). *Educational testing and measurement* (6th ed., pp. 223–262). New York: John Wiley & Sons.

Lynn, R. L., & Gronlund, N. E. (2000). *Measurement and assessment in teaching* (8th ed., pp. 507–522). Englewood Cliffs, NJ: Prentice-Hall.

Nitko, A. J. (1996). *Educational assessment of students* (2nd ed., pp. 449–462). Columbus, OH: Merrill.

Popham, W. J. (1999). *Classroom assessment: What teachers need to know* (2nd ed., pp. 66–97). Boston: Allyn and Bacon.

Thorndike, R. M. (1997). *Measurement and evaluation in psychology and education* (6th ed., pp. 23–50). Columbus, OH: Merrill.

Worthen, B. R., White, K. R., Fan, X., & Sudweeks, R. L. (1999). *Measurement and assessment in schools* (2nd ed., pp. 57–92). New York: Addison-Wesley Longman.

Analyzing Test Items, Tasks, and Tests

OBJECTIVES

- Define and interpret indices of item difficulty.
- Define and interpret indices of item discrimination.
- Define and interpret data for an item distractor analysis.
- Define and interpret indices of test internal consistency.
- Evaluate test items and tests.
- Calculate measures of item difficulty and discrimination and test internal consistency reliability.

In developing classroom tests, teachers must synthesize many factors related to the skills to be measured, the instruction delivered, and the characteristics of target students. The tests they develop reflect their perceptions of the best way to measure prescribed skills. Teachers often check their perceptions of the clarity and technical accuracy of items by asking a colleague and a few students to review new items. These reviews help them detect problems and revise the items before administering new tests.

Like classroom teachers, test specialists have content experts and sample students review new items they write. However, they also administer new tests to a large, representative group of students before the tests are finalized. They evaluate a new item using three quality characteristics, including (1) its *difficulty* for the group, (2) its ability to *discriminate* between those students who possess the most knowledge and skill in a domain and those students who possess the least, and (3) its *distractor* plausibility for the group. Using data from these field trials, test specialists usually find problems in the items that were not detected during item reviews. Defective items are then revised or eliminated before a new test is actually used.

Since defective items are commonly found during field trials, it is unfortunate that most teachers do not have the time or resources to conduct such trials before administering new tests in the classroom. Even though defective items cannot always be identified before a test is administered, teachers can use the item analysis procedures used by test specialists to locate defective items after the test is administered. Teachers who simply score, record, and return test papers without performing item analyses are missing opportunities to identify and discount defective items, improve their item-writing skills, and evaluate the quality of their test and instruction.

In spite of the importance of these item analyses for developing quality achievement tests, the technology for enabling classroom teachers to perform item analyses routinely was not available in schools until recently. Most schools today have computer-scoring services for selected-response tests that quickly calculate and summarize the data teachers need to perform item analysis. If computer-scoring services are available in your school, and your class is mature enough to manage a separate answer sheet, use them. When machine scoring is not feasible, item analysis can be performed using a spreadsheet computer program, although it is time consuming and typically not done.

This chapter describes item and test evaluation procedures for selected-response objective tests. The first section explains item difficulty analysis; the second, item discrimination analysis; the third, item distractor analysis; and the fourth, internal consistency measures for the overall test. Finally, the derivation of the indices used for each analysis is explained to aid your interpretation of them on test analysis reports generated by a computer. Classroom teachers typically do not have time to generate item and test data by hand, but relatively little time is required to interpret them from the test evaluation reports once their meaning is clear. Typical item analysis reports are included for practice in using them to evaluate items and tests.

One caution is necessary before beginning this chapter. The illustrations of calculating the various indices use very small numbers of items and students in order to simplify and clarify the calculation procedures. In reality, much larger samples of items and students would be required for the indices to reflect meaningful properties of the items or characteristics of a student group. Even when using these indices for a realistic classroom test and a typical size group, you should be cautious. The item and test data you obtain will differ from group to group due to factors such as differences in the groups' achievement characteristics and differences in instructional activities. Faulty, unclear items, scoring errors, and ineffective tests can often be detected using the data from only one class; therefore, item analysis procedures are appropriate for classroom teachers to use in the development and evaluation of their tests. It would not, however, be appropriate to use test data from one class to make generalizations about other classes or the students in an entire grade level.

▪ Item Difficulty Analysis

The first measure used to evaluate the quality of a test item is its difficulty for the group. The item difficulty index, p, is the proportion or percentage of students in the analysis group who answer the item correctly. Difficulty indices can be interpreted, with those expressed as proportions ranging from .00 to 1.00 and those expressed as percentages ranging from 0 to 100, as follows:

	Very Difficult	Fairly Difficult	Moderately Easy	Very Easy
Proportion	.00–.49	.50–.69	.70–.89	.90–1.00
Percentage	0%–49%	50%–69%	70%–89%	90%–100%

As you can see, the higher the *p* value, or difficulty index, the easier the item is for the group.

Evaluating Items Using the Item Difficulty Index

The *difficulty index* is a *measure* of each item's difficulty for the students tested. This measure can be used to describe the difficulty of the item (e.g., this item is very easy, moderately easy, fairly difficult, or very difficult for this group). It can also be used to evaluate or judge the quality of the item using criteria and standards. Evaluation requires that you identify variables that influence the difficulty index and standards for judging the quality of the item. In essence, you are judging the reasonableness of the measure considering the variables that influence it. When an observed difficulty index does not seem reasonable given the circumstances, then you have evidence to question the quality of the item. The following four variables can be used to evaluate the item using the difficulty index:

1. The complexity of the skill measured
2. The achievement characteristics of the group
3. The comparability of difficulty indices for multiple items that measure the same enabling skill
4. The comparability of difficulty indices for items that measure hierarchically related skills

Skill Complexity   To determine whether an observed difficulty index is reasonable, you should first estimate the complexity of the skill measured by the item and set expectations for the percentage of students likely to answer correctly. For example, if a test item requires students to recall simple verbal information, make a relatively obvious discrimination, or perform a simple calculation, you would expect most of the students to answer the item correctly. If, on the other hand, the item measures a complex skill, some students undoubtedly will miss the item. If many students miss an item you believe measures a simple skill, then you have reason to believe that something is wrong either with the item or with the instruction. Likewise, a very high proportion of correct responses for a relatively complex task may signal the presence of a clue in the item. Therefore, the reasonableness of an observed difficulty index depends in part on the complexity of the skill measured.

The Group's Achievement Characteristics   In addition to the complexity of the skill measured, interpreting difficulty indices requires considering the group's achievement characteristics. Given the same skill complexity and item to measure the skill, you would adjust the anticipated difficulty index depending on whether the group was heterogeneous or homogeneous. The expected proportion of students who answer the item correctly in a very heterogeneous group should be lower than that expected for a homogeneous group of high achievers. The expected difficulty index for a homogeneous, high-achieving group should be higher than one for a homogeneous group of average achievers. Likewise, a homogeneous group of average achievers should have a higher expected difficulty index than a homogeneous group of low-achieving students.

Using information about the complexity of the task measured and about the group's achievement characteristics, you can make decisions about the reasonableness of an observed difficulty index. In a group of high achievers, a large proportion of students would probably answer an item correctly, regardless of task complexity, if instruction was adequate and the item was clearly written. In a group of average achievers, items measuring easy skills would probably produce a high proportion of correct responses; items measuring more complex skills would produce a smaller proportion of right answers. You might expect most students in a group of low achievers to answer complex items incorrectly and to produce high difficulty indices only on very easy questions. Similarly, you would not expect all of the students in a heterogeneous group to answer an item correctly, unless the task was very simple or the item contained a clue. Item difficulty indices that seem unrealistically high, given the task's complexity and the group's characteristics, usually signal clues in the items; those that seem unreasonably low signal either defective items or inadequate instruction.

Multiple Items for the Same Objective   Comparing the difficulty indices for different items that measure the same enabling skill can usually help you determine whether problems detected are caused by the item or by instruction. Test items that measure the same skill should result in approximately the same difficulty indices. For example, if you include three items on a test to measure the same enabling skill, and all students answer one item correctly but only 60 percent answer the other two items correctly, you should look for a clue in the easy item. On the other hand, if only 55 percent of the students answer one of a set of three items correctly, and more than 90 percent answer the other two items correctly, it might signal a complexity in the difficult item not experienced by students in the easier ones. The following example illustrates this situation. The set of five items requires students to select words that are nouns. Notice that the difficulty index is at about the same level on all but one item.

Word	Difficulty Index, p
1. barn	.70
2. busy	.65
3. brown	.75
4. barrel	.70
5. barrister	.40

The first four items have difficulty indices between .65 and .75. Item 5, however, is obviously more difficult than the other four. The atypically low proportion of correct responses to this item suggests some sort of problem. From this example, you would probably conclude that most students did not know the meaning of the word *barrister,* which influenced their responses.

Locating an atypical difficulty index in a set of items does not always pinpoint the defective item. You should also use your estimation of a reasonable difficulty index in deciding whether the atypical item is the one posing the problem. Consider, for example, a set of three items that measures a rather complex skill administered to a very heterogeneous group of students. If you estimated that approximately two-thirds of the class had mastered the skill, yet observed difficulty indices of .60, .90, and 1.00 for the three items, you probably would not conclude that the more difficult item contained inadvertent complexity. Instead, you might review the two easier items to see whether they contained clues to the correct answer. Although this type of situation is possible, the atypical difficulty index usually reflects the problem item.

Hierarchically Related Items   In interpreting difficulty indices, it is also important to compare them for items that measure hierarchically related skills. For instance, students may be required to do the following:

1. State the identifying characteristics of nouns.
2. Select nouns from a list of words containing nouns and other parts of speech.
3. Select proper nouns from a list of nouns.
4. Capitalize proper nouns.

Obviously, students who do not know the characteristics of nouns cannot consistently separate nouns from other parts of speech. If they cannot recognize nouns, they will not be able to recognize proper nouns without clues. Also, if they cannot recognize proper nouns, they can only guess which nouns should be capitalized. Consider the reasonable difficulty indices for three test items based on each of the skills in Table 11.1.

In Table 11.1, 80 percent of the group correctly answered the item that required them to state the characteristics of nouns. Therefore, no more than 80 percent should

TABLE 11.1

Difficulty Indices for Hierarchical Tasks

Difficulty Indices			
Item 1	Item 2	Item 3	Skills
.60	.60	.65	Capitalize proper nouns.
.65	.60	.65	Select proper nouns from a list of nouns.
.70	.75	.70	Select nouns from a list of nouns and other parts of speech.
.80			State the identifying characteristics of nouns.

correctly answer higher-level skills. Notice that 70 percent correctly selected nouns, and fewer, or 60 percent, correctly selected proper nouns. All the students who were able to identify proper nouns could also capitalize them. Considering the hierarchical relationship among these skills, the difficulty indices for the items seem reasonable.

Now, compare these data with a second set of unreasonable difficulty indices in Table 11.2. Here, 90 percent or more of the students could locate proper nouns, yet only 80 percent knew the characteristics of nouns and only 70 percent could correctly select nouns from a list of words containing nouns and other parts of speech. These illogical percentages can be explained in two ways. First, proper noun items may have contained clues—for example, being capitalized when other words in the list were not. The other possibility could be faulty reasoning in establishing the relationship among skills in the hierarchy. If you encounter difficulty indices that imply that higher-level skills have been mastered by more students than have subordinate skills, you should look for (1) clues in items that measure higher-order skills, (2) errors in logic in identifying skills included in the hierarchy, and (3) errors in sequencing skills in the hierarchy.

In summary, interpreting the reasonableness of item difficulty indices requires the following:

- Comparing observed indices with those anticipated given the complexity of the skills measured and the achievement characteristics of the group
- Comparing difficulty indices for multiple items that measure the same enabling skill
- Comparing difficulty indices for items that measure hierarchically related skills

These comparisons should enable you to pinpoint items that either contain clues or introduce unintended complexity.

You can also use difficulty indices to evaluate the quality of your instruction. If many students incorrectly answer some or all of the items related to an important skill, you need to reconsider the instruction for these enabling skills. Although an analysis of item difficulty will not identify the instructional weaknesses, it will indicate where to look for problems.

TABLE 11.2

Unreasonable Difficulty Indices for Hierarchical Tasks

Difficulty Indices			
Item 1	Item 2	Item 3	Skills
.60	.60	.60	Capitalize proper nouns.
.90	.95	.90	Select proper nouns from a list of nouns.
.70	.70	.70	Select nouns from a list of nouns and other parts of speech.
.80	.80	.80	State the identifying characteristics of nouns.

Caution is required when interpreting item difficulty indices. In a small group, one wrong answer or a careless mistake will produce a different difficulty index. Therefore, in making your comparisons, you should look for a reasonable range of scores. A difference of as much as 10 to 15 percentage points in a small group will be due to chance errors on the part of students rather than to actual differences in item difficulty. Thus, you should be concerned only with large, obvious differences in your analysis.

Some measurement specialists recommend comparing the difficulty indices of items on pretests and posttests in order to evaluate the quality of items on criterion-referenced tests. To perform such an item analysis, you need to administer a pretest and posttest that contain the same items. Then calculate the difficulty indices for the items on each test and subtract each item's p value on the pretest from its p value on the posttest. The difference between these values is considered one indicator of item quality. This procedure is illustrated in Table 11.3.

Items that exhibit high, positive differences, such as 1, 3, and 4, supposedly reflect good technical characteristics. Items that have small or no differences, or negative differences, such as items 2 and 5, supposedly reflect technical problems with the item, the instruction, or both.

Using a pretest-posttest comparison to evaluate the quality of items on your criterion-referenced tests has several limitations. First, pretest data are not always available for comparison. Pretests are usually administered only when teachers have reason to believe that some students in the class already possess some of the enabling skills in the goal framework. When this is the case, pretests are administered to aid in grouping students for instruction or for differentiating between skills that need to be taught and those that simply need to be reviewed. Second, when pretests are used to aid planning, different or novel items should be used on posttests to measure students' accomplishment of the same enabling skills and objectives. When exactly the same items are included on pretests and posttests, it is impossible to determine whether students have learned the enabling skill or simply remember the example used in the previous measure. Third, when different items are used to measure the same skill on the pretest and posttest, comparing them would not make sense because it is impossible to ensure that different items are precisely equal in difficulty. Although comparing students' pretest and posttest performances is valuable for evaluating the quality of

TABLE 11.3

Comparing Item Difficulty on Pretests and Posttests

Item	Enabling Skill 1				
	1	2	3	4	5
Posttest $_p$	.60	.40	1.00	.85	.20
Pretest $_p$	.20	.40	.50	.50	.80
Difference (post − pre)	.40	.00	.50	.35	−.60

instruction, these comparisons are best made at the enabling skill level rather than at the item level. Procedures for judging students' progress at the enabling skill level are described in Chapter 12. Item analysis for criterion-referenced tests is best accomplished by comparing the reasonableness of observed difficulty indices against your perceptions of the complexity of the skill measured and the achievement characteristics of your class.

Sometimes teachers do not have time to perform all these comparisons between their expectations for item difficulty and their observed item data. When this is the case, and often it is, they set a minimum acceptable p value for all posttest items. A typical minimum acceptable p value is set at .50, reflecting that at least one-half the class answered correctly. This criterion is based on the assumption that items presented following instruction should be tailored to the ability level of the group; thus, if instruction was clear and the item was clear, then at least one-half of the group should be able to identify the correct answer. Using such a rule of thumb, all items on a test failing to meet the minimum difficulty criterion would be flagged for further analysis. Obtaining a difficulty index lower than .50 does not automatically reflect a problem with the item since it may instead reflect inadequate instruction for the enabling skill. Further analysis of the item should help you determine whether the problem is rooted in the item or in the instruction.

■ Item Discrimination Analysis

Item discrimination analysis is based on the assumption that students who receive high scores on the overall test should score better on an item-by-item basis than students who receive low scores on the overall test. An index of item discrimination permits a teacher to determine whether students' performances on individual items are consistent with their overall performances.

Discrimination indices can range from −1.00 to 1.00 as follows:

Maximum Negative Discrimination between Highest- and Lowest- Scoring Groups	*No Discrimination between Highest- and Lowest- Scoring Groups*	*Maximum Positive Discrimination between Highest- and Lowest- Scoring Groups*
−1.00	.00	1.00

A discrimination index of 1.00 for an item indicates maximum positive discrimination between the highest- and lowest-scoring students. To observe such an index, all students in the highest-scoring group would have to answer the item correctly, whereas all students in the lowest-scoring group would have to miss the item. An index of .00 indicates that the item does not discriminate at all between the highest- and lowest-scoring students. When the same number of students in each group answers an item correctly, a discrimination index of .00 results. Maximum negative discrimination is −1.00, which results when all students in the lower-scoring group answer an item correctly and all students in the upper-scoring group miss it. Generally, high negative discrimination indices reflect problems.

The highest-quality tests are those that contain all items that have positive discrimination indices. A positive discrimination index indicates that more higher-scoring than lower-scoring students answered the item correctly. When the reverse is true, and a test contains many negatively discriminating items, the overall test scores fail to differentiate as they should between those who know the most and the least in the domain. Thus, in evaluating the quality of test items and tests, teachers should flag negatively discriminating items for further analysis.

There are several different discrimination indices used to judge the quality of test items. Two are presented because they are the ones most commonly used on computer-generated item analysis reports for classroom tests. One is the discrimination index, d, and the other is the point-biserial correlation index, r_{pbi}. Both discrimination measures reflect whether students' performance on a single item is consistent with their overall test scores; however, there are some differences in the calculation procedures and interpretations.

Evaluating Test Items Using the Discrimination Index d

The discrimination index, d, reflects the difference between the difficulty of a test item for the upper- and lower-scoring subgroups in a class. The upper group is most frequently defined as the highest scoring 25 or 27 percent of the students in the class. In contrast, the lower group is the lowest scoring 25 or 27 percent of the students in a class. Ideally, the students who scored the highest on the overall test should score better than the students who earned the lowest scores on the test on an item-by-item basis. As noted earlier, the best discriminating items have positive discrimination values; however, there are some rules of thumb for interpreting the quality of an item using the discrimination index (d) beyond simply stating that all positive values are good and all negative values are not. The rules of thumb include the following:

Quality Category	d value for $p < .50$	d value for $p > .50$
Unacceptable test item discrimination	Any negative value of d	Any negative value of d
No discrimination	$d \approx .00$	$d \approx .00$
Moderate discrimination	$d \approx 1/2p$	$d \approx 1/2q$
Good discrimination	$d \approx p$	$d \approx q$
Excellent discrimination	$d \approx 2p$	$d \approx 2q$

Recall that the symbol p refers to the proportion of students who answer an item correctly. The value of q is the opposite, and it refers to the proportion of students who answer the item incorrectly. For example, if $p = .70$, then $q = .30$. When item difficulty indices are equal to or greater than .50, you should use q as the comparison value for the discrimination index.

Using this rule of thumb for quality standards, you can readily evaluate item discrimination quality for any item data that includes both the difficulty and the discrimination indices. To illustrate this point, see how the discrimination indices are evaluated for the test items in Figure 11.1.

Evaluating Test Items Using the Point-Biserial Correlation Index for Discrimination

Another discrimination measure provided in item analysis reports generated by the computer is the point-biserial correlation index (r_{pbi}). This index indicates how well you can predict the total test scores of students from an individual item on the test. An item is judged consistent with students' overall test scores when students who earn the highest overall test scores answer the item correctly and students who earn the lowest overall scores answer incorrectly. When more higher- than lower-scoring students answer an item correctly, a positive r_{pbi} index results; when the students who answer correctly are equally represented among the higher- and lower-scoring groups, a value near .00 results; and when more lower- than higher-scoring students answer correctly, a negative r_{pbi} index is obtained.

The possible scale for the point-biserial correlation index extends from -1.00 to 1.00, although obtaining values this high in either a positive or negative direction on classroom tests is unlikely. More typically, they are observed to range between $-.30$ and .70.

FIGURE 11.1

Evaluating Item Discrimination Using Quality Standards Based on the Difficulty Index

Item Indices*			Item Discrimination Quality Levels				
p	q	d	Unacceptable (Negative)	None (.00)	Moderate ($\approx 1/2p$ or q)	Good ($\approx p$ or q)	Excellent ($\approx 2p$ or $2q$)
.10	.90	.20					✓
.20	.80	.00		✓			
.45	.55	.45				✓	
.50	.50	−.50	✓				
.65	.35	.18			✓		
.80	.20	.20				✓	
.95	.05	.05				✓	

*$p + q = 1.00$ or 100% of the students in the item analysis.

Note: Use p as the standard for interpreting discrimination indices when $p \leq .50$ and q as the standard when $p \geq .50$.

Unlike the previously described discrimination index, *d*, the point-biserial correlation index does not compare the performance of only the upper and lower extreme subgroups; instead, it uses the item and total test scores for all students who complete the exam.

Additionally, only one standard or criterion is needed to evaluate the discrimination quality of an item. For typical classes containing 30 to 50 students:

- Negative point-biserial correlation indices reflect unacceptable item discrimination.
- Indices lower than .20 reflect very weak discrimination.
- Indices greater than .30 reflect good discrimination.

Comparing the Discrimination Indices *d* and r_{pbi} for Test Items

Two different indices of item discrimination have been described. Although they are calculated quite differently, they indicate the same characteristics: an item's ability to discriminate between those who performed the best and the least well on the exam. Comparing the information provided by each index for the same items and tests, you typically would reach the same conclusion about the items' discrimination quality. To illustrate this, review the item data presented in Table 11.4. All the item difficulty and discrimination indices described thus far are included. The first four rows contain various difficulty values for each item calculated from the total group and the upper and lower subgroups. The last two rows contain the discrimination indices.

Would your overall conclusions about the items' ability to discriminate be different if you used one or the other of the indices? No. All items besides 4 and 7 yield credible discrimination. Both indices for item 4 indicate that the item yielded no or negligible discrimination, and both indices for item 7 indicate a high level of negative discrimination.

TABLE 11.4

Sample Item Difficulty and Discrimination Indices

Difficulty/ Discrimination	Test Item									
	1	2	3	4	5	6	7	8	9	10
p (overall class)	.80	.70	.50	.60	.40	.50	.60	.60	.40	.50
p_u (upper group)	1.00	1.00	1.00	1.00	.33	1.00	.33	1.00	1.00	.67
p_l (lower group)	.33	.00	.00	1.00	.00	.00	1.00	.00	.00	.33
p_{ul} (upper/lower group)	.67	.50	.50	1.00	.17	.50	.67	.50	.50	.50
r_{pbi}	.66	.81	.84	−.05	.40	.84	−.48	.81	.83	.34
d	.67	1.00	1.00	.00	.33	1.00	−.67	1.00	1.00	.34

The d value and the r_{pbi} value for an item can sometimes provide conflicting evidence about an item's discrimination quality. When this occurs, the d value will reflect stronger discrimination for an item, whereas the r_{pbi} index will reflect weaker discrimination for the same item. What could cause this difference? It stems from the fact that the d value reflects the test performance of only the highest- and lowest-scoring students, whereas the r_{pbi} index is calculated using the scores of all students who completed the test. Discrimination indices calculated on only the extreme scoring groups will typically reflect higher discrimination for an item than those calculated using all group members.

Evaluating Test Items Using Difficulty and Discrimination Indices

In order to judge an item's quality using the difficulty and discrimination indices, you must consider several factors. The criteria established depend on multiple factors related to the inherent complexity of the skill measured and the characteristics of the students, including the variability of their performance on the overall test.

In a preceding discussion on item difficulty, a minimum p value of .50 was recommended for posttests under the assumptions that if (1) the instruction was clear, (2) the item was clear and was tailored to students' developmental level, and (3) the students were trying to succeed, then at least 50 percent of them should be able to identify the correct response. Under special circumstances, you may choose to lower or raise this criterion of $p \geq .50$, but it will serve as a good rule of thumb for quickly screening items for potential problems when you have not specifically identified reasons why the p values should be lower or higher for a particular group on a particular test.

In setting a minimally acceptable criterion for judging item discrimination using either of the discrimination indices, you need to consider the variability of the group's overall test performance. A group's performance would be considered homogeneous when there is a narrow range and standard deviation for test scores, and it would be considered heterogeneous when there is a wide range and standard deviation. This suggestion usually causes teachers to ask, How wide is wide, and how narrow is narrow? Obviously, there is no correct answer to such reasonable questions, so a rule of thumb can be cautiously applied to help you determine the homogeneity or heterogeneity of a group's test performance. Test performance can be considered homogeneous when you obtain a range of raw scores that spans approximately 25 percent or less of the total number of items on the test and a standard deviation that spans approximately 25 percent or less of the range. Test performance would be considered heterogeneous when the range spans approximately 33 percent of the total number of items on the test and the standard deviation spans approximately 25 percent or more of the range. Test performance would be considered very heterogeneous when the range is approximately 50 percent or more of the total number of items on the test and the standard deviation is approximately 25 percent or more of the range. When you obtain a relatively wide range and standard deviation for a test, you can reasonably expect the items on the test to yield high positive discrimination indices. Conversely, when you obtain a relatively narrow range and standard deviation, lower item discrimination generally can be expected.

What levels of discrimination should be considered minimally acceptable for typical class-size groups containing fewer than 50 students? When your group's overall test performance is homogeneous, then .00 or any positive value for d or r_{pbi} would be acceptable for all items. Heterogeneous group performance on a test means that you can expect higher levels of item discrimination.

■ Item Distractor Analysis

The third type of item analysis performed by teachers is the distractor analysis. Unlike the difficulty and discrimination indices that reflect the group's performance relative only to the correct answer, the incorrect answers chosen by group members are the focus of the distractor analysis. The index used is the proportion of students who select each incorrect response. Distractors chosen by a large portion of the group possibly reflect misconceptions, and those chosen by no one potentially reflect choices considered illogical by group members. Similar to the difficulty and discrimination analyses, the data required to perform this analysis are generated by the computer as the tests are scored, and they are printed in a summary table for teachers to interpret.

There are two main reasons why teachers perform an item distractor analysis: to facilitate instructional planning and to determine why the items yielded unreasonable difficulty and discrimination indices. Recall from Chapter 5 that distractors should reflect common misconceptions or incomplete learning observed among students during instruction. When item distractors do reflect common misconceptions, it is important to understand which ones students select so that instruction for correcting these errors can be provided in subsequent review sessions. Through performing a distractor analysis, teachers can diagnose the actual problems students are having and prescribe targeted instruction. Some items come to your attention because you judge the difficulty index to be too high or low for the inherent complexity of the skill measured or because they yield a negative discrimination index.

Items that all members of the group answer correctly ($p = 1.00$) are immediately suspect. If the skill measured is not extremely easy or one particularly emphasized during instruction, then you might conclude that the distractors did not reflect plausible alternatives, even for students who did not know the correct answer. Items that unskilled students can answer correctly by default are often called *"gimmes"* by students. Although students tend to like gimmes, tests that contain too many of them will not yield test scores that lead to valid decisions about the students' skill level in the domain. Each distractor for such an item should be analyzed carefully to ensure that it is a plausible alternative. Some potential problems are that distractors contain (1) information not studied in the lessons, (2) unfamiliar terminology, (3) grammatical mismatches between the stem and the distractors, or (4) obviously more or less information than the correct answer. You may also find that clues to the correct answer are in the stem of the question, the directions for a set of questions, or in other items on the test.

Items also attract attention because they are more difficult for students than anticipated based on the inherent complexity of the skill measured. Very difficult items may result from problems with item construction or inadequate instruction, and the distractor analysis will help you determine whether the root of the problem is the item.

Potential problems include (1) unfamiliar vocabulary in the stem or distractors, (2) two correct answers, (3) a distractor rather than the correct answer keyed as correct, or (4) a confusing, unclear question.

Negatively discriminating items with p values lower than .90 also signal that an item may be flawed, and an analysis of the response choices selected by the upper and lower subgroups may provide clues to the problem. Typical problems resulting in negative discrimination include (1) miskeyed items, (2) unfamiliar terminology, (3) a distractor that appears correct to the upper subgroup, or (4) a confusing, unclear question. If instruction was misleading, students in the upper subgroup could have actually learned an incorrect response. Inadequate instruction in the skill measured can also lead to negatively discriminating items. If the upper subgroup of students does not know the answer to the question, then they, like members of the lower subgroup, try to guess the correct answer, and the discrimination index is as likely to be negative as positive.

Interpreting Item Distractor Data

Table 11.5 illustrates different item data formats commonly provided by computers for distractor analysis. The item numbers are listed in the second column, and students' responses for five-option test items are illustrated in the columns to the right. The far right column, NR, indicates no response, or the number of students who did not answer the question. Data sets I and II report the proportion of the total group that selected each option. In set I, the correct answer is printed in the second column beside the item number, and in set II, the correct answer is indicated by an asterisk beside the proportion of students choosing it. The same format is used in set III, with the only difference being that both the frequency (f) and the proportion (%) of the students who selected each option are indicated.

Examining these item data in the first three sets will help you see what you can infer about the items. In set I, the difficulty index (p) for the first item is .40, indicating a very difficult item. The proportion of students choosing the keyed answer is the difficulty index. All distractors were chosen by some member of the group, which illustrates that the teacher had included distractors that were all plausible. You might also conclude from the data that the item was not miskeyed since the keyed answer was selected by the largest proportion of the class. For item 2 in set I, 100 percent of the class selected the keyed answer 4, reflecting either an easy item, a clue, or unreasonable distractors.

Now consider the data for the two items in set II. Both items appear to be functioning well, since they were moderately easy for the majority of the class ($p = .80$ and .70). In addition, both items contained distractors considered plausible by the group, which provides information for planning the review session. In set III, the majority of the class chose distractor 3 ($p = .60$) for the first item, providing a hint that this item may either be miskeyed or contain two correct answers. The item should be reviewed for both possibilities. The second item was moderately easy for the group ($p = .80$), and only one distractor was functioning.

Much information about the items can be obtained from analysis programs that provide whole group data, but the information provided in set IV is much more helpful. For each of the three items, three difficulty indices—p_u, p_l, and total group p— are provided. This analysis program reports separately the options chosen by the

TABLE 11.5

Item Data Useful for Performing a Distractor Analysis

Item	Key	Total Group Performance Responses					
		1	2	3	4	5	NR
I. 1	2	.20	.40	.10	.10	.20	.00
2	4	.00	.00	.00	1.00	.00	.00
II. 1		.00	.20	.80*	.10	.00	.00
2		.70*	.10	.00	.10	.10	.00
III. 1	f	0	16*	24	4	4	0
	%	.00	.40*	.60	.00	.00	.00
2	f	0	0	32*	8	0	0
	%	.00	.00	.80*	.20	.00	.00

		Upper-Lower Group Performance						
		1	2	3	4	5	NR	p
IV. 1	u	.50*	.00	.50	.00	.00	.00	.60
	l	.50*	.00	.20	.20	.10	.00	
2	u	.00	.80*	.00	.00	.20	.00	.60
	l	.20	.20*	.20	.30	.10	.00	
3	u	.60	.00	.40*	.00	.00	.00	.75
	l	.20	.00	.80*	.00	.00	.00	

Note: Decimal numbers reflect the proportion of students selecting each response, and asterisks reflect the correct response.

upper and lower 27 percent of the class. Notice that for item 1, one-half of both the upper and lower subgroups selected the correct answer. Based on this information, can you calculate the discrimination index d? It is .00. The distractor most attractive to the remaining upper subgroup students was 3, whereas members of the lower subgroup selected options 3, 4, and 5. This information should cause you to investigate the following:

1. Why was distractor 3 so attractive? Is it also a correct answer? Was adequate instruction provided to enable the students to correctly distinguish between responses 1 and 3?
2. What is wrong with distractor 2? Does it really reflect a misconception or problem students have?

Consider the pattern of responses for item 2 in set IV. The item was fairly difficult for the class ($p = .60$), and it discriminated well between the upper and lower subgroups ($d = .80 - .20 = .60$). Distractor 5 should certainly be explained to students during the test review, and overall instruction on the skill should be provided for the lower group since these students appear to have all the misconceptions identified by the item distractors. For item 3, you should first check to see whether it is miskeyed since the difficulty and discrimination data for distractor 1 seem more plausible than for the keyed response (1: p_{ul} = .40, d = 40; 3: p_{ul} = .60, d = −.40).

■ Evaluating Items Using Student Performance Data

As you can see, it is relatively easy to generate hypotheses about the problems students experience with your test items using only the item analysis reports. To check your hunches, however, you will need to transfer the item data to a copy of your test and examine the actual items using the data. This transfer can be accomplished easily by hand when it is not done for you by the computer. Figure 11.2 contains three sample multiple-choice items with the item analysis data inserted beside the item and responses. Beside each item number, you can see the difficulty (p) and discrimination (d) indices. To the left of each item response, you will find the proportion of the upper and lower subgroups who selected it. To the right of each distractor in parentheses, you will find the logic used to create the distractor.

Items 1 and 2 are both easy; verbal information recall items related to the paragraph instructional goal previously described. The teacher undoubtedly judged that both items would be very easy for the class on the posttest; however, item 1 was much more complex than anticipated, and it did not discriminate well. Reviewing the data, you can see that an equal number of students in the upper group selected the responses "First sentence" and "Topic sentence," possibly indicating that the students did not read the question carefully enough. The teacher would either emphasize this difference in subsequent instruction or replace the distractor "First sentence" with information more readily distinguished by the group for subsequent tests. The other two distractors chosen by members of the lower group were key terms repeated from the stem, which possibly reflects that students were reaching for an answer using clues. The distractor not chosen by anyone in the group was "Relevant sentence," a quality criterion for topic sentences.

The teacher would probably judge that the second item was quite good based on the p and d values of .80 and .50, respectively. Additionally, the distractors used were all considered plausible by some group members.

The third item relates to the standard deviation described previously. If these item p and d values (.20, .00) were obtained, they would surely reflect a mistake; however, just from these indices, you could not determine whether the error was in teaching the concept or in developing the item. The distractor analysis data indicate that both these hunches are wrong. Reviewing the data for the upper group, it becomes obvious that the item is miskeyed. The correct answer is 4 since the range, 8, divided by 2, is 4 rather than 5.

Using a distractor analysis report, you will be able to improve the quality of your feedback to students following the exam, and you will be able to improve the quality of items you use to judge students' performance—both worthwhile pursuits.

FIGURE 11.2

Item Analysis Data for Distractor Analysis

---

p_n/d 1. What is the sentence called that introduces the subject in a paragraph?
.60/.10

p_u p_l
.50   .30   A. First sentence   (physical criterion)
        .20   B. Introduction sentence   (repeat stem term)
        .00   C. Relevant sentence   (quality criterion)
        .10   D. Subject sentence   (repeat stem term)
.50   .40   *E. Topic sentence

p_n/d 2. What are the sentences in a paragraph called that elaborate the topic?
.80/.50

p_u p_l
        .10   A. Elaboration sentence   (repeat stem term)
        .20   B. Relevant sentences   (quality criterion)
        .10   C. Sequenced sentences   (quality criterion)
1.00   .50   *D. Supporting sentences
        .10   E. Topic sentences   (repeat stem term)

p_n/d 3. What is the largest standard deviation possible for a test that contains 20
.20/.00   items, has a mean of 10, and has a range of 8?

p_u p_l
        .10   A. 2   (divisor: $R/2$)
.90   .50   B. 4
.10   .10   *C. 5   ($\overline{X}/2$)
        .20   D. 10   (# of items/2)
        .10   E. None of these

---

* = Correct response.

Interpreting a Typical Item Analysis
Report Generated by a Computer

Prior to reviewing item analysis data, it might be helpful to list the steps a teacher would take in analyzing the data. The following procedure is recommended:

1. Determine whether the group's overall test performance is homogeneous or heterogeneous using the range and standard deviation.

2. Based on your perceptions of the group's achievement and motivation characteristics, the complexity of the skills measured, and the quality of the instruction delivered, set minimally acceptable criteria for difficulty and discrimination levels.

3. Scan the item analysis report to locate questionable items based on difficulty and discrimination. Mark any items that are more difficult than anticipated. Locate the

discrimination index column on the report, and mark any items that do not yield the established minimum criterion. For items that do not yield acceptable discrimination, locate the corresponding p value. If the p value is greater than .90, review the item to determine whether such high performance is reasonable for the skill measured. The negative and negligible discrimination indices can be ignored when the high difficulty indices are logical for the skill measured. If the p value is lower than .90, review each response to see whether you can identify problem distractors.

4. Check the distractors selected by upper and lower subgroup members to help locate potential problems within items.

Each of these steps is illustrated in the following example.

Determine Group Homogeneity   The first step is to determine whether the group's performance should be classified as heterogeneous or homogeneous. The following information from a report for an actual classroom test should be useful:

> *Number of test items:* 20
> *Range:* 20 – 12 = 8, or 38 percent of 20 items
> *Standard deviation:* 1.76, or 22 percent of the range
> *Number of students:* 34
> *Number of students in upper-lower subgroups:* 9 each group

The range is greater than one-third of the total items on the test, and the standard deviation is approximately one-quarter of the range. Based on these data, the group's overall test performance will be classified as heterogeneous, although the standard deviation is borderline. The small number (9) of students in the subgroups means that you should be cautious in interpreting the d index. If even one more or less student answers an item correctly, then the p_u and p_l values will change by 11 percent.

Set Criteria for Item Difficulty and Discrimination   The next steps are to set minimum criteria for the difficulty and discrimination indices. The minimum criterion for the difficulty index is set at $p \geq .50$ since the exam was a unit posttest, the instruction was considered good, and the group contained high-achieving students. Using the group's heterogeneous overall test performance, minimum standards for the discrimination index are based on the previously described rules of thumb for d and a value $\geq .20$ for the point-biserial correlation index. For items with $p \geq .90$, any positive or negative discrimination index will be considered acceptable if the high p value is reasonable for the skill measured.

Table 11.6 contains the item analysis data for a 20-item objective test that will be used for locating potential problem items. The item number is listed in the first column, and the keyed correct answer is listed in the second column. The next 10 columns contain the percentage of students in the upper and lower subgroups who selected each of the four response options. The columns corresponding to the keyed response for each item contain the p_u and p_l values. The two columns marked NR reflect the percentage of students who made no response or failed to answer the question.

TABLE 11.6

Computer-Generated Item Analysis Data for an Objective Test

Item	Key*	Upper Group						Lower Group						Difficulty/Discrimination		
		1	2	3	4	NR		1	2	3	4	NR	p_n	d	r_{pbi}
1	4			.11	.89				.22	.33	.33	.11	.68	.56	.481
2	3			1.00						1.00			1.00	.00	.000
3	4			.22	.78					.33	.67		.65	.11	.081
4	1	.67	.22	.11				.89		.11			.76	−.22	−.057
5	2		.78		.22				1.00				.82	−.22	−.270
6	4				1.00			.44	.11	.11	.33		.68	.67	.454
7	4				1.00			.11	.11	.33	.44		.76	.56	.652
8	1	1.00						1.00					.97	.00	.010
9	4				1.00			.22	.22		.56		.79	.44	.168
10	1	1.00						.89		.11			.94	.11	.334
11	2		1.00					.11	.22	.67			.68	.78	.696
12	3			1.00						1.00			.97	.00	−.064
13	4			.11	.89					.33	.67		.74	.22	.247
14	2	.22	.78					.22	.78				.65	.00	.029
15	2	.11	.89					.22	.67	.11			.76	.22	.342
16	3			1.00						1.00			.85	.00	−.047
17	4				1.00					.33	.67		.88	.33	.468
18	1	.78	.11	.11				.22	.33	.22	.22		.59	.56	.455
19	3			1.00				.11	.11	.78			.79	.22	.060
20	3	.11	.22	.67				.33	.44	.11	.11		.35	.56	.286

*Key = correct response.

The three columns on the far right of the table contain the difficulty index for the entire group of 34 students (p); the d item discrimination value based on performance of the 18 students in the upper and lower subgroups; and the r_{pbi} discrimination index based on the performance of all 34 students.

Locate Questionable Items Based on Difficulty and Discrimination   The next step is to locate the subset of items that have potential problems. Begin by locating the item difficulty column (p_n) in Table 11.6. Scan the difficulty indices in the column and mark all items in the table that were extremely difficult ($p < .50$) and extremely easy ($p > .95$) for the group. You should mark item 20 as very difficult and items 2, 8, 10, and 12 as extremely easy.

Next, locate the two item discrimination index columns on the right side of the table (d and r_{pbi}) and mark all items that do not yield acceptable discrimination. If one of the two indices indicate adequate discrimination, you may wish to accept this as evidence that the item discriminates adequately and not mark these items. You may also want to exclude items with difficulty indices greater than .90 since these very easy items may not discriminate well. Items with p values less than .90 that clearly produce inadequate discrimination include numbers 3, 4, 5, 14, and 16. Of the 20 items, 5 should be reviewed based on their difficulty levels for the group and 5 should be examined due to inadequate discrimination.

Examine Distractor Data for Questionable Items   Once you have pinpointed potentially flawed items, you should examine the proportion of upper- and lower-group students who selected each distractor for the items. This analysis may help you locate particular parts of the items that appear to cause the problem. Examine the distractor data for the 10 items you have checked in Table 11.6, and develop hunches about which distractor or distractors appear to warrant further examination. See whether the conclusions you reach about the distractors match those in Table 11.7.

Comparing Item Data for Multiple Class Groups

In order to illustrate the tentative nature of item data from one class group, the same test of 20 items was administered to another class studying the same unit, and the following test data were obtained:

	$\overline{X}$	Range	σ	σ/R	N	Subgroup #
Group 1	17.00	20 − 12 = 8	1.76	.22	34	9
Group 2	17.32	20 − 13 = 7	2.31	.33	28	8

The mean scores were very similar for the two groups, which indicates that you can expect the item difficulty indices (p) to be relatively similar for the two groups since $\Sigma p = \overline{X}$. The range is smaller for group 2, yet their standard deviation is larger, at 33 percent of their range. The larger standard deviation indicates a wider dispersion of test scores within the range for the second group; thus, you might expect better item discrimination for the second group than you observed for the first group.

Table 11.8 contains the item data for both groups. First, compare the groups' performance for item 20 that was judged too difficult for the first group. Notice that group 2 earned an acceptable difficulty index of .61, and their discrimination indices for the item would be judged excellent. The additional data from group 2 reflect that item 20 is a good test item and that the discrepant p values most likely stem from different instructional emphases in the two classes.

Now compare the item discrimination data for the two class groups. Items 3, 4, 5, 14, and 16 were observed to yield inadequate discrimination when the test was

TABLE 11.7

Analysis of Potentially Faulty Items Based on Student Performance Data

Item	Conclusions about Items Flagged for Difficulty	Analysis Procedure
20	Too difficult for group All distractors chosen Keyed response most selected Good discrimination	1. Check item vocabulary, context 2. Provide more emphasis on skills during instruction
2 8 10 12	Extremely easy for group No (or 1) distractors chosen by upper or lower subgroups	1. Check stem, distractors for clues 2. Check distractors for plausibility 3. Check distractors to determine whether they reflect common misconceptions

	Conclusions about Items Flagged for Discrimination		
Item	Nonfunctioning Distractors	Distractor Most Attractive for Upper Group	Analysis Procedure
3	1, 2	3	1. Examine nonfunctioning distractors to determine whether they reflect common misconceptions/problems and revise as needed.
4	4	2	
5	1, 3	4	
14	3, 4	1	
16	1, 2, 4		2. Check distractor most attractive for upper group to determine whether it also reflects a correct answer and revise as needed.

administered to group 1. Reviewing the discrimination indices from group 2, note that items 3, 14, and 16 again failed to yield acceptable discrimination, providing further evidence that these three items contain some type of flaw. A different item discrimination pattern emerges for the other two items. Items 4 and 5 yielded adequate discrimination indices for group 2.

Based on all item discrimination data from the two groups, you might conclude that only items 3, 14, and 16 appear inadequate. Examining the distractors chosen by members of the upper and lower subgroups from both classes may help determine where to look for problems in these items, and Table 11.9 includes the complete data for items 3, 14, and 16. One potential problem with these items is that they have only one distractor considered plausible by students in either group. The two nonfunctioning distractors might be revised to see whether the items' discrimination quality can be improved with subsequent class groups.

TABLE 11.8
Item Discrimination Data for Two Groups of Students

Item	Group	P_n	d	r_{pbi}
3	1	.65	.11	.081
	2	.82	.00	.007
4	1	.76	−.22	−.057
	2	.82	.25	.278
5	1	.82	−.22	−.270
	2	.71	.50	.285
14	1	.65	.00	.029
	2	.71	.13	−.012
16	1	.85	.00	−.047
	2	.89	.13	−.026
20	1	.35	.56	.286
	2	.61	.62	.684

TABLE 11.9
Distractor Analysis Data for Three Items with Consistently Inadequate Discrimination Indices

Item	Key	Group	Upper Group 1	2	3	4	NR	Lower Group 1	2	3	4	NR	P_n	d	r_{pbi}
3	4	1			.22	.78				.33	.67		.65	.11	.081
		2			.25	.75				.25	.75		.82	.00	.007
14	2	1	.22	.78				.22	.78				.65	.00	.029
		2	.13	.88				.25	.75				.71	.13	−.012
16	3	1			1.00					1.00			.85	.00	−.047
		2			1.00					.87	.13		.89	.13	−.026

Adjusting for Flawed Items

Finding faulty items on a test you have administered to your class means that you must decide what to do about the items. Of course, you will want to revise flawed items prior to using them again, but what about the class that was subjected to the problematic items? The scores students earn on your tests are used to describe their achievement in the course. When these test scores are based on some flawed items, they reflect your errors as well as the students' errors. There is no rule for solving these problems but ignoring them does not seem prudent. Many teachers give all students in the class credit for items that were too difficult. Others eliminate the items and rescore the exam.

When the items you use on a test are new, you should not be surprised to find that approximately 10 percent of them do not yield the anticipated difficulty indices. Even very experienced test developers find this to be the case. Take care in setting unreasonable standards for yourself as a test developer, and avoid holding your students responsible for your inadvertent errors.

An Example

Figure 11.3 contains the item analysis data for the topic sentence portion of the unit posttest on writing paragraphs. Enabling skill codes are included in the top row, and items that measure each skill are listed beneath the codes. The correct answers are located in the third row. Students' names are listed in the far left column, and an asterisk in the student-by-item cell indicates a correct answer. A number in the intersecting cell indicates the number of the distractor selected by the student. The teacher used an x in the intersecting cell to indicate unacceptable original topic sentences.

Item data are included in the last rows of the table. The names of indices are listed in the far left column, and the value calculated for each item appears in the intersecting index-by-item cell. These indices can be used to locate potentially flawed items on the test. First, examine the difficulty indices for all items to locate any items that are too difficult for the class. The total group difficulty indices illustrate that this portion of the test was quite easy for most class members; no items had difficulty indices lower than .50. Second, look for items that contain possible clues. All students in the class answered 4 of the 15 items correctly (3, 4, 6, 7). The text of these items should be examined to determine whether clues are present or the items are simply easy for class members. Items 3 and 4 reflect physical and functional characteristics, and items 6 and 7 are discrimination items requiring students to locate topic sentences in a paragraph. These should be easy enabling skills for students following instruction, and it seems reasonable that all students answered them correctly.

After examining items for potential problems related to item difficulty, you should examine the discrimination indices for potentially confusing items. All discrimination indices for all items with p values lower than 1.00 appear quite reasonable. One possible exception is item 8, with a point-biserial correlation index of .19. In contrast, the d index based on upper-lower group comparisons reflects adequate discrimination between the two extreme scoring groups for this item. Based on these item data, it appears that all topic sentence items are functioning well for this group of students. With the item data analyzed, you are ready to consider the internal consistency of the total test.

■ Test Internal Consistency Analysis

The preceding sections described procedures for evaluating the quality of individual items on a test. To check the discrimination quality of a particular item, the consistency

FIGURE 11.3

Item Analysis for the Topic Sentence Portion of the Paragraph Posttest (Enabling Skills II.A to II.F in Figures 3.6 and 4.2)

TOPIC SENTENCE OBJECTIVES							
Objective Codes	II.A	II.B	II.C	II.D	II.E.1	II.E.4	II.F
Items	3	4	5	6 7	8 9	10 11	12 13
Correct Answers	*4*	*4*	*4*	*1 1*	*2 4*	*1 4*	*Hand Scored*
Augustine	*	*	*	* *	* *	* *	* *
Prince	*	*	*	* *	* *	* *	* *
Deddens	*	*	*	* *	* *	* *	* *
Talbot	*	*	*	* *	* *	* *	* *
McComas	*	*	*	* *	* *	* *	* *
Rust	*	*	*	* *	* *	* *	* *
Carey	*	*	*	* *	* *	* *	* *
Cromer	*	*	*	* *	* *	* *	* *
Hager	*	*	*	* *	* *	* *	* *
McLaughlin	*	*	*	* *	* *	* *	* *
White	*	*	*	* *	* *	* *	* *
Otto	*	*	*	* *	* *	* *	* *
Lovejoy	*	*	*	* *	* *	* *	* *
Hill	*	*	*	* *	* *	* *	* *
Scragg	*	*	2	* *	* *	* *	* *
Gormley	*	*	3	* *	* 3	* *	* *
Bailey	*	*	2	* *	1 *	* *	* *
Deiters	*	*	2	* *	* 3	* *	* x
Stewart	*	*	3	* *	* *	2 *	* x
Smith	*	*	2	* *	* 3	2 2	x x

TOPIC SENTENCE OBJECTIVES							
Objective Codes	II.A	II.B	II.C	II.D	II.E.1	II.E.4	II.F
Items	3	4	5	6 7	8 9	10 11	12 13
Total Class p	1.0	1.0	.70	1.0 1.0	.95 .85	.90 .95	.95 .85
p_{ul}	1.0	1.0	.50	1.0 1.0	.90 .70	.80 .90	.90 .70
d	.00	.00	1.00	.00 .00	.20 .60	.40 .20	.20 .60
r_{pbi}	.00	.00	.79	.00 .00	.19 .63	.69 .67	.67 .72

* p_{ul} = The difficulty index for only students in the upper and lower groups in the class.

was judged between students' performance on that item and their performance on the overall test. This question of the consistency of students' performance can be expanded to apply to an entire test. A test is said to have good internal consistency if the students who answer each question correctly are the same students who tend to answer the other questions correctly. Stated in a different way, a test has good internal consistency when the pattern of student performance on the overall test matches the pattern of student performance on most items on the test, where the students who have the highest overall scores on the test comprise the group that has the highest rate of correct responses on most items on the test. In other words, a test will have good internal consistency if most of the items on the test show good, positive discrimination.

The measure of a test's internal consistency described is the Kuder-Richardson formula 20, referred to as K-R$_{20}$. This particular index is used with objective-style tests when answers are scored as either correct or incorrect.

Interpreting the K-R$_{20}$ Internal Consistency Reliability Index

The K-R$_{20}$ index typically ranges between .00 and 1.00, although negative values are possible. A K-R$_{20}$ index of .00 reflects no internal consistency for a test, and obtaining a value this low following instruction is highly unlikely. Indices greater than .90 reflect excellent internal consistency reliability. Obtaining a value this high or higher on a classroom test administered following instruction would be rare. Values this high are frequently observed for large standardized tests designed to discriminate among students. Indices near .80 are frequently obtained for classroom tests that measure complex skills and that are administered to heterogeneous groups of students. Values as low as .50 are also common for classroom tests administered following instruction to homogeneous groups of students. Values lower than .50 would be considered questionable unless one knows that the students tested were very similar in their skill levels.

Four main factors influence the size of the $K-R_{20}$ internal consistency reliability index:

1. Group homogeneity
2. Content homogeneity
3. Test length
4. Item difficulty

Group Homogeneity   The achievement characteristics of the group examined will affect internal consistency reliability. The same test will yield a lower $K-R_{20}$ index when it is administered to a homogeneous group than when it is administered to a heterogeneous one. Students who are very similar in skill level will achieve similar raw scores on an examination, resulting in lower item discrimination, a more narrow range of scores, and a smaller standard deviation. Thus, you should not be surprised when the same posttest yields different $K-R_{20}$ indices when administered to different student groups.

Group homogeneity is influenced by instruction, and the same test administered to a group as a pretest and again as a posttest will yield different $K-R_{20}$ indices. Suppose you administered a pretest covering unencountered skills to a heterogeneous group. Students typically guess on pretests, the raw scores are usually low, and test variance is usually low. On the pretest, students' performance would be homogeneous, and a low internal consistency index would undoubtedly result. Administering the test again following quality instruction, you would most likely observe a much higher $K-R_{20}$ index for the same group due to differential learning rates in heterogeneous groups.

Content Homogeneity   A second factor that influences measures of internal consistency is the homogeneity of skills measured on a test. A purely homogeneous test is one that measures only one skill. For example, a test measuring students' skill in capitalizing proper nouns would be considered homogeneous. Students who possess this single skill would be expected to answer all items correctly, and students who did not understand proper nouns or capitalization would be expected to miss all items. Such a skill-specific exam administered to a heterogeneous class would yield a relatively large test variance and corresponding large internal consistency reliability index. It probably would not yield a perfect index of 1.00 due to the presence of inadvertent errors and guessing behavior.

The more skills measured by a test, the less homogeneous the test content. Tests that include a variety of skills typically yield a lower internal consistency reliability index than those that cover only one. For example, a term examination that measures 10 different capitalization objectives would be considered heterogeneous in content. Some students may know most capitalization rules very well but not all 10, and they may be proficient in different rules. The resulting uneven pattern of responses across the items on the test will tend to yield a lower $K-R_{20}$ index than a test containing the same number of items that covers only 1 capitalization rule. Heterogeneity of test content is an important factor for classroom teachers to consider in judging their tests since most unit, term, and semester examinations contain a variety of instructional goals.

Test Length   The number of test items included on a test will influence the internal consistency reliability index. Basically, the longer the test, the better the internal consistency reliability indices. For example, a test on capitalizing proper nouns that contains 40 items will be much more reliable than one that contains only 10 items. With 40 items, you can adequately measure all four types of nouns with multiple examples and nonexamples for each type. Presenting only 10 items would limit the representativeness of items for the domain, thus potentially reducing the reliability. The correction factor in the formula ($n/n - 1$) will also differentially affect the K-R$_{20}$ index based on the number of items on the test.

Item Difficulty   The difficulty of the items and the overall test will affect the internal consistency reliability index. Tests that are extremely easy or difficult for a group yield little item and test variance, and lower K-R$_{20}$ indices will result. Very easy items are less problematic than very difficult ones since easy items tend to increase everyone's score by a constant. Extremely difficult items, on the other hand, tend to reduce reliability when guessing is rampant within the group.

■ Calculating Indices for Item and Test Evaluation

Teachers typically do not calculate difficulty, discrimination, and test reliability indices. These data are most often generated by a computer and then used by teachers to evaluate the quality of their tests. Teachers who use spreadsheet programs, however, can easily obtain these test quality indicators using the statistical functions in spreadsheets. To facilitate the work of these computer-based analysts and to help ensure that you understand the nature of these quality indicators and their interrelationships, the calculation procedures are included in this section.

Calculating Item Difficulty Indices

The item difficulty index, p, is easy to calculate. The number of students in the group who answer each item correctly is divided by the total number of students who took the test. The formula for calculating p is:

$$P = \frac{R}{N}$$

R represents the number of students who answer each item right, and N represents the total number of students in the class.

Suppose you administer a five-item test to a class that contains 40 students, and you obtain the item results displayed in Table 11.10. The first column contains each

TABLE 11.10

Item Difficulty Indices for a Five-Item Test

Item	R	N	p
1	40	40	40/40 = 1.00
2	36	40	36/40 = .90
3	32	40	32/40 = .80
4	20	40	20/40 = .50
5	15	40	15/40 = .375

item number; the second column, *R,* lists the number of students who answered each item right; the third column, *N,* indicates the number of students who took the test; and the last column, *p,* illustrates how the difficulty index is calculated for the five items.

Interpreting the difficulty indices for these five items, you would conclude that item 1, $p = 1.00$, was very easy for the group since all members answered it correctly. Each subsequent item is more difficult for the group, and item 5, $p = .375$, was extremely difficult.

Calculating *d* for Item Discrimination

Prior to calculating the discrimination index, *d,* two subgroups of class members must be identified. One subgroup selected typically contains approximately 27 percent of the class who earn the highest overall test scores, and it is called the *upper subgroup.* The other subgroup contains approximately 27 percent of the class who earn the lowest overall test scores, and it is called the *lower subgroup.* For example, if a class contains 40 students, the upper and lower subgroups would each contain 10 students, or about 27 percent of the total class of 40. Should a class contain 100 students, then the upper and lower subgroups would each contain 27 students. The performance of these two extreme subgroups is then compared on an item-by-item basis following the assumption that if an item differentiates between those who do and do not know the content, it will be most readily detectable by comparing the performance on that item of the extreme upper- and lower-scoring subgroups.

Although computer-generated reports typically include only 27 percent of the students in the subgroups, it is not incorrect to include more, and including 50 percent in each subgroup is acceptable. Discrimination indices calculated on only the highest- and lowest-scoring students tend to be higher than those obtained using all members of a class.

To identify the particular students included in each subgroup, the raw scores (total number of items answered correctly) of all students who took the test are calculated and then students are ranked by raw score from the highest to the lowest performance. From these ranked raw scores, the number of students required to complete the upper subgroup are selected from the high end of the raw score scale, and the number of students required for the lower subgroup are selected from the bottom end of the scale. Each subgroup must contain an equal number of students.

With these two subgroups identified, the discrimination index, d, can be calculated. The procedure is to (1) calculate the proportion of students in the upper subgroup who answer the item correctly (p_u), (2) calculate the proportion of students in the lower subgroup who answer the item correctly (p_l), and (3) subtract the proportion correct in the lower group from the proportion correct in the upper group to obtain the difference. The formula for this calculation is

$$d = p_u - p_l \quad \text{or} \quad \frac{R_u}{n_u} - \frac{R_l}{n_l}$$

where

p_u = the proportion in the upper subgroup who answers correctly
p_l = the proportion in the lower subgroup who answers correctly
R_u = the number in the upper subgroup who answers correctly
R_l = the number in the lower subgroup who answers correctly
n_u = the number of students in the upper subgroup
n_l = the number of students in the lower subgroup

This difference between subgroup difficulty indices reflects whether the item was easier for the upper- than the lower-scoring subgroup, as one would reasonably expect.

Table 11.11 contains a five-item test administered to 40 students. Columns II and III repeat the total group item difficulty (p) information from Table 11.10. Column IV contains the difficulty index for only the 10 students in the upper subgroup (p_u). This index is calculated by dividing the number of students in the upper subgroup who answered the item correctly (R_u) by the number of students in the upper subgroup (n_u). Column V includes the difficulty index for the lower subgroup (p_l) obtained by dividing the number of students in the lower subgroup who answered the item correctly by the number of students in the lower subgroup (n_l). Column VI contains the discrimination index (d) for each item. It is obtained by subtracting the difficulty index of the lower subgroup (p_l) from the difficulty index of the upper subgroup (p_u).

TABLE 11.11

Item Discrimination Indices for a Five-Item Test

I Item	II R	III p_n	IV $R_u/n_u = p_u$	V $R_l/n_l = p_l$	VI $p_u - p_l = d$
1	40	1.00	10/10 = 1.00	10/10 = 1.00	1.00 − 1.00 = .00
2	36	.90	10/10 = 1.00	8/10 = .80	1.00 − .80 = .20
3	32	.80	6/10 = .60	6/10 = .60	.60 − .60 = .00
4	20	.50	8/10 = .80	2/10 = .20	.80 − .20 = .60
5	15	.375	1/10 = .10	3/10 = .30	.10 − .30 = −.20

Recall that the discrimination index (d) reflects the difference between the difficulty of the item for the upper and lower subgroups. Notice that item 1 was very easy for the entire class ($p = 1.00$), for the upper group ($p_u = 1.00$), and for the lower group ($p_l = 1.00$). The discrimination index of .00 for item 1 reflects that there was no difference at all in the difficulty of the item for the two extreme subgroups; thus, it fails to discriminate between those who know the most (highest overall exam scores) and those who know the least (lowest overall exam scores) in the domain tested.

Item 2 was easy for the overall class ($p_n = .90$), yet it was easier for the upper subgroup ($p_u = 1.00$) than for the lower subgroup ($p_l = .80$), resulting in a discrimination index of .20 for the item. The third item was more difficult for the class ($p_n = .80$), although it was equally difficult for the upper subgroup ($p_u = .60$) and the lower subgroup ($p_l = .60$), resulting in no discrimination between the two extreme groups ($d = .00$). Item 4 was quite difficult since only one-half the class answered correctly ($p_n = .50$). The item, however, was relatively easy for the upper group ($p_u = .80$) and very difficult for the lower group ($p_l = .20$), resulting in good discrimination between those students who knew the most and the least on the overall exam. Quite a different result was observed for item 5. It was very difficult for the entire class ($p_n = .375$), extremely difficult for the upper group ($p_u = .10$), and very difficult for the lower group ($p_l = .30$). Since the lower subgroup performed better on item 5 than the upper subgroup, the discrimination index is a negative value, -.20, which occurs when an item is less difficult for the extreme lower subgroup.

The negative discrimination index of $-.20$ for the item 5 reflects some type of ambiguity in the item. The item is quite difficult for the class ($p_n = .375$) and even more difficult for the upper subgroup ($p_u = .10$). Such a difficult item with a negative discrimination index might reflect rampant guessing behavior, a distractor that was also correct, a miskeyed item, or any number of other problems. This illogical data for the item indicates that the item should be analyzed carefully prior to using it again. The p value of .375 indicates that there is either a problem with the item or the instruction was inadequate. The low p value, coupled with the negative discrimination index, indicates clearly that further analysis of the item is warranted.

The Item Difficulty-Discrimination Relationship

Undoubtedly, you noticed during the preceding discussion that the discrimination index was interpreted relative to the difficulty index. The discrimination index is partially a function of the difficulty index in that for each difficulty index, there is a limited range of discrimination indices possible. Figure 11.4 illustrates the relationship between the difficulty and discrimination indices. Difficulty indices are listed along the bottom of the figure from 0.00 on the left, indicating that no student answered an item correctly, to 1.00 on the right side of the scale, indicating that all students answered correctly. These difficulty indices are calculated based on the performance of the subgroups (p_{ul}) rather than the overall class (p_n). The numbers along the left side of the figure reflect the possible range of discrimination indices from

FIGURE 11.4

The Test Item Difficulty-Discrimination Relationship

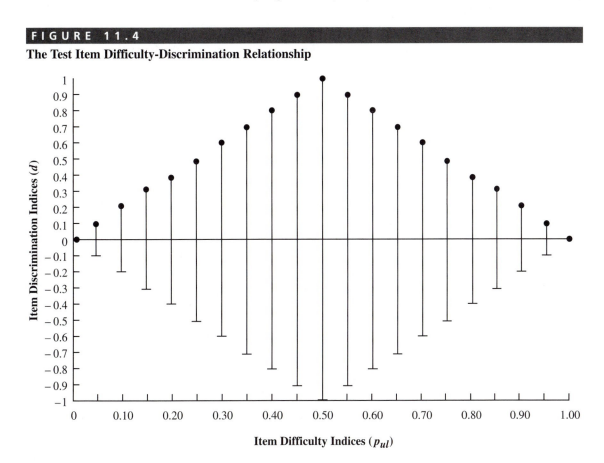

1.00 at the top through −1.00 at the bottom. Recall that discrimination values above .00 reflect that an item was easier for the upper group than the lower group, and negative values below 0.00 reflect that an item was easier for the lower subgroup than for the upper.

Directly above each difficulty index is a vertical line. The dot at the top of each line indicates the highest possible positive discrimination value for the given difficulty index, and the bar at the bottom of the line indicates the lowest possible negative discrimination index for the item difficulty level. Notice, for example, that for a difficulty value of .10, the highest positive discrimination value is .20 and the lowest negative value is −.20. The maximum discrimination values for a difficulty level of .20 are .40 and −.40. The vertical line connecting the two extreme discrimination values indicates that discrimination values may fall at points between the two extremes for any difficulty index, depending on the difference in item difficulty between the two extreme comparison groups. The horizontal line across the figure at $d = 0.00$ indicates the point at which there is no discrimination between the two groups, and $d = .00$ can occur across the range of difficulty indices.

Notice the symmetrical nature of discrimination values in Figure 11.4. For each difficulty value, the discrimination value range extends an equal distance above and below the $d = 0.00$, or no discrimination line. Notice also that the extreme possible values of discrimination increase steadily from a p_{ul} value of 0.00 to a p_{ul} value of 0.50 and then steadily decrease from $p_{ul} = 0.50$ to $p_{ul} = 1.00$. This symmetry is explained easily when you understand the relationship between the p_{ul} and d values.

Consider first the symmetry of the range of positive and negative discrimination indices for each p_{ul} value. Suppose your total class contains 40 students and that the upper and lower subgroups each contain 10 students. Based on these numbers, the possible range of discrimination indices for items with p_{ul} values of 0.30 and 0.70 will be examined. Notice in Figure 11.4 that the extreme values and the range of possible discrimination values are the same for these two difficulty indices.

Table 11.12 contains all the possible item discrimination data for the selected p_{ul} values. The left data set illustrates all the possible combinations of right responses to the item if 14, or 70 percent, of the upper and lower subgroups answer correctly ($20 \times .70 = 14$). The highest positive discrimination index will be observed when all 10 members of the upper subgroup answer correctly, while only 4 members of the lower subgroup answer correctly ($d = 1.00 - .40$, or $.60$). There are, however, six other combinations of upper- and lower-subgroup correct responses when the number of students answering correctly totals 14, and they are also illustrated in the table. Each time 1 less student from the upper subgroup responds correctly, 1 more in the lower subgroup must answer correctly since for a p value of .70, the total number of correct responses is fixed at 14. Each combination of R_u and R_l results in a different discrimination index. When each subgroup has 7 members responding correctly, then a d value of .00, or no discrimination between the upper and lower subgroups, results. The maximum negative discrimination index occurs when all members of the lower subgroup and only 4 members of the upper subgroup answer the item correctly.

You can see that the same phenomenon occurs in the right side of the table for items with difficulty indices (p_{ul}) of .30. In this instance, however, only 6 of the 20 students have answered the item correctly ($.30 \times 20 = 6$). Again, only seven different combinations of R_u and R_l are possible, and they are illustrated. The maximum positive discrimination index possible is .60 and the maximum negative is $-.60$. The remaining five discrimination values fall between these two extremes.

Table 11.13 illustrates the various levels of discrimination possible for difficulty indices of .60 and .40. Notice in Figure 11.4 that the vertical discrimination line above p_{ul} values of .60 and .40 are longer than the ones for items with p_{ul} values of .30 and .70. The longer length of the lines reflects that there are more combinations of R_u and R_l possible at p values of .60 and .40. When the analysis group contains 20 students and the p_{ul} value is .60, then 12 students have answered the item correctly ($.60 \times 20 = 12$). There are nine combinations of R_u and R_l possible in this case, and the discrimination index that would result from each combination is illustrated. Why

TABLE 11.12

The Possible Discrimination Indices for Difficulty Indices of .70 and .30 and an Analysis Group Containing 20 Students

		$P_{ul} = .70$					$P_{ul} = .30$		
R_u	R_l	P_u	P_l	d	R_u	R_l	P_u	P_l	d
10	4	1.00	.40	.60	6	0	.60	.00	.60
9	5	.90	.50	.40	5	1	.50	.10	.40
8	6	.80	.60	.20	4	2	.40	.20	.20
7	7	.70	.70	.00	3	3	.30	.30	.00
6	8	.60	.80	−.20	2	4	.20	.40	−.20
5	9	.50	.90	−.40	1	5	.10	.50	−.40
4	10	.40	1.00	−.60	0	6	.00	.60	−.60

Note: The total number of students in the upper and lower subgroups for each *p* value is calculated as: $p = .70$, $20(.70) = 14$; $p = .30$, $20(.30) = 6$.

TABLE 11.13

The Possible Discrimination Indices for Difficulty Indices of .60 and .40 and an Analysis Group Containing 20 Students

		$P_{ul} = .60$					$P_{ul} = .40$		
R_u	R_l	P_u	P_l	d	R_u	R_l	P_u	P_l	d
10	2	1.00	.20	.80	8	0	.80	.00	.80
9	3	.90	.30	.60	7	1	.70	.10	.60
8	4	.80	.40	.40	6	2	.60	.20	.40
7	5	.70	.50	.20	5	3	.50	.30	.20
6	6	.60	.60	.00	4	4	.40	.40	.00
5	7	.50	.70	−.20	3	5	.30	.50	−.20
4	8	.40	.80	−.40	2	6	.20	.60	−.40
3	9	.30	.90	−.60	1	7	.10	.70	−.60
2	10	.20	1.00	−.80	0	8	.00	.80	−.80

Note: The total number of students in the upper and lower subgroups for each *p* value is calculated as: $p = .60$, $20(.60) = 12$; $p = .40$, $20(.40) = 8$.

is there no $R_u - R_l$ combination of 12 and 0 or 11 and 1 listed in the table? These combinations are not possible since the upper and lower subgroups contain only 10 students; thus, the highest possible R value is 10 for either group. Notice the symmetrical nature of d values for a difficulty index of .40. Eight students have answered the item correctly with nine possible d values.

The fact that the highest possible discrimination index varies with the level of the difficulty index makes the discrimination index somewhat abstract to interpret. For example, you cannot set one value of discrimination to reflect good item discrimination. Suppose you established $d = .50$ as a value below which item discrimination is judged questionable. Notice in Figure 11.4 that it is impossible to obtain such a high value unless the item difficulty level is between .25 and .75. This criterion of $d \geq .50$ presents a problem since many quality items on classroom tests yield p_{ul} values of .80 or higher. To solve this dilemma, use the criteria based on p and q previously described to judge discrimination quality.

Calculating the Point-Biserial Correlation Index for Item Discrimination

The formula used to calculate the point-biserial correlation index is

$$r_{pbi} = \frac{\overline{X}_p - \overline{X}}{\sigma} \sqrt{\frac{p}{q}}$$

where

$\overline{X}_p$ = the mean or average overall test score for only the subgroup of students who answers the item correctly.

$\overline{X}$ = the mean or average overall test score for the total class.

σ = the standard deviation for the total test.

p = the proportion of the total class who answers the item correctly.

q = the proportion of the total class who answers the item incorrectly $(1 - p)$.

A quick look at the terms in this formula makes it clear that teachers do not calculate the r_{pbi} index by hand for items on their tests. Since the item analysis reports generated in your school are likely to include the point-biserial correlation index instead of the discrimination index, d, it is important for you to be able to interpret the r_{pbi} values provided. The following discussion is for those readers who want to understand the indices they are expected to interpret. The calculation of each element in the formula and the combination process are described in Table 11.14. Students are listed in Column A, and their responses to each of five test items are included in section B. For each item, correct answers are indicated with a 1, and incorrect answers are assigned a 0. Column C contains each student's raw score and the total group's mean score. The standard deviation for the test is calculated in Column D.

Column E illustrates the calculation of the mean test scores for only the students who answered each of the five items correctly ($\overline{X}_p$). Column F illustrates the calculation of the difficulty index (p) for the five items, and Column G shows the calculation of q, or $1 - p$, for each item. Column H illustrates the calculation of the point-biserial correlation index for each item.

TABLE 11.14

Calculation of the Point-Biserial Correlation Index

I.

A	B Test Item					C	D Standard Deviation		
Student	1	2	3	4	5	Raw Score	$(X - \overline{X})$	x^2	σ
1	1	1	1	1	1	5	5 − 3 = 2	4	$\sigma = \sqrt{10/5}$
2	1	1	1	1	0	4	4 − 3 = 1	1	
3	1	1	1	0	0	3	3 − 3 = 0	0	= 1.41
4	1	1	0	0	0	2	2 − 3 = −1	1	
5	1	0	0	0	0	1	1 − 3 = −2	4	
p_n	1.00	.80	.60	.40	.20	$\Sigma = 15$	$\Sigma x^2 = 10$		
r_{pbi}	.00	.70	.87	.86	.71	$\overline{X} = 15/5 = 3$			

II.

Item	E $\overline{X}_p$	F p	G q	H $r_{pbi} = \dfrac{\overline{X}_p - \overline{X}}{\sigma}\sqrt{\dfrac{p}{q}}$		
1	15/5 = 3	5/5 = 1	1 − 1 = .00	$[(3 - 3)/1.41]\sqrt{1.00/.00}$ =	.00(1.00)	= .00
2	14/4 = 3.5	4/5 = .80	1 − .80 = .20	$[(3.5 - 3)/1.41]\sqrt{.80/.20}$ =	.35(2)	= .70
3	12/3 = 4	3/5 = .60	1 − .60 = .40	$[(4 - 3)/1.41]\sqrt{.60/.40}$ =	.71(1.22)	= .87
4	9/2 = 4.5	2/5 = .40	1 − .40 = .60	$[(4.5 - 3)/1.41]\sqrt{.40/.60}$ =	1.06(.816)	= .86
5	5/1 = 5	1/5 = .20	1 − .20 = .80	$[(5 - 3)/1.41]\sqrt{.20/.80}$ =	1.42(.5)	= .71

The difficulty and point-biserial correlation indices are repeated in the bottom rows of the top portion of the table in section B. Notice that all students answered item 1 correctly; thus, the difference between the two means is .00, which can only result in a r_{pbi} discrimination index of .00. The remaining r_{pbi} indices are all high and positive. These results could have been predicted from the pattern of incorrect responses since all errors committed for any items were made by the lower-scoring students. Except for item 1, you could conclude that the items on this test discriminated well between those who earned the highest and lowest scores on the exam.

Table 11.15 contains another set of test scores with less than ideal discrimination for some items. The test scores range from 10 to 2, the overall mean is 5.6, and the standard deviation is 2.37. The highest difficulty index is .80, and the lowest is .40. The point-biserial correlation indices are calculated in the bottom portion of the table. Notice that two of the items, 4 and 7, have negative r_{pbi} indices. These negative

TABLE 11.15

The Point-Biserial Correlation Index Calculated for a Ten-Item Test

Student	1	2	3	4	5	6	7	8	9	10	Raw Score X	$(X - \bar{X})$	x^2
					Test Item								
1	1	1	1	1	1	1	1	1	1	1	10	4.4	19.36
2	1	1	1	1	0	1	0	1	1	1	8	2.4	5.76
3	1	1	1	1	0	1	0	1	1	0	7	1.4	1.96
4	1	1	1	0	1	1	0	1	1	0	7	1.4	1.96
5	1	1	1	0	0	1	0	1	0	1	6	.4	.16
6	1	1	0	0	1	0	1	1	0	0	5	−.6	.36
7	1	1	0	0	1	0	1	0	0	1	5	−.6	.36
8	1	0	0	1	0	0	1	0	0	0	3	−2.6	6.76
9	0	0	0	1	0	0	1	0	0	1	3	−2.6	6.76
10	0	0	0	1	0	0	1	0	0	0	2	−3.6	12.96
p_n	.80	.70	.50	.60	.40	.50	.60	.60	.40	.50	$\bar{X} = 56/10$		$\sigma = \sqrt{56.4/10}$
r_{pbi}	.66	.81	.84	−.05	.40	.84	−.48	.81	.83	.34	$= 5.6$		$= 2.37$

Item	$\bar{X}_p$	$\bar{X}_p - \bar{X}$	$\dfrac{\bar{X}_p - \bar{X}}{\sigma}$	$\sqrt{\dfrac{p_n}{q}}$	r_{pbi}
1	6.38	.78	.329	2.00	.66
2	6.86	1.26	.532	1.53	.81
3	7.60	2.00	.844	1.00	.84
4	5.50	−.10	−.042	1.22	−.05
5	6.75	1.15	.485	.82	.40
6	7.60	2.00	.844	1.00	.84
7	4.67	−.93	−.392	1.22	−.48
8	7.17	1.57	.662	1.22	.81
9	8.00	2.40	1.013	.82	.83
10	6.40	.80	.338	1.00	.34

values resulted from the fact that the average test score for students who passed these items is lower than the mean score for the class. For item 4, the means were very close, so the r_{pbi} index is slightly lower than 0 at −.05. For item 7, the difference between the two means is −.93, so the r_{pbi} index is much lower.

Consider the three items with p_n values of .50. Both items 3 and 6 yield a very high r_{pbi} index of .84, indicating that the items discriminate extremely well between the two groups. Item 10, on the other hand, has students at the upper and lower end of the raw score scale who answered the item correctly, so a much lower r_{pbi} index of .34 resulted. It remains a positive value because one more higher- than lower-scoring student answered correctly, which yielded a positive difference between the two mean scores.

Calculating the Kuder-Richardson Internal Consistency Reliability Index

The K-R$_{20}$ index is the internal consistency reliability measure most often reported on computer-generated test analysis reports. The following formula is used for computing it:

$$\text{K-R}_{20} = \frac{n}{n-1}\left(1 - \frac{\sum p_i q_i}{\sigma^2}\right)$$

where

n = the total number of test items.

p_i = the proportion of students who answer each item correctly.

q_i = the proportion of students who answer each item incorrectly, or $1 - p$.

$p_i q_i$ = the proportion answering correctly times the proportion answering incorrectly. This value is called the *item variance,* and it is sometimes symbolized as s_i^2.

Σ = sum the values for all test items.

σ^2 = the total test variance. This value is the square of the standard deviation. The variance is calculated as $\Sigma(X - \overline{X})^2/N$. When the group tested represents a sample rather than the population, this value will be written as s^2 and calculated using $N - 1$ in the denominator.

The subscript $_i$ refers to item data.

Table 11.16 illustrates the calculation of the K-R$_{20}$ internal consistency reliability index. Two tests are included in the table. Each test includes data for six items and six students. The bottom rows for each test list item difficulty and discrimination data. The far right side of each test's data includes the calculation of the mean, test variance, and internal consistency reliability index.

Test I has a perfectly U-shaped distribution of raw scores, maximum item variance for each item (pq), and perfect item discrimination for all items at 1.00 for the point-biserial correlation index. Such a configuration of item characteristics yields the maximum sum of item variances ($\Sigma p_i q_i$). It also yields maximum test variance given the range of scores since $[(6 - 0)/2]^2 = 3^2 = 9$. Notice that the maximum sum of item variances divided by the maximum test variance results in a K-R$_{20}$ index of .999. Such a high K-R$_{20}$ index reflects that the test is completely internally consistent.

Now review the item and test data in Table 11.16 for Test II. The items vary in difficulty and thus in item variances. This variability will reduce the internal consistency reliability index. These items probably do not measure the exact same skill since all students answered item 1 correctly and only one student answered item 6 correctly. Such item data usually reflect heterogeneous test content. In spite of test content differences, all items but the first one discriminate very well, which results in a wide range of scores and large test variance for a content-heterogeneous test containing only six items. The observed K-R$_{20}$ index of .80 reflects good internal consistency for a test measuring heterogeneous content.

TABLE 11.16

Two Tests with Good Internal Consistency Reliability

	Test I									Test Data		
		Item					**Data for Test Variance**					
Student	1	2	3	4	5	6	Raw Score	$x*$	x^2			
1	1	1	1	1	1	1	6	3	9	$\overline{X}$	= 18/6 = 3	
2	1	1	1	1	1	1	6	3	9	σ^2	= 54/6 = 9	
3	1	1	1	1	1	1	6	3	9	K-R$_{20}$	= 6/5[1 − (1.5/9)]	
4	0	0	0	0	0	0	0	−3	9		= 1.2(.833)	
5	0	0	0	0	0	0	0	−3	9		= .99	
6	0	0	0	0	0	0	0	−3	9			
p	.50	.50	.50	.50	.50	.50						
pq	.25	.25	.25	.25	.25	.25						
r_{pbi}	1.00	1.00	1.00	1.00	1.00	1.00						

	Test II									Test Data		
		Item					**Data for Test Variance**					
Student	1	2	3	4	5	6	Raw Score	$x*$	x^2			
1	1	1	1	1	1	1	6	2.5	6.25	$\overline{X}$	= 21/6 = 3.5	
2	1	1	1	1	1	0	5	1.5	2.25	σ^2	= 17.5/6 = 2.92	
3	1	1	1	1	0	0	4	.5	.25	K-R$_{20}$	= 6/5[1 − (.97/2.92)]	
4	1	1	1	0	0	0	3	−.5	.25		= 1.2(.668)	
5	1	1	0	0	0	0	2	−1.5	2.25		= .80	
6	1	0	0	0	0	0	1	−2.5	6.25			
p	1.00	.83	.67	.50	.33	.17						
pq	.00	.14	.22	.25	.22	.14						
r_{pbi}	.00	.65	.83	.88	.82	.66						

$*x = X - \overline{X}$.

Now consider the item and test data for the two tests illustrated in Table 11.17. These tests both have lower K-R$_{20}$ indices than the tests in Table 11.16. Notice that Test III has the same mean, range, and variance as Test II in Table 11.16, yet the internal consistency index is smaller. The smaller K-R$_{20}$ index results from the item characteristics. Item 2 discriminates negatively, and all items are relatively difficult, yielding higher item variances than those in Test II.

Test IV in Table 11.17 has an internal consistency reliability index of −.456, indicating internal inconsistency for the test. Students' responses were random, the items were difficult, and all six students obtained the same raw score of 3. In this case:

1. The mean score is 3.
2. The test variance and standard deviation are .00 since no score varies from the mean.
3. The item point-biserial correlation indices (r_{pbi}) are all .00 since there is no difference between means for item passers and the total group, and the test's standard deviation is .00.

TABLE 11.17
Two Tests Yielding Lower Internal Consistency

Test III

Student	1	2	3	4	5	6	Raw Score	x*	x^2	Test Data
1	1	1	1	1	1	1	6	2.5	6.25	$\overline{X}$ = 21/6 = 3.5
2	1	0	1	1	1	1	5	1.5	2.25	σ^2 = 17.5/6 = 2.92
3	1	0	0	1	1	1	4	.5	.25	K-R$_{20}$ = 6/5[1 − (1.41/2.92)]
4	1	1	1	0	0	0	3	−.5	.25	= 1.2(.52)
5	0	1	1	0	0	0	2	−1.5	2.25	= .62
6	0	1	0	0	0	0	1	−2.5	6.25	
p	.67	.67	.67	.50	.50	.50				
pq	.22	.22	.22	.25	.25	.25				
r_{pbi}	.83	−.42	.42	.88	.88	.88				

Test IV

Student	1	2	3	4	5	6	Raw Score	x*	x^2	Test Data
1	1	0	1	0	1	0	3	0	0	$\overline{X}$ = 18/6 = 3
2	0	1	0	1	0	1	3	0	0	σ^2 = 0/6 = 0
3	0	1	0	1	0	1	3	0	0	K-R$_{20}$ = 6/5[1 − (1.38/.00)]
4	1	0	0	1	0	1	3	0	0	= 1.2 (−.38)
5	1	0	1	0	1	0	3	0	0	= −.456
6	0	1	0	1	0	1	3	0	0	
p	.50	.50	.33	.67	.33	.67				
pq	.25	.25	.22	.22	.22	.22				
r_{pbi}	.00	.00	.00	.00	.00	.00				

$*x = X − \overline{X}$.

Notice the impact of these data on the K-R$_{20}$ index for Test IV. The first element in the formula remains 1.2 since there are six items. The item variances for the six items are relatively high since the items are difficult, yet the test variance is .00. Only the sum of the item variances is subtracted from 1, yielding –.38, which, multiplied by the correction factor 1.2, is –.456. This K-R$_{20}$ index reflects great internal inconsistency for the test. The difficult items are not accompanied by good item discrimination and reasonable test variance. Test inconsistency can be expected when students do not possess the skills measured by a test and are randomly guessing answers.

■ Computer Technology

The item and test analysis information described in this chapter is readily available from computer-based test scoring and item analysis programs. An example of a computer-generated report is illustrated in Figure 11.5. The portion of the report illustrated is for only 10 items of a 50-item test. Notice that the top of the report contains the teacher's name, class identification, and date. It also reports the test's total number of items and students, the group's mean and median scores, the range, the high score, the low score, the standard deviation, and the total test reliability (K-R$_{20}$) index.

The bottom portion of the table contains the item numbers in the far left column and the number of students choosing each response option in the next six columns. You can perform a distractor analysis using the information in these response columns. Following the response data, there are three difficulty indices and two discrimination indices listed for each item. Using this information, you can locate items that are too difficult for the class as well as items that do not discriminate adequately between the upper- and lower-scoring students.

These item difficulty and discrimination indices can be generated using a computer-based spreadsheet program when scanning services are not available or practical. The types of item data, however, are rarely available from commercially available gradebook programs.

■ Summary

Due to limited time and resources, teachers usually cannot field test and revise items before a test is administered to a class. However, analyzing test items after students have taken the test can help teachers locate faulty or ineffective items and identify areas where instruction might be improved.

The three types of item analysis are item difficulty analysis, item discrimination analysis, and distractor analysis. The difficulty index is a measure of the difficulty of an item for a given group of students; it is the proportion of students who answer the item correctly; and it can range from 0 to 1.00. To describe the difficulty of an item using this measure, the indices can be classified into four categories: very easy (p = .90–1.00), moderately easy (p = .70–.89), fairly difficult (p = .50–.69), and very difficult (p = .00–.49). The overall difficulty of a test depends on the number of items falling into each category. The difficulty index can be used to evaluate an

FIGURE 11.5

Sample Computer-Generated Test and Item Analysis Report

Report for: Ms. Hauser					Social Studies 10:00		November 12	
Total Points	50	Total Students	39		Mean	24.85	Median	23
Range Hi/Low	33 43/11	Standard Deviation	8.4		Reliability: K-R$_{20}$	.80		

	Response Frequencies (# of students choosing each response)						Difficulty Indices (p)			Discrimination Indices	
Item No.	A 1	B 2	C 3	D 4	E 5	none	Total Group	Upper Group	Lower Group	d	r_{pbi}
1	4	1	3	30*	1	0	.77	.82	.55	.27	.23
2	24*	3	2	2	8	0	.62	.91	.18	.73	.64
3	8	26*	5	0	0	0	.67	.82	.36	.46	.42
4	1	31*	4	2	1	0	.79	.91	.45	.46	.41
5	15*	13	6	3	2	0	.38	.73	.09	.64	.60
6	2	3	11	22*	1	0	.56	1.00	.18	.82	.70
7	13*	15	9	2	0	0	.33	.45	.09	.36	.28
8	18	5*	8	4	4	0	.13	.27	.09	.18	.29
9	3	10*	16	3	7	0	.26	.00	.27	−.27	−.25
10	4	2	18*	2	13	0	.46	.64	.27	.37	.27

*Correct response.

item by comparing (1) an item's difficulty with the difficulty anticipated, given the skill's complexity and the group's achievement characteristics; (2) the difficulty indices for items measuring the same objective; and (3) the difficulty indices for hierarchically related items. Difficulty measures that are very different from those anticipated signal a problem with the item, the instruction, or your perception of the circumstances.

Item discrimination analysis compares the performances of students who earn higher overall test scores with those of students earning lower total scores. Discrimination indices can range from 1.00 to −1.00. Positive numbers indicate that students with higher overall scores performed better on an item than did students with lower test scores. A discrimination index of .00 indicates that the upper and lower groups performed the same on an item; a negative index indicates that the lower-scoring group performed better.

Evaluating an item using the discrimination index depends on two factors: the difficulty level of the item and the group's achievement characteristics. For homogeneous groups, relatively little discrimination is anticipated for an item, regardless of its difficulty level. For heterogeneous groups, little or no discrimination is anticipated for items that are extremely easy or extremely difficult. However, moderate-to-high, positive values should be anticipated for midrange difficulty indices.

Distractor analysis is performed for selected-response items. It provides information about the plausibility of distractors, helps teachers identify common misconceptions, and pinpoints parts of an item that are causing problems. In performing a distractor analysis, the number or percentage of students in the upper and lower groups who select each response are identified and analyzed. If teachers have ample time, they analyze the distractors for all items. However, when time is limited, they analyze only items that were (1) less difficult or more difficult than anticipated, (2) negative discriminators, and (3) designed to measure relatively complex skills.

Item analysis data do not indicate what is wrong with an item. Instead, they suggest that an item and perhaps the related instruction need to be reconsidered. Before calculating students' grades, you should eliminate items found to be defective, as they tend to distort the results and affect the validity of your interpretations.

One measure, the $K\text{-}R_{20}$ index, can be used to evaluate the internal consistency of an objective test. The $K\text{-}R_{20}$ index compares the sum of the item variances with the total test variance. This index is affected by group homogeneity, content homogeneity, test length, and item difficulty. The maximum $K\text{-}R_{20}$ value is 1.00, though obtaining values this high for classroom tests is unlikely. Typically, $K\text{-}R_{20}$ indices around .80 reflect good internal consistency for classroom tests, given students' inadvertent errors, guessing behavior, and common instruction; $K\text{-}R_{20}$ values near .50 are common; but ones much below this level should be questioned.

Table 11.18 contains a summary of the indices used to evaluate test items and tests. It includes the purpose for each measure, its formula, and the criterion values for judging the item and test quality. These criterion values are appropriate for classroom posttests.

Calculating by hand the item and test indices described in this chapter is not feasible, but computer-based programs will calculate them for you. When you understand the indices included on computer-generated test reports, it is relatively easy to locate both the areas of strengths and problems in your tests, which is the first step in improving the quality of tests you use in your classroom.

■ PRACTICE EXERCISES

I. Types of Item Analysis

In the following exercise, Column A contains descriptions of item analysis activities and Column B names the three types of item analyses. Match each activity with its corresponding type of analysis.

TABLE 11.18

A Summary of Indices Used to Conduct an Item and Test Analysis

Analysis	Purpose	Measure	Formula	Criterion Values for Classroom Tests
Item Difficulty	Locate items more or less difficult than anticipated.	p	$p = \dfrac{R}{N}$ range $= .00$ to 1.00	Scanning Criterion: $p \geq .50$ $p \geq 90$: Very Easy $p = .70 - .89$: Moderately Easy $p = .50 - .69$: Fairly Difficult $p \leq .49$: Very Difficult
Item Discrimination	Determine consistency of students' item and total test performance.	d	$d = p_u - p_l$ range $= -1.00$ to 1.00	Scanning Criterion: $d \geq .00$ <table><tr><td>Quality</td><td>$p \leq .50$</td><td>$p \geq .50$</td></tr><tr><td>Inadequate</td><td>.00↓</td><td>.00↓</td></tr><tr><td>Moderate</td><td>$d \cong 1/2p$</td><td>$d \cong 1/2q$</td></tr><tr><td>Good</td><td>$d \cong p$</td><td>$d \cong q$</td></tr><tr><td>Excellent</td><td>$d \cong 2p$</td><td>$d \cong 2q$</td></tr></table>
		r_{rbi}	$\dfrac{\overline{X}_p - \overline{X}}{\sigma} \sqrt{\dfrac{p}{q}}$ range $= -1.00$ to 1.00	Scanning Criterion: $r_{pbi} \geq .20$
Item Distractor	Locate students' misconceptions for subsequent instruction. Locate faulty items for revision.	Proportion of students selecting each response		
Test Internal Consistency Reliability	Compare item variance with total test variance.	K-R$_{20}$	$\dfrac{n}{n-1}\left(1 - \dfrac{\sum pq}{\sigma^2}\right)$	K-R$_{20}$ > .80 Excellent K-R$_{20}$ < .50 Questionable

Column A	Column B
_____ **1.** Calculate the proportion of students who answer each item correctly.	a. Difficulty analysis
	b. Discrimination analysis
	c. Distractor analysis
_____ **2.** Summarize the number or proportion of students in the upper and lower groups who select each response option.	
_____ **3.** Compare the proportion of the upper and lower groups who answer each item correctly.	

_____ **4.** Compare the perceived item complexity with the proportion of students who answer correctly.

_____ **5.** Locate responses that were not plausible as well as common misconceptions.

_____ **6.** Compare the proportion of students who correctly answer items related to the same objective.

II. Using Item Data to Locate Potentially Flawed Objective Items and Distractors

In the preceding chapter on group performance analysis, the group's overall performance on the compound sentences posttest was described as somewhat heterogeneous (range $42 - 27 = 15$ or 36 percent of the total number of items on the test and standard deviation of 3.88 encompasses 26 percent of the range). Use the item data for only items 1 through 11 in Figure 11.6 to locate potentially flawed items based on their difficulty and discrimination indices, and record your answers in Figure 11.7. Check your analysis in Figure11.8F.

III. Interpreting Item Analysis Reports

Interpreting a computer-generated item analysis report using difficulty, discrimination, and distractor data. Table 11.19 contains 16 items selected from an item analysis report for a 56-item unit test. The following data were obtained for the test:

$\overline{X}$	R	σ	N Students	N Subgroups
47, 86%	$56 - 37 = 19$	5.6	28	8

The small number of students means that the data should be considered tentative.

A. Classify the group performance as heterogeneous or homogeneous, and set minimum values for the r_{pbi} and d indices.

B. Using Table 11.19, locate any items with total group difficulty indices (p) lower than .50.

C. Locate any items that all students answered correctly.

D. Locate all items with r_{pbi} and d indices lower than the established minimum criteria. Can any of these items be ignored based on the p value?

E. The same 56-item test was administered to a second class containing 32 students. Compare these overall test data to determine whether the two groups' performances were similar.

Group	$\overline{X}$	%	Range	Range as % of Total Items	σ	σ as % of Range
I	47	84	19	34%	5.6	29%
II	45.4	81	25	45%	5.6	22%

F. Using the selected data in Table 11.20, determine whether any items yielded consistently low r_{pbi} indices across class groups.

FIGURE 11.6

Item and Enabling Skill Data for Only the Coordinating Conjunction Portion of the Compound Sentences Posttest (Objectives III.A to III.F in Tables 3.5 and 4.11)

Mean = 37.5   Standard Deviation = 3.88

Enabling Skill Codes	COORDINATING CONJUNCTION ENABLING SKILLS															Overall Test Raw Score
	III.A	III.B	III.C	III.D				III.E		III.E		III.F				
Items	1	2	3	4	5	6	7	8	9	10	11	12	13	14	15	42
Correct Answers	2	3	1	3	2	4	1	4	2	1	4	Hand	Scored			
McComas	*	*	*	*	*	*	*	*	*	*	*	*	*	*	*	**42**
Talbot	*	*	*	*	*	*	*	*	*	*	*	*	*	*	*	**42**
Deddens	*	*	*	*	*	*	*	*	*	*	*	*	*	*	*	**41**
Prince	*	*	*	*	*	*	*	*	*	*	*	*	*	*	*	**41**
Augustine	*	*	*	*	*	*	*	*	*	*	*	*	*	*	*	**40**
Rust	*	*	*	*	*	*	*	*	*	*	*	*	*	*	*	40
Carey	*	*	*	*	*	2	*	*	*	*	*	*	*	*	*	40
White	*	*	*	*	*	*	*	*	*	*	*	*	x	*	*	40
Hager	*	*	*	*	*	*	*	*	*	*	*	*	*	*	*	40
McLaughlin	*	*	*	*	*	2	*	*	*	*	*	*	*	x	*	39
Cromer	*	*	*	*	*	2	*	*	*	*	*	*	*	x	*	39
Otto	*	*	*	*	*	2	*	*	*	*	*	*	*	x	*	38
Scragg	*	*	*	*	*	2	*	*	*	*	3	*	*	x	*	37
Hill	*	*	*	*	*	2	*	*	*	*	3	*	*	*	x	36
Lovejoy	*	*	*	*	*	*	*	*	*	4	3	*	*	x	*	35
Bailey	*	*	3	*	*	2	*	*	*	2	3	*	*	x	*	**35**
Gormley	*	*	*	*	*	2	*	*	3	*	3	*	*	x	x	**34**
Deiters	*	*	*	*	*	1	*	*	3	2	1	x	*	x	*	**33**
Stewart	*	*	2	*	*	1	*	3	3	*	2	x	*	x	x	**31**
Smith	*	1	*	*	*	1	*	1	1	*	1	x	x	x	x	**27**

(continued)

FIGURE 11.6   Continued

Enabling Skill Codes	COORDINATING CONJUNCTION ENABLING SKILLS														
	III.A	III.B	III.C	III.D				III.E		III.E		III.F			
Items	1	2	3	4	5	6	7	8	9	10	11	12	13	14	15
Total p	1.0	.95	.90	1.0	1.0	.45	1.0	.90	.80	.85	.60				
d	.00	.20	.40	.00	.00	1.0	.00	.40	.80	.40	1.0				
r_{pbi}	.00	.62	.39	.00	.00	.61	.00	.73	.81	.34	.84				

FIGURE 11.7

Chart for Summarizing Potentially Flawed Objective Test Items in Figure 11.6

Item Evaluation Criteria	Potentially Flawed Coordinating Conjunction Items	Potentially Problematic Distractors for Identified Items
1. Too difficult ($p < .50$)		
2. All students answering correctly (potential clues)		
3. Much more or less difficult than other items measuring the same objective		
4. Inadequate discrimination for a somewhat heterogeneous group		

TABLE 11.19

Difficulty and Discrimination Data for Selected Items from a Unit Test

Item	Key	Upper 27% Responses					Lower 27% Responses					Difficulty/Discrimination		
		1	2	3	4	NR	1	2	3	4	NR	p	d	r_{pbi}
1	3			1.00			.13	.26	.50	.13		.79	.50	.787
2	3		.13	.88			.25	.13	.63			.57	.25	.277
3	3		.13	.88			.25	.25	.25	.25		.64	.63	.460
4	1	.75		.13	.13		.50	.13	.13	.25		.57	.25	.162
5	3	.13		.88			.38		.63			.64	.25	.141
6	2		1.00					.50	.38	.13		.82	.50	.512
7	3	.13		.88			.25		.75			.82	.13	.130
8	3	.13		.88				.13	.75	.13		.86	.13	.016
9	2		.13	.88				.25	.63	.13		.25	−.12	−.260
10	3			1.00				.25	.75			.75	.25	.452
11	1	1.00					.88			.13		.86	.12	.052
12	3			1.00					.38	.63		.79	.63	.059
13	3	.13		.88			.25		.75			.75	.13	.114
14	4			.13	.88				.25	.75		.79	.13	.012
15	2		1.00				.13	.88				.93	.13	.393
16	2		1.00					.88		.13		.96	.13	.102

Note: A blank space indicates that no student selected the response, and the number beneath each response option indicates the proportion of the upper or lower subgroup that selected the response.

TABLE 11.20

Selected Data from Two Groups for Items That Yield Inadequate Point-Biserial Correlation Indices

Item	Key	Group	Upper 27% Responses				Lower 27% Responses				p	r_{pbi}
			1	2	3	4	1	2	3	4		
4	1	I	.75		.13	.13	.50	.13	.13	.25	.57	.162
		II	.89			.11	.78		.11	.11	.78	.082
7	3	I	.13		.88		.25		.75		.82	.130
		II			1.00				1.00		.91	−.013
8	3	I		.13	.88			.13	.75	.13	.86	.016
		II		.11	.78	.11		.11	.67	.22	.84	.172
9	2	I		.13	.88			.25	.63	.13	.25	−.260
		II	.11		.89			.33	.44	.22	.30	−.162
13	3	I	.13				.25		.75		.75	.114
		II	.11		.89		.44		.56		.72	.422
14	4	I			.13	.88			.25	.75	.79	.012
		II				1.00			.33	.67	.78	.379

G. Consider the distractors chosen by subgroup students for item 4. Based on this information, what might you conclude about the item?

H. Consider the distractors chosen by subgroup students for item 9. What might you conclude about this item?

I. Items 13 and 14 yielded inconsistent item discrimination data for the two groups. What might have caused these inconsistencies?

IV. Calculating Difficulty and Discrimination Indices

Figure 11.6 contains enabling skill and item data for the coordinating conjunction portion of the unit posttest prescribed in Figure 4.8F. The goal framework for this section of the exam is described in Figure 3.10. All item data are provided for items 1 through 11. For items 12, 13, 14, and 15, use your own paper to calculate the following indices and then insert them in the table in the appropriate cells.

A. Total group difficulty indices (p)

B. Discrimination indices (d)

C. Point-biserial correlation indices (r_{pbi})

V. Determining the Internal Consistency of the Overall Test

Using the item data and standard deviation reported for the coordinating conjunction items in Figure 11.6, calculate the K-R$_{20}$ index. (*Note:* This index is typically only calculated for the total test. There were 42 items on the total test, and that seems a few too many calculations for practice!)

VI. Enrichment

Obtain a computer-generated item analysis report for a test that either you or someone else has administered. If the test was administered to two different class groups, obtain both data sets to enable comparison of the data for two occasions. Obtain a copy of the examination.

A. Locate the mean, range, and standard deviation. (You may need to calculate the range since it frequently is not provided.)

B. Classify the group's performance as heterogeneous or homogeneous.

C. Set your minimum standards for difficulty and discrimination.

D. Locate the difficulty indices (p) for each item, and circle those items more difficult than your set criterion. Transfer the difficulty and discrimination data for these items to a copy of the test. Analyze the text of the test item and generate hunches about why the item was more difficult than anticipated.

E. Locate all items on the test that measure the same enabling skills. Compare the p values for item sets, and locate any items that are very much more or less difficult than others in the set. Copy difficulty, discrimination, and distractor data for items identified as potentially flawed onto the test copy, and examine the items carefully for inadvertent item construction errors.

F. Locate the discrimination index. Your report will typically include only one of the two indices described. If your report contains difficulty indices for upper and lower subgroups, you can use p_u and p_l to obtain d when it is not provided. Discrimination is usually considered acceptable when either of the discrimination indices reflects an adequate level. Circle all items that did not yield adequate discrimination. Copy difficulty, discrimination, and distractor data for these items onto the test form, and analyze the item context and content.

    G. In analyzing the content of items judged potentially flawed based on difficulty and discrimination indices:

        1. Locate and review distractors not chosen by any class members.

        2. Locate and review distractors selected by many of the students in the group.

        3. Locate and review distractors chosen by more students in the upper subgroup.

    H. Revise items you consider faulty.

■ FEEDBACK

  I. Types of Item Analysis

      1. a   **4.** a

      2. c   **5.** c

      3. b   **6.** a

  II. Using Item Data to Locate Potentially Flawed Objective Items and Distractors
    See Figure 11.8F.

  III. Interpreting Item Analysis Reports

    A. The range spans approximately 33 percent of the items, and the standard deviation spans 29 percent of the range. Based on these data, the group's performance would be classified as somewhat heterogeneous. The minimum value for r_{pbi} should be set at 20. Minimum values for d should be set at $1/2p$ or q depending on the p value. Any d value is acceptable when p values are .90 or greater.

    B. Item 9 has a p value of .25; thus, it does not meet the minimum difficulty criterion.

    C. There are no items that all students answered correctly; however, 96 percent answered item 16 correctly, and 93 percent answered item 15 correctly.

    D. Items with inadequate r_{pbi} indices include 4, 5, 7, 8, 9, 11, 12, 13, 14, and 16. Item 16 can be ignored based on its extremely high difficulty index (.96). Only one item, 9, yielded an inadequate d index.

    E. The two groups' average test performances were similar. Based on their ranges and standard deviations, both groups' performances would be classified as somewhat heterogeneous.

    F. Items that yielded consistently low discrimination indices across class groups are 4, 7, 8, and 9.

    G. For item 4, all distractors were chosen by at least one group member, indicating that they were plausible for students. The item does not appear to be miskeyed since the majority of both subgroups selected the keyed answer. Distractors 3 and 4 should be analyzed carefully to determine why they might be attractive to upper subgroup members.

    H. For item 9, all distractors were chosen by at least one member of the groups. The item is possibly miskeyed since distractor 3 had p_{ul} values of .76 (calculated as $[.88 + .63] \div 2$) and .67 and d values of .25 (calculated as $p_u - p_l$) and .45 for the two groups. If option 3 is not the correct answer, it should be analyzed carefully to determine why it was so attractive to students in both classes.

    I. The small number of students in each class and the even smaller number of students in the upper and lower subgroups undoubtedly resulted in item data that were not generalizable across groups. Notice in Table 11.19 that the d values for group I on these two

FIGURE 11.8F

Chart for Summarizing Potentially Flawed Objective Test Items in Figure 11.6

Item Evaluation Criteria	Potentially Flawed Coordinating Conjunction Items	Potentially Problematic Distractors for Identified Items
1. Too difficult ($p < .50$)	Item 6	Distractor 2 chosen by 8 students
2. All students answering correctly (potential clues)	Items 1, 4, 5, 7. These items are recalling verbal information and locating the coordinating conjunction within a sentence. It is reasonable for all members of the class to answer them correctly.	
3. Much more or less difficult than other items measuring the same objective	Item 6, more difficult Item 11, more difficult	▪ Distractor 2 chosen by 8 students ▪ All distractors functioning, 3 is the most chosen misconception
4. Inadequate discrimination for a somewhat heterogeneous group	None except those items answered correctly by all students	

items were acceptable at .13; thus, the higher discrimination values for group II were not completely unexpected.

IV. **Calculating Difficulty and Discrimination Indices**

	Item			
	12	13	14	15
A. Total p	.85	.90	.50	.80
B. d	.60	.20	1.00	.60
C. r_{pbi}	.78	.34	.70	.71

V. **Determining the Internal Consistency of the Overall Test**

The K-R$_{20}$ index is .95, and this value represents very good internal consistency for the co-ordinating conjunction portion of the unit posttest.

SUGGESTED READINGS

Gallagher, J. D. (1998). *Classroom assessment for teachers* (pp. 326–350). Columbus, OH: Merrill.

Lynn, R. L., & Gronlund, N. E. (2000). *Measurement and assessment in teaching* (8th ed., pp. 361–372). Englewood Cliffs, NJ: Prentice-Hall.

Nitko, A. J. (1996). *Educational assessment of students* (2nd ed., pp. 300–321). Columbus, OH: Merrill.

Popham, W. J. (1999). *Classroom assessment: What teachers need to know* (2nd ed., pp. 286–308). Boston: Allyn and Bacon.

Worthen, B. R., White, K. R., Fan, X., & Sudweeks, R. L. (1999). *Measurement and assessment in schools* (2nd ed., pp. 264–277). New York: Addison-Wesley Longman.

Evaluating Individual Performance and Instruction

- Perform a criterion-referenced analysis and an evaluation of an individual's test performances.
- Perform a norm-referenced analysis and an evaluation of an individual's test performances.
- Evaluate the quality of instruction for each goal.

Once you have analyzed a group's performance and the test, you need to interpret each individual's performance. A test score by itself has little meaning. To interpret a student's score, you can relate it to the number of skills measured by the test or compare it with scores of other students. Relating a student's test score to the number of skills measured is called *criterion-referenced analysis.* This term refers only to the interpretation of test scores obtained from criterion-referenced tests. Remember that the design of a criterion-referenced test is based on the carefully specified set of enabling skills that make up an instructional goal framework. Thus, a high score on a criterion-referenced test reflects that the student has mastered the criterion or set of skills embedded in the goal. Likewise, a low score reflects that a student has made little, if any, progress on the criterion. Relating a student's performance with that of other students is called *norm-referenced analysis.* Teachers use this type of analysis to determine whether a student's test performance is above average, average, or below average compared to classmates. Norm-referenced analysis can be used to interpret students' scores from any test, regardless of the logic used in the test design. Since the classroom tests described in this chapter are criterion referenced, both criterion-referenced and norm-referenced analyses can be performed.

Each of these analyses provides a different type of information. For example, if a criterion-referenced analysis indicated that a student had mastered only half of the skills measured, you might consider the student's performance inadequate. If you then performed a norm-referenced analysis and discovered that the same student's performance was well above average in the class, your interpretation of the score would probably change. In addition to evaluating individual performances, you should evaluate the group's performance on each goal and enabling skill. Information from this analysis will help you evaluate the quality of the instruction and identify lessons or portions of lessons that were not effective.

Conducting a Criterion-Referenced Analysis

All the performance analysis procedures presented thus far use students' raw scores. Raw scores alone do not provide the type of information you need to evaluate a student's progress on prescribed skills. Consider, for example, the test performances of J. Allen and T. Baker shown in Figure 12.1. The top row of the figure identifies the six enabling skills measured by the examination. The second row identifies the item numbers from 1 to 24. Notice that numbers 10 through 24 are written vertically. The third row identifies the keyed correct answer for each item. Notice that there are four items measuring each of the six skills. The rows for Allen and Baker contain the responses made by each student. A dot (.) indicates that the student's response matched the keyed correct response, and a number in a student-by-item cell indicates the particular incorrect response selected by the student. From the raw score column, you can see that both students answered 18 of 24 test items correctly. If the mean score on the test is also 18, you might conclude that their performances are the same and that they are average for the group. After looking at the students' prior performance records, you might also conclude that their test performances are typical for them. Now, compare the two students' responses by enabling skill and item.

Although both students answered 18 items correctly, their performances on the enabling skills were quite different. Allen correctly answered 3 of 4 items for each skill. Baker, however, correctly answered all of the items for four of the skills, failed skill 4 completely, and answered half the items correctly for skill 6. This information sheds new light on the divergence of the students' performances and suggests very different instructional needs.

FIGURE 12.1

Student Performance by Enabling Skill and Item

Enabling Skills	1	2	3	4	5	6	Total	
Item **Answer**	1 2 3 4 3 2 1 4	5 6 7 8 4 3 1 4	1 1 1 9 0 1 2 2 3 5 1	1 1 1 1 3 4 5 6 2 2 1 3	1 1 1 2 7 8 9 0 5 1 4 3	2 2 2 2 1 2 3 4 2 1 1 5	**Raw** **Score**	**%**
Allen, J.	. . 2 .	. 1 . .	. . 4 .	1 . . .	. 2 . .	. . 3 .	18	75
Baker, T.	. . . .	. . . .	. . . .	1 3 2 2	. . . .	3 . 3 .	18	75

Note: Item numbers are written vertically.

Reviewing your students' response patterns can help you determine their mastery of the enabling skills or goals you are measuring. By using such a mastery analysis, you can better judge the quality of each student's performance and prescribe appropriate follow-up activities.

To perform a mastery analysis, do the following:

1. Compare items by enabling skill or goal.
2. Determine the number of correct answers that will indicate minimal mastery of each skill.
3. Determine whether each student mastered each skill.
4. Prescribe follow-up activities.
5. Develop a student progress chart.
6. Evaluate students' performances.

Comparing Items by Enabling Skill or Goal

For the comparison, you can use the student response matrix you obtain when you use machine scoring. To separate items by enabling skills or goals, simply draw vertical lines in the matrix between items measuring different skills. Figures 12.1 and 12.3 both illustrate the way a test report can be subdivided by enabling skill. Teachers also create their own formats for organizing classroom test information by enabling skill to make it easier to determine whether students are mastering the content.

Establishing Mastery Criteria

After you have separated the test items by skill, decide the level of performance on each skill that you consider mastery. If a skill is represented by multiple test items, minimal mastery is generally defined as correctly answering a majority of the items. If a skill is measured by only one or two items, the student would need to answer one or both items correctly. For example, the test described in Figure 12.1 measured six different objectives with four items each. Students would have had to answer three of the four items correctly to master each skill. If a skill is extremely important or includes a variety of subskills, you might want to set the criterion at a level higher than a simple majority of correct items.

Determining Individual Mastery of Skills

To determine an individual student's mastery of the skills, you need to (1) count the items that the student answered correctly for each skill and (2) count the number of skills that the student mastered. Referring to the example test in Figure 12.1, if a student missed two or more items per objective, you should circle these items on your chart. Next, count the number of objectives mastered and record them in the right-hand column of your chart. Your mastery chart should look like Figure 12.2 for the two students.

According to the chart, Allen correctly answered a majority of the items for each skill, achieving at least minimal mastery on all six enabling skills. For Baker, skills 4

FIGURE 12.2

Describing Students' Mastery

Enabling Skills	1	2	3	4	5	6	Total		
Item Answer	1 2 3 4 3 2 1 4	5 6 7 8 4 3 1 4	1 1 1 9 0 1 2 2 3 5 1	1 1 1 1 3 4 5 6 2 2 1 3	1 1 1 2 7 8 9 0 5 1 4 3	2 2 2 2 1 2 3 4 2 1 1 5	Raw Score 24	%	OBJ. 6
Allen, J.	. . 2 .	. 1 . .	. . 4 .	1 . . .	. 2 . .	. . 3 .	18	75	6
Baker, T.	. . . .	. . . .	. . . .	(1 3 2 2)	. . . .	(3 . 3 .)	18	75	4

and 6 are circled. The number in the right-hand column indicates that this student mastered only four of the six enabling skills.

Prescribing Follow-Up Activities

To prescribe appropriate follow-up activities, you need to consider the importance of the skills that students failed and the students' previous achievement. For example, if subsequent lessons build on a particular skill, a student who failed to master the skill will undoubtedly have difficulty. The simplest way to avoid such problems is to divide the group into two categories: students who have mastered the goals and students who need more instruction and practice. You can then prescribe enrichment activities for the first group and developmental activities for the second, or you could organize peer-tutoring or cooperative learning activities to involve the entire group in bringing all students up to an acceptable level of mastery.

In establishing follow-up activities, also consider each student's previous achievement. If a student's test performance is inconsistent in terms of the number of goals or skills typically mastered, you may wish to interview the student to determine what factors contributed to the sudden decline or improvement in achievement.

Developing a Student Progress Chart

Some teachers like to keep a student progress chart that indicates the skills that remain to be mastered by each student. This type of chart usually lists all student names in the left-hand column and indicates the enabling skills or goals to be mastered across the top. The teacher can either post the chart on a bulletin board for student use or refer to the chart during private consultations with students or their parents.

Evaluating Students' Performances

Students' performances can be evaluated by comparing the raw scores and the number of skills mastered. Reviewing either of these scores independently does not provide the same insight. Earning a high test score and mastering all skills would obviously be considered a good test performance. Likewise, earning a low score and failing several skills would be judged an inadequate performance. However, it is not uncommon to find rather average test scores for students who have mastered all the skills, at least at a minimum level. When such a pattern is found, a student's overall performance can be judged as good because mastering all the skills reflects good work. However, the student may have a reading problem, may not be motivated to be very careful in answering questions, or may work too quickly. Such a pattern warrants a student conference to investigate and hopefully resolve the problem.

An Example

Figure 12.3 contains students' scores by item and by enabling skill for the topic sentence strand of the unit posttest on writing a paragraph. The item specifications are described in Figure 4.6, and the table of test specifications for the unit posttest are described in Figure 4.2. The top three rows of the table contain the enabling skill codes, the test item numbers, and the correct answers. Notice that skill II.F indicates that these test items were hand scored. This skill required students to write topic sentences for incomplete paragraphs. Students' names are listed in the far left column. Asterisks placed in the item columns reflect correct answers. The numbers listed in test item columns reflect incorrect responses, and the particular number indicates the distractor selected by the student.

Using the rule that minimal mastery requires answering a simple majority of the items correctly for each skill, you can see that students needed to answer all items correctly for skills II.A through II.F. Skills not mastered are highlighted in the table using a dark box. All students in the class mastered the recall skills related to the physical and functional characteristics of topic sentences (skills II.A and II.B). Six students did not demonstrate mastery of the skill related to the quality characteristics of topic sentences (II.C). All students mastered the skill related to discriminating between topic sentences and other sentences included in a paragraph (II.D). Considering the two skills for evaluating topic sentences, four students failed skill II.E.1 and two students failed skill II.E.2. Three students also did not master the skill for writing topic sentences when given incomplete paragraphs.

Figure 12.4 includes the original goal analysis matrix, and it is often used to summarize the names of students who require additional instruction on particular enabling skills in the unit. Comparing the students' names within each enabling skill cell in Figure 12.4 with the item data in Figure 12.3, you can see that only the names of students who did not master the skills are entered into the skills cells. Although only the mastery data for the topic sentence portion of the test is included in the table, the names of students who failed to master other enabling skills on the posttest can be inserted into the appropriate cells. The completed chart will provide the teacher with a good class summary for prescribing follow-up activities. As students master the skills following subsequent instruction, their names can be removed from the table.

Figure 12.5 includes a partial student progress chart for the instructional goal, "Write a paragraph." The summary chart lists the enabling skills from the goal analysis matrix to indicate learner progress. The far left column of the table lists students'

Mastery Analysis of Students' Performance for Only the Topic Sentence Portion of the Paragraph Posttest (Skills II.A to II.F in Tables 4.2 and 4.8)

Enabling Skill Codes	TOPIC SENTENCE OBJECTIVES							Total Objectives Mastered
	II.A	II.B	II.C	II.D	II.E.1	II.E.2	II.F	
Items:	3	4	5	6 7	8 9	10 11	12 13	7
Correct Answers:	*4*	*4*	*4*	*1 1*	*2 4*	*1 4*	*Hand Scored*	
Augustine	*	*	*	* *	* *	* *	* *	7
Prince	*	*	*	* *	* *	* *	* *	7
Deddens	*	*	*	* *	* *	* *	* *	7
Talbot	*	*	*	* *	* *	* *	* *	7
McComas	*	*	*	* *	* *	* *	* *	7
Rust	*	*	*	* *	* *	* *	* *	7
Carey	*	*	*	* *	* *	* *	* *	7
Cromer	*	*	*	* *	* *	* *	* *	7
Hager	*	*	*	* *	* *	* *	* *	7
McLaughlin	*	*	*	* *	* *	* *	* *	7
White	*	*	*	* *	* *	* *	* *	7
Otto	*	*	*	* *	* *	* *	* *	7
Lovejoy	*	*	*	* *	* *	* *	* *	7
Hill	*	*	*	* *	* *	* *	* *	7
Scragg	*	*	2	* *	* *	* *	* *	6
Gormley	*	*	3	* *	* 3	* *	* *	5
Bailey	*	*	2	* *	1 *	* *	* *	5
Deiters	*	*	2	* *	* 3	* *	* x	4
Stewart	*	*	3	* *	* *	2 *	* x	4
Smith	*	*	2	* *	* 3	2 1	x x	3
Number of Students Who Mastered	20	20	14	20	16	18	17	
Percentage of Students Who Mastered	100%	100%	70%	100%	80%	90%	85%	

FIGURE 12.4

Prescribed Instructional Activities Based on Mastery Analysis

CONCEPTS/ CONTENT	A State/Recall Physical Characteristics of:	B State/Recall Functional Characteristics of:	C State/Recall Quality Characteristics of:	D Discriminate between Examples and Nonexamples	E Evaluate Given Examples	F Produce Examples of:
II. Topic Sentence			Bailey Deiters Gormley Scragg Smith Stewart		Bailey Deiters Gormley Smith Stewart	Deiters Smith Stewart
III. Supporting Sentences						
IV. Concluding Sentence						

names, and the enabling skills for the paragraph unit are listed across the top of the chart. The teacher has placed an x in the intersecting student-by-enabling skill cells to indicate the students who have mastered each skill. In addition, an **M** for mastery is inserted in the total topic sentence column (**II**) for those students who mastered all topic sentence enabling skills. A **PM** is used to identify the students who mastered the majority of the enabling skills. The blank cells indicate nonmastery of a concept area, and they are used to identify the students who did not master the majority of enabling skills. In the example class group, Bailey, Gormley, and Scragg partially mastered the topic sentences area, whereas Deiters, Smith, and Stewart failed to master topic sentences. The other 14 students mastered all enabling skills for topic sentences.

■ Evaluating the Quality of Instruction

Analyzing individual performances provides useful information about each student's progress. To evaluate the quality of instruction, however, you need to analyze the entire group's mastery of each goal. To conduct a group mastery analysis, you need to do the following:

1. Establish a minimum standard for group mastery of each skill.
2. Describe the proportion of the group that mastered each skill.
3. Compare the group's performance to the minimum standards.
4. Evaluate the quality of the instruction for each skill.

FIGURE 12.5

A Partial Student Progress Chart for the Instructional Goal "Write a Paragraph"

Enabling Skills	Paragraph			Topic Sentences							
	I A	I B	I D	II A	II B	II C	II D	II E	II F	II	Etc.
Augustine	x	x	x	x	x	x	x	x	x	M	
Bailey	x	x	x	x	x		x		x	PM	
Carey	x	x	x	x	x	x	x	x	x	M	
Cromer	x	x	x	x	x	x	x	x	x	M	
Deddens	x	x	x	x	x	x	x	x	x	M	
Deiters	x	x	x	x	x		x				
Gormley	x	x	x	x	x		x		x	PM	
Hager	x	x	x	x	x	x	x	x	x	M	
Hill		x	x	x	x	x	x	x	x	M	
Lovejoy	x	x	x	x	x	x	x	x	x	M	
McComas	x	x	x	x	x	x	x	x	x	M	
McLaughlin	x	x	x	x	x	x	x	x	x	M	
Otto	x	x	x	x	x	x	x	x	x	M	
Prince	x	x	x	x	x	x	x	x	x	M	
Rust	x	x	x	x	x	x	x	x	x	M	
Scragg	x	x	x	x	x		x	x	x	PM	
Smith	x	x	x	x	x		x				
Stewart	x	x	x	x	x		x				
Talbot	x	x	x	x	x	x	x	x	x	M	
White	x	x	x	x	x	x	x	x	x	M	

Note: x = at least minimal mastery of enabling skill; **PM** = Partial Mastery of concept strand (e.g., topic sentences, supporting sentences, and concluding sentences); **M** = Mastery of concept strand.

Setting Minimum Standards for Group Performance

To set minimum standards for the group, again consider the achievement characteristics of the students and the complexity of the skills measured. In addition, consider each skill's importance as a prerequisite for subsequent goals. For example, if a class contains average and above-average students, and if the skills measured are relatively easy, you might reasonably expect 80 percent or more of the students to master each skill. However, if the skills are important prerequisites for subsequent lessons, you might raise your criterion to 100 percent. If you have a very low-achieving group of students who are learning rather complex skills, you might lower your criterion to 75, 70, or 60 percent of the group passing. The mastery criteria you set are relative and should reflect all the factors just described. You can set one mastery criterion for all skills measured or establish a different minimum standard for each.

Describing Group Performance on Each Skill

You can easily calculate a group's performance on each skill using a mastery analysis like the one in Figure 12.3. Simply count the number of students who mastered each skill and write the total in a row created at the bottom of the table. To find the percentage who mastered each objective, divide the number who passed the skill by the total number of students and then multiply the proportion by 100. The percentage of students in the class who mastered each objective can be inserted in the last row of the table. Notice the group performance figures in the last two rows of Figure 12.3. The physical and functional characteristics skills (II.A and II.B) and the examples discrimination skill (II.D) were mastered by 100 percent of the class. Only 70 percent of the group, however, mastered the quality characteristics skill (II.C), and 80 and 90 percent of the group mastered the two evaluation skills (II.E.1 and II.E.2 respectively). More emphasis on identifying quality characteristics and discriminating them in the paragraph context will undoubtedly improve students' achievement in these two areas. Finally, 85 percent of the class wrote acceptable topic sentences for the incomplete paragraphs presented on the objective unit posttest.

Comparing a Group's Performance to Minimum Standards

If 80 percent of the group passing each goal was set as the minimum acceptable standard for each skill, then you can see that group performance on only one objective, quality characteristics (II.C), did not meet the standard. The percentage of students passing the other six enabling skills was at or above the minimum standard.

Evaluating the Quality of Instruction

As the previous example shows, a group's performance reflects the quality of instruction much more than does individual achievement. When group performance on a skill exceeds your minimum criterion, you can conclude that instruction was very effective. If group performance barely meets the minimum standard, the instruction can be judged as acceptable. If a group fails to meet the established minimum, however, you should review and revise instruction that produced such a poor posttest performance. In the example, instruction related to the quality characteristics of topic sentences should be revised. By revising ineffective lessons throughout the year, you improve the quality of your instruction and, hopefully, raise the level of subsequent group performances.

Evaluating Instruction Using Product and Performance Tests

This same process can be used to evaluate group performance and instruction when you have administered product and performance tests. A portion of the group summary data is provided in Figure 12.6 for the instructional goal of writing descriptive paragraphs. Notice the enabling skills are listed across the top along with the number of points students could earn on their paragraphs for each skill. Students' names are listed in the far left column, and the intersecting student-by-skill cells contain the actual number of points earned by each student. The bottom three rows of the table contain the total number of points available for each enabling skill and the percentage of points earned by the total class.

Suppose you set a quality criterion that 80 percent of the total possible points should be earned by the group. Using a criterion of 80 percent, you can see that instruction should be reviewed for enabling skills I.C, description, and II.C.2, scope.

The summary data at the bottom of the table were obtained in the following manner:

Sum = Add the total points earned by all students for each enabling skill and record the sum at the bottom of the table.

Total possible = Multiply the points available for each enabling skill (fourth row from top of table) by the total number of students in the class.

Percentage = Divide the sum (points earned by all students) by the total number of students, and multiply by 100.

■ Evaluating Group Progress

Often, the types of skills measured using product and performance tests are evaluated multiple times during a term or semester using the same rating scale or checklist. Procedures similar to those just described for assessing students' performance on one occasion can be repeated to examine the quality of instruction indicated by

FIGURE 12.6

Group Summary Data from a Portion of the Paragraph Rating Scale Included in Figure 6.13

WRITE DESCRIPTIVE PARAGRAPHS (I.F.1)

Date: 11-23	Paragraph			Topic Sentence				
	Indent I.A	One Topic I.B	Description* I.C	Location II.A	Introduces II.B	Relevant II.C.1	Scope II.C.2	Interest II.C.3
Total Points:	1	2	3	2	2	2	2	2
Students								
Augustine	1	2	3	2	2	2	2	2
Bailey	1	1	2	2	1	1	1	2
Carey	1	2	3	2	2	2	2	2
Cromer	1	2	2	2	2	2	2	2
Deddens	1	2	3	2	2	2	2	2
Deiters	1	1	1	2	1	1	1	1
Gormley	1	1	1	2	1	1	1	1
Hager	1	2	3	2	2	2	2	2
Hill	1	2	3	2	2	2	1	1
Lovejoy	1	2	1	2	2	2	1	1
McComas	1	2	3	2	2	2	2	2
McLaughlin	1	2	3	2	2	2	2	2
Otto	1	2	2	2	2	2	2	2
Prince	1	2	3	2	2	2	2	2
Rust	1	2	3	2	2	2	2	2
Scragg	1	1	1	2	2	2	1	1
Smith	1	1	1	2	1	1	1	1
Stewart	0	1	2	2	1	2	1	1
Talbot	1	2	3	2	2	2	2	2
White	1	2	3	2	2	2	1	1
Sum:	19	34	46	40	35	36	31	32
Total Possible:	20	40	60	40	40	40	40	40
Percentage:	95	85	77	100	88	90	78	80
			**				**	

Note: This quality characteristic is used to judge whether students' paragraphs actually contained descriptions of something.

students' achievement each time the instructional goal is assessed. To illustrate how you might proceed, the general paragraph and topic sentence subcomponents of the paragraph goal are used to demonstrate the summary and analysis procedure. Other main components and subcomponents of the assignment would be evaluated in the same manner.

Figure 12.7 contains a summary form useful for evaluating group progress across time. The top of the table again identifies the enabling skill (I.F) for writing descriptive paragraphs, and the column headings name the subcomponents. Rather than listing individual students' names in the far left column, the dates on which the writing samples were taken are included. For each subcomponent, the percentage of possible points earned by the class is listed.

A summary table such as this will enable you to determine whether your students are progressing as a group on the main components and subcomponents of the instructional goal. For example, the teacher appears to have corrected the problem occurring with students not actually writing a description of something (I.C) in their paragraphs. Each time the writing sample was taken, students did a better job with descriptions. Likewise, problems with the scope of students' topic sentences (II.C.2) appears to be resolved for most students in the class. With data summarized in this manner, you can also monitor progress for skills not actually considered problematic. Notice that the group is making good progress in the area of writing to suit the interest of their intended audience (II.C.3).

Group performance summaries across time will also help you locate areas where the students' achievement was initially considered adequate, but no progress or improvement is being made. Consider the introductory quality of students' topic

FIGURE 12.7

Group Progress Data from a Portion of the Paragraph Rating Scale Included in Figure 6.13

	WRITE DESCRIPTIVE PARAGRAPHS (I.F)							
	Paragraph			Topic Sentence				
	Indent I.A	One Topic I.B	Descrip- tion I.C	Loca- tion II.A	Intro- duces II.B	Rele- vant II.C.1	Scope II.C.2	Interest II.C.3
Date: 11/23 Percentage:	95	85	77	100	88	90	78	80
Date: 12/18 Percentage:	100	85	80	100	85	86	80	95
Date: 1/21 Percentage:	100	86	86	100	86	88	84	90
Date: 2/28 Percentage:	100	88	90	100	88	89	86	92

Note: The number in the cell reflects the percentage of total possible points the group earned for each subcomponent.

sentences (II.B). The class has made no progress on this subcomponent, and the teacher may want to rethink the instructional strategy relative to this important characteristic.

■ Conducting a Norm-Referenced Analysis

To compare an individual's performance to the group's, you need to determine whether (1) the student's performance is above average, average, or below average and (2) the student's performance is consistent with her or his past performance.

Comparing Individual Performance to the Group

An easy way to compare a student's performance to the group is to divide the raw scores into categories of above average, average, and below average, and then compare the student's score with these categories. You can use the mean and the standard deviation to categorize the raw scores. Raw scores equal to and higher than one standard deviation above the mean are classified as above average. Raw scores equal to and lower than one standard deviation below the mean are classified as below average. Scores between these two anchors are categorized as average-level performance on the test. Raw scores equal to and greater than two standard deviations above the mean are classified as being well above average. Likewise, scores equal to and lower than two standard deviations below the mean are considered to be well below average compared to the class.

Notice in the following example how these categories of performance are created using the mean and standard deviation. If the mean score is 20 and the standard deviation is three, then:

$$\overline{X} - 1SD = 20 - 3 = 17 \text{ or } 1 \text{ standard deviation below the mean}$$
$$\overline{X} - 2SD = 20 - 6 = 14 \text{ or } 2 \text{ standard deviations below the mean}$$
$$\overline{X} + 1SD = 20 + 3 = 23 \text{ or } 1 \text{ standard deviation above the mean}$$
$$\overline{X} + 2SD = 20 + 6 = 26 \text{ or } 2 \text{ standard deviations above the mean}$$

Test Scores

Consider, for example, the following achievement categories for a 25-item test. Remember the following symbols: X_H = the highest earned score, X_L = the lowest earned score, $\overline{X}$ = the mean, and σ = the standard deviation. The standard deviation in the example is 4.73. This value is added to and subtracted from the mean score, 19.1, to locate the categories of above average, average, and below average. According to this chart, no scores would be classified as very high performance compared to the class, and scores of 24 and 25 would be considered above average in the group. Raw scores ranging from 15 to 23 would be classified as average-level performance compared to the class. Scores ranging from 11 to 14 would be classified as below average, and scores from 8 to 10 would be categorized as well below average for this group.

Score Category	Very Low Performance		Below-Average Performance	Average Performance	Above-Average Performance		Very High Performance
Scores	8	9.64	14.37	19.10	23.83	25	
	X_L	-2σ	-1σ	$\overline{X}$	$+1\sigma$	X_H	$+2\sigma$

Comparing a student's performance with the group's performance is sometimes accomplished through the use of standard scores and percentile scores. Standard scores and percentile scores are often reported on computer-generated reports.

Describing a Student's Achievement Using Standard Scores

Often, standard scores are used to compare an individual's test performance with that of the group. The most commonly reported standard scores on computer-generated test analysis reports are the z and T scores. Standard scores are derived from an individual's raw score, the group's average score, and the group's variability as measured by the standard deviation. Thus, students' raw scores are modified to reflect their group standing.

These norm-referenced z and T scores are called standard scores because they convert all posttest scores to a standard scale that has a constant mean and a constant standard deviation. Holding the mean and standard deviation constant enables interpreting students' relative performance on a single test and across tests using only the standard score. The z score has a constant mean of 0 and a constant standard deviation of 1, and the T score has a constant mean of 50 and a standard deviation of 10.

The standard score scale for z and T scores is illustrated in the following chart:

z Scores	-3	-2	-1	0	$+1$	$+2$	$+3$
T Scores	20	30	40	50	60	70	80
Standard Deviations	-3σ	-2σ	-1σ	$\overline{X}$	$+1\sigma$	$+2\sigma$	$+3\sigma$

A z score of 0 and a T score of 50 both reflect that the student earned the mean score on the test. A z score of 1 and a T score of 60 both are one standard deviation above the mean; therefore, they reflect the lower boundary of above average performance. Likewise, a z score of -1 and a T score of 40 both are one standard deviation below the mean and reflect the upper boundary of below average performance. Scores farther from the mean in either direction reflect performance farther removed from average. Thus, regardless of the original raw scores, original mean score, or original standard deviation on a test, the standard scores can be used to locate a student's comparative performance level. These standard scores can be related to the achievement level categories in the following way:

Score	Very Low Performance	Below-Average Performance	Average Performance	Above-Average Performance	Very High Performance
z	-2	-1.5	-1 $-.5$ 0 $.5$	1	1.5 2
t	30	35	40 45 50 55	60	65 70

Describing a Student's Achievement Using Percentile Scores

Percentile scores range from 1 to 99, and they reflect the percentage of students surpassed at each raw score in a distribution of test scores.

For example, a student who earns a percentile score of 13 is said to have scored better than 13 percent of the students in the class, and a student who earns a percentile score of 80 has surpassed 80 percent of the group. Percentile scores are related to the performance categories in the following way:

Score	Very Low Performance	Below-Average Performance	Average Performance	Above-Average Performance	Very High Performance
Percentile	1	4	25	50 75	96 99

Teachers need to be cautious and not confuse percentile scores with the percentage of items answered on a test. The percentage correct score reflects the proportion of *test items* answered correctly, and the percentile score represents the proportion of *students* surpassed on the exam.

One final comment should be made. Teachers cannot determine the percentage of items answered correctly using only norm-referenced scores. For example, a student may earn a *T* score of 70 and a percentile score of 99, yet only answer correctly 60 percent of the items included on a test. Norm-referenced scores indicate how well a student performed compared to classmates, but not how much of a domain a student has mastered. Percentile scores will be discussed again in Chapter 15.

Comparing Current with Past Performances

Comparing a student's performance with the group's performance provides a general indication of how the student is performing. To interpret properly a student's performance that is classified as above average, average, or below average, you need to compare it with his or her usual or typical performance level. For example, an average test performance can be considered as not good, typical, or excellent, depending on the student's previous record. An average-level performance would undoubtedly be considered good for a student who typically earns below-average scores. Likewise, an average performance would be viewed negatively for a student who typically earns one of the highest scores in the group.

The achievement characteristics of the group will also influence your interpretation of high, average, and low performance. An average performance in a high-achieving, homogeneous group is different than an average performance in a heterogeneous group. Because norm-referenced interpretations are relative, you should also evaluate students on the number of skills they have mastered.

An Example

Students' raw scores from the objective portion of the paragraph posttest are used to demonstrate norm-referenced analysis. Table 12.1 includes the test scores of all class members in the left portion of the table, and the right portion contains norm-referenced data with the mainstreamed student's outlier score removed. The first column contains students' raw scores, followed by the percentage of items correct for each raw score. The third column contains the frequency with which each raw score occurred for the exam. The remaining columns include the z, T, and percentile scores for each raw score.

TABLE 12.1

Norm-Referenced Analysis of Students' Achievement on the Objective Portion of the Paragraph Unit Posttest

$N = 20$ Mean = 38 Standard Deviation = 4.84						$N = 19$ Mean = 38.74 Standard Deviation = 3.71		
			Total Class Group			**Recalculated without Outlier**		
X	Percentage Correct	f	z	T	Percentile	z	T	Percentile
43	100	5	1.03	60	88	1.15	61	87
42	98	2	.83	58	70	.88	59	68
41	95	1	.62	56	63	.61	56	61
40	93	1	.41	54	58	.34	53	55
39	91	1	.21	52	53	.07	51	50
38	88	1	.00	50	48	−.20	48	45
37	86	2	−.21	48	40	−.47	45	37
36	84	1	−.41	46	33	−.74	43	29
35	81	2	−.62	44	25	−1.00	40	21
34	79	1	−.83	42	18	−1.28	37	13
33	77	1	−1.03	40	13	−1.55	35	8
32	74	1	−1.24	38	8	−1.82	32	3
24	56	1	−2.89	21	2			

Examine first the data in the left side of the table that includes all members of the class. Only students who earned perfect scores on the exam would be classified as above average in this class (z and T scores of 1.03 and 60, respectively). Raw scores of 34 and 42 set the boundaries for average-level performance on the test ($z = -.83$ to .83 and $T = 42$ to 58). Raw scores 32 and 33 are classified as below average with z and T scores lower than one standard deviation below the mean score. The mainstreamed student earned a raw score of 24, a z score of –2.89, and a T score of 21. This achievement level would be classified as well below average in this class since it is lower than two standard deviations below the mean.

The percentile scores are located in the last column for the total class. Notice that the highest percentile score is 88 and the lowest is 2. Even though students earned perfect scores on the exam (43 and 100% correct), they did not obtain a percentile score of 100 because they cannot surpass themselves. Why did these five students not receive percentile scores of 99? The percentile score of 88 was the highest on this test because there were five students who tied for a perfect raw score. All students earning scores lower than 43, plus one-half the students tied at 43, results in a percentile score of 88. The effect of tied scores on the percentile score is described in more detail in the calculation section later in this chapter.

Comparing the percentage of items correct and the percentile for each score should illustrate why it is important not to confuse these two scores when interpreting students' test performance. For a percentage correct score of 100, the corresponding percentile score is 88, and for a percentage correct score of 86, the percentile score is 40.

The right side of Table 12.1 includes the recalculated z, T, and percentile scores with the outlier score removed. Similar to the previous data, only a raw score of 43 is classified as above average in this class. Removal of the outlier score, however, resulted in decreasing the size of the average group and increasing the number of students classified as below average in the class. Average raw scores now range from 36 to 42 ($T = 43$ to 59) and below-average scores range from 32 to 35 ($T = 32$ to 40). Omitting the outlier score decreases the number of students classified as average from 12 to 9 and increases the number classified as below average from 2 to 5 (excluding the mainstreamed student). These recalculated data illustrate how the nature of the comparison group can influence the norm-referenced scores and the classification of students as above average, average, and below average.

Calculating Standard Scores (z and T)

The formulas for calculating the z and T scores are:

$$z = \frac{X - \overline{X}}{\sigma} \qquad T = 10z + 50$$

The z score is calculated by subtracting the mean score on the test from each student's raw score. This difference, or the amount the individual's score deviates from the mean, is divided by the standard deviation to determine how much larger or smaller the individual's deviation is than the group's standard deviation. In other words, a z score of .5 or –.5 indicates that a student's deviation from the mean score is half as large as the group's standard deviation. Negative numbers reflect deviation below the mean. A *z* score of 1 or –1 indicates that the student's deviation from the mean score is the same as the group's standard deviation. Scores of 1.5 and –1.5 indicate that a student's deviation from the mean is one and one-half times larger than the group's standard deviation.

The *T* score is calculated from the *z* score. The *z* score is multiplied by 10 to change the size of the standard deviation from 1 to 10. This product is added to 50 to change the size of the mean from 0 to 50. These *T* scores have the same meaning as the *z* scores. Scores of 45 or 55 indicate that a student's deviation from the mean is only half as large as the group's standard deviation. *T* scores rather than *z* scores are frequently used to report a student's relative performance to avoid using the negative and decimal numbers on the *z* score scale. Regardless of whether the *z* or *T* score is reported on your analysis reports, its indication of a student's group standing remains the same.

To illustrate the calculation procedure, suppose that you have a mean score of 35 and a standard deviation of 5 for your students' latest test. Calculate the *z* and *T* scores for students who earned raw scores of 37, 32, and 28.

$$z = (X - \overline{X})/SD \qquad\qquad T = 10z + 50$$
$$z = (37 - 35)/5 = .4 \qquad\qquad T = 10(.4) + 50 = 54$$
$$z = (32 - 35)/5 = -.6 \qquad\qquad T = 10(-.6) + 50 = 44$$
$$z = (28 - 35)/5 = -1.40 \qquad\qquad T = 10(-1.4) + 50 = 36$$

Table 12.2 illustrates the calculation of *z* and *T* scores for a hypothetical set of test data. The raw scores are listed in the first column and the frequency with which each score occurs in the set is shown in the second column. The *z* scores are provided in the third column and the corresponding *T* scores are listed in the last column. The mean for this set of scores is 19.1 and the standard deviation is 4.73. Notice that the raw score 24 is closest to one standard deviation above the mean, 23.83, and that this score has a *z* score of 1.04 and a *T* score of 60. The raw score 19 is closest to the mean score 19.1 and it has a corresponding *z* score of –.02 and *T* score of 50. The raw score nearest one standard deviation below the mean is 14 and its *z* and *T* scores are –1.08 and 39, respectively. The raw score 8 is lower than two standard deviations below the mean and it has *z* and *T* scores of –2.35 and 26, respectively. When standard scores are provided with computerized test analysis forms, you can simply use these scores to classify students' test performance as above average, average, or below average.

Calculating Percentile Scores

Table 12.3 contains hypothetical raw scores for 20 students. The first column contains the raw scores, and the highest possible score is 25. The second column contains the percentage of items correct for each raw score. The third column contains the frequency with which each raw score occurred in the class. The fourth column contains the *cumulative frequency of students* below each raw score, or the total number of students scoring *below* each raw score. The fifth includes one-half of the students

TABLE 12.2

Standard Scores for Hypothetical Objective Test Data

Mean = 19.1		Standard Deviation = 4.73		
X	f	z	T	
25	2	1.25	62	⎫ Above Average Compared to Classmates
24	1	1.04	60	⎭
23	2	.82	58	⎫
22	2	.61	56	
21	4	.40	54	
19	2	−.02	50	Average Achievement Compared to Classmates
18	1	−.23	48	
17	2	−.44	46	⎭
14	1	−1.08	39	⎫
12	1	−1.50	35	Below Average Compared to Classmates
10	1	−1.92	31	⎭
8	1	−2.35	26	Well Below Average Compared to Classmates

Note: The z score for a raw score of 25 is calculated as follows: $(25 - 19.1)/4.73 = 1.25$. The T score for a raw score of 25 is calculated as follows: $(10 \times 1.25) + 50 = 62$.

TABLE 12.3

Calculating Percentile Scores for Objective Test Data

N = 20							
1 Raw Scores X	2 Percentage Correct	3 f	4 cf below	5 1/2f within	6 cf at Midpoint	7 Proportion Surpassed	8 Percentile
25	100	2	18	1.0	19.0	.95	95
24	96	1	17	.5	17.5	.88	88
23	92	2	15	1.0	16.0	.80	80
22	88	2	13	1.0	14.0	.70	70
21	84	4	9	2.0	11.0	.55	55
20	80	−					
19	76	2	7	1.0	8.0	.40	40
18	72	1	6	.5	6.5	.31	31
17	68	2	4	1.0	5.0	.25	25
16	64	−					
15	60	−					
14	56	1	3	.5	3.5	.18	18
13							
12	48	1	2	.5	2.5	.13	13
11							
10	40	1	1	.5	1.5	.08	8
9							
8	32	1	0	.5	.5	.03	3

who earn each raw score. The sixth column contains *cumulative frequency at midpoint,* and it is the sum of values in columns 4 and 5. The cumulative frequency at midpoint value includes the total number of students scoring below each raw score and one-half the number of students who earn that raw score. The seventh column contains the proportion of students represented in the cumulative frequency at midpoint. This proportion is obtained by dividing the cumulative frequency at midpoint by the total number of students in the group. The eighth column contains the percentile score, and it is obtained by multiplying the proportion of students in column 7 by 100.

To illustrate how each percentile is calculated, the step-by-step procedures for calculating the percentile scores for raw scores of 12 and 21 are illustrated. Locate raw scores of 12 and 21 in Table 12.3, and notice that one student earned a raw score of 12 (information in column headed f), and 4 students earned a raw score of 21. To obtain the cumulative frequency below value (Column 4) for each raw score, sum the frequency of scores below each of these raw scores.

	Cumulative Frequency below (*cf* below) in Column 4	
	Raw Score = 12	Raw Score = 21
(*f* Column 3)	1 + 1 = 2	1 + 1 + 1 + 1 + 2 + 1 + 2 = 9

Next, you need to locate one-half the number of students who tied for each of these raw scores:

	One-half the Number of Students Tied for Each Raw Score (*1/2f* within) in Column 5	
	Raw Score = 12	Raw Score = 21
(*f* Column 3)	1 ÷ 2 = .5	4 ÷ 2 = 2

With this value, you are ready to calculate the cumulative frequency at midpoint, which is the sum of the frequency values in Columns 4 and 5.

	Cumulative Frequency at Midpoint (*cf* at Midpoint) in Column 6	
	Raw Score = 12	Raw Score = 21
(Columns 4–5)	2 + .5 = 2.5	9 + 2 = 11

You can now determine the proportion of students surpassed at each of the raw scores.

	Proportion Surpassed in Column 7	
	Raw Score = 12	**Raw Score = 21**
(Column 6)	2.5 ÷ 20 = .125	11 ÷ 20 = .55

From the proportion, you can obtain the percentile by multiplying the proportion of students surpassed by 100.

	Proportion Surpassed in Column 8	
	Raw Score = 12	**Raw Score = 21**
(Column 7)	.125 × 100 = 12.5 or 13	.55 × 100 = 55

◼ Computer Technology

When you use computer-based test scoring programs, you can readily obtain individual student test reports. Although these reports come in a variety of formats, they usually contain both criterion-referenced and norm-referenced individual student test data. Related to criterion-referenced information, they typically contain raw scores and percentage correct scores for the overall test as well as subtest percentage correct scores that can be used to obtain mastery scores for enabling skills. Related to norm-referenced analysis, these computer-generated reports often contain z scores, T scores, and percentile scores. Occasionally they will also report stanine scores. Recall from Chapter 2 that stanine scores range from 1 to 9, reflecting areas of below average, average, and above average performance.

Table 12.4 contains a sample format from a computer-generated class report. The first column identifies the student by name or number, followed by raw score and percentage correct columns. The next six columns, labeled Subtest Scores, are percentage correct scores for subsets of test items anchored to particular enabling skills. If you have set 70 percent correct as your criterion for minimal mastery of these subtests, then you can readily determine mastery levels from the student performance report without calculating this information by hand for each individual student in your classes.

The remaining three columns contain the norm-referenced information for each student. These norm-referenced scores are based on the student's overall test raw score. In this case the T score, z score, and percentile score are reported. Knowing that you can easily obtain all this criterion-referenced and norm-referenced information

TABLE 12.4

Computer-Generated Criterion-Referenced and Norm-Referenced Individual Student Test Information

Student	Raw Score	Percent Score	Subtest Scores						*T* Scores	*z* Scores	Percentile Scores
201	22	88	70	80	80	75	90	100	56	.61	70
202	24	96	90	95	80	100	80	100	60	1.04	88
203	12	48	40	50	60	50	30	70	35	−1.5	13
Etc.											

for your students should encourage you to seek computer scoring services whenever they are available in your school.

Spreadsheet programs can be used to easily summarize student's enabling skill and goal data for objective, essay, product, and performance tests. To evaluate student achievement, you can use these programs to create a data matrix of students-by-items or enabling skills. Students' raw scores, percentages correct, and skills mastered can be calculated easily using the functions within the spreadsheet. To evaluate instruction, you can readily calculate the number and percentage of students who mastered each enabling skill and goal by using data across students within a skill or goal area.

■ Summary

Test data can be used to analyze and evaluate an individual's performance, a group's performance, and the quality of instruction. An individual's scores can be evaluated using both criterion-referenced and norm-referenced analysis. Using criterion-referenced analysis, you can evaluate individual students' progress on prescribed instructional goals, or enabling skills. To conduct such an analysis, you need to organize items within enabling skills or goals, establish minimum criteria for mastering each, and determine whether each student mastered each skill. This information can be used to prepare follow-up activities and to judge the quality and consistency of each student's performance. Progress charts will help you keep track of skills that individual students still need to learn.

Evaluating the quality of instruction requires a second type of analysis. First, prescribe the minimum percentage of students who must master each skill for instruction to be considered adequate. Next, calculate the percentage of students who pass each skill and compare these figures with the established minimums. If the percentage of students who pass a skill exceeds the minimum standard, then instruction is considered good; if the minimum is met, instruction is considered adequate. However, if the proportion passing does not meet the minimum standard, the instruction is considered inadequate, and you should analyze and revise related lessons.

To evaluate instruction for product and performance tests, you will need to summarize the group's achievement data that were gathered using checklists and rating scales. The following steps are used to summarize a group's achievement on product, performance, and behavior rating scales:

1. Create a summary table that includes the points earned by all students for each component on your checklist or rating scale.
2. Use your professional judgment to set a standard for the minimum percentage of points that should be earned by your class on each subcomponent.
3. Calculate the percentage of points earned by the group for each subcomponent.
4. Locate any subcomponents where the percentage of points earned is less than the established standard.
5. Evaluate your instruction and instructional schedule for subcomponents where students' achievement does not meet the established standard.

Besides summarizing a group's achievement on one test, you should evaluate their progress across several work samples. The procedures for summarizing data to evaluate group progress are the same as those for evaluating group performance on one measure with one exception. To examine progress, you will need to summarize the percentage of points the total group earned for each subcomponent across the times the skills were assessed. Using these data, you can detect areas where the group is improving, maintaining status, or regressing. These progress assessments provide information about whether instructional interventions are effective.

To make norm-referenced comparisons, you need to create performance categories of above average, average, and below average. You can then compare each student's score with these categories and with the levels earned by the student on previous tests. The most basic way to make norm-referenced comparisons among students is to use the mean and standard deviation to classify raw scores as above average, average, or below average.

A second method is to calculate standard scores and use them to locate students' normative performance levels. The most commonly used standard scores are the z and T scores. Scores equal to and greater than 1.0 on the z score scale and 60 on the T score scale are classified as above average. Scores equal to and less than −1.0 on the z score scale and 40 on the z score scale are considered to be below average. Scores between these two anchors are classified as average-level performance.

The third norm-referenced procedure is to rank raw scores and convert them to percentile scores. The upper quartile and lower quartile on the percentile scale are classified as above and below average. Scores between these two anchors are classified as average level performance.

Although these analysis procedures may seem complex and time consuming, they are easily mastered with practice. Today, machine-scoring services or spreadsheet programs can provide most of the required data summaries that you need. Once you recognize the value of these analyses for aiding your evaluation and planning, you will want to use them whenever possible.

■ PRACTICE EXERCISES

I. **Criterion-Referenced Analysis of a Student's Performance**
Figure 12.8 contains the enabling skills from the coordinating conjunction portion of the compound sentences posttest. The item specifications for this unit are described in Figure 4.9F and the table of test specifications for the unit posttest is included in Figure 4.8F. Using the item-by-skill data included in Figure 12.8, perform the following tasks (check your work in Figure 12.14F in the Feedback section):

A. Determine the number of items that need to be answered correctly to master each enabling skill.

B. Examine the item data in the table and highlight (circle or square) the skills not mastered by particular students in the class.

C. Count the number of skills mastered by each student, and insert the sum in the last column on the right marked Total Skills Mastered.

D. Count the number of students in the class that mastered each skill, and insert the sum in the Number of Students Who Mastered row at the bottom of the table.

E. Calculate the percentage of students who mastered each objective and insert these percentages in the bottom row of the table. Suppose you set a criterion of 80 percent of the class mastering each objective. Are there any objectives for which instruction should be reconsidered?

F. Examine Smith's response pattern and compare it with the correct answers in the fourth row of the table. Based on the pattern, do you suspect that Smith really missed items 3, 7, and 10? What evidence makes you suspect this?

II. **Prescribing Instructional Activities Based on Mastery Analysis**
Figure 12.9 is a goal analysis framework for the instructional goal, "Write a compound sentence." Based on the mastery data in Figure 12.8, list the names of students who need more instruction in each of the coordinating conjunction enabling skills cells. Check your work in Figure 12.15F in the Feedback section.

III. **Monitoring Student Progress**
Figure 12.10 contains a sample student progress chart for the instructional goal, "Write a compound sentence." Using the mastery information summarized in Figures 12.8 and 12.9, complete the mastery chart for students in the class. Check your decisions in Table 12.16F in the Feedback section.

IV. **Evaluating Instruction Using Product and Performance Tests**
Using the group summary form for chapter outlines included in Figure 12.11, perform the following steps (assume a group score of earning 80 percent of the points available for each subcomponent as your minimum standard for evaluating instruction):

A. Sum the total number of points earned by the group for each subcomponent and insert this value in the Sum row at the bottom of the table.

B. Determine the total number of points possible for the group to earn for each subcomponent, and insert this number in the Total Possible row at the bottom of the table.

C. Calculate the percentage of possible points earned by the class for each subcomponent, and insert this percentage in the row marked Percentage Earned.

D. Locate subcomponents for which additional instruction and practice appear warranted. See Figure 12.17F in the Feedback section for calculations.

FIGURE 12.8

Mastery Analysis of Students' Performance for Only the Conjunction Portion of the Compound Sentences Posttest (Enabling Skills III.A to III.F in Table 3.5)

	CONJUNCTION OBJECTIVES							
Enabling Skill Codes	**III.A**	**III.B**	**III.C**	**III.D**	**III.E.1**	**III.E.2**	**III.F**	**Total Skills Mastered**
Items	1	2	3	4 5 6 7	8 9	10 11	12 13 14 15	7
Correct Answers:	2	3	1	3 2 4 1	4 2	1 4	*Hand Scored*	
McComas	*	*	*	* * * *	* *	* *	* * * *	
Talbot	*	*	*	* * * *	* *	* *	* * * *	
Deddens	*	*	*	* * * *	* *	* *	* * * *	
Prince	*	*	*	* * * *	* *	* *	* * * *	
Augustine	*	*	*	* * * *	* *	* *	* * * *	
Rust	*	*	*	* * * *	* *	* *	* * * *	
Carey	*	*	*	* * 2 *	* *	* *	* * * *	
White	*	*	*	* * * *	* *	* *	* x * *	
Hager	*	*	*	* * * *	* *	* *	* * * *	
McLaughlin	*	*	*	* * 2 *	* *	* *	* * x *	
Cromer	*	*	*	* * 2 *	* *	* *	* * x *	
Otto	*	*	*	* * 2 *	* *	* *	* * x *	
Scragg	*	*	*	* * 2 *	* *	* 3	* * x *	
Hill	*	*	*	* * 2 *	* *	* 3	* * * x	
Lovejoy	*	*	*	* * * *	* *	4 3	* * x *	
Bailey	*	*	3	* * 2 *	* *	2 3	* * x *	
Gormley	*	*	*	* * 2 *	* 3	* 3	* * x x	
Deiters	*	*	*	* * 1 *	* 3	2 1	x * x *	
Stewart	*	*	2	* * 1 *	3 3	* 2	x * x x	
Smith	*	1	*	* * 1 *	1 1	* 1	x x x x	
Number of Students Who Mastered								
Percentage of Students Who Mastered								

FIGURE 12.9

Prescribed Instructional Activities Based on Mastery Analysis

CONCEPTS/ CONTENT	A State/Recall Physical Characteristics of:	B State/Recall Functional Characteristics of:	C State/Recall Quality Characteristics of:	D Discriminate between Examples and Nonexamples	E Evaluate Given Examples	F Produce Examples of:
I. Comma						
II. Simple Sentence						
III. Coordinating Conjunction						
IV. Compound Sentence						

V. **Evaluating Instruction across Time**

Figure 12.12 contains a partially completed group progress chart for the instructional unit on outlining chapters in a textbook. Using this chart, perform the following steps:

A. Complete the table by inserting into the first data row the group's percentage of points earned from the bottom of Figure 12.11.

B. Examine trends in students' performance over the term, and identify subcomponents where students' learning appears to be:

1. Progressing (improving)
2. Staying about the same
3. Regressing (getting worse)

C. Using a minimum standard of 80 percent of the total points earned and lack of progress on subcomponents, identify subcomponents where additional group instruction appears necessary.

VI. **Norm-Referenced Analysis of a Student's Performance**

Figure 12.13 contains the raw scores from the objective portion of the compound sentences unit posttest. Using the raw scores, the mean score, and the standard deviation, calculate the following indices (check your calculations in Figure 12.19F in the Feedback section):

A. The raw scores comparable to one standard deviation above the mean, the mean, one standard deviation below the mean, and two standard deviations below the mean. Plot these scores on the scale provided at the bottom of the table.

B. The z score for each raw score in the first column.

C. The T scores for each raw score.

D. The percentiles for each raw score. Columns are provided in Figure 12.13 for the cumulative frequency below, one-half frequency within, cumulative frequency at midpoint, proportions, and percentiles.

E. Using the mean and standard deviation scale at the bottom of Figure 12.13, how would you interpret the performance of a student who earned a raw score of 42 on the test?

FIGURE   12.10

A Sample Student Progress Chart for the Instructional Goal "Write Compound Sentences"

COORDINATING CONJUNCTION ENABLING SKILLS									
Enabling Skills	III A	III B	III C	III D	III E.1	III E.2	III F	III	Etc.
Augustine									
Bailey									
Carey									
Cromer									
Deddens									
Deiters									
Gormley									
Hager									
Hill									
Lovejoy									
McComas									
McLaughlin									
Otto									
Prince									
Rust									
Scragg									
Smith									
Stewart									
Talbot									
White									

Note: x = at least minimal mastery of enabling skill; **PM** = Partial Mastery of concept strand (e.g., simple sentences, commas, coordinating conjunctions, compound sentences); **M** = Mastery of concept strand.

FIGURE 12.11

Evaluating Instruction Using Group Performance Data for Product and Performance Tests

Subcomponent	A	B	C	D	E	F	G
	Identify	Relate	Paraphrase	Parallel	Order	Label	Align
Students *Points:*	3	3	3	3	3	2	2
Augustine	3	3	3	3	3	2	2
Bailey	1	1	2	2	1	1	2
Carey	2	2	3	3	2	2	2
Cromer	2	2	2	3	2	2	2
Deddens	3	3	3	3	2	2	2
Deiters	1	1	1	2	1	1	2
Gormley	1	1	1	1	1	1	2
Hager	3	3	3	3	3	2	2
Hill	1	2	1	2	2	2	2
Lovejoy	1	2	1	2	2	2	2
McComas	3	3	3	3	3	2	2
McLaughlin	2	2	3	2	3	2	2
Otto	1	2	2	2	2	2	2
Prince	3	3	3	3	3	2	2
Rust	3	3	3	3	3	2	2
Scragg	1	1	1	2	2	2	2
Smith	1	1	1	1	1	1	1
Stewart	1	1	2	2	1	2	1
Talbot	3	3	3	3	3	2	2
White	2	2	3	2	2	2	2
Sum:							
Total Possible:							
Percentage:							
Review Inst.:							

INSTRUCTIONAL GOAL: OUTLINE TEXTBOOK CHAPTERS

II. Secondary Ideas

FIGURE   12.12

Evaluating Instruction Using Group Performance Data

OUTLINE TEXTBOOK CHAPTERS								
II. Secondary Ideas								
Subcomponent		**A**	**B**	**C**	**D**	**E**	**F**	**G**
		Identify	**Relate**	**Paraphrase**	**Parallel**	**Order**	**Label**	**Align**
Date	*Totals:*	3	3	3	3	3	2	2
1/12	Percentage							
1/19	Percentage	66	68	72	80	78	92	95
1/28	Percentage	72	67	78	81	80	90	94
2/10	Percentage	78	69	84	79	86	91	96

Note: Numbers in cells represent the percentage of points earned by the total class on each subcomponent.

    F. Using the z scores, how would you interpret the performance of a student who earned a z score of $-.39$ on the test?

    G. Using the T scores, how would you interpret the performance of a student who earned a 56 on the test?

    H. Using the percentile scores, how would you interpret the performance of a student who earned a score of 68 on the test?

VII. Enrichment

For a test you have developed and administered, complete the following:

    A. Establish criteria for minimal mastery of each skill measured and:

        1. Determine the number of skills each student mastered.

        2. Prescribe follow-up activities for each student. Identify students who should receive enrichment activities and those who need additional instruction and practice on each skill.

    B. Evaluate instruction:

        1. Establish a criterion for the minimal percentage of students who should master each skill.

        2. Calculate the percentage of students who master each skill.

        3. Compare the percentage who passed each skill to the criterion established and judge instruction as good, adequate, or inadequate.

        4. Revise lesson plans for ineffective instruction.

    C. Establish above-average, average, and below-average categories of scores using the mean and the standard deviation.

    D. Compare each student's score to the established categories and determine whether the performance is above average, average, or below average within the group.

    E. Calculate z, T, and percentile scores for each raw score. Using these scores, judge each student's performance level.

FIGURE 12.13

Norm-Referenced Analysis of Students' Posttest Scores for the Compound Sentences Unit

$N = 20$ Mean $= 37.5$ Standard Deviation $= 3.88$

X	f	z	T	fb	1/2 fw	cfmp	Proportion	Percentile
42	2							
41	2							
40	5							
39	2							
38	1							
37	1							
36	1							
35	2							
34	1							
33	1							
31	1							
27	1							

Score Anchors X_L -2 -1 X $+1$ X_H

Raw Scores

■ FEEDBACK

I. **Criterion-Referenced Analysis of a Student's Performance**
   A. See Figure 12.14F.
   B. See Figure 12.14F.
   C. See Figure 12.14F.
   D. See Figure 12.14F.
   E. See Figure 12.14F.
   F. Instruction should be reconsidered for skill III.E.2.
   G. It appears that Smith selected response option 1 for all items on the last half of the objective part of the test. Since the correct answer for items 3, 7, and 10 is 1, Smith may have inadvertently answered them correctly. It seems wise to follow up with some oral questions for Smith.

Mastery Analysis of Students' Performance for the Conjunction Portion of the Compound Sentences Posttest (Enabling Skills III.A to III.F in Table 3.5)

	CONJUNCTION OBJECTIVES															Total Skills Mastered
Enabling Skill Codes	**III.A**	**III.B**	**III.C**	**III.D**				**III.E.1**		**II.E.2**		**III.F**				**Total Skills Mastered**
Items	1	2	3	4	5	6	7	8	9	10	11	12	13	14	15	7
Correct Answers:	2	3	1	3	2	4	1	4	2	1	4	*Hand Scored*				
McComas	*	*	*	*	*	*	*	*	*	*	*	*	*	*	*	7
Talbot	*	*	*	*	*	*	*	*	*	*	*	*	*	*	*	7
Deddens	*	*	*	*	*	*	*	*	*	*	*	*	*	*	*	7
Prince	*	*	*	*	*	*	*	*	*	*	*	*	*	*	*	7
Augustine	*	*	*	*	*	*	*	*	*	*	*	*	*	*	*	7
Rust	*	*	*	*	*	*	*	*	*	*	*	*	*	*	*	7
Carey	*	*	*	*	*	2	*	*	*	*	*	*	*	*	*	7
White	*	*	*	*	*	*	*	*	*	*	*	*	x	*	*	7
Hager	*	*	*	*	*	*	*	*	*	*	*	*	*	*	*	7
McLaughlin	*	*	*	*	*	2	*	*	*	*	*	*	*	x	*	7
Cromer	*	*	*	*	*	2	*	*	*	*	*	*	*	x	*	7
Otto	*	*	*	*	*	2	*	*	*	*	*	*	*	x	*	7
Scragg	*	*	*	*	*	2	*	*	*	*	3	*	*	x	*	6
Hill	*	*	*	*	*	2	*	*	*	*	3	*	*	*	x	6
Lovejoy	*	*	*	*	*	*	*	*	*	4	3	*	*	x	*	6
Bailey	*	*	3	*	*	2	*	*	*	2	3	*	*	x	*	5
Gormley	*	*	*	*	*	2	*	*	3	*	3	*	*	x	x	4
Deiters	*	*	*	*	*	1	*	*	3	2	1	x	*	x	*	4
Stewart	*	*	2	*	*	1	*	3	3	*	2	x	*	x	x	3
Smith	*	1	*	*	*	1	*	1	1	*	1	x	x	x	x	3
Number of Students Who Mastered	20	19	18	20				16		12		16				
Percentage of Students Who Mastered	100%	95%	90%	100%				80%		60%		80%				

II. Prescribing Instructional Activities Based on Mastery Analysis

See Figure 12.15F. Note that Smith was added to the list for enabling skill III.C.

III. Monitoring Student Progress

See Figure 12.16F. In order to be judged "master," students had to master all enabling skills for the strand. Partial mastery was assigned for students who had mastered a majority of the enabling skills for the coordinating conjunction strand. Nonmastery (blank cells) was assigned for students who mastered half or less of the enabling skills in the strand.

IV. Evaluating Instruction Using Product and Performance Tests

For items A through D, compare your calculations with ones included in Figure 12.17F. More instruction and rehearsal are needed for subcomponents II.A, II.B, II.C, II.D, and II.E.

V. Evaluating Instruction across Time

   A. See Figure 12.18F.
   B. Subcomponents include the following:
       1. Progressing: II.A, II.C, and II.E
       2. Staying about the same: II.B, II.D, II.F, and II.G
       3. Regressing: none
   C. Additional instruction appears warranted for the following subcomponents: II.A, II.B, and II.D.

FIGURE 12.15F

Prescribed Instructional Activities Based on Mastery Analysis

CONCEPTS/ CONTENT	**A** State/Recall Physical Characteristics of:	**B** State/Recall Functional Characteristics of:	**C** State/Recall Quality Characteristics of:	**D** Discriminate between Examples and Nonexamples	**E** Evaluate Given Examples	**F** Produce Examples of:
I. Comma						
II. Simple Sentence						
III. Coordinating Conjunction		Smith	Bailey Stewart Smith?	Smith?	Bailey Deiters Gormley Hill Lovejoy Scragg Smith Stewart	Deiters Gormley Smith Stewart
IV. Compound Sentence						

FIGURE 12.16F

A Sample Student Progress Chart for the Conjunction Portion of the Instructional Goal: "Write Compound Sentences"

COORDINATING CONJUNCTION ENABLING SKILLS								
Enabling Skills	**III A**	**III B**	**III C**	**III D**	**III E**	**III F**	**III**	**Etc.**
Augustine	x	x	x	x	x	x	M	
Bailey	x	x		x		x	PM	
Carey	x	x	x	x	x	x	M	
Cromer	x	x	x	x	x	x	M	
Deddens	x	x	x	x	x	x	M	
Deiters	x	x	x	x			PM	
Gormley	x	x	x	x			PM	
Hager	x	x	x	x	x	x	M	
Hill	x	x	x	x		x	PM	
Lovejoy	x	x	x	x		x	PM	
McComas	x	x	x	x	x	x	M	
McLaughlin	x	x	x	x	x	x	M	
Otto	x	x	x	x	x	x	M	
Prince	x	x	x	x	x	x	M	
Rust	x	x	x	x	x	x	M	
Scragg	x	x	x	x		x	PM	
Smith	x		?	?				
Stewart	x	x		x				
Talbot	x	x	x	x	x	x	M	
White	x	x	x	x	x	x	M	

Note: x = at least minimal mastery of enabling skill; **PM** = Partial Mastery of concept strand (e.g., coordinating conjunctions); **M** = Mastery of concept strand. For partial mastery, students mastered four of the six enabling skills.

FIGURE 12.17F

Evaluating Instruction Using Group Performance Data

OUTLINE TEXTBOOK CHAPTERS							
II. Secondary Ideas							
Subcomponent	**A**	**B**	**C**	**D**	**E**	**F**	**G**
	Identify	**Relate**	**Paraphrase**	**Parallel**	**Order**	**Label**	**Align**
Students *Points:*	3	3	3	3	3	2	2
Sum:	38	41	44	47	42	36	38
Total Possible:	60	60	60	60	60	40	40
Percentage:	63	68	73	78	70	90	95
Review Inst.:	***	***	***	***	***		

FIGURE 12.18F

Evaluating Instruction Using Group Performance Data across Time

OUTLINE TEXTBOOK CHAPTERS							
II. Secondary Ideas							
Subcomponent	**A**	**B**	**C**	**D**	**E**	**F**	**G**
	Identify	**Relate**	**Paraphrase**	**Parallel**	**Order**	**Label**	**Align**
Date *Totals:*	3	3	3	3	3	2	2
1/12 Percentage	63	68	73	78	70	90	95
1/19 Percentage	66	68	72	80	78	92	95
1/28 Percentage	72	67	78	81	80	90	94
2/10 Percentage	78	69	84	79	86	91	96

Note: Numbers in cells represent the percentage of points earned by the total class on each subcomponent.

VI. Norm-Referenced Analysis of a Student's Performance

A. See Figure 12.19F.

B. See Figure 12.19F.

C. See Figure 12.19F.

D. See Figure 12.19F.

E. The two students who earned scores of 42 performed above average compared to their classmates.

F. A z score of $-.39$ reflects average level performance in the class.

G. A T score of 56 reflects average level performance in the class.

H. Students who earned a percentile score of 68 performed better than 68 percent of the students in the class.

FIGURE 12.19F

Norm-Referenced Analysis of Students' Posttest Scores for the Compound Sentences Unit

$N = 20$ Mean = 37.5   Standard Deviation = 3.88

X	f	z	T	fb	1/2 fw	cfmp	Proportion	Percentile
42	2	1.16	62	18	1.0	19.0	.95	95
41	2	.90	59	16	1.0	17.0	.85	85
40	5	.64	56	11	2.5	13.5	.68	68
39	2	.39	54	9	1.0	10.0	.50	50
38	1	.13	51	8	.5	8.5	.43	43
37	1	−.13	49	7	.5	7.5	.38	38
36	1	−.39	46	6	.5	6.5	.33	33
35	2	−.64	44	4	1.0	5.0	.25	25
34	1	−.90	41	3	.5	3.5	.18	18
33	1	−1.16	38	2	.5	2.5	.13	13
31	1	−1.68	33	1	.5	1.5	.08	08
27	1	−2.71	23	0	.5	.5	.03	03

Score Anchors	X_L	−2	−1	X	+1	X_H
Raw Scores	27	29.74	33.62	37.5	41.38	42

SUGGESTED READINGS

Dick, W., Carey, L. M., & Carey, J. O. (2001). *The systematic design of instruction* (5th ed., pp. 254–293). New York: Addison-Wesley Longman.

Gallagher, J. D. (1998). *Classroom assessment for teachers* (pp. 373–384). Columbus, OH: Merrill.

Lynn, R. L., & Gronlund, N. E. (2000). *Measurement and assessment in teaching* (8th ed., pp. 475–487). Englewood Cliffs, NJ: Prentice-Hall.

Nitko, A. J. (1996). *Educational assessment of students* (2nd ed., pp. 284–298). Columbus, OH: Merrill.

Oosterhof, A. (1999). *Developing and using classroom assessments* (2nd ed., pp. 197–208). Columbus, OH: Merrill.

Popham, W. J. (1999). *Classroom assessment: What teachers need to know* (2nd ed., pp. 412–422). Boston: Allyn and Bacon.

Thorndike, R. M. (1997). *Measurement and evaluation in psychology and education* (6th ed., pp. 51–65). Columbus, OH: Merrill.

Worthen, B. R., White, K. R., Fan, X., & Sudweeks, R. L. (1999). *Measurement and assessment in schools* (2nd ed., pp. 57–92). New York: Addison-Wesley Longman.

13

Developing and Using Portfolios

- Develop portfolios of individual students' work to demonstrate initial status and progress on instructional goals.
- Describe guidelines for choosing portfolio exhibits that are not related to instructional goals and objectives.
- Summarize students' progress on one instructional goal across time to evaluate their development.
- Write verbal descriptions of students' strengths and areas for continued development based on exhibits in the portfolios.

One of the most important tasks that teachers perform is to communicate clearly and accurately their students' progress in school. Teachers can have difficulty clearly communicating achievement to students and parents when using abstract numbers and grades, and many choose to supplement test scores and grades with portfolios that contain samples of a student's work throughout the term. Although teachers have used portfolios for decades to collect work samples and describe pupils' progress, there is increased interest among educators in encouraging their use to improve communication. Whether you personally decide to develop and maintain student portfolios or you are required to do so by school administrators, carefully planning will help ensure that your portfolios are useful.

As you studied the previous chapters on objective and alternative means of assessment, it may have become obvious to you that the most logical approach to reporting many of these assessments would be through organizing a collection of students' work for criterion-referenced analyses. Most of the conceptual work for producing quality portfolios was addressed in preceding chapters since portfolios do require ideas and materials that you studied on goal analysis, test development, and test analysis. Portfolios are unique, however, in that they enable you to pull everything together into a coherent picture of a student's development in your class. The design of portfolios should enable a balanced view of your students that includes (1) a picture of students' status at the outset of instruction on academic goals and documentation of their progress through instruction and posttests, (2) a broader picture of growth that is not tied to specific instructional goals and objectives, and (3) when viewed as a class set, a composite picture of strengths and weaknesses in the instructional program.

Developing Portfolios to Monitor Growth on Instructional Goals

Effective portfolios are not simply chronological collections of students' work from a particular time. Rather, their design should enable illustration of students' status at the outset of instruction and provide documentation of their progress through instruction and posttests. The following paragraphs describe planning and design activities for quality portfolios. An example portfolio assessment form for the instructional goal "Write a paragraph" is used to illustrate the process. In developing a portfolio, you might take the following steps:

1. Examine the instructional goals in the curriculum guide and identify the types of information that can illustrate students' status and growth on the goals.
2. Plan a testing strategy that will enable demonstration of students' progress.
3. Design the overall portfolio.
4. Develop a portfolio assessment form.
5. Select a container for your portfolios.
6. Enter information and work samples into the portfolio.
7. Compare students' pretest and posttest performance and assess development.
8. Write a descriptive summary of students' status and growth.

The following paragraphs describe each of these steps.

Examining Instructional Goals

Developing and maintaining portfolios can be quite time consuming, so you should ensure that the instructional goals you select for portfolio assessment are the most critical ones for analyzing and communicating your students' progress. Skills you might judge as most critical are ones that are foundational not only for your subject but also for the students' development in other subject areas. For example, a language arts teacher might choose to document oral and silent reading goals in a portfolio because reading is foundational for all school subjects; a math teacher might choose to document calculations as well as particular kinds of quantitative reasoning; and a physical education teacher might choose to demonstrate physical fitness and strength development goals. Basic life skills such as these warrant the additional time required for portfolio assessment. When you have selected the goals you believe should receive the most attention from you, your students, and their parents, you need to consider your strategy for examining students' skills on the goals.

Planning a Testing Strategy That Will Enable Illustration of Student Progress

Well-designed portfolios should illustrate students' progress during a term, semester, or year. It is unlikely that any portfolio system will enable you to store all the work samples your students produce, so samples chosen should be relevant for your instructional goals and they should illustrate students' progress on the goals.

To demonstrate students' progress during your course, you will need to have a measure of their status at the outset of instruction and then subsequent measures of their skill at various points across the term, semester, or year. Initial status assessments could include pretests (and perhaps readiness tests), observations, interviews, samples of work, and other formal and informal assessments, since students' achievement levels on these materials provide baseline data for reviewing progress. Students' achievement on practice tests can provide illustrations of interim progress, and posttest data, when compared with pretest information, will illuminate the skills changes that occur. Recall that the design of all these types of tests was described in Chapter 4. For the critical goals you select, planning methods to assess students' status before or during the beginning of instruction is the only way to guarantee that you have the information required to develop a good portfolio. Remember that such testing could include objective tests and any of the other alternative tests that you have studied.

Along with the work samples you choose for your students' portfolios, you might want to encourage your students to evaluate their own work and to volunteer samples for inclusion in their portfolios. Engaging in exercises to evaluate their own work and selecting samples they consider their best work can be very good learning experiences. Additionally, comparing initial products with those they develop after instruction and seeing their progress in the class can also be illuminating for students.

Designing the Portfolio

Portfolios can take many forms. In determining the best form for your subject area and students, keep three criteria in mind. The first criterion is *feasibility*. Do you have the time and resources to develop and maintain a portfolio for all students in your classes? If time is limited, which standards should you select for portfolio assessment? The second criterion is *utility*. Of what benefit will your portfolios be in communicating to students, parents, and colleagues the growth and development of students in your classes? The third criterion is *clarity*. Have you gathered the best assessment materials and provided enough documentation and explanation for others to understand the student's growth and current status?

The typical elements included in portfolios are illustrated in Figure 13.1. This language arts teacher has chosen a spiral notebook container for the students' portfolios. Following the portfolio cover, teachers often choose to develop a table of contents to guide the reader through the portfolio. For each instructional goal or standard selected, there is a portfolio assessment form that contains the student's scores on all assessments included in the portfolio for the goal. This summary form also contains the teacher's verbal assessment of the student's general progress in the goal during the time period and his or her status at the time the portfolio is completed for the goal. Exhibits of the student's actual work samples follow the portfolio summary form. In this case, the teacher has chosen an objective pretest, an objective posttest, and several products collected over time, each accompanied by its rubric.

FIGURE 13.1

Materials Typically Contained in One Student's Portfolio

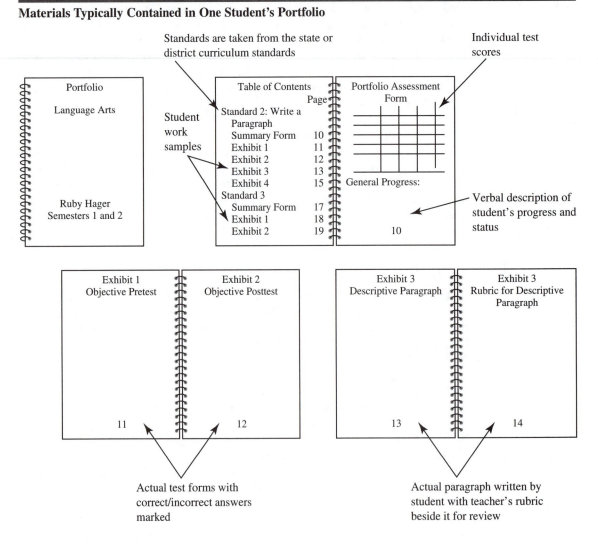

Developing a Portfolio Assessment Form

Designing an effective portfolio assessment form requires consideration of how to format the information you need. Since the purpose of portfolios is to communicate both status and growth, the manner in which you organize work samples and describe them is very important. Portfolios should *not* be only a chronological collection of students' papers and projects; instead, they should contain work samples organized to enable direct comparisons of initial work with work samples produced following instruction and practice. Early planning for organizing and describing materials in the portfolio can ensure that you identify the best way to display and describe students' progress.

Figure 13.2 contains a sample portfolio assessment form for the instructional goal "Write a paragraph." The first row of the form identifies the purpose; the second indicates the particular instructional goal from the curriculum guide; the third row names the student, grade level, and teacher; and the fourth row is used to identify the products the teacher plans to include in the portfolio. Notice that the objective-style pretest and posttest for paragraphs are listed as well as the four types of paragraphs students wrote during the unit. It is quite appropriate to include objective tests as work samples in portfolios.

The fifth row, labeled Exhibits, contains numbers that are used to identify and sequence students' products in the portfolio. The sixth row, labeled Purpose, identifies whether each work sample is a baseline measure or a measure obtained following instruction. In this example, only pretest and posttest samples are included; however, teachers can include interim work as well. The seventh row of the summary form identifies the date the student produced the work. Notice that work samples are sequenced in pretest/posttest pairs rather than chronologically. This ordering strategy will enable teachers, parents, and students to examine progress better since contiguous products are the same assignments collected early and late during the unit. The information described in these top rows is similar to a textbook's table of contents in that it informs readers of what they will find in the portfolio and where they will find it. Moreover, the information helps teachers classify and file information in the portfolio as it is completed by students and evaluated.

The criteria for judging students' paragraphs are listed in the far left column. Notice that only main paragraph components (I. through IV.) are included on the form. This is done because the purpose for this form is to provide a summary of the students' work. Listing each criterion within the components could create information overload for the reader. Notice also that this teacher has opted to include criteria other than paragraph structure on the summary form. Criteria related to the students' choice of content and ideas, as well as their sentence structure, grammar, punctuation, and spelling, are being monitored in the work samples. These criteria will not be considered in evaluating students' ability to structure paragraphs, but they are being monitored in the paragraph writing samples to enable communication of progress in these important skills.

The last two rows in the summary form are reserved for the teacher's descriptive comments. The first of these rows is for comparison of each pair of products, and the last row is reserved for the teacher's general impressions of the students'

FIGURE 13.2

A Sample Portfolio Assessment Form for the Instructional Goal "Write a Paragraph"

<table>
<tr><td colspan="7" align="center">PORTFOLIO ASSESSMENT</td></tr>
<tr><td colspan="7">Instructional Goal: Write a paragraph
Name _____ Grade _____ Teacher _____</td></tr>
<tr>
<th>Objectives</th>
<th>Paragraph
Objective
Tests</th>
<th>Rating
Scale
Totals</th>
<th>I.F.1
Descriptive
Paragraph</th>
<th>I.F.2
Time Series
Paragraph</th>
<th>I.F.3
Procedure
Paragraph</th>
<th>I.F.4
Feelings
Paragraph</th>
</tr>
<tr>
<td>Exhibits:</td>
<td>#1   #2</td>
<td></td>
<td>#3   #4</td>
<td>#5   #6</td>
<td>#7   #8</td>
<td>#9   #10</td>
</tr>
<tr>
<td>Purpose:</td>
<td>Pre Post</td>
<td></td>
<td>Pre Post</td>
<td>Pre Post</td>
<td>Pre Post</td>
<td>Pre Post</td>
</tr>
<tr>
<td>*Criteria   Date*</td>
<td>____ ____</td>
<td></td>
<td>____ ____</td>
<td>____ ____</td>
<td>____ ____</td>
<td>____ ____</td>
</tr>
<tr>
<td>I. Paragraph</td>
<td>____ ____</td>
<td>7</td>
<td>____ ____</td>
<td>____ ____</td>
<td>____ ____</td>
<td>____ ____</td>
</tr>
<tr>
<td>II. Topic Sentence</td>
<td>____ ____</td>
<td>10</td>
<td>____ ____</td>
<td>____ ____</td>
<td>____ ____</td>
<td>____ ____</td>
</tr>
<tr>
<td>III. Supporting
Sentences</td>
<td>____ ____</td>
<td>14</td>
<td>____ ____</td>
<td>____ ____</td>
<td>____ ____</td>
<td>____ ____</td>
</tr>
<tr>
<td>IV. Concluding
Sentence</td>
<td>____ ____</td>
<td>13</td>
<td>____ ____</td>
<td>____ ____</td>
<td>____ ____</td>
<td>____ ____</td>
</tr>
<tr>
<td>Raw Score
Percentage
Correct</td>
<td>____ ____

____ ____</td>
<td>44</td>
<td>____ ____</td>
<td>____ ____</td>
<td>____ ____</td>
<td>____ ____</td>
</tr>
<tr>
<td>V. Content</td>
<td>____ ____</td>
<td></td>
<td>____ ____</td>
<td>____ ____</td>
<td>____ ____</td>
<td>____ ____</td>
</tr>
<tr>
<td>VI. Sentence
Structure</td>
<td>____ ____</td>
<td></td>
<td>____ ____</td>
<td>____ ____</td>
<td>____ ____</td>
<td>____ ____</td>
</tr>
<tr>
<td>VII. Grammar</td>
<td>____ ____</td>
<td></td>
<td>____ ____</td>
<td>____ ____</td>
<td>____ ____</td>
<td>____ ____</td>
</tr>
<tr>
<td>VIII. Punctuation</td>
<td>____ ____</td>
<td></td>
<td>____ ____</td>
<td>____ ____</td>
<td>____ ____</td>
<td>____ ____</td>
</tr>
<tr>
<td>IX. Spelling</td>
<td>____ ____</td>
<td></td>
<td>____ ____</td>
<td>____ ____</td>
<td>____ ____</td>
<td>____ ____</td>
</tr>
<tr>
<td>Comments:</td>
<td></td>
<td></td>
<td></td>
<td></td>
<td></td>
<td></td>
</tr>
<tr>
<td colspan="7">General Progress:</td>
</tr>
</table>

development during the unit. These descriptive summaries serve to focus parents' and students' attention on facets of students' work that the teacher considers important.

Completing the design of your portfolio assessment summary form for a unit of instruction is, in essence, completing the design of that section of the portfolio. The assessment form can be attached in some manner to the front of the portfolio where it will be convenient to use. It is a good idea to keep it inside the cover, however, as students undoubtedly will consider the information it contains to be confidential. All that remains at this point is to collect students' work, score it, enter the scores on the summary form, assign each sample an exhibit number, and place it—along with a copy of the checklist or rating scale used to judge the work—into the portfolio.

Selecting a Container for Your Portfolios

Several criteria should be considered for selecting portfolio containers that best suit your needs. Some include the available storage space and facilities, the number of students you teach, and the type and size of appropriate work samples. If appropriate work samples are limited to paper-and-pencil products, you teach over 150 students a day, and you have very limited storage facilities, then the file folder will undoubtedly be the container of choice. On the other hand, if you teach a subject where products other than paper-and-pencil ones are common (e.g., computer discs, videotapes, notebooks, woodcuttings), then you will need to balance product size and storage capabilities in determining the best portfolio containers. It is important to remember that the type of container chosen will influence the nature of the work samples that can be stored.

Entering Information on the Summary Form and Placing Products into the Portfolio

Figure 13.3 contains the portfolio assessment form with all the pretest information inserted for one student. Ruby's objective pretest was administered on October 2. The number of questions she answered correctly for each main paragraph component is inserted in the form, along with the total number of items the pretest contained for each component. For example, she answered all four general paragraph questions correctly and 7 of 11 topic sentence questions correctly.

The writing sample pretests were administered on October 3, 4, 5, and 6. The points Ruby was awarded for each main component are inserted for each of these pretests. With her data from these different samples collected together, the teacher can analyze patterns in her initial work. For example, Ruby had already mastered the general idea of paragraphs since she earned all possible points in this category. She appears to need work, however, on topic sentences, supporting sentences, and concluding sentences. Her writing samples, with their rating scales attached, document her initial status on writing paragraphs. They should be numbered for reference and filed in the appropriate place in the portfolio. Notice that there are no general comments inserted on the assessment form since data from the posttests are unavailable at

FIGURE 13.3

A Sample Paragraph Portfolio Assessment Form for One Student

				PORTFOLIO ASSESSMENT		

Instructional Goal: Write a paragraph
Name _Ruby Hager_____   Grade _8____   Teacher _Ms. Jones_____

Objectives	Paragraph Objective Tests	Rating Scale Totals	I.F.1 Descriptive Paragraph	I.F.2 Time Series Paragraph	I.F.3 Procedure Paragraph	I.F.4 Feelings Paragraph
Exhibits:	#1 #2		#3 #4	#5 #6	#7 #8	#9 #10
Purpose:	Pre Post		Pre Post	Pre Post	Pre Post	Pre Post
Criteria Date	10/2 ___		10/3 ___	10/4 ___	10/5 ___	10/6 ___
I. Paragraph	4/4 ___	7	7 ___	7 ___	7 ___	7 ___
II. Topic Sentence	7/11 ___	10	6 ___	6 ___	7 ___	6 ___
III. Supporting Sentences	8/11 ___	14	7 ___	6 ___	7 ___	8 ___
IV. Concluding Sentence	7/11 ___	13	10 ___	9 ___	9 ___	10 ___
Raw Score	26 ___		30 ___	28 ___	30 ___	31 ___
Percentage Correct	70 ___	44	68 ___	64 ___	68 ___	70 ___
V. Content	___ ___		___ ___	___ ___	___ ___	___ ___
VI. Sentence Structure	___ ___		___ ___	___ ___	___ ___	___ ___
VII. Grammar	___ ___		___ ___	___ ___	___ ___	___ ___
VIII. Punctuation	___ ___		___ ___	___ ___	___ ___	___ ___
IX. Spelling	___ ___		___ ___	___ ___	___ ___	___ ___
Comments:						
General Progress:						

this point for comparison. As posttest measures are obtained, they can be scored and compared with these baseline data.

Comparing Pretest/Posttest Performance and Assessing Progress

Figure 13.4 includes Ruby's posttest scores for the paragraph unit. Dates the exams were administered are inserted at the top of the posttest columns, and her scores are listed beside the pretest scores. Notice that her performance on the objective posttest demonstrates good progress across all main components of a paragraph. Her total score changed from 70 percent of the items answered correctly on the pretest (26/37) to 91 percent on the posttest (40/44), which reflects marked improvement.

Ruby's performance on each of the four writing samples improved as well. She moved from earning 68 to 89 percent of the points on the descriptive paragraph, 64 to 91 percent on the time series paragraph, 68 to 91 percent on the procedures paragraph, and 70 to 100 percent on the feelings paragraph. From these data comparisons, the teacher can see that Ruby's overall development was at a consistent level across all writing samples. Examining her progress for each paragraph component, you can see that she was already proficient in general paragraph skills at the outset, and she made good progress during the unit in writing both topic and concluding sentences. She still has room for improvement in the supporting sentences area. The descriptive information included at the bottom of the form can provide insights into particular areas of supporting sentences that require additional instruction and practice.

Writing a Descriptive Summary of Students' Status and Progress

As you analyze a student's work and make descriptive comments about its features, it is important to point out uniqueness within and across work samples. Otherwise, these features may be missed by you, parents, and students when the portfolio is reviewed during conferences. Additionally, it is important to describe both strengths and areas that need to be improved in a student's work. Stressing strengths is important because it is discouraging to a student and parent to review a summary of work that stresses only faults and weaknesses. Calling attention to good points, and pointing them out *first,* often ensures that students and parents have a receptive mindset for accepting information about areas that need to be improved.

In writing your summaries, keep in mind that the nature and tone of words you use in your descriptions are important for the students and parents. Avoid using terms on these assessment forms such as *failed, inadequate,* or *unacceptable.* These terms are not only discouraging to students but they also connote a misleading sense of finality to skill development. Language that implies future development and growth is far more appropriate. Problematic areas in students' work samples might be positively described as skills that need improvement, future focus, or strengthening.

FIGURE 13.4

Paragraph Portfolio Assessment Form for One Student Completed for a Unit of Instruction

PORTFOLIO ASSESSMENT						
Instructional Goal: Write a paragraph Name _Ruby Hager_ Grade _8_ Teacher _Ms. Jones_						
Objectives	**Paragraph Objective Tests**	**Rating Scale Totals**	**I.F.1 Descriptive Paragraph**	**I.F.2 Time Series Paragraph**	**I.F.3 Procedure Paragraph**	**I.F.4 Feelings Paragraph**
Exhibits:	#1 #2		#3 #4	#5 #6	#7 #8	#9 #10
Purpose:	Pre Post		Pre Post	Pre Post	Pre Post	Pre Post
Criteria Date	10/2 11/22		10/3 11/23	10/4 11/24	10/5 11/25	10/6 11/26
I. Paragraph	4/4 7/7	7	7 7	7 7	7 7	7 7
II. Topic Sentence	7/11 11/11	10	6 10	6 10	7 10	6 10
III. Supporting Sentences	8/11 10/13	14	7 10	6 10	7 12	8 14
IV. Concluding Sentence	7/11 12/13	13	10 12	9 13	9 11	10 13
Raw Score	26 40		30 39	28 40	30 40	31 44
Percentage Correct	70 91	44	68 89	64 91	68 91	70 100
V. Content			✓ +	✓ +	✓ +	✓ +
VI. Sentence Structure			+ +	+ +	+ +	+ +
VII. Grammar			+ +	✓ +	+ +	+ +
VIII. Punctuation			+ +	+ +	+ +	+ +
IX. Spelling			n7 n7	n7 n7	n7 n7	n7 n7
Comments:	Good effort and improvement		Good desc. Needs to work on sequence	Topic sentence good improv.	Over generalized conclusions	Very good at expressing personal feelings
General Progress: *Ruby has a good concept of paragraph structure and purpose. She is imaginative and detailed in her descriptions. Her writing developed nicely over the term. She needs to work on transition and sequence. Her spelling needs attention—a personal dictionary may help.*						

Choosing Goal-Free Exhibits for Portfolios

When you consider the purpose for a portfolio, you can see why teachers often choose to include materials that are not directly related to a student's progress on a specific goal. These extras can help provide a richer picture of a student's intellectual and social growth. A problem arises when the portfolio becomes a cluttered catchall for *everything* that is cute, colorful, humorous, inventive, or unique in even the smallest way. Then the portfolio begins to resemble a bulletin board or the refrigerator door in households, and the value of the portfolio is diminished as a method of communication among teachers, students, and parents. There are three guidelines that will help ensure that extra material inserted into portfolios is useful for your periodic reviews of a student: focus, chronology, and documentation.

Providing a Focus

Sometimes it is fun to include a few things in a portfolio just because you want to, but usually what is included should focus on aspects of a student that you think deserve additional notice. Such aspects could include attitudes and behavior not listed on report cards, academic abilities or deficiencies not related to your subject area, artistic tendencies, social accomplishments, career goals, or a myriad of other areas that would help you communicate with students and their parents. If material does not focus on something that needs to be said about a student, then do not include it in the portfolio.

Portraying a Chronology

The most useful exhibits in a portfolio are those that sustain their focus across time, whether it be a grading period or an entire school year. Exhibits will occasionally be entered into a portfolio as isolated comments on a student, but those exhibits that have a sequence and demonstrate a pattern will have more value in your periodic reviews of students.

Providing Documentation

A good rule of thumb is that if it is not worth taking a moment to document a potential exhibit for a portfolio, then do not include it. Documenting what you include will help tie together the contents of a portfolio and emphasize the focus of the exhibits. Figure 13.5 is a generic form to use for documenting exhibits included in a portfolio. You could adapt the format to meet your needs in a particular classroom setting.

Assume that you have decided to include something in a student's portfolio; these are the steps you could take to document the exhibit:

1. In the heading for the first column on the top of the form, enter:
   a. An identifying number for the exhibit
   b. The date

FIGURE 13.5

Generic Form for Documenting Portfolio Exhibits

	DESCRIPTION OF EXHIBITS		
	No. _____ Date _____ Description _____	No. _____ Date _____ Description _____	
Focus of Exhibits			**Etc.**
1.			
2.			
⋮			

      c. A description of the exhibit that could include:
        (1) Notes from an interview or informal observation
        (2) A rating scale or checklist from some product or process
        (3) An objective test or quiz
        (4) An actual product
        (5) Anecdotal comments written on a slip of paper
        (6) A lab report or technical drawing
        (7) A sample of writing
        (8) Any other document or product that would support a focus on an aspect of a student

2. In the space in the left side of the first row on the form, enter a description of the focus of the exhibit. Remember that the focus is student centered. It is the particular aspect of the student that you have chosen to highlight by inserting this exhibit into the portfolio. The focus could be on:
   a. Career goals
   b. Social adjustment
   c. Athletic ability
   d. Academic skills
   e. Classroom behavior
   f. Any other aspect of the student that you have chosen

3. In the cell where the focus row intersects the description column, enter any notes that will add more meaning to this summary document or help you remember details of the exhibit. Such notes might include:
   a. Anecdotal impressions
   b. Test scores, grades, percentage correct, objectives mastered, and so on

      c. Comments on progress
      d. Other information that will help jog your memory so that you will not need to refer to the original exhibit each time you review the portfolio

When you decide to insert another exhibit into the student's portfolio, just move over one column to the right and down one row and repeat the three steps. On the other hand, if the new exhibit is focused on the same aspect of the student as exhibit number 1, then you would use the same row and just move over one column to the right for your new entry. By documenting your exhibits in this manner, you automatically create the focus and the sense of chronology that are so valuable in making a portfolio an effective tool for communicating with students and parents.

■ Computer Technology

Teachers are realizing that computer technology can be very helpful for developing and managing portfolios. Current computer technology is revolutionizing the manner in which students' work samples are catalogued, stored, and retrieved. Teachers who use word-processing and spreadsheet programs to develop their assessments and rubrics can simply transfer their files for individual students into each student's computer-based portfolio. Using readily available scanners, you can convert students' hand-written work samples into computer-based exhibits. Digital cameras are also useful for creating computer-based visuals of students' work samples, displays, projects, and even of the students themselves.

Using World Wide Web technology, teachers can create webpages for the class and for each individual student's portfolio. In addition to the typical products found in a portfolio, websites can be used to store videotapes of students performing skills, such as reading orally, delivering a speech, participating in a debate, or performing a motor skill. Web-based portfolios can be made available to parents who may access the site using a teacher-assigned password for confidentiality. These sites can be updated on a regular basis to keep parents informed of overall class activities as well as individual student progress.

If you are not yet skilled in using word processors, spreadsheets, scanners, digital cameras, or web-page technology, it is time! Your ability to monitor your students' work and communicate with them and their parents about their progress will be greatly enhanced when you have these skills. When selecting in-service activities for the upcoming year, consider requesting computer-technology workshops for portfolio development.

■ Summary

Procedures for evaluating students' progress using portfolio assessments are described in this chapter. Portfolios are collections of students' work that are used to document progress on instructional goals, and their main purpose is to improve communication with students and parents. Portfolios do not contain simply a chronological collection of random work samples; instead, they include carefully selected sets of materials that demonstrate students' initial status on key instructional goals and the progress they make on these goals during a course. The following procedures are recommended for designing and developing effective portfolios to demonstrate students' progress:

1. Examine the instructional goals in the curriculum guide and identify the types of information that can illustrate students' status and growth on the goals.
2. Plan a testing strategy that will enable demonstration of students' progress.
3. Design the overall portfolio.
4. Develop a portfolio assessment form.
5. Select a container for your portfolios.
6. Enter information and work samples into the portfolio.
7. Compare students' pretest and posttest performance and assess development.
8. Write a descriptive summary of students' status and growth.

Many teachers use the portfolio as an instructional tool by encouraging students to assist with selecting materials for inclusion. Moreover, many encourage students to evaluate their own progress during a course using the work samples collected.

Teachers sometimes choose to include in portfolios exhibits that do not relate directly to instructional goals or objectives. Guidelines for incorporation of such exhibits include: (1) having a clear focus for the materials selected, (2) portraying a chronology or focus across time, and (3) providing documentation of what is included and why.

■ P R A C T I C E   E X E R C I S E S

I. Portfolio Assessment
A. What is the *main purpose* for creating and maintaining portfolios of students' work?
B. What kinds of information are summarized in portfolio assessment forms?
C. What type of products can you use to document a student's initial skill status on instructional goals?
D. What type of products can you use to document students' progress and growth?

II. Develop a Portfolio Assessment Form
Design a portfolio assessment form for the chapter outline rating scale included in Figure 13.6. Compare your assessment form with the one included in Figure 13.8F in the Feedback section.

III. Describe a Student's Status and Growth
A. What is a good strategy for describing the strengths and weaknesses in a student's skills that become apparent in a portfolio?
B. Examine the test data for outlining text chapters in Figure 13.7. Using your own paper, analyze Ruby's status and growth and write information appropriate for the General Progress section at the bottom of the Portfolio Assessment form. In writing your summary, you will want to describe Ruby's strengths, her overall progress, and areas where she still needs practice.

FIGURE 13.6

Rating Scale for Evaluating Outlines

Name _____ Date _____ Score _____

Total   (35)

I. Main Ideas

	1	2	3
A. Main ideas identified	Secondary ideas included	Some ideas missing	All main ideas included
	1	2	3
B. Clearly paraphrased	Some meaning changed	Too brief/wordy	Clearly paraphrased
	1	2	3
C. Parallel structure	Mixed sentence/phrase	All sentences or phrases	Consistent word format
	1	2	3
D. Consistent order	Out of order	Most in order	All in order
	1	2	3
E. Consistent labels	Inconsistent	Consistent	
	1	2	
F. Alignment	Flush with left margin	Aligned	
	1	2	

II. Secondary Ideas

A. Secondary ideas identified	Main ideas included	Some ideas missing	All secondary ideas included
	1	2	3
B. Related to main idea	Scrambled placement	Most within right topic	All within right topic
	1	2	3
C. Clearly paraphrased	Some meaning changed	Too brief/wordy	Clearly paraphrased
	1	2	3
D. Parallel structure	Mixed sentence/phrase/word	All sentences, phrases, or words	Consistent word format
	1	2	3
E. Consistent order	Out of order	Most in order	All in order
	1	2	3
F. Consistent labels	Inconsistent	Consistent	
	1	2	
G. Alignment	Indented five spaces	Aligned	
	1	2	

A Sample Portfolio Assessment Form for the Instructional Goal "Outline Chapters in the Text"

PORTFOLIO ASSESSMENT						

Instructional Goal: Outline text chapters including main ideas and secondary ideas in the outline
Name _Ruby Hager_   Grade __8__   Teacher ___Ms. Jones___

Objectives		**Initial Chapter 4**	**Chapter 5**	**Chapter 6**	**Chapter 7**	**Etc.**
Exhibits:		#1	#2	#3	#4	
Criteria *Date*	*Total Points*					
I. Main Ideas						
A. Identified	3	1	2	2	3	
B. Paraphrased	3	1	1	2	2	
C. Parallel	3	1	2	3	3	
D. Consistent order	3	1	1	2	2	
E. Consistent labels	2	1	2	2	2	
F. Alignment	2	2	2	2	2	
II. Secondary Ideas						
A. Identified	3	1	1	2	2	
B. Related to main	3	1	3	3	3	
C. Paraphrased	3	1	1	2	2	
D. Parallel	3	1	2	3	3	
E. Consistent order	3	1	1	2	2	
F. Consistent labels	2	1	2	2	2	
G. Alignment	2	2	2	2	2	
Total	35	15	22	29	30	
Percentage of Total	100	43	63	83	86	
General Progress:						

IV. Enrichment

Select an instructional goal from a curriculum guide for the subject and grade level that you teach or plan to teach. For this goal:

A. Name possible work samples that could be used to provide baseline data for students' skills at the outset of instruction.

B. Name possible work samples that could be included to illustrate students' interim progress.

C. Name possible work samples that could provide outcome measures of students' achievement during the class.

D. Plan ways to organize the portfolio.

E. Develop a portfolio assessment form for recording performance data, contrasting work samples, describing students' strengths, and describing areas where they need additional instruction and practice.

F. Locate a teacher who has a good portfolio system developed and request permission to examine the following:

  1. The materials it contains that are anchored to instructional goals

  2. The materials that are unique to a particular student

  3. The assessment form(s) used to locate, contrast, and describe both goal-based and student-based materials included in the portfolio

■ FEEDBACK

I. Portfolio Assessment

A. The main purpose for creating and maintaining portfolios of students' work is to provide better communication to students and parents about students' learning and their progress in school. The letter grades and skills checklists typically provided to summarize students' progress cannot illustrate as clearly the instructional goals that students have mastered, partially mastered, or not mastered during a term. They also cannot communicate noncurricular aspects, talents, and characteristics of a student that should be recognized and communicated.

B. The kinds of information typically included in portfolios are samples of students' work that demonstrate their status on instructional goals at the outset of instruction and their growth on these goals during and following instruction. Many teachers also choose to include materials students produce that are not anchored to any particular instructional goal but that do illustrate students' status and growth on both cognitive and social skills. Moreover, many teachers frequently include samples of work that students choose to include in their portfolios, regardless of whether these student selected samples are anchored to the curriculum or are particularly good at illustrating the student's progress.

C. Students' initial skill status can be documented using any work sample produced at the outset of instruction. The samples can be formally or informally produced materials or they can be formally administered pretests for the instructional unit. Teachers sometimes use formal or informal readiness tests as a part of the initial documentation. These work samples can be objective-style exams, products students develop, active performances, and attitude rating scales or questionnaires.

D. Students' progress and growth can be documented using practice exercises (interim) and posttests designed to measure their goal-based knowledge and skill. These tests can be objective-style exams, product development tests, active performance tests, and attitude rating scales or questionnaires. The posttests can include unit exams, term exams, or semester exams. These formal assessment materials can be supplemented with other work samples the teacher considers unique and important for describing a student's progress.

II. Compare your portfolio assessment form with the example in Figure 13.8F. The students' baseline skills will be recorded in the column labeled Chapter 4. Space is included for data from their outlines for subsequent chapters. Notice that space is provided for recording the total points available for each subcomponent.

III. A. The best strategy for communicating students' strengths and weaknesses is to address the strengths first. After discussing all the strong points in a student's work, especially areas where the student is making strides and improving, the student will be more receptive to critical comments concerning how they can improve. Critiques should be phrased positively, connoting growth, progress, and future development.

B. "Ruby is exceptionally good at identifying main ideas in her chapter outlines. She is also good at keeping her statements parallel and relating her secondary and main ideas. She should also be commended for her formatting skills. She had no experience in outlining chapters when we started the unit in October, and her growth and progress are satisfying to her and to me. In continuing her development, she needs to work on paraphrasing ideas (much too long) and ordering her entries consistently."

FIGURE 13.8F

A Sample Portfolio Assessment Form for the Instructional Goal "Outline Chapters in the Text"

PORTFOLIO ASSESSMENT						
Instructional Goal: Outline text chapters including main ideas and secondary ideas in the outline Name _____ Grade _____ Teacher _____						
Objectives		**Initial Chapter 4**	**Chapter 5**	**Chapter 6**	**Chapter 7**	**Etc.**
Exhibits:		#1	#2	#3	#4	
Criteria *Date*	*Total Points*					
I. Main Ideas						
A. Identified	3					
B. Paraphrased	3					
C. Parallel	3					
D. Consistent order	3					
E. Consistent labels	2					
F. Alignment	2					
II. Secondary Ideas						
A. Identified	3					
B. Related to main	3					
C. Paraphrased	3					
D. Parallel	3					
E. Consistent order	3					
F. Consistent labels	2					
G. Alignment	2					
Total	35					
Percentage of Total	100					
General Progress:						

■ R U B R I C

A Rubric for Evaluating Portfolios

Not Included	Needs Work	Good	CRITERIA
			I. Container/Cover
			1. Suitable for subject matter and exhibits.
			2. Attractive.
			II. Table of Contents
			3. Names important state/district performance standards studied during the time period.
			4. Clearly organizes standards/goals from simple to complex to illustrate progress.
			5. Names materials and exhibits included for each standard.
			III. Portfolio Summary Form
			6. Names the student.
			7. Names the instructional goal or standard.
			8. Includes dates work samples were created.
			9. Includes type of test (readiness, pretest, practice, or posttest).
			10. Includes criteria used for scoring each exhibit.
			IV. The General Progress Comments on the Portfolio Summary Form
			11. Begin with the student's specific strengths related to enabling skills in the goal area.
			12. Describe the student's progress in the enabling skills and goal over the time period.
			13. Describe enabling skills where student needs more work or practice.
			V. Student Work Samples or Exhibits
			14. Are linked to curriculum standards or goals.
			15. Reflect formal or informal assessments (e.g., readiness tests, pretests, practice tests, posttests).
			16. Are scored by teacher with correct and incorrect work clearly marked.
			17. Product and performance tests are accompanied by their original rubrics.

Not Included	Needs Work	Good	CRITERIA
			VI. Goal-Free Exhibits
			18. Are clearly related to important aspects of the student's development during the course.
			19. Portray a chronology of development.
			20. Are clearly documented (exhibit number, date collected, description, focus or purpose for inclusion).
			VII. Technology
			21. Portfolio is created using appropriate computer technology.
			22. Portfolio is managed using appropriate computer technology.

SUGGESTED READINGS

Cook, R. E., Tessier, A., & Klein, M. D. (1996). *Adapting early childhood curricula for children in inclusive settings* (4th ed., pp. 125–126). Columbus, OH: Merrill.

Gallagher, J. D. (1998). *Classroom assessment for teachers* (pp. 288–323). Columbus, OH: Merrill.

Kubiszyn, T., & Borich, G. (2000). *Educational testing and measurement* (6th ed., pp. 181–201). New York: John Wiley & Sons.

Lynn, R. L., & Gronlund, N. E. (2000). *Measurement and assessment in teaching* (8th ed., pp. 289–313). Englewood Cliffs, NJ: Prentice-Hall.

Nitko, A. J. (1996). *Educational assessment of students* (2nd ed., pp. 278–282). Columbus, OH: Merrill.

Oosterhof, A. (1999). *Developing and using classroom assessments* (2nd ed., pp. 179–194). Columbus, OH: Merrill.

Schlam, L., & Cafetz, S. (1977). Using portfolios with language minority students. In R. B. Weiner & J. H. Cohen (Eds.), *Literacy portfolios.* Columbus, OH: Merrill.

Soodak, L. (1977). Using portfolios with students who have learning and behavioral-emotional problems. In R. B. Weiner & J. H. Cohen (Eds.), *Literacy portfolios.* Columbus, OH: Merrill.

Tombari, M., & Borich, G. (1999). *Authentic assessment in the classroom* (pp. 164–188). Columbus, OH: Merrill.

Weiner, R. B., & Cohen, J. H. (1997). *Literacy portfolios.* Columbus, OH: Merrill

Wortham, S. C. (1995). *Measurement and evaluation in early childhood education* (2nd ed., pp. 197–221). Columbus, OH: Merrill.

Worthen, B. R., White, K. R., Fan, X., & Sudweeks, R. L. (1999). *Measurement and assessment in schools* (2nd ed., pp. 301–308). New York: Addison-Wesley Longman.

chapter 14

Grading and Reporting Student Progress

- Design a record or gradebook to manage classroom records
- Create curriculum-based, mastery report cards
- Assign term grades
    a. Combine posttest scores into a term composite score
    b. Convert composite scores into term, semester, and annual grades
- Avoid confounding achievement grades
- Create a daily record
- Prepare for conferences with students, parents, and colleagues
- Use computer technology to manage classroom records

Teachers are usually expected to monitor and report three types of student behavior: achievement, attendance, and conduct. School districts use report cards to communicate this information to students, parents, school personnel, and other interested parties. Students use their achievement grades and other marks to verify the quality of their work and the acceptability of their conduct. Parents use report cards to help determine the amount of study time their children need and to make educational plans. School personnel also use grades, along with other information, for a number of purposes, such as the following:

1. To review the scope and sequence of the curriculum
2. To plan supplementary programs
3. To help students plan their education
4. To determine students' eligibility for special programs
5. To compare with standardized achievement test scores
6. To manage students' promotion

Employers and admission officers for colleges and universities use grades to determine whether an individual will be hired or admitted. Because grades can significantly influence decisions about a student's future, teachers should ensure that students' achievement grades and marks for conduct accurately reflect their behavior.

■ Managing Classroom Records

Teachers use gradebooks to document students' progress throughout a year. Although teaching assignments and information requirements vary, most teachers need a daily record of students' attendance and other information related to daily classroom management, a record of posttest scores, and a record of conduct scores obtained from behavior rating scales. Like most efficient accounting systems, your record should separate the different types of information to reduce the probability of recording and analysis errors.

Your record design should also reflect the nature of your teaching assignment. For example, an elementary teacher who teaches five different subjects to the same group needs to create one daily record, one conduct record, and a different posttest record for each subject. On the other hand, a teacher who is assigned five different groups needs a gradebook that contains a daily record, a posttest record, and a conduct record for each class.

Most schools have implemented computer-based information management systems to collect, synthesize, and communicate student information. The classroom records that you create should be compatible with the school's programs. Many commercially produced electronic gradebooks are available as shareware, and they can be obtained readily from the Internet. These programs are easy to use, and with the variety available, you can locate one that suits your classroom needs. If you are skilled in using a computer-based spreadsheet program, you can design a gradebook tailored exactly to your needs. Computer-based classroom records save teachers hours of clerical work and tedious calculations. Keep in mind the availability of these resources as you study the procedures recommended in this chapter.

■ Creating Curriculum-Based Mastery Report Cards

Many school districts use curriculum-based mastery report cards to communicate student achievement of district and state curriculum standards. These report cards name the instructional goals or standards studied during a term or semester, and they indicate whether the student mastered, partially mastered, or did not master each goal or standard. Mastery report cards are relatively easy to complete following criterion-referenced mastery scoring of the posttests administered during a grading term (see Chapter 12).

Figure 14.1 contains a generic form for a school district's mastery report card. Notice the top of the form contains information to identify the following:

- School
- Student

- Subject area
- Grade level
- Date and term
- Teacher

The body of the report contains the names of the instructional goals studied along with columns to report the students' mastery of each instructional goal or standard. Using such a report card, parents can see the instructional goals studied along with the teacher's judgment of their child's achievement in each curricular area.

These mastery report cards can be created easily for an entire class using a computer-based word-processing program. Simply create a table and add the common information including the instructional goals studied during a term. Then simply

FIGURE 14.1

Generic Curriculum-Based Mastery Report Card

GARFIELD SCHOOL

Student: _____   Subject: _____

Teacher: _____   Grade Level: ____ Date: _____ Term: ___

Mastery	Partial Mastery	Non-mastery	Instructional Goals	Mastery	Partial Mastery	Non-mastery	Instructional Goals
			1.				6.
			2.				7.
			3.				8.
			4.				9.
			5.				10.
			Conduct				
			Citizenship				
			Work Habits				

General Comments:

save the form using each student's name as the file name and complete the individual form using each student's unique information from your records (e.g., Figure 12.5).

Figure 14.2 contains a form completed for one student, Ruby Hager. Notice that the teacher has inserted the names of the instructional goals covered during the grading term and indicated Ruby's mastery level for each one. She has also added Ruby's mastery level in each attitude/behavior level monitored, and she has orally described Ruby's progress during the term. Many parents and school districts consider such mastery cards an improvement in communicating students' school achievement.

FIGURE 14.2

Sample Curriculum-Based Mastery Report Card

GARFIELD SCHOOL

Student: _Ruby Hager_   Subject: _Language Arts_

Teacher: _Ms. Jones_   Grade Level: _8_ Date: _2001–2002_ Term: _2_

Mastery	Partial Mastery	Non-mastery	Instructional Goals	Mastery	Partial Mastery	Non-mastery	Instructional Goals
✓			1. Writing Sentences	✓			6. Listening/ Responding
✓			2. Writing Paragraphs				7.
✓			3. Outlining Passages				8.
	✓		4. Presenting Orally				9.
✓			5. Writing Letters/ Journals				10.
	✓		Conduct				
✓			Citizenship				
✓			Work Habits				

General Comments: Ruby has mastered at a high level of achievement all of the "writing instructional goals" studied during the term. She is progressing in oral presentations. Related to conduct, she needs to talk less to her neighbors during classroom activities.

Many parents have not been completely satisfied with mastery report cards that do not include test scores or direct evidence of their child's achievement levels. As a result, some school districts are providing performance graphs illustrating students' posttest scores. Such graphs help parents interpret what a teacher means by the terms mastery, partial mastery, and nonmastery. Figure 14.3 includes such a report.

Although these mastery report cards describe a student's achievement quite well, many teachers, parents, and school districts still want to see composite grades that describe a student's overall achievement level for a term. The next section describes procedures you can use to calculate composite achievement scores that are used in creating term grades.

Combining Posttest Scores into a Composite Score

At the end of each term, you may need to combine posttest scores into a *composite score* that reflects each student's achievement throughout the term. A composite score is created by combining two or more test scores. The steps in creating a composite score include (1) analyzing the relationship among posttests administered during the term to determine the weight each posttest should contribute to the composite score, (2) identifying weighting factors, (3) calculating weighted scores so each test contributes the desired amount, and (4) combining weighted scores into the composite score. Although most computer-based gradebook programs will perform the calculations for you, let's walk through the process conceptually to ensure a complete understanding.

Analyzing the Relationship among Posttests

When combining scores from multiple tests in a composite score, you need to decide how much weight each test will contribute. Analyzing the relationship among the tests will help you determine an appropriate weight for each one. There are at least two factors to consider in analyzing tests: their interdependence and their complexity.

The first comparison is whether tests measure different or overlapping sets of instructional goals. For example, if only unit tests are administered, each will most likely measure a different set of goals. However, posttests are frequently interdependent because they overlap in the goals measured. Suppose you administer quizzes, unit tests, midterm exams, and a final exam. Unit tests will measure many of the goals previously measured by quizzes; midterm exams will overlap unit tests; and comprehensive finals will overlap all previous tests. When posttests are interdependent, you should compare them across these categories as well as within each category.

A second comparison is the relative complexity of the tests. Factors that influence a test's complexity are its scope and the difficulty level of goals it measures. The scope of tests can be compared using the number of goals measured and the length of time between instruction and testing. Difficulty can be compared using the relative complexity of the goals measured by each test.

FIGURE 14.3

Sample Curriculum-Based Mastery Report Card with Test Performance

GARFIELD SCHOOL

Student: Ruby Hager

Subject: Language Arts

Teacher: Ms. Jones

Grade Level: 8 Date: 2001–2002 Term: 2

Mastery	Partial Mastery	Non-mastery	Instructional Goals	Mastery	Partial Mastery	Non-mastery	Instructional Goals
✓			1. Writing Sentences	✓			6. Listening/ Responding
✓			2. Writing Paragraphs				7.
✓			3. Outlining Passages				8.
	✓		4. Presenting Orally				9.
✓			5. Writing Letters/ Journals				10.
	✓		Conduct				
✓			Citizenship				
✓			Work Habits				

General Comments: Ruby has mastered at a high level of achievement all of the "writing instructional goals" studied during the term. She is progressing in oral presentations. Related to conduct, she always tries, assists her classmates, and she needs to talk less to her neighbors.

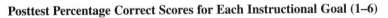

Posttest Percentage Correct Scores for Each Instructional Goal (1–6)

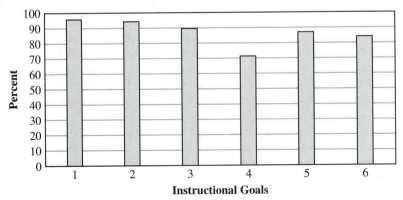

Comparing tests on the basis of scope, quizzes administered immediately following instruction that measure the enabling skills for only one goal are undoubtedly the least complex. A unit test that measures more goals and spans more time is more complex. Similarly, a comprehensive final exam that measures all the goals studied during the term and spans many weeks of study is more complex than any other test during the term. Based on these differences in complexity, you might decide that (1) a comprehensive final should contribute more to the composite score than any midterm exam, (2) a midterm exam should contribute more than any unit test, and (3) a unit test should contribute more than any quiz.

In addition to scope, the relative difficulty of goals measured is used to compare tests. Most likely, the goals measured by different tests are unequal in difficulty. For example, one test may measure students' skills in capitalizing the pronoun *I* and the first word of a sentence, whereas another measures their skill in capitalizing proper nouns and the titles of artistic works. Obviously, the goals measured by the second test are more difficult. The format of a test can sometimes provide a clue to the difficulty of the skills measured. For instance, essay tests, product development tests, and performance tests that require recall, analysis, organization, synthesis, and presentation skills might be judged more difficult than some objective tests. Based on differences in skill difficulty, you might decide to assign more weight to tests that measure more difficult goals.

Although tests may differ in the number and difficulty of goals measured, their overall complexity might be considered equal. For example, one test that measures several less difficult goals might be considered comparable in overall complexity to another that measures fewer more difficult ones. Thus, based on overall complexity, you might decide to assign them equal weight in the composite score.

You need to summarize information about posttests in order to compare them. Figure 14.4 contains two summary charts for nine tests administered during a term. The information required to create such a summary should be available in your achievement record. In the top chart, the left-hand column identifies the test, and the second column identifies its format. The next set of columns identifies the instructional goals studied during the term, and the particular goals measured by each test are identified using an X. The right-hand column lists the total number of goals measured by each test.

Using the information in the top chart, tests can be compared for interdependence. From the table, the following relationships are evident:

1. Tests 1, 2, 3, 5, 6, and 7 are independent in the goals they measure. They appear to be unit tests because each measures either 2 or 3 goals. Collectively, they measure all 16 goals.
2. Test 4 measures goals previously measured by unit tests 1, 2, and 3.
3. Test 8 measures the same goals as unit tests 5, 6, and 7.
4. Together, tests 4 and 8 measure all 16 goals.
5. Test 9 measures all 16 goals studied during the term.

This example includes three categories of interdependent tests: (1) six unit tests, numbers 1, 2, 3, 5, 6, and 7; (2) two midterm exams, tests 4 and 8; and (3) one

FIGURE 14.4

Summary of Posttests Administered during One Term

Test	Format	Goals Measured 1	2	3	4	5	6	7	8	9	10	11	12	13	14	15	16	Total Goals
1	Objective	X	X	X														3
2	Product				X	X	X											3
3	Performance							X	X	X								3
4	Objective	X	X	X	X	X	X	X	X	X								9
5	Product										X	X	X					3
6	Objective													X	X			2
7	Objective															X	X	2
8	Objective										X	X	X	X	X	X	X	7
9	Objective/ Product	X	X	X	X	X	X	X	X	X	X	X	X	X	X	X	X	16

	Test Categories Unit Tests						Midterm Exams		Comprehensive Final
Test	1	2	3	5	6	7	4	8	9
Number of Goals	3	3	3	3	2	2	9	7	16
Format	0	PD	PF	PD	0	0	0	0	PD
Difficulty of Goals					X	X		X	X

Note: An X reflects more complex goals. PD = essay or product assessments, and PF = live-performance assessments.

comprehensive final exam, test 9. Based on the fact that the tests are interdependent, you could first compare categories to determine how much weight each category should contribute to the term composite score. Once the weight for each category is selected, you can compare tests within each category to determine how much weight to assign each one.

To compare categories, consider the number and complexity of goals measured by tests across categories. In this example, all three categories measure the same 16 goals. Therefore, one category probably would not be considered more complex than another, and they would be weighted equally in the composite score. To weight the categories equally, the unit tests collectively would contribute one-third, or 33.3 percent, to the composite score; the two midterm exams together would contribute one-third; and the final exam would contribute one-third, as illustrated in Figure 14.5.

When you have determined the percentage each category is to contribute to the composite score, the next step in the analysis is to compare the tests within a category. The purpose for this comparison is to determine how much weight each test should contribute to the total percentage allotted for the category. The lower portion of Figure 14.4 contains information about the nine tests' scope and difficulty arranged by category.

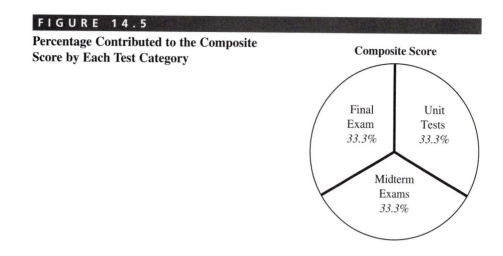

FIGURE 14.5

Percentage Contributed to the Composite
Score by Each Test Category

Comparing unit tests by scope, tests 1, 2, 3, and 5 all measure three goals, whereas tests 6 and 7 measure only two. Comparing them by the relative difficulty of goals measured, tests 6 and 7 are considered more difficult than the other four tests. If you decide that scope is balanced by skill difficulty and that the overall complexity of the six tests is approximately equal, then each test should contribute an equal percentage to the composite score.

Identifying Weighting Factors for Each Test

The percentage that each unit test will contribute to the composite score can now be determined. The total percentage allocated for unit tests (33.3 percent) is divided by the number of tests (6) to identify the percentage for each. Therefore, each unit test will contribute 5.55 percent to the term composite score.

The midterm exam category contains two tests to be compared. Test 4 measures nine skills, whereas test 8 measures only seven; however, the goals measured by test 8 are considered more complex. Thus, balancing scope and skill difficulty, you might decide to weight the two midterm exams equally.

To determine the percentage each midterm exam will contribute to the composite score, divide the percentage allocated for midterm exams (33.3 percent) by the number of exams (2). In this case, each midterm exam will contribute 16.65 percent to the composite score.

The percentage of weight assigned to categories and to individual tests is illustrated in Figure 14.6. Note that each of the three categories contributes an equal amount to the composite score (the six unit tests combined and the two midterm exams combined contribute equal amounts). Notice also that the final exam contributes more weight than either midterm exam and that each midterm exam contributes more weight than any unit test.

Usually, the manner in which you weight your tests is a matter of professional judgment. Some school districts, however, have grading policies that prescribe the

FIGURE 14.6

**Percentage Contributed to the Term Composite Score
by Each Test Category and Individual Test**

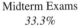

weight final exams are to contribute to the composite score. Should your district pre-scribe the percentage allotted to final exams, you would assign weights to individual tests using a procedure similar to the one described in the previous example.

Suppose your district's grading policies state that final exams must contribute 25 percent to the composite score. With this given, you need to determine how the re-maining 75 percent will be divided among the other tests. Using the nine tests in the preceding example and the same decisions about their relative weights, you could as-sign percentages to categories and to individual tests as follows:

1. Assign 25 percent to the final exam.
2. Divide the remaining 75 percent by the number of categories (2) and assign 37.5 percent to the unit test and the midterm exam categories.
3. Divide the percentage allocated for unit tests (37.5 percent) by the number of tests (6), and assign 6.25 percent to each unit test.
4. Divide the 37.5 percent allocated for midterm exams by 2, and assign 18.75 per-cent to each midterm.

Figure 14.7 illustrates the percentages assigned to each category and test. The unit test category and the midterm exam category each contribute more weight to the

FIGURE 14.7

Weight Assigned to Nine Tests Using School District Policy

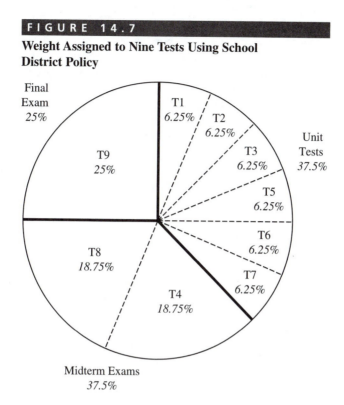

composite score than the final exam. However, the final exam contributes more than either midterm exam, and each midterm exam contributes more than any unit test. Thus, the assigned weights should reflect the relative complexity of the tests.

Calculating Weighted Scores

After selecting the weight each test will contribute to the term composite score, the next task is to calculate the weighted score for each test. This is accomplished using these steps:

1. When all tests within a category (e.g., unit tests) are to contribute *equally* to the category total, as in our example, do the following:
   a. Obtain a test category average score (percentage correct or *T* score) for each student by adding together the percentage of correct scores within the category and dividing the sum by the number of tests in the category. In the example, the average unit test score would be obtained by summing the scores for all six unit tests and dividing the total by six. The average midterm score would be obtained by summing the scores for the two midterm exams and

dividing by two. Since there is only one final exam, there is no need to obtain an average for this category.
   b. Obtain the weighting factor for each category of tests by dividing the percentage assigned by 100. For example, the 33.3 percent assigned in the example would become a weighting factor of .333
   c. Multiply each test category average score (percentage or T) by the designated weighting factor to obtain the category weighted score.
2. When tests within a category are not to contribute equally to the weight assigned for the category, do the following:
   a. Convert the percentage assigned for each test to a proportion by dividing the percentage by 100. For example, 5.55 percent becomes .056, 16.65 percent becomes .167, and 33.3 percent becomes .333.
   b. Multiply each test score (percentage correct and/or T score) by its designated proportion to obtain its weighted score.

Examine the sample gradebook created using a spreadsheet program in Figure 14.8. The first column identifies the names of two students, and rows are used to identify the particular tests and the dates they were administered. The first column within each test section, labeled X, contains the students' raw scores, and the next two columns contain the associated percentage correct (%) and T scores (T).

Notice the columns titled Term I Weighted Average Scores. There is a section for unit tests, midterms, and a final exam for both the percentage correct scores and the T scores. These columns are used at the conclusion of a grading term to record each student's test category average and weighted average scores. B. Allen's average scores were obtained in the following way:

B. Allen	*Average Percentage Correct*	*Weight %*
Unit Tests:	$(70 + 76 + 73 + 75 + 75 + 83)/6 = 75$	$75 \times .333 = 25$
Midterms:	$(86 + 87)/2 = 87$	$87 \times .333 = 29$
Final:	90	$90 \times .333 = 30$
	Average T Scores	*Weight T*
Unit Tests:	$(45 + 43 + 45 + 45 + 47 + 47)/6 = 45$	$45 \times .333 = 14.99$
Midterms:	$(50 + 53)/2 = 52$	$52 \times .333 = 17.32$
Final:	55	$55 \times .333 = 18.32$

Combining Weighted Scores into Term Composite Scores

You should create columns in your gradebook to record term composite scores and a term grade. You will need one column for the percentage correct composite score, one column for the composite T score, and one column for the earned grade. An example of the composite score section is illustrated in the bottom left section of Figure 14.8.

FIGURE 14.8

Term Summary for Nine Posttests

Students	Unit Test 1: 9/10			Unit Test 2: 9/17			Unit Test 3: 9/24			Midterm I: 10/1		
	X	%	T	X	%	T	X	%	T	X	%	T
Allen, B.	14	70	45	19	76	43	22	73	45	43	86	50
Baker, J.	18	90	55	25	100	63	28	93	63	47	94	60

Students	Unit Test 4: 10/8			Unit Test 5: 10/15			Unit Test 6: 10/22			Midterm II: 11/3		
	X	%	T	X	%	T	X	%	T	X	%	T
Allen, B.	15	75	45	15	75	47	25	83	47	39	87	53
Baker, J.	20	100	70	19	95	60	27	90	53	42	93	60

Students	Final Exam: 11/5			Term I Weighted Average Scores								
				Unit Tests		Midterms		Final	Unit Tests		Midterms		Final
	X	%	T	Avg. %	Wt. %	Avg. %	Wt. %	Wt. %	Avg. T	Wt. T	Avg. T	Wt. T	Wt. T
					0.333		0.333	0.333		0.333		0.333	0.333
Allen, B.	45	90	55	75	25	87	29	30	45	15	52	17	18
Baker, J.	5	100	66	95	32	94	31	33	61	20	60	20	22

Students	Composite		Grade			Straight Average Score (all tests equal)					
	%	T				%	T				
Allen, B.	84	51				79	48				
Baker, J.	96	62				95	61				

With the weighted test scores for each category of tests calculated and the summary columns designated in the record, you are ready to calculate the term composite scores. Term composite scores are calculated by summing the weighted scores for each category of tests. B. Allen's composite percentage correct score is 84 (25 + 29 + 30). Such criterion-referenced term composite scores generally reflect the percentage of test items or assessment tasks students performed correctly during the term, and they are used as the basis for students' grades when a school district's grading standards are defined using a 100-point scale. His score of 84 reflects good progress during the term, while J. Baker's score of 96 reflects very good achievement in the instructional goals studied. B. Allen's composite T score is 51 (14.99 + 17.32 + 18.32). This score reflects his norm-referenced standing in the class. Compared to his classmates, B. Allen's achievement was average during the term. J. Baker's composite T score of 62 reflects that his achievement during the term was above average compared to his classmates.

Converting Composite Scores into Term Grades

After calculating the composite scores, you need to convert them to grades. This conversion requires selecting a range of composite scores for each grade. These score ranges are called *grading standards*. Some school districts have policies that set common grading standards throughout the district. When this is the case, each grade and the range of composite scores required to earn it are described on the report card or in the teacher's manual. The three sets of grading standards shown in Table 14.1 are common.

These standards differ in the range of composite scores assigned for each grade. The first set assigns the highest eleven scores a grade of A, and the B, C, and D grade categories each contain 10 scores. It is the most lenient of the three standards. The grades in the second set have equal score ranges, but they include only 8 points instead of 10. The third set differs from the first two in that it has unequal score ranges for the grades. The range of scores for an A is only 6 points, the range for a B is 7 points, and the range for both C and D grades is 9 points. Therefore, this set is more rigorous at the high than at the low end of the scale.

Converting your students' composite scores to grades is easy when your district prescribes grade standards. You simply locate and assign the grade that corresponds to the earned composite scores. For example, if your district prescribed the first set of grade standards, B. Allen, who earned a composite score of 84, would receive a B.

TABLE 14.1

Three Sets of Grading Standards

| Grade | Standards and Ranges of Corresponding Composite Scores | | |
	Standard 1	Standard 2	Standard 3
A	90–100	93–100	95–100
B	80–89	85–92	88–94
C	70–79	77–84	79–87
D	60–69	69–76	70–78
F	59 and below	68 and below	69 and below

However, this student would be assigned a C if the second or third set of standards were applied. J. Baker, who earned a composite score of 96, would be assigned an A using any of the three grade standards.

When the district does not prescribe composite score ranges for grades, you need to set your own. There are two options to use in setting grade standards. One option is to set standards based solely on students' achievement of the goals, called *criterion-referenced grading*. The other option is to set standards based on students' relative performances, called *norm-referenced grading*. Criterion-referenced grading is preferable because it more clearly communicates the amount of information and skills each student has achieved.

Using Criterion-Referenced Standards

Setting standards for criterion-referenced grading is a matter of professional judgment. You need to select the composite score ranges that reflect outstanding, good, questionable, and inadequate achievement. You also need to select a score below which students will be assigned a failing grade. An outstanding, or A, grade should communicate to other people that a student has mastered all the skills covered and has done so at a high level. A grade of B should communicate that a student has mastered all or most skills, at least at a minimum level. A grade of C should reflect that the student has mastered the majority of the skills but is struggling. A grade of D should reflect that the student is having difficulty with many of the skills, and an F should reflect that the student has made little, if any, progress on the goals studied during the term.

To set your own grading standards, you need to select the lowest composite score that reflects each of the five grade levels. The minimum score for each grade can be set by (1) predicting a score range within which you believe the minimum score should fall, (2) reviewing the number of goals mastered by students who earn composite scores within the chosen range, and (3) selecting a cut-off score that best reflects that grade. For example, you might predict that the cut-off score for an A should be somewhere between 90 and 95. The total goals mastered column in the gradebook should be reviewed for students who earn composite scores in this range to determine whether they have mastered all the goals. If students who earn scores of 90 have mastered all the goals, then 90 could be set as the minimum score. However, if students who earn this score fail to master some of the goals, then you might want to set a higher cut-off score for an A. The same procedure can be followed to select the minimum score for each grade.

An alternative method for setting cut-off scores that is quicker, but not as thorough, is to (1) establish the lower limit for A and D grades, using the previously described method; (2) find the score range between the minimum A and D grades; and (3) divide this range by 3 to set the score ranges for the D, C, and B grades. For example, if you set 90 as the cut-off score for an A and 65 as the cut-off score for a D, the difference between these two scores is 25 points (90 minus 65). Dividing 25 by 3, you obtain 8.3 points. Therefore, the D, C, and B ranges will each contain about 8 points.

Next, you need to locate the minimum score for each grade. You can do so using the following steps:

1. Select the exact number of points for each grade. Assume you decide to make the D and B ranges equal 8 points and the C range equal 9 points.
2. Subtract the assigned number of points for a B (8) from the lowest A score (90) to identify the minimum score for a B ($90 - 8 = 82$).
3. Subtract the assigned number of points for a C (9) from the lowest B score to identify the minimum score for a C ($82 - 9 = 73$).
4. Subtract the assigned number of points for a D (8) from the lowest C score to identify the minimum score for a D ($73 - 8 = 65$). This score should match the one initially selected as the minimum D score, 65, which it does.

Thus, your grading standards would be the following:

Grade	Composite Score Range
A	90–100 (11 points)
B	82–89 (8 points)
C	73–81 (9 points)
D	65–72 (8 points)
F	64 and below

After establishing a range of scores for each grade, you can convert each student's term composite score to the matching letter grade. Using these standards, B. Allen, who earned a term composite score of 84 in the preceding example, would be assigned a grade of B; J. Baker, who earned a composite score of 96, would be assigned an A.

Using Norm-Referenced Standards

Although it is not recommended, some teachers choose to assign grades based on the relative performance of students in the class. If you want to use a purely norm-referenced grading system, you will need to base the grades you assign on term composite T scores. Recall that a T score is comprised of the student's raw score, the class's mean score, and the class's standard deviation. In essence, the T score reflects the student's relative performance on the test compared to the class. It is the ratio of the deviation of the student's raw score from the group's mean score compared to the group's standard deviation. The term composite T score reflects a student's achievement compared to the class on all tests administered during the term.

Rather than showing how much curriculum content the student has mastered, norm-referenced grades reflect a student's achievement level within a group. A norm-referenced grade of A should communicate to other people that a student's achievement is outstanding *compared to other students in the class*. A grade of B should indicate above-average achievement, and a grade of C should communicate average-level achievement in the group. A grade of D should reflect below-average achievement, and an F grade should communicate progress well below that of classmates.

Similar to criterion-referenced grading, setting standards for norm-referenced grades is a matter of professional judgment since there are no exact rules for establishing the range of T scores that should be equivalent to each letter grade assigned. Perhaps the best way to proceed in equating composite T scores with term grades would be the following:

1. Create a frequency distribution of term composite T scores.
2. Locate benchmark scores reflecting the mean and standard deviations below and above the mean (e.g., 20, 30, 40, 50, 60, 70).
3. Examine the shape of the distribution relative to the benchmarks (e.g., wide, tall, symmetrical, skewed).
4. Consider the achievement characteristics of the class (e.g., heterogeneous or homogeneous; high, average, or low).
5. Equate composite T score ranges with the letter grades that appear most reasonable based on the group's achievement characteristics and the distribution of T scores.

This list of steps implies that two factors—score distribution and group achievement characteristics—can influence the matching of composite T scores and letter grades. Consider first how the score distribution might influence your decisions. You might assign different grades to different scores for a distribution that is a symmetrical, narrow, bell-shaped curve than for a distribution that has an extreme negative skew. The two different distributions in Figure 14.9 illustrate this situation. In the top, bell-shaped distribution, T scores range from 30 to 70, whereas in the bottom, negatively skewed distribution, T scores range from 20 to 59. Obviously, the assignment of letter grades to T scores would differ for the two distributions.

The second factor to consider is the achievement characteristics of the class. Suppose you teach a homogeneous group of high-achieving students. Regardless of the shape of the distribution of T scores, does this mean that some students should be assigned grades of F simply because their scores are at the bottom in a high-achieving class? Should a student who earned a T score of 50 be assigned a C grade to reflect average performance in the class even though the T score of 50 equates to a composite percentage correct score of 85 or above? The answer to these questions is obviously no, and these examples illustrate the difficulties teachers encounter when trying to use purely norm-referenced standards for assigning term grades. They also illustrate why school districts typically specify percentage correct scores in their grading policies.

At this point you are probably wondering why teachers would want to calculate T scores for each test and for a term composite score when they are not particularly useful for assigning term grades. T scores help teachers communicate information about a student's performance that cannot readily be illustrated using percentage correct scores. For example, T scores are used to analyze a student's performance across time and tests since they have a common mean (50) and standard deviation (10). They help teachers determine and communicate whether students are holding their own, gaining ground, or losing ground compared to other students in the class. A downward trend in a student's T scores over the term could signal a problem that should be

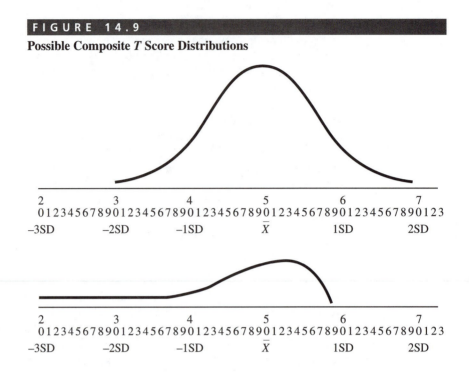

FIGURE 14.9

Possible Composite *T* Score Distributions

communicated to parents, whereas an upward trend would undoubtedly please the parents of a student who earned a low grade for the term.

Comparing Composite Score Outcomes Using Different Grading Systems and Weighting Plans

If you calculate both term composite percentage correct scores and term composite *T* scores, you should not be surprised to find that a student's rank in the class differs for the two types of composite scores. Differentially weighting tests administered during a term can also affect students' class ranks using either type of composite score. Figure 14.10 illustrates how using one or the other composite score and different weighting plans can affect the term rank of three students on two tests. The top portion of the table illustrates the outcome of composite percentage correct and *T* scores when the two tests are weighted equally, with each test contributing 50 percent to the composite score. For each student, the raw scores, percentage correct scores, weighted percentage correct scores (Wt.%), *T* scores, and weighted *T* scores (Wt.*T*) are listed for the two tests. The far right columns contain the students' composite scores. Notice that when using the percentage correct composite scores, all three students earn composite scores of 90, illustrating the same overall achievement level for the three students. In contrast, the composite *T* scores differ for the three students. Jones earned a *T* score of 52, Miller a score of 50, and Thomas a score of 49. Were grades to be

FIGURE 14.10

Comparison of the Rank of Composite Scores Using Percentage Correct Scores, *T* Scores, and Different Weights of Tests

TEST ONE WEIGHTED 50% AND TEST TWO WEIGHTED 50%

	Test One					Test Two					Term Composites	
	$\overline{X}$/SD	%	Wt.%	T	Wt.T	$\overline{X}$/SD	%	Wt.%	T	Wt.T	%	T
	18/3	20	.5		.5	18/5	20	.5		.5		
Jones	20	100	50	57	29	16	80	40	46	23	90	52
Miller	18	90	45	50	25	18	90	45	50	25	90	50
Thomas	16	80	40	43	22	20	100	50	54	27	90	49

TEST ONE WEIGHTED 80% AND TEST TWO WEIGHTED 20%

	Test One					Test Two					Term Composites	
	$\overline{X}$/SD	%	Wt.%	T	Wt.T	$\overline{X}$/SD	%	Wt.%	T	Wt.T	%	T
	18/3	20	.8		.8	18/5	20	.2		.2		
Jones	20	100	80	57	46	16	80	16	46	9	96	55
Miller	18	90	72	50	40	18	90	18	50	10	90	50
Thomas	16	80	64	43	34	20	100	20	54	11	84	45

TEST ONE WEIGHTED 20% AND TEST TWO WEIGHTED 80%

	Test One					Test Two					Term Composites	
	$\overline{X}$/SD	%	Wt.%	T	Wt.T	$\overline{X}$/SD	%	Wt.%	T	Wt.T	%	T
	18/3	20	.2		.2	18/5	20	.8		.8		
Jones	20	100	20	57	11	16	80	64	46	37	84	48
Miller	18	90	18	50	10	18	90	72	50	40	90	50
Thomas	16	80	16	43	9	20	100	80	54	43	96	52

assigned based on the composite *T* scores, the students could possibly be assigned different grades depending on where the established cut-off score was placed.

The middle set of scores contains the same raw score for the three students on the two tests with the same means and standard deviations. The second set of scores differs only in that Test One will contribute 80 percent and Test Two will contribute 20 percent to the composite scores. Using this weighting plan for the two tests, the students' composite percentage correct scores no longer equal 90; instead, they range from 96 to 84. Such large differences in term composite percentage correct scores would undoubtedly result in different term grades for the three students. Notice also the greater differences in the students' composite T scores. The resulting range $(55 - 45 = 10)$ is as wide as the standard deviation for T scores.

The third set of scores in Figure 14.10 contains the same raw scores, means, and standard deviations as the first two sets. In this set, however, the first test contributes 20 percent and the second test contributes 80 percent to the composite score. Using this weighting plan, the students' composite percentage correct scores are not equal at 90, as in the first set, and they are in the reverse order of the scores in the second set. Weighting the second test by .80 results in reversing the rank of Jones and Thomas for both the composite percentage and T scores.

One final observation about the test data in Figure 14.10 should be noted. It is not possible to use the norm-referenced T score to determine students' criterion-referenced skill levels in a domain. Notice in the first set of equally weighted scores that Miller earned a composite T score of 50. Such a score reflects that Miller's performance was quite average in the class. Now match this average-level T score with Miller's percentage correct composite score of 90. Obviously, Miller's average group performance reflects very good achievement of the skills taught during the term.

In summary, teachers need to be thoughtful about whether to use a criterion-referenced or a norm-referenced grading system. They also should take care in deciding whether and how to weight test scores differentially that are obtained during a term. Regardless of students' raw scores, different types of composite scores and different weighting plans can influence the final term grades assigned to students.

Calculating Semester and Annual Grades

At the conclusion of two or more terms, you may need to combine term grades into a semester grade; at the end of the year, you may need to combine semester grades into an annual grade. Suppose you teach in a school district that has two terms in a semester and a comprehensive semester exam that, by district policy, contributes 25 percent to the semester grade. In your record, you need to create semester summary columns for the composite score for each term; the semester exam raw score, percentage correct, and T score; the weighted scores for each measure; the semester composite score; and the semester grade.

The first step is to identify the percentage each measure is to contribute to the semester composite score. Since the semester exam contributes 25 percent to the semester grade, the term composite scores will contribute the remaining 75 percent. Undoubtedly, you will want to weight the terms equally, so each term composite score will contribute one-half the 75 percent, or 37.5 percent.

The second step is to convert the percentages assigned to weighting factors. The 25 percent assigned for the semester exam is converted to a weighting factor of .25, and the 37.5 percent for each term composite score is converted to a weighting factor of .375 to ensure that each measure contributes the desired amount to the semester composite scores. Next, you should (1) calculate the weighted scores and (2) sum the weighted scores to obtain the semester composite scores. These calculations for two students are illustrated in Figure 14.11. The last task is to convert these semester composite scores to semester grades using the scale established for term grades.

FIGURE 14.11

Semester I Summary

	Term I:		Wt. = .375		Term II:		Wt. = .375		Sem. Exam:		Wt. = .25			Sem. Summary		
	%	Wt.	T		%	Wt.	T		$\overline{X}$/SD	%	Wt.			%	T	Grade
	Comp	%	Comp	Wt. T	Comp	%	Comp	Wt. T	40/4	50	%	T	Wt. T			
Students									X							
Allen, B.	84	32	51	19	88	33	55	21	42	84	21	55	14	86	54	B
Baker, J.	96	36	62	23	93	35	60	23	45	90	23	63	16	94	62	A

A slightly different process is used to calculate annual grades. Usually, the two semesters are weighted equally when combined into a composite score for the year, and there is no comprehensive annual exam to be combined with the semester composite scores. Figure 14.12 illustrates how semester composite scores are combined to obtain the annual grade. The students' composite scores for the two semesters are added together and this sum is divided by 2 to obtain the annual composite score. These scores are then converted to the annual grade using the established grading scale.

Creating the Conduct Record

In addition to reporting achievement, teachers are often expected to measure and report students' conduct in such areas as study habits, attitude toward learning, and citizenship. The procedures for developing behavior rating scales to judge conduct are described in Chapter 8. During the grading period, you would follow an observation schedule and use the rating scales to score students' behavior. Similar to achievement test scores, these conduct scores should be recorded in the gradebook, combined into composite scores, and converted to the marks prescribed on the report card.

FIGURE 14.12

Annual Summary

	Semester 1 Composite		Semester 2 Composite		Total		Annual Composite		
Students	%	T	%	T	%	T	%	T	Grade
Allen, B.	86	54	80	55	165	109	83	55	B
Baker, J.	94	62	95	60	189	122	95	61	A

Recording Scores

Since different behaviors are reported separately, you can create an area for each in the conduct section of the gradebook. For example, if you are expected to report attitude toward learning, study habits, and citizenship, you would need three separate areas in the record. The number of columns required for each behavior depends on the number of times it was rated during the term. If you rated each behavior three times, you would need three columns to record students' scores. To accommodate your work at the end of the term, you should reserve three additional columns: one for the total score, one for the composite score, and one for the assigned mark. The record section for attitude toward learning might appear as follows:

Conduct:			Attitude toward Learning			
Date:	9-21	10-10	10-30	Total	Composite	Grade
Possible score:	18	18	18	54		
Allen, B.	12	13	14	_____	_____	_____
Baker, J.	18	16	18	_____	_____	_____

The conduct is identified in the top row, and the dates when students were rated and column titles appear in the second row. The third row is reserved for the total number of points included on the attitude-toward-learning instrument, and students' scores are listed in the remaining rows.

Combining Scores into a Composite Score

There are two factors to consider before combining conduct scores into a composite score: converting all scores to a common scale and determining the amount of weight each measure should contribute. Relative to a common scale, the same rating scale is usually used each time a behavior is scored, and no conversion should be necessary. Also, you will probably want each measure to contribute an equal amount of weight to the term composite score. Therefore, you will not assign any weights. If you want to weight the measures differently, you should identify weighting factors as you did for posttest scores, reserve space in the record for weighted scores, and convert raw scores to weighted scores before summing them.

Composite scores for conduct are calculated the same way as composite scores for achievement. For equally weighted measures, the steps are (1) sum the individual scores to obtain the total and (2) divide the total by the number of scores to obtain the average or composite score. The following example shows the calculation of composite scores for B. Allen and J. Baker:

Conduct:			Attitude toward Learning			
Date:	9-21	10-10	10-30	Total	Composite	Grade
Possible score:	18	18	18	54		
Allen, B.	12	13	14	39	13	
Baker, J.	18	16	18	52	17	

Converting Composite Scores to Marks

The final step in the procedure is to convert term composite scores into marks. The marks used to communicate conduct are generally described on the report card. Some school districts use a three-category scale, whereas others use four- or five-category scales. The three-category scale is often S for satisfactory, N for needs improvement, and U for unsatisfactory. The four-category scale might use E for excellent, G for good, N for needs improvement, and U for unsatisfactory. The five-category scale might use A through F, or 1 through 5, to communicate different levels of behavior.

One way to convert composite scores to report card marks is to (1) identify the possible range of composite scores, (2) divide this range by the number of grade categories prescribed by the district, and (3) assign a relatively equal number of scores to each category. Suppose the highest possible composite score for attitude toward learning is 18 and the lowest possible score is 6. You have a potential range of 13 points, including the lowest and highest scores. This range of 13 points might be divided in the following ways for scales that include three, four, and five categories:

Three-Category Scale		Four-Category Scale		Five-Category Scale	
Mark	Score Range	Mark	Score Range	Mark	Score Range
S	15, 16, 17, 18	E	16, 17, 18	A	16, 17, 18
N	11, 12, 13, 14	G	13, 14, 15	B	13, 14, 15
U	6, 7, 8, 9, 10	N	9, 10, 11, 12	C	10, 11, 12
		U	6, 7, 8	D	8, 9
				F	6, 7

Based on a three-category scale, B. Allen's composite score, 13, would be converted to an N; J. Baker's composite score, 17, would be S. On the four-category scale, Allen would receive a G and Baker an E. On the five-category scale, Allen and Baker would receive a B and an A, respectively. The standards you select should be recorded in the gradebook for reference.

■ Confounding the Achievement Grade

In their efforts to create a comprehensive index of students' progress, some teachers mix conduct and achievement. Although they may believe that mixing these variables improves the accuracy of students' grades, exactly the opposite occurs. The term used to describe mixing variables is *confounding*. When conduct is confounded with achievement, the meaning of the achievement grade is compromised, and valid interpretation becomes difficult, if not impossible. Four common ways that teachers confound achievement grades are (1) treating practice tests as posttests, (2) administering unannounced posttests, (3) reducing posttest scores for misbehavior, and (4) using extra-credit assignments to alter grades.

It is not uncommon to find teachers who treat practice tests and routine homework assignments as posttests. This is typically done to encourage students to complete their assignments and to do so carefully. When practice tests are used as posttests, students' initial attempts to perform skills are confounded with their progress following instruction, practice, and feedback. Since the purpose for practice tests is rehearsal, they are premature measures of achievement; and students' scores on practice tests tend to be lower than their scores on legitimate posttests. Thus, practice test scores negatively influence the composite score. Teachers who confound practice and achievement usually attempt to minimize this negative influence by reducing the percentage that practice tests contribute to the composite score, eliminating the lowest practice test score, providing opportunities for extra-credit work, or a combination of these three strategies.

A second confounding practice is administering unannounced posttests, sometimes called *pop quizzes*. The usual explanation teachers give for using such tests is to keep students studying on a regular basis rather than cramming just before a scheduled test. This practice, however, confounds study habits and actual achievement. Low scores could be attributed to the fact that either students did not study or they were experiencing difficulty learning the skills. The consequence of administering unannounced posttests is that these scores tend to be lower than scores on scheduled tests. Thus, they also have a negative influence on composite scores and grades. Like teachers who use practice tests as posttests, those who use unannounced tests generally need to develop strategies to counter their negative influence.

A third practice that confounds conduct and achievement is reducing earned posttest scores for unacceptable behavior. These unacceptable behaviors can include habitually submitting product development tests late, talking or being otherwise disruptive during a test, or cheating on a test. The reason usually given for altering the earned scores is to teach students that such misbehaviors will not be tolerated. However, this practice confounds achievement with lack of judgment and immaturity. Students caught cheating on a test should be required to take another form of the test so that a legitimate measure of their progress is obtained. Alternative strategies, besides reducing earned scores, should be sought for encouraging promptness, consideration, and honesty.

A fourth practice that confounds achievement and conduct is using extra-credit assignments to alter grades. Extra-credit assignments are those not required of all students in the regular conduct of the class. The reason typically given for altering grades using extra credit is to give students who are not satisfied with their earned scores an opportunity to improve their grades. However, this practice confounds students' achievement of the prescribed goals and their effort. For example, some students may want a higher grade than their test performance warrants. When given an extra-credit option, these students will complete the additional work to improve their grades. Suppose that students who demonstrated mastery at good (B) and questionable (C) levels are permitted to raise these grades one letter by completing an extra report, paper, or project. Does completing the assignment mean that they have now mastered the skills studied during the term at a higher level? Probably not. Instead, it means they have mastered the skills at the measured level but are willing to expend additional effort to obtain a higher grade. Thus, the higher grade masks their mastery level.

Any one of these confounding practices confuses the meaning of the grade. However, when two or more of them are used, the grade's meaning becomes increasingly distorted. The grade no longer reflects students' mastery level, but this level plus rehearsal, study habits, misbehavior, and effort. Parents and school administrators will undoubtedly misinterpret such grades. It is also unlikely that confounded grades will correlate very well with students' scores on districtwide or standardized tests that measure the same skills. The best practice is to assign achievement grades solely for achievement. You can communicate students' inadequate study habits, misbehavior, and outstanding effort using the space for such conduct on the report card.

Creating the Daily Record

The daily record is used to document information related to daily classroom management. It contains information about attendance, homework and classroom assignments, particular instances of conduct you want to record, and other school matters. This record helps you complete behavior rating scales throughout the term, complete the attendance section of the report card, and conduct conferences with parents, students, and others. Your notations can help you explain the term marks for study habits and conduct and can also help identify factors, such as attendance or lack of participation, that contributed to students' posttest scores.

Selecting Symbols

In creating this section of the classroom record, you need to select symbols to record information. For example, you can use symbols like those in Table 14.2 to record instances of behavior related to attendance, study habits, participation, and conduct.

TABLE 14.2

Legend of Symbols for Recording Behaviors

Attendance	Study Habits	Participation	Conduct
/ = Absent	H = Homework	M = Materials not present	A = Aggressive
Ⓙ = Unexcused absence	Ⓗ = Homework accurate	C = Clothing inadequate	D = Disruptive
X = Tardy	XH = No homework	P = Did not participate	CT = Cheating on test
Ⓧ = Unexcused tardy	IH = Inaccurate homework	T = Time wasted	
	CH = Homework not complete		
	LH = Late homework		

Symbols should be selected for their efficiency and convenience. Consider the symbols in the attendance column of Table 14.2. When you first record attendance, you can use the symbol / to note a student is absent. Should the student appear during the class session with an acceptable excuse for the lateness, the symbol can be converted to an X to indicate an excused tardiness. If the student does not have an adequate excuse, a circle can be placed around the X to signal an unexcused tardiness. However, if the student does not appear, the symbol / will indicate that the student was absent that day. If the student brings an acceptable excuse for the absence, no other mark is necessary. However, if the student does not present a legitimate excuse for the absence, a circle can be placed around the / to signify an unexcused absence.

Create a legend in the daily record that explains each symbol. Otherwise, you might use different symbols for the same behavior or forget what a particular symbol means. You can create new symbols as needed and add them to the legend. Should your district have common symbols in their information management system, learn and use them in creating your daily record.

Labeling Columns and Recording Information

In creating the daily record, you should reserve at least two rows at the top of the page to label columns. The date of each class session can be recorded in the top row. The second row can be used to label specific types of information—for example, homework due, parent permission slips due, laboratory fees paid, or materials borrowed from a class resource center. Since more than one column may be needed for some dates, it is best to complete this record on a day-to-day basis. An example of a daily record is shown in Figure 14.13.

Summarizing Information

At the end of the grading period, you need to summarize the information. The two rows at the top of this record can be used to organize the data. The first row can identify the behavior category, and the second row can label the particular type of behavior within each category. The total number of times a student exhibits each behavior can be recorded in the remaining rows. Figure 14.14 is a sample summary section of a daily record.

FIGURE 14.13

Sample Daily Record

Dates	9-1	2	3	4	5		8		9	10	11		12
Students							H					Trip	
Allen, B.					Ⓘ		X	IH	X	P		ok	
Baker, J.							H	/				ok	

Note: See Table 14.2 for symbol legend.

FIGURE 14.14

Sample Term Summary Section of Daily Record

Students	Attendance				Study Habits					Participation				Conduct		
	/	Ⓘ	X	Ⓧ	Ⓗ	XH	IH	CH	LH	M	C	P	T	A	D	CT
Allen, B.	0	1	1	0	12	2	1	0	0	1	0	0	0	0	0	1
Baker, J.	3	0	1	0	2	4	6	1	2	7	0	2	0	0	1	0

Note: See Table 14.2 for symbol legend.

■ Preparing for Conferences

Many school districts schedule parent-teacher conferences following the distribution of report cards. These conferences permit teachers to explain students' grades and answer questions parents may have about their child's achievement, conduct, and attendance.

To prepare for these individual conferences, you need to review each student's record, select the information to present, and decide how you will present your observations. Options that you may have include:

1. The portfolio of a student's achievement tests including readiness tests, pretests, practice tests, and posttests and your verbal assessment of the student's progress over the term
2. The behavior and conduct rating scales or observation forms that you have completed based on conduct that is reported
3. Samples of students' work that they have chosen to include in their portfolios (in addition to the portfolio, many teachers choose to create a summary table illustrating each student's criterion-referenced and norm-referenced progress over the term)

For those teachers who work in school districts that use mastery report cards such as the one illustrated in Figure 14.2, the summary table is virtually complete. They will only need to add the norm-referenced *T* scores for each assessment. Figure 14.15 illustrates such a summary table for Brian Allen whose achievement was summarized in Figure 14.8.

■ Computer Technology

Most school districts have student information management systems that administrators and teachers use to record student information and retrieve summary reports for individuals and groups. If you are unfamiliar with using your school's system, simply request assistance from the school's technology specialist. Accurate and timely use of the system helps protect the integrity of the school's student reports.

FIGURE 14.15

Term Performance Summary Form

HORACE MANN SCHOOL

Student: _Brian Allen_   Subject: _Language Arts_   Grade: ___B___

Teacher: _Ms. Dunn_   Grade Level: ___3___   Term: ___2___

Mastery	Partial Mastery	Non-mastery	Instructional Goals	Mastery	Partial Mastery	Non-mastery	Instructional Goals
✓			1. Group common words and objects.	✓			9. Use subordinating conjunctions.
✓			2. Name synonyms.	✓			10. Substitute pronouns for nouns.
✓			3. Name antonyms.	✓			11. Select adjectives to modify nouns.
✓			4. Add prefixes to root words.	✓			12. Select adverbs to modify verbs, adjectives, and adverbs.
✓			5. Add suffixes to root words.	✓			13. Write plural form of singular words and vice versa.
✓			6. Form contractions.	✓			14. Match singular subjects and verbs.
✓			7. Use coordinating conjunctions.	✓			15. Match plural subjects and verbs.
✓			8. Use correlative conjunctions.	✓			16. Select the correct verb tense.
✓			Conduct				
✓			Citizenship				
✓			Work Habits				

General Comments: Brian has mastered all of the writing instructional goals studied during the term. His journal and creative writing continues to improve and, as you must know, his stories are very creative. Related to conduct, he always tries, works very hard, and is a pleasant, responsible member of the class.

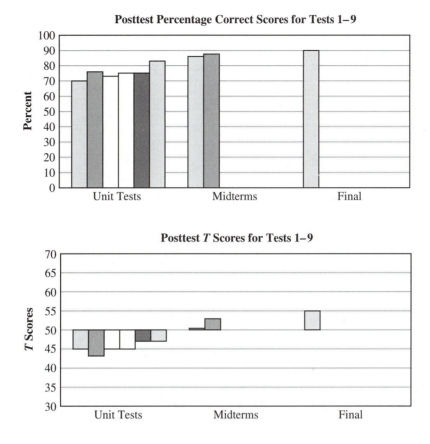

Note: Average class performance is *T* scores between 40 and 60. All Brian's posttest scores fall within the average range compared with his classmates.

In addition to the school's information management system, you may want to use one of the commercially available student information or gradebook programs to record and maintain your classroom information. These programs are widely advertised on the Internet, and you can often locate the perfect program for the type and age of your computer. Many of them are free, and others are available for examination and trial use. At the beginning of the school year, you should examine as many commercially available programs as possible, and select one that suits your teaching assignment and assessment program.

Should you not be able to locate a suitable gradebook program, you can design a record tailored to your class needs using a spreadsheet program. After entering raw scores for each student, you can use the formula functions within the spreadsheet to calculate a student's percentage correct scores, *T* scores, weighted scores, and composite scores. After checking the accuracy of your calculations for one student, you can copy your formulas across students' records to calculate the same scores for all class members. Using electronic record systems saves teachers hours of tedious record keeping and calculations. Computer-based records also help ensure more accurate and timely records for students, parents, and colleagues.

■ Summary

Each grading term, teachers are expected to evaluate and report students' progress in achievement and conduct as well as to report their attendance. To document and summarize student data, you need to design a gradebook that matches your teaching assignment.

Many school districts use criterion-referenced report cards. Such reports name the key instructional goals studied during a term and the student's mastery status on each one. Some also include the traditional composite score and letter grade.

In documenting student achievement, you should record general information about each test, such as (1) the format, title, and date; (2) the group's average score and standard deviation; (3) the number of items or points included on the test; and (4) the particular goals and number of goals measured. This information is used to compare tests at the end of the term and to interpret students' scores on each test. To document students' performance, record their raw scores, percentage correct scores, and/or T scores.

At the end of the term, you may need to synthesize individual test scores into a term composite score. The steps in this procedure include (1) analyzing the relationship among posttests to determine the weight each test should contribute to the composite score, (2) identifying weighting factors, (3) calculating weighted scores, and (4) calculating composite scores.

The next task is to convert composite scores to term grades using standards. Grade standards are often prescribed by district policy; when they are not, you need to set your own. Standards can be set using either criterion-referenced or norm-referenced methods, although criterion-referenced methods are preferred. Criterion-referenced standards are based on the level of students' performance on the goals studied during the term, and norm-referenced standards are based on relative group performance.

Most school districts also require you to assign marks for conduct in such areas as attitude toward learning, study habits, and citizenship. A third section of the gradebook should be reserved for recording students' scores from behavior rating scales. Similar to posttest scores, conduct scores should be combined into a composite score at the end of the term. These scores are converted to district-prescribed marks using standards you set yourself.

Some teachers confound achievement grades by combining conduct and achievement. This happens when posttest achievement is confounded with rehearsal, study habits, misbehavior, or effort. Such practices should be avoided because they make valid interpretation of the achievement grade impossible.

You should also maintain a daily record in which you document events that occur during each class session. To prepare this section, select the information you will document, choose symbols that represent each type of information, create a legend for the symbols, list class dates, and record the selected behaviors. You will also need a summary section in which to record the frequencies of selected behaviors. Information in the daily record will help you summarize attendance, complete behavior rating scales, and perhaps explain the grades and other marks students earn during parent conferences.

Teacher-parent conferences are usually scheduled after report cards are sent home. In preparing for these conferences, you need to select the information you want to communicate and decide how to present it. To save time, prepare a generic summary form that includes the selected information. The form can be completed for each student and used as a basis for discussion during scheduled conferences. Using portfolios of students' work can also facilitate communicating progress during the term to students, parents, and school personnel.

■ PRACTICE EXERCISES

I. The Gradebook

Identify the section of the record or gradebook (in Column B) in which each of the following types of information (in Column A) should be recorded.

Column A

_____ **1.** Scores from behavior rating scales

_____ **2.** Materials checked out from the resource center

_____ **3.** Dates of class sessions

_____ **4.** The title and dates of tests given

_____ **5.** Particular instances of conduct

_____ **6.** The number of items or points on a test

_____ **7.** Attendance

_____ **8.** Parent permission granted for a field trip

_____ **9.** Raw scores

_____ **10.** The percentage of items correct

Column B

a. The Daily Record

b. The Posttest Record

c. The Conduct Record

II. Identifying the Percentage Each Test Will Contribute to the Composite Score

Suppose that during one term you administered five quizzes, three unit tests, and a comprehensive final exam. Based on an analysis of the tests, you decide that:

1. The five quizzes together should contribute 25 percent to the composite score.

2. The three unit tests together should contribute 50 percent.

3. The final exam should contribute 25 percent.

4. The five quizzes should be weighted equally.

5. The three unit tests should be weighted equally.

A. What percentage will each quiz contribute to the final score?

B. What percentage will each unit test contribute to the composite score?

III. Identifying Weighting Factors for Each Category of Tests

Using the percentage allocated for each category of tests, identify in Table 14.3 the weighting factor for each quiz, each unit test, and the final exam named in II.

IV. Calculating Weighted Scores

A. The posttest record for the nine tests in II is included in Figure 14.16. Insert the selected weighting factors in the appropriate cell for each category of tests.

B. Calculate weighted percentage correct and T scores for each category of tests for the two students illustrated.

V. Calculating Composite Scores

A. A section, Composite, is located at the bottom of Figure 14.16.

B. Calculate the term composite scores for the two students and record them in this section.

VI. Setting Standards for Assigning Grades

A. Grade standards that are based on the number of goals mastered and points earned during a term are called _____.

B. Grade standards that are based on the relative position of students' composite scores are called _____.

C. In Table 14.4, describe the meaning of each letter grade for both criterion-referenced and norm-referenced grading systems. Check your definitions in Table 14.6F of the Feedback section.

D. Use the following information to determine the score ranges for grades B, C, and D.

Grade		Score Range
A	=	_93_ to _100_
B	=	_____ to _____
C	=	_____ to _____
D	=	_60_ to _____
F	=	_59_ and below

E. Using these grading standards, convert the students' composite scores in Figure 14.16 to grades.

TABLE 14.3

Weighting Factors for Posttests

Test Category	Percentage	Weighting Factor
Quizzes		
Unit Tests		
Final Exam		

FIGURE 14.16

Posttest Record for One Term

	Quiz 1: Jan. 15			Quiz 2: Jan. 24			Unit Test 1: 1/30			Quiz 3: Feb. 6			
Students	X	%	T	X	%	T	X	%	T	X	%	T	
Allen, B.	17	85	50	12	80	50	31	89	53	17	85	53	
Baker, J.	20	100	65	13	87	55	34	97	63	19	95	58	

	Quiz 4: Feb. 15			Unit Test 2: 2/10			Quiz 5: Feb. 28			Unit Test 3: 3/5			
Students	X	%	T	X	%	T	X	%	T	X	%	T	
Allen, B.	20	80	45	32	80	50	17	85	53	35	88	55	
Baker, J.	23	92	60	38	95	65	20	100	63	39	98	65	

				Term I Weighted Average Scores									
				Quizzes		Unit Tests		Final	Quizzes		Unit Tests		Final
	Final Exam: 3/15			Avg. %	Wt. %	Avg. %	Wt. %	Wt. %	Avg. T	Wt. T	Avg. T	Wt. T	Wt. T
Students	X	%	T										
Allen, B.	42	84	54										
Baker, J.	46	92	62										

	Composite		Grade								
Students	%	T									
Allen, B.											
Baker, J.											

Note: Try using a spreadsheet program to enter this data and calculate the average, weighted, and composite scores.

VII. Enrichment

    A. Obtain your school district's policies on grading and look for information that describes:
        1. The type and number of measures that are to be used to measure the students' progress
        2. The percentage a final exam is to contribute to the composite score
        3. The standards for converting composite scores to grades
        4. Whether grade standards are to be criterion-referenced or norm-referenced
    B. Review your school district's report card for your grade level and identify the categories of behavior that are to be reported.
    C. Design a gradebook that will enable you to document the required information.

TABLE 14.4
Grading Standards

Grade	Criterion-Referenced Standards	Norm-Referenced Standards
A		
B		
C		
D		
F		

D. Search for commercially prepared gradebooks on the Internet and compare them for utility given your recording needs, compatibility with your equipment, and school policies.

E. Select the behaviors you want to record in a daily record and identify symbols you can use to document each one.

■ FEEDBACK

I. The Gradebook

1. c	**6.** b
2. a	**7.** a
3. a	**8.** a
4. b	**9.** b
5. a	**10.** b

II. Identifying the Percentage Each Test Will Contribute to the Composite Score

A. Each quiz will contribute 5 percent.

$$\frac{\text{Total percentage allocated for quizzes}}{\text{Number of quizzes}} = \frac{25}{5} = 5 \text{ percent}$$

B. Each unit test will contribute 16.7 percent.

$$\frac{\text{Total percentage allocated for unit tests}}{\text{Number of unit tests}} = \frac{50}{3} = 16.66; 16.7 \text{ percent}$$

III. Identifying Weighting Factors for Each Test Category

See Table 14.5F.

TABLE 14.5F

Weighting Factors for Each Category of Tests

Test Category	Percentage	Weighting Factor
Quizzes	25	.25
Unit Tests	50	.50
Final Exam	25	.25

IV. **Calculating Weighted Scores**
   A. See Figure 14.17F. The weighting factors for each test category average are inserted in the cell beneath the titles Wt. % and Wt. *T*.
   B. The category average percentage correct and *T* scores are multiplied by the weighting factors to obtain the weighted scores.

V. **Calculating Composite Scores**
   A. See Figure 14.17F. Columns were created in the Term Composite section to record the composite scores and the term grade.
   B. The composite scores were calculated by summing the weighted percentage correct scores for each test category and by summing the weighted *T* scores for each category.

VI. **Setting Standards for Assigning Grades**
   A. Criterion-referenced standards
   B. Norm-referenced standards
   C. See Table 14.6F.

FIGURE 14.17F

Posttest Record for One Term

	Term I Weighted Average Scores										Term Composite		
	Quizzes		Unit Tests		Final	Quizzes		Unit Tests		Final	%	*T*	Grade
	Avg. %	Wt. %	Avg. %	Wt. %	Wt. %	Avg. *T*	Wt. *T*	Avg. *T*	Wt. *T*	Wt. *T*			
Students		0.25		0.50	0.25		0.25		0.50	0.25			
Allen, B.	83	21	87	43	21	50	13	54	27	14	85	53	B
Baker, J.	95	24	97	48	23	62	15	62	31	16	95	62	A

Note: These calculations were made using a spreadsheet program with the number of decimal places set at 0 for display. The decimals are still used by the program in calculating the numbers.

T A B L E 1 4 . 6 F

Grading Standards

Grade	Criterion-Referenced Standards	Norm-Referenced Standards
A	Outstanding number of goals mastered and points earned	Outstanding progress compared to classmates
B	Very good number of goals mastered and points earned	Above-average progress compared to classmates
C	Questionable number of goals mastered and points earned—student is experiencing some difficulty	Average progress compared to classmates
D	Inadequate number of goals mastered and points earned	Below-average progress compared to classmates
F	Unacceptable number of goals mastered and points earned	Very little progress compared to classmates

D. *Grade*   *Score Range*

    A = 93 to 100
    B = 82 to 92
    C = 71 to 81
    D = 60 to 70
    F = 59 and below

These scores were identified using the following steps:

1. Identify the range of scores between the lowest A and the lowest D ($93 - 60 = 33$).
2. Divide this range by 3 (there are three grade levels: B, C, and D) to obtain the range of scores for each grade ($33/3 = 11$).
3. Subtract 11 from 93 to identify the lower limit for a B grade ($93 - 11 = 82$).
4. Subtract 11 from 82 to identify the lower limit for a C grade ($82 - 11 = 71$).
5. Subtract 11 from 71 to obtain the lower limit for a D grade ($71 - 11 = 60$).

E. B. Allen would be assigned a B, and J. Baker would be assigned an A.

■ SUGGESTED READINGS

Gallagher, J. D. (1998). *Classroom assessment for teachers* (pp. 391–433). Columbus, OH: Merrill.

Kubiszyn, T., & Borich, G. (2000). *Educational testing and measurement* (6th ed., pp. 201–220). New York: John Wiley & Sons.

Lynn, R. L., & Gronlund, N. E. (2000). *Measurement and assessment in teaching* (8th ed., pp. 377–403). Englewood Cliffs, NJ: Prentice-Hall.

Nitko, A. J. (1996). *Educational assessment of students* (2nd ed., pp. 322–348). Columbus, OH: Merrill.

Oosterhof, A. (1999). *Developing and using classroom assessments* (2nd ed., pp. 209–220). Columbus, OH: Merrill.

Popham, W. J. (1999). *Classroom assessment: What teachers need to know* (2nd ed., pp. 400–412). Boston: Allyn and Bacon.

Tombari, M., & Borich, G. (1999). *Authentic assessment in the classroom* (pp. 207–227). Columbus, OH: Merrill.

Worthen, B. R., White, K. R., Fan, X., & Sudweeks, R. L. (1999). *Measurement and assessment in schools* (2nd ed., pp. 386–410). New York: Addison-Wesley Longman.

Gradebook software distributors on the Internet, including shareware and freeware:

Russ and Ryan Stevens. Edware <http://www.rredware. com>.

Softseek. <http://softseek.com/Education_and_Science/ Teaching_Tools>.

Interpreting Standardized Test Results

- Compare criterion-referenced achievement tests, norm-referenced achievement tests, and scholastic aptitude tests using their purposes, design characteristics, and uses.

- Describe the procedures for developing norm-referenced tests.

- Describe the normal curve and anchor points under the normal curve that are used to interpret standard scores.

- Describe scale scores and use them to analyze students' performance on standardized tests.

- Calculate and interpret the following standard scores: percentiles, percentile bands, and stanines.

- Interpret the following standard scores: normal curve equivalent scores and deviation IQ scores.

- Interpret grade equivalent scores and anticipated achievement scores.

- Describe the performance of individual students and class groups using their test records.

In addition to preparing and using classroom tests, teachers are usually expected to administer and interpret one or more standardized tests each year. These tests are called *standardized* because the same directions are used for administering them in all classrooms and standard procedures are used for scoring and interpreting them. This standardization permits comparing students' performance across classrooms, across schools, and across school districts. The three types of standardized tests used in schools include criterion-referenced achievement tests, norm-referenced achievement tests, and norm-referenced scholastic aptitude tests. These tests differ in purpose and in how they are developed and interpreted.

◼ Criterion-Referenced Achievement Tests

Criterion-referenced achievement tests are developed by school districts, state departments of education, and commercial testing companies. These tests measure students' progress in such subjects as language arts, mathematics, science, and social studies. The match between these tests and the prescribed curriculum for a particular grade level and subject is of primary importance. Because these tests correspond directly to the curriculum guide, they can be administered at the beginning of the school year to evaluate the appropriateness of the curriculum for the grade level and to plan instruction tailored to students' needs. At the conclusion of a semester or year, they can be used to evaluate students' progress during the course.

The procedures used to develop criterion-referenced achievement tests are similar to those teachers use to develop classroom tests. The goals prescribed in the curriculum guide are analyzed to identify their subordinate skills, which are divided into prerequisite and enabling skills for each grade. The conditions for performing each skill are identified; and item specifications are written to ensure that each item is at an appropriate level of complexity, elicits the appropriate behavior, and includes the intended content. Item specifications prescribe the characteristics of the stem (or question), the correct answer, and each distractor to be included. Multiple-choice items are often used because of their economy, versatility, and objectivity. Tables of specifications are developed to ensure an appropriate balance among goals and their subordinate skills. Using these specifications, a writing team writes many more items than needed for each skill.

The review process used to evaluate these items is more comprehensive than that used by teachers. In addition to the writing team, content experts review the items for congruence with item specifications. Language specialists evaluate the appropriateness of the vocabulary, reading level, and grammar. Representatives from different cultural groups evaluate the items for potential bias in vocabulary and context. Finally, target students are sometimes used to review the items to verify their readability. During the review process, many items are either eliminated or revised.

Items that survive these reviews are assigned to different test forms for a field test. A large, representative sample of students is selected to take each test, which is administered in regular classrooms by the teachers. Like classroom tests, the items are evaluated using their difficulty and discrimination indices. Related to difficulty, items that are more difficult than anticipated, given the complexity of the task, are eliminated. Likewise, those that do not discriminate well for the obtained difficulty levels are eliminated. Items that meet the criteria are stored in an item bank or item pool. Using the table of specifications, items are selected from the bank for tests as needed.

To help ensure the curricular validity of commercial criterion-referenced tests, publishers have begun to provide custom-made or tailor-made tests. Publishers follow the previously described procedure to create comprehensive item banks for each subject. Working in collaboration with a school district's representatives, they select the goals and objectives to be measured by a test and create a table of specifications tailored to the school's curriculum. Then, using the table of specifications, they select items from their item pool to create tests tailored to the district's curriculum.

Students' performance on criterion-referenced tests is usually reported as non-mastery, partial knowledge, or mastery of each objective. A criterion, or score needed for partial knowledge and mastery, is set using professional judgment. Scores used to report each student's level are either the percentage of items answered correctly for each objective or derived scores created using the number of items correct and other factors, such as the difficulty and discrimination levels of items in a set and the probability of guessing correct answers.

■ Norm-Referenced Achievement Tests

Norm-referenced achievement tests are used primarily to compare students' achievement to that of a large, representative group of students at the same grade level. This representative group is called a *norm group*. Norm groups can be made up of students from throughout a school district, the state, the region, or the country. The purpose for these tests is to determine whether a student's or a group's achievement level is above average, average, or below average when compared to that of the selected norm group. These tests typically measure students' achievement in basic skills, such as language and mathematics, although other subjects are sometimes included. Norm-referenced tests are extremely time consuming and expensive to develop; therefore, they are usually produced and distributed by commercial test publishers rather than by school districts or state departments of education.

A summary of the process used to develop norm-referenced achievement tests appears in Figure 15.1. There are five main stages in the process: designing, developing, field testing, creating norms, and writing test manuals. During the design of norm-referenced tests, those goals cited most often in curriculum guides throughout the nation are selected to ensure the test's relevance for most school districts. Tasks selected to measure each goal vary in difficulty; for example, some are prerequisite skills, some are enabling skills, and some are too complex for most students at each grade level. Tasks are chosen in this manner to ensure the wide range of scores necessary to discriminate among below-average, average, and above-average achievers.

The item writing and review processes are the same for both criterion-referenced and norm-referenced tests. However, the procedures used to field test and select items for norm-referenced tests are different. During the field test, the different test forms are administered to a large, representative sample of students. Students are selected according to specific characteristics, such as prior achievement or aptitude, age, gender, cultural group, socioeconomic level, school and community type, and geographic region. A sample of students from the grades immediately preceding and following the target grade may also be included. Teachers administer the tests in selected classrooms and follow the prescribed administration procedures, with one exception. Students are allowed ample time to finish the test. Teachers record the time each student requires, note any items or directions that cause confusion, and describe difficulties observed.

FIGURE 15.1

Process for Developing Standardized Achievement Tests

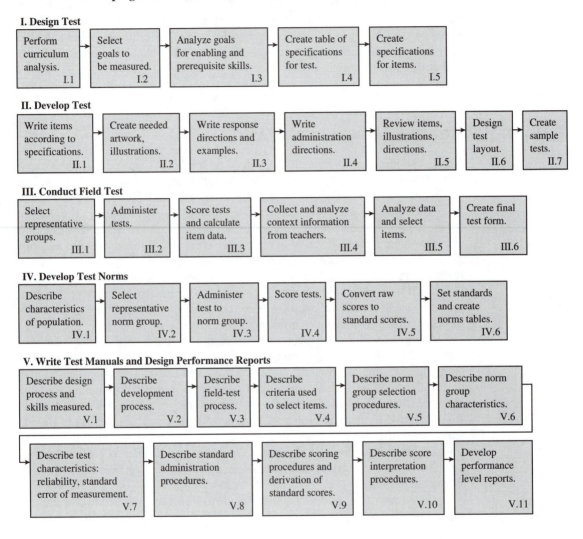

Data from the field test are analyzed, and items are selected for the final test version using the following four criteria:

1. Goal balance (inclusion of enough items for all skills)
2. Difficulty range (*p* values ranging from .90 down to .20, with a median value of about .55)

3. Discrimination indices (the highest positive discrimination index for the accompanying difficulty index)
4. Instructional sensitivity (a larger proportion of students answering items correctly at each higher grade level)

The items that best meet these criteria appear on the final test form, which is professionally formatted and produced.

Scores on norm-referenced tests are based on the performance of students in a reference group, or norm group. To select a representative norm group, the team must first define the population (e.g., all third-graders in the United States) and then select variables that accurately describe the group. If the norm group selected does not adequately represent the population, interpretations of individual students' performances are questionable.

To ensure that a cross-section of students is included, the team establishes categories of students and then determines the proportion of the population that falls into each category. For example, the team must know how the population is distributed according to the following characteristics:

1. Achievement or aptitude
2. Age, gender, race, and cultural group
3. Enrollment in public, private, and parochial schools
4. Enrollment in large, medium, and small schools
5. Residence in the different regions of the country
6. Residence in urban, suburban, and rural communities
7. Residence in high-, medium-, and low-income communities

Once the team has determined the characteristics of the population, a sampling plan is used to select the schools that will be included. The norm group usually includes thousands of students who, all together, are representative of the population.

Teachers then use the standardized procedures to administer the test to students in the norm group. At the same time, the team collects data on the group's characteristics. The tests are scored, and derived scores are calculated and reported in norms tables that appear in the test's technical manual and in the administrator's manual. Although raw scores are used to report students' achievement, they are converted to derived scores to facilitate comparing each student's performance to that of the norm group. Commonly used derived scores include scale scores, percentiles, percentile bands, stanines, normal curve equivalent scores, grade equivalent scores, and anticipated achievement scores. Procedures for interpreting these scores are described later in the chapter.

The team's final task is to develop the test manuals. These manuals usually describe the design and development process, the field test procedures, the item selection process, the sampling plan for the norm group, the characteristics of the norm group, and the group's test performance. They also include a list of the goals and objectives measured, directions for administering and scoring the test, and directions for interpreting the scores.

■ Scholastic Aptitude Tests

Scholastic aptitude tests are developed by commercial test publishers because they, too, are time consuming and expensive to develop. Unlike the two types of achievement tests, they do not measure students' achievement in school-related subjects. Instead, their main purpose is to measure students' thinking processes, sometimes called *reasoning skills.* These thinking processes include such skills as recall, concept discrimination, classification, analysis, sequencing, synthesis, inference, and generalization. Students' performances on aptitude tests are used to predict how well they will achieve in given subjects, special training programs, higher education, and careers that require similar reasoning skills.

The procedures used to develop scholastic aptitude tests are similar to those used to develop norm-referenced achievement tests because aptitude tests are norm-referenced. The skills measured vary widely in difficulty to enable discrimination among students who are below average, average, and above average in aptitude. The major difference between these tests is that the foundation or framework of skills measured by the aptitude test involves thinking or reasoning skills rather than curriculum-based skills.

Students' performances on aptitude tests are interpreted by comparing them to the performances of the representative norm group. The scores traditionally used to report performance on aptitude tests are deviation IQ scores and percentiles.

Table 15.1 summarizes the characteristics of criterion-referenced and norm-referenced achievement tests and scholastic aptitude tests. Because of the differences in these tests, school personnel carefully select the appropriate test for their purpose. For example, if they want to know how many students in each grade have mastered the skills prescribed in the curriculum guide, they should use a criterion-referenced test. However, if they want to know how their students' general achievement in a subject area compares to the achievement of a norm group, they should use a norm-referenced test. Finally, if they want to know which students are most likely to succeed in a particular subject, they should use an aptitude test that measures the reasoning skills required in the subject.

One type of test cannot serve all three purposes equally well; however, it is not uncommon to find a norm-referenced achievement test used for all three. For example, the publishers of norm-referenced tests have begun to report criterion-referenced or mastery scores in addition to traditional norm-referenced scores. Using these mastery scores, though, potentially can lead to inaccurate judgments about students' mastery. Remember that items are primarily selected for these tests to create a wide range of scores. Thus, many items are purposefully included that are judged to be too complex for most students at a given grade level. This design feature, which is necessary for norm-referenced achievement tests, will result in lower mastery scores for students than will scores produced from legitimate criterion-referenced tests. Norm-referenced achievement tests are also commonly used instead of aptitude tests to predict achievement. This practice is not as problematic since both previous achievement and aptitude have been found to be good predictors of future achievement. One potential problem with this practice is that the subject-based skills in the new curriculum may require different reasoning skills than those measured by previous achievement tests.

TABLE 15.1

Characteristics of Criterion-Referenced and Norm-Referenced Achievement Tests and Scholastic Aptitude Tests

	Criterion-Referenced Achievement Tests	Norm-Referenced Achievement Tests	Scholastic Aptitude Tests
Typical developers	School districts State departments of education Commercial publishers	Commercial publishers	Commercial publishers
Primary purpose	To measure students' achievement of curriculum-based skills	To measure students' achievement of curriculum-based skills	To measure students' general thinking or reasoning skills
Foundation or item basis	Grade or course-specific curricular goals and their subordinate skills	Curricular goals from multiple grade levels	Generic thinking or reasoning skills
Criteria for including items	Balanced representation of goals and objectives Measured difficulty levels are within bounds for perceived skill complexity Measured discrimination levels are high, positive for given difficulty levels	Balanced representation of goals and objectives Wide range of difficulty levels, from .90 to.20 with a median about .55 Measured discrimination levels are high, positive for given difficulty levels Sensitivity to instruction	Balanced representation of thinking or reasoning skills Wide range of difficulty levels, from .90 to .20 with a median about .55 Measured discrimination levels are high, positive for given difficulty levels
Scores typically reported	Minimum scores for partial and total mastery of main skill areas Number of items correct Percentage of items correct Derived score based on items correct and other factors	Percentile ranks Percentile bands Stanines Normal curve equivalent scores Grade equivalent scores Scale scores Anticipated achievement scores (in conjunction with aptitude scores)	Deviation IQ scores Percentiles
When administered	Before instruction After instruction	After instruction	With achievement tests Before selecting courses of study
Use	Assess the curriculum Plan instruction Evaluate progress Group students for instruction	Classify students' achievement as above average, average, or below average for a given grade Create homogeneous or heterogeneous class groups	Classify students' aptitude as below average, average, or above average for a given age Predict achievement in subjects and courses of study that require similar reasoning skills

Norm-Referenced Test Scores

Publishers of norm-referenced tests convert students' raw scores into derived scores that permit each student's performance to be compared to that of the norm group. These derived scores are created using only the raw scores of students in the norm group. Later, when students throughout the country take the test, their raw scores are matched with those of students in the norm group, and the corresponding preset derived scores are assigned to individual students.

Using the Normal Curve to Interpret Standard Scores

Most derived scores are based on the standard normal distribution of scores, frequently called the *normal curve*. This distribution is used to give the scores a common meaning that makes interpreting performance much easier. Obviously, if every standardized test used a different score distribution, interpreting the various scores would be a difficult task.

The area under the normal curve is divided into halves, with the mean score as the center. Notice that in Figure 15.2, the area between the mean score and one standard deviation above the mean score (+1SD) contains approximately 34 percent of the ranked scores in the distribution (.3413). Because a normal distribution is symmetrical, approximately 68 percent of the ranked scores fall between one standard deviation above (+1SD) and one standard deviation below (–1SD) the mean score (.3413 + .3413). Fourteen percent of the scores fall within the area between one and two standard deviations above the mean, and another 14 percent fall between one and two standard deviations below the mean. The remaining 4 percent of scores are evenly divided between the two remaining plus and minus categories. These percentages total 100 percent of the scores. If you add these percentages cumulatively from left to right, you can locate the proportion of scores that fall below each standard deviation. For example, about 2 percent of the scores fall below two standard deviations below the mean. About 16 percent of the scores fall below one standard deviation below the mean (2 + 14). Likewise, 50 percent fall below the mean (2 + 14 + 34). Eighty-four percent fall below one standard deviation above the mean, and 98 percent fall below two standard deviations above the mean. If you wanted to know the proportion of scores that fall below points between these standard deviation anchors, you could consult a table of areas under the normal curve. These tables are included in most basic statistics books.

It is important to become familiar with the normal curve anchor points illustrated in Figure 15.2 because the interpretation of the majority of derived scores reported for standardized tests depends on these anchor values. Recall how the mean and standard deviation are used in norm-referenced interpretations of students' performance on classroom tests. Scores within one standard deviation of the mean are considered to reflect average-level performance within the class. Scores equal to or greater than one standard deviation above the mean reflect above-average achievement compared to classmates. Scores equal to or lower than one standard deviation below the mean

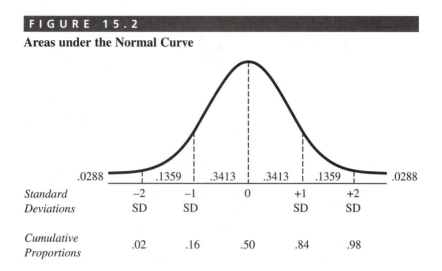

FIGURE 15.2

Areas under the Normal Curve

reflect below-average achievement in the group. On standardized, norm-referenced achievement tests, the same interpretation is given to scores located in each of these three areas. The main differences between norm-referenced, standard test scores and norm-referenced, classroom test scores is that standardized scores are interpreted relative to the areas under the normal curve. Scores equal to one standard deviation above the mean reflect above-average performance, and they indicate a score equivalent to the cumulative proportion .84 in Figure 15.2. Students earning scores at this level are comparable in achievement to the upper 16 percent of students in their norm group. Students earning scores within one standard deviation of the mean are comparable to approximately the middle two-thirds of their national norm group. Scores within one standard deviation of the mean are considered to reflect average performance. Students earning scores at one standard deviation below the mean on a standardized test are comparable in achievement to the lowest-scoring 16 percent of the norm group, and performance at this level is considered below average. Students at two standard deviations above the mean are comparable in achievement to the upper 2 percent of students in the norm group. Finally, the scores of students at two standard deviations below the mean are comparable to students in the lowest 2 percent of their national norm group.

In order to make the remainder of this discussion of standardized, norm-referenced tests more concrete, materials from the TerraNova Multiple Assessments, published by CTB/McGraw-Hill Publishing Company (1997), will be used as the example. Teachers' materials available from other well-established school test publishers are similar to those contained in the TerraNova materials. The TerraNova materials also provide a good example because they include a wide variety of the types of test scores reported for norm-referenced tests. The next section describes scale scores and how to use them for analyzing students' performance on standardized tests. Following this discussion are descriptions of various standard scores that are derived from scale scores.

Interpreting Scale Scores

The most basic score, or the first score often calculated for a standardized test, is called a *scale score.* The primary purpose of the scale score is to create other derived scores that are used to describe test performance. Scale scores are derived using either of two scoring methods: pattern scoring based on item response theory (IRT) and number correct scoring. A description of these two scoring methods is beyond the scope of this introductory text; however, readers interested in the process can consult advanced measurement textbooks and the publishers' technical reports that accompany their standardized tests. Generally, publishers use a series of test items that overlap grade levels and a complex, computerized, score-equating system to calculate scale scores for the fall and spring norm groups for each grade level. Factors such as the pattern of items answered correctly, item difficulty, item discrimination, and the likelihood of guessing the correct answer are often included in the scoring formulas.

Scale scores generally range from 0 to 999, with students' scores from all grade levels (K–12) placed within this range. Although different test publishers use a slightly different range of scale scores, students in the lower grades are assigned lower-scale scores, and students in higher grades are assigned higher-scale scores. Scale scores are equal interval scores, which means that the distance or interval between any two numbers is equal at any point on the scale. This equal interval property means that scale scores can be added, subtracted, and averaged.

The best way to become familiar with scale scores is to obtain the norms book for the standardized test that is administered in your school district and to study the range of scale scores used for the grade level(s) and subject(s) you teach. You should also examine the mean and standard deviation of scale scores for your grade level and subjects. Using these values for your grade level, scale scores can then readily be interpreted on each student's report.

Consider the scale score mean, standard deviations, and norm-referenced interpretations in Figure 15.3. Related to the normal curve, scores within one standard deviation of the mean are considered to be within the average range of achievement compared with students in the national norm group. Scores at and above one standard deviation above the mean are interpreted as above average, and those at or above two standard deviations above the mean are judged to be well above average for the grade level. At the other end of the scale, scores at or below one standard deviation below the mean are judged to be below average, and those at or below two standard deviations below the mean are interpreted as well below average.

When we do not have the administrator's manual handy to locate the mean and standard deviation for each subject in our class, we can compare a student's assigned scale score with the national percentile score assigned for the same test. Percentile ranks will be described in a later section of this chapter.

The following paragraphs provide descriptions of how to use scale scores for (1) summarizing students' achievement within a skill area and across the total test battery, (2) analyzing students' achievement within a skill area across grade levels, (3) analyzing a student's achievement across skill areas within a grade level, and (4) evaluating a student's progress from grade to grade.

FIGURE 15.3

Interpreting Scale Scores for your Subject and Grade Level

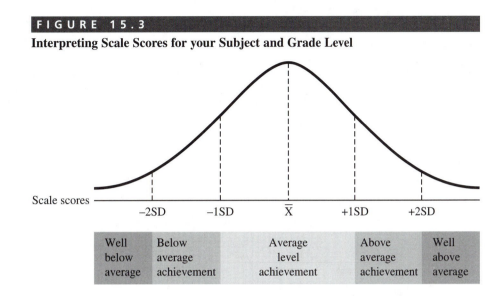

Summarizing Students' Scale Scores across Subtests   For the TerraNova Assessment series (CTB/McGraw-Hill, 1997), scale scores are initially calculated for each subtest within a basic skill area. These scores are then averaged to create composite scale scores for general areas such as reading, language, and mathematics. These composite scale scores are again averaged across the three content areas to create the total battery scale scores.

Table 15.2 contains an example of how scale scores from subtests are combined into content area scale scores and how content area scale scores are combined into total battery scale scores. For the reading area, the reading and vocabulary subtest scale scores are summed and then divided by two to obtain the reading composite scale score ([778 + 774]/2 = 776). The language area scale score is the average of the mechanics and language subtest scale scores ([786 + 780]/2 = 783), and the total mathematics scale score is the average of the computation and the concepts/applications scale scores ([813 + 797]/2 = 805). The total scale score for a student is the average of the total reading, total language, and total mathematics scale scores ([776 + 783 + 805]/3 = 788). Skill areas other than reading, language, and mathematics are typically not included in the total scale score. You will need to study the instructor's manual for the standardized tests used in your district to determine how subtest scores are combined to create skill area and total battery scores.

Analyzing Students' Progress across Grade Levels within a Subject   The best way to interpret scale scores for any subtest across grade levels is to relate the scale scores to comparable anchor scores from the normal curve. Figure 15.4 contains a selected sample of scale scores from the reading subtests of the TerraNova published

TABLE 15.2

Summarizing Subtest Scale Scores into Composite Scores and a Total Battery Scale Score

Reading Subtests	Reading Scale Scores	Language Subtests	Language Scale Scores	Math Subtests	Math Scale Scores	Total	Total Scale Scores
Reading	778	Language	786	Math	813	Reading	776
Vocabulary	774	Mechanics	780	Computation	797		
						Language	783
Reading		*Language*		*Math*			
Composite 1552/2 = 776		*Composite* 1566/2 = 783		*Composite* 1610/2 = 805		Math	805
						Total Score	2364/3 = 788

Source: TerraNova Spring Norms Book (Monterey, CA: CTB/McGraw-Hill, 1997).

by CTB/McGraw-Hill. Scale scores appear in the far left column of the figure. The labels beneath the graph represent the grade-level norms. The vertical lines above each grade level indicate the scale scores that correspond to normal curve anchor points for that grade. (See Figure 15.3 for normal curve anchor point values and their interpretation.) The highest scale score indicated for each grade level reflects the score equivalent to two standard deviations above the mean on the normal curve, and the next score down represents the scale score equivalent to one standard deviation above the mean. The center score reflects the score corresponding to the mean, and the lower two scores reflect those corresponding to one and two standard deviations below the mean, respectively. Notice the first vertical line in Figure 15.4 (first-grade students). The scale score corresponding to two standard deviations above the mean is 657, the mean scale score for first-graders is 576, and the scale score corresponding to two standard deviations below the mean is 495.

What interpretive principles can we glean from the sample scores in Figure 15.4 that will help us interpret students' reading achievement across grade levels? The first principle relates to the consistent increase in scale scores at each normal curve anchor point across grades. For example, the scale score corresponding to two standard deviations below the mean for first-graders is 495, for second-graders it is 527, for third-graders it is 545, and it increases for each grade through grade 12. Notice that the mean scale score for each subsequent grade is higher than the one for the preceding grade. Following the same pattern, the scale score equivalent to two standard deviations above the mean is likewise higher than the one for the previous grade.

The second interpretive principle relates to the overlap in the scale scores across grade levels. Notice in Figure 15.4 that the scale scores overlap from first grade, to second grade, to third grade, and so forth. In other words, students in different grades can be assigned the same scale scores on a standardized test. The meaning attributed to a particular scale score, however, depends on the student's grade level. You can see

FIGURE 15.4

Scale Scores Corresponding to Normal Curve Anchor Points for the Reading Subtest,
Grades 1 through 12

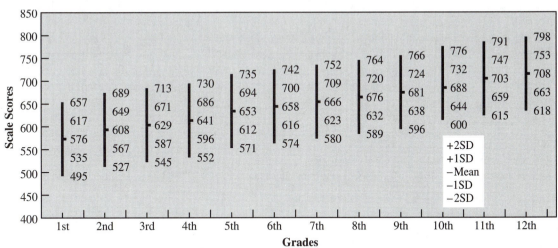

Source: Synthesized from materials in *TerraNova Technical Bulletin 1* (Monterey, CA: CTB/McGraw-Hill,
1997), pp. 225–230.

that a scale score of 620 represents above-average achievement for a first-grade
student since it is more than one standard deviation above the mean for this grade. A
score of 620 reflects average-level performance for a second-grade student since it is
near the mean for second-graders. The same score depicts below-average achievement
for a student in the higher grades since it is more than one standard deviation below
the mean for these grades.

The third principle is that there are greater achievement gains from grade
to grade in the lower grades than in the upper grades. Notice that the difference in
mean scale scores for reading from first to second grade is greater (608 – 576 = 32
points) than the difference in mean scale scores from eleventh to twelfth grade
(708 – 703 = 5 points).

Analyzing Achievement across Subjects within a Grade Level   We can also
increase our understanding of scale scores by comparing them across various subtests
within a particular grade level. Scale scores tend to fall in the same general region of
the score distribution for subtests within a grade level. A set of scale score ranges for
selected subtests based on sixth-grade norms appear in Table 15.3. Anchor scores for
the normal curve are in the far left column, national percentiles are located in the second column, and the subtest names are across the top of the table. The scale score corresponding to each normal curve anchor and subtest is included in the intersecting

TABLE 15.3

Scale Scores Corresponding to Normal Curve Anchors for Selected Subtests (Sixth Grade, Spring Norms)

Normal Curve Anchors	National Percentiles	Reading Composite	Language Composite	Mathematics Composite	Total Score*	Science	Social Studies
+2	98	735–741	728–736	738–747	732–738	742–754	743–751
+1	84	696–697	691	697–698	696–697	700	701
Mean	50	661	658	661	662	663	664
−1	16	620–621	621–622	619–620	622	621	623–624
−2	2	563–571	560–575	551–563	564–576	559–573	574–583

*Total score consists of reading, language, and mathematics.

Source: Synthesized from materials in TerraNova Spring Norms Book (Monterey, CA: CTB/McGraw-Hill, 1997), pp. 84–85.

cell. For example, a scale score of 735 in reading composite is two standard deviations above the mean and represents a score well above average in the sixth-grade spring norm group. A score of 661 corresponds to the mean and represents average-level achievement for a sixth-grader.

Notice that the scale score ranges across all subtests are in the same general region of the total distribution: Scale scores corresponding to two standard deviations below the mean are located in the mid 500s, the mean scale scores are all about 660, and the scores corresponding to two standard deviations above the mean are all in the mid-700s region of the distribution. The same pattern is true for subtests within each grade level. Although not illustrated here, the scale scores across subtests for ninth-graders provide an alternative example. The scale scores corresponding to two standard deviations below the mean are in the mid to high 500s across all subtests, the mean scale scores across all subtests are all within the high 600s area, and the scale scores corresponding to two standard deviations above the mean are in the mid-800s across all subtests. This common area pattern basically means that students in your class who receive scale scores toward the lower end of the distribution in any subtest would be considered to be below average in that subject compared to students in the national norm group. Students who receive scale scores toward the mean score would be considered average, and students who receive scale scores toward the top of the scale for their grade level would be considered above average compared to students in the national norm group.

Interpreting scale scores for an individual student across subtests is relatively easy when you know the region in which scale scores fall for students at your grade level. Using the publishers' norms tables to study the ranges of scale scores possible and the location of the scores relative to the normal curve anchor points for each subtest at your grade level will help you interpret the achievement level of students in your classes.

Suppose you teach sixth grade and have a student in your class who receives the following scale scores: reading composite, 735; language composite, 658; and math composite, 610. Using the normal curve anchor scores for the sixth-grade norms in Table 15.3, how would you interpret the achievement of the student? The student's reading composite is above average compared to the sixth-grade norm group since the scale score 735 is more than one standard deviation above the mean. The student's achievement is average in language since the scale score 658 is equal to the mean score. The student's math achievement is below average since the scale score 610 is more than one standard deviation below the mean. In interpreting the student's achievement across subtests, you could conclude that the student performed better in reading than in language, and better in language than in math.

Interpreting Scale Scores Using the Standard Error of Measurement (SEM)

Similar to other forms of human performance, the scores students earn on standardized achievement tests are not perfectly reliable. *Imperfect reliability* means that, upon retesting, students are not likely to earn the same raw score or scale score they obtained the first time they took the test. This phenomenon is best understood when you consider the difficulty we occasionally experience when trying to recall specific facts or procedures on demand. Sometimes we can readily recall details previously learned and other times we have difficulty remembering a familiar name or the steps in a procedure. Furthermore, we commonly forget the names of acquaintances when we introduce them in social situations. The more nervous we are about stating everyone's name correctly, the more likely we are to make errors in recalling names. It is impossible to create perfectly reliable achievements tests for our unreliable minds.

The standard error of measurement (SEM) is the index test publishers use to estimate the degree of score reliability for their standardized tests. Each scale score has its own standard error of measurement; scores toward the center of the distribution for each grade level have smaller standard errors of measurement than those toward the top or bottom of the distribution. The smaller the standard error of measurement, the more reliable the scores from the test. A student's performance level on a standardized test should be interpreted as falling within a range or band of scale scores that is established using the student's earned scale score and the standard error of measurement for that particular score. The standard error of measurement helps teachers avoid overinterpreting the precision of students' scores on standardized tests.

The standard error of measurement works conceptually much like the mean and standard deviation of a set of test scores. The student's earned scale score functions like the mean score since it is located toward the center of the band. The standard error of measurement functions similarly to the standard deviation because it is used to create the intervals around the earned score. A band, sometimes called a *confidence interval,* is placed around the student's earned scale score that is one standard error of measurement above and one standard error of measurement below the earned score. Hypothetically, the student's true score, or true achievement level, on the test is likely to fall within this ±1 SEM band approximately 68 percent of the time. The student's true score is likely to fall within ±2 SEMs approximately 95 percent of the time. (Recall from Figure 15.2 that under the normal curve, approximately 68 percent of the cases fall within ±1 standard deviation from the mean, and approximately 95 percent of the cases fall within ±2 standard deviations from the mean.) The earned scale score should be interpreted as a point within the SEM confidence band where the student's true score is likely to fall.

The standard error of measurement is calculated and reported in the norms tables by test publishers. The size of the standard error of measurement varies from test to test; and within a test, it varies across the range of test scores. The SEM is smallest toward the center of the distribution of scores for each norm group. It is larger toward the highest scores, and it is largest toward the lowest scores on the test. This phenomenon reflects that very high and very low test scores lack the same degree of reliability that scores toward the center of the distribution possess.

To illustrate how the size of the standard error of measurement varies across the range of scale scores within a single test, scores comparable to the normal curve anchor points and their SEM bands are plotted in Figure 15.5. The scale scores in the example are from the TerraNova reading composite scores (Form A, Level 16). The first vertical line on the left side of the figure reflects the SEM confidence band for a scale score equivalent to two standard deviations below the mean. The scale score located at this very low point in the normal distribution is 563, its published SEM is 19 points, and the corresponding confidence band ranges from 544 to 582. Notice that this confidence band is one of the largest in the set. At the scale score corresponding to the mean (661), the SEM is only 10 points, and the confidence band ranges from 651 to 671. At two standard deviations above the mean (SS 735), the published SEM is 20, and the confidence band ranges from 715 to 755. For students earning these particular scale scores, their true scores are expected to fall within these confidence bands 68 percent of the time. Generally, this indicates that you can have the most confidence in the reliability of scale scores in the center of the distribution and less confidence in score reliability toward the top and bottom of the distribution. Although this general rule applies, scale scores and their confidence intervals vary across subtests. The best way to determine the amount of measurement error associated with a particular scale score on a given test is to consult the norms book provided by the test publisher.

Although scale scores are useful to teachers for analyzing a student's standardized test performance, they are difficult to explain to students and parents. In fact, they are difficult for teachers to interpret without the aid of the publisher's norms book. For this reason, scale scores are converted to other derived scores that are more easily interpreted. The most common scores derived from the scale scores are the percentile ranks and percentile bands, stanines, normal curve equivalent scores (NCE), and deviation IQ scores.

Interpreting Percentile Ranks

The first derived score created from scale scores is the national percentile rank, and this score is used to anchor scale scores to the normal curve. The range for percentile ranks is 1 to 99. This score indicates the percentage of students in the norm group

---

FIGURE 15.5

Width of Standard Error of Measurement (SEM) Bands at Normal Curve Anchor Points for the *TerraNova Multiple Assessments* (Form A, Level 16, Reading Composite Score)

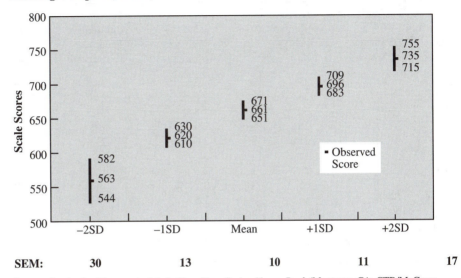

Source: Synthesized from materials in *TerraNova Spring Norms Book* (Monterey, CA: CTB/McGraw-Hill, 1997), pp. 45, 84–85.

who earned scale scores below the cumulative frequency at midpoint for each scale score in the distribution. Recall that the cumulative frequency at midpoint includes all the students who earned scale scores below a given score plus one-half of the students who earned that scale score. For example, if 38 students earned scale scores lower than 540 and 10 students earned a scale score of 540, the cumulative frequency at midpoint would be 38 plus 5, or 43. Suppose this value, 43, is equivalent to the 62nd percentile. A student who earns a percentile rank of 62 is said to have performed better than 62 percent of the students in the norm group.

Knowing how publishers convert scale scores to percentile ranks is helpful in interpreting them. Although publishers work with a wide range of scale scores and thousands of students, the simplified frequency distribution in Table 15.4 illustrates the process.

First, the scale scores are listed from highest to lowest (Column 1), and the number of students who earned each score is tallied (Column 2). Although there are several ways to proceed from this point, the most commonly used method is:

1. Sum the frequencies of scores falling below each scale score to obtain the cumulative frequency of scores below each scale score (Column 3).
2. Divide the frequency of scores at each scale score in half (Column 4).

TABLE 15.4

Derivation of Percentiles from Scale Scores

N = 36

(1) Scale Scores	(2) Frequency of Scores	(3) Cumulative Frequency below		(4) 1/2 Frequency within		(5) Cumulative Frequency at Midpoint	(6) Proportion	(7) Percentile Rank
450	1	35	+	.5	=	35.5	35.5/36 = .99	99
449	2	33	+	1	=	34	34/36 = .94	94
448	3	30	+	1.5	=	31.5	31.5/36 = .88	88
447	4	26	+	2	=	28	28/36 = .77	77
446	5	21	+	2.5	=	23.5	23.5/36 = .65	65
445	6	15	+	3	=	18	18/36 = .50	50
444	5	10	+	2.5	=	12.5	12.5/36 = .35	35
443	4	6	+	2	=	8	8/36 = .22	22
442	3	3	+	1.5	=	4.5	4.5/36 = .13	13
441	2	1	+	1	=	2	2/36 = .05	5
440	1	0	+	.5	=	.5	.5/36 = .01	1

3. Add the frequency of scores below to half the scores at the scale score to obtain the cumulative frequency at midpoint (Column 5).
4. Divide this figure by the number of students in the group to obtain the proportion of students at midpoint (Column 6).
5. Multiply this proportion by 100 to obtain the percentile rank for each scale score (Column 7).

For example, the percentile rank for a scale score of 445 in Table 15.4 is 50. This conversion was made by:

1. Summing the frequencies of scores falling below 445 (1 + 2 + 3 + 4 + 5 = 15).
2. Dividing the frequency of scores at 445 in half (6/2 = 3).
3. Adding the frequency of scores below to half the scores at a scale score of 45 (15 + 3 = 18).
4. Dividing the cumulative frequency at midpoint (18) by the total number of students in the group (36) to obtain the proportion at midpoint (18/36 = .50).
5. Multiplying this proportion by 100 to obtain the percentile rank (.50 × 100 = 50).

There are several factors to consider in interpreting percentiles. One is the distinction between the percentage of correct items and the percentile, since these indices are different. The percentile rank is based on the number of students surpassed, and the percentage correct is based on the number of items correctly answered by an individual student.

Another factor to consider in interpreting percentile ranks is that they are not equal interval scores. An increase of one point on the scale score distribution does not correspond to a similar size increase on the percentile scale. For example, in Table 15.4, a 1-point increase in scale scores (from 445 to 446) results in a 15-point increase on the percentile rank scale (from 50 to 65). An increase in scale scores from 446 to 447 results in a 12-point increase on the percentile scale (from 65 to 77). Similarly, an increase in scale scores from 447 to 448 results in an increase on the percentile rank scale of 11 points. This phenomenon occurs because percentile ranks are based on the frequency of students who earn each scale score, and this number varies across the scale score distribution.

Notice in Table 15.4 that the frequency of students earning each scale score is greater toward the middle of the range than toward the ends of the distribution. This uneven pattern of scores across the range influences the correspondence between scale scores and percentile ranks. Because there are many tied scores in the center of the distribution, small increases in scale scores result in large increases in percentile scores. As the number of tied scores decreases toward the ends of the scale score distribution, increases in percentile ranks become less dramatic. This uneven correspondence between scale score and percentile increments is not problematic if you know why it occurs and how to explain it to inquiring parents.

Another factor to consider in interpreting percentiles is that the scale scores of the norm group are the basis for the percentiles. Percentiles based on the performance of a nationwide norm group are called *national percentiles*. If other reference groups, such as all the students in a district, are used, then percentiles based on this group would be called *district* or *local percentiles*. Percentiles based on different norm groups are likely to be different even though the underlying scale score is the same for the test. Consider the following data:

Scale Score	National Percentile	District Percentile
640	60	75

When compared to the national norm group, a scale score of 640 reflects lower achievement than it does when compared to the district norm group. This difference reflects that a scale score of 640 ranked higher in the district group than in the national group. As this comparison shows, any interpretation of percentile ranks depends on the reference group for the scores.

The final factor to consider in interpreting percentile ranks is their relationship to the normal distribution. Because percentile scores reflect the percentage of people in the norm group who earned scores below the midpoint for a scale score, and the areas under the normal curve reflect the percentage of scores falling below a given point on the normal distribution of scores, percentiles can be equated directly to the proportions under the normal curve. The second percentile corresponds to the normal curve cumulative proportion of .02, or two standard deviations below the mean (−2SD). The sixteenth percentile corresponds to the normal curve cumulative proportion of .16, or one standard deviation below the mean (−1SD), and so on. The same correspondence is true for all percentile scores and for all cumulative normal curve proportions. Figure 15.6 illustrates this correspondence. Points between these anchors can be located using a table of areas under the normal curve.

The implication of this correspondence between the percentiles and the normal distribution is that percentiles between plus and minus one standard deviation from the mean are generally interpreted to reflect average test performance. Thus, percentile ranks between 16 and 84 are considered within the average range. Those at one standard deviation above the mean (percentiles of 84) are judged above average. Those at one standard deviation below the mean (percentile scores of 16) are judged below average.

Interpreting Percentile Bands

Test publishers use scale scores and the standard error of measurement to create percentile confidence bands. These percentile confidence bands, often simply called *percentile bands,* have the same meaning as the scale score confidence intervals. This means that due to measurement error, a student's true percentile rank can be expected to fall within the percentile confidence band 68 percent of the time. Although these two types of confidence intervals have the same meaning, students' test profiles contain percentile bands because they are easier to explain to parents.

Percentile bands are created directly from scale scores using the standard error of measurement and the percentiles calculated for each scale score. Generally, the procedure is the following:

1. Locate the earned scale score and its corresponding percentile rank in the publisher's norms table. The earned scale score and its percentile rank are the anchor points for calculating both the scale score confidence interval and the percentile confidence band.
2. Add and subtract one standard error of measurement from the earned scale score to create the scale score confidence internal. For example, the mean scale score for reading is 661 for the sixth-grade norm group. The standard error of measurement published for this scale score is 10, and the confidence interval extends 10 points in either direction from 661. This creates a scale score confidence interval around the mean score from 651 to 671.
3. Equate these boundary scale scores of 651 to 671 to their calculated percentile ranks in the norms book to locate the outer boundaries of the percentile confidence band. For example, the scale score 651 is equivalent to a percentile rank of 40, and the scale score 671 corresponds to a percentile rank of 60.
4. Plot the percentile band for the mean percentile 50 from percentile 40 to 60. You can interpret this percentile confidence band for an earned percentile rank of 50 as the area within which a student's true score is expected to fall 68 percent of the time.

Figure 15.7 contains the percentile bands that correspond to the scale score confidence intervals and normal curve anchor points illustrated in Figure 15.5.

FIGURE 15.6

Relationship of Percentiles to the Normal Curve

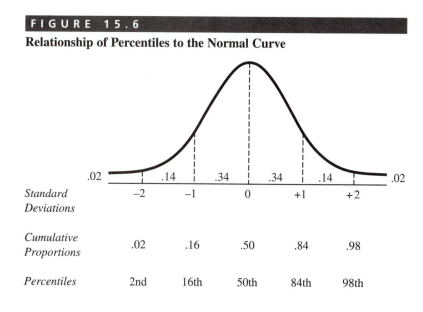

FIGURE 15.7

Percentile Confidence Bands Corresponding to the Scale Score Confidence Intervals and Normal Curve Anchor Points for the *TerraNova Multiple Assessments* (Form A, Level 16, Reading Composite) Depicted in Figure 15.5

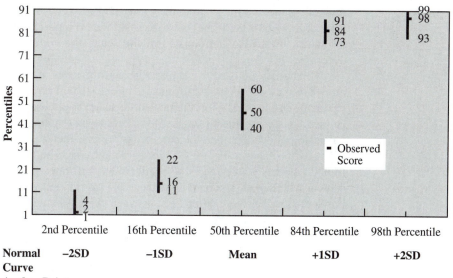

Source: Synthesized from materials in *TerraNova Spring Norms Book* (Monterey, CA: CTB/McGraw-Hill, 1997), pp. 45, 84–85.

There are two characteristics of percentile bands to consider: (1) the observed percentile score may not fall in the center of the percentile band and (2) the width of percentile bands varies for different percentiles. These characteristics both result from the fact that there are an unequal number of tied scores at each scale score. The obtained percentile does not fall in the center of the percentile band because there are unequal intervals between percentiles. The area of the band between the observed percentile and the center of the scale, the 50th percentile, will be wider than the area between the observed percentile and the outer edges of the scale. This occurs because there are more tied scale scores toward the center of the distribution. This characteristic can be observed in the five percentile bands in Figure 15.7. Consider the location of the percentile score 98 within its percentile band. There is a difference of only one percentile point between the observed score, 98, and the upper boundary, 99, yet there is a difference of five percentile points between the observed percentile and the lower boundary. The same characteristic can be observed for the band surrounding the second percentile. There is a one percentile point difference between the lower boundary and the second percentile. Toward the mean, there is a 2-point difference between the observed second percentile and the upper boundary of the band.

The second characteristic is that the width of the percentile band varies for different percentile scores. Generally, percentile bands are wider toward the center of the distribution (the 50th percentile). This occurs because there are more tied scores at each scale score toward the center of the distribution than there are toward the outer edges of the scale score distribution. Remember that many tied scale scores result in dramatic increases on the percentile scale for each increase of one point in the scale scores. This characteristic can also be observed in the five percentile bands in Figure 15.7. The percentile band for a percentile rank of 98 is narrower than the one for a percentile score of 84. Likewise, the percentile band for a percentile score of 84 is narrower than the one for a percentile of 50. Moving from the mean toward the bottom end of the scale, the width of the bands gradually decreases.

Percentiles are used to compare the performances of several students in a class on one test, as well as the performances of one student across several subtests. When percentile bands overlap on the percentile scale, then observed differences between percentiles are considered negligible or due to measurement error. However, if the bands do not overlap, then the percentiles are considered significantly different. For example, the bands in Figure 15.7 for percentiles of 50 and 84 do not overlap. Therefore, the student who earned a percentile of 84 performed significantly better than the student who earned a percentile of 50. This overlap rule provides an important reminder that rather large differences between percentile ranks, or group standing, can be based on small differences between scale scores.

There is a general rule for comparing percentiles when percentile bands are not provided on students' records. The rule is based on the fact that percentile bands are wider toward the center of the percentile scale than toward the ends. Percentile scores in the center of the distribution (between 30 and 70) should be at least 15 percentile points apart before you consider them different. Percentile scores above 70 and below

30 should be at least 10 percentile points apart. Although this procedure permits only general estimates of differences, it is preferable to assuming that small differences in percentile ranks are meaningful.

Interpreting Stanines

Stanine scores are another type of standard score used to report students' performance. This discussion of how publishers create them, their characteristics, and their relationship to the normal curve and percentile scores will help you interpret them.

There are nine scores on a stanine scale; a score of 1 reflects low performance, and a score of 9 reflects high performance. The mean stanine score is 5, and the standard deviation is 2. Each stanine score represents a set proportion of students in the norm group. The proportion of students that corresponds to each score is as follows:

Stanine scores	*1*	*2*	*3*	*4*	*5*	*6*	*7*	*8*	*9*
≈ Proportion of students assigned each score	.04	.07	.12	.17	.20	.17	.12	.07	.04
≈ Cumulative proportions	.04	.10	.22	.40	.59	.77	.89	.95	.99

Publishers create stanine scores directly from a table of proportions under the normal curve. Using cumulative proportions, all students in the norm group who fall at or below the cumulative proportion of .04 are assigned a stanine score of 1. The next 7 percent of the group, from .04 to .10, are assigned a stanine score of 2. The next 12 percent, from .11 to .22, are assigned a stanine score of 3, and so on.

Besides having only a nine-point scale, there are three characteristics of stanine scores you should consider when interpreting them. First, each stanine score represents a band of scale scores and percentile scores; thus, a different stanine score does not exist for each of the other types of scores. Second, stanine scores toward the center of the distribution include a wider band of percentiles than those toward the outer edges of the scale. Finally, stanines 2 through 8 are each one-half a standard deviation wide and have a fixed position on the normal distribution. Thus, they directly correspond to the normal curve and percentile scores.

Figure 15.8 illustrates the relationship among the stanine scores, the normal distribution, and the percentile scores. Stanine 5 extends one-quarter of a standard deviation on each side of the mean, making it one-half a standard deviation wide. Stanines 2 through 4 and 6 through 8 are also one-half a standard deviation wide. Stanines 1 and 9 are wider and extend to the ends of the distribution. Given this position of each stanine on the normal curve, you can equate stanine scores to the normal curve's standard deviation anchors and to percentile scores. For example, a stanine score of 1 is equivalent to standard deviations –3 and –2 and to percentiles 1 through 4. A stanine score of 2 is equivalent to percentile scores 5 through 10. Likewise, a stanine score of 5 is equivalent to the mean and to percentile scores 41 through 59. Because of this relationship, if you know the stanine score, you can locate the percentile scores corresponding to it and vice versa.

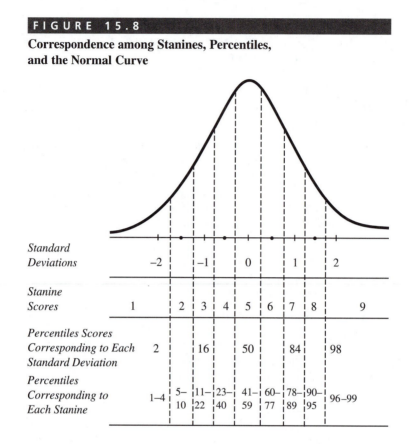

FIGURE 15.8

Correspondence among Stanines, Percentiles, and the Normal Curve

Interpreting stanines is rather straightforward. Generally, stanines of 1, 2, and 3 reflect below-average performance compared to the norm group. These scores include the bottom 22 percent of the students in the norm group. Stanines 4, 5, and 6 reflect average performance; these scores include the central 54 percent of the norm group. Stanines 7, 8, and 9 reflect above-average performance; these scores include 22 percent of the students at the top end of the scale. School personnel generally use stanines to classify below-average, average, and above-average performance. Although most publishers use both a percentile and a stanine to report students' performance on each subtest, these scores do not provide different information. Instead, they provide the same information in different forms.

Interpreting Normal Curve Equivalent Scores (NCE)

You might also encounter a standard score called the *normal curve equivalent score (NCE)*. As its name implies, this score is also based on the normal curve. It has a fixed mean of 50, a fixed standard deviation of 21.06, and a range from 1 to 99. Thus, an NCE score of 29 is equivalent to one standard deviation below the mean (50 − 21.06), and an NCE score of 71 is equivalent to one standard deviation above the mean (50 + 21.06). Additionally, NCE scores are equal interval scores, meaning that the difference between any two adjacent scores on the scale is equal.

Given these properties, NCE scores are easy to interpret. Those scores between 1 and 29 are considered below average; those between 29 and 71 are considered average; and those of 71 and above reflect above-average performance. The proximity of these scores to their mean and the standard deviation anchors can be used to make inferences about the performance level of each score. The NCE scores corresponding to the normal curve standard deviation anchor points are the following:

	Very Low	Below Average	Average Performance	Above Average	Outstanding
Normal Curve Standard Deviations	−2	−1	0	+1	+2
NCE Scores	7.88	28.94	50	71.06	92.12

When using these scores to compare individual students' performances, be cautious not to attribute undue measurement precision to them. Like scale scores and percentiles, these scores should be interpreted as reflecting a probable area of performance rather than a precise point on a scale.

Interpreting Deviation IQ Scores

The deviation IQ score is a standard score used to report students' performance on scholastic aptitude tests. Since it is a standard score, it is interpreted using the properties of the normal distribution. Publishers of aptitude tests use a common mean score of 100; however, some publishers use a standard deviation of 16 points and others use one of 15 points. The technical manual for each publisher's test will report which standard deviation value is used in making score conversions.

When the standard deviation is 16, a deviation IQ score of 84 is located one standard deviation below the mean (100 − 16). Thus, scores of 84 and below are considered to reflect below-average performance compared to the norm group. Scores between 84 and 116 are interpreted as reflecting average-level performance. Scores of 116 and above (100 + 16) are considered above average because they reflect scores that are one standard deviation or more above the mean. Scores of 132 are two standard deviations above the mean and reflect performance at the 98th percentile; these scores reflect outstanding performance compared to the norm group. At the opposite end of the scale, scores of 68 are two standard deviations below the mean and correspond to the 2nd percentile; therefore, they reflect very low performance compared to the norm group. These anchor points for interpreting deviation IQ scores are illustrated in the following diagram on performance level:

	Very Low	Below Average	Average Performance	Above Average	Outstanding
Normal Curve					
Standard Deviations	−2	−1	0	+1	+2
Deviation IQ Scores	68	84	100	116	132

Interpreting Grade Equivalent Scores

Grade equivalent scores enable educators to compare students' variability in each subject within and across grades. Unlike the previously described scores, these scores are not based on the performance of one norm group. Instead, the same test is administered to the norm groups for two or three contiguous grade levels. The mean or median score earned by each group is located and used as the basis for creating all the grade equivalent scores. For example, suppose that the same test is administered to the fourth-, fifth-, and sixth-grade norm groups in September. The grade equivalent scores are matched to scale scores for the test using a chart similar to the one illustrated in Figure 15.9. A hypothetical range of scale scores is used in the example.

Scale scores are ranked vertically from highest to lowest on the left side of the chart. Grade equivalent scores are listed from lowest to highest along the bottom. To begin, three data points are plotted: one at the intersection of the fourth-graders' median score 709 and the grade equivalent score 4.0; a second at the intersection of the fifth-graders' median score 728 and the grade equivalent score 5.0; and the third at the point intersecting the sixth-graders' median score 741 and the grade equivalent score 6.0.

All the remaining grade equivalent scores reported for the test are obtained by interpolation and extrapolation. *Interpolation* is used to match scale scores and grade equivalent scores between the three obtained scores. *Extrapolation* is used to match scale scores and grade equivalent scores outside the measured area (fourth, fifth, and sixth grades).

To match grade equivalent scores and scale scores within the grades tested, a line is drawn to connect the three observed data points. The area between each set of points is divided into nine equal segments. Each higher segment is assigned a grade equivalent score. For example, between 4.0 and 5.0, the first segment is assigned the grade equivalent score 4.1, the second is assigned the grade equivalent score 4.2, and so on to 4.9. The segments between 5.0 and 6.0 are assigned grade equivalent scores 5.1 through 5.9. Each grade equivalent score is matched to a scale score by assigning the scale score directly across from the intersecting point for each grade equivalent score.

FIGURE 15.9

Matching Grade Equivalent Scores to Raw Scores Using Obtained Mean or Median Scores and the Processes of Interpolation and Extrapolation

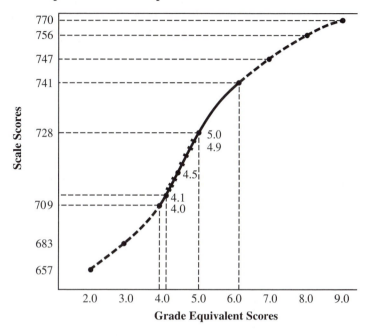

The next step is to use extrapolation to match estimated grade equivalent scores and scale scores for grades outside the three grade levels measured. Points to reflect median scores for grades lower than the fourth and higher than the sixth are estimated because students in these grades did not take the test. In order to match scores outside the measured area, the line connecting the three measured points is extended at both ends. In Figure 15.9, these extensions are illustrated using a broken line. Points on the line that reflect the mean or median score for these outside grades are estimated using the observed distances between the three actual scores. The point on the line that is estimated to locate the median point for each grade is used as the intersecting point on the two scales to equate the grade equivalent scores (2.0, 3.0, 7.0, 8.0, 9.0) to particular scale scores. The interpolation procedure described previously for matching scores between these points is used to complete the matching process.

An important assumption made in creating and interpreting grade equivalent scores is that each grade equivalent score reflects the mean or median score that students in the norm group would earn if they took the test in a given month. For example, a grade equivalent score of 4.0 reflects the mean or median score earned by the norm group in September of the fourth grade. A grade equivalent score of 4.1 reflects the group's expected mean or median score in October; 4.2 reflects the expected mean or median score in November; and so forth to 4.9, which reflects the group's expected score in June. Research has shown that the amount students progress is not equal from month to month within a year, or from year to year. However, the assumption of even progress will undoubtedly be used until a more realistic, yet systematic, method to describe progress is developed.

There are several important characteristics of grade equivalent scores that you should consider before interpreting them. One is that the observed mean or median score for each grade level in September is set at .0, such as 5.0. This implies that 50 percent of the students in the fifth-grade norm group are assigned a grade equivalent score below this level. A second characteristic is that, because norm-referenced tests are designed to yield a wide range of scores within each grade level, a wide range of grade equivalent scores is assigned to students within each grade. Thus, many students within a given grade will earn grade equivalent scores that are many grade levels lower or higher than their actual grade in school. One way to avoid misinterpreting a low or high grade equivalent score is to equate it to the percentile and stanine assigned to the same scale score. This will help remind you that a grade equivalent score that appears extreme might be within the average performance range for the norm group.

Consider some sample scale scores and their corresponding grade equivalent, percentile, and stanine scores for four subtests of the Comprehensive Tests of Basic Skills TerraNova Multiple Assessments (CTB/McGraw-Hill, 1997). These norms are for the eighth grade and for tests administered in the spring of the year. The first column in Table 15.5 lists the subtests. The second column contains a range of selected scale scores for each subtest. The third, fourth, and fifth columns contain the corresponding grade equivalent, percentile, and stanine scores for each of the scale scores. Since the norm group took the test in the spring, the median grade equivalent score should be 8.8 and correspond to a percentile of 50. Note that the third column contains grade equivalent scores of 8.8 and that the corresponding percentiles are 50. This means that 50 percent of the students in the eighth-grade norm group earned grade equivalent scores below 8.8.

Note the wide range of grade equivalent scores for each subtest. The grade equivalent scores for the reading test range from 1.7 to 12.9+. Using the corresponding percentile scores, you can see that a grade equivalent score of 1.7 reflects below-average performance for an eighth-grader because it corresponds to a percentile of 2 and a stanine of 1. However, a grade equivalent score of 3.8, which might be misinterpreted as very low for an eighth-grader, corresponds to a percentile of 16 and stanine of 3, reflecting below-average performance for eighth-graders. A grade equivalent score of 12.9+, which corresponds to a percentile of 84 and a stanine of 7, is just within the above-average range for eighth-grade students. This correspondence is the same between the grade equivalent scores and the percentile and stanine scores for each of the other three tests. Before you interpret a grade equivalent score as reflecting either above- or below-average achievement, check its corresponding percentile and stanine scores to verify your interpretation.

Educators who do not understand these characteristics of grade equivalent scores can make many mistakes in interpreting them. A statement such as, "Our goal is to have all students in Garfield School performing at or above grade level," is usually

TABLE 15.5

Selected Scale Scores and Their Corresponding Grade Equivalent Scores, Percentiles, and Stanines (Eighth Grade, Spring)

Subtest	Scale Score	Grade Equivalent Score	National Percentile	National Stanine
Reading	756	12.9+	98	9
	718	12.9+	84	7
	679	8.8	50	5
	631	3.8	16	3
	575	1.7	2	1
Vocabulary	760	12.9+	98	9
	717	12.9+	84	7
	679	8.7	50	5
	634	4.8	16	3
	585	2.7	2	1
Mathematics	785	12.9+	98	9
Computation	728	12.9+	84	7
	691	8.8	50	5
	636	5.6	16	3
	555	3.1	2	1
Mathematics	783	12.9+	98	9
	731	12.8	84	7
	691	8.8	50	5
	644	5.5	16	3
	583	3.1	2	1

Source: Synthesized from materials in TerraNova Spring Norms Book (Monterey, CA: CTB/McGraw-Hill, 1997), pp. 66–69, 88–89.

made by someone who does not understand grade equivalent scores. Reaching this goal is only possible in schools that have no below-average students enrolled. Such a statement as, "Although John is in the eighth grade, he is only working at a third-grade level," also demonstrates a misunderstanding of the grade equivalent score. No third-graders took the eighth-grade form of the test. In addition, very few, if any, of the skills measured by the eighth-grade test would be found in a third-grade curriculum guide or instruction targeted for third-grade students. John's low grade equivalent score simply reflects low performance compared to that of the eighth-grade norm group.

A third characteristic to be aware of is that grade equivalent scores are more variable in some subjects than others. This feature is important to the score's main purpose, which is detecting the norm group's performance patterns in a subject within and across grades. However, these scores should not be used to compare students' performances across subjects. The variability of the norm group's performance across subjects will lead you to conclude that differences exist when they may not.

To illustrate this point, consider the data in Table 15.6. These are scale scores and corresponding grade equivalent and percentile scores from the sixth-grade norms tables accompanying the TerraNova tests (CTB/McGraw-Hill, 1997). If you used the grade equivalent score to compare a student's performances on the language, reading, and mathematics subtests, you would undoubtedly conclude that the student performed best in reading and language skills (12.9+), and less well in mathematics (10.9 and 11.1). This conclusion would be incorrect, however, because all six of these grade equivalent scores correspond to a percentile of 91.

The differences among these grade equivalent scores simply reflect that the sixth-grade norm group was most variable in language, which resulted in a very wide range of grade equivalent scores. Their performance was less variable in mathematics, which resulted in narrower grade equivalent score ranges in these subjects.

Because parents are not familiar with the characteristics of grade equivalent scores and may misinterpret them, school districts and teachers should not use them to communicate students' achievement. If they are included in students' report forms, the easiest way to interpret them to parents is to equate them to their corresponding percentiles and stanines.

Interpreting Anticipated Achievement Scores

Anticipated achievement scores are quite different from those previously described. These scores are calculated separately for each student tested and indicate the student's expected score for each test. Anticipated scores are compared to the obtained scores to determine whether the student's performance was as expected, atypically high, or atypically low.

The publisher establishes anticipated scores for each student by matching the student to a subset of students from the norm group with the same characteristics. Characteristics typically used to match students are grade, age in months, year and month in school, and scores earned on an aptitude test administered at the same time as the achievement test. Sometimes gender is also used as a matching factor.

TABLE   15.6

Selected Scale Scores and Their Corresponding Grade Equivalent Scores and Percentiles (Sixth Grade, Spring Norms)

Test	Scale Score	Grade Equivalency	National Percentile
Vocabulary	712	12.9+	91
Reading	716	12.9+	91
Language	707	12.9+	91
Mechanics	711	12.9+	91
Computation	710	10.9	91
Mathematics	715	11.1	91

Source: Synthesized from materials in TerraNova Information Systems (Monterey, CA: CTB/McGraw-Hill, 1997), pp. 68–69, 88–89.

Once a matched set of students is selected from the norm group, their achievement test scores are ranked from highest to lowest and their mean score is calculated. The anticipated achievement score reported for each student is the mean score earned by the matched set of students from the norm group. Using a measure of the subgroup's variability, a confidence band is placed around the mean score to set boundaries above and below which scores can be considered atypical. The individual's obtained score is then compared to the matched group's score distribution. If the student's score falls within the confidence band, then the obtained score is considered typical. However, if the student's score falls outside the band, then the score is considered atypical or significantly different than anticipated. A plus sign is often used to indicate atypically high scores, and a minus sign is used to indicate atypically low scores.

Derived scores used to report anticipated achievement are the scale score, percentile, grade equivalent score, and normal curve equivalent score. The publisher clearly labels anticipated scores by placing the letters *AA* before the abbreviations for each type of score. *AAGE* is an anticipated grade equivalent score, *AASS* is an anticipated scale score, *AANCE* is an anticipated normal curve equivalent score, and *AANP* is an anticipated national percentile.

Test Records for Individual Students

Different publishers use different formats to report an individual's test performance. The report forms, sometimes called *profiles,* usually contain the names of the subtests in the battery and a variety of derived scores that match the student's performance to that of the norm group. The derived scores reported often include scale scores (SS), the national percentile (NP), the national stanine (NS), the normal curve equivalent score (NCE), the grade equivalent score (GE), and the anticipated achievement score (e.g., AAGE). The report form includes an anticipated achievement score only if both achievement and aptitude tests were administered at the same time. The form usually includes a chart that illustrates the position of the student's percentile and stanine scores and the percentile bands.

Figure 15.10 contains an individual student's record from the TerraNova Multiple Assessments (CTB/McGraw-Hill, 1997). (See p. 481.) Biographical information appears in the left margin. It identifies the student, teacher, grade, school, city, state, date of testing, particular test form used, and scoring method used to obtain the scale score. In this section, it is important to note that Mary took the test in November of the seventh grade (7.2).

Sections A and B list the subtests and Mary's derived scores. The names of the scores are at the top of each score column. Consider Mary's scores on the reading test. Her scale score is 751. Basically, we are interested in determining whether this scale score represents above-average, average, or below-average achievement compared to students in the seventh-grade norm group. Locate first her national percentile score. Her percentile of 65 reflects average achievement for students in the seventh-grade norm group since it is within one standard deviation of the mean. It also means that her scale score is better than the scale scores earned by 65 percent of the students in the national norm group. All the other derived scores reported for the reading test simply represent alternative ways of expressing the same level of average achievement. Her national stanine score is 6, which is near the mean for stanine scores. Although her grade equivalency score is 8.5, or one grade level above hers (7.2), information from the other derived scores means that this GE score is average compared to students in the seventh-grade norm group.

Notice the column in section B, labeled NP Range. The scores in this column indicate the boundaries of the percentile confidence band for her earned percentile, 65. This means that due to the calculated standard error of measurement for a scale score of 751, Mary's true score can be expected to fall within the percentile range of 55 to 75. Section C includes a graph of the percentile confidence bands. The percentile scores are listed along the top of the chart from 1 to 99. The first band at the top of the graph is the one depicting her reading achievement. You can see her observed percentile of 65 represented as a dot toward the center of the band. The lower boundary of the band extends to percentile 55, and the upper boundary reaches percentile 75. The bottom of the graph lists stanine scores. You can look down the chart from her percentile score of 65 (the dot in the center of the confidence band) to see that it falls within stanine 6. This graph of national percentile bands and stanines simply provides a picture of the percentile and stanine scores that appear in the columns of derived scores in section A.

Now consider Mary's performance on the language test. Her scale score is 742, which corresponds to a national percentile score of 53. This match means that her language score is also average compared to students in the seventh-grade national norm group. Her national stanine score of 5, and grade equivalency score of 7.4 are alternative ways of expressing her average achievement in language.

We can compare her achievement in reading and language using the percentile bands in section C. Notice that the bands are in the same average region and overlap on the scale, indicating that there is no significant difference in her achievement in the two areas.

Now consider her achievement in mathematics. Her scale score is 779, which corresponds to a national percentile score of 82. These scores are located in the above-average performance area. Her stanine score of 7, and grade equivalent score of 10.9, also reflect above-average achievement.

We can use her total score and her area scores in reading, language, and mathematics to summarize Mary's achievement compared to the seventh-grade national norm group. Her total battery scale score is 757, which corresponds to a national percentile of 72. She performed better on the total battery than 72 percent of the students in the national norm group, and her performance is average since it is slightly above the mean (stanine, 6; grade equivalent score, 9.1; and percentile band, 60 to 81. In comparing her percentile bands for reading, language, and mathematics in section C,

---

FIGURE 15.10 ➤

A Sample Student Interpretive Report from the TerraNova Multiple Assessments

Source: TerraNova Information Systems (Monterey: CA: CTB/McGraw-Hill, 1997), p. 9.

TerraNova

MULTIPLE ASSESSMENTS

Individual Profile Report

MARY BROWN

Grade 7

Purpose

This report provides a comprehensive record of this student's achievement. It is a source of information for instructional planning specific to the student and a point of reference for the teacher during a parent-teacher conference. It can contribute to the student's cumulative record.

Simulated Data

Birthdate: 09/11/83
Special Codes:
A B C D E F G H I J K L M N O P Q R S T
4 0 2 2 6   1 2 1
Form/Level: A-17
Test Date: 11/01/96   Scoring: IRT (Pattern)
QM: 07   Norms Date: 1996

Class: Parker
School: Winfield
District: Winfield

City/State: Winfield, CA

A Norm-Referenced Scores

	Scale Score	Grade Equivalent	National Stanine	National Percentile	NP Range	National Percentile
Reading	751	8.5	6	65	55-75	
Language	742	7.4	5	53	43-60	
Mathematics	779	10.9	7	82	74-89	
Total Score*	757	9.1	6	72	60-81	
Science	747	7.6	5	55	45-66	
Social Studies	746	7.8	5	58	48-68	

B

*Total Score consists of Reading, Language, and Mathematics.

C National Percentile / National Stanine (Below Average, Average, Above Average)

D Performance on Objectives

E Objectives Performance Index (OPI)
○ Non-Mastery   ◑ Partial Mastery   ● Mastery

Obj. No.	Objective Titles	Mastery Level	OPI
	Reading		
02	Basic Understanding	●	91
03	Analyze Text	●	92
04	Evaluate & Extend Meaning	◑	65
05	Identify Reading Strategies	◑	70
	Language		
07	Sentence Structure	◑	63
08	Writing Strategies	◑	59
09	Editing Skills	●	78
	Mathematics		
10	Number & Number Relations	◑	71
11	Comp. & Numerical Estimation	●	83
13	Measurement	◑	66
14	Geometry & Spatial Sense	◑	71
15	Data Analysis, Stat. & Probability	◑	61
16	Patterns, Functions, Algebra	◑	77
17	Problem Solving & Reasoning	◑	71
	Science		
19	Science Inquiry	○	47
20	Physical Science	○	49
21	Life Science	○	46
22	Earth & Space Science	◑	52
23	Science & Technology	○	48
24	Personal & Social Persp.	◑	52

Obj. No.	Objective Titles	Mastery Level	OPI
	Social Studies		
26	Geographic Perspectives	●	75
27	Historical & Cultural Perspectives	◑	65
28	Civics & Government Perspectives	◑	72
29	Economic Perspectives	◑	61

F / **G** Objectives Performance Index (OPI)
○ Non-Mastery   ◑ Partial Mastery   ● Mastery

Mastery Level OPI

Copyright © 1997 CTB/McGraw-Hill. All rights reserved.

CTBID392123B821460001-04-00262-000064
V1 IPR P1 final:1/10

CTB McGraw-Hill

Page 1

481

we find that two of her percentile bands overlap in the three areas. We can conclude from this comparison that her achievement in mathematics is superior to her language achievement; however her achievement in mathematics is not superior to her achievement in reading when compared to the seventh-grade national norm group.

Section D provides information about Mary's performance on particular objectives within each of the main test areas. The test areas and objectives are listed in the left column followed by a mastery level symbol and an objectives performance index (OPI) for each objective. Related to the symbols, a completely darkened circle represents mastery of the objective, a one-half darkened circle reflects partial mastery, and a blank circle stands for nonmastery. The OPI score provides the same information as the symbols but in numerical form. The OPI score represents the number of items on each objective, out of 100 hypothetical items, Mary can be expected to answer correctly. Using these indices, you can see that Mary mastered one-half of the reading objectives, one-third of the language objectives, one-fourth of the mathematics objectives, none of the science objectives, and only one-fourth of the social studies objectives. The graph in section G illustrates the confidence band placed around the OPI score.

Once you understand derived scores and how they are interpreted, you can interpret the performance of students on standardized achievement tests, regardless of how the scores are formatted on a student's profile sheet. Sometimes publishers provide verbal explanations of a student's performance on the report. These descriptions are typically brief, and they cannot substitute for teachers' ability to interpret the derived scores for themselves. Section G indicates the student's particular strengths and weaknesses for particular objectives within each subtest. This information can be helpful to both teachers and parents who want to help students progress.

Class Records

The performance of a class is typically summarized for teachers using a class record form. The norm-referenced scores on these forms are the same as those reported on individual students' records. Although norm-referenced achievement tests focus on language and mathematics skills, teachers of all subjects can use the class record to describe the achievement characteristics of their groups. Knowing whether a class is homogeneous or heterogeneous in basic skills can aid both instructional planning and the assessment of any group's progress. Teachers of subjects other than language and mathematics typically use students' scores on the aptitude, total reading, total language, and total math tests to describe a group's achievement characteristics. Teachers of language and mathematics also use students' performances on the subtests to describe the achievement characteristics of their classes.

One good way to describe a group's achievement characteristics is to locate the highest and lowest scores earned by class members and the group's mean score on all tests of interest. If the highest and lowest scores reflect the same general level of performance, then the group can be considered homogeneous. However, if these extreme scores reflect different performance levels, then the class can be described as heterogeneous. The location of the group's average score compared to the two extreme scores provides information about the distribution of the group's scores.

A Sample Class Record Sheet from the TerraNova Multiple Assessments (CTB/McGraw-Hill, 1997) appears in Figure 15.11 (see p. 485). The teacher's name (Jones) and grade level (6) appear in the top left corner of the report. Information about the test form, test date, and scoring procedures is located in the bottom left corner. The far left column, labeled A, contains an alphabetical list of students in a class, each student's date of birth, and the test form. Although only three students are illustrated, an actual form would include all members of a class. The second column from the left identifies the types of scores reported. Notice that the class record includes national percentiles, national stanines, grade equivalents, normal curve equivalents, and scale scores for each student. The remaining columns, located in section C, contain the derived scores for all subtests. The bottom portion of the table contains summary data for the class group.

The information provided for each student on the Class Record Sheet is very similar to that provided on the individual student profile form. The main benefit of the class record is to synthesize information across students to enable teachers to describe the class as a whole. The class summary information located at the bottom of the report in section D is additional information not provided on the individual profiles. Using these summary scores, teachers can describe the group's achievement in each of the subtests, area tests, and on the total test. On the basis of the total scores provided in section D of Figure 15.11, how would you describe the class in the example? The central tendency scores reported for the class (means and medians) indicate that their average or central achievement is comparable to the national norm group's average or central achievement. For example, their median national percentile of 60 is slightly higher than the norm group's center of 50, and their average stanine of 6 is also slightly higher than the norm group's average of 5.

■ School Records

Another type of form teachers find useful is the Objectives Performance Summary. This form, illustrated in Figure 15.12 (see p. 487), is especially helpful for curriculum planning and evaluation, since it describes the percent of students mastering each objective within subtests for the total school, national norm group, and for separate classes within each grade level. The far left column contains descriptive information about the school, grade level and test form, test date, and scoring plan. The second column, section A, contains instructions for interpreting the Objectives Performance Index, and section B is used to name the subtests and the objectives within each that are summarized. Section C reports the percent of students in the school, national norm group, and individual classes in the school who mastered each objective. The third column in section C, labeled *Difference,* indicates whether the students in the school performed better or worse than the national norm group. In the example, slightly fewer students in the school mastered the reading objectives; however, they appear to have performed better in language and mathematics than students in the national norm group.

Comparing the students' achievement for the three teachers reported, it appears that the students in Ottenwalter's and Smith's classes took turns being ranked first in the reading and language objectives, while Polk's class trailed each time. In the mathematics objectives, Smith's class was ranked first for both objectives, Polk's class was ranked second, and Ottenwalter's class was ranked third. Care must be taken in comparing classes using such data, since several factors can account for the observed, and often small, class differences, including the manner in which students are assigned to teachers by achievement levels and the actual significance of the differences observed.

Section D reports the Average Objectives Performance Index for the school, national norm group and individual classes within the school. Using these symbols, you can see that the students in Taft school are comparable to students in the national norm group, and students across classes within the school are also comparable.

The individual and class profile forms illustrated in this chapter represent only a sample of those available from commercial test publishers. Regardless of the test publisher or the particular format of the report, the tables and graphs within a report simply indicate whether a student or class group is above average, average, or below average compared to a representative sample of students at the same grade level. Before administering a standardized test to your students, you should study the examiner's manual carefully to ensure that you are following standard procedures in administering the test. Before interpreting student and class profiles for yourself, your colleagues, or parents, you should review the teacher's and administrator's manuals and the norms book to refresh your memory on the derivation and interpretation of the derived scores used with standardized tests.

■ Using Standardized Test Results for Personal Value-Added Assessment in Your Classroom

In business, the idea of value-added assessment means comparing the value of raw materials going into the manufacturing process with the value of the product produced. The goal is to have a product worth more at the end of the process than at the beginning of it. Within education, many support a similar idea of comparing students' achievement gains from one grade level to the next. True value-added assessment in education requires standardized, valid, and reliable tests that are linked and administered across contiguous grades. It also requires very sophisticated multivariate statistical methods. As classroom teachers, we can create estimated value-added indices of our students' achievement growth while in our classes. We can estimate our effectiveness as teachers by determining the average of all student growth indices in our

FIGURE 15.11 ▶

A Sample Class Record Sheet from the TerraNova Multiple Assessments

Source: TerraNova Information Systems (Monterey, CA: CTB/McGraw-Hill, 1997), p. 15.

TerraNova

MULTIPLE ASSESSMENTS

Class Record Sheet

Class: JONES

Grade 6

Title one
Title two

Purpose

This report provides a permanent record of test results for students in a class, or some other specified group. The summary data may be used to evaluate individual and group achievement compared to the nation, determine overall performance, and identify areas of strength and need.

| Simulated Data |

No. of Students: 26

Form/Level: A-16
Test Date: 04/01/97   Scoring: IRT (Pattern)
QM: 29   Norms Date: 1996

Class: Jones
School: Winfield
District: Green Valley

City/State: Winfield, CA

CTB McGraw-Hill

Page 1

Students [A]   Scores [B]   [C]

Students	Scores	Reading	Lang.	Math	Total Score*	Science*	Social Studies
Abby, Karen Birthdate: 2/26/86 Special Codes: ABCDEFGHIJKLMNOPQRST. ...12222221. Form: A Level: 16	NP NS GE NCE SS	68 6 9.1 60 758	36 4 4.7 42 723	67 6 8.4 60 758	59 5 7.7 55 748	71 6 9.6 62 763	41 5 5.9 45 734
Arnold, Stephen A Birthdate: 6/21/86 Special Codes: ABCDEFGHIJKLMNOPQRST. 12122222. Form: A Level: 16	NP NS GE NCE SS	57 5 7.8 52 743	41 5 5.2 45 728	91 8 12.+ 82 797	45 5 6.4 47 735	56 5 7.8 54 749	33 4 5.6 39 721
Brown, Susan J Birthdate: 8/22/86 Special Codes: ABCDEFGHIJKLMNOPQRST. 12222221. Form: A Level: 16	NP NS GE NCE SS	55 5 7.7 53 741	18 3 3.3 31 699	70 6 9.7 61 765	49 5 7.1 49 736	42 5 5.9 46 734	37 5 5.6 43 729
Chong, Louisa A Birthdate: 8/07/86 Special Codes: ABCDEFGHIJKLMNOPQRST. 22222222. Form: A Level: 16	NP NS GE NCE SS	89 7 11.7 77 786	71 6 9.5 60 758	75 6 9.6 64 766	79 7 10.1 67 767	56 5 7.4 53 749	62 6 8.4 56 756
Number of Students		26	26	23	23	25	26

Class Summary [D]

FormLevel: A-16

		Reading	Lang.	Math	Total Score	Science	Social Studies
Group (Summary) Scores	MDNP MNS GME MNCE MSS	60.0 6.0 8.8 55.0 750	37.2 4.5 5.1 43.8 724	68.2 6.8 8.8 60.4 759	52.0 5.3 7.3 51.8 742	60.3 6.0 8.1 55.1 752	49.2 5.2 7.2 49.8 743
Number of Students		26	26	23	23	25	26

Group (Summary) Scores

MDNP: MEDIAN NATIONAL PERCENTILE
MNS: MEAN NATIONAL STANINE
GME: GRADE MEAN EQUIVALENT
MNCE: MEAN NORMAL CURVE EQUIVALENT
MSS: MEAN SCALE SCORE

Individual Scores [E]

NP: NATIONAL PERCENTILE
NS: NATIONAL STANINE
GE: GRADE EQUIVALENT
NCE: NORMAL CURVE EQUIVALENT
SS: SCALE SCORE

* TOTAL SCORE consists of Reading, Language, and Mathematics.

CTBID:9212388214600001-04-00052-000054
W1 CRS P1 final:12/20

classroom. While we should interpret these indices cautiously, they can provide a general notion about our effectiveness.

Many school districts will provide you with the standardized test scale scores for students in your classes for the current year and for previous years. When you can obtain this information from district records, simply request the data you wish to use in making your own personal analysis. When districts cannot not provide the information you wish, you can obtain it yourself from the standardized test profile reports in your students' cumulative records. Simply investigate within your own district to determine the most efficient method of obtaining your students' test scores.

Value-Added Assessment of Your Students' Achievement

Evaluating Students' Progress from Grade to Grade   You can use the composite scale scores for subject area tests and the total test to analyze the progress of your students over the school year from fall to spring. For this analysis, you should first determine the amount of progress made from one year to the next by students in the comparable norm groups and then use this value as a standard for analyzing the growth of students in your class.

There are two factors that influence the amount of scale score gain we might expect for students from one grade to the next. As we saw previously, students progress differentially from grade to grade, with greater gains in scale scores expected during the early school years. Second, there is typically a wider range of scale scores between −2SD and the mean than there is between the mean and +2SD. (Do not confuse this scale score characteristic with the differential learning progress that occurs between above- and below-average students in your class.) These two characteristics of scale scores mean that we cannot expect to see the same gains in scale scores from one year to the next for younger and older students. We also cannot expect to see the same gains for students who are above and below the mean scale score. Since we know about these features of scale scores, it would be illogical to use one value as the amount of gain you anticipate for all students in a heterogeneous class or for students in lower and upper elementary grades.

The chart in Table 15.7 was constructed from the fourth- and fifth-grade spring norms for the total reading test. Scale scores for both grades were located in the norms tables that corresponded to the normal curve anchor points. Notice that students in the norm group whose scores were two standard deviations below the mean in total reading at the end of the fourth grade (SS = 522) gained 20 scale score points by the end of the fifth grade (SS = 542). Students who were at the mean gained 13 scale score points during the fifth grade, and students who were one standard deviation above the

FIGURE 15.12 ➤

A Sample Objectives Performance Summary from the TerraNova Multiple Assessments

Source: TerraNova Information Systems (Monterey, CA: CTB/McGraw-Hill, 1997).

TerraNova

CTBS COMPLETE BATTERY

Objectives Performance Summary

School: TAFT

Grade 4

Purpose

This report provides an analysis of group objectives mastery using the percent of students mastering each objective and average Objectives Performance Indexes (OPI) for this group. The information may be used to analyze curriculum strengths and areas of need.

Simulated Data

No. of Students: 65

Form/Level: A-14

Test Date: 04/24/97 Scoring: IRT (Pattern)
QM: 31 Norms Date: 1996

District: Green Valley

City/State: Winfield, CA

CTB / McGraw-Hill

Page 1

A Objectives Performance by School/Class

Objectives Performance Index (OPI)
OPI is the estimated number of items correct out of 100

- ● Mastery (Range: 75 – 100 correct)
- ◐ Partial Mastery (Range: 50 – 74 correct)
- ○ Non-Mastery (Range: 0 – 49 correct)

** National Reference Group Grade 4.8

C Percent of Students Mastering Each Objective   **D Average Objectives Performance Index (OPI)**

Objective	C: Total School	National **	Difference	CLASS OTTENWALTER	POLK	SMITH	D: Total School	National **	Difference	CLASS OTTENWALTER	POLK	SMITH
Reading												
02 Basic Understanding	43	45	-2	42	36	48	71	70	+01	69	72	72
03 Analyze Text	43	47	-4	38	36	52	66	67	-01	45	65	63
04 Evaluate & Extend Meaning	28	30	-2	38	21	22	61	63	-02	60	64	59
05 Identify Reading Strategies	18	16	+2	29	7	15	48	44	+04	54	42	45
Language												
07 Sentence Structure	62	47	+15	63	57	63	76	67	+09	78	75	75
08 Writing Strategies	57	39	+18	58	57	56	73	63	+10	75	71	71
09 Editing Skills	45	32	+13	50	36	44	68	61	+07	71	69	68
Mathematics												
10 Number & Number Relations	58	40	+18	46	64	67	74	67	+07	71	77	76
11 Computation and Numerical Estimation	35	19	+16	21	29	52	62	53	+09	56	58	71
12 Operation Concepts	77	55										
13 Measurement	51	23										
14 Geometry & Spatial Sense	98	95										
15 Data Analysis, Statistics, Probability	85	65										
16 Patterns, Functions, Algebra	95	87										
17 Problem Solving & Reasoning	85	62										
Number of Students:	65											

TerraNova

CTBS COMPLETE BATTERY

Objectives Performance Summary

School: TAFT

Grade 4

Purpose

This page gives administration information to interpret this report. This page is a narrative description of the data in the other side.

Simulated Data

No. of Students: 65

Form/Level: A-14

Test Date: 04/24/97 Scoring: IRT (Pattern)
QM: 31 Norms Date: 1996

District: Green Valley

City/State: Winfield, CA

CTB / McGraw-Hill

Page 2

E General Interpretation

The Objectives Performance Summary shows how your students performed on each educational objective compared to other groups. Usually several different objectives are measured in one content area. The TerraNova objectives represent groups of related skills, usually comprising several specific skills or instructional goals. Each reported TerraNova objective is measured by four or more items. Information from these items and the students' overall performance is used to determine a mastery score. A score indicating mastery does not necessarily mean that all related skills have been mastered. This score is a general indication of strength or potential need for that objective.

The Mastery categories are defined by the Objectives Performance Index (OPI). The OPI is an estimate of the number of items that a student could be expected to answer correctly if there had been 100 such items for that objective. These estimates have been averaged for the group. An OPI of 75 and above indicates Mastery. An OPI from 50 to 74 indicates Partial Mastery, and an OPI below 50 indicates Non-Mastery. Further explanation of the OPI can be found in the TerraNova Technical Bulletins.

F Observations

The report is organized with the content areas and corresponding objectives listed down the left side. The number preceding the objective title identifies the objective, which is described in the *Teacher's Guide to TerraNova*. The data are in two parts, both referring to objectives mastery ("Percent of Students Mastering Each Objective" and "Average Objectives Performance Index.")

The Percent of Students Mastering Each Objective includes data for three groups. The first column on the left shows the percent of students mastering each objective for your Total School. In the second column, the percent mastering each objective for the nation is given. The difference between the two is shown in the Difference column. For example, in Reading, Objective 02 Basic Understanding, 43% of your students demonstrated mastery of that objective compared to 45% nationally, for a difference of –2%, as shown in the Difference column. Data are shown for each class within TAFT School for purposes of comparison.

The data on the right show the average OPI number and corresponding mastery category reached for the same three groups (Total School, Nation and Classes). The difference between the average OPI for your students (Total School) and students nationally is shown in the Difference column. For example, in Reading, Objective 02 Basic Understanding, your students' average OPI score is 71 compared to an average OPI of 70 for students nationally. The difference is +1. Comparisons are also shown for each class within TAFT School.

The number of students in each group is displayed in the last row of information.

TABLE 15.7

Value-Added Assessment: Typical Class Gains at the Normal Curve Anchor Points

Reading Composite Scores	Normal Curve Anchors				
	-2SD	-1SD	Mean	+1SD	+2SD
Fifth-Grade Scale Scores	542	584	651	708	737
Fourth-Grade Scale Scores	522	560	638	698	722
Gains Spring Fourth Grade to Spring Fifth Grade	20	24	13	10	15

Source: TerraNova Information Systems (Monterey, CA: CTB/McGraw-Hill, 1997).

mean at the end of the fourth grade gained 10 scale score points during the fifth grade. These typical scale score gains in reading for norm group fifth-graders will help you determine whether students in your class are generally keeping pace, falling behind, or surpassing the gains of students in the norm group.

Value-Added Assessment of Individual Students

With the current press for teacher accountability, you may well wonder whether the achievement gains of students you teach are outpacing, keeping up, or lagging behind the growth of students in the national norm group at the same achievement levels as your students. As you have seen, students at various achievement levels have different achievement growth expectations as measured by scale scores. Assessing each student's achievement growth is best accomplished by using the student's scale score in a given subject from a prior grade as the anchor point. The standard for growth is established as the growth of the norm group from one grade to the next at a particular scale score. The student's actual growth is a comparison of the norm group's and the individual student's achievement growth accounting for the test's standard error of measurement in the process. In conducting this type of assessment, be sure that the scores you compare are compatible (e.g., the same company's test both years and same norming time of the year or spring to spring and fall to fall).

Locate Each Student's Expected Score   The first step in the value-added assessment procedure is to identify an expected scale score for each student in your class. The *expected scale score* is defined as the scale score your student would obtain this year if his or her achievement growth was equal to that of norm group students who were at the same achievement level last year.

For each student in your class, you can identify the expected scale score for the current year, or the scale score earned by the norm group at the same achievement level last year, using the following procedure:

1. Using your student's previous year's scale score, locate the national percentile score associated with it in the test publisher's norms tables for the previous grade level. You can locate your students' previous year's scale scores and percentiles in their permanent records.
2. Locate the national percentile score equivalent to your student's previous scale score in the current year's norms tables.
3. Identify the observed scale score for the norm group by locating the scale score associated with the same national percentile score in the current year's norms tables. The norm group's observed score is your student's expected score.

Consider the three sample fifth-grade students' expected scores illustrated in Figure 15.13. The students' names are listed in the far left column, and Column A contains the scale scores earned by these fifth-grade students in the spring of their fourth-grade year. Column B contains the national percentile scores equivalent to their observed scale scores. For example, Joey's scale score of 585 is equivalent to a national percentile score of 16. Column C contains the students' expected scale scores for the fifth grade. The teacher obtained these scores by linking the fourth-grade national percentile scores to the same fifth-grade percentile scores. This ensures that the scale scores selected as the expected ones represent the same achievement level or group standing across the two years. For Joey, who earned a percentile score of 16, the scale score equivalent to a percentile score of 16 in the fifth grade is 602. If Joey achieves as well as students in the norm group at the same achievement level, or the 16th percentile in the fifth grade, he will achieve a fifth-grade scale score of 602.

FIGURE 15.13

Students' Expected Scale Score in the Spring of Fifth-Grade

EXPECTED GROWTH

Students	A Observed Scale Scores, 4th Grade	B Equivalent 4th Grade National Percentile Scores for Observed Scale Scores	C Scale Scores Equal to Same National Percentile, 5th Grade
Joey	585	16	602
Megan	631	60	651
John	648	80	670

Source: Synthesized from materials in TerraNova Spring Norms Book (Monterey, CA: CTB/McGraw-Hill, 1997), pp. 80–83.

Locate the Standard for Student Growth   The second step in the process is to identify a standard or criterion for norm group growth that you can use to evaluate the observed growth of your own students. One convenient standard is the scale score band that surrounds the expected scale score for any given student. The scale score band is similar to the percentile band that we studied in a previous section, and it is defined as the expected scale score plus and minus one standard error of measurement (SEM). The following list contains the steps that you can use to identify the scale score band for each student:

1. Locate the expected scale score for individual students in your classes (Column C in Figure 15.13).
2. Locate the standard error of measurement for the expected scale score in the current year's norms tables.
3. Create the expected scale score band by adding and subtracting 1 SEM to the expected scale score.

The scale score bands for the three sample students are illustrated in Figure 15.14. Checking in the fifth-grade spring norm tables, the SEM for the expected scale score of 602 is 12 scale score points. The value 12 added to and subtracted from the observed score creates a band from 590 to 614. This band of scale scores defines the area where norm group students' and Joey's scale scores are likely to fall. In other words, this is the expected achievement growth region. If a student's score falls outside the band, it can be considered meaningfully higher or lower achievement growth than that observed for the norm group. If the student's scale score falls within the band, it is considered keeping pace with the norm group or growth as expected. Remember, the band created using the standard error of measurement indicates an area where students' true scores are likely to fall. If your student's observed score falls above or below the scale score band, then the achievement gain is considered to be meaningfully higher or lower than that of the norm group.

Evaluating the Achievement Growth of Individual Students   With the standards established using the standard error of measurement and the expected scale score, you are ready to evaluate the growth of individual students compared to the norm group.

Figure 15.15 contains expected scale score bands for each of the three students in the sample. The scale scores are named along the bottom of the figure and each student's expected scale score band is plotted beside the name. Notice that John's observed scale score of 663, although lower than his expected score of 670, falls within the expected scale score range for the norm group. This indicates that his achievement growth is comparable to the growth of students in the norm group, and he can be classified as keeping pace. Comparing Megan's observed scale score with her expected scale score band, you can see that she, too, is keeping pace with the norm group. Joey's growth, however, is meaningfully better than that anticipated for the norm group, since his score is higher than the highest score in the expected scale score band. His meaningful growth undoubtedly reflects his diligence and hard work as well as that of his teacher.

FIGURE 15.14

Expected Scale Score Bands Based on the Expected Scale Score and Related Standard Error of Measurement

Student	A Observed Scale Scores 5th Grade	B Expected Scale Scores 5th Grade	C SEM for Expected Scale Scores 5th Grade	D Expected Scale Score Bands 5th Grade
Joey	618	602	12	590–614
Megan	652	651	10	641–661
John	663	670	10	660–680

Source: Synthesized from materials in TerraNova Spring Norms Book (Monterey, CA: CTB/McGraw-Hill, 1997), pp. 44, 82–83.

FIGURE 15.15

Using Scale Score Expected Growth Bands to Evaluate the Achievement Growth of Individual Students

Source: Synthesized from materials in TerraNova Spring Norms Book (Monterey, CA: CTB/McGraw-Hill, 1997), pp. 44, 82–83.

Value-Added Assessment of Teacher Effectiveness

You can use information about your students' expected and observed achievement growth to create a measure of the quality of your instruction. The teacher effectiveness index, or the Instructional Quality Index, reflects the degree to which your collective students are keeping pace with those in the national norm group at the same achievement levels. Before using this index to evaluate your instruction, there are a few cautions to keep in mind. These value-added instructional quality indices are a general reflection of trends, and should not be the only information used to evaluate the quality of your instruction. Likewise, your index for only one year can be attributed to the characteristics of a particular class. Your indices aggregated across several years, however, begin to provide a pattern of the effectiveness of your instruction. You should also be cautious that factors such as congruence between the skills measured by the standardized test, your local curriculum, and your instruction will influence your Instructional Quality Index. Finally, keep in mind that your personal value-added study is much less sophisticated than the one your school district may use as a variable in your instructional evaluation. School districts' value-added assessment of teacher effectiveness uses many factors and sophisticated multivariate statistical methods to derive their quality indices. The ones recommended here, however, should point you in the same general direction as the ones used at the district level.

The Instructional Quality Index is a measure of a teacher's effectiveness that is based on the collective achievement growth of students assigned to his or her classes. These indices range from –1.00 to 1.00, with positive values reflecting higher performance. Rules of thumb for interpreting these indices are the following:

–1.00 ◄————————————— .00 ————————————► 1.00

| A teacher whose students' collective achievement gains are lower than that of the national norm group | A teacher whose students' collective achievement gains are similar to that of the national norm group | A teacher whose students' collective achievement gains are higher than that of the national norm group |

Calculating the Instructional Quality Index   In calculating this index for a teacher, information about the standard error of measurement for each student's expected scale score is used, and points are assigned that signal whether the gains and losses observed across students in a teacher's class are meaningful compared to the norm group's gains. The Teacher Effectiveness Index is obtained in the following manner:

1. Assign 1.00 for each student's gains that are meaningfully better than expected (e.g., greater than the upper boundary of the ±1SEM scale score band).
2. Assign .00 for each student's gains that are comparable to that of the norm group (within the scale score band).
3. Assign –1.00 for each student's gains that are meaningfully less than the norm group's gains (lower than the lowest score in the scale score band).
4. Sum the assigned scores.
5. Divide by the number of students in the group.

The highest Teacher Effectiveness Index, 1.00, is the score earned if all students in the class obtain gains greater than the upper boundary of the scale score (SS) band. The lowest score possible, −1.00, is the score that would result if all students in the class earn scale scores lower than the lowest value in the expected scale score band.

To illustrate the calculation of the Instructional Quality Index, reconsider the student scale scores illustrated in Figure 15.15. For these three students, the teacher would earn the following quality points:

Student	Quality Points	Rationale
Joey	1.00	His score of 618 is above the ±1SEM SS band
Megan	.00	Her score of 652 is within the ±1SEM SS band
John	.00	His score of 652 is within the ±1SEM SS band

To obtain the Instructional Quality Index, simply sum the quality points and divide by the number of students in the class. For our small sample, the index is:

$$TQI = 1/3 = .33$$

Assessing Instructional Quality across Achievement Levels of Students   Research indicates that some teachers are more effective in teaching students who are at one or another achievement level. You can use this value-added assessment procedure to judge your effectiveness with your students across the achievement spectrum. Examine the data for one teacher shown in Figure 15.16. The first column identifies the achievement levels of students in three groups: below average as 1 standard deviation

FIGURE 15.16

Instructional Quality Indices for One Teacher across Students' Achievement Levels

INSTRUCTIONAL QUALITY INDICES

Student Achievement Level	Reading Composite	Language Composite	Math Composite	Science	Social Studies
Below Average −2 to −1 SD	.33	.40	.00	.10	.20
Average Mean ±1 SD	.25	.28	−.12	.00	.18
Above Average ≤ 1SD	.00	−.05	−.40	−.20	−.10

*For the Instructional Quality Index, values greater than .00 reflect collective student growth greater than that of students in the norm group who earned the same scale score the previous year. Values at .00 reflect collective growth comparable to the norm group's. Values less than .00 reflect growth less than the norm group's.

below the mean and lower, average as within 1 standard deviation of the mean, and above average as scores at and above 1 standard deviation above the mean.

The remainder of the columns identify the specific test composite scores used in the analysis. The intersecting cells contain the Instructional Quality Indices calculated for the teacher using only the students in the class whose performance falls in the named achievement level. For example, the Instructional Quality Index of .33 beneath the Reading Composite title is based only on the students in the class who are classified as below average. Suppose these indices in Figure 15.16 are ones that you have derived for yourself. Do you believe that you are more or less effective with any achievement level group in your class? Do you believe that you are more effective in teaching some areas of the curriculum than others? Is your instruction, based on collective student growth, outstanding, keeping up, or lagging behind other teachers?

If you were the teacher in the example shown in Figure 15.16, unfortunately, you appear to be less effective with above-average students across all the disciplines that you teach. Your above-average students' growth lags behind that of students in the national norm group at their same level in all areas besides reading. Related to content areas, you appear to have been less effective this year in teaching mathematics across the three achievement group levels. Related to your general effectiveness, you appear to be best in reading, language and social studies for below-average and average-level achievers.

Assessing Instructional Quality across Years Using the student growth data for only one year provides a snapshot of your effectiveness rather than quality patterns or trends. You can repeat the process described for obtaining Instructional Quality Indices for your classes for multiple years. Studying your indices across years helps you discover your own status and growth as a teacher. Suppose that you teach all students of average-level achievement and you have summarized your indices for three years across several subject areas. Imagine that the data presented in Figure 15.17 reflects your indices and trends. Is your instruction better in some disciplines than others? Are you improving as you go along?

FIGURE 15.17

Instructional Quality Indices for One Teacher across Subjects and Years

INSTRUCTIONAL QUALITY INDICES

Year	Reading Composite	Language Composite	Math Composite	Science	Social Studies
1	.33	.18	.00	.10	.20
2	.35	.25	−.15	.08	.25
3	.38	.40	−.22	.00	.28

Note: For the Instructional Quality Index, values greater than .00 reflect collective growth greater than that of students in the norm group who earned the same scale scores the previous year. Values at .00 reflect growth equal to the norm group's. Values less than .00 reflect growth less than the norm group's.

If you were the teacher in the example, it appears that your students' growth is quite good in reading, math, and social studies, and that you have a positive student achievement growth trend in these areas. In contrast, your students do not achieve as well in math and science, and your instruction does not appear to be improving in either area.

In summary, if there is a pattern of being ahead of, keeping pace with, or falling behind norm group growth, you as a teacher should question your instruction related to the standardized test content. When a potential problem appears, such as many students' indices below the norm group's indices, you should look for potential causes. Areas you might address include the match between the curriculum assessed and that prescribed at your grade level, the timing of the test relative to the scheduling of instruction for skills assessed using the test, whether the test was administered as prescribed, and whether your instructional skills lag behind those of teachers across the country.

■ Summary

Due to the increasing emphasis on data-based decision making in schools, school personnel must be able to interpret and use information from standardized achievement and scholastic aptitude tests. Achievement tests, which may be either criterion referenced or norm referenced, measure students' knowledge and skills in school subjects. Scholastic aptitude tests measure students' general mental-processing skills.

School districts that intend to use test results for instructional planning, instructional evaluation, or grading students' progress generally select a criterion-referenced test that focuses on the school's curriculum. Districts that want to use test results to compare the performance of individuals or groups to a nationwide sample of students use norm-referenced achievement tests. Those that want to determine which students will probably succeed in a particular program use scholastic aptitude tests to predict students' achievement.

Scoring methods and scores used to report students' performance on the three types of tests differ. Performance on criterion-referenced tests is generally reported as nonmastery, partial knowledge, and mastery. These levels can be based either on the number and percentage of items students answer correctly for each objective or on scores derived using a variety of factors besides the number of correct items. Professional judgment and statistical tests are used to set the cut-off scores for each of the three levels. Performance on norm-referenced tests is reported using derived scores that enable comparisons among students. These scores include scale scores, percentiles, percentile bands, stanines, normal curve equivalent scores, and grade equivalent scores. An anticipated achievement score is also used when both aptitude and achievement tests are administered. Performance on aptitude tests is reported using a deviation IQ and percentile score. Table 15.8 summarizes the characteristics and interpretation of these scores.

Teachers of all subject areas use aptitude scores and total scores from the achievement tests to describe the characteristics of their assigned classes. Teachers of

---

TABLE 15.8

Scores Commonly Used to Report Students' Performances on Norm-Referenced Tests

Scores	Characteristics	Interpretation
Scale Scores	These scores range from 0 to 999 on an arbitrarily set common scale used to measure students' variability in a subject and their progress across grades in a subject. Mean scale scores and standard deviations vary for each subtest and grade level. These measures must be obtained from the test's technical manual for each grade and subject.	Scores 1 standard deviation below the mean and lower reflect below-average performance. Scores within 1 standard deviation from the mean reflect average performance. Scores 1 standard deviation above the mean and higher reflect above-average performance. Students' progress in one subject should be compared using scale scores appropriate to each student's achievement level because students at different levels progress at different rates.
Percentiles	Range from 1 to 99 Midpoint 50 $\overline{X} + 1SD = 84$ $\overline{X} - 1SD = 16$ There are unequal intervals between percentiles.	Percentiles reflect the percentage of students in the norm group surpassed at each raw score in the distribution.
Percentile Bands	These are confidence bands placed around each percentile using the test's standard error of measurement. The width of percentile bands varies across the percentile scale. Those in the center of the distribution are wider than those toward the ends.	A student's score on retesting could fall anywhere within the band. Overlapping bands reflect no significant differences between observed percentile scores.
Stanines	Range from 1 to 9 Midpoint is 5 $\overline{X} + 1SD = 7$ $\overline{X} - 1SD = 3$ Stanines are band scores and encompass several scale scores and percentiles. Stanines in the center of the distribution encompass more percentiles than those toward the ends.	Stanines 1, 2, and 3 reflect below-average performance. Stanines 4, 5, and 6 reflect average performance. Stanines 7, 8, and 9 reflect above-average performance.
Normal Curve Equivalents	Range from 1 to 99 $\overline{X} = 50$ $SD = 21.06$ $\overline{X} + 1SD = 71.06$ $\overline{X} - 1SD = 28.94$	Scores of 28.94 and lower reflect below-average performance. Scores between 29 and 71 reflect average performance. Scores of 71.06 and higher reflect above-average performance.

Scores	Characteristics	Interpretation
Deviation IQ Scores	$\overline{X} = 100$ $SD = 15$ or 16 $\overline{X} + 1SD = 115, 116$ $\overline{X} - 1SD = 85, 84$ These scores are used to report performance on scholastic aptitude tests.	Scores of 85, 84 and lower reflect below-average performance. Scores between 85, 86, and 114, 115 reflect average performance. Scores of 115, 116 and higher reflect above-average performance.
Grade Equivalent Scores	These are scores based on the median score earned by the norm group in two or three consecutive grades. These scores are decimal numbers; the first digit reflects a grade and the second reflects a month within a grade. All scores are derived from the two or three median scores using the processes of interpolation and extrapolation. Grade equivalent scores reflect the estimated median score earned by a group in a given grade and month.	A wide range of grade equivalent scores are assigned to students in each grade level. Match grade equivalent scores to their corresponding percentiles and stanines to determine whether they reflect below-average, average, or above-average performance for students in a particular grade. Do not use these scores to compare one student's performance across subtests. Do not use these scores to describe students' performance to parents and the community.
Anticipated Achievement Scores	These scores are the mean scores earned by a subset of students in the norm group who are matched to each student using aptitude scores and other characteristics. Confidence intervals are placed around these mean scores to differentiate between typical and atypically high or low observed scores.	Although anticipated and observed achievement scores are often different, the differences are considered insignificant unless a plus or minus sign is used to reflect atypically high or low performance.

language and mathematics use subtest scores and scores on each objective measured by the subtests to aid instructional planning.

It is becoming increasingly popular for school districts to conduct value-added assessments or studies of students' achievement growth on standardized tests from year to year. Although value-added assessments conducted by districts are very sophisticated statistically, teachers can conduct their own personal value-added assessments for the students in their classes. These personal assessments should provide comparable growth indicators to those calculated by the district. Using expected scale score bands, an individual student's achievement growth is judged as better than expected, as expected, and lower than expected. Teachers can calculate an Instructional Quality Index for their own work by summing students' quality points within a class and dividing the sum by the number of students in the class.

■ P R A C T I C E   E X E R C I S E S

I. Matching Test Types and Purposes
Three types of tests are listed in Column B. Indicate the type of test you would use to complete the tasks described in items 1 through 8 of Column A:

Column A

_____ **1.** Compare the performance of students in your school district to the performance of a nationwide sample of students in basic skills.

_____ **2.** Plan lessons covering the punctuation of declarative, interrogative, exclamatory, and imperative sentences.

_____ **3.** Predict which students are likely to be most successful in an advanced mathematics program.

_____ **4.** Compare a student's performance across reading, language, and mathematics skills.

_____ **5.** Analyze the variability of students' performance in mathematics within and across grades.

_____ **6.** Diagnose problems a student or class has in performing district-prescribed instructional goals.

_____ **7.** Predict the students most likely to succeed in a special mathematics program for gifted students.

_____ **8.** Determine students' mastery of selected language usage skills.

Column B

a. Criterion-referenced achievement test
b. Norm-referenced achievement test
c. Scholastic aptitude test

II. Converting Scale Scores to Percentiles
Items A through E list the steps you would follow to convert scale scores to percentiles. Use the frequency distribution in Table 15.9 to make these conversions. Check your work using Table 15.11F in the Feedback section.

   A. Beginning at the bottom of the table, calculate the cumulative frequency of scale scores below each scale score and record this number in Column 3.
   B. Divide the observed frequency for each scale score by 2 and record this number in Column 4.
   C. Sum the frequency below and one-half the frequency within (Columns 3 and 4) for each score and record the total in Column 5.
   D. Divide the total in Column 5 by the total number of students in the group to obtain the proportion of students whose scores fall below the midpoint for each scale score.
   E. Multiply these proportions by 100 to obtain the percentile for each scale score and record this value in Column 6.

TABLE 15.9

Worksheet for Converting Scale Scores to Percentiles

(1) Scale Scores	(2) Frequency	(3) Cumulative Frequency below	(4) 1/2 Frequency within	(5) Proportion	(6) Percentile
640	1				
639	1				
638	2				
637	2				
636	3				
635	3				
634	2				
633	2				
632	2				
631	1				
630	1				

III. **Interpreting Percentile Scores**

Judge whether each of the following statements about the characteristics of percentile scores and their interpretation is true.

A. There are equal intervals between percentile scores.

B. Percentiles reflect the percentage of items answered correctly.

C. Percentiles correspond to the standard normal distribution of scores.

D. Percentiles are created using the processes of interpolation and extrapolation.

E. There is an equal number of percentile points between the mean and one standard deviation above the mean and between one and two standard deviations above the mean.

F. There are larger intervals between the percentiles in the center of the distribution than between those toward the ends of the scale.

G. Percentiles range from 0 to 100.

H. Relatively small differences between percentiles toward the center of the scale are not meaningful.

I. Percentiles reflect the percentage of students surpassed at the midpoint for each scale score.

J. One standard deviation above the mean is equivalent to the 60th percentile.

K. Each increase of one scale score point can result in an increase of several percentile points.

IV. **Calculating and Plotting Percentile Bands**

Use the scale score-to-percentile conversions made in Table 15.9 to complete this exercise. Table 15.10 contains three scale scores and their corresponding percentiles from Table 15.9. Follow the directions in items A through C to plot the percentile bands for these three scores. Check your work using Table 15.12F in the Feedback section.

A. Using a standard error of measurement (SEM) of 2, calculate the scale score corresponding to +1 SEM and −1 SEM for each obtained score.

TABLE 15.10

Worksheet for Calculating and Plotting Percentile Bands

SEM = 2

	−1 SEM	Obtained Score	+1 SEM	Percentiles													
				1	5	10	20	30	40	50	60	70	80	90	95	99
Scale Score		639														
Percentile		93														
Scale Score		635														
Percentile		48														
Scale Score		632														
Percentile		15														

B. Locate the corresponding percentile scores in Table 15.9 for each extended scale score.

C. Using the chart on the right-hand side of Table 15.10, plot the percentile bands for each obtained percentile score. Mark the position of the obtained percentile score within the band.

V. Interpreting Percentile Bands

Judge whether each of the following statements about the characteristics of percentile bands and their interpretation is true.

A. Percentile bands for percentiles throughout the scale are of equal width.

B. Percentile bands reflect that norm-referenced tests are imprecise measures of achievement.

C. The obtained percentile score usually falls in the center of the percentile band.

D. Percentile bands can be used to compare one student's performance on various subtests.

E. The performance of several students in the class can be compared on one test using percentile bands.

F. Scores that have a small standard error of measurement have wider percentile bands than scores that have a large standard error of measurement.

G. Overlapping bands reflect meaningful differences in obtained percentile scores.

H. Percentile bands are confidence intervals that reflect the range of scores where a student's score is likely to fall on retesting.

VI. Interpreting Stanine Scores

A. What percentage of the norm group is assigned each stanine score?

Stanine Scores	*1*	*2*	*3*	*4*	*5*	*6*	*7*	*8*	*9*
Percentage									

B. If there were 1,000 students in the norm group, how many students would be assigned each stanine score?

Stanine Scores		1	2	3	4	5	6	7	8	9
Number of Students										

C. Judge whether each of the following statements about the characteristics of stanine scores and their interpretation is true.

1. An equal number of students is assigned each stanine.
2. Each stanine encompasses a range of scale scores and percentile scores.
3. An equal range of scale scores corresponds to each stanine.
4. Stanines correspond to the standard normal curve.
5. One standard deviation above the mean corresponds to a stanine score of 7.
6. A stanine of 3 corresponds to one standard deviation below the mean.
7. All nine stanines are one-half a standard deviation wide.
8. A stanine score is more similar to a percentile band than to a percentile.

VII. Selecting Scores from the Report Form

Select the score or scores (from Column B) that best answer the questions from Column A.

Column A

_____ 1. What two scores are used to compare the variability of students' achievement across grade levels?

_____ 2. What scores are used to determine whether a student's obtained score is atypical?

_____ 3. What score is used to report students' aptitude levels?

_____ 4. Of all the scores associated with achievement tests, which one is most likely to be misinterpreted?

_____ 5. Which score is created using the processes of interpolation and extrapolation?

_____ 6. Which achievement scores should not be used to compare a student's achievement on different subtests?

_____ 7. Which score should not be used to report students' performance to parents?

Column B

a. Anticipated achievement scores
b. Deviation IQ scores
c. Grade equivalent scores
d. Normal curve equivalent scores
e. Normalized z and T scores
f. Percentile scores
g. Scale scores
h. Stanine scores

VIII. Interpreting Test Records

A. Use the Individual Profile Report in Figure 15.18 to answer the following questions:

1. When did Steven take the test (grade, month)?

2. His scale score on the language test is 767. What level of performance does this score reflect?
   a. Above average
   b. Average
   c. Below average
3. How did you reach this conclusion?
4. On a retest, his language percentile score would probably fall within which range?
5. Which of Steven's scores could you use to compare his performance on the reading, language, and mathematics tests?
6. On which of these tests did he perform best?

FIGURE 15.18

Sample Individual Profile Report Adapted from the TerraNova Multiple Assessments

Student: _____Steven Jones_____   Grade: ___11___   Date of Test: ___May 14___

Tests	Scale Score	Grade Equivalent	National Stanine	Normal Curve Equivalent	National Percentile	NP Range
Reading	756	12.9+	8	78	90	81–96
Language	767	12.9+	9	86	96	90–99
Mathematics	762	12.9+	7	71	85	77–89
Total Score	762	12.9+	8	77	90	
Science	777	12.9+	8	82	93	91–98
Social Studies	738	12.9+	7	69	82	74–89

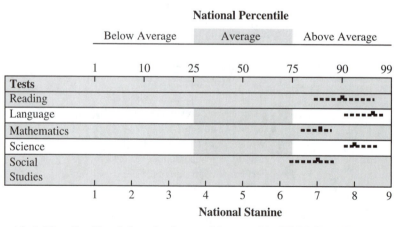

Source: Adapted from TerraNova Information Systems (Monterey, CA: CTB/McGraw-Hill, 1997).

7. Is his performance in language superior to his performance in reading?

8. How do you know this?

9. Steven's national percentile score on the reading test is 90, and his percentile score on the mathematics test is 85. On which test did he perform better?

10. His normal curve equivalent score (NCE) in language is 86. Is this score greater than one standard deviation above the mean NCE score?

11. Use Steven's stanine scores to describe his overall performance on the test.

B. Use the Class Summary Report in Figure 15.19 (see p. 505) to complete the following exercises:

1. Use the group's mean national stanine (MNS) to describe the group's standing in reading.

2. Use the group's median national percentiles (MDNP) in composite reading, language, and mathematics to describe their overall achievement.

IX. Value-Added Assessment

The expected scale score bands illustrated in Figure 15.20 (see p. 506) are based on the tenth-grade spring norms for the composite mathematics score from the TerraNova Multiple Assessments. Assume that your school district provided you with this set of expected scale score bands for your students. Also assume that you received the students' actual scale scores following the spring administration of the tests to your students.

A. Using the students' observed scale scores listed in Figure 15.20, plot the observed score of each student on or beside her or his expected scale score band. Check your scale score plots in Figure 15.21F.

B. Using the expected scale score bands and the location of the students' earned scale scores on the bands, name the students whose achievement gains were greater than the norm group's from the spring of ninth grade to the spring of tenth grade.

C. Name the students whose mathematics achievement growth was less than anticipated in the tenth grade.

D. Using data for all the students in the class, calculate their tenth-grade mathematics teacher's Instructional Quality Index.

E. Based on the teacher's Instructional Quality Index, evaluate the teacher's instruction. How did you reach this evaluative conclusion?

X. Enrichment

A. Make an appointment with a school guidance counselor to discuss the norm-referenced achievement and aptitude tests used by the district. Ask the following questions:

1. How are tests selected?

2. Which tests are used at each grade level?

3. When are the tests administered?

4. How do administrators and teachers use the test results?

B. If district policy permits, review samples of the following test materials:

1. The administrator's guide for a test used at your grade level. Find a description of the objectives measured, the norm group, administration procedures, and sample report forms.

2. Sample individual and group report records from the most recent test. The counselor may want to cover or block out students' names before you review these records.

C. If you have kept your own test records or those of your students, analyze these reports and interpret the scores.

■ F E E D B A C K

I. Matching Test Types and Purposes

1. b	**5.** b
2. a	**6.** a
3. c	**7.** c
4. b	**8.** a

II. Converting Scale Scores to Percentiles
For items A through E, see Table 15.11F (p. 507).

III. Interpreting Percentile Scores
The following statements are correct: C, F, H, I, and K.

IV. Calculating and Plotting Percentile Bands
For items A through C, see Table 15.12F (p. 507).

V. Interpreting Percentile Bands
The following statements are correct: B, D, E, and H.

VI. Interpreting Stanine Scores

Stanine Scores	*1*	*2*	*3*	*4*	*5*	*6*	*7*	*8*	*9*
A. Percentage	4	7	12	17	20	17	12	7	4
B. Number of Students	40	70	120	170	200	170	120	70	40

C. The following statements are correct: 2, 4, 5, 6, and 8.

VII. Selecting Scores from the Report Form

1. c and g	**5.** c
2. a and b	**6.** c and g
3. b	**7.** c
4. c	

VIII. Interpreting Test Records
A. Referring to Figure 15.18 will give you the following answers:
1. 11.9
2. a
3. By determining the performance level indicated by the corresponding percentile or stanine score.
4. It should fall between the 90th and 99th percentiles. This information was obtained by locating the percentiles that correspond to the outer edges of his percentile band for language.

F I G U R E   1 5 . 1 9 ➤

Class Record Summary Sheet for the Comprehensive Tests of Basic Skills, Fourth Edition

Source: TerraNova Information Systems (Monterey, CA: CTB/McGraw-Hill, 1997), p. 27.

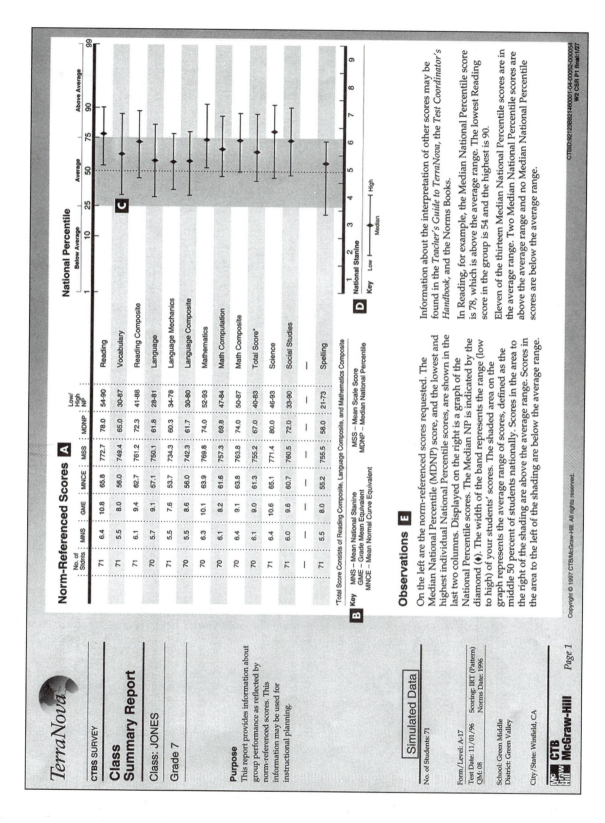

TerraNova

CTBS SURVEY

Class
Summary Report

Class: JONES

Grade 7

Purpose

This report provides information about group performance as reflected by norm-referenced scores. This information may be used for instructional planning.

Simulated Data

No. of Students: 71

Form/Level: A-17
Test Date: 11/01/96
QM: 08
Scoring: IRT (Pattern)
Norms Date: 1996

School: Green Middle
District: Green Valley

City/State: Winfield, CA

McGraw CTB
Hill McGraw-Hill

Page 1

Norm-Referenced Scores **A**

	No. of Stdnts	MNS	GME	MNCE	MSS	MDNP	Low/High NP	
Reading	71	6.4	10.8	65.8	772.7	78.0	54-90
Vocabulary	71	5.5	8.0	56.0	749.4	65.0	30-87
Reading Composite	71	6.1	9.4	62.7	761.2	72.3	41-88
Language	70	5.7	9.1	57.1	750.1	61.8	28-81
Language Mechanics	71	5.5	7.6	53.7	734.3	60.3	34-78
Language Composite	70	5.5	8.6	56.0	742.3	61.7	30-80
Mathematics	70	6.3	10.1	63.9	769.8	74.0	52-93
Math Computation	70	6.1	8.2	61.6	757.3	69.8	47-84
Math Composite	70	6.4	9.1	63.8	763.8	74.0	50-87
Total Score*	70	6.1	9.0	61.3	755.2	67.0	40-83
Science	71	6.4	10.6	65.1	771.4	80.0	46-93
Social Studies	71	6.0	9.6	60.7	760.5	72.0	33-90
—			—		—	—	—
Spelling	71	5.5	8.0	55.2	755.5	58.0	21-73

*Total Score Consists of Reading Composite, Language Composite, and Mathematics Composite

B **Key**
MNS – Mean National Stanine
GME – Grade Mean Equivalent
MNCE – Mean Normal Curve Equivalent
MSS – Mean Scale Score
MDNP – Median National Percentile

National Percentile

| Below Average | Average | Above Average |

D **Key** Low ├──◆──┤ High
Median

Observations **E**

On the left are the norm-referenced scores requested. The Median National Percentile (MDNP) score, and the lowest and highest individual National Percentile scores, are shown in the last two columns. Displayed on the right is a graph of the National Percentile scores. The Median NP is indicated by the diamond (◆). The width of the band represents the range (low to high) of your students' scores. The shaded area on the graph represents the average range of scores, defined as the middle 50 percent of students nationally. Scores in the area to the right of the shading are above the average range. Scores in the area to the left of the shading are below the average range.

Information about the interpretation of other scores may be found in the *Teacher's Guide to TerraNova*, the *Test Coordinator's Handbook*, and the Norms Books.

In Reading, for example, the Median National Percentile score is 78, which is above the average range. The lowest Reading score in the group is 54 and the highest is 90.

Eleven of the thirteen Median National Percentile scores are in the average range. Two Median National Percentile scores are above the average range and no Median National Percentile scores are below the average range.

CTB/D:92123882146000f1-04-00082-000054
W2 CSR P1 final:1/27

FIGURE 15.20

**Students' Expected Scale Score Bands and Observed Scale Scores
in the Tenth Grade**

Student	Observed Scale Scores	Student	Observed Scale Scores	Student	Observed Scale Scores
JP	787	Katy	760	Jim	735
Ben	788	Jeff	767	Patty	747
Darcy	779	Molly	774	Bob	766
Tom	747	Amy	764	Betsy	737

Source: Synthesized from materials in TerraNova Spring Norms Book (Monterey, CA: CTB/McGraw-Hill, 1997), pp. 49, 92.

5. Percentile bands, stanines, or normal curve equivalent scores.
6. Language and science were better than mathematics and social studies because these percentile bands did not overlap.
7. No.
8. Because the percentile bands for these tests overlap.
9. His performance is equivalent on the two tests since the percentile bands overlap.
10. Yes. For the NCE score, the mean is 50 and the standard deviation is 21.06. His score of 86 is greater than 50 + 21.06, or 71.06.
11. In comparison with the national norm group, Steven's performances in reading, language skills, and mathematics are above average.
B. Referring to Figure 15.19 will give you the following answers:
1. The group's mean national stanine of 6.4 in reading indicates average group performance compared to the national norm group.

TABLE 15.11F

Scale Scores and Their Corresponding Percentiles

(1) Scale Scores	(2) Frequency	(3) Cumulative Frequency below	(4) 1/2 Frequency within	(5) Proportion	(6) Percentiles
640	1	19	.5	19.5/20 = .98	98
639	1	18	.5	18.5/20 = .93	93
638	2	16	1	17/20 = .85	85
637	2	14	1	15/20 = .75	75
636	3	11	1.5	12.5/20 = .63	63
635	3	8	1.5	9.5/20 = .48	48
634	2	6	1	7/20 = .35	35
633	2	4	1	5/20 = .25	25
632	2	2	1	3/20 = .15	15
631	1	1	.5	1.5/20 = .08	8
630	1	0	.5	.5/20 = .03	3

TABLE 15.12F

Percentiles and Their Corresponding Percentile Bands

SEM = 2

	−1 SEM	Obtained Score	+1 SEM	Percentiles 1 5 10 20 30 40 50 60 70 80 90 95 99
Scale Score	637	639	640	
Percentile	75	93	98	· xxxxxxxxxxxx
Scale Score	633	635	637	
Percentile	25	48	75	· xxxxxxxxxxxxxxxxxxxxx
Scale Score	630	632	634	
Percentile	3	15	35	· xxxxxxxxxxxxxxx

Note: The narrow range of scale scores in the example resulted in abnormally wide percentile bands. Because norm-referenced tests are designed to yield a wide range of scores, the percentile bands are narrower.

2. The group's median percentiles (MDNP) in composite reading (72.3), language (61.7), and mathematics (74.0) all reflect high average performance compared to the national norm group.

IX. **Value-Added Assessment**
   A. See scale scores plotted in Figure 15.21F.
   B. The students whose achievement gains were greater than the norm group's from ninth to tenth grades are Ben, Darcy, Molly, and Bob.

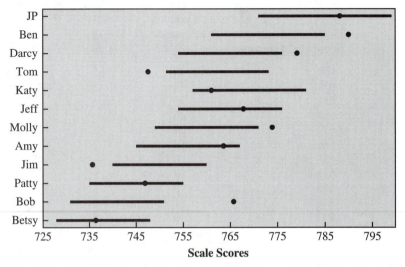

Note: Dots within the graph represent students' earned scale scores for the tenth-grade math composite score.

Source: Synthesized from materials in TerraNova Spring Norms Book (Monterey, CA: CTB/McGraw-Hill, 1997), pp. 49, 92.

C. The students whose mathematics achievement growth was less than anticipated in the tenth grade include Tom and Jim.

D. The tenth-grade mathematics teacher's Instructional Quality Index is .17, and it was calculated as follows:

Students	Above Expectations, As Expected or below Expectations	Individual Growth Score
JP	As Expected	.00
Ben	Above Expectations	1.00
Darcy	Above Expectations	1.00
Tom	Below Expectations	−1.00
Katy	As Expected	.00
Jeff	As Expected	.00
Molly	Above Expectations	1.00
Amy	As Expected	.00
Jim	Below Expectations	−1.00
Patty	As Expected	.00
Bob	Above Expectations	1.00
Betsy	As Expected	.00
Total		**2.00**
Instructional Quality Index		**2.00/12 = .17**

E. The teacher's instructional effectiveness was good. This judgment is based on the students' achievement gains as either anticipated or above anticipated levels for the majority of students (83 percent) in the class. The Instructional Quality Index (.17) is a positive value.

REFERENCES

CTB/McGraw-Hill. (1997). *Teacher's guide to Terra-Nova*. Monterey, CA: CTB/McGraw-Hill Publishing Company.

CTB/McGraw-Hill. (1997). *TerraNova norms book, spring*. Monterey, CA: CTB/McGraw-Hill Publishing Company.

CTB/McGraw-Hill. (1997). *TerraNova technical bulletin 1*. Monterey, CA: CTB/McGraw-Hill Publishing Company.

CTB/McGraw-Hill. (1997). *TerraNova information systems*. Monterey, CA: CTB/McGraw-Hill Publishing Company.

CTB/McGraw-Hill. (1997). *TerraNova multiple assessments*. Monterey, CA: CTB/McGraw-Hill Publishing Company.

SUGGESTED READINGS

Gallagher, J. D. (1998). *Classroom assessment for teachers* (pp. 444–473). Columbus, OH: Merrill.

Kubiszyn, T., & Borich, G. (2000). *Educational testing and measurement* (6th ed., pp. 265–280, 323–415). New York: John Wiley & Sons.

Lynn, R. L., & Gronlund, N. E. (2000). *Measurement and assessment in teaching* (8th ed., pp. 405–505). Englewood Cliffs, NJ: Prentice-Hall.

Nitko, A. J. (1996). *Educational assessment of students* (2nd ed., pp. 350–428). Columbus, OH: Merrill.

Oosterhof, A. (1999). *Developing and using classroom assessments* (2nd ed., pp. 221–234). Columbus, OH: Merrill.

Popham, W. J. (1999). *Classroom assessment: What teachers need to know* (2nd ed., pp. 156–180). Boston: Allyn and Bacon.

Thorndike-Christ, T. (1997). Assessment and educational decisions. In R. M. Thorndike (Ed.). *Measurement and evaluation in psychology and education* (6th ed., pp. 263–286). Columbus, OH: Merrill.

Worthen, B. R., White, K. R., Fan, X., & Sudweeks, R. L. (1999). *Measurement and assessment in schools* (2nd ed., pp. 95–97, 411–480). New York: Addison-Wesley Longman.

Sample Matrix Diagram

FIGURE 3.6

Sample Matrix Diagram for the Instructional Goal "Write a Paragraph"

CONCEPTS/ CONTENT	A State/Recall Physical Characteristics	B State/Recall Functional Characteristics	C State/Recall Quality Characteristics	D Classify Examples and Nonexamples	E Evaluate Given Examples	F Produce Examples
I. Paragraph	Series of sentences Indented	Express ideas on one topic		Correct vs. not indented Many topics		Time Series Feelings Procedure Description
II. Topic Sentence	Typically first Indented	Introduce topic	Relevance Scope Interest	Topic vs. Supporting Concluding	Correct vs. flawed by: Relevance Scope Interest	Time Series Feelings Procedure Description
III. Supporting Sentences	Middle sentences	Elaborate topic	Relevance Sequence Transition	Supporting vs. Topic Concluding	Correct vs. flawed by: Relevance Sequence Transition	Time Series Feelings Procedure Description
IV. Concluding Sentences	Typically last	Conclude/ summarize topic	Transition Relevance Sums up Scope	Concluding vs. Topic Supporting	Correct vs. flawed by: Transition Relevance Conclusion Scope	Time Series Feelings Procedure Description

Sample Table of Test Specifications

FIGURE 4.2

Tables of Test Specifications for the Intellectual Skill "Write a Paragraph," Based on the Goal Framework in Figure 3.6

PRETEST

		RECALL-LEVEL SKILLS						HIGHER-ORDER SKILLS				
Skills	**# Items**	**Item Task General Format***			**Time**	**Skills**	**# Items**	**Item Task General Format**			**Time**	
		OB	**PD**	**PF**				**OB**	**PD**	**PF**		**Totals****
I.A	1	X			.5	I.D	2	X			1.0	**Sk: 18**
I.B	1	X			.5							**Itm: 28**
II.A	1	X			.5	II.D	2	X			1.0	**Mn: 20**
II.B	1	X			.5	II.E	3	X			3.0	
II.C	1	X			.5							
III.A	1	X			.5	III.D	2	X			1.0	
III.B	1	X			.5	III.E	3	X			6.0	
III.C	1	X			.5							
IV.A	1	X			.5	IV.D	2	X			1.0	
IV.B	1	X			.5	IV.E	3	X			3.0	
IV.C	1	X			.5							

UNIT POSTTEST

		RECALL-LEVEL SKILLS						HIGHER-ORDER SKILLS				
Skills	**# Items**	**Item Task General Format**			**Time**	**Skills**	**# Items**	**Item Task General Format**			**Time**	
		OB	**PD**	**PF**				**OB**	**PD**	**PF**		
I.A	1	X			.5	I.D	2	X			1.0	

UNIT POSTTEST

RECALL-LEVEL SKILLS						HIGHER-ORDER SKILLS						
Skills	# Items	Item Task General Format			Time	Skills	# Items	Item Task General Format			Time	Totals*
		OB	PD	PF				OB	PD	PF		
I.B	1	X			.5	I.F	4		X		40.0	Sk: 22
II.A	1	X			.5	II.D	2	X			1.0	Itm: 41
II.B	1	X			.5	II.E	4	X			3.0	Mn: 69
II.C	1	X			.5	II.F	2		X		3.0	
III.A	1	X			.5	III.D	2	X			1.0	
III.B	1	X			.5	III.E	3	X			2.0	
III.C	1	X			.5	III.F	3		X		6.0	
IV.A	1	X			.5	IV.D	2	X			1.0	
IV.B	1	X			.5	IV.E	3	X			2.0	
IV.C	1	X			.5	IV.F	3		X		3.0	

PRACTICE TEST 1: Topic Sentence, Relevance

RECALL-LEVEL SKILLS						HIGHER-ORDER SKILLS						
Skills	# Items	Item Task General Format			Time	Skills	# Items	Item Task General Format			Time	Totals*
		OB	PD	PF				OB	PD	PF		
II.A	1	X			.5	II.D	1	X			1.0	Sk: 6
II.B	1	X			.5	II.E	7	X			3.0	Itm: 14
II.C	1	X			.5	II.F	3		X		3.0	Mn: 18

PRACTICE TEST 2: Topic Sentence, Scope, and Relevance

RECALL-LEVEL SKILLS						HIGHER-ORDER SKILLS						
Skills	# Items	Item Task General Format			Time	Skills	# Items	Item Task General Format			Time	Totals*
		OB	PD	PF				OB	PD	PF		
												Sk: 2
						II.E	12	X			24.0	Itm: 15
						II.F	3		X		9.0	Mn: 33

(continued)

FIGURE 4.2   Continued

PRACTICE TEST 3: Supporting Sentences, Relevance

RECALL-LEVEL SKILLS						HIGHER-ORDER SKILLS						
Skills	# Items	Item Task General Format			Time	Skills	# Items	Item Task General Format			Time	
		OB	PD	PF				OB	PD	PF		Totals*
III.A	1	X			.5	III.D	2	X			1.0	**Sk: 6**
III.B	1	X			.5	III.E	4	X			8.0	**Itm: 11**
III.C	1	X			.5	III.F	2			X	9.0	**Mn: 19**

PRACTICE TEST 4: Supporting Sentences (Sequence)

RECALL-LEVEL SKILLS						HIGHER-ORDER SKILLS						
Skills	# Items	Item Task General Format			Time	Skills	# Items	Item Task General Format			Time	
		OB	PD	PF				OB	PD	PF		Totals*
						III.D	2	X			1.0	**Sk: 3**
						III.E	4	X			8.0	**Itm: 8**
						III.F	2		X		9.0	**Mn: 18**

PRACTICE TEST 5: Supporting Sentences (Transition)

RECALL-LEVEL SKILLS						HIGHER-ORDER SKILLS						
Skills	# Items	Item Task General Format			Time	Skills	# Items	Item Task General Format			Time	
		OB	PD	PF				OB	PD	PF		Totals*
						III.D	2	X			1.0	**Sk: 3**
						III.E	4	X			8.0	**Itm: 8**
						III.F	2		X		9.0	**Mn: 18**

PRACTICE TEST 6: Concluding Sentences

RECALL-LEVEL SKILLS					HIGHER-ORDER SKILLS					
Skills	# Items	Item Task General Format			Time	Skills	# Items	Item Task General Format		Time	
		OB	PD	PF				OB	PD	PF		Totals*
IV.A	1	X			.5	IV.D	1	X			5.0	**Sk: 6**
IV.B	1	X			.5	IV.E	7	X			7.0	**Itm: 14**
IV.C	1	X			.5	IV.F	3		X		9.0	**Mn: 18**

PRACTICE TEST 7: Concluding Sentences, Scope, and Relevance

RECALL-LEVEL SKILLS					HIGHER-ORDER SKILLS					
Skills	# Items	Item Task General Format			Time	Skills	# Items	Item Task General Format		Time	
		OB	PD	PF				OB	PD	PF		Totals*
												Sk: 2
						IV.E	12	X			24.0	**Itm: 15**
						IV.F	3		X		9.0	**Mn: 33**

PRACTICE TESTS 8–11: Writing Paragraphs

	HIGHER-ORDER SKILLS					
	Skills	# Items	Item Task General Format		Time	
			OB	PD	PF		
8. Writing descriptive paragraphs			OB	PD	PF		**Totals for Each Test**
9. Writing time series paragraphs							**Sk: 2**
10. Writing procedural paragraphs	IV.E	12	X			24.0	**Itm: 15**
11. Writing expression of feeling paragraphs	IV.F	3		X		40.0	**Mn: 64**

*For general item formats, OB = objective-style items, PD = essay or product assessments, and PF = live-performance assessments.

**For Totals, Sk = enabling skills, Itm = items, and Mn = minutes. Time estimate totals are rounded up to nearest minute.

FIGURE 4.3

A Sample Table of Test Specifications for Term and Semester Exams for the Instructional Goal "Write a Paragraph"

COMPREHENSIVE TERM EXAM

RECALL-LEVEL SKILLS		Item Task General Format				HIGHER-ORDER SKILLS		Item Task General Format				
Skills	# Items	OB	PD	PF	Time	Skills	# Items	OB	PD	PF	Time	Totals**
						I.F	2		X		40.0	Sk: 7
						II.E	1	X			2.0	Itm: 8
						II.F	1		X		6.0	Mn: 64
						III.E	1	X			2.0	
						III.F	1		X		6.0	
						IV.E	1	X			2.0	
						IV.F	1		X		6.0	

COMPREHENSIVE SEMESTER EXAM

RECALL-LEVEL SKILLS						HIGHER-ORDER SKILLS						
Skills	Items	OB	PD	PF	Time	Skills	Items	OB	PD	PF	Time	Totals**
						I.F	2		X		40.0	Sk: 4
						II.F	1		X		3.0	Itm: 5
						III.F	1		X		5.0	Mn: 51
						IV.F	1		X		3.0	

*Sk = enabling skills, Itm = items, and Mn = minutes.

Sample Table of Learning Objectives (Test Item or Task Specifications)

FIGURE 4.6

Table of Test and Test Item Specifications for the Paragraph Unit Posttest Illustrated in Figure 4.2

UNIT POSTTEST

		RECALL-LEVEL SKILLS				
Skills	**# Items**	**Item Task General Format**			**Time**	**Test Item Specifications (Performance Objectives)**
		OB	**PD**	**PF**		
I.A	1	X			.5	I.A.1 Given a description of the appearance (or physical characteristics) of a paragraph, and a list of terms related to paragraphs, *select the paragraph as the term being described.*
I.B	1	X			.5	I.B.1 Given a description of the purpose (functional characteristics) for a paragraph, and a list of terms related to paragraphs, *select the term being described.*
II.A	1	X			.5	II.A.1 Given a description of the appearance (physical characteristics) of topic sentences, and a list of terms related to paragraphs, *select the term being described.*
II.B	1	X			.5	II.B.1 Given a description of the purpose (functional characteristics) of a topic sentence, and a list of terms related to paragraphs, *select the term being described.*
II.C	1	X			.5	II.C.1 Given a description of the quality characteristics of a topic sentence, and a list of terms related to paragraphs, *select the term being described.*

(continued)

FIGURE 4.6 Continued

RECALL-LEVEL SKILLS						
Skills	**# Items**	**Item Task General Format**			**Time**	**Test Item Specifications (Performance Objectives)**
		OB	**PD**	**PF**		
III.A	1	X			.5	III.A.1 Given a description of the appearance (physical characteristics) of supporting sentences, and a list of terms related to paragraphs, *select the term being described.*
III.B	1	X			.5	III.B.1 Given a description of the purpose (functional characteristics) of supporting sentences, and a list of terms related to paragraphs, *select the term being described.*
III.C	1	X			.5	III.C.1 Given a description of the quality characteristics of supporting sentences, and a list of terms related to paragraphs, *select the term being described.*
IV.A	1	X			.5	IV.A.1 Given a description of the appearance (physical characteristics) of concluding sentences, and a list of terms related to paragraphs, *select the term being described.*
IV.B	1	X			.5	IV.B.1 Given a description of the purpose (functional characteristics) of concluding sentences, and a list of terms related to paragraphs, *select the term being described.*
IV.C	1	X			.5	IV.C.1 Given a description of the quality characteristics of concluding sentences, and a list of terms related to paragraphs, *select the term being described.*
HIGHER-ORDER SKILLS						
Skills	**# Items**	**Item Task General Format**			**Time**	**Test Item Specifications (Performance Objectives)**
		OB	**PD**	**PF**		
I.D	2	X			1.0	I.D.1 Given a series of complete and incomplete paragraphs, correctly indented, *locate the complete paragraphs.*
II.D	2	X			1.0	II.D.1 Given a complete paragraph, correctly indented, *locate the topic sentence.*

HIGHER-ORDER SKILLS						
Skills	**# Items**	**Item Task General Format**			**Time**	**Test Item Specifications (Performance Objectives)**
		OB	**PD**	**PF**		
II.E	4	X			3.0	II.E.1 Given an incomplete paragraph with the topic sentence, omitted, and given three to four optional sentences to complete the paragraph, *choose the best sentence to complete the paragraph.* II.E.2 Given (1) a complete paragraph with the topic sentence flawed by *relevance,* (2) a list of possible judgments about the sentence that includes "no flaw present," as well as (3) the criteria for quality sentences, *choose the problem with the sentence.*
II.F	2		X		3.0	II.F.1 Given an incomplete paragraph, missing the topic sentence, *write the sentence to complete the paragraph.*
III.D	2	X			1.0	III.D.1 Given a complete paragraph, correctly indented, *locate the supporting sentences.*
III.E	3	X			2.0	III.E.1 Given (1) a complete paragraph with the supporting sentences flawed by *interest value for reader,* (2) a list of possible judgments about the sentences that includes "no flaw present," as well as (3) the criteria for quality sentences, *choose the problem with the sentences.* III.E.2 Given (1) a complete paragraph with the supporting sentences flawed by *relevance,* (2) a list of possible judgments about the sentences that includes "no flaw present," as well as (3) the criteria for quality sentences, *choose the problem with the sentences.* III.E.3 Given a complete paragraph with either supporting sentences flawed by *transition,* and given a list of possible judgments about the sentences that includes "no flaw present," as well as the criteria for quality sentences, *choose the problem with the sentences.*
III.F	3		X		6.0	III.F.1 Given an incomplete paragraph, missing the supporting sentences, *write the sentences to complete the paragraph.*
IV.D	2	X			1.0	IV.D.1 Given a complete paragraph, correctly indented, *locate the concluding sentence.*

(continued)

F I G U R E   4 . 6   Continued

		HIGHER-ORDER SKILLS			
Skills	**# Items**	**Item Task General Format**			**Time**
		OB	PD	PF	

Skills	**# Items**	**Item Task General Format** OB	PD	PF	**Time**	**Test Item Specifications (Performance Objectives)**
						HIGHER-ORDER SKILLS
IV.E	3	X			2.0	IV.E.1 Given an incomplete paragraph with the concluding sentence omitted, and given three to four optional sentences to complete the paragraph, *choose the best sentence to complete the paragraph.* IV.E.2 Given (1) a complete paragraph with the concluding sentence flawed by *relevance,* (2) a list of possible judgments about the sentence that includes "no flaw present," as well as (3) the criteria for quality sentences, *choose the problem with the sentence.*
IV.F	3		X		3.0	IV.F.1 Given an incomplete paragraph, missing the concluding sentence, *write the sentence to complete the paragraph.*
						INSTRUCTIONAL GOAL
Skills	**# Items**	OB	PD	PF	**Time**	**Test Item Specifications (Performance Objectives)**
I.F	4		X		40.0	I.F.1 Given a topic requiring a description of something, *write a 4- to 6-sentence paragraph.* I.F.2 Given a topic requiring a time series (chronology), *write a 4- to 6-sentence paragraph.* I.F.3 Given a topic that is a procedure for doing something, *write a 4- to 6-sentence paragraph.* I.F.4 Given a topic that is an expression of feelings or attitude, *write a 4- to 6-sentence paragraph.*

Note: OB = objective-style items, PD = essay or product assessments, and PF = live-performance assessments.

Entry Behaviors Test
for Writing Paragraphs

Name_____ Date _____

Directions: Place a check mark (✓) in the space before each **complete** sentence.

_____ 1. Once when I was going to the store.
_____ 2. There are eight kinds of fish in the pond.
_____ 3. John, a friend of mine, likes to camp.
_____ 4. The more people there are in a circus tent.
_____ 5. Both Sarah and Susan enjoy working in the lab.

Directions:
A. Locate the subject or subjects in the following sentences and draw one line under it.
B. Locate the predicate in the following sentences and draw two lines under it.

Example: The big dipper sparkles on clear nights.

6. Bears hibernate in the winter.
7. Ants are very social insects, and they live in colonies.
8. George helped his parents clean the yard.

Directions: Write two complete sentences about any topic you choose.

9. _____
10. _____

Pretest for Writing Paragraphs
(I. Paragraphs and II. Topic Sentences)

Name _____ Date _____

Directions: Use a #2 pencil to grid your name and student number on the answer sheet provided. Mark your answers to the following questions about paragraphs on your answer sheet.

I. Paragraphs

I.A **1.** Which of the following descriptions bests fits a paragraph?
    A. One complete sentence that is either declarative or exclamatory
    B. A set of three or more sentences with the first sentence indented
    C. A compound, complex sentence that is indented
    D. A topic sentence

I.B **2.** Which of the following descriptions best fits a paragraph?
    A. A series of sentences on many topics
    B. A series of sentences on three topics
    C. An indented sentence on one topic
    D. A series of sentences on one topic

I.C.1 **3.** Which of the following paragraphs is correctly indented?

A	B
I don't think it will ever stop raining. It was raining Friday when I came home from school. It rained all day Saturday. It rained so hard Sunday that the picnic was canceled. The sun, if it ever shines again, will certainly be a welcome sight.	I don't think it will ever stop raining. It was raining Friday when I came home from school. It rained all day Saturday. It rained so hard Sunday that the picnic was canceled. The sun, if it ever shines again, will certainly be a welcome sight.

I.C.2 **4.** Which of the following is a paragraph?

A	B
The largest trees grow from very small seeds. Usually the children in my class exchange valentines. If I do my chores without complaining, I get to choose something special I like to do each weekend.	It seems that strawberries are ripe before blackberries. I like raspberries, especially in ice cream. Some people put blueberries in their cereal. Apples ripen after berry season.

C	D
Hot air balloons of all colors soared across the sky last weekend. They reminded me of a hawk sailing along on air currents. I got a pair of stilts last weekend, and I almost broke my neck trying to learn to walk on them.	Sometimes I feel very lonely. I feel lonely when I look across a large, empty pasture. The feeling stirs when I look up and see thousands of stars in the sky or walk at the beach. It is not an unpleasant feeling . . . just a lonely one.

II. TOPIC SENTENCES

II.A 5. Which of the following descriptions best fits a topic sentence?
  A. Usually the first sentence in a paragraph, indented
  B. Usually the middle sentence in a paragraph
  C. Usually the last sentence in a paragraph

II.B 6. Which of the following descriptions best fits a topic sentence?
  A. It introduces the subject in a paragraph
  B. It expands the subject or ideas in a paragraph
  C. It summarizes the topic in a paragraph

II.C 7. Which one of the following qualities is important for topic sentences?
  A. Transition to the topic
  B. Sequence of ideas in the paragraph
  C. Relevant to the ideas presented in the paragraph

II.D *Directions:* Locate the topic sentences in paragraphs 8 and 9. Mark the letter before the topic sentence on your answer sheet for each question number.

Question 8	Question 9
(A) Spring is the Season of beginnings. (B) The spring winds carry the smell of new blossoms through open windows and help birds return to build new homes. (C) Gentle rains nudge buds on trees and lilac bushes. (D) Bright sunshine encourages children to come outside to make new friends and learn new games. (E) These beginnings are so welcome after the long winter.	(A) "This is my first dance, and it seems a little weird. (B) The lights in the gym are dim and romantic, but I can't see who is standing across the room. (C) The music is loud and great, but it's pretty hard to talk without shouting. (D) We all said we were going to dance, but we're just standing here and watching. (E) Would you like to dance? (F) I said, would you like to dance?"

II.E *Directions:* Read the following incomplete paragraphs carefully and then choose the best topic sentence for each one from among the sentences provided.

10. _____ . An isosceles triangle has two sides that are the same length. An equilateral triangle has three sides that are the same length, while a scalene triangle has three unequal sides. A right triangle has two sides that are perpendicular and form a 90 degree angle.

Topic Sentences:
  A. There are lots of types of triangles
  B. There are only four kinds of triangles.
  C. Triangles are described by the length of their sides and the angles they form.

11. _____. They are the
    queen, the workers, and the drones. The queen bee is the only bee in the colony
    that can lay eggs, and she can lay enough eggs to form an entirely new colony. The
    worker bees are female bees, and they gather food, clean the hive, feed the young
    bees, and tend the queen bee. The drones are the male bees, and their role is to
    mate with the queen bee.

    Topic Sentences:
    A. There are three types of bees in a colony, and they differ by gender and role.
    B. Entirely new bee colonies are created by the queen bee.
    C. Drone bees appear to have an easy life compared to other bees.
    D. If it weren't for the workers, members of a bee colony might go hungry.

12. _____. Inside the state,
    the governor chooses citizens for important jobs in the state government. He or she
    develops and proposes a budget for determining how state revenues will be spent each
    year. Nationally, the governor works with governors from other states to plan and im-
    plement cross-state programs. He or she is also the coordinator between federal and
    state programs. The governor has many jobs as head of the executive branch.

    Topic Sentences:
    A. The governor and lieutenant governor are a team.
    B. The federal and state governments are a team.
    C. The governor must work very hard.
    D. The governor of a state has many responsibilities.

II.F.1 *Directions:* Write topic sentences for each of the following incomplete paragraphs. Use
your own paper to write the topic sentences. Write your name in the upper left corner
and today's date in the upper right corner of your paper. Put the question number (e.g.,
13, 14, 15) on your paper, and write the topic sentence for each paragraph beside the
correct question number.

13. _____. Hunting tribes moved often, and they lived in "portable" homes
    that could be built quickly. They moved their homes and villages several times during
    a year to match the hunting seasons. Farming tribes, on the other hand, stayed in one
    place to tend their crops. Since the farmers were not mobile, they built sturdy, perma-
    nent homes. The type of homes the tribes built depended on their needs.

14. _____. We can have fluoride treatments for our teeth at the dentist's
    office. We can brush our teeth carefully using a fluoride toothpaste after each meal.
    Before bedtime, we can floss our teeth, brush with a fluoride toothpaste, and rinse
    our mouth with a mild salt-water solution. Good dental hygiene saves smiles,
    money, and pain.

15. _____. Valentine's Day isn't about candy and flowers. The Fourth
    of July isn't about picnics and fireworks. Thanksgiving isn't about turkey and pie.
    These are the ways in which we celebrate and not the reasons why we celebrate.

HAVE YOU CHECKED YOUR WORK?
DID YOU ANSWER ALL QUESTIONS?
DID YOU ERASE CLEANLY?

IS YOUR NAME ON YOUR ANSWER SHEET AND ON YOUR TOPIC SENTENCES PAPER?

First Practice Test for the Topic Sentence Area (II.A–E)

Name _____ **Date** _____

II.A   **1.**   Within a paragraph, the first sentence that is indented is called the _____ sentence.

II.B   **2.**   The sentence that introduces the subject of a paragraph is called the _____ sentence.

II.C   **3.**   Name three quality characteristics of topic sentences. _____, _____, _____.

II.D   **4.**   Underline the topic sentence in the following paragraph.

> Many claim that besides tasting good, garlic has several benefits for people. First, it is believed to help us digest our food after meals. Second, it just might help lower blood pressure and reduce the risk from strokes. Third, some think it is an antiseptic that kills germs. Finally, its use in warding off vampires has been well documented in novels and films.

II.E.1   *Directions:* Judge the quality of the topic sentences in the following paragraphs. After reading each paragraph, circle the letter before the statement that best describes the topic sentence in the paragraph.

    5.   The quality of our school depends on the motivation and skills of many different people in our community. As students, we must want to learn new ideas and skills, and we need to try our best in order to learn. Our teachers must truly want to help us learn and to work with us until we do. Our principals and counselors must work hard to assist teachers in their quest to help us learn. Although not present in the school, the citizens and tax payers of our town must work hard to support our school. When all these different people pull together as a team, an excellent school is the result.

    The topic sentence is:
    A. Good as it is written
    B. **Not relevant** to the information contained in the paragraph
    C. **Too narrow in scope** for the paragraph
    D. **Too broad in scope** for the paragraph
    E. Missing in the paragraph

Note: Answers to verbal information items (1–3) are readily discernible from other items on the test. This cueing problem is difficult to avoid in tests at the lesson (single-concept) level; however, it is not a problem since the test is designed as a practice exercise. Those students who do not yet know the terminology will certainly get a good reminder from the test.

6. Maps are abstract pictures of the earth. The flat shape of maps makes them very convenient to use. They can be bound into books for study, or they can be folded to take along on a journey. The round shape of a globe provides a more realistic view of the earth in its natural form. Globes, however, are not as convenient to use since they cannot be bound into books or carried along on vacation. Both maps and globes help us view our world.

    The topic sentence is:
    A. Good as it is written
    B. **Not relevant** to the information contained in the paragraph
    C. **Too narrow in scope** for the paragraph
    D. **Too broad in scope** for the paragraph
    E. Missing in the paragraph

7. It is amazing that birds can find their way home after migrating so far each winter. One type of feather grows closest to the bird's body, and it is short, soft, and fluffy. The purpose for these inner feathers is to keep the bird warm. The feathers covering these soft feathers are longer and stiffer. These cover feathers give the bird its unique color and shape, and they keep water off the bird's body. A third type of feather can be found on the bird's wings and tail. These feathers are longer still and stiff, and they are necessary to help birds fly. Each type of feather is textured, colored, and shaped for its use.

    The topic sentence is:
    A. Good as it is written
    B. **Not relevant** to the information contained in the paragraph
    C. **Too narrow in scope** for the paragraph
    D. **Too broad in scope** for the paragraph
    E. Missing in the paragraph

8. I do many special things when I visit my grandfather's farm. I take walks in the woods and identify the different types of plants that grow there. I pet the kittens that live in the barn and the horses as they graze in the fields. I watch the pigs try to root out a cool spot on a hot summer day. I follow the cow paths to meet the cows and walk them back to the barn in the evening. A visit to his farm is like a visit to nature itself.

    The topic sentence is:
    A. Good as it is written
    B. **Not relevant** to the information contained in the paragraph
    C. **Too narrow in scope** for the paragraph
    D. **Too broad in scope** for the paragraph
    E. Missing in the paragraph

II.E.2 *Directions:* Study the following paragraphs and **rewrite** the topic sentences to meet the quality criteria. Write your sentences in the space provided at the bottom of each paragraph.

9. Dogs, cats, birds, and fish make very good pets. Dogs serve as companions and friends for children, adults, and elderly people. They greet you at the door to welcome you home in the evening. They often accompany you on walks around the neighborhood. Many dogs play with you by chasing sticks and balls. They can even work for you by barking when strangers come into your yard or near your house. Having a good dog is like having a good friend.

    Revised topic sentence:

10.   Roses are very pretty. First, locate a spot in your yard that gets at least five hours of sun daily. Next, dig a hole big enough to hold the rose planter. Line the bottom of the hole with good soil and a small bit of fertilizer. Then, remove the rose from the pot and lower it gently into the hole. Hold the bush upright with one hand while you fill around it with soil. Water around the plant with a hose, and fill any holes that develop in the soil as you water. Water and dust weekly, fertilize monthly, and soon you will have your own roses.

Revised topic sentence:

_____

11.   Houses have windows. Windows are measured in square inches. To find the area of a window, measure the height of the window in inches. Then, measure the width of the window in inches. Multiply the window's height by its width and you have the area of the window. For example, if the window is 30 inches tall and 20 inches wide, its area is 600 square inches.

Revised topic sentence:

_____

Paragraph Unit Posttest
(Topic Sentence Portion)

Name _____ Date _____

II.A **3.** In a paragraph, what is the first, indented sentence typically called?
  A. Concluding sentence
  B. Declarative sentence
  C. Supporting sentence
  D. Topic sentence

II.B **4.** What sentence introduces the subject presented in the paragraph?
  A. Concluding sentence
  B. Declarative sentence
  C. Supporting sentence
  D. Topic sentence

II.C **5.** What sentence in a paragraph is (a) relevant to the topic, (b) appropriate in scope for the information that follows it, and (c) interesting to attract the reader's attention?
  A. Concluding sentence
  B. Declarative sentence
  C. Supporting sentence
  D. Topic sentence

II.D *Directions:* Locate the topic sentences in the following paragraphs. Place the number before the topic sentence on your answer sheet for each question.

Question 6	Question 7
(1) In order to determine how heavy an object is, we can measure it in ounces, pounds, or tons. (2) There are 16 ounces in a pound and 2000 pounds in a ton. (3) Some measuring scales only measure in ounces, some in pounds and ounces, and others in tons and pounds. (4) Regardless of the size of an object, there is usually a scale that can be used to measure its weight.	(1) The state fair started Saturday. (2) This year there will be sewing contests, vegetable growing contests, cooking contests, art contests, animal contests, and much more. (3) There is lots of food for sale in the booths along the midway. (4) Besides all this, there are great rides to enjoy. (5) If you have time, you should come to the fair.

Note: The verbal information question on the posttest (3–5) would be located with the verbal information questions from general paragraph, supporting sentence, and concluding sentence objectives. Placing items together from all the verbal information objectives will eliminate the problem of clueing terminology from other items related to topic sentences.

II.E.1 *Directions:* Read the following incomplete paragraphs carefully and then choose the best topic sentence for each one from among the sentences provided.

8. _____. My piano teacher says that I am really getting better. The recital is only a month away, and I plan to practice very hard each day. With lots of practice, I can be even better by the time the recital is here. Playing the piano and getting better all the time are very enjoyable to me.

Topic Sentences:
A. Piano is fun.
B. I have been practicing the piano a lot lately.
C. Recitals make me nervous.
D. My piano teacher expects too much of me.

9. _____.
Mother says that one way I can show others that I am responsible is always to be on time. She said I should be on time for school, and I should always be on time when I come home from school. She said I should arrive at a friend's house or a game at the time I said I would be there. She believes that I should also leave a friend's house at the designated time and not over-extend my welcome. I think I will get a watch and at least try to be on time.

Topic Sentences:
A. There is never enough time.
B. Responsibility is important at home and school.
C. Dad said that I was irresponsible, but I really didn't mean to be.
D. I enjoy visiting at a friend's house as long as I don't stay too long.

II.E.2 *Directions:* Evaluate the topic sentences in the following paragraphs. After reading the topic sentence and the complete paragraph, select the one description from beneath the paragraph that you believe best fits the topic sentence.

10. Many people in our neighborhood have garage sales. You should begin planning your sale a week or two in advance. First, scour your room, the family room, the attic, the basement, and the garage to find old toys and games that you have out-grown. Second, go over your sale items with your parents to see that they do not have other plans for the items you picked. Next plan a sale price for each item with your parents and tag the items. When you are ready, move your items outside, post signs, and begin the sale!

The topic sentence is:
A. Good the way it is written
B. Not relevant
C. Too broad
D. Too specific

11. Tennis is a game that is very hard to play. With a lot of practice, some people can get pretty good, but most people never quite get the swing of it. No matter how hard I try, I just do not seem to get better. I think I will try golf instead!

The topic sentence is:
A. Good the way it is written
B. Not relevant
C. Too broad
D. Too specific

II.F   *Directions:* Write topic sentences for each of the following incomplete paragraphs. Use your own paper to write the topic sentences. Write your name in the upper left corner and today's date in the upper right corner of your paper. Put the question number (e.g., 12, 13) on your paper, and write the topic sentence for each paragraph beside the correct question number.

12.   _____. I can sleep in. I can help others who need it at home or in my neighborhood. I could come up with a scheme to earn some money. I could have a friend over or go to a friend's house. I could walk alone along a stream and watch the water go by. Oh, so much to do . . . so few Saturdays.

13.   _____. We can all play an important part in conserving energy at home and at school. We can turn lights off when we leave a room. We can take shorter showers and turn off the water while we brush our teeth. We can recycle paper, bottles, and plastic. If we all try, our natural resources will last longer.

Sample Rating Scale

FIGURE 6.13

A Sample Rating Scale for Evaluating Students' Original Paragraphs

WRITING PROCEDURAL PARAGRAPHS (WASHING A DOG)					
Name _____	Date _____		Score _____ (44) _____ %		
Criteria	**No** **0**	**Vaguely** **1**	**Mostly** **2**	**Well** **3**	**Comments**
I. Paragraph (7)					
A.1 Four to six sentences	0	1 (Yes)			
A.2 Indented	0	1 (Yes)			
B.1 Only one topic		1	2		
C.1 Describes procedure		1	2	3	
II. Topic Sentence (10)	0	1 (Included)			
A.1 Location (first)	0	1 (Yes)			
B.2 Introduces topic		1	2		
C.1 Relevant to paragraph		1	2		
C.2 Appropriate scope		1	2		
C.3 Interest for reader		1	2		
III. Supporting Sentences (14)	0	1 (Included)			
A.1 Location (middle)	0	1 (Yes)			
B.2 Elaborates topic		1	2	3	
C.1 Relevant to topic		1	2	3	
C.2 Sequence of ideas		1	2	3	
C.3 Transition		1	2	3	

(continued)

FIGURE 6.13 Continued

Criteria	No 0	Vaguely 1	Mostly 2	Well 3	Comments
IV. Concluding Sentence (13)	0	1 (Included)			
A.1 Location (last)	0	1 (Yes)			
B.1 Summarizes		1	2	3	
C.1 Transition		1	2	3	
C.2 Relevance		1	2	3	
C.3 Scope		1	2		
Totals		( ) +	( ) +	( )	= _____

Sample Group Performance Measures

FIGURE 10.13

Group Performance Measures for a Paragraph Unit Posttest

$N = 20$

X	f	fX	x	x^2	fx^2
43	5	215	5	25	125
42	2	84	4	16	32
41	1	41	3	9	9
40	1	40	2	4	4
39	1	39	1	1	1
38	1	38	0	0	0
37	2	74	−1	1	2
36	1	36	−2	4	4
35	2	70	−3	9	18
34	1	34	−4	16	16
33	1	33	−5	25	25
32	1	32	−6	36	36
24	1	24	−14	196	196

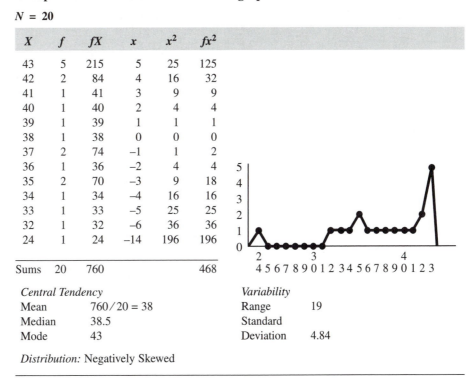

Sums	20	760			468

Central Tendency
Mean $760/20 = 38$
Median   38.5
Mode   43

Variability
Range   19
Standard
Deviation   4.84

Distribution: Negatively Skewed

FIGURE 10.14

Paragraph Unit Posttest Data Recalculated after Eliminating Outlier Student's Raw Score

X	f	fX	x	x^2	fx^2
43	5	215	4.26	18.75	90.75
42	2	84	3.26	10.63	21.26
41	1	41	2.26	5.11	5.11
40	1	40	1.26	1.59	1.59
39	1	39	.26	.07	.07
38	1	38	−.74	.55	.55
37	2	74	−1.74	3.03	6.06
36	1	36	−2.74	7.51	7.51
35	2	70	−3.74	13.99	27.98
34	1	34	−4.74	22.47	22.47
33	1	33	−5.74	32.95	32.95
32	1	32	−6.74	45.43	45.43

Sums   19   736   261.73

```
              2        3              4
              4 5 6 7 8 9 0 1 2 3 4 5 6 7 8 9 0 1 2 3
```

Central Tendency

Mean   736/19 = 38.74

Median   39

Mode   43

Variability

Range   43 − 32 = 11

Standard

Deviation   3.71

Distribution: Negatively Skewed

Sample Item Analysis

FIGURE 11.3

Item Analysis for the Topic Sentence Portion of the Paragraph Posttest (Enabling Skills II.A to II.F in Figures 3.6 and 4.2)

Objective Codes	TOPIC SENTENCE OBJECTIVES						
	II.A	**II.B**	**II.C**	**II.D**	**II.E.1**	**II.E.4**	**II.F**
Items	3	4	5	6 7	8 9	10 11	12 13
Correct Answers	*4*	*4*	*4*	*1 1*	*2 4*	*1 4*	*Hand Scored*
Augustine	*	*	*	* *	* *	* *	* *
Prince	*	*	*	* *	* *	* *	* *
Deddens	*	*	*	* *	* *	* *	* *
Talbot	*	*	*	* *	* *	* *	* *
McComas	*	*	*	* *	* *	* *	* *
Rust	*	*	*	* *	* *	* *	* *
Carey	*	*	*	* *	* *	* *	* *
Cromer	*	*	*	* *	* *	* *	* *
Hager	*	*	*	* *	* *	* *	* *
McLaughlin	*	*	*	* *	* *	* *	* *
White	*	*	*	* *	* *	* *	* *
Otto	*	*	*	* *	* *	* *	* *
Lovejoy	*	*	*	* *	* *	* *	* *
Hill	*	*	*	* *	* *	* *	* *
Scragg	*	*	2	* *	* *	* *	* *

(continued)

FIGURE 11.3 Continued

	TOPIC SENTENCE OBJECTIVES							
Objective Codes	II.A	II.B	II.C	II.D		II.E.1		II.E.4		II.F	
Items	3	4	5	6 7		8 9		10 11		12 13	
Correct Answers	*4*	*4*	*4*	*1 1*		*2 4*		*1 4*		*Hand Scored*	
Gormley	*	*	3	* *		* 3		* *		* *	
Bailey	*	*	2	* *		1 *		* *		* *	
Deiters	*	*	2	* *		* 3		* *		* x	
Stewart	*	*	3	* *		* *		2 *		* x	
Smith	*	*	2	* *		* 3		2 2		x x	
Total Class *p*	1.0	1.0	.70	1.0 1.0		.95 .85		.90 .95		.95 .85	
p_{ul}	1.0	1.0	.50	1.0 1.0		.90 .70		.80 .90		.90 .70	
d	.00	.00	1.00	.00 .00		.20 .60		.40 .20		.20 .60	
r_{pbi}	.00	.00	.79	.00 .00		.19 .63		.69 .67		.67 .72	

* p_{ul} = The difficulty index for only students in the upper and lower groups in the class.

Sample Norm-Referenced Analysis and Mastery Analysis

TABLE 12.1

Norm-Referenced Analysis of Students' Achievement on the Objective Portion of the Paragraph Unit Posttest

$N = 20$ Mean = 38	Standard Deviation = 4.84					$N = 19$ Mean = 38.74	Standard Deviation = 3.71	
	Total Class Group					Recalculated without Outlier		
X	Percentage Correct	f	z	T	Percentile	z	T	Percentile
43	100	5	1.03	60	88	1.15	61	87
42	98	2	.83	58	70	.88	59	68
41	95	1	.62	56	63	.61	56	61
40	93	1	.41	54	58	.34	53	55
39	91	1	.21	52	53	.07	51	50
38	88	1	.00	50	48	−.20	48	45
37	86	2	−.21	48	40	−.47	45	37
36	84	1	−.41	46	33	−.74	43	29
35	81	2	−.62	44	25	−1.00	40	21
34	79	1	−.83	42	18	−1.28	37	13
33	77	1	−1.03	40	13	−1.55	35	8
32	74	1	−1.24	38	8	−1.82	32	3
24	56	1	−2.89	21	2			

FIGURE 12.3

Mastery Analysis of Students' Performance for Only the Topic Sentence Portion of the Paragraph Posttest (Skills II.A to II.F in Tables 4.2 and 4.8)

TOPIC SENTENCE OBJECTIVES								
Enabling Skill Codes	II.A	II.B	II.C	II.D	II.E.1	II.E.2	II.F	Total Objectives Mastered
Items:	3	4	5	6 7	8 9	10 11	12 13	7
Correct Answers:	*4*	*4*	*4*	*1 1*	*2 4*	*1 4*	*Hand Scored*	
Augustine	*	*	*	* *	* *	* *	* *	7
Prince	*	*	*	* *	* *	* *	* *	7
Deddens	*	*	*	* *	* *	* *	* *	7
Talbot	*	*	*	* *	* *	* *	* *	7
McComas	*	*	*	* *	* *	* *	* *	7
Rust	*	*	*	* *	* *	* *	* *	7
Carey	*	*	*	* *	* *	* *	* *	7
Cromer	*	*	*	* *	* *	* *	* *	7
Hager	*	*	*	* *	* *	* *	* *	7
McLaughlin	*	*	*	* *	* *	* *	* *	7
White	*	*	*	* *	* *	* *	* *	7
Otto	*	*	*	* *	* *	* *	* *	7
Lovejoy	*	*	*	* *	* *	* *	* *	7
Hill	*	*	*	* *	* *	* *	* *	7
Scragg	*	*	2	* *	* *	* *	* *	6
Gormley	*	*	3	* *	* 3	* *	* *	5
Bailey	*	*	2	* *	1 *	* *	* *	5
Deiters	*	*	2	* *	* 3	* *	* x	4
Stewart	*	*	3	* *	* *	2 *	* x	4
Smith	*	*	2	* *	* 3	2 1	x x	3
Number of Students Who Mastered	20	20	14	20	16	18	17	
Percentage of Students Who Mastered	100%	100%	70%	100%	80%	90%	85%	

Prescribed Instructional Activities Based on Mastery Analysis

CONCEPTS/ CONTENT	A State/Recall Physical Characteristics of:	B State/Recall Functional Characteristics of:	C State/Recall Quality Characteristics of:	D Discriminate between Examples and Nonexamples	E Evaluate Given Examples	F Produce Examples of:
II. Topic Sentence			Bailey Deiters Gormley Scragg Smith Stewart		Bailey Deiters Gormley Smith Stewart	Deiters Smith Stewart
III. Supporting Sentences						
IV. Concluding Sentence						

FIGURE 12.5

A Partial Student Progress Chart for the Instructional Goal "Write a Paragraph"

| Enabling Skills | Paragraph | | | Topic Sentences | | | | | | | |
	I A	I B	I D	II A	II B	II C	II D	II E	II F	II	Etc.
Augustine	x	x	x	x	x	x	x	x	x	**M**	
Bailey	x	x	x	x	x		x		x	**PM**	
Carey	x	x	x	x	x	x	x	x	x	**M**	
Cromer	x	x	x	x	x	x	x	x	x	**M**	
Deddens	x	x	x	x	x	x	x	x	x	**M**	
Deiters	x	x	x	x	x		x				
Gormley	x	x	x	x	x		x		x	**PM**	
Hager	x	x	x	x	x	x	x	x	x	**M**	
Hill		x	x	x	x	x	x	x	x	**M**	
Lovejoy	x	x	x	x	x	x	x	x	x	**M**	
McComas	x	x	x	x	x	x	x	x	x	**M**	
McLaughlin	x	x	x	x	x	x	x	x	x	**M**	
Otto	x	x	x	x	x	x	x	x	x	**M**	
Prince	x	x	x	x	x	x	x	x	x	**M**	
Rust	x	x	x	x	x	x	x	x	x	**M**	
Scragg	x	x	x	x	x		x	x	x	**PM**	
Smith	x	x	x	x	x		x				
Stewart	x	x	x	x	x		x				
Talbot	x	x	x	x	x	x	x	x	x	**M**	
White	x	x	x	x	x	x	x	x	x	**M**	

Note: x = at least minimal mastery of enabling skill; **PM** = Partial Mastery of concept strand (e.g., topic sentences, supporting sentences, and concluding sentences); **M** = Mastery of concept strand.